INVESTMENT BANKING HISTORY

NATIONAL AND COMPARATIVE ISSUES
(19th-21st CENTURIES)

P.I.E. Peter Lang
Bruxelles · Bern · Berlin · Frankfurt am Main · New York · Oxford · Wien

EUROCLIO is a scientific and editorial project, a network of research institutions and researchers, and an ideas forum. EUROCLIO as an editorial project consists of two aspects: the first concerns studies and documents, the second concerns tools. Both are aimed at making the results of research more accessible, and also at opening up paths through the history of European construction/integration/unification.

The EUROCLIO series meets a dual objective:

- to provide reference tools for research,
- to provide a platform for this research in terms of the publication of results.

The series thus consists of two sub-series that satisfy these requirements: the STUDIES AND DOCUMENTS series and the REFERENCES series. These two series are aimed at general libraries and/or university history departments, teachers and researchers, and in certain cases, specific professional circles.

The STUDIES AND DOCUMENTS series consists of monographs, collections of articles, conference proceedings, and collections of texts with notes for teaching purposes.

The REFERENCES series consists of bibliographies, guides and other tools. It thus contributes to the creation of a database making up a "Permanent catalogue of sources and bibliographies on European construction".

Edited by
Éric Bussière, Université de Paris-Sorbonne (France),
Michel Dumoulin, Louvain-la-Neuve (Belgique),
& Antonio Varsori, Universitá degli Studi di Padova (Italia)

INVESTMENT BANKING HISTORY

NATIONAL AND COMPARATIVE ISSUES
(19th-21st CENTURIES)

Hubert BONIN & Carlo BRAMBILLA (eds.)

Euroclio No. 78

The book was subject to a double blind refereeing process.

Éditions scientifiques internationales
Brussels, 2014
1 avenue Maurice, B-1050 Brussels, Belgium
pie@peterlang.com; www.peterlang.com

ISSN 0944-2294
ISBN 978-2-87574-115-8
D/2014/5678/19

CIP available from the British Library, UK and from the Library of Congress, USA.

"Die Deutsche National Bibliothek" lists this publication in the "Deutsche Nationalbibliografie"; detailed bibliographic data is available on the Internet at <http://dnb.de>.

Acknowledgments

* The two authors and participants of the book thank:

- The *Università dell'Insubria* (*dipartimento di Economia*) in Varese (Italy), for its participation to the financing of the publication;
- The various banking archives centers all over Europe for their welcoming support to the enquiries conducted by the authors;
- Cognizant-Equinox Consulting for their explanations and developments about the "model" of investment banks or of investment banking within universal commercial banks;
- The team of PIE-Peter Lang for it constant cooperation throughout the process of publishing.

* Hubert Bonin thanks:

- The research centre UMR CNRS GRETHA from Bordeaux University and the research programme *Aquibanque* financed by the Région Aquitaine, for their support to the researches of professor Bonin, to the translations, and to the sponsorship of research missions in Paris;
- Sciences Po Bordeaux for its daily support to Pr. Bonin's researches;
- The Historical Archives of BNP Paribas, of *Crédit agricole*-CASA-*Crédit lyonnais-Banque de l'Indochine* (from Roger Nougaret to Anne Brunterch, and their team), and of *Société générale* (Marjolaine Meschaert and Sylvie Guillaudeau), for the availability of their records;
- The Association for the history of BNP Paribas (and Pierre de Longuemar), for the opening of its own archivistic records and documents (oral history, etc.).

Table of Contents

List of Tables

Chapter 10. L. J. Coronas-Vida

Part I

Introductive Issues

CHAPTER 1

Varieties in Investment Banking Evolutions and Functions

Hubert BONIN & Carlo BRAMBILLA

Our book is the concrete expression of issues raised during a session on investment banking history held in Utrecht in August 2009 at the congress of the World Economic History Association; but it prolonged a middle-term research programme which Hubert Bonin, Carlo Brambilla and Giandomenico Piluso had set up as soon as a EBHA (European Business History Association) congress in Copenhagen (2007) and developed afterwards (Geneva: 2007; Bergen: 2008). Since then, our informal academic "club" deepened its analysis and moreover; it could confront its analysis about the past to the arguments among academics fuelled by the present crisis, where investment banks were suspected to play altogether as triggers to the krash (Bear Stearns, Lehman Brothers) and the greedy sharks swallowing the fundamentals of capitalism and even market economy. But the final version of the collective process which gave birth to this book was completed under the Franco-Italian guidance of professors Bonin and Brambilla.

1. Varieties of investment banking: How to unify our prospects?

Sure, one might pretend that everything has already been told about investment banking history, models, strategy, and even prospects… A few books brought rich materials and arguments to this topics, line those of Vincent Carosso, in his time one of the founders of such investigations about US investment banks (1970),[1] Samuel Hayes and Philip Hubbard

[1] Vincent Carosso, *Investment Banking in America: A History*, Cambridge, Mass., Harvard University Press, 1970. Also see: Vincent Carosso, *More than a Century of Investment Banking: the Kidder, Peabody & Co. Story*, New York, McGraw Hill, 1979. Vincent Carosso, *The Morgan's: Private International Bankers, 1854-1913*, Cambridge, Mass., Harvard University Press, 1987.

(1990),[2] Alan Morrison and William Wilhelm, a perfect handbook (2007),[3] like that of Richard Roberts (1988).[4] Anyway, banking and business historians can enrich the analysis of banking and economic experts, of researchers in banking and finance management, because they confront archives recently scrutinised – thus renewing somewhat narrative history – with the business models and the evolution of the finance system. Throughout the process of maturing our programme, we could observe once again the extreme variety of investment banking and the adaptive character of strategies carried out by financial actors in relation to widely different contexts, circumstances and institutional frameworks. Our debate has shown that it is hard to rely upon a too strict definition of investment banking and that the sector is susceptible to changes stemming out both from autonomous strategies and external regulation or interventions. Moreover, economic historians are aware that, as a matter of fact, investment banking ever modified its characters, profiles, and rules over time as well as it differs, say, between the US and Europe, advanced economies and "followers", core countries and peripheries or emerging markets. The emphasis on the variety of business models and practices – *in lieu* of the idea of the "one best way" or model – is probably the main point of our specific contribution to the comprehension of the evolution of this peculiar industry, from which all major financial innovations have often spun off. And we know that such variety has even fostered arguments about the very vocabulary used to nominate and define investment banks[5]...

Our attention to regulation, national contexts and peripheral or emerging markets thus tries to add to the analysis of investment banking and its main tendencies in history.

To put it in a nutshell, we think that the very core of this book is the extreme variety of investment banking and the adaptive character of strategies carried out by financial actors in relation to widely different contexts

---

2 Samuel L. Hayes & Philip M. Hubbard, *Investment Banking: A Tale of Three Cities*, Boston, Harvard Business School Press, 1990. Also see: Samuel Hayes, "Investment banking: Power structure in flux", *Harvard Business Review*, No. 49, 2, 1971, pp. 136-152. Samuel Hayes, "The transformation of investment banking", *Harvard Business Review*, No. 57, 1, 1979, pp. 153-170. Samuel Hayes, A. Michaël Spence & David van Praag Marks, *Competition in the Investment Banking Industry*, Boston, Harvard University Press, 1983.

3 Alan Morrison & William Wilhelm, *Investment Banking. Institutions, Politics and Law*, Oxford, Oxford University Press, 2007.

4 Richard Roberts, *Inside International Finance*, London, Orion Business Books, 1998 [Chapter 3: "International commercial banking (pp. 46-56); chapter 4: "Global investment banking" (pp. 57-79)]. Also see: Richard Roberts (ed.), *International Financial Centres: Concepts, Development and Dynamics*, Aldershot, Edward Elgar, 1994.

5 Richard Roberts, "What's in a name? Merchants, merchant bankers, accepting houses, issuing houses, industrial bankers and investment bankers", *Business History*, 35/3, 1993, pp. 22-38.

and circumstances. The underlying evolutionary approach will help us putting together all various chapters and cases in a coherent frame. As we all know, investment banking took the stage during the last years of financial turmoil, raising worries and being blamed for the part it took in the crisis. Many voices have been calling for a tougher regulation of this segment of the financial industry, though, more recently, others have been arguing for lower controls and supervision, especially major investment banks, which claimed for their peculiar functions and specific status.

Investment banks are today in the eye of a storm, of an extensive and devastating crisis. They had huge responsibilities in igniting it, and a part of the public opinion blames them for the derailment of the world economy from "Main Street toward Wall Street", and for all the consequences such a turn has had. Some of them, such as Bear Stearns and Lehman Brothers,[6] paid a steep price for it, though nothing compared to the huge costs the crisis imposed to so many countries. This notwithstanding, nothing of what happened in the last few years was implicit in their very original nature, in intrinsically distorted mechanisms of management of a risky business. The choice of many investment banks to venture in highly risky operations is due to the historical evolution of the banking industry as a whole and to relevant institutional changes, that can be understood in the light of the historical evolution of the industry during the last thirty or forty years. The current crisis has been ascribed to the greedy sharks swallowing the fundamentals of capitalism and even of the market economy. Nonetheless, we think a better explanation lies in structural and operational changes in the financial industry that increasingly weakened global capitalism because they did not provide for protection nets and disincentives to adopt hazardous behaviours and to build major conflicts of interests, finally resulting in huge information asymmetries.

Here we would emphasise two main aspects that we consider particularly relevant in the understanding of the past and, in its light, of the present, too. They indeed emerge more or less explicitly in all the contributions to the book, and seem to have had an important role in shaping the peculiar evolutions of investment banking in the various contexts. The first one is regulation, also meant as the interaction between banks and non-bank institutions and the financial markets. The second one is the deeper and deeper chasm that might divide the "real" from the "financial" economy. The processes of steep "financialisation" of the economy can lead to the accumulation of distortions in the propensity to invest, shorten the investors' time horizon, and subvert the "natural" and sound

6 Alan Greenberg (with Mark Singer), *The Rise and Fall of Bear Stearns*, New York, Simon & Schuster, 2010. Peter Chapman, *Lehman Brothers, 1844-2008. The Last of the Imperious Rich*, New York, Portfolio Penguin, 2010.

hierarchy of the industrial and financial capital yields, and the prospects of the programmes of investments into manufacturing or services infrastructures. Investment banks place themselves on the faulty lines, they can contribute to stitch up as well as they can widen the divide between the two worlds. The history of finance of modern industrial capitalism shows alternate phases of conjunction and disjunction.

Investment banks do have some common features: they have usually enjoyed wide degrees of freedom in their activities, wider than those granted to banks; the long-lived ones were founded by merchant-bankers at the end of the 19th century, or even before, and they kept many of their original characters over time, in particular their specialisation in activities such as corporate finance,[7] corporate control, originating, issuing, underwriting and trading financial assets, etc.; they have seldom entered the business of deposit taking; they have often been protagonists in promoting financial innovations connected with market activities, a role that became progressively more relevant since banks had been excluded from regularly and massively operating on the stock exchanges, or in those countries where the universal bank had been banned.

These being the scope and framework "defining" investment banks, their evolutionary paths show an increasing variety of patterns over time and places, that further deepened differences among national cases. Why was that? Some hypothesis can be suggested, in the light of the chapters contributing to this book. Investment banks playing a growing role in granting highly specialised services and funds to industrial companies were confined to some countries, where a few but relevant institutional conditions were present: financial markets were able to grow bigger and deeper, not being constrained by strict regulation on monetary fluxes; state bonds did not have relevant effects of crowding out; markets for corporate control were relatively open and contestable, transparency and publicity of information relatively high.

In the last decades of the 20th century many things have changed. The demise of the Bretton Woods' system put an end to the long run stability of the monetary variables resulting in the diffusion and increase of risks, both on credit activities and on financial trading operations. The necessity to handle higher risks fostered financial innovation aimed at securing against them, and triggered an increase in the volume of hedging operations that eventually had the effect of boosting risk. The development of the markets for future contracts and other derivatives resulted in an opportunity of growth for investment banks and other similar financial intermediaries. Deregulation then was a further

---

[7] See Jonathan Barron Baskin, *A History of Corporate Finance*, Cambridge, Cambridge University Press, 1997, 1999 & 2003.

incentive to the growth of this kind of activities and services. More recently in some countries, especially in the US, investment banks transformed into big corporations, characterised by large dimension in terms of capital, asset volumes, number of employees, scope: many among them became multi-business firms and global players. The variety of 'flavours' of investment bankers, the differences in the craft are grown further.

2. Investment banking as leverage to financing firms

One of the most important differences among financial systems is probably the way by which firms' extraordinary financial operations are organised and realised. In this respect, as recent literature points out, financial systems are relevant in order to shaping, at least to some extent, various corporate governance national models.[8] Above all, firms need financial intermediaries during the most difficult phases of discontinuity in their life cycle, such as crisis, merger and acquisitions, changes affecting their major shareholders or management, active or passive takeovers, critical readjustment processes to contrast dramatic environmental changes (for example, typically, technological/product or market changes).[9] Under these circumstances, financial intermediaries enable firms to overcome such a difficult phases assuring them long term resources and stability, both in their capital structure and management. These functions are generally exerted by financial institutions whose main characteristics can vary according to the specific functional and regulatory structures of the national systems.[10] From this point of view, it does not matter whether the financial system is a market oriented or a bank oriented one: Market and bank oriented financial systems[11] have broadly the same functions, even if they act very differently and, indeed, they reach non homogenous degrees of success in providing resources to the economy, both to micro- and to macro-levels. Even though along

---

8 See Asli Demurgiuç-Kunt and Ross Levine (eds.), *Financial Structure and Economic Growth. A Cross Country Comparison of Banks, Markets, and Development*, Cambridge (Mass.), MIT Press, 2000. Franklin Allen and Douglas Gale, *Comparing Financial Systems*, Cambridge (Mass.), MIT Press, 2000.

9 See Mary O'Sullivan, "Finance and Innovation", in Jan Fagerberg, David Mowery and Richard Nelson (eds.), *The Oxford Handbook of Innovation*, Oxford, Oxford University Press, 2005.

10 See Bernard Amable, *The Diversity of Modern Capitalism*, Oxford, Oxford University Press, 2003.

11 See Daniel Verdier, *Moving Money. Banking and Finance in the Industrialized World*, Cambridge, Cambridge University Press, 2002. Douglas Forsyth & Daniel Verdier (eds.), *The Origins of National Financial Systems. Alexander Gerschenkron reconsidered*, London, Routledge, 2003.

different ways and methods, both these systems need special intermediaries for attaining a more efficient functioning of markets and firms.[12]

Probably, it is possible to attribute a part of responsibility to the financial system which has not been able to provide resources to new firms and emerging technologies. The relationship bias implicit in the merchant banking activities in Continental Europe has had some role in rationing credit to emerging entrepreneurs and sectors: indeed, a sharp contrast with the Schumpeterian attitude supposed to be the cornerstone of the banking activities.[13] During the 1950s and the early 1960s large industrial firms could finance medium and long-term investments essentially by self financing or, especially in Italy, through the domestic bonds market. From the late 1960s, instead, large firms needed more external financial support and French and Italian banking systems became to diverge: the first one modified its regulatory architecture in 1965, with a new banking law which allowed universal banks to operate, even if *banques d'affaires* – such as the most prestigious Lazard, Paribas or Indosuez – continued to exert their role. The second one did not modify its fundamental banking law and long term finance was exclusively committed to the so-called "*istituti di credito speciale*", such as *Istituto Mobiliare Italiano* (IMI) and Mediobanca, a well international linked institution and probably the only real merchant bank in Italy. Due to the lack of an effective market for corporate control, supporting firms' long-term growth and dynamic efficiency was assured by these merchant banking institutions, through issuing bonds or equity capital, providing advisory assistance in merger and acquisition, consulting for long term strategic alliances (both for financial or production and technological goals), assuring ownership or management turn over *vis-à-vis* firms' difficulties or crisis.

3. Specialisation vs. despecialisation

Traditional banking activity, that performed by merchant-bankers between the 18th century and the beginning of the 19th century, is basically un unspecialised activity in the sense that every banker would enter any financial business he is able to, unless he finds a comparative advantage in specialisation (e.g. in financing international trade, or in issuing activities), or he is constrained by institutional or consuetudinary restrictions,

---

12 As stated in Franklin Allen and Douglas Gale, *Comparing Financial Systems*, *op. cit.* This does not mean, of course, that every firm or sector need in the same measure external finance for growing, as underlined by Raghuram Rajan and Luigi Zingales, "Financial Dependence and Growth", *American Economic Review*, Vol. 88, 1998, No. 3, pp. 559-586.

13 Carlota Perez, *Technological Revolutions and Financial Capital*, Cheltenham, Elgar, 2002.

or finally by regulation. The institutionalisation of banking that took place around the mid-19th century, known as 'financial revolution' made some of those bankers gradually leave the old business to become promoters of new banks in the form of joint-stock companies, gathering deposits, mobilising them and lending on large scale. From then on, others further specialised their competences and skills to become 'pure' financiers.

These banking intermediaries had their particular traditions and features. They evolved over time according to practices, scope, and techniques in the United States, in Great Britain and in Continental Europe. The range of functions has been historically exerted by New York "investment banks" in United States, London "merchant banks" in Great Britain[14] and "*banques d'affaires*" in France, while in the rest of Continental Europe had been generally attributed to universal banks – even if some *Privat Banken* did assume activities in investment banking (Oppenheim, Bleichröder, Warburg, etc.).

It is worthy to observe that, nevertheless, the role played by these institutions in the international markets – in order to finance international trade, underwriting foreign and domestic public debts, organising syndicates for equity issuing or structured financing, etc. – induced the formation, so to speak, of a common stock of knowledge and the sharing of similar practices and techniques.

Moreover, this process of sharing worldwide instruments and techniques had naturally been enhanced by the cosmopolite character of the investment and merchant bankers.[15] It may be enough to remember, for example, that a German merchant banker, Paul Warburg, was the real promoter of the Federal Reserve after the 1907 crisis and of the Glass-Steagall Act during the Great Depression,[16] or similarly, after the second world war, that a French banker, André Meyer, was a prominent figure of the New York scene[17] until the 1970s and almost in the same period a German banker, Sigmund Warburg, was a leading

14 Joseph Wechsberg, *The Merchant Bankers*, New York, Pocket Books, 1986. Bo Bramsen & Kathleen Wain, *The Hambros, 1779-1979*, London, 1979. Stanley Chapman, *The Rise of Merchant Banking*, London, 1984. Kathleen Burk, *Morgan Grenfell, 1838-1988. The Biography of a Merchant Bank*, Oxford University Press, 1989-1990. Richard Roberts, *Schroders. Merchant and Bankers*, London, MacMillan, 1992. Jehanne Wake, *Kleinwort Benson. The History of Two Families in Banking*, Oxford University Press, 1997. Niall Ferguson, *The World's Banker. The History of the House of Rothschild*, London, Weidenfeld & Nicolson, 1998. Niall Ferguson, *The House of Rothschild. Money's Prophets, 1798-1848*, London & New York, Penguin Books, 1998.

15 Youssef Cassis, *La City de Londres, 1870-1914*, Paris, Belin, 1987. Youssef Cassis, *Les banquiers de la City à l'époque édouardienne, 1890-1914*, Geneva, Droz, 1984.

16 See Ron Chernow, *The Warburgs*, New York, Random House, 1993.

17 See Cary Reich, *Financier. The Biography of André Meyer*, New York, Wiley and Sons, 1983.

and innovative London banker.[18] A number of investment and merchant banks have had a typical transnational origin, structure and history: the Rothschilds had a five-countries structure from the early 19th century, being present in Frankfurt, Vienna, Paris, London and Naples; the Morgans operated on the two sides of the Atlantic with JP Morgan in New York and Morgan Grenfell in London; similarly, the Lazards were established in New York, Paris and London; the Warburgs were based in Hamburg but had strong personal links with the Kuhn Loeb of New York and, after the Second World War, SG Warburg became a brilliant operator in London; from the beginnings Paribas used three bases in Paris, Amsterdam and Brussels.[19]

Investment and merchant banks were generally independent intermediaries in financial systems in which a credit specialisation principle is affirmed. Otherwise, universal or mixed banks played more or less the same role *vis-à-vis* financed firms by relating to them along side the position of a "*Hausbank*", according to a scheme of long term inside relations: according to some scholars, this kind of scheme was more effective in promoting the long run growth of industrial firms through a better screening and monitoring of the borrowers.[20] Our study therefore determines why and how these networks of relationship were more developed and active by the investment banks than by the commercial banks, why they were more able to confront the asymetry of information about projects requiring huge amount of middle and long term money, although the commercial banks did practice "industrial finance", e.g. intensified their relations with a core of key entreprise clients and accompanied them on the long run for their banking and financial needs. Why did the process of "specialisation"[21] take shape in several countries on several periods and led to a somewhat binary[22] division of tasks within the banking system?

---

18 Jacques Attali, *Sir Siegmund Warburg, 1902-1982. Un homme d'influence*, Paris, Fayard, 1985. Niall Ferguson, *High Financier: The Lives and Time of Siegmund Warburg*, London, 2010.

19 Éric Bussière, *Paribas, l'Europe et le monde, 1872-1992*, Anvers, Fonds Mercator, 1992.

20 Charles W. Calomiris, "The Costs of Rejecting Universal Banking: American Finance in the German Mirror, 1870-1914", in Naomi Lamoreaux & Daniel Raff (eds.), *Coordination and Information: Historical perspectives on the Organization of Enterprise*, Chicago, University of Chicago Press, 1995, pp. 257-315.

21 See Maurice Lévy-Leboyer, "La spécialisation des établissements bancaires", in Fernand Braudel & Ernest Labrousse (eds.), *Histoire économique et sociale de la France*, Paris, PUF, III, first volume, 1976.

22 If we don't consider local banks (saving banks, cooperative banks, petty family banking), which constituted everywhere a third (and influent) sector of the banking system.

For instance in Britain, commercial banks[23] enlivened their own deposit banking activities instead of competing directly with merchant banks. Even in West-Germany, the decline of the *Privat Banken* in the first third of the 20th century[24] was followed in the 1950s-1970s by the emergence of mixed banking[25] with a large part dedicated to "*banque d'affaires à la française*", that is a mixture of commercial banking and investment banking – even with actual proprietary investments in the equity of large customers.[26]

Our chapters achieved thus some kind of a process of "disaggregation" of investment banks' portfolio of skills in order to gauge their key specialties. Using present models of analysis of banking activities, we determine how much difference appeared in the past between investment banks and commercial banks, what was the degree of specialisation for each key sector of activity. Several questions have been raised: Did investment banks assume a key role in the structuration of the economy of their country and thus assume a "historical function" within its banking system? What was their "historical usefulness" or even "necessity" as a leverage to growth and as parts of the financial machinery? As tools or lubricants to help money to "circulate" (from piled up assets to investing facilities or to financial markets) and to be "transformed" (from short term cash to middle and long term investments)? Such key questions find answers throughout the various chapters there.

Sure, regulation, monetary policies and overall economic policies of the State were equally or more important in the building of each

23 See Margaret Ackrill & Leslie Hannah, *Barclays. The Business of Banking, 1690-1996*, Cambridge, Cambridge University Press, 2001. Weyer Vander, *Falling Eagle: The Decline of Barclays Bank*, London, Weidenfeld & Nicolson, 2000. J.R. Winton, *Lloyds Bank, 1918-1969*, London, Oxford University Press, 1982. A.R. Holmes & Edwin Green, *Midland. 150 Years of Banking Business*, London, Batsford, 1986. Michael Collins & Forrest Capie, "Industrial lending by English commercial banks, 1860s-1914: Why did banks refuse loans?", *Business History*, Vol. 38, No. 1, 1996, pp. 26-44. David Kynaston, *City of London: Illusions of Gold, 1914-1945*, London, Chatto & Windus, 1999. Bernardo Batiz-Lazo & Douglas Wood, "A case study on the strategy and stock market performance of Lloyds Bank Group, 1980-1993", *Journal of European Financial Services*, 4(1), 2000, pp. 31-63.

24 Youssef Cassis, "Banque et industrie en Grande-Bretagne et en Allemagne, 1870-1939", *Entreprises et histoire*, No. 2, 1992, pp. 7-18.

25 See Harold Wixforth & Dieter Ziegler, "Bankenmacht: Universal banking and German industry in Historical perspective", in Youssef Cassis, Gerald Feldman & Ulf Olsson (eds.), *The Evolution of Financial Institutions Markets in 20th century Europe*, Aldershot, Ashgate, 1995. Caroline Fohlin, "Universal banking in pre-World War I Germany: Model and myth", *Explorations in Economic History*, 36, 1999, pp. 305-343.

26 Lothar Gall, Gerald Feldman, Harold James, Carl-Ludwig Holtfrerich & Hans Büschgen, *The Deutsche Bank, 1870-1995*, London, Weidenfeld & Nicolson, 1995.

banking system, whilst the process of internationalisation and integration of the markets (foreign exchange, international credit, stock exchanges, then futures markets or else) fixed the background for banking and finance activities. But, within such patterns, specialised investment banks became among the main developers of the banking system, owing to the transformation of "ancient banks" into "modern banks" (French *maisons de Haute Banque* joining into Paribas or *Banque de l'union parisienne*;[27] British merchants banks into investment banking business, US investment bank houses contributing to the building of big corporate banks, etc.) or institutions created from scratch thanks to financiers and institutional investors – like Italian *Mediobanca*.

4. From specialisation to differentiation: Business models challenged

In 2008, arguments among economists challenged the re-establishment of the "business model" of "universal banking" which had been suspended by national laws (US Glass-Steagall act in 1933, Swiss and Belgian laws in 1934-1935, French 1941-1946 laws, etc.) or limited by cultural and historical habits separating banks alongside patterns of liquidity, in the UK or in Germany. New impetus has been thus be given to reflections about the "business model" of investment banking ("*banque de financement et d'investissement*" or "*banque d'affaires*", in French; "merchant banking" in the UK, etc.). Historians have therefore to take part to the present debates and bring their contribution through analysis of the very nature, the portfolio of skills, the corporate culture, the advantage edge, of investment banks.

A first flow of books had been published in the 1960s-1970s, which provided a first mainframe for a comprehensive understanding of the factual history of investment banks. Since then a fresh flow of researches gathered momentum, thanks to new generations of historians (and economists), to the access to large amounts of archives, and even to the collection of testimonies. A reconsideration of the history of investment banking seemed relevant, through the confrontation of historians and economists, and of national histories, through the assessment of the degree of internationalisation of investment banks and thus of the reality of a money and banking market within a transatlantic business community, then at the scale of a worldwide and now globalised business community. Key issues could be: Was there a business model of internationalised investment bank? How much

27 Hubert Bonin, *La Banque de l'union parisienne (1874/1904-1974). De l'Europe aux outre-mers*, Paris, Publications de la SFHOM, 2011.

investment bankers were able to be "ground-setters", "path-breakers", "trendsetters", or "rainmakers" of national and international economy and growth? What core competences were those of investment bankers?

Banking history has considerably benefited from numerous individual and collective studies: deposit banking, merchant banking, family banking, local and regional banking, and thematic approaches (industrial banking, etc.) complemented such breakthroughs. But investment banking might seem to have escaped to such deepening of knowledge and analysis – beyond the fate of merchants or investment banks about which monographs have already been published (Kleinwort-Benson, Schroders, Morgan Grenfell, Goldman Sachs, Lazard, Baring,[28] etc., and in France: *Banque de l'union parisienne*, Paribas and a few merchant houses of the *Haute Banque*[29] community). In the meanwhile anyway, micro-economists did gauge the business model of investment banking, their portfolio of "functions", their leverage force on the range of commercial, market and merchant banking, their part on the big banking and financial places, which can lead banking historians to a better understanding of these issues between the past and the present times.

Such issues may join one key issue, about "differentiation". We mean there the distinction between commercial banks and investment banks. The present krach revealed how far commercial banks did practice what is commonly called "investment banking", that is commitment to

28 Peter Austin, *Baring Brothers and the Birth of Global Finance*, London, Pickering & Chatto, 2007.

29 David Landes, "Vieille banque et banque nouvelle: la révolution financière du dix-neuvième siècle", *Revue d'histoire moderne*, III, July-September 1956, pp. 204-222. Herbert Lüthy and Alain Plessis, *Mallet frères et Cie: deux cent cinquante ans de banque*, Paris, Mallet, 1963. Bertrand Gille, *Histoire de la maison Rothschild (1817-1870)*, Geneva, Droz, 1965 & 1967. Jean-François Belhoste & Henri Rouquette, *La maison Seillière-Demachy, banque de l'industrie et du commerce depuis le XVIIIe siècle*, Paris, Floch, 1977. Jean Bouvier, *Les Rothschild*, Paris, Fayard, 1967; second edition, Brussels, Complexe, 1985. Christian Grand, *Trois siècles de banque. De Neuflize, Schlumberger, Mallet, de 1667 à nos jours*, Paris, E/P/A Éditions, 1991. Frédéric Barbier, *Finance et politique. La dynastie des Fould, XVIIIe-XXe siècles*, Paris, Armand Colin, 1991. Jacques Wolff, *Les Perier. La fortune et les pouvoirs*, Paris, Economica, 1993. Geneviève Daridan, *MM. Le Couteulx et Cie, banquiers à Paris. Un clan familial dans la crise du XVIIIe siècle*, Paris, Loysel, 1994. Robert Hentsch, *Hentsch. Banquiers à Genève et à Paris au XIXe siècle*, Paris, self-edition, 1996. Alain Plessis, "Une maison de la Haute Banque parisienne: les Mirabaud et le financement des entreprises de la fin du XIXe siècle à la Seconde Guerre mondiale", in Philippe Marguerat, Laurent Tissot & Yves Froidevaux (eds.), *Banques et entreprises industrielles en Europe de l'Ouest, XIXe-XXe siècles*, Geneva, Droz, 2000, pp. 239-250. Isabelle Chancelier, *Messieurs Mirabaud et Cie. D'Aigues-Vives à Paris, via Genève et Milan*, Paris, Éditions familiales, 2001. Alain Plessis, "The Parisian '*Haute Banque*' and the international economy in the nineteenth and early twentieth centuries", in Youssef Cassis & Philip Cottrell (eds.), *The World of Private Banking*, London, Ashgate, 2010, pp. 127-140.

financial markets (proprietary trading, M&A, secondary markets) beyond their classical portfolio of commercial banking dedicated to companies, that is "corporate banking". On several periods of banking history (and also business history), bank managers often followed "fads",[30] along with sheepish trends or herding behiavours. Some chapters ponder how far deposit and commercial banks did practice investment banking whilst extending their range of services in corporate banking, to propose them the engineering of schemes about project financing, issuing of securities, international credits, middle and long term banking or financial products adapted to the development of equipments and investments – which had been the "prehistoric" purpose of new types of investment banking in the mid-19th century, to supply means of growth to emerging big firms of the first industrial revolution (1780s-1880s).

5. The "originality" of investment banking?

Such arguments about differentiation cannot but foster reflections about the historical "necessity" of investment banking will also be a key issue. Despite the recent trend towards "universal banking" on one side, and towards "financialisation", on the other side, which somewhat short-circuited banking intermediation from the 1980s in favour of investment funds and direct access to stock exchanges, our book assess how investment bankers – within universal banks or elsewhere – preserved their ability of being influential and active on the markets of mergers & acquisitions, of project financing, in issuing. Despite the building of huge corporate and investment banking bodies (mainly in the US, with a very few "national champions" in each European countries and in Japan), the resurgence of "*boutiques*" – little investment banks – in the 21st century draws attention to such an issue of the "necessity" of investment bankers. This led our book to a long term argument about the "usefulness" of investment banking, to determine in conclusion why such competences kept momentum through three industrial revolutions, and also through the various stages of banking history and even through what we can call "banking revolutions".[31] At each period of growth or at each cyclical "boom", new instruments to act on the fields of financial markets and medium-long term credit were set up, and new actors were created by speculators, feeling the windows of opportunities for profit, and more frequently by innovators or

---

30 See Hubert Bonin, "Fashion trends in banking business models since the 1850s", *Business & Economic History On-Line*, Vol. 7, 2009 <http://www.thebhc.org/publications/BEHonline/2009/beh2009.html>.

31 Hubert Bonin, "Peut-on parler de révolution bancaire (XIXe-XXe siècles)?", in Éric Bonhomme (ed.), *Les révolutions industrielles et scientifiques à l'époque contemporaine*, Bordeaux, SCEREN-CRDP Aquitaine, 2007, pp. 13-29.

followers of the move: that was the case during the ultimate boom of the first industrial and banking revolutions in France in the 1870s-1880s with a burst of *maisons de Haute Banque*, during the *Gründerzeit* in Germany, during both booms in the US in the 1890s-1900s or in the 1920s, for instance. "Fever" provoked such initiatives on every banking and finance place, all the more that emulation guided ground-setters among "capitals of capital".[32]

Our table there under could appear as an attempt to summarise what paths of differentiation could be followed to identify pure investment banking, investment and corporate banking, and mere commercial banking, along with the various functions and fields of activity – the very issue being that of their "identity" indeed.[33]

Table 1. Towards a process of "disaggregation" of investment banks' portfolio of skills: A first assessment of specialisation

Managing the primary market	issuing and underwriting (as co-lead-managers of syndicates) brokering equity and bonds assessing the market's ability of absorbing fresh financial paper committing insider trading buying the financial press negotiating with the state entertaining networks of family merchant banks, etc. managing special relationship with a few states for bonds issuing
Managing the secondary markets	Trading on equity and bonds Managing of speculative trends, etc. Managing discreetly emerging bids or counter-bids operations Lead-managers of syndicates helping to maintain the value of the equity of enterprises as customers
Money markets management	Managing debt assets and liabilities for customers (with rates risks); swaps of debts FOREX (with exchange risks), swaps of currencies

32 Youssef Cassis, *Capitals of Capital. A History of International Financial Centers, 1780-2005*, Cambridge, Cambridge University Press, 2006. Youssef Cassis, *Les capitales du capital. Histoire des places financières internationales, 1780-2005*, Geneva, Slatkine & Pictet, 2005; Paris, Honoré Champion, 2008.

33 See Éric Bussière, "Les banques d'affaires françaises au xxe siècle: des établissements en quête d'identité?", in Maurice Lévy-Leboyer (ed.), *Les banques en Europe de l'Ouest de 1920 à nos jours*, Paris, Comité pour l'histoire économique & financière de la France, 1995, pp. 223-235.

Assets management	[Linked with the above sectors] Proprietary management of assets Assets management for institutional investors (insurance companies, retirement funds, etc.) Development and management of real estate assets "Research" (financial analysis) and economic studies
Wealth management ("private banking")	In favour of family business, of well established fortunes, of rich managers, etc. Managing inheritance processes within privately-owned companies Managing (blinded or not) investment trusts
Tailor-made advice activities	Mergers and acquisitions advice Managing bids Conceiving structured financement: project financing (huge equipments, plants, ship then planes, etc.) Conceiving syndicated credits Advice in "haut de bilan" operations, banking engineering
Financing innovation	Raising funds to finance: start-up companies innovative specialised credits units companies involved in industrial revolutions
Investing in companies' capital	Practicing industrial finance for proprietary investments [see above] Stabilising the equity of partner companies and being part of their stakeholding Managing financial groups, with industrial and services "partners" or almost "subsidiaries" Helping investors to become stakeholders in companies (today: "private equity investments")
Sustaining internationalisation	Managing Foreign Exchange activities Networking the City (then also in New York or in Asia) Financing and managing the spreading of banking managerial skills on emerging banking markets (Central Europe, colonial areas, Latin America, Asia, etc.) Project Financing [see above]
Taking part to classical corporate commercial banking, but with trends towards:	Financing commodities trading Structuring credits for export or import Conceiving middle and long terms credits

6. Delving into investment banking in the making

Several issues were raised through our book. We applied the methods of business history to banking history, that is we questioned the history of investment banking through the spectrum of issues raised about stakeholders, strategies, internationalisation, innovation, corporate culture, portfolio of management skills, knowledge capital, differentiation, performance, and competitiveness, which required questioning the data and facts accurately. Despite our focus on the relevant balance of the "organisation of firm" and its overall portfolios of strategic activities and of skills, we provided sometimes biographical approaches, to assess how much investment bankers as personalities did orient the fate investment banks, as innovators, go-betweens, managers, financiers, "market markers", etc.

We focused on the portfolio of skills of investment banks along with some kind of "an inside outlook", that is *grosso modo*: How did it function? How did they do it? What was their capital of knowledge and competence? What did characterise actually investment banks in front of deposit banks? This led the authors to determine what achieved an investment banker in his day to day activities, and how he was working (teams, access to information, networks of relationship, links with the State, international minds) and how he used his networks of communication.

But, meanwhile, our collective and comparative investigation considered one key issue: What type of organisation did characterise and today characterise investment banking firms? How managers of such companies succeeded in balancing creativity, reactivity, resiliency, openness to information, trust building, closeness to innovative entrepreneurs, action through moving connections on one side, and the drastic (and classical) management of firm organisation, the building of an array of processes to assess risks, and the development of auditing balance sheets, especially in proprietary trading and proprietary investment portfolios. And such paths were followed to gauge the process of building business models, portfolio of skills and corporate cultures through an evolutive analysis, about each "*Belle Époque*" of booming investment banking.

Classically but methodically, our chapters pondered how investment banking did constitute to the conception and to the development of new financial and banking products. We linked banking history and the history of innovation, because we dedicated studies on the part played by investment banks and a few investment bankers or teams in the emergence and structuration of some activities, like: leasing, specialised credits, industrial banking, collateralisation, mutual funds, financing of real estate development, financing of developing or emerging countries, structured project financing, public-private project financing, the creation and functions of investment funds, etc. We focused on the entertainment of networks of capital, to reconstitute how investment bankers succeeded in mobilising "sleeping" capital, assuming a function of intermediation between wealthy industrialists or estate owners, institutional investors, family entrepreneurs with available cash, then the assets of mutual funds, on one side, and the course of financial markets. How did they exert such a capacity of leverage, within the circuits of capital?

We have indeed to question the role played by investment banks in setting up tools to invest funds into the equity of (quoted or unquoted) firms. Did investment banks became key stakeholders of their national capitalism through direct investment in national companies? How much did they become "financial holdings" or "financial groups" (like in France in the 1960s-1970s)? Did they exert any influence on the industrial or services strategy of their national capitalism and firms? Were they bankers of influence? Or only of intermediation? How did they create, develop and manage investment funds? Did they play a key role in the strategies of customers' firms? Did they control their boards? How did function this interlocking of individuals, finance, influence? Proprietary investment and trading will be a crucial issue. Did investment banks used their own capital (either owned or borrowed) to become global players on the secondary stock trading markets and foster "speculative moves" in order to broaden their revenues? Can we estimate the weight of proprietary trading within the activities of investment banks? How much did they live and earn through such market finance activities? Several chapters enhanced the function of investment banks as cornerstones of financial innovation; the became market makers for many functions: those shown in the previous table, but also, at key stages of the financial history, they especially vitalise and foster the new markets, as they did very recently (OTC, futures; diffusion of derivatives and so forth).

Internationalisation has been one core issue too. We determined how investment banks entertain some specific corporate culture within their country because they were steadfastly oriented toward foreign perspectives, relationships, and markets. We precised whether they were some kind of an "off-shore" pole of services in their country, dedicated to European, transatlantic or worldwide markets; or how much they contributed to the opening of their national economies to internationalised scopes.

Competitiveness drew consideration because, on the long term, the ability of national market places was at stake; the future of the financial power was challenged. We argue about the ability of some market places to keep pace with the changes of the banking industry, to adapt to financial, technological and commercial revolutions. We question thus the frailness of investment banks to keep momentum in front of new competitors; and we determine whether the size and prosperity of national economies had effects on the existence and the strength of national investment banks: could such banks still be active in countries of which the economy was declining? In contrary, were all powerful countries destined to be equipped with powerful investment banks? The apex then the decline of British merchant banks, the fate of German and Swiss investment banking between *Privat Banken* and universal banks, the uncertainty about Dutch and Belgian investment banks to keep momentum in face of considerable competition, the rapid upsurge of American investment bankers, the limits to Asian types of investment banking, fuel analysis.

Banking "business models" mobilised the book, because the competitiveness and performance of investment banks relied on the relevance of their strategy, on the efficiency of their organisation, and on the effectiveness of their management. Monographs and comparative studies can help determine "the best ways" to get relevant business models at investment banks, perhaps also in comparison with deposit banks.

The durability of the model of family investment banking has been gauged, in order to determine how the capital of skills and relationships could be renewed within family banks, or had to be transmit to larger institutions – as in France when merchant banks (*Haute Banque* houses) created large investment banks. What business model could preserve the existence and competitiveness of family investment banks?

The importance of investment banking within deposit banking drew attention to precise how much competence in issuing, brokerage and M&A had been acquired by specialised divisions of deposit banks. Such a trend towards "universal banking", within managerial or law limits, will be somewhat analysed, explained and assessed.

The key roles assumed by investment banks in the development of national economies and in their involvement into international markets led to crucial positions within the circles of national power. Our book reconstituted the relations between investment banks and national authorities, to precise how much they exerted influence on the State or political circles, how much the State could orient they choices, for instance in favour of the reinforcement of the national economy and companies.

Banking economic models are presently at stake: "universal banking" and "specialised banking" are once more been challenged during the crisis of the recent years 2007-2008, even with the Glass-Steagall Act reconsidered. Historians will thus contribute to the debate through arguments about investment banking portfolio of skills, range of risks, and business models – therefore fuelling analysis about the firm organisation, governance and strategy, and about patterns of business management in banking – mixing banking history and business history, and the institutionalised economy of the firm too.

Such issues allow a comprehensive approach to the history of investment banking. Comparative approaches were tackled, long term considerations also. But monographs and moreover biographies play a significative role in a few chapters. Fresh access to archives and/or testimonies foster several developments, in order to renew our understanding of the innovations of path-breaking bankers and the key role on several market-places of trendsetters. One key originality of our book might be the confrontation of historians and of economists, to ponder about the business models, the strategies, the issue of universal banking, etc.

Chapter 2

Summaries

Janette Rutterford

Sir Everard Hambro, born in 1842, was a fourth generation banker who held a dominant position in the London banking world during the late nineteenth and early twentieth centuries. He died in 1925, with net wealth of £2,132,340 [*Financial Times*, 20 April 1925]. Hambro was a personal friend of John-Pierpoint Morgan, the American investment banker, helping him to recruit Clinton Dawkins as a partner in the British Morgan firm, J.P. Morgan. However, Hambro's attitude to helping British industry was very different from that of his American counterpart. For a limited number of British companies seeking to raise finance on the stock market, Hambro provided legal, financial and Stock Exchange regulatory expertise but did not build up long-term relationships with the directors of the companies involved, nor did he invest personally in these concerns. This chapter explores in detail Everard Hambro's input into two new issues of London-based firms: Thames Ironworks in 1899 and Trollope, Colls & Co. in 1903. This is done by using archives which include correspondence between Hambro and the chairmen of the two companies, as well as draft prospectuses and press cuttings. The chapter first looks at the input of Hambro into the following aspects of the Thames Ironworks & Trollope, Colls & Co. new issues: capital structure, disclosure of financial and other information in the prospectus; the role of the broker, and underwriting and new issue costs. It then compares Hambro's role with that of J.P. Morgan in the US, and concludes with a brief analysis of Hambro's personal investments in the context of investments in British industry.

Peter Hertner

Railways, invented during the earlier part of the 19th century, were an essential tool of transport and communication during the following decades. By the 1880s practically each angle of Europe had been opened up through their construction. In South-Eastern Europe this process had started during the 1870s, and by 1888 Constantinople/Istanbul could be reached by rail from Paris or Vienna. There were, however, still large gaps in the transport system of this part of the continent. The chapter tries to show how a railway line was eventually built between 1893 and 1896 which was to link Salonica/Thessaloniki to Dedeagatch/Alexandroupolis. Thus a Southern connection through Eastern Macedonia and Western Thrace with the Ottoman capital city was created. The two most important founders of this railway company were the Imperial Ottoman bank, essentially an Anglo-French institution, and *Banque de Paris et des Pays-Bas*. A third important partner was the Frankfurt private banking house of Bethmann Brothers. With the British partners refusing at the end to participate in this venture the bank became rather a Franco-German affair with the French side dominating the matter. The *Compagnie du chemin de fer ottoman Jonction Salonique-Constantinople*, as it was finally called, was founded as an Ottoman company in March 1893 with the issue of a huge amount of bonds and a rather small part of shares, only 7.2 per cent of the entire capital. Construction and running of the railway were handed over to the Paris-based *Régie générale pour la construction et l'exploitation de chemins de fer*, a prominent French group which had built railways all over Europe. The entire business could not have been started without a sizeable kilometrical guarantee offered by the Ottoman state, a guarantee which was also granted at different levels to the other Ottoman railway companies, almost all of them financed by Western European – French, German, British – capital. The aim of the Ottoman authorities, connected with the concessions given to the *Jonction Salonique-Constantinople* railway company, was above all strategic: thus, in the case of an armed conflict, troops from Anatolia could be rushed to all possible war theatres in the Balkans. As a matter of fact, this was done successfully during the war with Greece in 1896. Until 1911 the *Jonction Salonique-Constantinople* developed slowly and its profit situation remained more modest than the results of the other two railway companies built by foreign capital in the European South-East (not counting Rumania). One of the reasons for this must have been the fact that navigation on the Mediterranean remained a strong competitor for this railway company. Everything changed during and as a result of the two Balkan wars in 1912-13: The Ottoman Empire lost most of its European possessions and the line ended up to be situated on territories handed over to Greece and Bulgaria. As was to be expected, the share and bond holders had to negotiate with these two powers, and it took them more than a year to get at least part of the money claimed. WWI, the 1929-33 economic crisis and then WWII complicated everything and it took another fifty years to find a compromise which seems to have given at least a partial compensation for the *Jonction Salonique-Constantinople* bondholders. Through this case study, the chapter determines how investment banking worked concretely in a sector, the railways, which proved to be fundamental for economic growth during most of the 19th century, along cross-borders projects joining Berlin and Vienna places and Eastern and Balkanic Europe. First, the overall issues of financing railway infrastructures are recalled, which opened doors to "project financing" design at investment banks, relying on their teams of experts, engineers and financiers. Second, the various types and origins of banking stakeholders have been precised, through the balance of power between European places and big banks of the second half of the century and the turn of the 20th century. But, thirdly, the chapter insists on the permanent *modus operandi* within the communities of banking and business competing to gain contracts, concessions, building and equipment orders, and, finally, finance issues and banking credits. On one side, competition prevailed, but connections were established among the competitors to share information and alleviate the load borne by each bank, thanks to syndicates. The organisation and way of life of these latter are scrutinised, and the chapter insists on the close cooperation between "old bank", that is the merchant banks at the apex of their role on a European level, and "new banks", the joint-stock firms which scrambled for issuing and distribution missions throughout the successive project financing operations to be conceived. The portfolio of skills of investment bankers are therefore detailed and assessed, to contribute to insights into the very nature and function of investment banking.

Juan Flores

The historiography on the Baring crisis, both in Britain and Argentina, is vast and rich. The interactions between banks in Europe on the one hand, and the national, provincial and municipal governments in Argentina, on the other, have been described and analysed in a number of works since the very moment of the crisis. The cycle of capital flows to the so-called "new countries" experienced an inflexion point in 1885. During this year, a currency crisis erupted in Argentina, ending the gold standard regime that had been set up only two years before. Far from deterring new capital to be invested in Argentina, the effect was precisely the opposite. The true boom of foreign investment to the country really took off during that year, and peaked in 1888 before its sudden collapse in 1889 and mainly in 1890. This chapter aims to explain this apparent paradox through an analysis of London's underwriting strategies, their business structure and their risk management. Their implication in the issuing of bonds also affected investors' risk perception. In particular, the involvement of Baring, the historical underwriter of Argentina's bonds in London, was regarded as a seal of approval by financial markets. However, overindebtedness in Argentina, along with political instability and a number of external shocks contributed to freeze the demand for new bonds, triggering thereby Baring's own fall in 1890. We argue that despite the general environment of competition between underwriting banks, in 1885 they colluded to impose on Argentina a set of conditions to continue borrowing. Among them, two conditions were particularly relevant, one related to Argentina's fiscal policy and another on the suspension of new external borrowing. Financial markets' reacted positively to the announcement of the agreement, although in the medium term none of these conditions were met. Moreover, they served to open up Europe's capital markets to Argentina's provinces and municipalities. We speculate on the possible perception of the market on Baring's acting as a lender of last resort to Argentina.

Piet Geljon & Ton de Graaf

In this chapter, investment banking is defined as including the following activities: new issue business, both national and international; securities trading and holding of securities portfolio's; investment advice and fund/asset management; advice and intermediation regarding company formations, mergers, acquisitions and restructuring (corporate finance); special forms of credit and financial innovation. The origin of the Dutch securities sector lies with the establishment of the VOC (United East India Company) in 1602, the shares of which were traded on the exchange. The wealth accumulated by the Dutch merchants was later on used for the granting of loans to foreign sovereigns or countries. Among a number of merchants/bankers active in this field, Hope & Co. gained prominence, in particular with its Russian loans. The decline in commerce and industry, followed by the French occupation in 1795, was a severe blow to the financial activities. After 1815 international issues became rare. As far as domestic issues occurred banking or securities houses were not used; subscriptions took place via a notary public or the Nederlandsche Bank (in particular state loans). The stock exchange continued its activities, including trading in the new shares and bonds. Since 1774 also investment funds were known. From about 1860 economic growth in the Netherlands started to accelerate and gradually an industrialisation process took place. The Dutch remained active investors, in particular abroad, but given the relative size of the economy they could only occupy a minor place internationally. Domestic issue activity increased slowly, but began to grow after the turn of the century. The stock exchange flourished with a.o. American and Russian railway companies. New banks were also established (Rotterdamsche Bank, Amsterdamsche Bank), which under foreign influence Crédit mobilier) combined from the beginning commercial banking (deposits and credits) with new issues and securities trading. Institutions that were initially active in another field, ventured in the securities business to increase their profitability (the pure commercial bank Twentsche Bank, the trading company Nederlandsche Handel-Maatschappij). Apart from Amsterdamsche Bank, which became prominent in the new issue business, smaller private banking houses developed investment banking activities of various kinds. Already before 1914 a banking concentration movement had started, in which the bigger commercial banks not only spread over the whole country by taking over local banks/cashiers, but also strengthened their position in the securities business by mergers with older firms. The revival of economic activity after WWI caused an increase in the demand for capital, both in the form of bank credits and new issues. The ensuing crisis of 1921/1922 led to heavy problems for the most expansionary banks. In this period there were many newcomers in the securities business, mostly smaller firms, but also the Dutch overseas banks expanded in this field. In the 1920s, the Netherlands as a political stable and liberal country acted as a save haven for foreign capital. For a short period the international accepting business flourished. Foreign issues on the Dutch capital market also grew substantially. The turmoil of the 1930s brought largely an end to these international activities, while also domestic issues decreased strongly. After WWII, investment banking activities were restricted by regulation of the capital market and of international capital flows. As the economy gathered steam after a number of years and personal wealth rose rapidly, the emphasis fell on the expansion of banking services for the general public. As a result, even those banks that were rather strongly involved in investment banking tried to expand in commercial banking. So, what specialisation still existed disappeared and the general banking concept gained more and more ground. From the 1960s, however, the securities business was rather depressed and banks even thought of ending this activity. All this changed in the 1980s. The economic boom, together with the liberalisation of financial markets, led to a renewed and very strong expansion of investment banking activities, further stimulated by strong rises in share prices. New players appeared, both from abroad and domestically, where new financial conglomerates were formed. As a result, investment banking activities were more and more performed by big units within financial groups, which competed heavily with each other and with foreign institutions. As a result of the financial crises, over the past few years a completely new situation has arisen in investment banking. Conglomerates had to be split up, new groups were formed and new regulations were introduced. As yet, the situation is still not completely cleared up and the prospects of investment banking remain uncertain.

Hubert Bonin

The chapter is focused on the function of French investment banks as "pathbreakers" to accompany and stimulate the rebirth of French economy after WWII. First it finds out why investment banks escaped to the move of nationalisation which was achieved in 1944-1946 and which involve Banque de France, banks and insurance companies. The balance of powers, the networks of influence, the commitment of investment bankers to the rebuilding of France within an internationalised economy, and the issue of the connections to be re-established with the City and the US bankers and financiers are at stake through the scrutiny. Second, it assesses the strengths and weaknesses of investment banks (Paribas, Banque de l'union parisienne, Rothschild, Lazard), precises the emergence of new competitors (Banque de l'Indochine, the Jack Francès group, etc.), and as a consequence determines the strategy followed by these players. For example it precises the effects of the nationalisation of numerous big companies and the dwindling of the financial market on their issuing and brokering activities. Third it considers the evolution of the portfolios of strategic activities and skills within the "classical" investment banking services. It gauges their ability to regain momentum in favour of corporate customers (merchant banking, corporate banking), either nationally or internationally. It reconsiders the "path-breaking" activities of investment bankers on the international market of structured finance, as a leverage force of French industrial investments abroad. Fifth, it reconstitutes the competitive edge of investment banks on the imperial/colonial market, and argue about the priorities fixed, either "obsolete strategies" or the involvement of colonial sectors into internationalised and modern business models. Sixth, it tackles the issue of investment bankers as "pioneers" about the new credit and financial products and techniques which were being either transferred mainly from the US or engineered in Paris, as a way to find out new sectors of activity to balance those being assumed by the public institutions, or as a way to establish bridges on promising activities in connection with real estate development, the restart of outlets for bourgeois building, and the construction of the society of affluence.

Carlo Brambilla

The banking crisis of the early 1930s put an end to investment banking in Italy and led to a radical reform that almost "nationalised" the banking system and entrusted state-owned special credit institutions with industrial financing and investments. This chapter traces the development of investment banking in Italy from its appearance in the 1860s to its collapse in the early 1930s. Following shortly other European experiences, big joint stock investment banks played a relevant role both in supporting investments in infrastructures and public utilities, and in fostering the first wave of industrialisation. This chapter argues that the affirmation and consolidation of Italian investment banking was an evolutionary process of innovation aimed at allowing big banks to root in a newly emerging financial system, tweaking to the developments of markets and institutions, as they gradually came forth, mainly in response to crises. Financial innovation, however, was not always attended and steered by "regulative" and "institutional" innovation, thus compelling banks to adapt their strategies to the specific kinds of guarantees and risks they can rely upon and have to cope with. Big universal joint stock banks had to face up to an institutional framework that did not provide incentives for information disclosure by companies, did not limit the speculative attitudes and prices' volatility of the stock exchanges, thus allowing for high degrees of opacity as for the quality of investments and for overly high risks connected with capital investments. Moreover, persistent segmentation of the banking system and the presence of large shares of non-contestable financial intermediaries limited universal banks' external growth and curtailed their ability to collect resources. Big banks' responses to those issues tended to improve capital markets weaknesses and instability, and to expose the banks themselves to liquidity risks and financial crises. Indeed hazardous credit policies and highly risky asset-liability management strategies they adopted in the 1920s transformed universal banks into quasi-holding companies, an "innovation" in the pattern of investment banking that eventually led to its failure in the early 1930s.

Luis J. Coronas-Vida

The 'Six big banks' group, consisting of a genuine investment bank, four mixed-type banks and a commercial bank, dominated the financial sector in Spain until the 1970s. The nature and evolution of this group is analysed and characterised during the interwar period and the Franco regime. Spanish banking grew up in a very protectionist environment in which relations between banks and companies were established in several ways. The big banks of Madrid and Bilbao acquired shares and participated in the launch of some of the most important firms in Spain. Their directors also sat on the boards of numerous companies and exercised voting rights on behalf of individuals with shareholdings in their banks. Banks also helped to finance firms through short-term credit; although renewable, there was always a risk that these loans might be refused at any time. The Bank Regulation Act of 1962 introduced greater specialisation, in an attempt to achieve better long-term credit facilities. Nevertheless, the performance of industrial and investment banks, as company shareholders at least, during the 1960s and 1970s, failed to meet the objectives that had been expected of them. The economic crisis of 1973, the Spanish banking crisis (1977-1985) and the entry of Spain into the EEC (1986) all changed the banking panorama in Spain. Nowadays there are two big banks which hold securities portfolios, but their nature is far from the former mixed-type of banking.

Sofya Salomatina

The chapter analyses investment banking in pre-revolutionary Russia. In the focus of its attention there are banking services on initial public offering for private companies' securities. This activity became a mass phenomenon in the 1890s for the first time. This research is an attempt to investigate making and evolution of Russian investment banking in the aspect of banking models' development. It proves that investment banking for private companies appeared throughout traditional activity of several commercial banks in St. Petersburg, dealing with services to public and mortgage bond market and intensive currency speculation caused by fiduciary standard. However, private companies' demand for investment banking appeared persistently in the peak of pre-revolutionary economic growth by 1895, and the Petersburg banks switched over to private stock as a new subject for exchange transactions. In the beginning of the 20th century the crisis revealed weak points of the 1890s investment banking, and they were overcame by universal banking development by the 1910s.

Gergana Taneva

This chapter presents a model of development of Franco-Bulgarian financial and economical relations in the late of 19th and early 20th century. The chapter explores the role and impact of French banking groups in the Bulgarian foreign loans, consolidation of the banking structure and their influence on the Bulgarian economy and industry. The French banking groups occupied an important place in Bulgarian history due to their structure and their influence on social organisation. They entered the market to promote its development through a portfolio of skills. Such a study, dealing with investment banks (*Paribas*, Bup) and the financial activities of commercial banks (*Crédit lyonnais*, *Société générale*) intends therefore to examine the role and the impact of financial groups, first in the formation of a Bulgarian State, and then in its institutional reorganisations. To study the impact of French financial institutions in Bulgaria means analysing their strategies and their operations on stock exchange and financial markets, whose competition and collaboration represent the form of bank investments.

Chris Kobrak

Deutsche Bank's acquisition of Bankers Trust was an important milestone in the creation of multi-service, transnational mega banking institutions. This chapter traces the major steps in and justifications for the acquisition. The narrative is put into both its German and American social and political context, including short histories of both banks. It highlights the mixture of technological, regulatory and general economic changes that led to the purchase and suggests some insights about contemporary financial architecture that can be gleaned from this cross-cultural event.

Giandomenico Piluso

As it is well known, banks have liquid liabilities against potentially illiquid assets. Normally, such a "maturity mismatch" does not affect financial stability, as it is unlikely that all depositors would request their money back exactly at the same moment. Yet, when a wider lack of trust occurs a run could follow by menacing the very financial stability, possibly with a serious impact on capital formation and, in the end, on economic growth. Such a problem was particularly apparent up to the first decades of the last century, when financial systems were loosely regulated and central banks were rather reluctant to intervene during liquidity crises as they were tied up by gold standard constraints. In the 1930s, as the financial crisis hit hardly all major economies, maturity mismatch and related instability issues were dealt with by central authorities and lawmakers. The emerging idea was that financial intermediaries needed to be set in a more regulated environment, where commercial banking was to be separated by investment banking, in order to preserve stability. In Italy the Banking Act of 1936 was accordingly conceived. The new Banking Law mirrored the vision of a group of technocrats, connected to the Bank of Italy, who experienced directly to which extent universal banking could degenerate and produce systemic instability that could affect capital formation in the long term. It adopted specialisation as its cornerstone and, therefore, investment banking was rigidly separated from commercial banking and universal banking was at least formally banned up to the reforms of the early 1990s. The chapter aims to sketch a general picture of dynamics of forms, institutions and mechanisms of long-term financing in Italy from the mid-1930s to the mid-1970s. It offers a short illustration of the genealogy of the regulatory model and its main principles depicting the main evolutionary dynamics of the model during the Golden Age when it was regarded as substantially fitting to investments and firms' demand. The chapter illustrates what factors were mostly responsible for the decreasing allocative efficiency of the model since the mid-1960s and, especially, during the 1970s when it entered a major crisis. It concludes discussing whether the model implied a trade-off between stability and efficiency or, instead, other factors, such as monetary policy, affected the efficiency of investment institutions and, in the very end, the overall allocative performance of financial intermediaries up to the late 1970s.

PART II

PORTFOLIO OF SKILLS AND NETWORKS: INVESTMENT BANKERS, AND INSTITUTIONAL AND PRIVATE INVESTORS

CHAPTER 3

Everard Hambro, between Investment Banker and Investor

Janette RUTTERFORD

Professor of Finance at the Open University Business School

"I confess that personally I have a horror of all industrial companies and that I should not think of placing my hard-earned gains into such a venture":[1] Sir Everard Hambro, born in 1842, was a fourth generation banker who held a dominant position in the London banking world during the late nineteenth and early twentieth centuries. He died in 1925, with net wealth[2] of £2,132,340. Hambro's bank was truly international, involved in numerous overseas government bond issues and also in mining and American railroads. Hambro was also a personal friend of John-Pierpoint Morgan, the American investment banker, and helped him to recruit Clinton Dawkins as a partner in the British Morgan firm, J.S. Morgan.[3] However, his attitude to helping British industry was very different from that of his American counterpart. For a limited number of British companies seeking to raise finance on the stock market, Hambro provided legal, financial and Stock Exchange regulatory expertise; help on drafting the prospectus; access to brokers; and underwriting if required, but did not build up long-term relationships with the directors of the companies involved, did not help on corporate strategy nor with access to government officials, and did not invest personally in these concerns.

This chapter will explore Everard Hambro's input into two new issues, those of two domestic companies, Thames Ironworks ('Thames Iron')

1 Quote in 1911 by Lord Revelstoke of Barings, cited in Peter Ziegler, *The Sixth Great Power, Barings, 1762-1929*, London, Collins, 1988, p. 186.

2 See *Financial Times*, 20 April 1925.

3 Mira Wilkins, *The History of Foreign Investment in the United States to 1914*, Harvard, Harvard University Press, 2004, p. 863 and p. 58. One third of Hambro's Bank's investments in 1898 were in American railroads.

and Trollope, Colls & Co. ('Trollope, Colls'), both London-based firms, in 1899 and 1903 respectively. This is done through the prism of correspondence archives which include correspondence between Hambro and the chairmen of the two companies, as well as various drafts of the prospectuses, newspaper clippings, etc.[4] The role of Hambro as an investment banker will be compared with that of JP Morgan. Finally, the portfolio of Hambro at death will be analysed with respect to the types of investment held, showing that Hambro held only a handful of investments in companies operating in Britain and concentrated his portfolio on foreign bonds and companies with foreign operations.

The chapter looks at the Hambro's input into the following aspects of the Thames Iron and Trollope, Colls new issues: capital structure, disclosure of financial and other information in the prospectus; the role of the broker, and underwriting and new issue costs. It then compares Hambro's role with that of J.P. Morgan in the US, and concludes with a brief analysis of Hambro's personal investments in the context of investments in British industry.

1. Hambro structuring new issues for companies

We intend to gauge the reality of the portfolio of skills of Hambro merchant bank in tackling one main activity of an investment bank, that is, the issuance and underwriting of equities and bonds. The case studies will help our understanding of how the emergence and development of the London Stock Exchange required the extension and intensification of investment bankers' skills, in particular the balancing of the interests of their clients, the companies whose securities were being issued and possibly underwritten, and the interests of the subscribers and investors who might also be wealth management clients of the bank.

A. Hambro as senior adviser to Thames Iron

Established by Charles J. Mare in 1846, Thames Iron was one of the leading shipbuilding firms on the Thames from the 1850s, building the first ironclad warship, the Warrior, in 1859, thereby becoming a household name.[5] It suffered a number of downturns,[6] being re-formed in 1864 and 1870.

---

4 Janette Rutterford, "The merchant banker, the broker and the company chairman: A new issue case study", *Accounting, Business & Financial History*, 2006, 16, 1, pp. 45-68.

5 Sidney Pollard, "The decline of shipbuilding on the Thames", *The Economic History Review*, New Series, 1950, 3, pp. 72-89.

6 *Ibidem*, 1950. A.J. Arnold, *Iron Shipbuilding on the Thames 1832-1915*, Aldershot, Ashgate, 2000, pp. 72-89.

a. Background

Its banking relationships were problematic, with Prescotts bank pressed to lend £50,000 when a Turkish debtor had defaulted following the banking crisis initiated by the collapse of Overend Gurney in 1866. Prescotts did so reluctantly, noting that it only did so as "many of our customers are shareholders". In 1870, after the restructuring, Prescotts refused to become the new company's banker, being replaced by London & Westminster.[7] Originally run by Mare and his father-in-law, Peter Rolt, MP, influence had shifted by the 1870s to F.C. Hills, a successful Deptford chemist. His son, Arnold Hills, joined the board in 1880 and later became managing director; one of three sons, he attended Harrow and Oxford, was a champion footballer and held the record for the mile in 1878, although his official biographer was grudging in praise, commenting that he won the three-miles race at the inter-university championship in 1879 in "creditable time". Concerned with worker welfare, A. Hills spent the first five of his years at Thames Iron living in the East End of London, "devoting his days to the shipyard and his evenings to the recruitment and recreation of his workpeople".[8] He organised many educational and recreational clubs, of which the most famous later became West Ham United Football Club. He was president of the London Vegetarian Society and of the Vegetarian Cycling and Athletic Club. He funded the first vegetarian restaurant in Britain and was a firm teetotaller, arguing that he had been "led to the conclusion that it is the American habit of abstinence from alcohol that is one fundamental cause for their commercial prosperity".[9]

In the 1880s and early 1890s the firm suffered industrial unrest. Although the Thames shipbuilding workers were better paid than their counterparts on the Clyde and the Tyne,[10] they were still prepared to down tools. Hills believed in having the freedom of choice of labour, and Thames Iron endured a number of strikes[11] with Hills having a proposed profit-sharing scheme voted down. He took this to heart, writing later in the *Thames Ironworks Quarterly Gazette* (*TIQG*) that he would "not easily forget the brutal rejection. I was assumed to possess some

7 D. Souden, *The Bank and the Sea. The Royal Bank of Scotland Group and the Finance of Shipping since 1753*, Edinburgh, The Royal Bank of Scotland Shipping Business Centre, 2003, p. 128.

8 *The Times*, 8 March 1927.

9 *Thames Ironworks Quarterly Gazette*, 1895, 3, p. 152.

10 Bids by Thames shipbuilding firms were on average 9.4 per cent higher than the successful bids in the period 1889 to 1996 (Hills, 1896, cited in A.J. Arnold, *Iron Shipbuilding*, *op. cit.*, p. 136.

11 Including, at different times, (a) boilermakers, (b) shipwrights, (c) engineers, (d) carpenters, (e), labourers, Directors' Report for 1898, CLC/B/110/MS19096, London Metropolitan Archive.

Machiavellian instinct of tyranny".[12] However, in 1892, Hills was able to introduce a Good Fellowship Scheme that paid out bonuses to groups of workers if contracts came in under budgeted cost and, in 1894, an eight-hour day.[13] By 1899, Hills was able to comment, with satisfaction:

> The Good Fellowship system (which gives to every workman a direct interest in the work he has in hand) was established with the consent of the Directors to create a more friendly order of things in the Works. It has proved in every way satisfactory beyond our anticipations. Our business has increased [...]. Our costs have decreased by some 17 to 18 per cent while [...] monthly dividends have been paid to the workmen in addition to the highest wages paid in the Kingdom, and in addition to the Eight Hours Day, which the success of the Good Fellowship System justified us in introducing.[14]

By the 1890s, the shipbuilding industry was becoming more dependent on warship construction as government orders increased. As a result, a number of mergers between shipbuilders and armaments manufacturers took place, notably Vickers Barrow and Maxim, and Armstrong Mitchell with Whitworth.[15] Thames Iron, operating on a smaller scale, although the largest shipbuilding firm on the Thames at the time, chose to merge with a small local firm, John Penn & Sons, engine-makers and engineers. The sums involved were not disclosed, although later correspondence hints at an asset value for Penn[16] of £100,000.

b. Capital structure

We now examine how the capital structure for the flotation of Thames Iron, after the merger with John Penn & Sons, was decided upon by Hills and by Hambro. The first evidence of written contact between Hambro and Arnold Hills of Thames Iron is a letter dated 14 May 1899 from the latter, in which Hills discusses Canadian mining companies in which he was an investor, inviting Hambro to also invest, as well as inviting Hambro to stay at his holiday home in Cromer: "The links are charming, and tho' a bad player, I shall some day like to have a round with you." In a letter dated four days later, on 18 May 1899, Hills produced a first draft of a prospectus outlining a proposed preference share issue for Thames Iron.[17] This draft was clearly based on previous discussions which are not minuted in the archive. The

---

12 *Thames Ironworks Quarterly Gazette*, 1895, 1, p. 23.

13 *Thames Ironworks Quarterly Gazette*, 1897, 9, pp. 99-101. A.J. Arnold, *Iron Shipbuilding*, *op. cit.*, p. 138.

14 Thames Iron Directors' Report for 1898, London Metropolitan Archive (LMA), CLC/B/110/MS19096.

15 Sidney Pollard, *art. cit.* A.J. Arnold, *Iron Shipbuilding*, *op. cit.*, p. 124.

16 Letter from Hambro to Hills, 12 June 1899, LMA CLC/B/110/MS19096.

17 Both letters are in LMA, CLC/B/110/MS19096.

then authorised capital of Thames Iron was £500,000, split equally between ordinary and preference shares, with an issued capital of £200,000 of ordinary shares and £150,000 of 5 per cent preference shares, preferred as to dividend only and not cumulative. These shares were all held by the directors of the Company. The new issue was to consist of a further £100,000 of the 5 per cent preference shares and £150,000 of new debentures.

In his draft prospectus, Hills was honest enough to state that the preference share issue was "to meet the convenience of the Chairman who is the principle [*sic*] holder of the company's shares". It is likely, therefore, that the issue was intended to repay loans made by Hills to the company,[18] or at least to provide additional working capital required after the merger with John Penn & Sons.[19] The new issue was of a security already in circulation and should therefore have been a relatively simple matter. However, Hambro perceived a problem: the market did not like non-cumulative preference shares.[20] Hambro replied to Hills, thanking him for his enclosure which

> reads well as regards all but one thing. We had understood that the preference shares were really preferred in every sense, both capital and interest, and in fact would be a first lien on everything after the Debentures were satisfied and it was under that idea we had been talking but if they are really ordinary shares, but preferred as to dividends, each year for itself only, they have all the risk of the ordinary and none of the sweets ... I am very sorry that we have given you so much trouble but as now put, tho' I think the Co. could quite offer them themselves to the public, I do not see how we could.[21]

Thus, Hills had a choice: he could issue new non-cumulative preference shares under the company name or he could restructure the company, replacing the existing preference shares with cumulative preference shares, and issue the new securities with Hambro's name on the prospectus. In the former case, he might have difficulty when trying to underwrite the issue; in the latter, the restructuring would be more costly but he would have the benefit of the Hambro name and advice. It was important that any "scheme of combination of [...] classes of capital be well thought out".[22]

---

18 As was the case with later issues.

19 See the Thames Iron prospectus, LMA, CLC/B/004/F/01/MS18000/63B/562.

20 See, for example, J.-B. Jefferys, *Trends in Business Organization in Great Britain since 1856, with Special Reference to the Financial Structure of Companies, the Mechanism of Investment and the Relationship between the Shareholder and the Company*, PhD Thesis, University of London, 1938, p. 225, on how, by the 1880s and 1890s, the market favoured cumulative preference shares.

21 Letter from Hambro to Hills, 19 May, 1899, LMA, CLC/B/110/MS19096.

22 G.H. Le Maistre, *Investments for All, Their Importance, Selection and Management*, London, John Murray, first edition, 1926, p. 147.

Hills wrote to Hambro on 31 May 1899, trying to persuade him of the case for not restructuring by including a copy of the latest, glowing, Directors' report – "in all Departments and in all directions the Thames Iron Works and Shipbuilding Co. are more busily and profitably engaged than in any previous period of their existence".[23] Hambro was not convinced; he had taken legal advice, which had confirmed that the existing preference shares could not be made cumulative.[24] He had also sent his legal expert, Broad, to visit the company at Thames Iron's offices in Deptford, attend the General Meeting and try to persuade the directors of the need for a new capital structure, to include cumulative preference shares. He wrote back, thanking Hills, "but as all preference shares of similar companies so far offered to the public, have been cumulative in every sense of the word, I do not see how I can come back on my last letter and make any public issue of your company's preference shares".[25]

In the face of Hambro's adamancy, Hills wrote to Hambro the same day conceding the need for a new capital structure and suggesting £375,000 each of cumulative preference shares and ordinary shares. "This issue would provide capital £600,000 for the purchase of the present company's properties (premises, plant, contracts, goodwill, etc.) and leave £100,000 for the purchase of stocks (say £50,000) and working capital. Of this issue, which would remove any necessity for the proposed debenture issue of £150,000, I should wish to retain £75,000 in preference shares and £325,000 of the ordinary shares."[26] Hills provided support for his proposed capital structure with a recent valuation of the aggregate assets of the merged company of "over £600,000, which with loose tools & will be increased by say £50,000".[27]

Hambro did not agree with Hills' proposed capital structure. Assuming that ordinary shares were to be issued to the public, he designed an alternative capital structure according to interest cover and to the dividend yield on the ordinary shares, starting from the estimated profit. He replied, again the same day: "I consider that taking the valuation of your assets, which you name as £600,000, and the profits, which you say could be certified by an auditor averaging £50,000 a year, the capital you propose would be too large, and that you should rather follow the lines of Messrs. Vickers, Son & Maxim, and most other companies, and show at least 10 per cent on your ordinary stock. Then your company would have a capital of

23 Thames Iron prospectus, LMA, CLC/B/004/F/01/MS18000/63B/562.

24 Letter from Cheston & Sons to Hambro, 30 May 1899, LMA, CLC/B/110/MS19096.

25 Letter from Hambro to Hills, 12 June 1899, LMA, CLC/B/110/MS19096.

26 Letter from Hills to Hambro, 12 June 1899, LMA, CLC/B/110/MS19096.

27 *Ibidem.*

£200,000 debentures 4 per cent – £8,000 a year

£200,000 preference 5 per cent – £10,000 a year

and £300,000 ordinary showing 10 per cent.

If you approve of this, and if an issue were made, you could get a quotation for the whole if you offered £133,333 of the preference stock and £200,000 of the ordinary stock, always supposing the issue were a success and that the public subscribed for a good portion of it."[28] Hambro was perhaps also referring to the draft prospectus which Hills had sent with his original 18 May letter to Hambro and which had included the statement: "while the last balance sheet (April 1899) enabled the Directors to declare a ten per cent dividend upon the then capital of the Company (£100,000)'".[29] In Hambro's view, the proportion of preference shares and ordinary shares depended on the profit and the desired yield on the ordinary shares. The greater the proportion of low interest senior securities, the higher the possible dividend on the ordinary shares.[30]

As well as offering the required dividend yield on the ordinary shares, which was then key to determining equity values,[31] Hambro's suggested capital structure had the added advantage of being close to the then norm: in 1898, an official report had found that a capital structure of one third debentures, one third preference shares and one third ordinary shares was "almost universal".[32] Hills had suggested issuing preference shares and debentures in his 18 May letter to Hambro: Hambro had also included debentures as well as preference shares in his counter-proposal. By the turn of the century, debentures were a popular form of low risk investment – in 1896, the yield on debentures was as low as that on consols twenty years previously.[33] Debentures had been considered attractive as alternatives to equity investment in earlier decades, as they did not have the disadvantage attached to many shares of the time of being partly-paid.[34] The success of railway debentures, limited to no more than one-third of

28 Letter from Hambro to Hills, 12 June 1899, LMA, CLC/B/110/MS19096.

29 Letter from Hills to Hambro, 18 May 1899, LMA, CLC/B/110/MS19096.

30 In the same year, W. Cotton, *Everyone's Guilde to Money Matters*, London, 1898, in a book on investment, commented: "There is no denying that loan capital has been an important factor in the making of dividends" (cited in J.-B. Jefferys, *Trends in Business Organization*, 1938, p. 192).

31 See Janette Rutterford, "From dividend yield to discount cash flow: A history of US and UK equity valuation techniques", *Accounting, Business and Financial History*, 2004, 14, pp. 115-149, for a description of how equities were valued at that time.

32 J.-B. Jefferys, *Trends in Business Organization*, thesis cit., 1938, p. 227.

33 K. Watson, "Banks and industrial finance: The experience of brewers, 1880-1913", *Economic History Review*, XLIX, 1996.

34 J.-B. Jefferys, *Trends in Business*, thesis cit., p. 192.

the authorised capital, also helped their reputation.[35] Investment trusts and insurance companies, widely regarded as cautious investors, concentrated their portfolios on debentures[36] (May, 1912). And, furthermore, there was an increasing demand by retail investors, as well as investing institutions, for relatively low-risk securities, such as debentures and preference shares.[37] Including both types of security in the capital structure was more likely to make the issue a success.

The other limiting factor on capital structure was the Stock Exchange requirement that, in order to obtain an official quotation, at least two thirds of the securities intended for public subscription had to be subscribed and allotted.[38] This explains Hambro's requirement for £133,333 preference shares and £200,000 ordinary shares to be offered to the public. It is worth noting that, at this point, both Hills and Hambro appeared happy to issue Ordinary shares to the public, although Hills clearly wished to retain control whereas Hambro was following Stock Exchange quotation rules. Hills wanted to retain 20 per cent of the preference shares and 87 per cent of the ordinary shares under his capital structure proposal whereas Hambro needed two thirds to be offered to the public for a Stock Exchange listing to be granted. This Stock Exchange listing was important for any security issue in the eyes of investors: "Investors laid special emphasis on companies which received a special settlement and quotation on the Stock Exchange", despite the fact that the Stock Exchange was concerned only with liquidity and legality.[39] Size was also a factor, with companies having to satisfy the Stock Exchange that they were of "sufficient magnitude" and, in any case, investors were warned by brokers against investing in any company with a capital[40] of less than £100,000.

There were significant changes in the proposed capital structure throughout the period from the initial approach from Hills on 14 May 1899 to the final issue on 26 July 1899. Hills had originally suggested £200,000 ordinary shares, £350,000 of preference shares, and £150,000 of debenture stock, a total of £700,000, with only £100,000 of preference shares being issued to the public. After agreeing to the need to recapitalise the company in view of

---

35 Jonathan P. Baskin & Paul Miranti, *A History of Corporate Finance*, Cambridge, Cambridge University Press, 1997, p. 146.

36 J.B. Jefferys, thesis cit., 1938.

37 Philip Cottrell, *Industrial Finance 1830-1914*, London, Methuen, 1980.

38 G.R. Gibson, *The Stock Exchanges of London, Paris and New York*, New York and London, The Knickerbocker Press, 1889, p. 37. J. Armstrong, "The rise and fall of the company promoter and the financing of British industry", in Jean-Jacques Van Helten and Youssef Cassis (eds.), *Capitalism in a Mature Economy, Financial Institutions, Capital Exports and British Industry, 1870-1939*, Aldershot, Edward Elgar, 1990, p. 117.

39 Philip Cottrell, *op. cit.*, p. 147.

40 *Ibidem*, pp. 148, 151.

the need to have cumulative preference shares, Hills then proposed £375,000 each of ordinary and preference shares, a total of £750,000. Hambro responded with a counter-suggestion of £200,000 debentures, £200,000 preference shares and £300,000 ordinary shares, a total of £700,000. The draft prospectuses show subsequent changes in the capital structure and pricing. The fifth proof, dated 11 July 1899, has £250,000 of 5 per cent cumulative preference shares, £350,000 of ordinary shares and £200,000 of irredeemable 4 per cent mortgage debentures, all to be issued at par, a total of £800,000. A corrected proof dated 14 July 1899 changed the amount of preference shares back up to £300,000, and reduced the Ordinary shares to £300,000, leaving the debentures unchanged at £200,000. The final prospectus, dated 26 July, has these amounts. No ordinary shares were to be issued to the public: the Hambro and Hills requirements had been incompatible. They were instead to be retained by vendors, notably Hills. This was not viewed as a negative by potential investors in the debentures and preference shares. Indeed, it was seen to be a positive factor: "It should be added that confidence in all issues of this class [of companies being sold by vendors], is much strengthened when the original owners of the property agree to take a large part of the purchase price in shares, preferably ordinary shares, in the new company and thus demonstrate their belief in its future prosperity."[41]

B. Hambro as senior adviser to Trollope, Colls

In this section, we now look at the second correspondence archive, that relating to the new issue of securities by Trollope, Colls under the aegis of Hambro's Bank.

a. Background

On 5 February 1903, George Trollope wrote to Hambro, asking for help in a new issue involving Trollope, Colls, a company to be formed by the merger of two firms involved in building and decorating. The story was a common one, of illness and merger, and the tone was respectful: "Since the great gap left in the firm by my brother Frank's death following that of another partner, we have been considering what best to do for the future welfare of the business and we have thought – after much deliberation – that for the purposes of continuity – and convenience – it would be better to convert this part of the business – that is the building decorating and furnishing – into a limited company. This we proposed doing in conjunction with our friends […] Colls of Coleman St. City, well-known builders doing a first class business and who are thinking of the same thing. We propose to keep the capital to a very modest £300,000 half preference and half ordinary shares, keeping the ordinary shares ourselves. The assets would

[41] G.H. Le Maistre, *op. cit.*, p. 233.

be upwards of £225,000 and the average profits about £45,000. If this is not too small a matter for you, I need hardly say, I am yours."[42]

b. Capital structure

The correspondence is less rich on the stages of the capital structure process than the Thames Iron archive. However, greed was clearly not a factor in the capital structure proposal, since Trollope's original suggestion of £300,000, half in preference shares and half in ordinary shares, was replaced in the final prospectus by £200,000 5½ per cent cumulative preference shares and £250,000 of ordinary shares, with the whole of the ordinary shares (apart from £3,000 of directors' shares) retained by the vendors, Trollope, Colls. No debentures were issued, or intended to be issued, which doubtless reflected the relatively small asset base, primarily work in progress and a limited amount of tools and stock-in-trade. Hambro had intervened on the legal side with respect to the debentures: "As regards Trollope, Colls, they have no intention at all of putting anything in front of the preference shares, but I stipulated there should be a clause in the articles of association prohibiting them from ever doing so without the consent of a large majority of the Preference shareholders."[43] He also arranged for Trollope, Colls, with their lawyers, to meet Broad, Hambro's lawyer, who "will then go into the whole legal part of the business and will assist them in drawing up a prospectus for our approval".[44]

It is not clear who took the decision to increase the total capital of the company from £300,000 to £450,000, although it was Hambro who had the final word on the total and on the proportions of preference shares and ordinary shares. An undated note in Hambro's handwriting has £225,000 ordinary shares and £225,000 preference shares.[45] A later Hambro memo to Richard Heriot of Hambros comments: "I think I have also arranged with them to reduce the amount of the preference capital to £200,000, increasing the ordinary to £250,000. Nothing could be nicer than the way Trollope behaved."[46] With this, the final capital structure, the three vendors, George Trollope, H. Trollope and J.H. Colls, received £247,000 in ordinary shares and £152,999 in cash, a total of £399,999. Under Trollope's original suggestion, the maximum they could have received, after allowing for £50,000 working capital would have been £300,000.

---

42 Letter to Hambro from George Trollope, 5 February, 1903, LMA, CLC/B/110/MS19097.

43 Letter from Hambro to Heriot, dated 29 June 1903. The prospectus stated that a majority of three-fourths of the preference shareholders would have to approve at a special meeting LMA, CLC/B/110/MS19097.

44 Letter from Hambro to Heriot, dated 29 June 1903, LMA, CLC/B/110/MS19097.

45 *Ibidem.*

46 *Ibidem.*

As a result of discussions with Hambro and their brokers, the vendors were £100,000 better off. The capital raised was £200,000 in cumulative preference shares and £250,000 in ordinary shares, a total of £450,000.

2. Disclosure and the prospectus

We now turn to key matters of interest to potential investors, in particular, disclosure as to asset values, profitability, and other aspects such as details as to workers and management.

A. *Asset values at stake*

The art of evaluating balance sheets and understanding accounting was a prerequisite for the investment banker who could not rely only on his connections, "nose", and an intuitive perception of the situation of his clients. At this time, bankers had to prove themselves as acute practitioners of some kinds of financial intelligence, an aspect of the banker's role which would later become "research".

a. Hambro assessing Thames Iron

For Thames Iron, Hambro expressed interest in the asset valuation figures. These were relevant in providing asset backing for the proposed capital of the company, the latter for covering interest and dividend payments. Hambro responded cautiously to Hills' 12 June suggestion of £375,000 each of preference and ordinary shares, trying to avoid "watering the stock": "I am bound to say that even these figures which I suggest seem to me large, because your old capital was £300,000 [*sic*] and you are adding to it Penn's Works for £100,000."[47] Stock was considered "watered" if it was not backed by tangible assets or if it were backed by assets which were over-valued in the balance sheet:

> 'Watered stock' was repeatedly inveighed against as a deception practised upon the stock-buying public, who were misled by a fictitious statement of the asset values existing behind the shares. Hence one of the functions of security analysis was to discover whether the value of the fixed assets, as stated on the balance sheet of the company, fairly represented the actual cost or reasonable worth of the enterprise.[48]

Akroyd, of the major stockbroking firm of Cazenove, Akroyd & Co., had been consulted by Hambro on this topic. Hambro reported back to Hills

---

[47] Hambro had doubtless deduced this from Hills' letter of 18 May 1899 in which he had referred to a 'then' ordinary share capital of £100,000 and 'now issued' £200,000 of ordinary shares.

[48] Benjamin Graham & David L. Dodd, *Security Analysis*, New York, McGraw-Hill Book Company Inc, 1934, p. 306.

that Akroyd "thinks it important that the valuation of the accountant clearly showed £600,000 was the actual value of the property, not including tools". Thus, both Hambro and Akroyd were concerned that the asset value should be robust, and seen to be robust in the prospectus, which at the time was accorded great importance by potential investors.[49] Under Hambro's proposal of £700,000 of securities (£200,000 debentures, £200,000 of preference shares and £300,000 of ordinary shares), and with a solid asset valuation of £600,000, only £100,000 of ordinary shares would be "watered". This could be tolerated in the context of the ordinary shares, provided they offered a dividend of 10 per cent. This was a more conservative view than that expressed by the firms amalgamating to form Imperial Tobacco in 1901, when the merged firm was valued in terms of earning power (eight times net profits) plus the value of the tangible assets[50] or by Le Maistre, who later wrote about company flotations that "it is now generally accepted that goodwill should not ordinarily exceed 1¼ to 3 years' purchase of the net profits of a business, after provision for depreciation has been made, based on the average of the last five years".[51] Hambro did not consider profit in the sense of years' purchase, but in the context of being able to generate a dividend yield.[52]

The various proofs of the prospectus show that the asset value remained a bone of contention. The proof dated 11 July included an estimate of the gross (pre-depreciation) aggregate value of the combined premises, buildings, fixed plant, etc. of Thames Iron and John Penn of "£800,000, this valuation not including the many costly tools in the various yards".[53] The valuation by Fuller, Horsey & Co., included in the final prospectus dated 26 July 1899, reduced that figure to £587,500, less than the original £600,000. However, the total assets acquired were given as just over £800,000, achieved by adding to the valuation figure a further £51,534 for tools and utensils (certified), £51,507 for stocks, stores & c. (uncertified), £69,015 working capital and £50,000 to be provided by the issue itself. It is worth noting that the purchase price paid to the vendors was given in the final prospectus as £750,000, payable as to £300,000 in ordinary shares and the rest in cash. This purchase price was £50,000 higher than given in the 14th July proof.

b. Hambro assessing Trollope, Colls

There was little debate between Hambro and George Trollope as to the value of Trollope, Colls. The asset value (in the usual course of

---

49 J.B. Jefferys, thesis cit., 1938.

50 J. Armstrong, *op. cit.*

51 G.H. Le Maistre, *op. cit.*, p. 149.

52 For discussion of how company valuation techniques changed over time, see J. Rutterford, *op. cit.*, 2004.

53 Draft prospectus, proof, 11 July 1899, LMA, CLC/B/110/MS19096.

business) was £236,060 excluding goodwill, somewhat above £225,000 (as Trollope had stated in his original letter). This, with the traditional £50,000 of working capital from the issue proceeds, gave a total asset value of £286,060, more than covering the preference shares and contributing £86,060 of asset cover to the ordinary shares. There is no discussion in the correspondence over the asset valuation itself, merely of the capital structure to be applied to it. This is doubtless because the asset valuation was much less contentious than in the case of Thames Iron. In Trollope, Colls's case, assets were made up of tools, stock-in-trade, and work in progress.

B. The investment banker confronted with profit disclosure

The investment banker had to estimate the profit potential of his clients, considering likely profitability but more importantly, their ability to pay future dividends or interest on the securities to be issued.

a. Hambro gauging the profitability of Thames Iron

On profits in the Thames Iron prospectus, Hambro also reported the views of Akroyd, of Cazenove, Akroyd & Co., that "the certificate of profits for 3 years lumped together would not be very satisfactory, because underwriters would immediately ask why it had not been divided; and he thinks that, even if one of the years was slightly inferior to the other two, it would be better to show all three than lump them together".[54] The final version of the prospectus, dated 19 July, included a statement of profits earned by the vendor company (excluding those of John Penn & Sons) of £146,064 for the four years 1895 to 1898, or an average of £36,516 per annum. However, the auditor's certificate, which was included in the prospectus, went into more detail, in particular showing an increasing trend of profits: £27,407 in 1895; £29,677 in 1896; £41,462 in 1897; and £47,518 in 1898. Although audited, the profit figures given were misleading for a number of reasons. First, as Arnold has pointed out,[55] the profit figures given were operating profits, before deduction of interest charges on loans (not disclosed in the prospectus), directors' fees and managing director's remuneration although after "extensive expenditure" to keep buildings, plant and tools "all in a state of complete efficiency". They were thus not the profits available for payment of interest and dividends on the debentures, preference and ordinary shares. The auditors pointed this out in

54 Letter from Hambro to Hills, 14 June 1899, LMA, CLC/B/110/MS19096.

55 A.J. Arnold, *op. cit.*, p. 141.

the first paragraph of their report, although they did not give figures for the missing items.[56]

As well as the problem of profit definition, determining annual profits for a company such as Thames Iron over time was fraught with difficulty given the size of the shipbuilding contracts and the relatively low profit margins. For example, the auditors reported a work in progress figure as at January 1895 of £140,000 compared with £877,000 at end 1898. They commented: "The length of time over which the carrying out of large construction work necessarily extends, involves that the ascertainment of their results can be arrived at only at irregular intervals."[57] They then apportioned the profits between each of the four years 1895, 1896, 1897 and 1898 by using the wages paid in each as an indication of work done. In practice, the press, commenting on the new issue, picked up only the profit figures for the four years 1895 to 1898. No comment was made on the problem of profit estimation in such a business. *The Economist* was the most sceptical, reporting that the auditors, when looking at the four year profit total, "think this may be divided as follows".[58] *The Economist* then went on to recommend both the debentures and the preference shares as a "sound investment". A typical comment was that of *The Statist*: "Profits last year of over £47,000, and even in the dull time of 1895 they were £27,000."[59] Most newspapers preferred to make no comment on the figures and to concentrate on the nature of the business. As the *Newcastle Daily Journal* observed, "demand for war vessels seems to be on the increase all over the world".[60]

b. Hambro gauging the profitability of Trollope, Colls

The Trollope, Colls prospectus differed from that of Thames Iron in one important point. The auditors did not give either an annual or an average profit figure, but they limited themselves to an estimate of dividend cover: "The joint profits of the two firms have during each of the last three years been more than four times the amount of the dividend on the present issue of the preference shares. Such profits for the year 1902 were greater than those of either of the two preceding years." From the correspondence between

56 In fact, directors' fees were, in 1900, £315, less than the £433 2s 6d paid to the debenture trustees. They were also not necessarily a fixed cost. Reaching a high of £630 in the years 1904 to 1907, in the loss-making year of 1908 the directors chose to waive their fees altogether. See the Thames Iron Annual Report and Accounts, 1900 to 1910, Iron and Steel Company Annual Report and Accounts, London Metropolitan Archive.

57 Letter from auditors, James & Edwards, included as auditors' report in the prospectus, LMA, CLC/B/004/F/01/MS18000/63B/562.

58 Press cuttings file, LMA, CLC/B/110/MS19096.

59 *Ibidem*.

60 *Ibidem*.

Hambro and Colls, we know that the average profit was in fact £45,000. After payment of the preference share dividend of £11,000 (as stated, less than one quarter of average profits) this, in theory, left £34,000 for Trollope ordinary shareholders. If a 10 per cent dividend were paid on ordinary shares (the rate given as desirable by Hambro for Thames Iron), there would still have remained £9,000 profit that could be set aside as reserves. This was in line with the average for new issues of the period where three quarters of profits were paid out in dividends on preference and ordinary shares. It was also usual to assess preference shares in the context of the earning power of the company, rather than on asset backing.[61] Given their earnings cover, the Trollope, Colls preference shares, paying 5½ per cent, were clearly less risky than those of Thames Iron, paying 5 per cent.

c. Other prospectus disclosures

As far as reasons for the Thames Iron issue were concerned, the various drafts did not alter much. The key reasons given were the general increasing nature of the business, the need to pay off temporary loans, the extension of plant and machinery, and a catch-all "general purposes". No profit forecast was given although "good results are anticipated. Another feature of the prospectus was the importance given to Hills' leadership. The potential investor was reassured that Hills, who had been managing director for the past fifteen years, had entered into an agreement with the company to act in a similar manner for five years. Hills wanted to include a seven-year history of the wages-bill,[62] which had increased from £99,066 in 1893 to £242,838 in 1898. He was proud of the wages-bill increase since it reflected the benefits of the Good Fellowship Scheme and lack of industrial unrest.[63] Hambro quashed the inclusion of the wages bill in the prospectus: "Unless the auditors could show an increasing profit, I do not think if the fact that the Wages Bill had been going up would be taken as of any value, in fact, unless the auditors' certificate showed the profit increased in the same proportion it would be a disadvantage to give it." In the prospectus, Hills was limited to an indirect mention of the Good Fellowship Scheme, with no numbers provided. "The vendor company has adopted the plan of interesting its staff and employees in the profits earned. This arrangement has proved to work with every satisfaction to both sides, and since its initiation in 1892 there has been complete immunity from labour troubles."[64] For Trollope, Colls, the prospectus was much easier. Since

61 J.B. Jefferys, thesis cit., 1938.

62 Letter from Hills to Hambro, 12 June 1899, LMA, CLC/B/110/MS19096.

63 See the introductory article in the first issue of the *Thames Ironworks Quarterly Gazette*, 1895, p. 1.

64 Final prospectus, LMA, CLC/B/004/F/01/MS18000/63B/562.

the preference shares to be issued were to be marketed to clients, reasons for the issues were given as to enable the directors to give employees a greater financial interest and to allow customers to share in the success of the firm.[65]

3. The role of Hambro as a broker

A key role of the investment bankers was to sponsor the new issue, by providing its name on the prospectus and also to "sell" the securities to be issued. Hambro had private clients whose portfolios they managed, but these portfolios were focussed on overseas government bonds and corporate securities, and Hambro's clients did not expect to invest in low risk preference shares in domestic companies. Investment banks, and UK merchant banks too, struggled to broaden and entertain their connections among potential purchasers of equity and bonds, For brokerage, merchant banks relied on a separate firm, in both cases under consideration, this was Akroyd & Co., a member of the Stock Exchange, able to deal with listing requirements. The broker also gave valuable advice to Hambro as to the pricing and timing of each new issue.

A. Hambro's role in "selling" Thames Iron equity

Hambro viewed his own role as being to comment and improve upon the suggested capital structure, taking into account market demand, and to be aware of Stock Exchange regulation and company law. His role was also, in conjunction with the broker, to comment on the prospectus which, in 1899, was required by the Stock Exchange rather than by law.[66] For such issues as this, Hambro deferred to his Stock Exchange broker on detail such as pricing of securities and market timing of the issue as, on these topics, the opinion of a good broker was paramount. It was the broker who knew what the underwriters would or would not accept. Hambro ended his 12 June letter to Hills saying that he had not yet consulted any broker as to the possible success of such an issue, warning only that recent issues had not gone well for shares in relatively small companies, so that a prospectus would have to be very attractive before people could be induced to subscribe.

Hills, in promoting his proposed capital structure of £375,000 each of preference shares and ordinary shares, argued that, in the absence of a debenture issue of any kind, the preference shares should be issued at a premium as this would reflect well on both the issuing house and the company concerned.[67] Hills argued for a premium by sending Hambro a press

---

65 Letter from Trollope to Hambro, 5 February 1903, LMA, CLC/B/110/MS19097.

66 J. Armstrong, *op. cit.*

67 As Hambro later commented in his letter to Trollope, 2 July 1903, LMA, CLC/B/110/MS19097.

cutting of a 5 per cent cumulative preference share issue by William Cory & Son [coal merchants and shippers]: "From the very first the five per cent cumulative preference shares of William Cory and Son were recognised as a good thing. Large applications were sent in when the prospectus was issued, and they were immediately quoted at a premium which has gradually increased until the £5 share is worth about £6 5s."[68] By 14 June, Hambro had consulted the broker, Akroyd, and reported back, in a letter to Hills, on his views. Akroyd had taken note of Hambro's preferred capital structure for Thames Iron and commented on how these could be made attractive to underwriters: "Mr Akroyd thinks that in ordinary times and under ordinary circumstances the debentures and preference shares of the proposed company could be underwritten [...]. His idea is that if the debentures were perpetual debentures they might be issued at 102 [...] and that the preference would have to be issued at par."[69]

The 5 per cent to be offered on the preference shares was in line with other issues and thus could only be offered at par. With a debenture issue now ranking ahead of the Preference shares, Hills lost the premium he had hoped to achieve. There was also a change in the nominal value: the 11 July prospectus referred to £5 nominal preference shares – by 14 July, these were £1 nominal. The lower nominal value reflected the general trend towards low denomination shares which allowed small investors access to such issues.[70] It is also likely that the decision to reduce the nominal value of the preference shares was taken in the light of the successful 1897 Vickers, Son & Maxim Limited new issue, referred to by Hambro in his letter to Hills dated 12 June 1899, which also involved the issue of £1 preference shares.[71] Just as preference shares then had to be cumulative in order to be successfully issued, so irredeemable debentures

68 Enclosed press cutting with letter from Hills to Hambro, 31 May 1899, LMA, CLC/B/110/MS19096.

69 Letter from Hambro to Hills, 14 June 1899, LMA CLC/B/110/MS19096.

70 See J.B. Jefferys, "The denomination and character of shares, 1855-1885", in E.M. Carus-Wilson (ed.), *Essays in Economic History*, London, Edward Arnold, 1954, pp. 344-357. W.A. Thomas, *The Finance of British Industry, 1918-1976*, London, New York, Methuen, 1978, p. 33 for discussion of the general downward trend in nominal values of shares. The 1897 Vickers, Son & Maxim Limited new issue referred to by Hambro in his letter to Hills dated 12 June 1899, also involved the issue of £1 preference shares, with £1 ordinary shares already in issue. The prospectus for this issue is included in LMA, CLC/B/110/MS19096.

71 The prospectus for the Vickers, Sons & Maxim Limited 1897 new issue is included in LMA, CLC/B/110/MS19096. It may also be the case that Hills hoped to persuade Thames Iron Employees to purchase a few preference shares. The first issue of the *Thames Ironworks Quarterly Gazette* in January 1895 included an issue by directors to "workmen in their employ" of £5,000 of 5 per cent redeemable Thames Iron debentures "to encourage habits of thrift and providence" (*Thames Ironworks Quarterly Gazette*, 1895, 1).

were then considered more attractive in the British market than fixed maturity debentures. Irredeemable debentures resembled preference shares and ordinary shares in their lack of redemption date, and were thus considered to be part of the long-term capital of the firm.[72] An early (undated) draft Thames Iron prospectus had specifically mentioned "redeemable" debentures. Making the Thames Iron debentures perpetual would, according to Akroyd, allow them to be offered at a £2 premium. The Thames Iron debentures were also to be first mortgage debentures, secured by a floating charge on the freehold and leasehold property, and on all other property including uncalled capital, the floating charge feature having become general by this time.[73]

The debentures, when issued, had a 4 per cent per annum coupon, to be paid semi-annually on 15 April and 15 October of each year, and were indeed, irredeemable. However, Hambro and his lawyer, Broad, failed to spot a flaw in the wording describing the debentures in the prospectus, which said that they were "irredeemable, unless the company goes into liquidation, in which case the debentures will be repayable at the rate of 110 per cent" of their par value.[74] The secretary of the Stock Exchange Committee which met to approve the listing of the new Thames Iron debentures and preference shares, noted that "insufficient care has been taken in the statement of those terms in the prospectus [...]. Unless, therefore, the expression 'goes into liquidation' is voluntary, it is probable that the stockholders could enforce the more favourable terms of the prospectus and claim the premium of 10 per cent in case of a liquidation, whether favourable or otherwise".[75] The principal indenture of the mortgage debt had to be altered.

Another key role of both Hambro and the broker was to decide exactly when the new issue could be launched to best effect. For the London market, this meant knowing about demand for domestic industrial and commercial securities, such as Thames Iron, in the context of international issues taking place. Hills, writing his initial letters to Hambro in May 1899, had hoped to get the issue away before the holidays. Hambro reported that Akroyd's opinion was that "the business might be done if everything was ready to come out at a favourable moment, but he hardly seems to think that that favourable moment will come until after the holidays", given the fact that "at the

72 See Philip Cottrell, *op. cit.* This was not true of the American market where the preferred maturity of debentures was under ten years; see Jonathan B. Baskin and Paul J.J Miranti, *A History of Corporate Finance*, Cambridge, Cambridge University Press, 1997.

73 J.B. Baskin & P.J.J. Miranti, *op. cit.*, p. 147.

74 Note dated 20 December 1899 by J.A. Torrens-Johnson of the Stock Exchange Committee considering the application for listing of the debentures and preference shares. LMA, CLC/B/004/F/01/MS18000/63B/562.

75 *Ibidem.*

present moment, underwriters are smarting from the results of the Japanese issue".[76] However, Hills had his way; the prospectus was dated 26 July 1899.

B. Hambro's role in "selling" Trollope, Colls equity

For Trollope, Colls, there was a question mark over the coupon to be paid on the preference shares. As with Thames Iron, the broker's view was paramount on pricing. In an internal note, Hambro commented: "Henderson [a broker] would not take Trollope preferently at 5 but we agreed we would at 5½ – if T[rollope] wants 5 per cent then you must ask H[enderson]."[77] At some point, Hambro must have suggested a 6 per cent coupon on the preference shares and Colls wrote to Trollope saying that this was too high. Trollope forwarded the Colls letter (missing from the archive) to Hambro, who replied: "I return your enclosure. As regards 6 per cent interest on your preference shares, the last thing I meant to do was to do anything that in sense could be considered damaging to your firm's credit. I said 6 per cent, because the only thing I could compare it to was Waring's 6 per cent preference shares. While it is true they command a premium now, I should be sorry, both for your sake and ours, if the issue of your preference shares did not go to a premium also."[78]

In a note to Heriot, two months later, and three months before the issue, Hambro commented: "I thought the type of interest was to be 5 per cent but if they will pay 5½ or 6 per cent, the issue will be more attractive."[79] The final prospectus shows that 5½ per cent was the coupon agreed upon. There was, however, no discussion of the nominal value, which was £10 for both ordinary and preference shares, in contrast to the £1 for Thames Iron ordinary and preference shares. The Trollope, Colls preference shares were aimed at Trollope, Colls customers and to enable the directors to "give a greater interest to several of our people who have served us well".[80] There was no perceived need to reduce the nominal value to £1 to attract small investors.

4. The investment banker and underwriting and new issue costs

Underwriting was legalised by the Companies Acts of 1900 and 1907 although, in 1899, underwriting was possible, so long as paid for by the vendor (in this case Hills) rather than the company itself and provided

76 Letter from Hambro to Hills, 14 June 1899, LMA, CLC/B/110/MS19096.

77 Undated note by Hambro, LMA, CLC/B/110/MS19097.

78 Letter from Hambro to Trollope, 2 July 1903, LMA, CLC/B/110/MS19097.

79 Note from Hambro to Heriot, 1 September 1903, LMA, CLC/B/110/MS19097.

80 Letter from Trollope to Hambro, 5 February 1903, London Metropolitan Archive, CLC/B/110/MS19097.

the shares were not issued at a discount to par value.[81] The 1900 Act required disclosure of the underwriting details but, to some extent, made underwriting less necessary, as minimum subscription payments were laid down, as was a minimum number of shares to be applied for before shares could be allotted.[82] Underwriting ensured that the entire issue was sold at the price given in the prospectus. Failure to underwrite could mean that some capital was not issued, the proceeds were reduced, and could also mean failure to gain a quotation for the securities, given the requirements imposed by the Stock Exchange.

A. Hambro and the underwriting of Thames Iron equity

Hills initially expected to have the new issue underwritten: "If this preference issue in your opinion requires underwriting, I shall be willing to pay a commission of up to 5 per cent for the service."[83] Hambro replied with the opinion of Akroyd of Cazenove, Akroyd, who believed that perpetual debentures could be underwritten for 3 per cent, to include the broker's commission of ½ per cent, and the preference shares for 3½ per cent, also to include the broker's commission.[84] A letter to Hills five days later enclosed an introduction to Akroyd, at the same time giving Hills the estimated costs of the issue without underwriting: ½ per cent for Hambros (minimum £1,250), ¼ per cent brokerage on debentures placed, 6d per share brokerage on the preference shares placed, £100 for getting quotations on the Stock Exchange (which had to be paid by Hambros), about £600 to £700 on advertisements, depending on the number of papers, and legal expenses.[85] Hills wrote on 4 July 1899 to say that he would call on Hambro about the underwriting "which should be arranged in the course of the next week".[86] None of the draft proofs mention underwriting but the actual prospectus, dated 26 July 1899, rather surprisingly states: "Nothing whatever is charged or paid for goodwill and the issue is not underwritten." There is no record of what took place at the meeting in early July. One possibility is that Hills believed that the issue would be so successful that it would be a waste of money to underwrite it. The fact that he had specifically arranged with an advertising agency to publish the prospectus in the religious press may have encouraged this belief.[87] Another possible

---

81 J.B. Jefferys, *op. cit.*, p. 344.

82 P.L. Cottrell, *op. cit.*, pp. 70-73.

83 Letter from Hills to Hambro, 12 June 1899, LMA, CLC/B/110/MS19096.

84 Letter from Hambro to Hills, 14 June 1899, LMA, CLC/B/110/MS19096.

85 Handwritten note from Hambro to Hills, 19 June 1899, LMA, CLC/B/110/MS19096.

86 Letter from Hills to Hambro, 4 July 1899, LMA, CLC/B/110/MS19096.

87 Letter from Cheston & Sons, solicitors, to Thames Ironworks, 18 July 1899, LMA, CLC/B/110/MS19096.

reason is that he had, when meeting Hambro in person, become unconvinced of the arguments in favour of underwriting. The archive is silent on this point. Without underwriting, however, the cost of raising capital was low – at around 1 per cent excluding legal costs.

In the event, the 4 per cent debentures were issued at par and were oversubscribed, with applications for £312,400 of stock, 56 per cent more than the £200,000 issued. Akroyd had been right in that there was substantial demand for perpetual 4 per cent debenture stock, with Northern Assurance Company, Edinburgh Life Assurance Company, and the Standard Life Assurance Company applying for £20,000 each. However, the 5 per cent cumulative preference shares were less popular. Only £229,643 were applied for and subscribed out of the £300,000 on offer, forcing Hills to take the balance of £70,357 in lieu of cash as part payment for the sale of the company.[88] It had originally been agreed that Hills would take one third of the initially proposed £250,000 issue, later changed to £75,000 of a proposed £375,000. The £70,357 taken up by Hills represented 23.5 per cent of the £300,000 issued.[89] Perhaps Hills had decided that, even if the issue were not fully subscribed, a risk with an issue which was not underwritten, he was more than happy to bridge the gap.

B. Hambro and the underwriting of Trollope, Colls equity

Despite the fairly conservative capital structure and despite the fact that, following legislation,[90] the prospectus stated that the minimum subscription on which the directors would proceed to allotment was £200,000, the Trollope, Colls issue was underwritten. There was, however, some discussion with Trollope as to the fees, after negative comment by Colls, clearly a thrifty businessman. Hambro felt obliged to explain the charges in a letter to Trollope dated 1 July 1903:

> As regards the second part of Mr Coll's [*sic*] letter, when I named 3 per cent for underwriting, you must remember I named a figure much lower than that which is customary in similar cases, because I hoped and believed that a great number of your customers and merchants would subscribe for the shares at issue, and certainly there would be no difficulty in sending them the prospectus so that it would arrive to them as quickly as to anybody else, or in allotting them as much as possible in the interests of your firm. The 5 per cent named by me was to cover brokerages and everything else, except legal, advertising expenses and stamps.[91]

88 National Archives, BT31/62972.

89 LMA, CLC/B/004/F/01/MS18000/63B/562.

90 P.L. Cottrell, *op. cit.*, p. 73.

91 Letter from Hambro to Trollope, 2 July 1903, LMA, CLC/B/110/MS19097.

The issue, which became dormant, was resuscitated in September when Hambro wrote an internal note saying that he had found Trollope's letter in a drawer. His memory of previous discussions with Trollope and Henderson's, "was that the following was agreed: Commission to Hambro's 2 per cent out of which we pay the brokerage. Underwriting commission 3 per cent and Henderson and we share the underwriting. Trollope to pay all expenses".[92] In the actual prospectus, Henderson's were not mentioned, with the 3 per cent underwriting commission and 2 per cent commission (to cover the cost of printing, issuing and advertising the prospectus, brokerage and all other charges) attributed to Hambros. The vendors were to pay the preliminary expenses, estimated at £4,500, for company registration, solicitors' and accountants' fees, as well as stamp duties. The total costs, expressed as a percentage of the nominal value of the £200,000 preference shares issued, and including underwriting, came to 7¼ per cent of the total, in line with estimates made by Chapman[93] and slightly above the 5-6 per cent estimate of Cairncross.[94] After an initial approach in February 1903, the issue was finally launched in December of the same year.

In a note dating from the time when Hambros Bank had been due to underwrite only half the issue, Hambro commented that the directors wanted £20,000 of the preference shares (as well as their ordinary shares), and that a further £10,000 was required for the pension fund and that Dick (presumably Richard Heriot) wanted £1,000. "So our own half is going fast."[95] In addition, lists were provided by both Colls and Trollope of people to whom the prospectus should be sent, forming part of the minimum 3,000 prospectuses to be issued and circulated by Hambro under the final underwriting agreement. The prospectus had said that special consideration would be given to applicants connected with or customers of the business. In the end, £265,370 were applied for and £200,000 allotted. The issue was a success, perhaps due to the reputation of the 'thoroughly practical men' who ran the two businesses begun in 1778 and 1840, and without the need for full profit disclosure. As *The Economist* commented, "the firms undoubtedly enjoy a good reputation and it is upon this and upon the ability of the partners [...] to conduct the business with the same success as in the past that investors must mainly rely if they decide to take an interest in the concern".[96]

---

92 Note from Hambro to Heriot, 1 September 1903, LMA, CLC/B/110/MS19097.

93 Stanley Chapman, *The Rise of Merchant Banking*, London, Allen & Unwin, 1984.

94 A.K. Cairncross, *Home and Foreign Investment, 1870-1913*, Cambridge, Cambridge University Press, 1953.

95 Undated note in Hambro's handwriting, LMA, CLC/B/110/MS19097.

96 *The Economist*, 5 December 1903, p. 1029.

5. The overall role of Hambro as investment banker

The behaviour of Hambro, and that of his associates in the City, can be compared with that of JP Morgan and his investment bank, JP Morgan & Co., in promoting and directing major US companies at around the same time. "Morganisation", described as "the extraction of monopoly rents from consumers", consisted of amalgamating firms in the same industry to give them economies of scale and the ability to charge higher prices.[97] Charging relatively high fees (between 4 and 10 per cent of the (inflated) value of the businesses involved,[98] this approach to investment banking can be said to have three advantages, one for vendors of the businesses and two for potential investors. Book values of "Morganized" companies represented not the cost of the physical assets but Morgan's assessment of their earning power.[99] This meant, for the vendors, that they received a higher price for their companies than they otherwise would have. De Long argues that the lack of such a mechanism in the UK can explain the failure of British companies to make the transition from "paternalistic capitalism" to "professionally managed" organisations with diversified stock ownership.[100] The second advantage, put forward by Moody, was that J.P. Morgan & Co. did not walk away from the companies they promoted after the issue. They put directors on the Board, thereby ensuring effective monitoring of the firm's managers and signalling to investors that management was both competent and industrious, thereby making it more likely that the firm would survive. Incompetent managers could be fired.[101] The third advantage, suggested by a partner in J.P. Morgan, was that promotion by firms such as J.P. Morgan provided a guarantee to the "thousands of investors [...] seeking securities" who "have neither the knowledge nor the opportunity for investigating a great [...] enterprise".[102] Morgan invested in the companies he promoted (even if at advantageous prices) and thus provided a signal to the market. De Long argues that the commissions charged by J.P. Morgan were high but still worth the advantages brought by "Morganisation".

---

97 James Bradford De Long, "Did J.P. Morgan's men add value? An economist's perspective on financial capitalism", in Peter Temin (ed.), *Inside the Business Enterprise: Historical Perspectives on the Use of Information*, Chicago, Chicago University Press, 1991, pp. 205-236.

98 *Ibidem*, p. 3.

99 A. Dewing, *The Financial Policy of Corporations*, New York, Ronald Press, 1914.

100 J.B. De Long, *op. cit.*, p. 233.

101 John Moody, *The Truth about Trusts: A Description and Analysis of the American Trust Movement*, New York, Moody Publishing Co. J. Moody, *How to Invest Money Wisely*, New York, Office of John Moody, 1912.

102 J.B. De Long, *op. cit.*, p. 14.

By contrast, Hambro charged lower fees than his American counterpart but adopted a relatively hands-off approach to the two businesses. He treated each flotation as an independent event, not having been involved in events leading up to the flotation and not being involved afterwards. For example, Hambros Bank, and Hambro in particular, were not involved in the company mergers which had led to the creation of both Thames Iron and Trollope, Colls. In Thames Iron's case, Hambro did comment on the Thames Iron merger with John Penn, but more in terms of the price paid rather than the economic rationale behind the merger, for which he deferred to Hills' judgment: "Of course I do not know whether the valuation you give of £600,000 includes Penn's, nor do I know whether you could show that Penn's business was an increasing one, and that its past profits would justify the price you have paid, though I thoroughly understand that their works may be worth the sum to you to join them to your own."[103] This lack of involvement occurred despite the fact that, from the correspondence, there is some sense of social equality with Hills, who had been to public school and Oxford.[104] They spoke of their holidays and met several times, albeit at Hambro's Bank rather than at Thames Iron's offices.[105] There is no evidence of any personal relationship or sense of equality between Hambro and Trollope. The tone of the correspondence between Trollope and Hambro is more distant, with no mention of social activities or points of common interest, and the damning "found letter in desk" forgetfulness on the part of Hambro.

What was the advantage of issuing securities using the name of Hambro? First of all, Hambro provided access to the City network of lawyers and, in particular, stockbrokers and the Stock Exchange. Hambro knew what was required for securities to be accorded a Special Settlement Day and thus to be able to be traded on the Stock Exchange. Hambro, and his broker, were aware of which issues had been successful and why. Hambro could organise underwriting, if need be. Second, Hambro acted in the short-term financial interests of the vendors, ensuring the best prices for the vendors in the reconstructions and flotations, within the requirements of the Stock Exchange and of marketability. In particular, Hambro could advise on how best to make the issues attractive to a public not particularly keen on domestic industrial or commercial securities. This involved ensuring that the stock to be issued was not "watered", that the preference share dividends and debenture interest payments were sufficiently covered

103 Letter from Hambro to Hills, 12 June 1899, LMA, CLC/B/110/MS19096.

104 However, Hills, despite his contributions to the Thames shipbuilding industry, to vegetarianism, and to the social welfare, pay and benefits of his workforce, was never given recognition in the form of an honour, unlike the key figures in the City (Youssef Cassis, *City Bankers*, Cambridge, Cambridge University Press, 1994).

105 Hambro sent his lawyer colleague, Broad, to visit Thames Iron.

by profits – at least those disclosed in the prospectus, and that the coupons offered on the securities were comparable to those on comparable recent issues. Hambro did not invest in, nor expect clients of his bank to invest in, either firm's securities although Richard Heriot of Hambros does appear to have invested £1,000 in Trollope, Colls. By contrast, a stockbroker might have access to a private client list more attracted to such issues.[106]

6. The role of Hambro as an investor

Hambro, head of Hambro's Bank since 1877, was a prominent banker in the City of London, as evidenced by the fact that he was a appointed a director of the Bank of England from 1893 and remained so until his death[107] in 1925. His bank specialised in raising funds for overseas governments, particularly the Nordic countries, as it had been court bankers to the Danish throne and Everard's father had been created Baron of the Kingdom of Denmark.[108] For example, Hambro's bank raised £6.5 million in loans for Sweden and Denmark[109] in the 1870s. The links with northern Europe were consolidated by amalgamation with the British Bank of Northern Commerce in 1920. Hambros raised substantial funds for Italy in the 1880s, to enable Italy to return to a convertible currency, and, later raised funds for Russia, Finland and Greece.[110] Indeed, just before his death, Hambro had led a £7.5 million loan issue for Greece, which was oversubscribed twenty times.[111] Hambro was knighted in 1908 but not made a peer, unlike the head of N.M. Rothschild & Sons, Lord Rothschild, and of Barings Bank, Lord Revelstoke. Everard Hambro died on 26 February 1825, aged 82.

He had amassed substantial wealth, valued at £2,323,710 excluding settled property (which was already settled on his eldest son, Charles Eric). The *Financial Times*[112] estimated that death duties would amount to £943,400. Hambro, who had been heavily involved in charitable enterprises, most

---

[106] Lance E. Davis & Robert A. Huttenback, *Mammon and the Pursuit of Empire: The Politican Economy of British Imperialism, 1860-1912*, Cambridge, Cambridge University Press, 1987, pp. 196-198, in their survey of share registers between 1883 and 1907, show how elite investors (those likely to use Hambro's Bank) preferred foreign and empire securities to home industrials whereas lawyers, accountants, and other professionals were more inclined to buy domestic securities.

[107] *Morning Post*, 13 April 1893. *The Times* Obituary of Hambro, 25 February 1925, p. 17. His role in the Barings crisis of 1890 will doubtless have been a factor in his appointment.

[108] *The Times* obituary of Hambro, 27 February 1925, p. 17.

[109] Kathleen Burk, *Morgan Grenfell, 1838-1988: The Biography of a Merchant Bank*, Oxford, Oxford University Press, 1989, p. 46. See also *The Times* obituary of Hambro, *art. cit.*

[110] *Idem.*

[111] *Financial Times*, 27 February 1925, p. 5.

[112] *Ibidem.*

notably as Chairman of the Royal National Pension Fund for Nurses (as well as a member of the Committee of the Home Hospitals Association and the Society of the Friends of Foreigners in Distress, to name but a few), left nothing to charity.[113] Instead he transmitted to his eldest son all unsettled freehold and leasehold properties and some personal effects, his wife a £50,000 trust fund and some personal effects, and his four sons – Charles Eric. Ronald Olaf, Harold Everard, and Angus Valdemar, 7/20, 5/20, 4/20 and 4/20 of the remainder, respectively, with nothing for his married daughter, Violet Mary Smith.[114]

Table 1. Portfolio of Sir Everard Hambro in probate documents

Valueless holdings	Nominal Value £
New Florence Holding Co	70
do ordy	76
Aberdare Merthyr collieries	426
do a preference	15
do b preference	38
Norris Tube Anc. & Safety Rifle Company	94
Empire Mine	500
Potosi Mine	500
Channel Tunnel	395
Smelting Co. of Mexico	500
Golden Chance Founders	500
Coronation syndicate	150
Peruvian Tobacco Monopoly Founders	1
Burma Ruby Mines Founders	5
British Columbia Phoenix	1,100
Railways & General	34
North American Transport and Trading	575
British Uralite ordy	1,860.3
Durham Collieries preference	9177
Foreign Press Review	500
Potchefstrom Exploration	1,000
Agric & Hortic assn	5
Brilliant Gold Mining Co	500

113 For example, see *The British Medical Journal*, 1st March 1879, p. 327 and 21 June 1913, p. 1355. For more on the philanthropic endeavours of London investment bankers, and how this was linked to being close to the royal family, in particular, Edward VII, see Pat Thane, "Private bankers and philanthropy: the City of London, 1880s to 1920s", in Youssef Cassis & Philip Cottrell (eds.), *The World of Private Banking*, Farnham, Ashgate, 2009, pp. 247-263.

114 See Hambro's obituary in *The Times*, 27 February 1925; details of probate in the *Financial Times*, 20 April 1925.

Valueless holdings	**Nominal Value £**
Phillips River Gold & Copper	2,000
American Association Inc	
do of $5.25	219
do ordy of £1	1,600
do preferences of £1	500
do cons stock	1,400
New Rhodesia Mines	210
Caledonian Copper	83
Naponite	350
Swaziland Corporation	1,000
Société de golfe du Touquet	1
Luipards Vlei	62
Transvall Exp & lnd & Mining	4,000
St Clements House	100
New England Farm Stock	100
Brevets Dolter	400
Sun Fuel Co	500
Rock Island Coy	500
Mexican Internal Devs Int Warrants $	1,530
do southern do	17 4s
National Railway of Mexico 1d sh	90
Dansk Ostindisk Plance preference Kr	120,000
Probate for Sir Everard Hambro, LMA, CLC/B/110/MS1921	

What is striking about Hambro's portfolio at death (shown in Table 1) is the relatively small investment in British registered companies, and of that, the almost total absence of investments in British registered companies operating in Britain. Of the total portfolio of £2,218,038, Hambro had £291,227 invested in stocks and funds of the United Kingdom and £77,131 in overseas government bonds. Investments in companies were primarily in overseas companies and primarily in fixed income securities. Hambro's largest holdings of ordinary shares were in Shell (worth £37,001 at death), Imperial Tobacco (£25,198), Rio Tinto (£25,200), Royal Dutch (£19,564), British American Tobacco (£11,917) and Swedish Match (£10,687) out of a total of 44 non-government bond holdings. The only British investments which had a market value were in the London Produce Clearing Company, the Army and Navy Cooperative Society and debentures and shares in his own Dorset estate. Included in the probate documents is a list of 45 valueless stocks of Sir Everard Hambro's estate, shown in Table 2. Only eight of these are domestic in nature and include holdings of securities of a Welsh and a Durham colliery, the Channel Tunnel Company, British Uralite, a railways investment trust, and two charitable holdings: £5 in the Agricultural and Horticultural Association and £100 in St Clement's House. The only British industrial – and worthless – holding is in Norris Tube Ancillary and Safety Rifle Company.[115]

Table 2. Valueless holdings in Everard Hambro's probate documents

Stocks, shares, bonds, or debt of companies	Currency	Nominal value	Price	£	shillings	
Hambros Bank ltd shares		196,079	7 and 15/16	1,556,377	1	3
5% Salmias of Mexico Debs	£	8,400	32	2,688	0	0
6% Railway of Central America notes	$	14,400	88,25	2,541	12	0
7.5% Borneo company preference shares		1,000	1 7/32	1,218	15	0
Mid European corporation 7 10s prefs		5,000	7	35,000	0	0
Chinese Shanghai Banking Corporation		146	12 3/8	1,806	15	0
Mexican north western railway cons. shares		500	0,25	125	0	0
National railway of Mexico 2nd preference		190	2,25	85	0	0
Railway of Central America preference		1,280	63	16,128	0	0
Hambros Bank Ltd. Shares		400	20,25	1,620	0	0
British Portland Cement		890	26 6d	1,179	5	0
Garland Steam Ship co		187	2s3d	21	0	0
Huronian Belt co		6,600	49s6d	16,335	0	0
VOR holding co ordinary		4,000	63s1d	12,616	13	4
Mexican Eagle		2,450	17s7.5d	2,159	1	3
Pan American Petroleum B		390	79¾	6,220	10	0
Shell Transport		8,000	4 41/64	37,001	5	0
Royal Dutch Petroleum		563	34¾	19,564	5	0
Arizona Copper		424	16s10d	357	15	0
San Francisco Mines of Mexico		3,021	23s3d	3,511	18	3
Rio Tinto ordinary		600	42	25,200	0	0
American Cellulose & Chemical company ordinary		500	19 5/16	9,656	5	0
British American Tobacco ordinary		2,100	113s6d	11,917	10	0

115 Probate for Sir Everard Hambro, LMA, CLC/B/110/MS19219.

Stocks, shares, bonds, or debt of companies	Currency	Nominal value	Price	£	shillings	
Imperical Tobacco co of GB		5,333	94s6d	25,198	8	6
Sudan plantations syndicate		1,333	7 7/16	9,914	3	9
Swedish Match co B		1,000	10 11/16	10,687	10	0
4% Mexican Southern debs	£	430	15½	66	13	0
Maraivan Rubber co shares	sh	3,730	2s0d	373	0	0
United Sumatra Rubber		8,441	3s 1 1/2d	1,318	18	1
Golconda Malay Rubber	sh	1,000	1 5/16	1,312	10	0
Oriental Cons Hdg co	sh	2,000	13s 1 1/2d	1,312	10	0
Johannesburg Cons Investment	sh	100	39/-	195	0	0
Alaska Treadwell Gold Mining	sh	500	2 1/32	1,015	12	6
Do Mexican	sh	500	6s 9d	168	15	0
Do United	sh	1,000	1s 7 1/2d	81	5	0
London Produce Clearing ordinary		100	3 13/16	381	10	0
Do founders		5	110	550	0	0
Army and Navy coop soc		13	1 13/16	23	11	3
Dorset Estates deb stock		30,000	55	16,500	0	0
D0 second issue		25,000	25	13,750	0	0
Do sh shillings		19,999	2s6d	2,499	17	6
5% American Assn incorp B income stock deb £		4,000	25	1,000	0	0
			Sub-total	1,849,679	15	8
Stocks or funds of the UK						
5% National Loan 1929/47		150,000	101 7/16	152,156	5	0
4% Victory Bonds		130,000	92 3/8	120,087	10	0
5% National War Loan 1928/33		13,000	105 5/8	13,731	5	0
Bank of England stock		2,010 7s 2d	261¼	5,252	1	2
Bonds of foreign countries transferable in GB						
6% Norwegian bonds 1921	£	1,000	103½	10,350	0	0
5% Italian Marmara bonds 1862		6,580	63	4,079	12	0
4½% Finland bonds 1909		500	64¾	3,237	10	0
do 1923		7,000	88	6,160	0	0
6% Japanese Bonds 1924		25,000	89¾	22,437	10	0
4% Brazil 1911		4,500	51½	2,317	10	0

Stocks, shares, bonds, or debt of companies	Currency	Nominal value	Price	£	shillings	
7% German 1924		10,500	99¼	10,421	5	0
7% Greek 1924 60% pd		25,000	63½	15,875	0	0
4% City of Copenhagen 1910		500	75¾	378	15	0
Jutland Land		89,5	72	19	16	0
5% Argentine port of the capital Buenos Ayres		2,000	89½	1,790	0	0
Mexican Internal 1894	$	3,600	9	64	16	0
				77,131	14	0
			Total	2,218,038	10	10

Probate for Sir Everard Hambro, LMA, CLC/B/110/MS19219

Conclusion

This chapter has explored the role of Hambros Bank in two new issues around the turn of the 20th century, those of Thames Iron and Trollope, Colls. It has examined the role of Sir Everard Hambro as an investment banker in the two new issues for domestic companies. It is clear from the correspondence between Hambro and the chairmen of the two companies that Hambro, himself, was heavily involved in the capital structure decision which was jointly discussed in both cases, with the chairmen making initial suggestions and Hambro having the last word as far as the capital structures of the two companies were concerned. Similarly, the choice of coupon and type of security was very much influenced by Hambro and the broker he consulted in each case. This was not the case for underwriting which appears to have been left to the discretion of the chairmen, with Hills choosing not to underwrite and Trollope choosing so to do. Hambro was also influential in ensuring that Stock Exchange rules were adhered to, for example, the minimum amount of free float required by the Stock Exchange and the contents of the Articles of Association. Hambro relied on the broker, Akroyd, to ensure that the new issues were priced according to market norms established with recent and comparable new issues. Hambro also intervened in terms of prospectus content and disclosure of accounting information, in particular historic profits and asset values. The prospectus provided information to reassure investors that the proposed securities were well-backed in terms of income and asset cover, with Hambro acting to prevent too much 'stock watering' and to ensure a high enough yield was offered on fixed-rate securities.

Hambro did not, though, take account of the particular risks of the businesses in formulating his advice. This did not matter to Trollope, Colls, which did not need external funding to survive, but it was important for Thames Iron which operated in a capital-intensive, competitive industry. Despite the relative social ease between the chairman of Thames Iron and Everard Hambro, no long-term financial advisory relationship was established nor ongoing financial advice offered. The new issue advantages which were offered by Hambro, notably access to experts, speed of issue and relatively low costs, were not sufficient to ensure repeat business. Neither Thames Iron nor Trollope, Colls used Hambros Bank again for new issue finance.

In both cases, Hambro kept his distance from the firms which he introduced to the stock market. Cairncross attributes this attitude to a lack of industrial expertise: 'The London merchant banks did not possess the apparatus of investigation necessary for home industrial flotations, but were admirably placed for the handling of loans to foreign governments and corporations [...]. They were under no temptation to dabble in home industrial issues (except the very largest).'[116] Indeed, Everard Hambro's own portfolio shows a disdain for domestic investment and a preference for overseas government issues rather than corporate issues. This view seems to have been shared with Lord Revelstoke of Barings, whose derogatory comments about investing in domestic concerns form the introductory quotation of this chapter.

116 Alexander K. Cairncross, *Home and Foreign Investment, 1870-1913*, Cambridge, Cambridge University Press, 1952, p. 90.

CHAPTER 4

Investors, Investment Banks, and Governments between Cooperation and Competition

A Short History of the Salonica-Constantinople Railway (1892-1914)

Peter HERTNER

(Universität Halle-Wittenberg at Halle/Saale, Germany)

Not fundamentally different from what happened in the late 20th century, the financing of investment activities during the last two thirds of the 19th century was typical of a certain type of banking business which was mainly concerned with the creation and the sale of securities, private and public. To a certain extent these early private banking houses were also busy with the founding of firms, particularly joint-stock companies, as well as with mergers and acquisitions of commercial and industrial property.[1] Not much later the so-called "mixed" or "universal" banks – following a pattern established first by the Belgian Société générale and the French Crédit mobilier – sprang up in central Europe as a new type of credit institution, particularly between the 1850s and the early 1870s. This new type of banking considered investment banking to be an essential, but not an exclusive part of its business. During the last decades quite a lot has been written on investment and "universal" banking and its peculiar way of business,[2] and the following chapter cannot pretend to give new and original insights into such an important topic. In a more modest way it wants to

1 See for the French case the short study by Alain Plessis, "The Parisian 'Haute Banque' and the international economy in the nineteenth and early twentieth centuries", in Youssef Cassis and Philip Cottrell (eds.), *The World of Private Banking*, Farnham, Surrey, and Burlington, Vermont, Ashgate, 2009, pp. 127-140.

2 See for the British and the US case: Stanley Chapman, *The rise of Merchant Banking*, London 1984. Vincent P. Carosso, *Investment Banking in America. A History*, Cambridge, Mass. and London 1970.

show, with a small case study at hand, how investment banking worked concretely in a sector, the railways, which proved to be fundamental for economic growth during most of the 19th century.

1. Banks and railway construction in South-Eastern Europe in the late 19th century

As a matter of fact, railways were exactly the industry that had given birth to the rise of investment banking starting in the 1820s and 1830s in Britain and then quickly moving over to the European continent and to North America.[3] In Europe, railways did not only support the rapid growth of industrialising countries in its Western parts, they also "served as a strategic tool for the development of hitherto backward areas; they helped to penetrate regions far away from the political and economic centres".[4] In Western, Southern and Central Europe, the main railway lines had already been constructed by the end of the 1860s. In the European East, however, by far the largest part of the Russian Empire was then not yet covered by a railway network, and South-Eastern Europe was lagging still further behind. From the 1830s there had been plans for developing a railway link between Central Europe and its South-East but only during the 1860s two isolated and relatively short lines were built in the European parts of the Ottoman Empire: one in what was later to become Bulgaria, the other one was situated in the Dobrucha region which at a later stage was to be annexed by Romania.[5] A real break-through was achieved only by baron Moritz von Hirsch, a Bavarian banker established in Brussels, later in Paris, who managed in 1869 to sign a concession agreement with the Ottoman government. It was meant to provide "for the construction and operation of a railway network in European Turkey which was to connect

---

3 With the French example of the reciprocal relationship between railways and the banks at hand, François Caron has written: "L'histoire financière de la France est [...] incompréhensible sans référence à celle des chemins de fer: la mobilisation de capital qu'ils ont rendu nécessaire en permanence a fait évoluer l'activité des banques d'affaires et élargi la sphère d'appel à l'épargne" (François Caron, "Quels modèles pour une histoire des chemins de fer?", in *L'économie française du XVIIe au XXe siècles. Mélanges offerts à François Crouzet*, Paris, PUPS, 2000, pp. 687-704, quote on p. 694).

4 Peter Hertner, "The Balkan railways, international capital and banking from the end of the 19th century until the outbreak of the First World War", in Gerry D. Feldman and Peter Hertner (eds.), *Finance and modernisation. A transnational and transcontinental perspective for the nineteenth and twentieth centuries*, Farnham, 2008, pp. 125-153, quote on p. 125.

5 *Ibidem*, p. 126. See also Alexandre Kostov, "Les Balkans et le réseau ferroviaire européen avant 1914", in Alberto Carreras, Andrea Giuntini and Michelle Merger (eds.), *European Networks, 19th-20th Centuries. New Approaches to the Formation of a Transnational Transport and Communication System*, Milano, 1994, pp. 93-103, and specifically p. 97.

Constantinople with Vienna".[6] The original concession was planned for a railway network of about 2,500 kilometres. The main line should have run from Constantinople/Istanbul to the Austro-Hungarian border via Edirne (Adrianople) – Plovdiv-Sofia-Nish-Pristina-Sarajevo to Sisak. Besides, four connecting branches were planned: from Edirne to Dedeagatch on the Aegean coast; another one from Plovdiv to Burgas on the Black Sea; one from Nish to the border with Serbia; and finally one from Pristina to Salonica.

The concession-holder was pledged by the Ottoman government of an annual rental of FRF 14,000 per completed kilometre, payable by the Ottoman government, for the entire period of 99 years, and to be financed with a state loan, and an annual rental of 8,000 francs per kilometre to be paid by the operator."[7] Not all of these projected lines came to real life: The Bosnian trunk had been partly completed by 1872 but due to the difficult financial situation of the Turkish government and because of the technical problems caused by the Bosnian mountains completion of this particular part of the line was abandoned in 1876.[8] Nevertheless, in 1872, the construction of Hirsch's so-called *Oriental Railways* had been well under way: starting from Constantinople and from the Aegean coast at Salonica 387 kilometres had already been put into operation. Furthermore, "102 [were] ready for operation and 661 under construction – altogether 1,150 kilometres".[9]

In 1875, when the Ottoman State suspended all its payments, 1,179 kilometres, "all the lines entrusted to Hirsch were completed, but not those which were to be built by the Turks. Thus the railway project meanwhile consisted of three isolated lines".[10] From 1875 the railway construction in the European part of the Ottoman Empire came to a virtual standstill, not least because of anti-Turkish revolts in Bosnia and Bulgaria between 1875 and 1878, and also as a consequence of the Russo-Turkish War of 1877-78. The 1878 Congress of Berlin, in the article 10 of the treaty, entrusted the newly created Bulgaria as a successor state to the Ottoman Empire with the task of providing for a railway link with Austria-Hungary.[11] But only in 1882 did the delegates of the

6 Kurt Grunwald, *Türkenhirsch. A Study of Baron Maurice de Hirsch, Entrepreneur and Philantropist*, Jerusalem, 1966, p. 28.

7 *Ibidem*, p. 34.

8 *Ibidem*, p. 40.

9 *Ibidem*, p. 39.

10 *Ibidem*, p. 41. See also Charles Morawitz, *Die Türkei im Spiegel ihrer Finanzen. Nach dem französischen Original "Les finances de la Turquie"*, Berlin, 1903, pp. 417-418.

11 See C. Morawitz, *Die Türkei, op. cit.*, p. 419. Kurt Grunwald, *Türkenhirsch*, p. 46. W.N. Medlicott, *The Congress of Berlin and after. A diplomatic history of the Near Eastern settlement 1878-1880*, 2nd ed., London 1963, p. 411.

Ottoman Empire, Bulgaria, Serbia and Austria-Hungary meet in Vienna and reached an agreement in March 1883. It provided for the construction of two missing railway links: one from Bellova via Sofia, Nish and Belgrade to Semlin in Hungary, the other from Nish to Vranje and from there to Skopje – Üsküb in Turkish – and thus to the line connecting Mitrovitza and Salonica.[12]

It took another five years until the completion of the missing links between East and West. Finally, on 12 August 1888, almost twenty years after the signing of the original concession, the first train left Vienna for Constantinople.[13] The distance covered amounted altogether to 1,686 km.[14] Once the *Orient-Express*, which had been tentatively installed already in 1883 as a luxury train,[15] had been definitively established, it took 57 hours to go from Berlin via Budapest to Constantinople/Istanbul.[16] The same trip with the *Orient-Express* from Paris required 62 hours in 1914.[17] The line from Belgrade to Salonica had already been inaugurated in May of the same year 1888.

These spectacular achievements should however not let us forget that South-Eastern Europe – the Balkans, as railway historian Alexandre Kostov defined them – in 1912 could muster only a mere 4% of the length of the entire European railway network and that on these 13,900 kilometres just 2% of the entire amount of European passengers and goods were transported during the same year.[18]

2. The *Salonique-Constantinople*: the financial issues

It was precisely from Salonica that a new line linking this city directly with Constantinople was projected at the beginning of the 1890s.

---

12 See W. Rechberger, *Zur Geschichte der Orientbahnen. Ein Beitrag zur österreichisch-ungarischen Eisenbahnpolitik auf dem Balkan in den Jahren von 1852-1888* (unpublished Ph.D. thesis, Universität Wien 1958), pp. 195-208.

13 Kurt Grunwald, *Türkenhirsch*, p. 58.

14 P.F. Sugar, "Railroad construction and the development of the Balkan village in the last quarter of the 19th century", in R. Melville and Harm-J. Schröter (eds.), *Der Berliner Kongreß von 1878. Die Politik der Großmächte und die Probleme der Modernisierung in Südosteuropa in der zweiten Hälfte des 19. Jahrhunderts*, Wiesbaden, 1982, p. 488.

15 See Werner Sölch, *Orient-Express. Glanzzeit, Niedergang und Wiedergeburt eines Luxuszuges*, 4th ed., Düsseldorf, 1998, pp. 17-19.

16 Karl Baedeker, *Konstantinopel. Balkanstaaten, Kleinasien, Archipel, Cypern. Handbuch für Reisende*, 2nd edition, Leipzig, 1914, p. 25.

17 Werner Sölch, *Orient-Express*, *op. cit.*, p. 20.

18 Alexandre Kostov, "Les Balkans et le réseau ferroviaire européen avant 1914", p. 95. For A. Kostov, the so-called Balkans consist of Bulgaria, Greece, Rumania, Serbia, the Turkish part of Europe, Montenegro, Croatia, Bosnia-Hercegovina and Dalmatia (*ibidem*, p. 94).

There is quite an interesting report from 1913, done by the financial research department of *Crédit lyonnais*,[19] then the biggest French bank, on this railway line which was officially named *Compagnie du chemin de fer Ottoman Jonction Salonique-Constantinople*.[20] According to this report and to the Paris stock exchange yearbook[21] the *Jonction Salonique-Constantinople* Railway had been founded provisionally as a joint-stock company according to Ottoman law on 8 October 1892 when a French banker, René Baudouy, living in Constantinople, had obtained an imperial decree ("firman" of the Sultan) which conferred to him a concession of 99 years for a railway line from Salonica to Dedeagatch of a total length of 511 kilometres.[22] Dedeagatch is nowadays part of Greece, close to today's border with Turkey and called Alexandroupolis. According to a German travel guide of 1908 at that moment, this small town counted 5,500 inhabitants and had been founded only in the 1870s.[23] Its importance as a quickly developing commercial centre and Aegean harbour, particularly for Adrianople, was the motive for the Imperial Ottoman Bank (IOB) to establish, in 1904, an agency in this town.[24]

Coming back to the railway concession of Baudouy one should note that it was handed over quickly to the new company which was officially established with a nominal capital of FRF 15 million through its shareholders' meeting of 23 March 1893. Baudouy, the seller of the concession, was paid in shares which amounted to a nominal value of FRF 3m. The principal founders of this new railway company were IOB and the *Banque de Paris et des Pays-Bas* (or Paribas), the big French investment bank. It seems as if IOB had been rather sceptical as to the chances of its participation in this business. The fact that some of its leading figures as well as the French government were quite pushing from behind – the Paris government principally because it did not want to leave all railway projects

19 As to the structure and development of this financial and economic studies department of Crédit lyonnais, see Marc Flandreau, "*Caveat emptor*. Coping with sovereign risk under the international gold standard, 1871-1913", in Marc Flandreau *et al.* (eds.), *International Financial History in the Twentieth Century. Systems and Anarchy*, Washington, DC, 2003, pp. 17-50.

20 Archives historiques du Crédit agricole, Paris. Fonds Crédit lyonnais, DEEF 24189: Report of February 1913 (See this report for the following details).

21 Compagnie des agents de change près la Bourse de Paris. Chambre syndicale (ed.), *Annuaire des valeurs admises à la cote officielle*, année 1894, Paris 1894, p. 1188.

22 See André Autheman, *La Banque impériale ottomane*, Paris, CHEFF, 1996, p. 128.

23 *Meyers Reisebücher: Türkei, Rumänien, Serbien, Bulgarien*, 7th edition, Leipzig/Wien, 1908, p. 69.

24 See Christopher Clay, "The origins of modern banking in the Levant: the branch network of the Imperial Ottoman Bank, 1890-1914", *International Journal of Middle East Studies*, Vol. 26, 1994, pp. 589-614, and particularly p. 603.

in the European part of Turkey in German hands – must have helped to persuade IOB, initially rather reluctant, to participate in this venture with quite an important amount of capital.[25]

The proportion between the company's share capital of only FRF 15 million and an issue of bonds which ran up to 160 million seemed to be quite extraordinary – in the case of the Salonica-Monastir railway there were 20 million francs issued for the shares and only 60 million for the bonds – but André Autheman explains it underlining the quite higher profitability of the bonds if compared with the shares.[26] Immediately after the establishment of the company its founders transferred the construction and, after this had been done, the management of the railway to the *Régie générale pour la construction et l'exploitation des chemins de fer*, a firm still dominated by the family of its creator count Philippe Spiridon Vitali (1830-1909) and then, from the end of the 1890s, Georges Vitali (1861-1925).[27] Compared to the Oriental Railways, the *Jonction Salonique-Constantinople* enterprise was certainly much smaller but it was essentially a French investment and belonged thus to the most important investing nation in the Ottoman Empire. According to Jacques Thobie, in the summer of 1914, just before the outbreak of WWI, about 60 per cent of foreign capital invested in Turkey were of French origin. Seen from France, it was almost as much as the capital invested in the French colonial empire.[28] We should of course not forget that both Balkan wars of 1912 and 1913 had just been over and with them the *de facto* loss of the railway line from Salonica to Dedeagatch to Greece and Bulgaria. The overall proportions of foreign investment and the importance of French capital in the Ottoman Empire which, as a consequence of these two wars, had by and large become confined to its Asiatic parts, had barely been altered by these events.

One and a half years after the official establishment of the company, on 22 October 1894, the first 97 km of its line could be inaugurated. The entire network was opened to traffic on 1st April 1896 as a single-track and normal gauge line. A German railway review reported in the same year that, once two short connecting lines to the network of the Oriental Railways had been completed, it would take only 24 hours to get from Salonica to

25 *Ibidem.*

26 See André Autheman, *La Banque impériale ottomane*, *op. cit.*, p. 128f. See also von Wiczlinski, *Im Zeichen der Weltwirtschaft*, p. 266f.

27 See Dominique Barjot, "La mise en place des infrastructures européennes de transport: le rôle des entrepreneurs français de travaux publics (1857-1974)", in Michelle Merger, Alberto Carreras, and Andrea Giuntini (eds.), *Les réseaux européens transnationaux, XIXe-XXe siècles. Quels enjeux?*, Nantes, 1995, pp. 61-76, particularly pp. 64f.

28 See Jacques Thobie, "Intérêts économiques, financiers et politiques dans l'Empire ottoman (1895-1914)", *Le Mouvement social*, No. 86, January-March, 1974, pp. 43-53, particularly pp. 49f.

Constantinople whereas before a large detour had to be taken which, until this moment, had required not less than 62 hours in order to arrive on the shores of the Bosphorus.[29] According to a German travel guide, published in 1908, four through-going trains ran each week from Salonica to Istanbul over a distance of 840 km. The trip from Salonica to Dedeagatch, offered by the *Jonction Salonique-Constantinople* company, took twelve hours and was, with its 444 km, about half as long.[30] The Ottoman government guaranteed a yearly gross income of FRF 15,500 per kilometre to the company[31] and provided this subsidy with the income from the tithes of four districts in Western Thrace. These tithes were to be administered by the Ottoman Public Debt and paid to IOB in favour of the railway company.[32] As soon as the income from this line would had gone beyond the limit of 15,500 francs the additional receipts would have to be evenly shared between the company and the Ottoman government. Once thirty years had elapsed after the initial concession the Ottoman government was allowed to buy back this line at any time.

In its report on the company the experts of *Crédit lyonnais* stressed the fact that the line from Salonica to Dedeagatch linked the fertile valleys of the small rivers which descended from the Rhodopian mountains to the Aegean Sea but that there existed no transversal railway lines and only insufficient roads. This "harms the development of these valleys and the transport of local products to the stations of the [Salonica-Dedeagatch] railway".[33] "From the point of view of transit, the line Salonica-Dedeagatch is the only link between the Constantinople network of the Oriental Railways and the Salonica network of the same company and the line Salonica-Monastir which it is also running. On the other side, it is neglected by all the international traffic which is frequenting the ports of Constantinople and Salonica. Income from transit traffic amounts to about a third of total income of the company. In order to meet the needs of this traffic the Company offers the services of one daily train in each direction between Salonica and Dedeagatch. In that city the track got connected with the trains of the Oriental Railways going to Constantinople".[34]

With a closer look at the same report we also arrive at a figure for the construction costs of the entire company network. The costs of the

29 See a note in the *Archiv für Eisenbahnwesen*, Vol. 19, 1896, p. 789.

30 See *Meyers Reisebücher, Türkei. Rumänien, Serbien, Bulgarien*, p. 373f.

31 See for this policy: Donald Quataert, "The age of reforms, 1812-1914", in Halil Inalcic and Donald Quataert (eds.), *An Economic and Social History of the Ottoman Empire, 1300-1914*, Cambridge, Cambridge University Press, 1994, p. 806f.

32 Compagnie du chemin de fer Jonction Salonique-Constantinople. Rapport du conseil d'administration pour l'exercice 1894, Constantinople 1895, p. 4.

33 Source as above in note 20, p. 9.

34 *Ibidem*, p. 10. Beside these daily long distance trains there were two other two daily "regional" trains running each on the two opposite parts of the line.

concession and of the preliminary studies paid in advance by the already mentioned Baudouy – including certainly also the customary bribes to be paid to the Ottoman administration[35] – amounted altogether to FRF 81.7 million. Subtracting the pure concession costs the amount which had to be spent per kilometre reached a sum of FRF 154,000 on average. The author of the report thought that this sum "did not seem to be exaggerated given the nature of the terrain" with all its difficulties; "after all, it was comparable to the corresponding figures for the various railway networks in Algeria and Tunisia".[36] The rolling stock was worth FRF 6.3m. It comprised 848 wagons of different types and 34 locomotives, including five new ones which the Ottoman Government obliged the company to buy in 1903.[37] The pressure exercised by the Turkish authorities in this particular case can probably explained by the usefulness this line – as well as the German-financed line from Salonica to Monastir – had for the army. As a matter of fact, the Ottoman government could, as soon as the two lines had been completed, send large amounts of troops at short notice from the Bosphorus and from Anatolia to the European parts of the Ottoman Empire, particularly to ever-rebellious Macedonia.[38] The "Constantinople Junction railway", wrote the British correspondent William Miller in 1898, "enabled the Turks to strike hard and quickly at their foes", and he was certainly referring to the war between Greece and Turkey which had broken out in 1897 and which had quickly been won by the Ottoman forces.[39]

There can be little doubt that the services which these new railways delivered to the Ottoman Empire and its economy were important.[40]

---

35 For the Oriental Railways project, Grunwald has already pointed out that "Hirsch had to pay his way in Turkey, as was customary" (Grunwald, *Türkenhirsch*, p. 52). See also for the corresponding Egyptian case in the 19th century: David S. Landes, *Bankers and Pashas. International Finance and Economic Imperialism in Egypt*, London, 1958, p. 29, note 1.

36 See source as in note 16 above, p. 11.

37 *Ibidem*, p. 12.

38 See Basil Gounaris, *Steam over Macedonia, 1870-1912. Socio-Economic Change and the Railway Factor*, Boulder, Colorado, 1993, pp. 55-58. Meropi Anastassiadou, *Salonique, 1830-1912. Une ville ottomane à l'âge des Réformes*, Leiden/New York/Köln, 1997, p. 175f. See also André Autheman, *La Banque impériale ottomane*, Paris, Comité pour l'histoire économique et financière. Ministère de l'Économie et des Finances-CHEFF, 1996, p. 128f.

39 William Miller, *Travels and Politics in the Near East*, London, 1898, p. 363. Yves Ternon, *Empire ottoman. Le déclin, la chute, l'effacement*, Paris, Éditions du Félin & Éditions Michel de Maule, 2005, pp. 218f.

40 Frithjof Benjamin Schenk maintains that – if one looks at the example of the Russian Empire since the 1860s – railways were used by all European empires as "motors of economic development but also as instruments of political power". Territories in the periphery could thus be controlled much more efficiently. Frithjof Benjamin Schenk, "Imperiale Raumerschließung. Die Beherrschung der russischen Weite", *Osteuropa*, Vol. 55, 2005, pp. 33-45, quote on p. 39.

Certainly much more problematic were the targets which these new means of transport offered to terrorist attacks. In this respect one might for instance quote the yearly report of the Oriental Railways for 1903: "A certain number of atrocities were perpetrated with infernal machines against moving trains, and a number of passengers were killed or injured."[41] The majority of these attacks occurred probably in Macedonia, and there they hit the Oriental lines and the Salonica-Monastir Railway. But such fearful events have also been registered on behalf of the Salonica-Constantinople Junction Railway in Thrace,[42] which leads Peter Mentzel to the conclusion that "the activities of the terrorists had indeed succeeded in disrupting the normal functioning of the Ottoman Balkan railway system by 1911."[43]

3. *Compagnie de chemin de fer Salonique-Constantinople*: Co-operation and competition between French and German banks in the Ottoman Empire

It has been quite often described how Deutsche Bank and its allies got a concession, founded a company and started to build the first kilometres in 1888/89 of what was to become the Anatolian and later on the Baghdad Railway.[44] Less known is their purchase of the Oriental Railway[45] and even less the concession which Deutsche Bank obtained in 1890 for a railway from Salonica to Monastir,[46] today's Bitolj in the Republic of Macedonia. As a counterpart, and possibly with a view to give compensation to the financial group headed by IOB, a French syndicate prepared the creation of a railway linking

41 Betriebsgesellschaft der Orientalischen Eisenbahnen. Vierundzwanzigste ordentliche Generalversammlung abgehalten in Wien am 31. Mai 1904. Betriebsjahr 1903, Wien [1904], p. 3.

42 In 1903 a bridge near the Anghista station had been seriously damaged, in 1904 another bridge was blown up at kilometre 395; Compagnie du chemin de fer Ottoman Jonction Salonique-Constantinople: Rapport à l'assemblée générale, Exercice 1903, p. 5. *Idem*, Exercice 1904, p. 5.

43 Peter Mentzel, "Accidents, sabotage, and terrorism: Work hazards on Ottoman railways", in Colin Imber, Keiko Kiyotaki and Roads Murphey (eds.), *Frontiers of Ottoman Studies: State, Province, and the West*, tome 2, London/New York, IB Tauris, 2005, pp. 225-240, quote on p. 231.

44 See among many others Karl Helfferich, *Georg von Siemens. Ein Lebensbild aus Deutschlands großer Zeit*, tome 3, 2. Aufl. Berlin, 1923, pp. 15ff. Boris Barth, *Die deutsche Hochfinanz und die Imperialismen. Banken und Außenpolitik vor 1914*, Stuttgart 1995, pp. 76ff.

45 See Karl Helfferich, *Georg Siemens*, Vol. 3, p. 48ff. H. Feis, *Europe, the World's Banker 1870-1914*, New York, 1965 [Erstausgabe, New Herbert, 1930], pp. 293ff. B. Barth, *Die deutsche Hochfinanz*, pp. 76ff. Peter Hertner, *The Balkan Railways*, pp. 126ff.

46 See Karl Helfferich, *Georg Siemens*, Vol. 3, p. 50f.

Salonica directly to Constantinople/Istanbul as has already been shortly described above.

Preliminary meetings for the foundation of this new line – which at that point was still called *Chemin de fer de Salonique à Dédéagatch* – were held in London on 29th and 30th of June 1892 and in Paris exactly a month later.[47] Several groups met on that occasion: There was on the one side the concession holder, the already mentioned Baudouy, a French banker established in Constantinople. There was a British group, headed by the marquess of Tweeddale – William Montagu Hay, 10th marquess of Tweeddale (1826-1911) – which had already founded a London-based construction company for the projected line. Participating was also a group from Paris represented by Noël Bardac. Both, the London and the Paris group, represented "*un syndicat financier*" [a finance pool], and at its centre must certainly have been IOB. This multinational bank, during the 1880s, "was not just the state bank, but also [...] the only significant European financial institution operating in the Ottoman capital" but its "virtual monopoly of Ottoman finance" had just recently been threatened by Deutsche Bank and its allies.[48] The London and Paris meetings were also attended by Albert de Biedermann, administrator of the *Régie générale pour la construction et l'exploitation de chemins de fer*, the Paris-based construction group of Vitali, well known for its activities in the South-Eastern European area. Among the results of these three meetings was the decision to create a railway company with a capital of FRF 15m, and to establish it in Constantinople under Ottoman law. The British construction company would have to prepare the necessary provisional planning which would then have to serve in order to obtain the definitive Ottoman concession.

Several meetings were then held in Paris at the end of 1892. One on 15th December and another one called together four days later had seen three groups which would direct this enterprise also in the future: IOB, headed then by its general manager Sir Edgar Vincent, the Bardac financial syndicate, directed by Paris private banker Bardac, and the already mentioned *Régie générale*, lead by Vitali and Biedermann. The total cost of the future line was estimated to amount to 86.8 million francs of which

47 The minutes of these meetings can be found in: Institut für Stadtgeschichte, Frankfurt-am-Main (IfSF). Bethmann-Archiv, V 866. *Eisenbahn Saloniki-Konstantinopel, 1893-1896*, Vol. I: Chemin *de fer de Salonique à Dédéagatch. Protocole et résolutions des conférences réunies à Londres les 29 et 30 juin et à Paris le 30 juillet 1892.*

48 Christopher Clay, "The Imperial Ottoman Bank in the later nineteenth century: a multinational ‚national' bank?", in: Geoffrey Jones (ed.), *Banks as Multinationals*, London/New York, Routledge, 1990, pp. 142-159, quotes on pp. 146-147. See also Jacques Thobie, "Les choix financiers de l'Ottomane en Méditerranée orientale de 1856 à 1939", in *Banque et investissements en Méditerranée à l'époque contemporaine*, Marseille 1985, pp. 57-89.

68.8m had been calculated as pure construction expenses. As a matter of fact, the definitive building contract was concluded with *Régie générale* on 1st June 1893 – the British construction group had obviously dropped out in the meantime. In a second round *Régie générale* then employed various local subcontractors.[49] The concession holder Baudouy would receive 6,000 shares for the transfer of his concession. He declared himself ready to take another 5,600 shares for himself and his group. 9,200 shares each would be taken over by IOB and by *Régie générale*.

Thus the total share capital would consist of 30,000 shares with a nominal share value of FRF 500 each. On top of this the need for an additional 74.8m had to be covered by the issue of a total number of 310,000 bonds, each one of them with a nominal value of 500 francs and paying an interest of 3 per cent. 265,000 of these bonds would be taken over by IOB and its allies, the rest by Baudouy and his group. All shares and bonds had to stay with IOB as long as the railway would not have been finished and technically approved by the Ottoman authorities.[50] The "London Committee" of IOB – which until May 1894 was still called the "London Agency" – discussed the matter in various meetings between May 1891 and the end of 1892. At the beginning the London members of IOB just refused flatly to participate in that "undertaking".[51] Finally, in November 1892 they "decided that the Paris Committee be left full liberty to settle what responsibility the Bank shall assume as Bankers to the Company and financial managers of the Syndicate to be formed for dealing with the shares [and, P.H.] bonds and what interest the Bank itself shall take in the affair."[52]

Further details were settled in a meeting which took place also in Paris at the IOB headquarters on 28th December 1892.[53] Essentially this meeting served to confirm the financial decisions discussed and taken already ten days before. *Régie générale* agreed to accept a comprehensive price of FRF 141,635 for each kilometre it was supposed to build. A large part of this discussion seems to have been dedicated to the problem of the bonds' issue which in principle had been decided already before. It was an important problem because only 7.2 per cent of the company's total

49 See Compagnie du chemin de fer Ottoman Jonction Salonique-Constantinople, Rapport du conseil d'administration pour l'exercice du 23 mars 1893 au 31 décembre 1893, Constantinople 1894, p. 14.

50 IfSF, Bethmann-Archiv, V 866: Procès-Verbal de la réunion du Comité provisoire en date du 19 décembre 1892. See also Centre des Archives du Monde du Travail (CAMT), Roubaix, 207 AQ 329, fasc. 14: "Combinaison financière".

51 Guildhall Library, London: Imperial Ottoman Bank papers, Ms 23,967 (Minute books of the meeting of the London Agency), Vol. 5, p. 199 (6th May 1891), p. 260 (18th May 1892), p. 276f. (17th August 1892).

52 *Ibidem*, p. 293 (8th November 1892).

53 *Ibidem*: meeting on 28 December 1892.

capital would consist of shares – all the rest, more than nine tenths, would have to be covered by bonds. The definitive result of these discussions on the bond question was then agreed upon in another meeting on February 28 of the following year:[54] The 310,000 bonds were distributed among IOB which took 115,000 of them. To Baudouy and his group a number of 80,000 bonds was assigned, and there appeared a completely new name, Baron Hugo von Bethmann, who engaged himself and his group – and among its members we find again the Paris private banker Bardac – for an amount of 115,000 bonds, the same amount as IOB had promised to take. This was no less than 37 per cent of the entire bonds issue. Hugo von Bethmann was the brother of Ludwig Simon Moritz von Bethmann, the head of one of the most important Frankfurt private banking houses which however by 1900, had – as practically all other private banks in Germany – been overtaken by the big German joint-stock banks.

Despite these developments the house of Bethmann still played an important role in German and international finance and was frequently involved in common undertakings with Deutsche Bank.[55] H. von Bethmann, who lived in Paris since 1883, had his own private bank in Paris. He had taken it over from his father-in-law, and in 1893 it was still known under the name of *Veuve Kinen & Cie*. Later on it took the name of H. de Bethmann but inevitably it had to be wound up as a consequence of WWI.[56] The sister of the two Bethmanns was married to baron Rodolphe Hottinguer, an important private banker in Paris as well as one of the key directors of IOB, and from 1902 the chairman of its Paris committee,[57] a fact which might at least in part explain Bethmann's excellent connections with several Parisian private banks.[58]

When *Compagnie du chemin de fer ottoman Jonction Salonique-Constantinople* had been finally founded in Istanbul on 23rd March 1893 and its prospectus published shortly afterwards, the houses which offered the subscription of the 3 per cent bonds were of course IOB at Paris and Constantinople – as well as at its other agencies in the Ottoman Empire –, Paribas, always closely linked to IOB, and Gebrüder Bethmann – the bank

---

54 Minutes of the meeting of February 28, 1893.

55 Boris Barth, *Die deutsche Hochfinanz und die Imperialismen: Banken und Aufienpolitik vor 1914*, Stuttgart, Franz Steiner Verlag, 1995.

56 See Johann Philip Freiherr von Bethmann (ed.), *Bankiers sind auch Menschen. 225 Jahre Bankhaus Gebrüder Bethmann*, Frankfurt-am-Main, 1973, p. 245. See also the excellent study done by Verena von Wiczlinski, *Im Zeichen der Weltwirtschaft. Das Frankfurter Privatbankhaus Gebr. Bethmann in der Zeit des deutschen Kaiserreichs, 1870-1914*, Stuttgart, 2011, p. 244f.

57 See A. Autheman, *La Banque impériale ottomane*, *op. cit.*, p. 169.

58 See Claus Helbing, *Die Bethmanns. Aus der Geschichte eines alten Handelshauses zu Frankfurt-am-Main*, Wiesbaden, Gericke, 1948, pp. 129-131.

of the Bethmann brothers – in Frankfurt which likewise could count on excellent relations with IOB, particularly during the 1890s.[59]

The fact that the Bethmann bank figured on this official document was however not only a result of family relations and of long-term business connections, it was also due to the ongoing efforts of H. von Bethmann and Carl Borgnis, another member of the Bethmann family, who both kept on talking and proposing to their French colleagues. The first letter concerning this matter which has been handed down to posterity dates from the end of October 1892 and had been written by H. von Bethmann to Borgnis. There Bethmann told him that the talks on the Salonique-Dedeagatch affaire had now arrived at a point where a meeting of the representatives of the different banking groups seemed to make sense and had therefore been arranged.[60] Borgnis, who in the meantime had travelled from Frankfurt to Paris, stated only two days later in a letter to L.S.M. von Bethmann, the head of the family bank at Frankfurt, that he had met already quite a lot of bankers and that, from what he had heard so far, there "seems to lie a large profit in the business [...]. To me and also to Hugo this business seems to be very tempting".[61] Three days later, Borgnis was still in an optimistic mood, and recommended that *Gebrüder Bethmann* should try to let "once again" its friends participate in the Frankfurt banking scene at the sale of the Salonique-Constantinople securities.[62] Several months later, at the end of February 1893, Hugo told Moritz that the 3 per cent bonds would be given to the Bethmanns at a price of 52 per cent of its nominal value – which in fact meant that their real interest rate would then be only slightly below a 6 per cent line.[63]

Two weeks later Hugo informed Moritz in Frankfurt that the Ottoman Debt Administration had declared to accept the kilometrical subsidy payments by the Ottoman government to the railway company – something which was absolutely essential for the future functioning of the railway firm.[64] In this letter Hugo was also quite confident that the contract with the construction company, *Régie générale*, and the other formalities, for instance the creation of the company board, would be successfully dealt with within the next few weeks. He also hoped that Crédit lyonnais would give a hand in the efficient marketing of the bonds even if this would

59 See B. Barth, *Die deutsche Hochfinanz*, *op. cit.*, p. 83. V. v. Wiczlinski, *Im Zeichen der Weltwirtschaft*, *op. cit.*, pp. 245-259.

60 IfSF, Bethmann-Archiv, V 866: Hugo v. Bethmann to Carl Borgnis (Paris, October 26, 1892).

61 *Ibidem*: Carl Borgnis to Ludwig Simon Moritz v. Bethmann (Paris, October 28, 1892).

62 *Ibidem* (Paris, October 31, 1892).

63 *Ibidem*: Hugo v. Bethmann an Ludwig Simon Moritz v. Bethmann (Paris, February 28, 1893).

64 *Ibidem* (Paris, March 14, 1893).

have to be paid somewhat better. "I would be very much interested in this because they [*Crédit lyonnais*] really manage to place such bonds" – quite an interesting statement coming from a professional banker and which underlines the high esteem enjoyed by the placement power of this very important French bank.[65] In a letter written a week before Hugo had mentioned among others that the subscribers of the bonds should in some way or another also participate in the issue of shares. Maybe, he admitted, the actual proposal was "not totally satisfactory." On the other hand, he argued, the future of the company shares would not be that clear since prospects for "big dividends" were not really that bright.[66]

Finally, on 23rd March 1893, the first general shareholders meeting of the *Jonction Salonique-Constantinople* railway company met in the IoB premises in Paris. It nominated the first ten members of the Board, among them three members of the Council of the Ottoman Debt Administration – one of them was Ham-di-Bey, a high Ottoman administrator.[67] There was also a representative of IoB and one of Paribas in the Council, and there was H. von Bethmann and his bank *Veuve Kinen & Cie*,[68] who, together with IoB, would negotiate the conditions of the sale of the Company's bonds with the syndicate formed for that purpose.[69] At the end of March and the beginning of April 1893 three meetings of this syndicate took place in Paris: It was first of all decided to issue for the moment only part of the 310,000 bonds, i.e. 100,000, to offer them in France, as already mentioned, through Paribas and IoB, in Frankfurt through Bethmann brothers and finally to try to involve *Crédit lyonnais* and its hundreds of sale points, as H. von Bethmann had already considered.[70] By the middle

65 See Hubert Bonin, "Le Crédit lyonnais, la Société générale et les autres: essai d'appréciation des rapports de force (1864-1966)", in Bertrand Desjardins, Michel Lescure, Roger Nougaret, Alain Plessis and André Straus (eds.), *Le Crédit lyonnais, 1863-1986*, Geneva, Droz, 2003, pp. 725-749.

66 IfSF, Bethmann-Archiv, V 866: Hugo v. Bethmann to Ludwig Simon Moritz v. Bethmann (Paris, March 7, 1893).

67 As to the administration of the Ottoman Debt, see Jacques Thobie, "Finance et politique extérieure: L'administration de la dette publique ottomane, 1881-1914", in Jacques Thobie, *La France et l'Est méditerranéen depuis 1850*, Vol. 1, pp. 337-352. See also Ehdem Eldem, *A History of the Ottoman Bank*, Istanbul, 1999, pp. 157, 276f.

68 Not everybody was as cosmopolitan as the members of the founding group of the *Salonique-Constantinople* railway: The Paris newspaper *Paris Bourse* of April 20, 1893, criticised the election of Hugo von Bethmann to the Board "because all these names of foreign noblemen add a bad German taste to your business" (*ibidem*, open letter to Monsieur J. Henri Thors, manager of Paribas).

69 *Ibidem*: *Compagnie du chemin de fer Jonction Salonique-Constantinople. Assemblée générale des actionnaires du jeudi 23 Mars 1893. Procès-Verbal.*

70 See the minutes of the syndicate meetings on 28th March, 30th March and 10th April 1893, in: *Archives nationales (AN), Centre des archives du monde du travail (CAMT)*, Roubaix, 207 AQ 329, fasc. 15.

of April 1893 the Frankfurt Bethmann bank had managed to place almost two thirds of the 15,000 *Jonction* bonds it had subscribed to with its partners, mostly private bankers of the same city.[71]

Until the end of 1893 there were two further developments in this business. One was quite normal and was practiced regularly when new securities were pushed into the market: Bethmann and Bardac tried to stabilise the price of *Jonction* bonds at the Paris and Frankfurt stock exchanges through frequent buying and selling.[72] The other initiative was a child of Bardac who thought that it might be a good idea to put all three railways – the *Oriental*, the *Salonique-Monastir*, and the *Jonction Salonique-Constantinople* – under one hat and sell them afterwards to the Sultan who, in search of finance, would then create a single new security, "*Chemins de fer consolidés*", which could then be traded on an international scale.[73] This idea remained in discussion for the rest of the year 1893[74] and seems to have disappeared afterwards, probably because nobody could imagine that the Ottoman government would have wanted or would have been able to take such an initiative.

Apart from such far flung projects, the sale of the *Jonction* bonds went ahead very well. Thus, in January 1894, Bardac informed M. von Bethmann in Frankfurt: "About the *Salonique*, the issue is faring perfectly well. We have now one sold over hundred thousand bonds, and I presume that since a little while we will complete it, except an unexpected event."[75] By the middle of February 1894, of the 310,000 bonds to be sold 200,746 had found their buyers. A "new syndicate", which probably consisted of the old members, had been formed in order to sell the remaining 109,254 bonds.[76] The company's 320,000 bonds had been admitted to the official listing at the Paris stock exchange in four different moments: the first 100,000 in July 1893, the following two tranches of 50,000 each in February and April 1894. The last 120,000 were admitted in August of the same year – and there were

71 IfSF, Bethmann-Archiv, V 867: List of subparticipations, dated April 13, 1893.

72 *Ibidem*: see the numerous letters exchanged between Banque Bardac and Bethmann Bank during the second half of 1893.

73 *Ibidem*: "Visite de M. Noël Bardac, 12 Juillet 1893". There is a commentary in this report on Bardac's visit to Frankfurt which underlines that Bardac is wrong when he proposes a possible acquisition of the Oriental Railways by the Sultan because they already belong to him. He probably confounded them with the *Betriebsgesellschaft* which is running the lines.

74 See for example the "*Note sur la fusion des lignes de la Turquie d'Europe*", 25 November 1893 (*ibidem*).

75 *Ibidem*: Letter of January 18, 1894 (in French).

76 Syndicate meeting of 10 February 1894 (Source as indicated in note 62 above).

to be no further initiatives of this kind until the outbreak of WWI.[77] These bonds had also been listed in Frankfurt and Amsterdam, but not in London.[78]

If we are to believe several lists of subscribers to *Jonction Salonique-Constantinople* shares and bonds – lists originating from the IOB archives and unfortunately not dated but most probably from 1893/94 –, there must have been thirty banks and individuals participating in the subscription of the 24,000 shares on sale.[79] The most important subscribers were *Régie générale* with a subscribed amount of 9,150 shares, followed by Baudouy, the original concession holder, with 5,600 shares, IOB with 2,786 shares, the Bardac bank, Paris, with 2,600 pieces, Paribas with a number of 1,590, Veuve Kinen & Cie., Paris, the bank of H. von Bethmann, with a subscription of 600 shares, and Bethmann Brothers, Frankfurt, with an identical amount. The rest was subscribed at quotas of not exceeding 100 shares by a certain number of Paris private banks and a few British ones. Another undated list contains the name of the subscribers to 95,000 bonds: The most important subscriptions – which were written on a sheet called *Liste de la Maison Veuve Kinen & Co.* – came from Noël and Sigismond Bardac (26,500 bonds) and from H. von Bethmann's bank Veuve Kinen & Cie (15,000 bonds). They were followed by the Disconto-Gesellschaft and S. Bleichroeder, both from Berlin (each of them 5,000 bonds). James Saloschin, whom we could not identify, was next with 4,000 bonds followed by the Geneva banking house of Velay, Hentsch, Odier & Cie (3,500 bonds) and the Austrian Credit-Anstalt, Vienna, the *Allgemeine Depositen Bank*,[80] N. & E. Léon and the Trustees Executors Securities Insurance Corporation, probably from London, with 3,000 bonds each. There were then other names – more private customers than banks – with subscription orders starting from 2,500 bonds downward. There is also a subscription list for a total of 80,000 bonds of the "*Groupe Baudouy-Zogheb*". Baudouy at Constantinople and Baudouy at Paris started with subscription orders for 8,240 and 6,360 bonds. There was the viscount of Zogheb and his friends with a sum of 14,005, and we

---

77 See the various yearbooks of the Paris stock exchange between 1894 and 1913 (Compagnie des agents de change près la Bourse de Paris, Chambre syndicale (ed.), *Annuaire des valeurs admises à la cote officielle*, Paris, *ad annos*).

78 See Guildhall Library, London: Imperial Ottoman Bank papers, Ms 23,967 (Minute books of meetings of the London Agency, Vol. 5), p. 321 (19 April 1893).

79 See (also for the following): AN, CAMT, 207 AQ 329, fasc. 15.

80 In 1873, Deutsche Bank had liquidated an *Allgemeine Depositenbank*, Berlin (Manfred Pohl, *Konzentration im deutschen Bankwesen* (*1848-1980*), Frankfurt/Main, 1982, p. 130), so it could not have been this one: On the other hand, it is quite surprising to find another bank twenty year later with exactly the same name.

find *Société ottomane de change et de valeurs*, with an order for 4,000 bonds followed by *Banque de Constantinople* with 2,500, and Crédit général ottoman with 2,000 bonds. There were various customers of IOB in Cairo (4,020), Beyrouth (4,500), Alexandria (3,500), Smyrna (1,020), Sofia (325) and even Rustschuk (250). And finally a collective order for 18,450 bonds came from "about thirty high Ottoman civil servants connected to IOB, the accounts of whom present serious guarantees".[81]

Despite being obviously incomplete these lists reveal some interesting insights: They show that particularly about the bonds there was quite an interest shown by banks and individuals active or even resident in the Ottoman Empire. One can also find some first-rate addresses in Paris, London, Geneva, Berlin, and Vienna – many of them private bankers but also some joint-stock banks, most of them probably ready to sell these new bonds as soon as possible to their customers. Interest in the new shares was obviously much more limited – understandably, because for years they would yield not more than 2 per cent per year. It is also not really astonishing that *Régie générale* took a huge part, 38 per cent, of the shares right from the beginning. As the constructor and the future manager of the railway it wanted to occupy a strong position and have its say in all matters financial and technical.

Apart from all that the sources we have consulted on the first two years of the *Jonction* company reveal a lot of information on the complexity of founding such a firm which were valid still at the end of the 19th century: the time necessary to deal with the Ottoman administration, the attitudes of the local population, the *milieu* of Parisian finance and its international connections, the time it took to create a new title of finance and to find its necessary buyers in France and in the rest of Europe – all these factors had their importance and had to be taken into consideration. Still, the founders of the *Jonction* company must have been people who believed in the essential quality of their line, which meant that they saw it as an important link between West and East and, indirectly, also between North and South. A proof of this conviction is certainly the fact that, as far as we know, at no moment a narrow-gauge line through Thrace was envisaged. This was quite different from the original solution adopted in Thessaly after it had become a part of Greece in 1881. There a narrow-gauge network was constructed first, to be transformed into a full-gauge line only two decades later.[82]

81 "About thirty high Ottoman officials in relationship with the Imperial Ottoman Bank and whose accounts give all the desired guarantees."

82 See Catherine Bregianni, "Réseaux techniques et concepts de modernisation", *Cahiers de la Méditerranée* [on-line], 78, 2009, pp. 291-306.

4. Finance through years of routine and gradual development (1896-1911)

Once the entire line from Salonica to Dedeagatch had been officially opened – on 1st April 1896, as already mentioned above –, investors' expectations could be fulfiled only up to a certain extent. One of the reasons was certainly that travellers and tourists from Western and Central Europe did not use the line of the Oriental Railways to Salonica as much as had been hoped, and this of course meant also less traffic on the line Salonica-Dedeagatch-Constantinople. A German consular report from Salonica, dated 2nd April 1900, noted among others that most travellers from Central Europe still took the boat from Trieste to Constantinople without passing through Salonica. In the meantime however, the new railway line to the Bosporus via Dedeagatch had become an "important competitor" to traditional coastal navigation from Salonica to Constantinople.[83]

It cannot be the aim of this short chapter to follow the development of the Salonique-Constantinople line year by year and in all possible detail. But if we want to get a rough idea of its position and relative importance within the Ottoman railway system we might have a short look at the relevant statistics published for the year 1907.[84] Following these data the minimum income from this line was guaranteed by the Ottoman state to the company, and it had to be FRF 15,500 per kilometre and year. Given that the entire network had a length of 510.6 km, the total minimum sum in 1907 was FRF 7,914m. The total revenue of the line amounted to FRF 2,738m in the same year, and thus the Ottoman state had to pay a subsidy of 5,176m francs to the owners of this railway. Compared with another railway line in the European part of the Ottoman Empire, the line from Salonica to Monastir, which was less than half as long (218.9 km) and had been completely inaugurated in 1894, there the yearly income guaranteed by the Ottoman state amounted only to FRF 14,300-1,200 less than in the case of the *Jonction Salonique-Constantinople* railway. This latter company had transported 332,835 persons and 129,473 tons

83 *Bundesarchiv Berlin*, R 901/53748: Annual reports of the German consulate in Salonica, part 1, fol. 68. Likewise, the German vice-consul at Dedeagatch registered – for the following year – a small increase of imports into this town. According to him this was due to the impact of the new railway line coming from Salonica (*ibidem*, R 901/53777: Report of the German vice-consul of 11th February 1901, folio 12).

84 See "Die Eisenbahnen der Türkei im Jahre 1907", *Archiv für Eisenbahnwesen*, Vol. 33, 1910, pp. 459-477. This article is based on the publication by Alexis Rey, *Statistique des principaux résultats de l'exploitation des chemins de fer de l'Empire ottoman pendant l'exercice 1907*. It is not totally clear if the figure for the transport of passengers includes military personal but it seems probable.

of goods in 1907[85] whereas the much shorter Salonica-Monastir line had shown a quite more intense activity with 207,821 persons and 103,983 tons of merchandise shipped in the course of 1907. This relatively better performance of the Salonica-Monastir railway can be underlined by the fact that it was achieved by only eight locomotives, 22 passenger cars, 6 baggage cars and 190 cars for merchandise and cattle. In comparison the *Jonction Salonique-Constantinople* line owned no less than 32 locomotives, 90 passenger cars, 30 baggage cars and the impressive number of 728 cars for the transport of merchandise. Two years later the situation had not changed a lot: In 1909 the Jonction *Salonique-Constantinople* line transported 407,359 persons; 85,959 of them belonged to the military. That was quite an increase from 1907. On the other hand, 126,155 tons of goods had been carried by this railway in 1909. At the same time the Salonica-Monastir track had increased the number of its travellers to 242,885 and the transported goods to 109,924 tons, a growth which was altogether not very impressive.[86]

Among the railways of European Turkey already in 1896 there had been spectacular differences in their revenues per kilometre: the oldest one among them, the Oriental Railways, could show a revenue per kilometre and year of FRF 9,811. They were followed by the Salonica-Monastir line with a revenue of FRF 6,381. At a considerable distance behind them came the *Jonction Salonique-Constantinople* company with only FRF 2,064.[87] Three years later, in 1899, this latter railway had improved its income per kilometre with a yearly result of 3,073 francs. Salonica-Monastir showed a small increase by earning FRF 6,668. Only the Oriental lines had fallen back to FRF 8,139 but they were still leading the field.[88]

It is certainly not easy to explain this very important difference between at first the two and then the three railway companies keeping in mind their respective capacities, their performance and, as a consequence, their individual productivities. So far we lack or we have not yet seen the source material which would enable us to come to clear-cut conclusions. A possible answer might be found in the interest shown by the Ottoman authorities which probably "persuaded" the *Jonction*

85 Between 1895 and 1897 more than half of the revenues achieved on this line originated from the transport of travellers, a tendency which was increasing over time. Most of the transported goods were grain and melons, not tobacco. A large part of the tobacco was exported by ship from Kavalla (Die Anschlussbahn Salonik – Konstantinopel, in: Archiv für Eisenbahnwesen, Vol. 21 (1898), pp. 1375-1377).

86 See "Die Eisenbahnen der Türkei im Jahre 1909", *Archiv für Eisenbahnwesen*, Vol. 35, 1912, pp. 246-254, and particularly 248f.

87 "Die Eisenbahnen in der Türkei im Jahre 1899", *Archiv für Eisenbahnwesen*, Vol. 24, 1901, pp. 865-867 (figures on p. 867).

88 *Ibidem*, p. 867.

Salonique-Constantinople company to enlarge its transport capacities beyond reasonable limits since this was, as we have seen above, a "strategic" line.[89] A certain compensation for these requirements may be found in a larger kilometrical subsidy for the *Salonique-Constantinople* line: as a matter of fact it was about 8 per cent higher than the corresponding sum for the Salonica-Monastir railway. Another reason for the lower cost of constructing and running the Salonica-Monastir line might be the fact that after its inauguration it was run by the Oriental Railways, which had already quite a long experience in managing railways in the Ottoman Empire. The Oriental Railways also put their railway station in Salonica at the disposal of the Salonica-Monastir enterprise which therefore did not have to build a new one. Both of these measures must have helped to reduce Salonica-Monastir's total expenses.[90]

The economic and finance research unit of *Crédit lyonnais*, its body to prepare and conceive financial operations and issues, as part of its corporate and investment banking activities, in its careful analysis of the *Salonique-Constantinople* company[91] delivered in 1913, came, at the end of the report, among others back to the problems of profitability of the company. Quite apart from the lack of "vertical" i.e. North-South lines coming down from the mountains or up from the seaside to join the main (West-East) line the research report stressed the fact that the near-distance traffic of this railway – "*le trafic de la petite vitesse*" – remained comparatively underdeveloped whereas its passenger traffic was growing much faster. Thus the transport of merchandise at short distance had increased by about 10 per cent on average during the last years. On the contrary the revenue from passenger transportation had grown from FRF 1,207m in 1906 to 2,853m in 1911, an average increase of 18 to 20 per cent.

89 The structure of the Salonique-Constantinople company's revenues demonstrates this quite clearly: In 1895 and 1896 its income from the transport of persons and merchandise went from 1,999 francs per kilometre to 2,065 francs. In 1897, the year of the Greek-Turkish War, this figure went down to 1,786 francs per kilometre whereas there was now an amount of 8,483 francs, paid by the Ottoman Government for military transports (See "Über die Anschlussbahn Salonik-Konstantinopel", *Archiv für Eisenbahnwesen*, Vol. 21, 1898, p. 1376). The annual report of the Compagnie du chemin de fer ottoman Jonction Salonique-Constantinople for the year 1897 referred to this conflict in the following way: "*Au cours de cet exercice, l'exploitation de notre réseau a été effectuée dans les conditions exceptionnelles motivées par la guerre dont la Thessalie et l'Épire ont été le théâtre. Nous avons dû, en effet, assurer, de fin février à mi-juin, les transports de mobilisation, de concentration, de renforcement, de ravitaillement et d'évacuation des blessés des armées Ottomanes qui opéraient dans ces régions*", Compagnie du chemin de fer ottoman Jonction Salonique-Constantinople: Rapport à l'assemblée générale, exercice 1897, Constantinople, 1898, p. 5.

90 See "Salonik-Monastir Eisenbahngesellschaft", *Archiv für Eisenbahnwesen*, Vol. 21, 1898, pp. 1377-1380, and particularly p. 1378.

91 Archives historiques du Crédit agricole, Paris. Fonds Crédit lyonnais, DEEF 24189.

The passenger tariff had remained more or less stable, so the growth of income from that category must have been due to a larger number of persons using the line. On the contrary, the merchandise tariff per ton was, according to the report, "very high" – which would be at least part of the explanation for the lower growth in this sector.[92]

The railway company had entrusted already in 1895 the daily business of running the line to *Régie générale*, the same firm which had built its line. According to the report the financial means which had been reserved for the maintenance of the network by *Régie générale* might possibly have been "a bit too small".[93] Finally, the company had paid a yearly dividend of 2 per cent from 1899 to 1910 on its small share capital. In 1911 no dividend was paid to the shareholders – to whom normally half of the net profit had been distributed – because revenues had increased so favourably that the Ottoman state could reduce its guarantee payment.[94] The rule was that, beyond a limit of a yearly gross revenue per kilometre of FRF 15,500, the additional income had to be shared equally between the company and the Ottoman government.[95] This could be called an economically perverse mechanism but probably it was just a consequence of short-term considerations of the company's founders when they decided to create it almost two decades earlier.

The best proof for the assumption that the original investors might not really have been that happy with the situation of the *Jonction Salonique-Constantinople* – and the same was more or less true for the banks engaged in the other two railways running through the European parts of Turkey – is the fact that they wanted these three networks to be united. Such ideas seem to have come up for the first time in October 1893 – when the construction of the *Jonction* line was not even

92 *Ibidem*, p. 14. This argument is surprisingly similar to how Ahmet Akarli describes the situation on the Oriental line between Salonica and Skopje and further north of it: He talks of "exorbitant railway tariffs" (Ahmet O. Akarli, "Growth and retardation in Ottoman Macedonia, 1880-1910", in Şevket Pamuk and Jeffrey G. Williamson (eds.), *The Mediterranean Response to Globalization before 1950*, London/New York, Routledge, 2000, pp. 109-133, quote on p. 118.

93 *Ibidem*, p. 16.

94 "Les clauses de la garantie sont telles que, jusqu'à des recettes brutes de 15,500 francs par km, plus le trafic augmente, plus le produit net disponible diminue." (*ibidem*, p. 23).

95 *Ibidem*, p. 5. This had been shown already in a calculation which must have been developed by the IOB staff, probably in 1892, shortly before this bank decided to participate in the foundation of the *Jonction Salonique-C*onstantinople. It demonstrates very clearly that higher revenues were apt to endanger – with smaller or no subsidies paid by the Ottoman government – the payments for the bonds issued by the company (NA, CAMT: 207 AQ 329, fasc. 14).

terminated – and they foresaw the union of the three lines as well as the unification of the Ottoman debt for these three railways. In this early case it was the *Wiener Vereinsbank* together with the other two allied credit institutes, Deutsche Bank and Crédit suisse, who had bought the Oriental Railways from baron Hirsch in 1890 and who now believed that such a strategy of unifying lines and debts would be a good affair and talked about it with the management of IOB.[96] Nothing seems to have come out of this but the next meeting took place only a year later, in December 1894 in Paris, between two top representatives of Deutsche Bank, Siemens and Gwinner, Bauer of the *Wiener Bankverein*, the Paris committee of IOB and Vincent, Hugo von Bethmann, Bardac as well as Biedermann of *Régie générale*.[97] There the "general principles" of a compromise concerning the putting together of the three mentioned railway companies were fixed: *Compagnie d'exploitation des Chemins de fer orientaux* should continue its negotiations with the *Sublime Porte* in Constantinople. Once these talks had been carried ahead the *Banque des chemins de fer orientaux* at Zurich should buy the shares of the *Jonction Salonique-Constantinople* railway and of the Salonica-Monastir line.[98] As soon as this operation had been finished Deutsche Bank and *Wiener Bankverein* would offer to IOB a "new" participation of 15 per cent in the share capital of the Oriental Railways at a fixed price. Once all this had been done, the "German group" would demand from the Ottoman government that questions pending with the Oriental Railways had to be solved and that the long expected harbour construction works at Salonica and Dedeagatch had to come finally to an end. As before, this idea remained just a project.

There were other plans coming up during the following years, each of them different but having also many points in common. So for instance the "programme for the merger of the three railway companies of European Turkey", dating from 24 December 1895, which proposed the acquisition, by the Ottoman government, of the entire share capital of those three companies. In this case, the original shareholders would be compensated with newly issued bonds. The original bonds would then be guaranteed by the Ottoman Government. The network, once it had been united, would be run by a new Ottoman company. According to this

96 Letter of Théodore Berger, membre of the Paris committee of IOB, to Sir Edgar Vincent, general manager of the same bank, on 10 October 1893 (AN, CAMT, 207 AQ 333, fasc. 22). About Berger, see André Autheman, *La Banque impériale ottomane*, *op. cit.*, p. 88, note 74. About Vincent, *ibidem*, p. 123.

97 See the minutes of a meeting in Paris on 6th December 1894 (AN, CAMT, 207 AQ 333, fasc. 22).

98 About the *Banque des chemins de fer orientaux*, see Peter Hertner, *The Balkan Railway*, *op. cit.*, pp. 140-142.

project important savings could be made by concentrating the administration and the management as well as by combining and better organising the use of the existing rolling stock.[99] Another study, dated 26 February 1896, dealt with the possible acquisition, by the Ottoman government, not only of the three "European" lines but also of the Smyrna-Cassaba Railway, since 1894 under the control of the Imperial Ottoman Bank,[100] and of the German-built Anatolian Railway.[101] In this case again the calculation tried to show that by unifying all those companies under the roof of the Zurich-based holding, *Banque des chemins de fer orientaux*, quite considerable savings could be achieved.

Finally, in February 1902, there arrived another project, developed by Deutsche Bank, which proposed the creation of a *Société ottomane des chemins de fer de l'État* (*Régie co-interessée*). A new syndicate would have to be founded in equal parts by Deutsche Bank and IOB. It would issue a loan of FRF 145 million which would serve to place bonds for an amount of 116m. The rest of the money could then be used for buying shares of the three railway companies of European Turkey. "The instrument [...] for putting this whole operation to work" would be again the Zurich-based *Banque des chemins de fer orientaux*, as Arthur von Gwinner (from Deutsche Bank) informed Gaston Auboyneau (at the Paris committee of IOB) in his answer of 27 February 1902. In a letter of 24 February 1902 to Gwinner, Auboyneau made some critical remarks on behalf of his committee. Among others he just noted that it might be quite difficult to get such a large amount of money from the capital market for an object which in any way would go to the Turkish state only after 90 years. Apart from that, and given the particular proportions between the share capital of the bank and its issue of bonds, the future of the shares (FRF 25m) would in this specific case be much less important than the outlook for the bonds (FRF 116m).[102] As in all other cases proposed before this time again the plans for the unification of rails and capital did not succeed. The Paris committee of IOB did not want to get involved in a "combination" which it considered to be favourable above all for the Oriental Railways and the Zurich holding, of which IOB was also a shareholder, but this would not compensate the risks IOB estimated to run in case it subscribed half of the FRF 140m loan.[103]

---

99 *Ibidem*.

100 Jacques Thobie, "Conjoncture et stratégie: Le groupe financier de l'Ottomane en 1914", in Jacques Thobie, *La France et l'Est méditerranéen depuis 1850*, Vol. 1, Istanbul, 1993, pp. 261-277, particularly pp. 267f.

101 AN, CAMT, 207 AQ 333, fasc. 22.

102 *Ibidem*: Auboyneau to Gwinner (24/2/1902), Gwinner to Auboyneau (27/2/1902).

103 *Ibidem*: Auboyneau to Gwinner (1/3/1902 and 13/3/1902).

Ten years later, in 1912, the idea of putting the various participations together was again discussed but this time preference was given to strictly national or even company solutions. The general climate had obviously changed and international cooperation in business of that kind had become less desirable.[104] Thus in August 1912 the London committee of IOB sent a note to the Paris committee in which it pleaded for a more coherent policy in the Bank's way of participating in different railways and other infrastructural undertakings.[105] The answer from Paris was positive: The Parisian committee proposed to unite all railway shares and bonds possessed by IOB "and its friends" in a single company with shares worth more or less FRF 32m and bonds for 80m. The railways involved would have been the *Smyrne-Cassaba, Jonction Salonique-Constantinople, Damas-Hamah & Prolongements* as well as the IOB participation in the Baghdad line. This could not be done immediately but "in the autumn", i.e. within the next two or three months.[106]

Two months later, on 5 October 1912, a new document, most probably done by IOB staff, appeared. It proposed, quite in line with the preceding projects, the foundation of a holding company, a so-called *Omnium franco-ottoman*, which would "assemble all French interests in order to provide them with the indispensable cohesion and unity as well as with the power to treat on an equal level with the Ottoman government."[107] As a decade before, nothing of this kind was realised. If in the earlier years close cooperation between the various international groups seemed to be too complicated and full of unknown risks, now international politics had created much more intricate scenarios and the retreat to purely national solutions – even if IOB formally still carried the character of a bi-national institution – appeared clearly safer and for the moment more promising.

---

104 See for instance the opinion of the French ambassador at Constantinople who expressed such a view in a report of 3rd December 1912 to the French Prime Minister and minister of Foreign Affairs, Raymond Poincaré. Referring to the idea of the minister of finance Joseph Caillaux to create a holding for all French companies and participations active in the infrastructural sector of Syria – which then was still part of the Ottoman Empire –, the ambassador wrote: "Le trust des affaires françaises en Syrie doit avoir, dans les circonstances actuelles, une allure nettement et exclusivement française." (AN, CAMT, 207 AQ 333, fasc. 23). See also Jacques Thobie, "Conjoncture et stratégie", *op. cit.*, pp. 273-277.

105 AN, CAMT, 207 AQ 333, fasc. 23: The IOB London to the IOB Paris committee (8/8/1912).

106 *Ibidem*: IOB Paris committee to IOB London committee (9/8/1912).

107 Document *Omnium Franco-Ottoman*, dated 5th October 1912, p. 1 (AN, CAMT, 207 AQ 333, fasc. 23.

5. Wars and nationalism putting an end to the commitment of western finance in Balkanic international railways

For the railway companies the two Balkan Wars in 1912/13 and their results changed everything.[108] As is well known, the first one put an end to Ottoman power in almost all of South-Eastern Europe. Serbia, Greece, and Bulgaria together with a formally independent Albania inherited almost all of the former Ottoman territories. During the hostilities the railway lines of the three international companies were occupied by the different armies. Once the conflict had ended new borders were drawn up which in most cases did not at all correspond to the needs of travel and transportation.

These unforeseen developments could not leave the shareholders and the banks who had issued the bonds of the three international railway companies undisturbed. Thus, already in May 1913 *Compagnie de Jonction Salonique-Constantinople* prepared a paper on the problem of the bonds and the connected interest payments to the bondholders. It was supposed to be submitted to the French government and to the International Financial Conference which the Great Powers had set up in view of the future peace treaty between the Balkan countries and the Ottoman Empire.[109] Four months later, in September, the management of *Compagnie de Jonction* became increasingly nervous since the next payments for their bonds had to be done by 15 October 1913 and the problems of their railway had become more and more visible. After the start of the hostilities, the income which the Company normally gained from its transports had declined dramatically. On the other hand the kilometrical subsidy payments by the Ottoman state had been stopped and would be paid, if everything went well, only two months after the end of the current business period by those Balkan states who would then have become the territorial successors to the Ottoman Empire.[110] In a meeting of the representatives of *Compagnie de Jonction* with some of the leading figures representing *Société générale*, Paribas, IOB, the private banking house Bardac and *Régie générale* on 19 September, it was decided to remind the French government that it should intervene strongly on behalf of the French bondholders and that it should declare that the reimbursement by the Balkan states and Turkey of the money advanced so far by the banks,

---

108 See Peter Hertner, "The Balkan railways", *op. cit.*, p. 147. For a general history of these two wars see among others Egidio Ivetic, *Le guerre balcaniche*, Bologna, Il Mulino, 2006.

109 "Obligations du Chemin de fer Jonction Salonique-Constantinople" (BNP Paribas. Archives historiques, 6\DFOM-221\493).

110 Document "Obligations *Salonique-Constantinople*" (AN, CAMT, 207 AQ 333, fasc. 22).

and *Régie générale* would be a fundamental condition for the listing of the loans of these countries at the Paris stock exchange.[111]

Given the importance of the French capital market before 1914 for these countries this was certainly quite an efficient threat. In a note written a few days later it was emphasised that the French government had informed IOB, *Société générale* and Paribas of its desire that a financial group be formed in order to provide the necessary means for the interest payments for the bonds due on next 15 October.[112] Finally, on 3rd October 1913 a contract was signed between these three banks plus *Régie générale* and the private bank N.J. & S. Bardac, Paris, on the one side, the *Jonction Salonique-Constantinople* on the other. It provided for the payment of the interest due for the railway company's bonds and for the payment of those bonds which had been sorted out by a lottery. Altogether this would have been a sum of FRF 2.7m which was to be advanced by the mentioned financial group.[113]

It must have been clear that it might be difficult to get regular payments from the Greek government which had occupied and then annexed the Western part of the *Jonction Salonique-Constantinople* railway, and it was probably quite a surprise when the Greeks paid for military transports on the line during the two Balkan Wars.[114] A month later a "provisional arrangement" between the Greek Government and *Compagnie de Jonction* was signed,[115] and at the beginning of April 1914 the Greeks handed over the money needed for the service of the bonds which had been due on 15 November 1913 and which had been provisionally financed by the syndicate mentioned above.[116] Things were much more difficult with the Bulgarians. The French Foreign Office, via the French legation at Sofia, had put pressure on the Bulgarian Minister of Finance already in November 1913, and the Bulgarian Foreign Ministry had accepted these demands "in principle" making however clear at the same

111 "Compagnie du Chemin de fer ottoman Jonction Salonique-Constantinople. Réunion du 19 septembre 1913" (*ibidem*). A fundamental contribution to the history of this use of "*l'arme financière*" (the financial weapon) is Raymond Poidevin, *Finances et relations internationales, 1887-1914*, Paris, Armand Colin, 1970, particularly chapter 1.

112 "Note Aide-Mémoire" of 24th September 1913, in: AN, CAMT, 207 AQ 333, fasc. 22.

113 Contract of 3rd October 1913 (*ibidem*). Another copy of this contract is in BNP Paribas, Archives historiques, 6\DFOM-221\493.

114 *Jonction Salonique-Constantinople* to *Banque impériale ottomane* on 3rd February 1914, in: AN, CAMT, 207 AQ 333, fasc. 22.

115 "Arrangement provisoire entre le gouvernement royal hellénique et la Compagnie du chemin de fer Salonique-Constantinople" (5 March 1914), in: BNP Paribas, Archives historiques, 6\DFOM-221\493.

116 BIO to private bank Bardac (3 April 1914), in: AN, CAMT, 207 AQ 333, fasc. 22.

time that the Sofia government still needed to be given "a certain delay" for the payment.[117]

When terms of agreement began to become gradually settled, WWI broke out. During the French and British intervention in the Salonica area part of the railway was used by them first and by the Greeks later, the other part by the Bulgarians who had joined the opposite camp. As a consequence of this war Bulgaria had to cede the part of the Aegean coast it had conquered in the First Balkan War, and thus the entire part of Thrace through which ran the *Jonction* railway had become Greek territory.

The final outcome of this newly changed situation was a contract concluded between the railway company and the Greek government on 3rd March 1920 by which the railway would be sold to the Greeks. It meant that the Hellenic government would pay 15 million francs plus some further money for the outstanding guarantee payments to *Compagnie de Jonction* which would use it then in part to pass it to its bondholders who had not received anything during the war. In the future, the interest payments for the bonds would be done by the Greek government. For each bond a sum of FRF 76.50 would be given for the arrears accumulated during the war years.[118] The railway itself was to be handed over by the French army which had used it since the armistice with Turkey to the Greek authorities by the end of May 1920.[119] At the end of April 1921 a letter of the French Foreign Office to the Ministry of Finance informed that the payments due by the Greek Government to the bondholders of *Compagnie de jonction* would in the future be transferred by the International Financial Commission – created in 1898 by the European Great Powers in order to administrate the Greek default of 1893 – and no longer by the Greek Government itself. The financial transactions linked to the interest payments would then be entrusted to *Comptoir national d'escompte de Paris* which would then pay the bondholders. That was the solution desired by the *Compagnie de Jonction* which evidently did not show an unlimited trust in the Greek willingness and capability to pay.[120]

---

117 Letters of the French Ministry of Foreign Affairs of 12 and 20 November 1913 to the *Compagnie Jonction Salonique-Constantinople* (*ibidem*).

118 See "Note sur les obligations de la Compagnie Salonique-Constantinople" (28/12/1920), in: BNP Paribas, Archives historiques, 6\ DFOM-221\493.

119 See *Procédure de règlement transactionnel de la Compagnie du chemin de fer ottoman Jonction Salonique-Constantinople* […]. *Communication de l'Administrateur à Messieurs les créanciers*, Paris, 1920, p. 10.

120 French Foreign Office to French Ministry of Finance (27 April 1921) and Compagnie du chemin de fer Salonique-Constantinople to French Foreign Office (30 April 1921), at: Centre des Archives économiques et financières (CAEF), Savigny-le-Temple (Seine-et-Marne), No. 43.878.

Bulgaria was, as seen by the bondholders, not better. Quite on the contrary: When a Bulgarian delegation came to Paris in the summer of 1921 in order to negotiate a loan with a group of French banks the *Compagnie de jonction* wrote a letter to the French Foreign Office underlining that Bulgaria owed FRF 47m as "reparations" to the *Compagnie* and that this would be the moment to ask the Bulgarians to recognise their existing debt with it. In its letter the *Compagnie* underlined as well that "our bondholders are, so to say, exclusively French"[121] – thus, but this was not explicitly said, an engagement of the French State in their favour would be almost obligatory.[122] At the same time the Compagnie Jonction wrote also to the Minister of Finance emphasising the fact that the opening of the French capital market to an "ex-enemy nation" would be the occasion of resolving all pending financial matters with that particular country.[123] We do not know if this initiative was successful but we have found a note telling us that on 23rd October 1923 a contract was signed between the Bulgarian Government and the two firms, the *Compagnie Jonction* and *Régie générale*, which reduced the amount due from Bulgaria from FRF 44.9m to 20m and established that the payments would be done in treasury bonds marked in French francs – which would eliminate the problem of currency fluctuations.[124]

The results of these negotiations were shown in a short note published by the newsletter *Agence économique et financière* of 2nd April 1930 saying that the Jonction Salonique-Constantinople Railway – now qualified with the adjective "*en liquidation*" – had received a sum of FRF 10m in early 1930 from the Bulgarian Government.[125] The remaining 10m would be sent in 1932. They never came because, as the Bulgarian Debt Administration at the end of December 1932 wrote to the *Compagnie Jonction Salonique-Constantinople*, the world economic crisis had hit Bulgaria to such an extent that it could not guarantee the transfer of the

121 This statement does not go fit to a letter from the Paris "Bureau allemand des biens et intérêts privés" to the French authorities from August 1921 in which its director clearly mentions "la partie des obligations qui se trouve en Allemagne" (letter of 6 August 1921), *ibidem*. A note of the "Agence économique et financière" of 14th March 1930 speaks also of the German Salonique-Constantinople bondholders who would have to get at least part of the outstanding payments to the bondholders of this company (*ibidem*).

122 Compagnie du chemin de fer Jonction Salonique-Constantinople to French Foreign Office (28 July 1921) (*ibidem*).

123 Compagnie du chemin de fer Jonction Salonique-Constantinople to French Minister of Finance (28 July 1921).

124 Note of 8 February 1933 (*ibidem*).

125 *Agence économique et financière*, 2 April 1930.

money it owed *Compagnie Jonction* and *Régie générale*, i.e. FRF 10m and 500,000, the latter for interest arrears.[126]

Based on a decision taken by the Financial Committee of the League of Nations and faced with an ongoing precipitation of the crisis the Bulgarian Government reduced the payments for the moment being to 40 per cent, the rest being transferred on a national account in leva, the national currency.[127] On 30 March 1934 a new contract was done between *Compagnie Jonction* and the Bulgarian Minister of Finance: It reduced the 40:60 proportion to 25:75 where 25 per cent meant the amount of debt which would be received until the end of 1934 and could eventually be changed into French francs; the 75 per cent would be paid in ten half-year portions within five years starting in 1935.[128] The same happened with the Greek Government which, already in April 1932, declared that – basing itself on the decision of the Financial Committee of the League of Nations – it would not produce any payments for its foreign debt.[129] This time the Bulgarians were more polite, but in the very end the result was the same for both debtor countries and for this moment it simply meant: default.

This is not the occasion for going ahead in detail with the further history of the 1893 Salonique-Constantinople bonds. It should be sufficient to say that WWII again interrupted all payments and that, after the war, it took more than two decades to obtain any payments from Greece – whilst for the bondholders Bulgaria, firmly established in the Soviet Bloc since 1944/45, was beyond all hopes anyway. A note from 25th July 1945 which tried to resume the newest information on the Salonique-Constantinople bonds did not come to very encouraging results.[130] Still in July 1964 the information sheet of the *Association nationale des porteurs français de valeurs mobilières* noted that the 3 per cent bonds of *Compagnie Jonction Salonique-Constantinople* were in suspense. There had been payment

126 The Balkan countries were hit particularly strongly by the world economic crisis, as has been shown among others by M.-L. Recker, "Großbritannien, Deutschland und die südosteuropäischen Staaten 1919-1939", in Marie-Luise Recker (ed.), *Von der Konkurrenz zur Rivalität/From Competition to Rivalry*, Stuttgart, Steiner Verlag, 1986, pp. 51-100, and especially pp. 68-70.

127 "Direction de la Dette publique" (Sofia) to Compagnie du chemin de fer Jonction Salonique-Constantinople: letters of 27 December 1932 and 6 January 1933 (CAEF, No. 43 878).

128 Compagnie du chemin de fer Jonction Salonique-Constantinople au gouvernement français (10 April 1934), *ibidem*.

129 Comptoir national d'escompte de Paris to French Minister of Finance (15 and 18 April 1932) (*ibidem*).

130 "Obligations 3% 1893 *Jonction Salonique-Constantinople*", 25 July 1945 (CAEF, B 0055818).

promises of the Greek Government since 1961 but nothing had come out of it. The Association regarded this attitude as highly discriminatory since Greece served the holders of Greek loans if they had been issued in dollars or British pounds.[131] Finally, in July 1969, the Greek Government declared that it would accept to buy these bonds. And that is how the story of this French investment ended. As far as we know the railway is still running between Salonica and Alexandroupolis, formerly Dedeagatch.

Together with the Oriental Railways and the *Salonique-Monastir* line the example of the Salonique – Constantinople Railway demonstrates quite clearly that railway building in this part of Europe – and the same was of course true for the lines running through the Asiatic parts of the Ottoman Empire – was an intricate entanglement between the lenders of capital – and above all the banks as their intermediaries – on the one side and a single host government first and – after 1912 – different host governments on the other. Capital and technology were, as in Western Europe, the two essential ingredients to this new strategic tool but without the political blessing – and the financial support – coming from the Ottoman government not much would have really happened. Once this overall political guarantor had disappeared in that region the situation became much more intricate and the original calculations of profitability were no longer valid. Now the successor states – Greece, Bulgaria, Serbia – took possession of the networks situated within their new borders but, once WWI had ended, foreign finance had virtually left the scene. Without its help technology and national politics were, generally speaking, incapable of expanding and modernising the railway networks which the successor states had inherited in this part of Europe.

131 *Association nationale des porteurs français de valeurs mobilières*, No. 1,839 (22 July 1964): Informations. *Dette extérieure hellénique* (*ibidem*).

CHAPTER 5

Moral Hazard and Investment Banking

Qualitative and Quantitative Evidence from the Baring Crisis (1880-1890)

Juan FLORES

Assistant professor at the Paul Bairoch Institute of Economic History, University of Geneva

The origins of speculative bubbles remain a sort of mystery. This is probably a side effect from the general disagreement on the precise meaning and measurement of bubbles.[1] However, the literature on economic crises is full of accounts where credit booms are followed by violent crashes, with asset prices rapidly raising during the boom only to collapse in the bust. Economists and historians frequently blame investors' irrationality, whose recurrent behaviour is faithfully described in works such as Charles Kindleberger's famous *Manias, panics and crashes*. This chapter aims to describe the origins of one of these episodes, the years that preceded the investment boom of 1885 to 1890. Unlike most of the traditional historiography of this period, we demonstrate that investors did not behave irrationally and rather responded to the actions of financial intermediaries. The underwriting banks' continuous involvement in Argentina's bond issues nourished the confidence in their investments. This feeling was motivated by the banks' supposed superior information on the country and by the fact that, in case of trouble, banks would act as lenders of last resort. In fact, the period ended with the so-called

1 Olivier Blanchard and Mark W. Watson, "Bubbles, rational expectations and financial markets", in Paul Wachtel (ed.), *Crises in the Economic and Financial Structure*, Lexington, MA, D.C. Heathand Company, 1982, pp. 295-316. Franklin Allen and Douglas Gale, "Bubbles and crises", *The Economic Journal*, 2000, No. 110, pp. 236-255. Franklin Allen, Stephen Morris and Hyun Song Shin, "Beauty contests and iterated expectations in asset markets", *Review of Financial Studies*, 2006, Vol. 19, No. 3, pp. 719-752.

"Baring crisis", as investors' strong demand for Argentina's financial assets rapidly weakened before underwriting banks could get rid of the bonds they still held in their portfolio. The most active of them, Baring Brothers, could only survive after this episode thanks to a bailout organised by the Bank of England in 1890.

The historiography on the Baring crisis – both in Britain and Argentina – is vast and rich. The interactions between banks in Europe on the one hand, and the national, provincial and municipal governments in Argentina, on the other, have been described and analysed in a number of works since the very moment of the crisis.[2] The year 1885 marked a turning point in the cycle of capital flows to the so-called "new countries". During that year a currency crisis erupted in Argentina, ending with the gold standard regime that had been set up only two years before. Far from deterring new capital from being invested in Argentina, the effect was precisely the opposite. The true boom of foreign investment into the country really took off during that year and peaked in 1888, before its sudden collapse in 1889 – and mainly in 1890.

This chapter will explain this apparent paradox through an analysis of London's underwriting strategies, their business structure and their risk management. Their implication in the issuing of bonds also affected investors' risk perception. In particular, the involvement of Baring as the historical underwriter of Argentina's bonds in London was regarded as a seal of approval by financial markets. However, overindebtedness in Argentina, along with political instability and a series of external shocks, contributed to freeze the demand for new bonds thus triggering Baring's own fall in 1890. We argue that despite the general environment of competition between underwriting banks, in 1885 they colluded to impose on Argentina a set of conditions before providing additional financial support. Among them, two conditions were particularly relevant. One was related to Argentina's fiscal policy and the other to the suspension of new external borrowing. Financial markets reacted positively to the announcement of the agreement, although in the medium term none of these conditions were met. Moreover, they served to open up Europe's capital markets to Argentina's provinces and municipalities. We speculate on the possible perception in the market that Baring could act as a last resort lender for Argentina. Such developments will contribute to fuel arguments about the portfolio of skills of investment banks at the end of the

2 Comprehensive literature reviews can be found in Juan Flores, *Lorsque le leader suit la foule. La crise Baring dans une perspective microéconomique*, Unpublished PhD Dissertation, Sciences-Po, Paris, 2004. Juan Flores, "Competition in the underwriting markets of sovereign debt: The Baring crisis revisited", *Law and Contemporary Problems*, 2010, Vol. 73, No. 4, pp. 129-150.

19th century within the overall financial architecture structured around international financial centers.[3]

1. The historiography of the Baring crisis and the agreement of 1885

In July 1885, a preliminary contract was signed between seven European banks – two of them British and five French – and Argentina's government. It established the general terms on which banks agreed to issue the largest loan ever granted to a Latin American country until then. The conditions accepted by the Argentina's government agent attempted to regulate the expansionary debt policy practiced by the government since 1880. However, the agreement had the opposite effect: The years between 1886 and 1889 were characterised by the acceleration of the loans contracted in Europe. Most of them were to be used for infrastructure building and the establishment of new banks, encouraged by the free banking law of 1887.

Historians have tried to explain the contradictory effects of the 1885 agreement.[4] They have identified this contract as a main factor leading to the investment process that resulted in the Baring crisis. Two clauses in that contract have been scrutinised. In the first clause, the government had agreed to provide revenues from customs duties, the most important revenue at the time, as a security for the loan. In the other one the Argentinian government had accepted to temporarily suspend any further negotiations for new loans and to request the banks' approval if it decided to restart one. Strikingly, a few months before the final signature of the contract the Argentinian Congress had strongly opposed the inclusion of both clauses. The Treasury's pressing needs may have been the cause for this change of stance on behalf of the Argentinan policymakers. It is considered that the final form of the agreement had a positive effect on investors' risk perception. According to H. Ferns,[5] for instance, investors had the feeling that Argentina's economic situation was being closely watched, within a sort of monitoring procedure conducted by the banks. This may have restored

3 See Marc Flandreau, "*Caveat Emptor*: Coping with sovereign risk without the multilaterals", CEPR Discussion Paper No. 2004, 1998. Marc Flandreau, "Crises and punishment: Moral hazard and the pre-1914 international financial architecture", CEPR Discussion Paper 3742, 2003. Marc Flandreau, Juan Flores, Norbert Gaillard & Sebastian Nieto-Para, "The end of gatekeeping: Underwriters and the quality of sovereign debt markets, 1815-2007", chapter in the NBER International Seminar on Macroeconomics 2009, 2010.

4 Henry Stanley Ferns, *Britain and Argentina in the Nineteenth Century*, Oxford, Clarendon Press, 1960. Andrés Regalsky, *Mercados, Inversores y elites. Las inversiones francesas en la Argentina, 1880-1914*, Buenos Aires, Eduntref-Editorial de la Universida nacional de Tres de Febrero, 2002.

5 H.S. Ferns, *op. cit.*

the confidence amongst investors, thereby increasing their demand for new bonds from Argentina.

In our view, some works on the Baring crisis have underestimated the importance of this agreement. Yet, its inclusion in any analysis of the Baring crisis would adequately highlight the importance of Europe's financial markets structure on Argentina's own borrowing policy. Even though the economists have been providing all sorts of explanations for the Baring crisis since its inception, no consensus has emerged regarding the main reasons for Argentina's economic crisis or Baring's near bankruptcy.[6] Moreover, most works on the Baring crisis have focused on the macroeconomic aspects of the crisis, and have left important microeconomic elements unexplained, such as the incentives of investors and banks and the way they responded to the events that led to the crisis. This chapter aims to fill this gap.

Most authors consider 1880 as the starting point of the capital export cycle and highlight 1885 as its turning point. The classic work by John Williams[7] separates the periods between 1881-1885 and 1886-1890, underlining the years 1884 and 1885 as the time in which there was a shift in Argentina's balance of payments. He argued that Argentina's transition to a permanent deficit in its current account rendered the country dependent upon external capital. This shift also obliged Argentina to abandon the gold standard in 1885, though this measure was initially conceived to be temporary. In 1887, despite a brief but considerable effort to balance both the fiscal and the current account deficit, Argentina's peso initiated a strong depreciation along with a continued increase in imports financed through foreign capital.

The year 1885 is also important for a number of reasons. Looking at Argentina's business cycles, Anna-Maria Cerro[8] situates an upward phase beginning at the second quarter of 1881 and ending in the second quarter of 1885, though it rapidly rebounds in the last quarter of 1886. From a political perspective, 1885 was the last year of general Julio Argentino Roca's government (1880-1886); he had played a decisive role in the country's unification, mainly through the federalisation of Buenos Aires and the extension of fertile lands to the south for colonisation.[9] His

6 For a literature review on the main theories on the Baring crisis, see J. Flores, 2010.

7 John H. Williams, *Argentine International Trade under Inconvertible Paper Money, 1880-1900*, Cambridge, Harvard University Press, 1920.

8 Anna-Maria Cerro, *La conducta cíclica de la economía argentina y el comportamiento del dinero en el ciclo económico. Argentina 1820-1998*, mimeo, 2000.

9 José Terry described the crisis in 1885, when banks experienced massive withdrawals and convertibility had to be suspended. He argued that a main mistake in Argentina's fiscal policy was to have refused the reduction of expenditures, many of which were unnecessary. See: José A. Terry, *La crisis, 1885-1892. Sistema bancario*, Buenos Aires, Imp. M Biedma, 1893.

successor, Miguel Angel Juarez Celman, led a government (1886-1890) marked by the adoption of an expansionary economic policy, along with a liberal perspective on banking and currency – all of which intended to accelerate the development of the country.[10]

As a main catalyser for this development strategy, foreign loans played a prominent role. Railway construction was at the heart of this strategy, but many other investments – public works, ports and mortgage banks amongst the most popular – were equally financed through new loan issues. Admittedly, this was nothing new neither for Latin American governments nor for European investors. The novelty was the rediscovered destination. Argentina had been a frequent yet risky borrower since its independence. In the 1880s the country was already well known in the European financial markets, and its repayment record was a combination between resound defaults but also unexpected and punctual repayment periods. Argentina had in fact avoided the fate of default in the world crisis of 1876, unlike many other Latin American borrowers. Moreover, in the early 1880s, its economic performance made the country particularly attractive for investors, as did its exports growth, immigration flow and perceived potential.

This lending boom was also encouraged by merchant banks of the main financial centres in Europe. The relationship between banks and South American governments was complex, volatile and unstable. This might explain why it has been such a popular topic among historians – besides the fact that it was a key element to understand the volume of capital exports from Europe to that region.[11] Some of the authors provided a detailed analysis of the 1880s international financial architecture. Amongst

---

10 Tim Duncan, "La política fiscal durante el gobierno de Juarez Célman, 1886-1890", *Desarrollo Económico*, April-June 1983, Vol. 23, No. 89, pp. 11-34.

11 Among the most relevant works we can mention: L.H. Jenks, *The Migration of British Capital to 1875*, New York, Knopf, 1927. Alec K. Cairncross, *Home and Foreign Investment, 1870-1913*, series "Studies in Capital Accumulation", Cambridge, Cambridge University Press, 1953. Alec George Ford, "Argentina and the Baring crisis of 1890", Oxford Economic Papers, 1956, Vol. 8, No. 2, pp. 127-150. Alec George Ford, *The Gold Standard, 1880-1914: Britain and Argentina*, Oxford, Clarendon Press, 1962. Alec George Ford, "British investment in Argentina and Long Swings", *Journal of Economic History*, Vol. 31, 1971, pp. 650-663. H.S. Ferns, *op. cit.*, 1960 and 1992. Harold Edwin Peters, *The Foreign Debt of the Argentine Republic*, Baltimore, John Hopkins Press, 1934. And more recently: Carlos Marichal, "Los Banqueros europeos y los empréstitos argentinos: rivalidad y colaboracion, 1880-1890", *Revista de Historia Economica*, 1984, No. 2, pp. 47-82. Carlos Marichal, *A century of Debt Crises in Latin America: From Independence to the Great Depression*, Princeton, N.J., Princeton University Press, 1989. Marc Flandreau & Juan Flores, "Bonds and Brands. Lessons from the 1820s", *Journal of Economic History*, 2009, No. 69, pp. 646-684. Juan Flores, "Information asymmetries and conflict of interest during the Baring crisis, 1880-1890", *Financial History Review*, 2011, Vol. 18, No. 2, pp. 191-215.

them, some works have described the particularities of the relationship between British merchant banks and Argentina. Carlos Marichal[12] defines this cycle of capital exports as one where interactions between European banks and Argentina were complex and multinational. British banks were not the only ones to seek for new business in Argentina. French and German banks were increasingly active, with other European banks also participating in diverse activities related to trade and the syndication of new loans. Whilst competition was strong, some scope for collaboration which was strongly dependent on the specific situation of Europe's financial centres emerged. During those years, Argentina also developed a position of external financial dependency.

Charles Jones[13] and Andres Regalsky[14] have analysed the negotiations that took place in 1885 between the government of Argentina and the banks that had acted as main underwriters for its loans. Some divergences emerge when comparing their main conclusions. A. Regalsky emphasised the strong financial necessities of the government of Argentina during that year. He argued that it had already exhausted all possibilities for internal funding; under these circumstances, its bargaining power before European banks was weak. Therefore, it is hardly surprising that banks were able to impose their conditions on the 1885 loan, as we describe below. According to A. Regalsky's analysis, the 1885 agreement was the final result of the debt policy followed by Argentina's government, which exploited competition between banks to obtain new loans at the best possible terms. From the beginning of 1881 this policy proved to be a complete failure.

C. Jones' analysis differs from A. Regalsky's mainly in its appreciation of Argentina's bargaining power. He nevertheless admits that the government of Argentina was obliged to accept the terms imposed by the banks, which responded to their short-term interests. C. Jones claims that the 1885 agreement was strongly criticised in London and Argentina especially because it allowed the banks to disburden their portfolios from the bonds they had previously been unable to place into the market. Furthermore, the conditions also implied some kind of control over the Argentinian government's finances through the well-known guarantee of the customs duties engaged for the repayment of the loan. C. Jones stated however that this agreement had failed and proceeded to analyse the main causes for such a

12 Carlos Marichal, *op. cit.*, 1984.

13 Charles Jones, *European Bankers and Argentine, 1880-1890*, Working Papers, "Business Imperialism Series", Centre of Latin American Studies University of Cambridge, No. 3, 1972.

14 Andres Regalsky, "Exportaciones de capital hacia los países nuevos: los bancos franceses y las finanzas publicas argentinas, 1881-1887", *Revista de Historia economica*, 1987, No. 1, pp. 73-97. Andres Regalsky, *Mercados*, *op. cit.*, 2002.

failure. He suggests mainly that banks did not have the means to enforce the contract. After the signing of the agreement, Argentina's government was in a more privileged position than the banks. Even if these financial institutions were the seven most active underwriting banks of Argentina's securities, the government was able to negotiate new loans with other banks. C. Jones considered the syndicalisation strategy of the banks as an inefficient measure of defence, first against the market – as it increased the likelihood of placement for the bonds it had already underwritten – and subsequently against Argentina's government, which saw its bargaining power increased. This did not deter the Argentinian government from ignoring the clause establishing a temporary suspension of borrowing. Not only did borrowing take off, but it did so at an accelerated pace. C. Jones argued that this harmed Argentinian credit in Europe, as Argentina had to accept worse terms than countries such as Brazil or Chile.

H. Ferns had also argued in this vein. He maintained that, if the objective was the rational control of the investment process, the agreement had exactly the opposite effect. He agreed with C. Jones on the banks' incapability to exercise any kind of control not only on the federal, provincial or municipal Argentinian governments, but also on the activities of new competitors. Whereas the number of banks participating in the syndicate that signed the agreement of 1885 was high (seven banks), after that year nine additional banks underwrote new loans to Argentina's provincial and municipal governments. According to H. Ferns, a main reason for this contradictory effect was the spurious atmosphere of confidence created in the bankers' minds due to the belief that Argentina's government had given them a safe basis for the loans in the form of a guarantee from the customs duties. This belief was strengthened by the fact that these loans were payable in sterling pounds (with fixed exchange clauses with other hard currencies) and the assumption that the contracts provided an effective mean to protect their own interests. More importantly, H. Ferns argued that the agreement had a positive effect on investors' perception of the risk involved. This perception was based on the general impression that the investment process was under the supervision of institutions that were well informed about its features and necessities. However, H. Ferns explained that the agreement was not a control scheme, but rather a medium to assure a reduced group of banks and their clients a first claim on Argentina's government revenues.

2. Government, banks and investors: Passing the buck

From our perspective, an analysis on the manner in which foreign government loans were issued in the main financial centres of Europe provides several elements to disentangle the different incentives and the behaviour of each agent participating in the market. In short, the main incentive behind the actions of governments, banks and investors was to obtain the highest revenue while minimising the risk involved. How was this achieved? The risk of a new issue was primarily assumed by the borrowing government; a bank would act as an intermediary and investors would decide whether to purchase the new bonds or not. Competition, however, encouraged banks to provide additional services to governments. Additionally, investors would also take into account the behaviour of underwriting banks and their reputation in their risk assessment.

Governments seeking for financial funds in Europe's financial markets were motivated by attractive interest rates – compared to their level at home – because of increased liquidity at times of more pressing needs or simply because their own capital markets were not fully developed. On the other hand, a main feature in the underwriting business in Paris and London was the increased practice of firm commitment where banks would directly purchase the bonds from the governments and resell them to investors.[15] French banks could successfully compete with their British counterparts thanks to this innovative offer. Governments seeking for security on the proceeds from loan issues would prefer this modality as they avoided the risk of a placement failure; this risk was then assumed by the underwriting banks. In the 1880s, most of Argentina's loans were issued under the firm taking modality. Although the commissions the government was obliged to pay were high in the beginning, they decreased considerably as competition for new loans increased in the following years.[16]

Banks, on the other hand, were only occasionally interested in issuing foreign loans, precisely due to the high risk involved. Stanley Chapman[17] mentioned a set of possible reasons for which a (merchant) bank would engage in the business of foreign loans. Firstly, merchant banks could offer to issue loans on behalf of governments of prosperous countries, as they offered a safer business with the promise of rapid gains.[18] Secondly, trade expansion coincided with stronger economic activity and higher funds availability, and thus, the opportunities for new business in both activities were highly correlated. Thirdly, specific links with railway contractors or other merchants (and even without them) often meant that the

15 On the different modalities on underwriting, see J. Flores, *op. cit.*, 2010.

16 Underwriting fees were as high as 9% in 1881 and decreased to a 4.5% in 1889. See Flores (2004).

17 Stanley D. Chapman, *The Rise of Merchant Banking*, London, G. Allen & Unwin, 1984.

18 S. Chapman (1984) observed that issuing activities were generally regarded as risky and with low profitability. However, a precise analysis of the evolution of underwriting fees in the 19th century for "safe" governments indicate that fees were a permanent, albeit low source of profits. Fees for risky countries were high, up to 15% in some cases. To avoid the high risk that this involved, syndicalisation became recurrent use by the end of the century.

funds raised from the loans would translate into the exports of specific goods. S. Chapman quoted James Rothschild, for instance, ascertaining, in 1866, that "seven-eighths or fifteen-sixteenths of any loan issued are employed in buying goods".[19] C. Marichal[20] also argued that much of the expansion of trade between France and Argentina was nourished by the loans raised in Paris by Argentina's government by the 1880s. Finally, issuing a loan also meant the expansion of commercial business, because they were interpreted as an official recognition of foreign governments which was helpful to obtain commercial connections.

Paul Cauboué[21] also argued that the main reason for entering that business was the high levels of benefits that banks obtained from these operations. Jean Bouvier[22] quoted Henri Germain, the founder of *Crédit lyonnais*, who provided a classification of the different bank activities. The banker placed foreign loan business within the group of "extraordinary operations", as opposed to ordinary operations – defined as those activities related to the use of deposits that the bank channeled for commercial purposes. Extraordinary operations were those with high expected benefits but whose participation the banks would only occasionally undertake. These were difficult operations, involving tough competition, and a high level of risk; thus, these activities had to be subjected to a strict assessment before a bank engaged in them.

These rather idealistic features of foreign lending were however only occasionally met. For some authors, the departure from these basic principles laid behind Baring's problems in 1890. H. Ferns, for instance, accused Baring of "imprudent behaviour" in its operations in Argentina: Baring did not respect the principle under which the decision of investment should depend on a previous estimation of the payment capacity of the borrower made by professional bankers. However, J. Flores showed that the level of information on Argentina was even lower for other underwriting banks;[23] he mentioned a striking example of Paribas inquiring in 1890 on the value of some securities from the Mortgage Bank of the Province of Cordoba, which were held at the bank's portfolio as guarantee for a loan they had underwritten and that was about to default. Whereas imprudence may have been related to Baring's near bankruptcy, this was not limited to Baring, nor was its level of information the lowest. And yet, it was the hardest hit from its position in Argentina.

19 Stanley Chapman, *op. cit.*, p. 104.

20 C. Marichal, *op. cit.*, 1984.

21 Paul Cauboué, *La conduite des banques*, Paris, Garnier & Bonamy, 1931.

22 Jean Bouvier, *Histoire économique et histoire sociale. Recherches sur le capitalisme contemporain*, Geneva, Droz, 1968, p. 121.

23 Juan Flores, *op. cit.*, 2011.

A main feature of the 1880s was the general incentive for banks to engage in underwriting activities given investors' high demand for Argentinian securities. Obviously, some of this demand seems to have had rather speculative origins: for instance, H. Ferns mentioned the case of mortgage bonds (*cedulas hipotecarias*) issued in the late 1880s which were mostly payable in paper pesos. The yields of these securities were highly dependent on the behaviour of the gold premium, whose fluctuation continuously increased, mainly after 1887, partly due to increased monetary issues but also to the occasional interventions of Argentina's Treasury in the exchange market. Moreover, municipalities and provinces that issued their own loans for the first time in Europe were by definition completely unknown among investors. Still, they could all place their bonds in a relatively short time.

The fact that banks were not investing in information production and yet continuously issuing new bonds should not be surprising given the issuing mechanism, which was very similar to the "originate and distribute" system of the 2000s, much criticised during the "subprime crisis" of 2007-2012. Most of the participating banks were new entrants into Argentina's underwriting markets and it seemed unclear whether this participation had long-term purposes. Banks could engage in an underwriting agreement, place the bonds and then limit their relationship to the payment of interests during the duration of the loan. In other words, this meant a big, short-term gain from a short-term activity. Still, although this behaviour was common among most of the participating banks, this was not a generalised practice for all banks. Some of them, those characterised as having the highest market share, developed long-term relationships with the borrowers.[24] In financial theory this is known as relationship banking.[25] The intuition is straightforward. A bank would have incentives to invest in the production of information from a firm if it expects to obtain the long-term gains from its financial support at initial stages or in periods of financial distress. Competition would erode this incentive thereby worsening the general level of information available to the firm's main bank.[26]

---

24 See Juan Flores, *op. cit.*, 2002.

25 Arnoud Boot, "Relationship banking: What do we know?", *Journal of Financial Intermediation*, 2000, No. 9, pp. 7-25. Arnoud Boot & Anjan V. Thakor, "Can relationship banking survive competition?", *The Journal of Finance*, Vol. LV, No. 2, April 2000, pp. 679-713. Also see: Arnoud Boot & Anjan Thakor, "The many faces of information disclosure", *Review of Financial Studies*, Vol. 14, No. 4, 2001, pp. 1021-1057.

26 Marc Flandreau & Juan Flores developed this issue for the mid-19th century London capital market in: Marc Flandreau & Juan Flores, "Bondholders vs bondsellers: Investment banks and conditionality lending in the London market for foreign government debt, 1815-1913", *European Review of Economic History*, 2012.

In most of Baring's historiography and its relationship with Argentina, Baring has been regarded as Argentina's main banker. Contrary to this common belief, however, H. Ferns[27] argued that archival evidence does not show that Baring considered themselves as the "bankers of the Argentine Republic". The reason for this common belief, argued Ferns, was the long-term relationship that Baring had developed almost involuntarily. They had been the first highly regarded firm to float a loan on behalf on the new born United Provinces of Rio de la Plata in 1824. This loan defaulted as did most Latin American issues in the 1820s. In contrast to the attitude of most underwriters, Baring persisted in protecting the interests of the bondholders.[28] Its persistence bore fruit in 1857 with the signing of an agreement with the Province of Buenos Aires. However, this did not mean that they were enthusiastic about lending to Argentina, as it was not until 1866 that they floated a new small loan. Other English banks became active in Argentinian affairs only in the 1870s.

Nonetheless, Baring did care about obtaining accurate information on Argentina. Since 1876 the bank sent one of its own employees, Nicholas Bower, to Buenos Aires. His task was to report on the projects for which loans had been floated: a waterworks and drainage system, the state of the Provincial Bank of Buenos Aires, and the Western Railroad (*Ferrocarril Oeste*). During the following years, Bower developed strong ties with the government of Argentina. This relationship cannot be underestimated, as it generated the kind of soft information that constituted a main advantage for Baring compared to other banks and to investors.[29] Unfortunately for Baring, and probably for Argentina, this relationship deteriorated considerably in the early 1880s. This situation appears to be strongly related to the entry of French banks as underwriters for the first loans issued during that decade. In fact, none of the banks issuing Argentina's securities in Europe during the 1880s developed a similar relationship with that country's government. They did not send a permanent agent either, although some of them did operate through commercial houses in Argentina that acted as their agents, particularly regarding the offers and negotiations on new loans. On the other hand, Bower's reports on their assessment on Argentina provide accurate and detailed descriptions on a number of topics, from public finances and transportation to migration. The only bank which systematically gathered statistics on trade, public finance, debt, or

27 Henry Stanley Ferns, "The Baring crisis revisited", *Journal of Latin American Studies*, 24, 1992, pp. 241-273.

28 On the relationship between banks, governments, and loan performances of the 1820s, see Marc Flandreau and Juan Flores, *op. cit.*, 2009.

29 Obviously, this information advantage could give place to possible conflicts of interests. This has been analysed in Juna Flores (*op. cit.*, 2011), though he found no evidence that Baring exploited his position to his own benefit.

currency issues was *Crédit lyonnais*, a bank[30] which was not directly involved in sovereign lending with Argentina but that developed these activities as a service for its clients mainly after the crisis in 1890. In other words, other banks' level of information was scattered or non-existent. As competition increased during the decade, the uncertainty on future business did not provide any incentives to improve the quantity nor the quality of this information. But as long as the market demanded Argentinian securities, banks continued floating loans on behalf of the country.

This situation was by no means underestimated by investors. From Argentina's view, competition had produced a combination of effects: while the government could improve the terms of the loans offered by the banks, investors perceived those securities as riskier. Alec Carincross[31] summarised this point for the London market. Investors considered that competition between issuing houses existed when the borrower was a new entrant to the market. Some authors argue that competition could increase the marketing risks of the loans, given the unsuccessful bankers' efforts to cry them down. Foreign governments who did not have a permanent agent in London had to negotiate on worse terms. A recent study[32] has also shown that countries who switched underwriter frequently had to pay the highest interest rates for their loans in the late 19th century.

3. Investment banks and Argentina in 1881-1884

The beginnings of this lending boom to Argentina have different origins. Some authors have argued that there was a shift in the perception of risk in investments in Argentina since the beginning of the decade. Peters[33] noticed that between 1876 and 1879 the country was "unworthy of any confidence" and that "their loans lacked any value", which was reflected in the market's loan prices: This was certainly a side effect from the crisis of 1873-1876 where defaults worldwide caused several losses to European investors; in Latin America, most countries defaulted during these years (this was the case for Bolivia, Colombia, Costa Rica, Guatemala, Honduras, Paraguay Peru, Uruguay) or continued in default (such as Mexico or Ecuador), Argentina did not default, but the prices of the bonds quoted in London and Paris were strongly affected by these events; Argentina's 1868 bond[34] fell to a low of 36 per cent of its nominal value, but gradually increased up to 91.5 in December of 1879. This shift

30 See Marc Flandreau, *op. cit.*, 200.

31 Alec Cairncross, *op. cit.*, 1953.

32 Marc Flandreau *et al.*, *op. cit.*, 2010.

33 Harold Edwin Peters, *The Foreign Debt of the Republic of Argentin*, 1934.

34 Data from the *Investors' Monthly Manual.*

can be explained by several factors: by the positive news arriving from that country (political unification, increase in exports and expansion of the territory), the country's punctual debt payments despite the wave of defaults in the 1870s; or the general recognition of the country's potential, as shown by the increased number of immigrants and merchants looking for new opportunities. It is therefore not surprising that banks competed for the issue of new loans. There was a general confidence among them that markets would open out their arms to Argentina's securities.

This perception shift is considered as one of the main reasons for the resulting increase in foreign investment received by Argentina[35] since 1880. But it was obviously not the only one, and literature has provided a set of factors that can be separated in two groups, depending on whether they are related to the supply or the demand side of funds. Amongst the factors related to the supply side worthy of mention are the low yields offered by European bonds[36] and the positive perception of growth in the "new countries". With regard to the demand of funds, a series of factors can be identified.[37] First, the expansion of lands available for agriculture and livestock resulting from the wars against the indigenous people. This encouraged primary exports and stimulated the railway and urban development. Second, the federalisation of the capital, Buenos Aires, which opened a new period of political stability. Finally, the reduction of maritime freights that increased the variety of products that could be placed on the European markets. C. Marichal[38] makes a distinction between Argentina and other Latin American countries; he argues that the situations in these countries were less attractive than that in Argentina: Chile and Peru were at war; Bolivia was negotiating its debt with its European bondholders; Costa Rica, Ecuador and Paraguay had ceased to pay amortisation and interests since 1873; Mexico had repudiated its debt since 1873. In our opinion, these differences do not provide an adequate explanation: As mentioned above, in the decade previous to the 1880s Argentina seemed to be as unattractive as the other Latin American countries, and the decade began with internal war between the province of Buenos Aires and the Confederation. If there was a country that had shown political stability and a clean external default history,

---

35 Irving Stone's data on capital exports shows this increase in 1880 (Irving Stone, *The Global Capital Export from Great Britain, 1865-1914: A Statistical Survey*, New York, St. Martin's Press, 1999). A. Regalsky (*op. cit.*, 1987, 2002) also identifies 1880 as the departure year of French investment in Argentina.

36 See Jan Tore Klovland, "Pitfalls in the estimation of the yield on British Consols, 1850-1914", *Journal of Economic History*, 1994, Vol. 54, No. 1, pp. 164-187.

37 These factor scan be found in A. Regalsky (*op. cit.*, 1987) or Mario Rapoport, *Crisis y liberalismo en la Argentina*, Buenos Aires, Editoriales de América Latina, 1998.

38 Carlos Marichal, *op. cit.*, 1989.

it would have been Brazil: If we compare the yields of the bonds of both countries, the market did perceive Brazil as less risky. An alternative factor not very often mentioned is the cultural factor, which takes into account that Argentina was the first country in Latin America to receive European immigration. Some studies have analysed the relation between immigration and capital flows.[39] To further underline this point, *Comptoir d'escompte de Paris* reflected the attitude of German bankers at the time when they entered the market of Argentinean bonds: "*Les Allemands* […], *surtout attirés vers la République argentine par le mouvement d'émigrants, qui sont pour la plupart de nationalité allemande, ont ouvert des suggestions aux Cahen d'Anvers pour cette affaire.*"[40]

Increased demand for capital and a sudden shift in risk perception opened up new profit opportunities for financial intermediaries participating in the business of foreign government loans. For practical purposes, both factors meant additional potential profits and manageable levels of risks. This incentive was further nourished by the increased interest by the financial press in London and Paris, and the increased number of publications specialised in foreign investments. Michael George Mulhall, who recurrently published a set of statistics[41] on wealth, trade and production in several countries in the press, in books and papers, had only favourable statistics to share. The country had become one of the main cereal exporters and its trade balance became positive; the construction of railways and telegraphs seemed to be one of the most profitable in the world and the public works and colonisation policies attracted a growing number of European workers.

Between 1881 and 1884, Argentina's federal government negotiated several loans with European bankers for a nominal amount of 8 million pounds (without taking into account another £8m that ended up being issued in 1886 and 1887), along with the provinces of Buenos Aires and Santa Fe, which negotiated a total of £11m. These amounts were to be increased, between 1886 and 1889, to reach a total of £17m to the federal government and 26m between both provinces and municipalities.

---

39 Ragnar Nurske, "International investment today in the light of 19th experience", *The Economic Journal*, 1954, Vol. 64, No. 256, pp. 744-758.

40 Archives of *Comptoir d'escompte de Paris*, January 29th 1886, Historical archives of BNP Paribas, Entry number 102 955. Box 637. Also see A. Regalsky, *op. cit.*, 1984.

41 See for instance his *Handbook of the River Plate*, published for the first time in 1863 and actualised several times in 1869, 1875 and 1892. Michael Georges & Edward Thomas Mulhall, *Handbook of the River Plate*, Buenos Aires, Buenos Ayres Standard, 1886. Michael Georges & Edward T. Mulhall, *Mulhall's Dictionary of Statistics*, London, G. Routledge & Sons, 1886. About Argentina's financial history in the 1880s, also see: Corporation of Foreign Bondholders, Press Clips, "Argentina, 1885-1890", Guildhall Library, London.

The first loan the government negotiated was the Railway Loan of 1881, for a nominal amount of £2,4m at 6%, marking the entry of the French bankers to a former English dominated market. The French could enter the market and successfully compete with the English thanks to their modality of syndication, facilitated by the French banking system; this contrasted with the English bankers, which acted in an individual way.[42] The innovative feature of the loan was the acquisition of the whole amount in firm. Argentina's government had used a system of auctioning, which forced the banks to compete amongst themselves. Competition may be the reason why, for the first time in Argentina's foreign lending history, the banks took on the risk for the loan's issue. Nevertheless, the purchase price agreed was relatively low (at 82%), compared to the issue price of 91%, resulting thereby in a high profit for the banks – or a high cost for Argentina's government – due to the risk involved in the loan's issue.

The same syndicate underwrote a second loan of £800 000 at a 6% rate, issued at the end of 1882. As seen previously, it was a firm loan in its totality, although this time the agreed price was 90.5%, and for the bankers' disappointment the issue price was only of 92.5% (the bank's benefits fell therefore to a low of 2%). At the same time, the province of Buenos Aires continued to negotiate with the English bankers. It issued two loans during 1881 and 1882, for a total amount of £2,3m; the banks who issued the loans were Stern and Baring respectively. We shall keep in mind, as S. Jones argues, that the second half of the last loan (offered by Baring) was issued only four years later. The loans of this province were particularly important to the eyes of the European investors and bankers as we can confirm from different sources, first in a report of the Paris' branch director of the Comptoir d'escompte de Paris about the state of the Argentinian confederation:

> *Cet État a actuellement trois emprunts en cours de remboursement, non compris les emprunts de Buenos Ayres de 1824 et 1857, qui sont cependant, sous tous les rapports de véritables emprunts nationaux.* Yet this government has been a very frequent borrower here lately, for although the last nominally Argentine loan was that of December 1882, Buenos Ayres, that province so predominates in the confederation, that its indebtedness cannot be ignored in considering Argentine finance. Indeed, various of the Buenos Ayres loans are really chargeable upon the national exchequer.[43]

The overall limited profit margin could be the result of three factors: first, that the constant competition between the different syndicates had a positive impact on the purchase price, and profits almost eroded; also,

[42] See Andres Regalsky, *op. cit.*, 1987. The participants in the syndicate were: Paribas, *Comptoir d'escompte de Paris* and Cahen d'Anvers (a Haute Banque house).

[43] *The Economist*, 29th March 1884.

bankers erroneously estimated the price at which the market would take the issue (the situation of the market had become adverse that year); and finally, the new Argentinian bonds were appearing on the market too frequently to be able to "prepare the market". Whatever the reasons, the disappointing results of the issue was a first warning that the banks initially retained in subsequent loans.

On the 31st March 1884, Baring issued in London a loan in order to inject capital into the National Bank of Argentina. Although it was the French syndicate who underwrote the loan, the bulk of the issue took place in London; the syndicate had delegated the issuing task to Baring, though it was not part of the underwriting syndicate. The nominal amount of the loan was £1,7m at a 5% interest rate. This time, the risk taken by the banks was lower: Instead of buying the loan at firm, the banks made a nine hundred thousand pounds advance directly to the government, with 6% interests and a 4% commission for each quarter; in addition, the bankers had the option to take firm the total of the loan one month after the issue date at an 85% of its price.[44] The issue of this loan was successful, so the banks took the option; about the skepticism of the Paris bankers about the success of the issue, we could read in the correspondence from the director of Paribas to *Comptoir d'escompte de Paris* the 4th April 1884: "The subscription for the Argentinean Loan of 5% 1884, opened in London on March 31st by Mr. Baring was a great success. The loan was covered a couple of times [...]. Would you let us know before the eighth of this month if your intention is to liberate immediately all or a part of your bonds."[45] However, this was to be the last loan to be well received by the market. Two additional loans were negotiated: the same syndicate underwrote one more loan on September 1883 for the construction of the "Sanitation Works and the Port of Riachuelo". Almost at the same time, another syndicate headed by Morgan & Co. and *Société générale* (from Paris) acquired in June 1884 another loan for public works. A. Regalsky[46] explained that Argentina's negotiations with this new syndicate were due to the difficulties encountered by Paribas' syndicate to place the loans: taking into account the installments for the delivery of the funds, in twelve quarters, discounted at 5% yearly at the end of the option, the real price was actually 79.6%, what seems to us quite logic, because the issue price had been of 84½.

The loan for the Sanitation Works amounted to a total of £2,4m, at a 5% interest rate; the syndicate underwrote a third of the total amount of the loan firm at 80%, and the rest was to be offered to the public with a commission of 2.5% and every surplus of 82.5% would be shared

44 A. Regalsky.

45 Historical Archives of BNP Paribas, Entry number 102.955, Box 404.

46 A. Regalsky, *op. cit.*, 2002.

between the banks and the government. Baring was included in the syndicate later, with a 30 per cent participation and the issuance of part of the loan in London. It was to be floated along with the National Bank's bonds, but it had to be postponed due to a legal dispute with the Stern Bank regarding the loan's guarantees: under the law of 28th October 1881, the federal government expropriated the work of Riachuelo Barracas, which were practiced under the government of the Province of Buenos Aires; this latter had contracted an internal loan that was sold to a British bank in Buenos Aires, and was issued in London by Stern Brothers in 1881; as guarantee for the loan the provincial government offered the product of the port works, exactly the same guarantee as the one foreseen by the law of 28th October for the new loan with the French syndicate.[47] Later in September 1884, the Morgan syndicate issued the bonds they had acquired at firm (a third of the 6 million pounds), at a price of 84%. This appeared to be, at first glance, as a profitable business, due to the fact that the agreed price was 81.5%, although the terms for the installments and delivery of the funds further reduced this figure.[48] However, the news on the increasing difficulties affecting Argentina as well as the rumors about the possible suspension of convertibility caused the bonds to be retained in the bankers' hands.

4. The 1885 agreement between Argentina and investment bankers

Argentina started off the year of 1885 with a currency crisis and ended it with an investment boom. While this seems paradoxical, a chronology of the events regarding the relations between Argentina's national government and the banks highlights the importance of the agreement on the significant volume of new loans. In January, the Provincial Bank of Buenos Aires, which was then the most important bank of the country, announced the suspension of payments in kind. The financial press in Europe reacted with a combination of surprise and disappointment. For instance, as soon as the gold premium revealed its first increases, *L'Économiste français* voiced concerns about its impact on Argentina's reputation amongst investors.[49] However, financial market's perception did not seem to be altered. The yields on Argentina's government bonds did increase (about 5% from their average value in December), though this alteration was mild and lasted a short period of time. *The Economist* summarised probably the market's general perception and optimism

47 See Peters, *op. cit.*, 1934.

48 A. Regalsky (*op. cit.*, 2002) estimates this price at 78.3%. The complete delivery of the funds had to be done one year after the government began paying interests.

49 *L'Économiste francais*, 10 January 1885.

regarding the near future: "The news that the Argentine Confederation had authorised the suspension of specie payments was a great surprise. The accounts of the increasing prosperity of the country had been of the most glowing character, and the only indicators of anything being amiss was a slight fall in the exchange [...] the rate continued to fall, causing a demand for gold to export, resulting in a run upon the banks, and the forced suspension of payment in coin and we confess to not having been prepared for a sudden collapse." On the reasons of such an event, it explained that "yet, the cause is not, we think, far to seek. Excessive imports, following on large borrowings, both public and private, have created a foreign indebtedness, the discharge of which has broken down of currency founded on a slender basis". But confidence in the country remained unaltered: "The disaster, it appears to us, is unconnected with the question of the prosperity of the country, and is likely, therefore, to be only of temporary nature."[50]

This confidence may explain why the price of Argentina's national government bonds experienced only a mild and temporary fall during those years. But difficulties did exist in Argentina, and from the government's perspective, their financial position experienced some problems regarding the need for the funds to complete the projects for which they were intended and to compensate the increased amount of debt. The government was already used to resort to short-term loans in Buenos Aires to meet its most immediate needs[51] whilst awaiting the proceeds from the foreign loans. The long delay of the 1884 issues and the pressing needs of the Treasury motivated the government to send Dr. Carlos Pellegrini as its official agent to Europe in order to conduct negotiations with both syndicates. A. Regalsky[52] explained that, at the same time, the banks had already agreed to adopt a common position towards Argentina's government. Former minister of Finance Pellegrini's arrival in London faced a situation that was best summarised in a report to Argentina's Parliament published in the press: "Once there, he found himself in an embarrassing situation; the French syndicate, who took $4,000,000 at firm from the loan of $12,000,000 for the Sanitation Works and Riachuelo could not place it in the market and had it still in its hands. Mr. Morgan, who took $10,000,000 at firm of the $30,000,000 loan, launched it to the market and was only able to place 300,000 pounds, having kept the remaining sum until today [...]. Antagonisms were created between these two syndicates, preventing reciprocal actions. In these circumstances, the

50 *The Economist*, 17 January 1885.

51 See Roberto Cortès Conde, *Dinero, Deuda y Crisis: Evolución Fiscal y Monetaria en la Argentina, 1862-1890*, Buenos Aires, Editorial Sudamericana, 1989.

52 Andres Regalsky, *op. cit.*, 2002.

commissioned began his negotiations to unify both syndicates and incorporate the respectable Baring."[53]

What did the agreement stipulate? In fact, there were two agreements. On the 6th and 7th July 1885, Pellegrini signed with seven European bankers a first draft of the contract. The participants were: *Banque de Paris & des Pays-Bas*, *Comptoir d'escompte de Paris*, Cahen d'Anvers, *Société générale*, *Crédit industriel & commercial*, Baring and Morgan. This agreement was provisional, and was subject to the approval of the Argentinean Congress. The government agreed to cancel two loans, the one voted by the law of 20th June 1884, for £2.4m and the second by the law of 25th October 1883 for £6m. They were replaced by a new one, of £8,4m: The government committed to buy the part being acquired at firm by the bankers. This money, amounting to £2,3m on June 1885, was converted into a deposit from the bankers to the Argentinian government, bearing a 6% yearly commission and a six-monthly commission of 50%; to this amount an additional sum of £1,8m was added. The service was guaranteed "in general by the nation's revenues and especially by the customs duties",[54] and the President committed himself to refrain from "authorising" or "sanctioning" the issue of any loan without a previous and formal agreement with the bankers. No loan already approved by the Congress could be negotiated during this period, and the agreement specifically mentioned the 16 million pesos loan created for the Provincial Bank of Buenos Aires.

The Banks reserved the right of decision regarding the date of issue of the total or partial amount of the loan, with the only condition that the price would not be lower than 75%, which was an amount reserved for the government. If the price was higher, half of the gap would be for the bankers. In addition, the banks were to be paid a 2.5% commission over the nominal amount of the sold bonds. On 11 August, Pellegrini informed the bankers that the Congress had refused the agreement, meaning that, as stipulated, it had to be cancelled. The main reason for this refusal was the clause on the customs duties guarantee, which Argentina's Congress considered as "harmful for the dignity of the country". During August and

---

53 Report to the Deputies' Chamber, published in *La Prensa*, 21st October 1885. Vice-president Carlos Pellegrini acceded later at the presidency (from 6 August 1890 till 12 October 1892).

54 We could find the agreements at the Historical Archives of Paribas (Entry number 102.955, Box 404). In 1884 the proportion of the revenues from duties out of the total revenues was about 62%. About the solidity of the duties fee, the CEO of *Comptoir d'escompte de Paris*, Eugène Denfert-Rochereau, wrote to Paribas: "*Les douanes ont produit, en 1884, une somme de 135 millions de francs, environ, et l'annuité nécessaire pour le service de l'emprunt total ne dépasse pas 12 millions et demi.*" Historical Archives of Paribas, Box 603.

September the negotiations were resumed. The bankers agreed to sign the agreement in "more acceptable terms" for the government, but only if the new agreement had the approval of the Congress. The financial position of the government may have worsened, because on the 16th October a new law was voted authorising the executive power to contract an additional loan for £4m, only a few days before the 21st October, when a new law was voted for the signature of the new agreement with the banks. In fact, there were no real differences with the previous agreement which had been discarded. The Congress even began its session by discussing the constitutionality of voting a law that had already been refused. The final agreement was signed on the 8th December.

On the London Stock Exchange, the juggling involved in the negotiation of the agreement was barely perceived and Argentina's government bond prices remained stable. However, C. Jones[55] mentioned that the results of the negotiations were reflected by the gold premium at the Buenos Aires Stock Exchange.[56] We have gathered their weekly movements from the annual reports published by the Chamber of Commerce of Buenos Aires. As expected, there is a strong increase in the first weeks of 1885, when inconvertibility was declared, to be followed by fluctuations over the next months. Some events marked however the behaviour of the risk premium, such as the bank's own previous agreement – when they decided to adopt a common position on behalf of Argentina's unplaced bonds – or Argentina's Congress refusal of the agreement. Still, even if a reduced influence would have been noticeable, the depreciation of the Argentinian paper peso was relatively stable in the second half of 1885, and remained that way until the first months of 1887 [see figure 1].

5. The 1885 agreement's effects on investment bankers' action

The bonds were issued in two parts. A first half was issued in January 1886, at a price of 80, and the second half was issued one year later, at a price of 85. On January 1886, the *Buenos Ayres Standard* published that "Messrs Baring Brothers telegram to the National Government states that the loan was subscribed for in its totality the very first day offered to the public. This is a great success and we compliment the Government on the results. It is perhaps, the most brilliant financial operation ever carried through by a South American state".[57] The success of the first issue

[55] Charles Jones, *op. cit.*, 1972.

[56] The gold premium reflected the exchange rate between Argentina's paper peso and the convertible gold peso.

[57] *Buenos Ayres Standard*, 10th January 1886.

established the confidence in Argentina's investments, as they were supported by seven of the most important underwriters who had assumed the risk and responsibility of the new loan. Baring could finally place on the market the second half of a loan for the province of Buenos Aires that was issued in 1881. Moreover, the agreement had allowed the banks that underwrote the loans of 1884 to avoid any losses. They had also minimised the risk of a placement failure in 1886, due mainly to the customs duties guarantee and the fact that all competitors were part of the same underwriting syndicate. But the profitability of the business had other unforeseen effects.

Figure 1. Gold premium

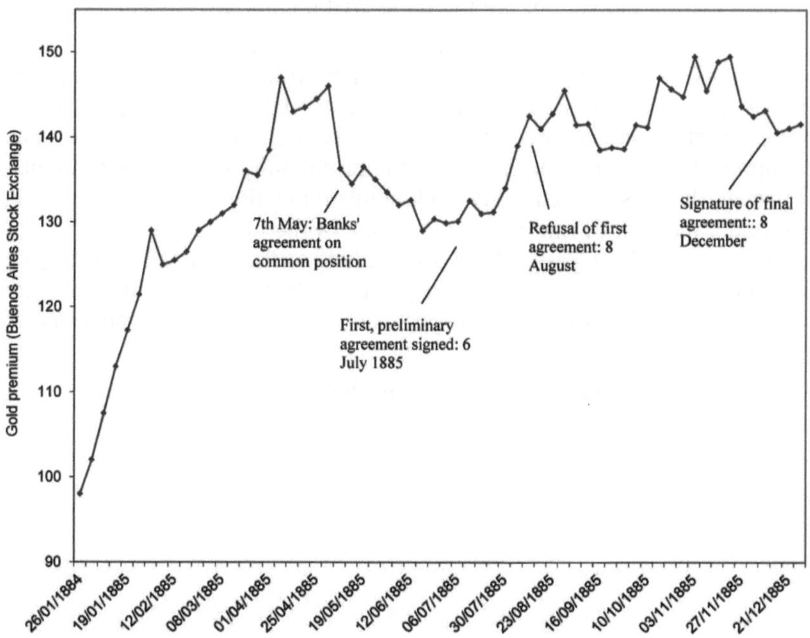

Source: Chamber of Commerce of Buenos Aires Stock annual reports.

Argentina's national government agreed to issue a new foreign loan in October 1886. The law was passed by the government during that month for the construction of new railroads. The total amount was £4m at a 5% interest rate. The underwriting bank was Murrieta, a bank that had not participated in the 1885 agreement. The contract was also signed under the new government, as Roca's government had ended just some days before. Furthermore, a loan for the Provincial Bank of Buenos Aires that had been negotiated by Argentina's national government in 1885 was finally contracted by the provincial government and a German syndicate, whose banks had not taken part in the 1885 agreement either (Mendelssohn, Bethmann and *Deutscher Effecter & Wechsel Bank*).

The national government reduced its share in Argentina's total borrowing after 1885. It continued financing public works at a large scale, while provinces borrowed to capitalise their new banks and municipalities did so to finance basic urban infrastructure. The national government also encouraged the formation of new public utilities or railway companies. The result of this borrowing policy can be appreciated in figure 2: It shows the sudden increase in the amounts issued, in London, and the number of underwriting banks and their average underwritten amount. Overall, the higher amounts issued were correlated with a higher number of participating banks, but not the underwritten amounts by each bank.

The impact of this massive arrival of new bonds to Europe's main financial centres was initially welcome, as evidenced by the general success of the new issues. This remained so until 1888, when the first failed placements began. In all cases, however, Baring's involvement in the new issues was enough to reassure the market about the profitability of their investments. However, the press increasingly evoked this reputation effect while it worried about the lack of information for some of the new issues. In 1886, for instance, when Baring issued the second half of the loan for the province of Buenos Aires, *The Statist Newspaper* published the following: "We are surprised to see this week the prospectus of a loan [...] for the province of

Figure 2. Banks and loans issued, 1881-1889

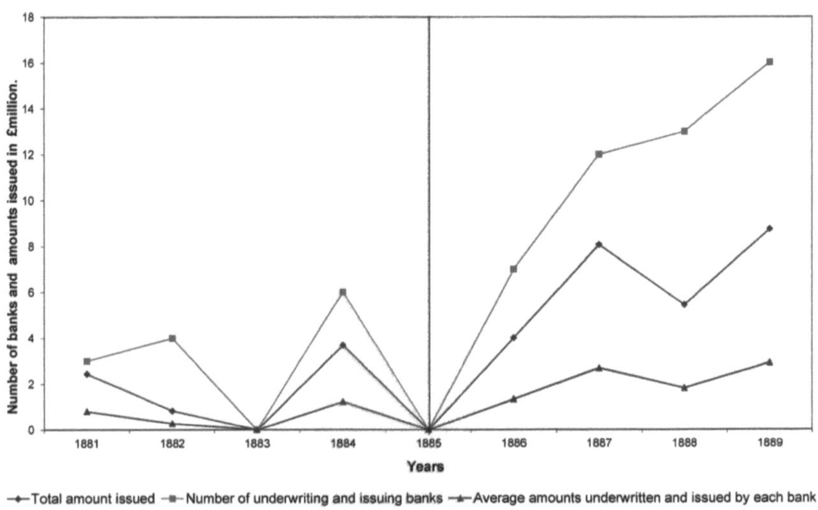

Source: Author computations from J. Flores (2004) and C. Stone (1999).

Buenos Ayres, issued by Messrs Baring Brothers & Co., without one word of explanation as to its object, or the slightest reference to the indebtedness and resources of the State."[58] The main reason for the continuous success was given through articles such as the one published in 1889 by *The Daily News*, on a loan to be issued on behalf of Argentina's national government: "As the matter is understood to be in the hands of Messrs Baring Brothers & Co. a successful result may be hoped for. The mere fact that an important syndicate is willing to negotiate is good for Argentine credit. Had matters been as bad as pessimists have been inclined to make out late, eminent firms would not have been disposed to trust the Argentine Republic more money."[59]

The participation in an underwriting syndicate (or as a mere issuer) of a loan appeared therefore as an important element on investors' risk assessment[60] [see figure 3]. We have calculated the spreads at issue of all new loans on behalf of national, provincial and municipal government loans as

Figure 3. Spreads of bond issues in the 1880s on behalf of Argentina's national, provincial and municipal governments and railways and public utilities companies. Classification by underwriting banks

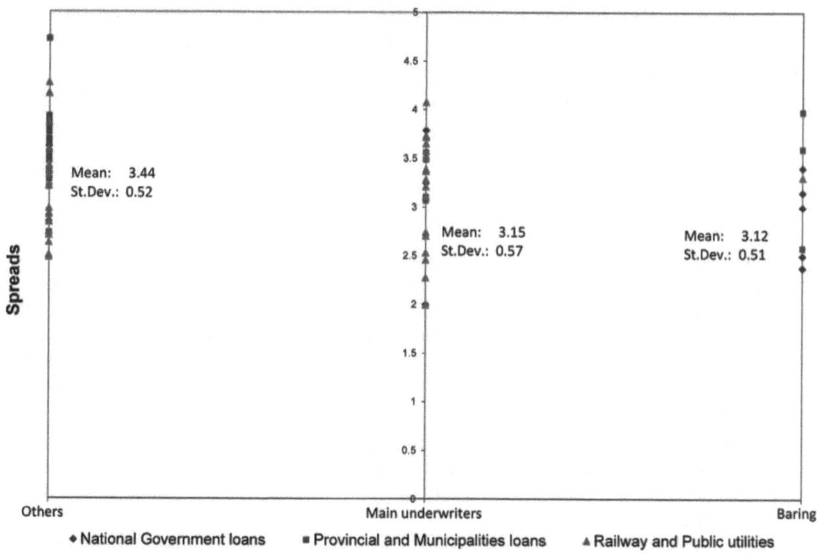

Source: see text.

58 *The Statist*, 27 March 1886.

59 *The Daily News*, October 5th 1889.

60 Juan Flores (*op. cit.*, 2011) demonstrated that, during this period, loans underwritten by Rothschild had a lower risk premium even controlling for macroeconomic fundamentals.

well as those for the railway and public utility companies for the period between 1881 and 1889 in London, Paris and Berlin.[61] The information on these loans can be found in the Burdett's Official Intelligence of 1890 and *The Statist Newspaper* (27 March 1887). We have divided the sample between those issues underwritten by "other banks" – those banks that had not been underwriters prior to 1880 –, those underwritten by the "main underwriters" – those that had been underwriters before the said date –, and those underwritten by Baring. We observe a difference in the average spread for each of the groups, but it is mainly significant between the group of the new banks and those banks that had underwritten before Argentinian securities.[62] Figure 3 also differentiates the issues between national, provincial, and public utilities and railway companies, many of which benefited from guarantees provided by Argentina's national government. An additional feature is the fact that the bulk of the less risky issues were mostly underwritten by Baring, and this partly explains the differences in the levels of spreads at issue.[63] Nevertheless, the private companies' issues of Baring were lower than those underwritten by "other banks", and the spreads at issue for national and provincial loans not underwritten by Baring were also higher on average than those underwritten by this bank.[64]

There are several reasons behind the investors' confidence generated by Baring (and to a less extent, by other main underwriters). H. Ferns[65] and M. Flandreau & J. Flores have suggested that a main reason was the support that could be provided by Baring in a period of financial distress. H. Ferns justifies this through the history of the relationship between Argentina and Baring between 1823 and 1857, whereas M. Flandreau and

61 Spreads at issue are defined as the differences between the yields at issue of the new bonds and the yield of a UK consol at the same date.

62 We have also tested and confirmed the statistical significance of the mean differences for each group through a t-test. This test had a value of 2.12 for the mean differences between "other banks" and "main underwriters". This value exceeds the critical value of 1.984 needed for a statistically significant difference at a 0.025 level. This test resulted non-significant for the mean differences between the main underwriters and Baring.

63 On the differences in the risk level for national and provincial bonds, see Gerardo Della Paolera & Martin Grandes, "The true measure of country risk: A primer on the interrelations between solvency and the polity of emerging markets: Argentina, 1886-1892", in Sebastian Edwards, Gerardo Esquivel & Graciela Márquez (eds.), *The Decline of Latin American economies: Growth, Institutions, and Crises*, Chicago, University of Chicago Press (and National Bureau of Economic Research & Net Library), 2007, pp. 195-211.

64 Baring average spread at issue for national government loans was 2.88, for "main underwriters" it was 3.23 and for "other banks" 3.01. We did not test for statistical significance in mean differences because the number of observations is low, but this confirms the general result obtained above.

65 H. Ferns, *op. cit.*, 1992.

J. Flores argue that Rothschild and other prestigious banks did provide this support during the long 19th century, though the costs that borrowing governments paid for this support was high – in terms of conditionality and financial costs. In fact, as the crisis of 1890 approached, the press speculated with the possibility of a bailout loan organised by Baring. It also reported on the banks' interest in participating in this new loan, something regarded to some extent as a repetition of the 1885 agreement – even if this time the situation was much more complicated. The *South American Journal* ventured even to name the banks implicated: Baring, Rothschild Paris, *Disconto Gesellschaft*, the North German Bank and Oppenheim.[66]

Archival evidence does demonstrate that Baring negotiated with Argentina's government a loan to support it through its difficulties to service its debt.[67] However, it was having difficulties to convince other banks to underwrite the loan and to make the government accept the conditions attached to the support. Whilst Samuel Hale, who acted as Baring's agent in Buenos Aires, repeatedly communicated with London on the continuous refusals of the government to accept Baring's conditions, the merchant bank also received the refusal from banks in France and Germany to participate in a new loan for Argentina. Those banks justified their refusal on the high risk of a new issue given the conditions in the South American country.[68] At the end, Baring was obliged to pursue with the loan alone, once the government accepted the conditions. However, political instability in Argentina and Baring's own difficulties prevented it from proceeding with the issue.

Concluding remarks

In broad terms, the 1880s were a distinct period in Argentina's external debt history given the competitive context of its foreign loan underwriters. This situation seems to have triggered a deterioration of the information held on Argentina's foreign investments. Admittedly, obtaining accurate and complete information was costly and therefore underwriting banks were hardly encouraged to assume these costs. As a result, Argentina ceased to retain a permanent bank to issue its loans in London, even if the country had been traditionally associated with Baring. As the 1885 agreement was ratified by Argentina's government in 1885, a deputy declared that "he desired to make a solemn manifestation, so that it could be recorded in the Congress's minutes, greeting with an applause vote and sympathies the reconquest of the respectable and powerful house of Baring

66 *South American Journal*, 19th October 1889.

67 On the conditions of this planned loan, see J. Flores, *op. cit.*, 2011.

68 See for instance the letter by Betzold to Baring of the 1st July 1890, ING Baring Archives, HC4 1_113.

for the national credit [...] whose friendship and services were abandoned by a fatal mistake of pour financial policy, who gave heavy operations to occasional syndicates, without the enough respectability in the financial world, and whose results we are now painly feeling".[69] Before the 1880s, the last loans issued on behalf of Argentina were negotiated with Baring in 1868, and with Murrieta in 1870 – or eleven years before the first loan of the 1880s. The novelty of the 1880s was the system the government implemented by making the banks compete and by prioritising the firm offers. This preference seemed to continue along with the decade, although bankers, alerted by the first failed issues in 1884, reduced their risk exposure by minimising their firm offers to such an extent that on the 1885 agreement the terms were completely different from those applied to the 1881 loan. After the success of the 1886 issue, however, this last situation reversed again and the government continued to favour the policy of competition. This time there was a new entrant to the business, the German bankers, who took the first loan after 1885. A major issue was precisely the 1885 initial credibility. Taking into account the poor results of the issues previous to the agreement, each agent – signing banks and government – had an incentive to adhere to the contract's terms. On the one hand, Argentina's government faced seven of the biggest European banks. Any action taken against their interests would have been highly harmful for their credit.[70] On the other hand, banks had no interest in taking additional risks through further committing to issue new bonds.

However, once the first bonds were placed on the market, the incentives of the bankers changed: the success of the bonds' placement in 1886, along with the results of the Buenos Aires second issue by Baring – the bonds had been kept in Baring's hands since several years before –, reopened new profit opportunities for the bankers. The entry of the German banks exerted more pressure on the syndicate members, so that every competitor took even greater risks issuing more bonds, also on behalf of Argentina's provinces and municipalities. Moreover, the growing demand for Argentina's securities further nourished the expansive debt policy pursued by the Argentinian government, which seized the opportunity to place new loans with the best terms offered. In sum, both parties had interests in continuing to float new loans as long as the market absorbed them.

A final question analysed concerns the reasons for the success in the 1886 issue, a result that contrasted with the previous failures. The agreement

69 Citation from *La Prensa*, 21st October 1885.

70 The Argentinean government understood, in general, the position with which they had to handle, as shown by the following observation from the same session on 21st October 1885: "The syndicates dispose of great resources, and they are not affected having a small part of them in good sovereign bonds, just like the argentines'."

provided all the elements to guarantee a positive outcome: first, the risk from competition between banks was dismissed, because the main competitors formed a common-interests syndicate; second, the temporary cessation of new issues provided by one of the agreement's clauses eliminated the risks of "being too fast to prepare the market" or the possible negative effects of additional issues; and third, the country's risk seemed to be more attractive due to the guarantee of the customs duties, and monitoring seemed to be assured through the common interest by the group of banks. Investors' risk perception could only improve, creating a virtuous circle nourished by a positive conjuncture in Europe's financial markets.

Finally, investors were rational: They assumed that even if fiscal problems persisted, underwriting banks, and mainly Baring, would support Argentina and avoid any losses to investors, as shown by the contradiction between the pessimistic articles published by the London's financial press and the stable behaviour of that country's government bonds. This perception seemed justified by Baring's efforts to secure a bailout loan to support Argentina's fiscal situation one year before the crisis.[71]

71 I thank comments from Marc Flandreau and Mary O'Sullivan on previous drafts of this chapter. The usual disclaimer applies. I also acknowledge financial support from the Swiss National Science Foundation.

Part III

National Paths for Pathbreaking Investment Bankers

CHAPTER 6

Investment Banking in the 19th and 20th Centuries

The Dutch Way

Piet GELJON & Ton DE GRAAF

Economic adviser to Mees Pierson bank
and *Corporate historian/curator of ABN-AMRO*
History Department in Amsterdam

Writing on investment banking in the Netherlands presents some specific problems. Although from time to time specialist firms or companies operated in this field – in particular in the 18th century – there has never been a strictly defined group of specialised institutions that can be compared with the British merchant banks, the American investment banks or the French *banques d'affaires*. Investment banking activities were in general performed by diverse institutions like private banking houses, stock broking firms, commercial banks, affiliates of foreign banks or joint ventures. Consequently, comparisons between groups of banks or individual institutions with a view to investment banking are hardly possible. In general, there are few sources available for comparing various activities like investment banking and commercial banking within one institution in terms of initiation, profitability or relative importance. Archives of private firms or smaller companies have mostly disappeared and where they have been kept they are far from complete. For example, minutes of partners' meetings (if there were several members of a firm, which was not always the case) were not recorded, since decisions on important transactions were often made over lunch or in personal conversations. For the larger banks more archival material is preserved, but as of yet no up-to-date histories have been written.[1] Against this background we can do no more than give a historical description of the Dutch

1 However, studies on Nederlandsche Handel-Maatschappij (Netherlands Trading Society) and Twentsche Bank are now in preparation. The archives of Rotterdamsche Bank were largely destroyed in the Second World War.

banking sector and try to identify how and by whom investment banking activities were undertaken.

First of all, some remarks on the terminology have to be made. In Dutch there is no good equivalent to the foreign names that have come into use. In the past, the French *banque d'affaires* was used; it had the connotation of institutions holding shares in (industrial) companies and/or engaged in granting long-term credits. With the internationalisation of the banking sector during the last decades the phrases *merchant bank* and *investment bank* are often used untranslated, with the latter becoming more and more common. In Dutch newspapers the translation *zakenbank* is often used, but that is hardly a clarification; it is also the translation of *corporate bank*, that is a bank for corporate clients. Literally *zakenbank* means *business bank*, just as the *Financial Times* is a business journal. The question of course is then: what kind of business?

In the few publications that have appeared in Dutch on this subject, merchant banking and investment banking are used alternatively, and are considered to have the same meaning, although the exact definitions vary.[2] One definition used is: "Investment banking is the granting of advice with a view to financial transactions that may give rise to temporary positions for the adviser." This definition seems rather narrow, but the activities mentioned include financial engineering (all kinds of financial innovations), new issues and syndicates and intermediation in the market for capital control (mergers, acquisitions, buy-outs etc.).[3] Another description, this time under the heading of merchant banking is as follows:

> The core of merchant banking has always been the issue of securities, with the bank acting as intermediary between companies and institutions [...] and the capital market [...]. Initially the emphasis was on the public market, but the activities have gradually expanded [...] with the managing of private issues and subsequently with the arrangement of mergers. For a number of years now, the banks have also been advising on the dismantling of conglomerates and on the buy-out and spin-off of parts of businesses [...]. Since the beginning of the eighties, the banks have become increasingly active in the venture capital market.[4]

Both definitions give important elements of investment/merchant banking, but leave aside other activities that were or are performed by institutions of this kind. Once, the accepting business was one of the primary tasks of merchant banks, together with the related foreign exchange transactions; the former has dwindled, but the latter have gained very

2 Banks still use the terms in different ways; sometimes merchant banking is part of investment banking, sometimes the reverse.

3 O.A. Waterlander and J.W.R. Schuit, *Investment Banking in Nederland*, Den Haag/Rotterdam, Staal Bankers/Erasmus University, 1990, p. 4.

4 Bank Mees & Hope, *Annual Report 1986*, p. 30.

much in importance. Furthermore, is securities trading for the banks' own account (proprietary trading) or for clients' account part of the job? From the beginning, in the UK it was not, in the USA it was.[5] What about investment advice for clients and the management of investment portfolios and investment funds? From the 1960s activities like leasing and factoring were added and this list is still incomplete. We may suggest that the terms investment banking and merchant banking are interpreted differently by different authors, but also that the meaning shifts over time.[6] So it would seem dangerous to start from a preconceived definition and try to model banking history accordingly. In the Dutch situation in particular that would be impossible. We prefer to mention the major activities that are considered to be part of investment banking – the term we will henceforth use in this chapter – and to see by what banks or other institutions these have been undertaken since the 19th century. These activities are:

- new issue business, both national and international;
- securities trading and holding of securities portfolios;
- investment advice and fund/asset management;
- advice and intermediation regarding company formations, mergers, acquisitions and restructuring (corporate finance);
- special forms of credit and financial innovation.

More or less this list is in chronological order, as the beginning of investment banking lies – apart from acceptances – with new issues and stock exchange transactions (the securities business). This will become clear from a historical sketch of the Netherlands. We distinguish the following periods:

- the rise and decline of the Dutch securities business up to 1860;
- the revival of the capital market and the establishment of new banks 1860-1914;
- war, banking crises and depression 1914-1945;
- regulation, concentration and liberalisation 1945-2000.

In a final section we make a few remarks on the Dutch banks during the recent turmoil in the financial markets and the positioning of investment banking. To this general description we add some boxes that give as a personal touch short biographies of prominent (investment) bankers.

5 Richard Roberts, *The City. A Guide to London's Global Financial Centre*, London, Profile, 2008, p. 43, speaks of the 'integrated American investment banking model'.

6 For the UK, see Richard Roberts, "What's in a name? Merchants, merchant bankers, accepting houses, issuing houses, industrial bankers and investment bankers", *Business History*, 35/3, 1993, pp. 22-38.

1. The rise and decline of the Dutch securities business up to 1860

The origin of the Dutch securities sector lies with the establishment of the Verenigde Oost-Indische Compagnie (United East India Company, VOC) in 1602. The issue of its large capital of Dutch florins abbreviation. 6.4 million received great interest and its shares were soon actively traded in Amsterdam. Because of the complicated settlement of transactions through entries in the share register only a few times per year, the practice of delivery at a future date arose. This not only offered the opportunity to compensate buying and selling orders, but it also made speculative transactions possible, which were indeed often used. Premium affairs – the precursors of the modern options – were also introduced. So, in the course of the 17th century a well-developed securities trade arose. From 1611 this took place in the general merchants exchange built by the municipal government. Apart from the VOC, shares in other companies and loans of various public bodies were dealt in. Later on, shares of some British companies were also introduced in Amsterdam. With the increasing wealth of the Dutch merchant population and a relatively low domestic rate of interest, investment in foreign securities – British government debt, later on French *rentes* – arose. In these cases it concerned local issues in foreign countries and denominated in their own currencies. In addition, in Amsterdam an international issuing business developed, i.e. the placing of loans on behalf of foreign monarchs and governments denominated in guilders. In particular in the second half of the 18th century, Amsterdam became the centre of the international capital market.

Although in an earlier phase money was already lent to other countries, the first foreign issue was probably a loan to the emperor of Austria in 1695. This was placed by the Amsterdam firm of Wed. Deutz & Co., which at the same time acquired a monopoly for trade in Austrian mercury. In the 18th century this country was followed by a number of other debtors, such as Sweden, Denmark, German states and princes, Spain, Poland and Russia, besides the loans that were issued on behalf of plantation owners in the West Indies. Financial relations with countries mostly ensued from earlier trade contacts and it is no wonder that Amsterdam merchants were very active in this field, thereby developing a certain kind of specialisation on regions they already knew from trade and trade financing (Deutz for Austria, followed by Goll & Co., Clifford & Zoonen for Denmark, J. & C. Hasselgreen for Sweden). However, these relations were not exclusive, because debtors did not hesitate to choose another house or another market if it suited better. Issuing houses could also break with a client debtor. Hope & Co. for example in 1787 acquired a loan mandate from Russia in stead of De Smeth & Co., but had then to give up its business with Sweden. During the years 1787-1793 Hope issued no fewer than eighteen Russian loans totaling Dfl. 53.5 million. At about the same time, the young United States borrowed Dfl. 30.5 m. through the houses of W. & J. Willink, N. & J. van Staphorst and De la Lande & Fynje.

The houses mentioned before can certainly be regarded as merchant bankers in the original sense of combining trade in various commodities with financial operations as trade financing, accepting business and issuing activities. At the time they were at the centre of the international capital market. Apart from a sufficient capital to sustain setbacks that occurred from time to time, they needed diplomatic skills and political insight to arrange large capital operations for countries with often conflicting interests. A problem for them was to get the necessary information on the financial capacity of their debtors, which was not an easy task as details on government finances were considered a state secret. So, the 'monitoring' of debtors was certainly not perfect, but it is an exaggeration to speak of the "systematic neglect by the banking houses of the interests of their customers-investors".[7] The experiences with foreign loans were initially not bad, security or guarantees were required, risks were reflected in the conditions of the loans and governments were often pressed to supply the money for payments. For investors, a major factor was the record on the payment of interest and redemptions on earlier loans.[8]

The merchant banking houses could arrange the loans mostly on their own, but for the placement of the debentures they needed the support of bankers or commission houses in various parts of the country. Sometimes these firms acted as issuing houses themselves, for example A. & S. Boas in The Hague or Joan Osy in Rotterdam. Other firms in places like Utrecht, Haarlem or Leyden acted only as commission houses for the placing of the securities with the investing public, not only private individuals, but also institutions such as churches and charities. The loans were mostly traded on the Amsterdam exchange through broking or commission houses. A listing from 1796 gives prices of fifty-seven domestic and thirty-nine foreign securities.

---

7 Joh de Vries and A. van der Woude, *The First Modern Economy. Success, Failure and Perseverance of the Dutch Economy, 1500-1815*, Cambridge, Cambridge University Press, 1997, p. 197. See also M.G. Buist, *At Spes non Fracta. Hope & Co., 1770-1815*, The Hague, Nijhoff, 1974, p. 30.

8 There is a vast literature, also in English, on the Dutch 'golden age' and the Amsterdam capital market. We mention in particular James C. Riley, *International Government Finance and the Amsterdam Capital Market, 1740-1815*, Cambridge, Cambridge University Press, 1980. L. Neal, "How it all began: The monetary and financial architecture of Europe during the first global capital markets, 1648-1815", *Financial History Review*, 7, 2000, pp. 117-140.

As a result of this early development, "Amsterdam merchants became the first masters of the various financial techniques and developments which, in the course of the 19th century, became identified with the emergent profession of merchant bankers".[9] However, as is very well known, the further growth of merchant banking mainly took place in England and Dutch (merchant) bankers had to content themselves with a secondary role in the international financial field. In the decades around the turn of the 18th to the 19th centuries most houses mentioned disappeared. Financial crises in 1763 and 1772-1773 took their toll; subsequently wars and the French occupation (1795-1813) further undermined an already weakening economic position and saw the fall of still more merchant houses. The value of Dutch investments abroad declined substantially as a result of the whole or partial defaults of foreign governments. The still available savings were in large part absorbed by the needs of the domestic government, which also introduced restrictions on international lending. Surviving houses like Van Eeghen, Insinger and Goll scaled down their activities.[10] Also Hope & Co., in this period mostly operating from London, lost its former power, its capital declining from Dfl. 15 m. in 1800 to Dfl. 1.5 m. in 1814. Nevertheless, during the first decades of the 19th century the firm continued to play a considerable role, mostly in cooperation with Barings (Louisiana deal 1803, French reparations loan 1817), but it lost a substantial part of its Russian business. Apart from internal developments within the firms mentioned – lack of successors or shortage of capital – it must be taken into account that the economic and financial position of the Netherlands itself had considerably changed since the 18th century, it being surpassed by bigger countries, in particular the UK. So it is no wonder that also in the international capital market it had to be content with a smaller role. London firms now took the lead, in particular Barings and Rothschild. Until 1860 foreign issues in the Netherlands were few and far between, which does not mean that Dutch investors lost their interest in foreign stocks.

Despite its weakened international position, the Dutch securities sector could recover in other fields. One was the marketing of foreign securities through investment funds and *administratiekantoren* (administrative offices). The latter issued bearer certificates against foreign loans when these were entered in a register in other countries, such as the French *rentes*. In the 1770s already, a few investment funds – the first ones in the world – were started for foreign debentures, later on followed by vehicles

9 Stanley Douglas Chapman, *The Rise of Merchant Banking*, London, Allen & Unwin, 1984, p. 1.

10 See, for the various houses, Joost Jonker, *Merchants, Bankers, Middlemen. The Amsterdam Money Market during the first Half of the 19th Century*, Amsterdam, NEHA, 1996, pp. 187-228.

for US bank shares and Austrian and Spanish loans. Apart from Hope and the old firms of De Smeth, Willink and Van Staphorst (the latter three would soon disappear), a number of younger firms were active in this field, such as Stadnitski & Van Heukelom (1785), Willem Borski (1789) and Ketwich & Voombergh (1790). Activity in the securities sector was further stimulated by the growth and the restructuring of government debt, which in 1809 was registered in the name of the owners in a *Grootboek* (Register of national debt). To enhance transferability, a number of *administratiekantoren* were established, the certificates of which were traded on the exchange. Apart from the placing of state loans, subscriptions for which were handled by the Nederlandsche Bank (1814), in the period till 1860 domestic issue activity remained subdued. Some major issues were looked after by a notary public (*Nederlandsche Bank*) or the Chambers of Commerce (*Nederlandsche Handel-Maatschappij*, Netherlands Trading Society, NHM, 1824).

The activities that took place in the various fields, though not impressive in comparison with earlier times, nevertheless apparently offered room for new firms to enter the securities business. Around 1800, in Amsterdam Joukes & Oyens (later on H. Oyens & Zonen) appeared, followed by Kerkhoven & Co. (1812), Gebr. Boissevain (1836) and the Jewish houses Gebr. Teixeira de Mattos (1822) and Wertheim & Gompertz (1834). Outside Amsterdam, cashiers and small banking firms played a part, which also maintained the connections with the capital. Only in Rotterdam and The Hague more important houses arose, such as the cashiers R. Mees & Zoonen (dating back to 1720) and Lissa & Kann (1806). These and other firms would all venture into various forms of investment banking. Against this background it is a little bit surprising that various international Jewish houses did not see a more permanent place for them in the Netherlands. The firms of Julius Königswarter (1817), L.R. Bischoffsheim (1820) and Gebr. Oppenheim & Co. (1836) sooner or later withdrew, continuing their business in other countries, where they probably saw more opportunities.

Box 1. The Laboucheres and Hope & Co.

In 1790, when Pierre César Labouchere (1771-1839) joined Hope & Co. as a clerk at the age of eighteen, this house had risen to first place in the world of international trade and finance. It dealt in many goods all over Europe and North America and it was the leading firm in issuing loans for foreign powers, at that time in particular for Russia. It had a capital of nearly Dfl. 12 million and made profits of between Dfl. 500,000 and Dfl. 1 million. In the personal sphere, however, it had to cope with problems. Of the 1762 partners only Henry Hope (1735-1811) had survived, after the death of the brothers Thomas (1779) and Adrian (1781) and of Thomas' son John (1784). There were no others Hopes to fill their places. In 1782 John Williams – later called John Williams Hope or John Hope – more or less adopted by Henry Hope as a son and married to his niece, had become a partner, but he was not a strong leader. A partnership of two outsiders did not last very long. So in 1790 it was foremost Henry Hope who was the driving force of the business. In this situation, the intelligent Pierre César Labouchere could deploy all his capacities. He was born in The Hague, but came from an originally French family of cloth merchants and had an apprenticeship in his uncle's house in Nantes. His entry into Hope & Co. turned out to be the beginning of a long lasting relationship between the Laboucheres and the banking business in the Netherlands and England.

In 1793 Pierre César was given power of procuration, which became the more important when the two partners left for England in October 1794 as the French troops neared the Dutch border, but only a few months later he had to follow them. In London, Hope & Co. worked closely together with Baring Bros & Co., a house with which there had already been close contacts before. This relationship deepened in 1796 when Labouchere married Dorothy Baring, daughter of Sir Francis and sister of Alexander Baring. Whether this was a condition for a partnership is not clear – earlier on a clerk had become a member of the firm – but it no doubt helped. Nevertheless, it was not until 1802 after the Treaty of Amiens, when the house was re-established in Amsterdam, that he appeared as a partner. In the following years Labouchere played a significant role in the various international transactions of the firm. He was, in the words of Vincent Nolte,[11] *'most of all remarkable for the chivalric idea of honour in mercantile transactions'.*

After the death of Henry Hope in 1811 and of John Williams Hope in 1813, the firm was on the brink of liquidation. Alexander Baring took over the remaining interests of the Hopes, the affairs in Amsterdam being placed into the hands of four managers, among them Labouchere. From England, where he had meanwhile settled, he undertook a number of foreign missions on behalf of the new Hope & Co., again in close cooperation with Baring Bros. In Amsterdam they had the active support of the firm Wed. W. Borski, which had substantial resources at its disposal and acted foremost on the Amsterdam stock exchange. In 1823 Alexander Baring transferred his interests in Hope to the acting managers, as a result of which the firm again became Dutch-owned. Pierre César now

[11] Vincent Nolte, *The Memoirs of Vincent Nolte, or Fifty Tears in both Hemispheres*, New York, G.H. Watt, 1934.

also broke his (nominal) ties with the firm, but two other Labouchere came in: his son John Peter Labouchere (1799-1863) and his brother Samuel Pierre Labouchere (1778-1867). At the same time Thomas Baring also became a partner, together with the old members Adriaan van der Hoop and Hieronymus Sillem. Five years later, John Peter Labouchere and Thomas Baring left the firm, both settling in England. The young Labouchere had meanwhile become a partner in the new banking house Williams, Deacon,[12] *Labouchere, Thornton & Co., emerging from two other banks that had got into difficulties in the 1825 banking crisis. The new house was a precursor of Williams & Glyn's Bank. Thomas Baring became a partner in the old family banking house. The formal links between Hope and Baring Brothers herewith came to an end, although their close cooperation would continue for a long time. The relationship between Hope and the Labouchere family continued well into the 20th century. Samuel Pierre Labouchere served until his death in 1867, his son Henri Matthieu (1807-1869) was a partner in the years 1839-1869, while his grandson Charles Henry (1863-1916) followed in his steps in 1887, acting as a partner until his death. After 1815 five members of the Sillem family also became partners of Hope. The younger generations kept the house well in order, but it lost much of its earlier dynamism. It leaned heavily on Wed. W. Borski, which brought in its own men, J.B. Stoop in 1833 and H.M.J. van Loon in 1852, while the mighty Willem Borski II (1799-1881) became a sleeping partner, without whom not much could be done.*

The story of the Labouchere family is a clear illustration of succession that often took place in banking family firms. We see the same with H. Oyens & Zonen, for example. In partnership agreements a new partner often claimed a place in the firm for one of his sons (often the eldest), if he proved capable. Sometimes another son could enter into a related firm. Thus, another grandson of S.-P. Labouchere, Ernst Samuel (1856-1932), became a partner in Labouchere, Oyens & Co., when in 1881 this firm took over the affairs of the old firm (1790) Ketwich & Voombergh (the Laboucheres were related to the Voombergh family). His companion was A.D. de Marez Oyens, for whom there was probably no place in H. Oyens & Zonen. The name Labouchere disappeared from the banking scene in 1913, the firm being taken over by Rotterdamsche Bank. It would reappear a few years later, when a son of Ernst Samuel, Henry Louis (1887-1954) started a new firm Labouchere, which after WWII changed hands many times.[13]

12 See *Williams Deacon's Bank, 1771-1970*, Manchester, 1971.

13 E.J.T. Acaster, "Banking with the Laboucheres", *The Three Banks Review*, 100, December 1973, pp. 29-42.

2. The revival of the capital market and the establishment of new banks (1860-1914)

Favoured by the accelerating growth of the economy, the years 1860-1914 saw a marked expansion of the Dutch securities sector, both in volume of trade and new issues and in the number of participating institutions.[14] The Dutch remained active investors in securities and supply on the capital market could grow substantially, emanating from new savings, redemptions of old loans and easy credit facilities. With regard to the latter, in particular the *prolongatie* – one month, renewable advances against securities – and lombard credits which ran for three months, played a part. All parties in the securities field were active in this credit market, both as lenders and as borrowers. The volume of outstanding credits in 1914 is estimated at Dfl. 660 m, not insignificant in comparison with a total investment in securities of Dfl. 5 to 6 billion. In an international context Dutch foreign investment now only occupied a minor place, however, amounting to about Dfl. 3 billion or $ 1.25b. compared with $ 19.5b. for Great Britain, $ 8.6b. for France and $ 6.7b. for Germany.[15] As a result, Dutch institutions could not regain the prominent position they once had in the international capital market; they now mainly acted in cooperation with the leading banks in England, France and Germany. Besides the international market, a growing domestic issue market developed as more businesses began to seek capital, apart from public authorities that also raised higher amounts. Correspondingly, the stock exchange, which also became better organised, saw its trading volume rise rather strongly, both in newly issued funds and securities issued elsewhere and introduced in Amsterdam. All this offered much room for new intermediating parties to enter the business as well as for existing institutions to expand in size and in diversity. Before describing the various investment banking activities, we first turn to the market participants that were active in this period. A general characteristic of the more important players was that they combined a broad range of activities, both in securities/investment banking and in commercial banking. This can be attributed to two general factors: the impact of the early development of the securities sector in the Netherlands, which continued also in the more difficult years up

14 This part of our chapter is mainly based on Piet Geljon, *Geschiedenis van de algemene banken in Nederland, 1860-1914*, Vol. III, Amsterdam, NIBE, 2005, a summary of which appeared in the *Bulletin of the European Association for Banking and Financial History*. See also Joh de Vries, W. Vroom and Ton de Graaf (eds.), *Worldwide Banking. ABN-AMRO Bank, 1824-1999*, Amsterdam, ABN-AMRO, 1999.

15 Charles F. Kindleberger, *A financial History of Western Europe*, London, Allen & Unwin, 1984, p. 225. His figure for the Netherlands compares well with the Dutch estimates for 1910/1915.

to 1860, and as a result of which many people were familiar with this kind of business, and influences coming from abroad, in particular the *credit mobilier* movement.

A. Old and new institutions

The link with the past is illustrated by the already established firms that continued their business in the new period and also broadened their activities. Apart from Hope, which mainly continued to rely on its Russian business, we mentioned earlier some firms from the first decades of the 19th century. Also the firm of Adolphe Boissevain (1875, in 1917 name changed in Pierson & Co.), stemmed directly from the securities business, starting in arbitrage in American funds. There were furthermore numerous smaller commission houses, both in Amsterdam and other places, which from time to time ventured in the introduction of foreign securities and/or smaller domestic issues. That the securities business remained attractive is made clear by the development of two institutions, originally operating in other fields but later on entering this sector. The first is Twentsche Bankvereeniging B.W. Blijdenstein & Co. (hereafter *Twentsche Bank*), stemming from a textile region in the east of the country, then establishing in London (1858) and Amsterdam (1861). From its origin it specialised in the financing of textile exports. To increase profitability on an enlarged capital, in 1871 it started with small participations in issuing syndicates, commission business in securities, arbitrage, the building of its own securities portfolio and the granting of *prolongatie* credits. In these new activities the bank had to cope with older parties on the stock exchange who were less friendly, but it succeeded in expanding its business.

Nederlandsche Handel-Maatschappij (Netherlands Trading Society, NHM) was slower to get started in the securities business. Established in 1824 under royal protection to stimulate trade and industry, particularly through the Dutch East Indies, NHM did not succeed in adapting well to the trade liberalisation after the mid-century. In 1880 it decided hesitantly to take part in issuing syndicates, initially in the Netherlands and its colonies, but soon also in international loans. The strength of NMH was its large capital, which enabled it to hold substantial parts of new issues in its own portfolio. The technical dealing with issues, such as subscription, payment etc., was mostly left to friendly parties. Only in 1912 a separate securities department was established. A full banking service did not arise before 1903, when the company started to accept deposits in the Netherlands (this had already been the case in the East Indies by 1883).

Against this background, it can easily be understood that the English type of pure deposit bank did not take root in the Netherlands. A more important and enduring influence emanated from France, where the *crédit mobilier* movement took ground after 1850 and also began to spread internationally. In 1856 already there were several plans to establish large *crédit mobilier* institutions in the Netherlands, but these were turned down by the government for being too speculative. Another early connection with the *crédit mobilier* sphere came along through the International Bank in Luxembourg. This bank was founded in 1856 with the help of Abraham Oppenheim of Sal. Oppenheim and G. Mevissen of the *Bank für Handel und Industrie* (*Darmstädter Bank*), the latter being formed in 1853 in cooperation with French *Crédit mobilier*. Leo Lippmann and George Rosenthal were connected with the International Bank and when they established their own firm Lippmann, Rosenthal & Co. in Amsterdam in 1859, this bank acted as a silent partner. A few years later French parties became more directly involved in the Dutch banking scene. In 1863 the *Algemeene Maatschappij voor Handel en Nijverheid* (General Company for Trade and Industry) was formed, in which *Crédit mobilier* had a 50 per cent interest. The remaining capital was taken up by Belgian and Dutch parties. The aforementioned Leo Lippmann was a member of the supervisory board, together with Isaac Pereire. The company started up quickly, setting up a bank and a railway company in the East Indies. Furthermore it was active in international loans. Its policy, however, was not very prudent and it soon got into difficulties, aggravated by fraud committed by the general manager. After a few years it was liquidated.

A rival French group with E. Hentsch and A. Pinard of *Comptoir d'escompte de Paris* and L.R. Bischoffsheim was involved in the *Nederlandsche Credit- en Deposito-Bank* (Netherlands Credit and Deposit Bank). The Dutch originator of this initiative was Samuel Sarphati, an ardent promoter of economic development of the Netherlands in general and Amsterdam in particular, who's earlier plan for a kind of *credit mobilier* bank had failed. He knew Bischoffsheim, who had stayed in Amsterdam up to about 1850, very well and through him the contacts with the French bankers came no doubt along. A.C. Wertheim, who moved in the same Jewish circles in Amsterdam, was appointed general manager. It would seem that the intentions of Sarphati differed from those of his French partners, who were entangled in a fierce competition with the Pereires in several European countries. Lacking attractive investment opportunities in Holland, the bank soon became active in the international capital market. After the death of Sarphati and the resignation of Wertheim – who concentrated on his own firm Wertheim & Gompertz – the company came more and more under French influence. In 1872 it merged with *Banque de Paris* to form *Banque de Paris et des Pays-Bas*, established in Paris with a branch in Amsterdam. The latter would act in particular as a link between the international market and the Amsterdam stock exchange.[16]

Although the original, far-reaching purposes of both institutions were not realised, their establishment meant a real break-through in the small-scale and rather closed Dutch financial world. It set new developments in motion, for example in Rotterdam, where *Rotterdamsche Bank* was established in 1863. Although this was intended to be a colonial bank, it had some investment banking characteristics. It ventured into securities and arbitrage transactions, but with disastrous results. The bank then concentrated on the short-term banking business and it was not until the last decade of the century that it returned to the securities trade and new issues. A last – indirect – connection with the *crédit mobilier* is visible in the establishment of Amsterdamsche Bank in 1871. This was set up with German and Austrian capital; the *Bank für Handel und Industrie*, *Oesterreichische Credit-Anstalt für Handel und Gewerbe* and A. *Schaaffhausen'scher Bankverein* were among its founders. *Amsterdamsche Bank* was a combination of a commercial bank and an investment bank, especially active in the securities trade and new issues. Soon after, in the crisis of 1873, the bank suffered losses on its securities portfolio and on participations in banking ventures in other countries. Thereafter following a cautious policy, it succeeded in occupying an important place in the financial world.

Box 2. *Van Nierop and the Amsterdamsche Bank*

Frits S. van Nierop (1844-1924) was a young lawyer interested in economic and financial affairs, when he happened to meet the manager of the Bank für Handel und Industrie, who visited Amsterdam with a view to founding a bank there. As a result he got involved in the creation of the Amsterdamsche Bank (1871), of which he became one of the managers and soon the leading personality. Besides the foreign institutions the Amsterdam firms of Lippmann, Rosenthal & Co., Wertheim & Gompertz, Becker & Fuld and H. Oyens & Zonen took an interest in the new bank, together with R. Mees & Zoonen and Rotterdamsche Bank. A.C. Wertheim and M. Mees became members of the supervisory board. Because of these and other relations the bank did not meet with the unfriendly attitude that Twentsche Bank had to overcome. At the start of the new organisation of the Amsterdam stock exchange in 1876, Van Nierop became a member of

[16] The part of the Dutch in founding the Amsterdam bank is mostly neglected by foreign authors, either Eric Bussière, *Paribas, Europe and the World 1872-1992*, Antwerp, Fonds Mercator, 1992, p. 20; or Youssef Cassis, *Capitals of Capital. A History of International Financial Centres, 1780-2005*, Cambridge, Cambridge University Press, 2006, p. 50. See also B. van Marken and Piet A. Geljon, "La Banque de crédit et de dépôts des Pays-Bas/Nederlandsche Credit- en Deposito-Bank" (forthcoming).

its governing board and he held this seat until 1915. One of the other two Dutch managers of Amsterdamsche Bank – the third was a representative of the German shareholders – was also well-known in banking circles, having started his career with the firm of Königswarter. The connections with the foreign founders gave ample access to the international capital market, where Amsterdamsche Bank soon became active, in addition to its domestic issues, mainly handled in cooperation with other institutions. One of its first transactions was the founding of Koninklijke Stoomweverij (Royal Steam Weaving Mill) at Nijverdal and the issue of its shares. The relations with Dutch trade and industry partly went through the Finantiëele Maatschappij voor Nijverheids-Ondernemingen (Financial Company for Industrial Enterprises), of which Amsterdamsche Bank was one of the founders in 1883, along with some ten smaller banking and commission houses. It was a real example of a credit mobilier institution, practically the only one in the Netherlands. Apart from floating new issues, mostly in cooperation with its shareholders, it acquired concessions in coal mining and public utilities, thus contributing to the development of these sectors. Van Nierop became chairman of the managing board and he was also appointed in the supervisory boards of a number of companies in which the Financiëele Maatschappij was involved. After the turn of the century, the Finantiëele Maatschappij retreated into the background, concentrating on participations in issuing syndicates.

In 1914 Van Nierop played an important part in the organisation of financial affairs, which were stymied by the outbreak of WWI. He was also active in spheres other than the financial one. He was a member of the Amsterdam municipal council during the years 1879-1905, but he refused to become an alderman as he was foremost dedicated to his work at the bank. From 1899 to 1922 he was a member of the First Chamber of parliament. He also held a number of leading positions in Jewish organisations. Although he was himself a secular Jew, he deemed it his duty to contribute to the well-being of the Jewish community and the emancipation of the Jews. Van Nierop remained a general manager of Amsterdamsche Bank until 1920, when he had to withdraw due to poor health. It is worth mentioning that his original two colleagues also served a long period, until 1900 and 1907 respectively, which can be seen as proof of the harmonious way in which the management of the bank worked. Van Nierop then became a member of the supervisory board until his death in 1924. He saw his son Henk van Nierop appointed general manager in 1916, a position he occupied until 1939.

During the last quarter of the 19th century quite a number of new banks and commission houses were founded. Banks mostly were of the general (mixed) type, combining the banking business with securities transactions.

On the other hand, larger securities houses started to act as bankers with the granting of credits, first of all for the purchase or the holding of securities (*prolongatie*). In this climate there was presumably little room for individual institutions to become large enough to specialise in a certain sector. Moreover, securities trade, new issues and credits were complementary services, and their combination surely had advantages. This may help to explain why specialist investment banks did not arise in the Netherlands. We can only give a few names of all the newcomers, which does not do justice to the extensiveness and the variety of the Dutch financial world up to 1914. In Amsterdam, the Incasso-Bank originated (1891) from a commission house and a banking/cashier firm. In the dynamic years around 1900 it grew very fast, also in the issuing business. The same holds true for Labouchere, Oyens & Co., founded in 1881 to take over the activities of an older firm. In 1902 it added the word 'bank' to its name, underlining its development in banking. The managers of both institutions could compete easily with the bigger banks in the number of seats they occupied in the supervisory boards of other companies. In Rotterdam the old cashiers also extended their activities in the securities sector, foremost R. Mees & Zoonen. Two dynamic institutions were Marx & Co.'s Bank, originating in 1906 from an older securities firm, and *Deposito- en Administratie-Bank* (Deposit and Administration Bank), established in 1900 with American and Belgian capital. The Hague saw a number of securities houses and banks, mostly serving private clients, but from time to time also participating in new issues for local companies. We only mention Heldring & Pierson (1879) and Schill & Capadose (1886). A regional centre arose in Groningen with some active firms. All in all, around the turn of the century there were more than 1,500 banks, bankers, cashiers and commission houses across the whole country.

B. *Investment banks and securities trading*

It is not easy to describe the activities of all these parties in the field of investment banking. In any case, trading in securities on behalf of clients or for own account (proprietary trading) occurred with practically all of them. From early times, trading in securities was free, although a few associations tried to bring order to the exchanges, to increase transparency in price formation and to exclude bunglers from the trade. A strengthening of the organisation in Amsterdam took place when in 1876 the *Vereeniging voor den Effectenhandel* (Association for the securities trade) was founded. From the start it tried to acquire its own room for the securities trade in the general (municipal) exchange, in which it succeeded in 1903 with a separate room in the new exchange building and with its own building in 1913. In Amsterdam, trade was dominated by a large number of small commission houses, which were not always sympathetic to newcomers, in particular not the (larger) banks. Nevertheless, banks took part in the formation of the Vereeniging and became members. So managers of Amsterdamsche Bank, Twentsche Bank and Paribas joined the Association, and were even elected in the governing board. Later on NHM and newly founded banks were also admitted. Of course, the older houses of Wed. W. Borski, Wertheim & Gompertz, Lippmann, Rosenthal & Co. and others were prominent members. A more monopolistic tendency arose after 1900, when with the opening of a separate trading room a new tariff structure was also introduced with higher rates for non-members. So a tendency arose to join the Association, also with institutions that had only a small interest in securities. This was the case with some colonial and overseas banks, which were denied membership in 1911, a decision that was revoked two years later. At that time Rotterdamsche Bank with its head office outside Amsterdam – which previously was an impediment for membership – was also admitted.[17] In numbers the banks were a minority, twenty out of a total of 415 institutions, but some of them were indeed the largest parties. On the floor of the stock exchange, Rotterdamsche Bank and its Amsterdam affiliate had twelve employees, Twentsche Bank and Incasso-Bank had nine each, the overwhelming number of members had fewer than five.

In Rotterdam there had also long been a securities trade on the exchange. Newly formed banks in the decades around 1900 in general had no difficulty in being admitted. Trade was much smaller than in Amsterdam and – apart from a small number of Rotterdam companies – the same stocks were traded. Gradually, the Rotterdam exchange became a place for compensating buying and selling orders, with only the remaining balance placed in Amsterdam, which saved commission payments there. The same holds true for the still smaller stock exchange in The Hague, which was created in 1905. Apart from that, firms in The Hague mostly had a direct correspondent relationship with an Amsterdam house, as was the case with firms elsewhere.

Considering the increasing number of stock exchange members and of the listings – in Amsterdam this rose from 95 in 1860 (of which seventy-eight were foreign) to nearly 1,800 in 1914 (840 foreign) – this period was a rather busy time for the securities business. Initially mostly debentures were traded, from about 1895 shares became more prominent, with a sharply rising trend in prices. Occurring crises, particularly in 1873 (American railways), 1884 (the so-called sugar crisis), 1903 and 1907 caused only temporary setbacks, although they took their toll. In the latter

17 Ranald C. Michie, *The Global Securities Market. A History*, Oxford, Oxford University Press, 2006, p. 139, mistakenly claims that banks were excluded until 1913. Only some banks encountered difficulties in the years 1911-1913.

two crises a number of provincial firms failed, partly as a result of heavy speculation and fraud. The bigger houses, which in general operated more cautiously, were able to overcome difficulties that arose. We may conclude that the securities trade was an important part of the business of banks and commission houses, smaller and bigger, all over the country. This included the settlement of the transactions, payment of interest, dividends and redemptions and after 1900 also facilities for the keeping of securities and the renting of safe deposits. Credits against securities were also usually part of the business. With regard to the latter, firms in the country could fall back on their correspondents in Amsterdam or on the agencies in the provinces of the Nederlandsche Bank, which at that time was still a private, commercial institution, although it exercised influence through its lending and exchange rate policies. Other parts of the investment banking business, besides the securities trade, were performed by a much smaller group of institutions. We will deal first with the issuing business, both in the international and in the domestic market.

C. Investment banks and foreign issues

Foreign securities partly consisted of bonds and shares issued in other countries – where Dutch investors could subscribe freely – and introduced in Amsterdam, partly these were issued directly to the investing public in the Netherlands. The latter mostly concerned international issues floated in various countries at the same time, Dutch institutions taking part in the issuing syndicates. The issues were denominated in the currency of the debtor or of a third country – mostly pound sterling – or in two or more different currencies with a fixed exchange rate. Foreign issues directed specifically to the Netherlands and expressed in guilders hardly took place. In a world with stable exchange rates under the gold standard this posed few problems, with some exceptions like Austria. Participating in international syndicates required above all good relations with issuing houses abroad, as well as a sufficient amount of capital to bear the risks. It is not always clear whether the Dutch syndicate members shared in the issuing risks or were merely acting as a subscription office. The latter was obviously the case where the Dutch agents of the Rothschild firms – including Becker & Fuld, A.S. Valentin and L. Auerbach – or the Amsterdam office of Paribas accepted the subscriptions. In other cases risk sharing in the syndicates is most likely.

It was only a limited number of Dutch institutions that operated internationally. Hope had been long dominant in Russian loans, from 1820 in cooperation with Baring. From 1860 – the issue of *Grande Société des chemins de fer russes* – this combination was extended with Mendelssohn & Co. from Berlin and Hottinguer & Co. from Paris. Domestically, Hope & Co. was challenged in particular by Lippmann, Rosenthal & Co., which obtained a large share in Russian state and railway issues, often in co-operation with Wertheim & Gompertz.[18] The arising tensions between Hope and Lippmann could only be resolved around 1900, when a new generation of partners took over in both firms. Meanwhile, Lippmann had manifested itself in many other areas too, from Austria to Egypt and South America. Quite another story is that of the American railways, first introduced in Amsterdam in 1856 with the Illinois Central Railroad.[19] By 1875 another eighty-eight stocks were introduced, which were severely hit by the crisis of 1873. Nevertheless, in the period 1876-1895 more than 150 new securities were floated, followed by another 111 in 1896-1914. As a result of the active promotion of their stocks by representatives of the American railway companies, many Dutch firms got involved in this trade. Only Hope stood aside until about 1890, as did Lippmann, Rosenthal. Most active in this field were Wertheim & Gompertz, followed by Teixeira de Mattos, Boissevain and Adolphe Boissevain. H. Oyens & Zonen and Kerkhoven were also involved in American railways, partly through their *administratiekantoren* which issued Dutch certificates for the original American stocks. H.J. de Marez Oyens of H. Oyens & Zonen played an active role in the management of some US railway companies.

The introduction of the Canadian Pacific Railway Company by Adolphe Boissevain and H. Oyens & Zonen in 1883 is also worth mentioning. After 1900 new types of American securities, such as industrial and shipping companies, found their way to Amsterdam. In addition to Russia and the United States, most of the rest of the world was represented on the Amsterdam stock exchange. South American countries were introduced by Wertheim & Gompertz, Lippmann, Rosenthal, Teixeira de Mattos and Labouchere, Oyens, and furthermore by the Amsterdam agents of the Rothschilds and Paribas. Of the other institutions Amsterdamsche Bank soon occupied a position in the international issue market, thanks to the relations with its German and Austrian shareholders. It was mostly involved in European countries, where Hope, Lippmann, Rosenthal and Wertheim & Gompertz also played a role, together with Paribas. Rotterdamsche Bank was, with a few exceptions, hardly active in this field. Twentsche Bank and NHM, which entered the issuing business only later on, primarily acted as sub-contractors in the Dutch part of international syndicates. All in all it can be said that Dutch issuing houses after 1860 became more and more active on the international capital market, taking part in thirty to forty issues a year in the period 1900-1914. The number of houses

---

18 See Boris V. Anan'ich and Valeri I. Bovykin, "Foreign banks and foreign investment in Russia", in Rondo Cameron and Valeri I. Bovykin (eds.), *International Banking, 1870-1914*, New York/Oxford, Oxford University Press, 1991, pp. 253-290.

19 See Arthur J. Veenendaal, *Slow Train to Paradise. How Dutch Investment Helped Build American Railroads*, Stanford, Stanford University Press, 1996.

operating in this field was, however, limited. Lippmann, Rosenthal & Co., Wertheim & Gompertz, Hope, Teixeira de Mattos, Paribas, Labouchere, Oyens, and Amsterdamsche Bank in particular were the most prominent.

D. Domestic issues and related activities

Still more expansive than the international market was the domestic issue market. Whereas in 1860 only a few issues were floated, in the years before 1914 their number often surpassed one hundred.[20] From year to year, however, there were large fluctuations in the number and size of issues, depending on the economic and financial situation and whether certain large debtors were present. The largest borrower was the central government, although after the reconstruction of its finances in the 1840s, it did not issue any loans until 1878 and took out only ten loans before 1914. Initially, and occasionally later on, the state came with issues for its own account. In 1884 for the first time a syndicate was formed that underwrote the issue. NHM, Amsterdamsche Bank and Paribas were the members. They mostly participated also in later issues, as did Hope & Co., Lippmann, Rosenthal & Co., Twentsche Bank or Wertheim & Gompertz. A special case was a loan in 1886, which was taken over by Rothschild, much to the chagrin of the Dutch banks. The Dutch municipalities also became active borrowers, partly with own issues. In so far as issuing houses were called in, Amsterdamsche Bank was often used, followed by the smaller houses Oppenheim & Van Till from The Hague and Wurfbain & Zoon from Amsterdam. NHM frequently took part in sub-syndicates.

Issues in the private sector were, when these were not for the company's own risk, supported by a rather large number of banks, bankers and commission houses, in part the houses already mentioned, but also smaller local firms. There was, however, great diversity between the various sectors of trade and industry. The railway companies offered their loans without assistance of the banks – they were older than the banks and already well-known – with a few exceptions when Hope and NHM were called in. In shipping, on the other hand, the banks played an important role. As early as 1856 a kind of syndicate was formed for a share issue of a shipping company. Subscriptions were handled by a few bankers and commission agents in the Netherlands and abroad, although they did not underwrite the issue. Later on, banks participated in establishing and financing companies, in particular R. Mees & Zoonen in Rotterdam and NHM in Amsterdam, followed by the *Finantiëele Maatschappij/*

20 As official statistics are not available, amounts are difficult to give. Just before 1914 domestic issues totaled Dfl. 125-200 million per year, foreign issues less than Dfl. 10 million (only issues of which a fixed amount was placed in the Netherlands, which is only part of the total).

Amsterdamsche Bank and Hope, other institutions mostly acting as syndicate members. Marx's *Bank and Deposito- en Administratie-Bank* in Rotterdam introduced smaller shipping companies to the exchange. Financing of the manufacturing industry has been a topic in the literature, and banks have been blamed for standing aside.[21] Industry indeed was only a minor sector on the stock exchange. Nevertheless, the first industrial issues already took place around 1860, although without a stock exchange listing. An important step was an issue of Heineken's *Bierbrouwerij Maatschappij* in 1873 and of *Koninklijke Stoomweverij* (already mentioned) in 1874, for which syndicates were formed and subscriptions invited in a large circle. The first official listing occurred in 1880 for a dry dock company, by 1895 followed by seventeen others. After 1895 more issues came out with larger amounts. Among the issuing houses were smaller firms in Amsterdam and other places, where they had easy contact with their clients. The big banks mostly entered this field only after 1900. It is remarkable that banks were also absent from the oil industry for a time. The first issue of Royal Dutch in 1890 was supported by the firms of Dunlop & Van Essen and Gebr. Boissevain, whereas later on Schill & Capadose in The Hague and Adr. Offers & Zoon and Jan van der Hoop & Zoon in Rotterdam were included in the syndicate. It would seem that personal factors were important here. Some of the bankers were members of the supervisory board of Royal Dutch and Henry Deterding was not sympathetic towards the banks.[22] It can also be asked whether the banks themselves were enthusiastic about this rather speculative new industry; in any case, Amsterdamsche Bank did not participate in the issue syndicates. Only around 1910 closer contacts between Royal Dutch and NHM and Twentsche Bank developed. With another oil company, Dordtsche Petroleum, NHM declined to introduce it to the stock exchange in 1897, then Hope & Co. was invited. Already soon, however, NHM did take part in a number of other syndicates. A host of mostly smaller oil companies appeared on the capital market around 1895, mostly introduced by smaller houses such as Dunlop & Van Essen and Leembruggen, Guépin & Muysken. In a few larger issues Labouchere, Oyens, Paribas and Amsterdamsche Bank played a role.

Having discussed Royal Dutch, it is worthwhile to consider the entrance on the capital market of the other companies that became the Dutch multinationals. One of the predecessors of Unilever, Anton Jurgens'

21 For a discussion see Joost Jonker, *Merchants, Bankers, Middlemen. The Amsterdam Money Market during the First Half of the 19th Century*, Amsterdam, NEHA, 1996, pp. 121-129, and the literature given there.

22 The new history of Royal Dutch does not shed light on the various issues (ten in the period 1890-1910). See Jan Luiten van Zanden, Stephen Howarth, Joost Jonker and Keetie Sluyterman, *A History of Royal Dutch Shell*, Oxford, Oxford University Press, 2007.

Vereenigde Fabrieken, was introduced on the stock market with a debenture issue in 1906 by Amsterdamsche Bank, Labouchere, Oyens and Rotterdamsche Bank. These institutions were also involved in subsequent issues of the company, including its shares. The later partner of Jurgens, Van den Bergh, chose another way, going to London for the issue of its shares in 1895, in which the company's strong orientation on the UK market played a part. The case of Philips is also interesting. In 1912 there were intensive contacts with Twentsche Bank and NHM, but there were differences of opinion on the form and the size of an issue. When both banks did not react quickly to new proposals by Philips, Labouchere, Oyens stepped in and soon came to an agreement. It formed a large syndicate of more than sixty participants (but not including Twentsche Bank and NHM!), that could place the shares easily.

Companies operating in the Dutch East Indies started to tap the capital market as early as 1863, followed by a host of other colonial enterprises after 1895. In this, the big banks participated, but only in a few sectors, such as railway and tramway companies and sugar factories. They mostly refrained from the many, often speculative, issues of tobacco and rubber companies that were left to smaller firms such as Wurfbain & Zoon, Dunlop & Van Essen and Kerkhoven. In both sectors, speculative bubbles arose in 1907-1913, followed by sharp price declines when the high expectations did not come through.

Box 3. Wertheim and Mees as investment bankers

If anyone in the 19th century deserves the designation investment banker (or more appropriately for that time merchant banker), it would be Abraham Carel Wertheim (1832-1897), although his firm was not a merchant bank in the English tradition. Wertheim & Gompertz, established in 1834 by an uncle of A.C. Wertheim, had its origin in the securities trade. At the age of thirteen, the young Wertheim was placed as a junior clerk in the firm, where he did well. He had an apprenticeship with the firm of Königswarter, then returned to the family firm, married the daughter of his uncle and became a partner in 1858. Soon he proved himself as the key partner, transforming the modest securities house into a leading player in the national and international capital market. In the Netherlands he was considered as the most influential and creative Jewish banker of his time. He was actively involved in the Nederlandsche Credit- and Deposito-Bank, of which he was a general manager in the years 1863-1865, as well as in the establishment of the Amsterdamsche Bank, becoming a member of the supervisory board (1871-1881). He also had a leading role in the founding of the Vereeniging voor den Effectenhandel, which from 1876 organised the Amsterdam stock exchange. He was a member of the board until his death. In particular Wertheim was able to mobilise substantial amounts of capital for the industrial and transport sectors, taking part in the establishment of several Amsterdam shipping lines. He was the central figure in the endeavours to overcome the effects of the sugar crisis in 1884 and involved in reorganisations of some railway companies and a machine factory. He was elected as a member of the supervisory board of many companies, among which the Nederlandsche Bank and NHM. Besides his economic activities he put much effort in charitable and social work, had a leading position in the Jewish community (although he did not practice the religion) and acted as a member of the First Chamber of parliament. After the death of A.C. Wertheim in 1897, Wertheim & Gompertz lost much of its dynamism, as his son and successor lacked the financial capabilities of his father. In 1918 the firm entered into an unlucky merger with the Credietvereeniging of Amsterdam, the new Bank-Associatie ultimately being taken over by the Incasso-Bank.

In many respects the position of Marten Mees (1828-1917) in Rotterdam was comparable to that of Wertheim in Amsterdam, although their backgrounds were quite different. R. Mees & Zoonen was an old insurance broker and cashier that entered the securities business only after 1850. The family which managed the firm since its inception in 1720 stood in the protestant tradition. Not destined for a place in the family business – for which his father considered three of his brothers – Marten studied law, specialising in insurance, and acted for some time as a lawyer. When unexpectedly a vacancy arose in the firm, he was invited, becoming a partner in 1858. He gradually became the primus inter pares in the firm and also gained a central position in the Rotterdam financial world, partly owing to his membership of the Chamber of Commerce (1865-1895). Just like Wertheim in Amsterdam Mees was involved in the establishment of many companies in Rotterdam, primarily in shipping, but also in other cases as the Rotterdamsche Bank (1863) and a tobacco firm. He supported Lodewijk Pincoffs in his endeavours to develop the Rotterdam harbour and was very disappointed when this initiative ended in fraud, costing Mees and his firm a lot of money. But with many other companies he was successful indeed. Outside Rotterdam he also assisted and financed new enterprises, such as a machine factory in Hengelo and a yeast and spirit factory in Delft. He was even involved in the Amsterdamsche Bank, of which he became a member of the supervisory board (1871-1916), where he could meet Wertheim. He published many articles on economic subjects, supported initiatives to improve social conditions and housing of the labour force and was invited twice to become minister of finance, which he declined.

In his later years, the firm lost a number of older but also younger partners, so Marten felt obliged to stay on. For the same reason in 1902 an outsider was invited to become a member of the firm, the Rotterdam merchant and politician G.H. Hintzen. Marten ultimately withdrew in 1909, leaving his house in such a condition that it survived as an independent firm until the 1960s, with members of the family still acting as managers.

Quite often the issue of shares or debentures was part of the establishment, restructuring or even rescue of companies. NHM, for example, was cofounder of the tobacco company Deli Maatschappij in 1869 and later on participated in many other colonial enterprises, sometimes accompanied by a public issue. This company also held a large portfolio of securities. In general, however, banks rarely participated in other companies, after earlier bad experiences. Nevertheless, banks and other issuing houses assisted businesses in different ways. In 1884, a crisis arose around some colonial banks as a result of falling sugar prices (the "sugar crisis"). A committee of prominent Amsterdam business men, guided by A.C. Wertheim, endeavoured to place substantial loans to restructure these banks, and succeeded with the help of NHM and other banks. R. Mees & Zoonen had strong relations with several industrial and shipping companies. Around 1900, banks especially NHM, got heavily involved in shipping, in particular to prevent foreign lines from penetrating or taking over Dutch companies, which were deemed vital for the overseas connections. As a more general solution to preserve Dutch influence, in 1908 *Nederlandsche Scheepvaart Unie* was established by three major lines to act as a holding company of their capital. New issues were then floated by the holding, which made the capital available to the subsidiary shipping lines.

A important phenomenon in the Dutch securities sector was the *administratiekantoren*, mentioned before. They received a new boost with the introduction of the American railways, the shares of which were registered in the US. An intermediary between the company and the Dutch shareholders made transactions easier and moreover it could act as their representative in cases of failure or reorganisation. Mostly smaller firms, often in combination, founded and managed such offices. In the domestic market these institutions were also used to facilitate dealing in registered shares or in shares with a high nominal value. It is only a small step from an *administratiekantoor* to an investment fund or company. From about 1870 a new generation of such vehicles – after their first appearance a century earlier – was introduced, sponsored by smaller firms, established also in Rotterdam, The Hague and Groningen, since it was easier for investors in these cities to buy shares in a fund. In general, these funds were not very successful and they were mostly liquidated before 1920. The

Dutch private investor liked doing things himself, for which he could get advice from his banker or a number of publications. Smaller houses in particular edited or published weekly or monthly papers or sometimes circular letters. Management of securities portfolios on behalf of clients only appeared after WWI. In this period investors regularly went to their bank or commission house to cut in the safe deposit the coupons of their shares or debentures to cash them at the counter.

3. Investment bankers through war, banking crises and depression (1914-1945)

The period now to be reviewed differs in many respects from the previous era. The political and economic upheavals of these years had of course a profound influence on the Dutch financial and banking scene, including the investment banking business. The historiography of Dutch banking in this period has concentrated on the banking side of its business, i.e. the acceptance of deposits and the granting of credits. From this angle the years around WWI saw a rather spectacular development. Dutch industry started to grow faster, stimulated by the isolation of the Netherlands as a neutral country during the war and the boom period after the cessation of hostilities. The inflationary tendencies during these years also were of influence. The economic upswing was, however, short-lived and the ensuing reaction caused severe difficulties for a number of banks. This episode has given rise to extensive discussions on the character of the banks and their relation with industry. One author forcefully states that there was a "completely new stature of the banks [and that] the Dutch banking system made a decisive move towards mixed banking, granting advances and supplying capital to industry".[23] In the more modest terms of another historian, "in search of profitable outlets for their booming funds, the banks experimented with the model of the universal or mixed banks, combining traditional short-term business with the long-term business of investment banking".[24] Both authors probably refer to the granting of long-term loans to the business sector. As the ensuing problems with a number of banks arose from frozen credits, this may be true, although no figures are available to substantiate this; we only know that credits rose

23 G. Vanthemsche, "State, banks and industry in Belgium and the Netherlands", in Harold James, Hakan Lindgren and Alice Teichova (eds.), *The Role of Banks in the Interwar Economy*, Cambridge/Paris, Cambridge University Press/Éditions de la Maison des Sciences de l'Homme, 1991, p. 107.

24 Jan Luiten van Zanden, "Old rules, new conditions, 1914-1940", in M. 't Hart, Joost Jonker and Jan Luiten van Zanden (eds.), *A Financial History of the Netherlands*, Cambridge, Cambridge University Press, 1997, p. 125.

substantially and were granted in a less prudent way. However that may be, in our terminology this was not an introduction of mixed banking, which was already practiced for a long time. In this sense there was no change in the character of the banks, which continued their investment banking activities.[25]

A. Developments in the banking sector

The years after the war saw an acceleration of already existing tendencies in the Dutch financial sector, the concentration in banking and the emergence of nationwide institutions. We saw earlier that some of the big banks had developed as the largest parties on the Amsterdam stock exchange. In the issuing business Rotterdamsche Bank, Amsterdamsche Bank, Twentsche Bank and NHM also began to outstrip the older banking houses. This resulted partly from autonomous growth made possible by their larger resources, and partly from mergers and takeovers. It is noteworthy that the first mergers were related to the securities business. Amsterdamsche Bank was a forerunner, absorbing the small firm of Stadnitski & Van Heukelom in 1904. The Rotterdamsche Bank in particular was a driving force in the merger movement. In 1911 it amalgamated with its local competitor Deposito- en Administratie-Bank, which had a strong position in the securities business, changing its name into Rotterdamsche Bankvereeniging (Robaver for short). It soon sought its way to the financial capital Amsterdam with the absorption of Determeyer Weslingh & Zoon, followed by the merger with the well-known Labouchere, Oyens' Bank in 1913. Robaver was also active in taking over a number of provincial banking firms, thus building a network of affiliated banks or branches over the country. Other banks too started with establishing branches or taking over local institutions, in many cases when the latter needed help from a stronger partner. NHM in 1916-1921 joined forces with the *Geldersche Credietvereeniging* and took over the old Rotterdam houses of Ian Havelaar & Zoon and Gebr. Chabot. Twentsche Bank already had a connection with the Wissel- en Effectenbank in Rotterdam, when it took over this institution in 1917. In 1919, the already fast-growing Incasso-Bank merged with Wiegman's Bank, and later on (1934) with the Disconto-Maatschappij in Rotterdam. A special case was the integration of Van Loon & Co. (up to 1881 Wed. W. Borski) and Hope. Both firms had already close personal and business relations and when the managing partner W.H. van Loon died in 1935, a decision was made to merge the two houses.

[25] The balance-sheet item *Participations* does not give reason to speak of a change in character of the banks. Although this did rise in amounts, relative to total assets it declined to below 5% for all the banks together.

In this way, a number of old names disappeared from the investment banking scene. This was also the case with Wertheim & Gompertz, which was already loosing strength when it amalgamated in 1918 with the *Credietvereeniging* in Amsterdam. The newly formed *Bank-Associatie* soon got into difficulties as a result of imprudent lending and it did not really recover, the viable parts being bought by the Incasso-Bank in 1934. More dramatic still was the fate of Marx Bank in Rotterdam. It could not be saved and had to be liquidated in 1922. In contrast, the much bigger Robaver, which suffered heavy losses in 1924, was rescued and reorganised with the help of the Nederlandsche Bank, backed by a guarantee from the government. In these and a number of other failures of minor provincial and small-business banks (*middenstandsbanken*) the problem lay in a too great expansion of lending to businesses that were hit by the economic crisis of 1921/1922. After this experience, banks became more cautious in their lending, thus avoiding much trouble in the 1930 crisis. As the authors cited before note: they withdrew from investment banking. Nevertheless, the banks were hit by the depression, but they succeeded in surviving, albeit with a much reduced level of activity. A heavy blow was dealt to NHM, which incurred severe losses on its substantial interests in agrarian enterprises in the Dutch East Indies. A large part of its capital had to be written off, but with a new share issue it could continue its business.

Against the disappearing houses there was a relative great number of newcomers. Mostly these were small businesses and many of them again disappeared sooner or later. More important was that some older institutions which previously had concentrated on their banking business now entered the field of securities. After their entry on the stock exchange, the colonial and overseas banks started to expand their securities business with transactions for their private clients and new issues for companies in their areas of operation. In particular *Nederlandsch-Indische Handelsbank* (NIHB) became an active party in the new issue business, but Nederlandsch-Indische Escompto Maatschappij (also a colonial bank) and *Nederlandsche Bank voor Zuid-Afrika* also developed their securities departments. Savings banks and farmer cooperative banks on the other hand were not yet involved in this sector (apart from their own investments), nor was the newly created (1927) *Nederlandsche Middenstandsbank* (Dutch small business bank, NMB). A few new names are worth mentioning. The first is Pierson which was the old firm of Adolphe Boissevain after a name change in 1917. An old name that revived was Labouchere. A really new foundation in Amsterdam was Mendelssohn & Co., established in 1920 as a subsidiary of the Berlin firm. After a start in foreign exchange trading, it specialised more and more in international issues, in which it gained an important place under its manager Fritz Mannheimer, until his death and the collapse of the house in 1939.

For the sake of completeness we also mention the establishment of a number of other German banks after the war, mostly affiliates of the big German banks which sought a new entry to the international market. They were active in investment management for German clients, foreign exchange and trade financing. In the 1930s these subsidiaries disappeared or developed into Dutch institutions. The affiliate of the Credit-Anstalt, the Amstelbank, failed after the collapse of its parent company, contributing to the turmoil in the markets just before the fall of sterling on 20 September 1931. In the 1920s a new boost was also given to the acceptance market in Amsterdam, in which Dutch banks had been active for a long time. Cooperation between Dutch, German and other institutions led to the establishment of a number of special accepting houses, but the crisis of the 1930s brought an end to their existence.

B. Investment bankers and foreign issues

The first consequence of the outbreak of war was the closure of the stock exchanges on 29 July 1914. This was a severe blow to the functioning of the *prolongatie* market, where it became impossible to get repayment of outstanding loans or to sell the underlying securities. To ease the difficulties of money lenders, a consortium of the *Nederlandsche Bank* and a number of other institutions was created to give help, which contributed to an orderly liquidation of outstanding credits. Nevertheless, this market never fully recovered. It was replaced by other forms of credit on securities. Before the reopening of the exchanges in February 1915, a special law was introduced which gave the Minister of Finance authority in a number of stock exchange matters, in particular opening and closing and the listing of securities. In practice, close cooperation developed between the authorities and the exchanges. Still more disturbing was the disruption of international relations as a consequence of the war. Not only did the new issue market come to a virtual standstill, many foreign governments also stopped the debt service on outstanding loans, including Germany and a number of central European countries. A few years later, the new Soviet regime in Russia cancelled all foreign loans, which was a heavy blow to the Dutch investors. In the best cases the arrears were included in later rescheduling agreements, in the worst case – that of Russia – nothing was ever paid back.

Since the Netherlands was a neutral country and the government now decided on the listing of securities, the issue of loans on behalf of the belligerent countries was impossible. Only towards the end of 1917 a French government loan was introduced, followed by a reconstruction loan in 1919, both managed by the Amsterdam branch of Paribas. For the rest only a few foreign companies appeared on the Amsterdam market during the war. Among them was Van den Berghs, the English financing vehicle of the Dutch Van den Bergh factories, which cooperated with Anton Jurgens. Its three- and five-year notes were issued through their Rotterdam bankers, Robaver. After the war it took several years before the international issue activity started to recover again, which is quite understandable with the prevalent unstable financial and monetary conditions. Loans by Belgium (in francs, via Robaver) and the City of Sao Paulo (in guilders, via Lippmann, Rosenthal & Robaver) in 1921 seemed the first indications of a revival. Remarkable was the issue of both shares and debentures denominated in marks for some German companies, as that currency was not yet stabilised. These were introduced by two small and unknown commission houses.

The efforts to rebuild the European economy after the war led to the new phenomenon of international stabilisation loans on behalf of a number of countries. An important figure in this field, including activities within the League of Nations, was C.E. ter Meulen, a partner of Hope from 1901 until death in 1937. No wonder that his firm played a leading role in arranging and placing the Dutch components of the various issues, starting with £ 500,000 for Czechoslovakia in 1922. The following year Dfl. 3m. were issued as part of an Austrian loan by a consortium consisting of Twentsche Bank, Incasso-Bank, Lippmann, Rosenthal, R. Mees & Zoonen, Nederlandsch-Indische Handelsbank, Pierson, Teixeira de Mattos and Vermeer, in addition to Hope. The same houses, now joined by NHM, Amsterdamsche Bank and Robaver, arranged a Dlf. 5m. issue on behalf of Hungary in 1924. Substantially larger was the German foreign loan of 1924 – the Dawes loan – the Dutch part of which was fixed at £ 2.5m. (Dfl. 28.5m.). The issue syndicate was again somewhat different, this time without Pierson, Lippmann & Vermeer. It may be remarked here that without further knowledge of the issue process it is difficult to understand how in a particular case a syndicate was formed. Parties might be invited, but decide to decline, there might be quarrels on the size of the participations or other details or an aversion to cooperate with some other participant. It is known for example that Hope always insisted on having the subscriptions routed via its affiliate Van Loon. This caused tensions in the long-time cooperation with NHM, which during the 1920s developed a cordial relation with the new firm of Mendelssohn. For the last of the stabilisation loans – the 1930 Young loan with a Dutch tranche of Dfl. 73m. – NHM and Mendelssohn initiated its own consortium, but the issue again went through the Hope group, which now also included the Amsterdam affiliates of the German banks.

The 1924 Dawes loan and the restoration of the gold standard in the following year much contributed to the stabilisation of monetary conditions which, together with the world economic recovery, initiated lively activity on the international capital market. Foreign loans of Dfl. 300 to 400m. a year during 1924-1930 were sometimes higher than domestic issues. One of the major borrowing countries was Germany, which needed much capital for the rebuilding of its economy. Both public authorities and private enterprises tapped the Dutch market for large amounts. Companies like August Thyssen and Siemens & Halske were among the first to issue dollar bonds in Amsterdam, together with municipalities like Cologne and Bremen. It was here that the new firm of Mendelssohn became active as an issuing house, first in cooperation with Pierson, and soon in a more stable syndicate also with NHM and R. Mees & Zoonen of Rotterdam, to which one or more other participants were occasionally added. But more houses in various combination were active on this front (Amsterdamsche Bank, Twentsche Bank, Hope, Lippmann, Rosenthal, Teixeira de Mattos, Robaver and the young firm Labouchere). In addition to Germany, governments and companies from other countries in Europe and overseas showed much interest in the Dutch market, just as before 1914. To mention only a few: Belgium (through Mendelssohn and Paribas), Denmark (Twentsche Bank), Poland (Hope, Lippmann, Rosenthal, Twentsche Bank), Uruguay (Amsterdamsche Bank), Peru (Teixeira de Mattos). The issues were denominated in dollars, pounds sterling and marks, but also in guilders. Foreign securities were also introduced on the stock exchange without a new issue, mostly by smaller stock broking firms.

From 1930 – not long after the Young loan – the ongoing depression completely changed the picture of the foreign issue market, when demand from companies dwindled and currency unrest made international financial relations hazardous. Also, Dutch authorities began to discourage foreign loan operations when the guilder – one of the last currencies tied to gold – came under speculative pressure. As a defensive measure, in 1933 the Nederlandsche Bank informally requested the banks to refrain from the introduction of long-term foreign loans on the Dutch market. This was not a full-fledged exchange restriction, as the purchase of foreign securities through the stock market or the participation in issues abroad remained possible. This unofficial embargo was terminated soon after the country left the gold standard in 1936. Although capital now started to flow back, only a small number of foreign debtors, notably from France and Belgium, were brought to the market. But not all went well. In particular the difficult placing of two French state loans totaling Dfl. 125m. directly led to the fall of Mendelssohn in August 1939, since it could not finance the heavy positions it was forced to take. At the same time the outbreak of WWII brought an end to international operations on the Dutch capital market.

Box 4. C.J.K. van Aalst and the NHM

When C.J.K. (Karel) van Aalst (1866-1939) joined the Nederlandsche Handel-Maatschappij (NHM) in 1889, this company was still in a period of transition. Its monopoly in the trade with the Dutch East Indies on account of the government was gradually abolished after 1870. It tried to compensate for this by increasing its own trade and its interests in agricultural enterprises in the East, the produce of which it could finance and sell at home. Moreover, NHM started to venture in banking, first in its office in Batavia (now Jakarta). In the Netherlands, it initially concentrated on taking part in new issue syndicates, proceeding with the general banking business in 1903. Van Aalst was first placed in Batavia and Surabaya, and was appointed manager of the Singapore branch in 1898. He was a hard working and ambitious young man and succeeded in increasing the NHM business in his region, among other things by putting the harbour and bunker station at Sabang to the North of Sumatra on a sound footing. Back in the Netherlands in 1902 he was appointed as a general manager, charged in particular with the banking side. In this capacity he did much to stimulate business and finance in Amsterdam, for example in the shipping sector. He was already an influential figure, representing the biggest financial institution in the country, when he became president of NHM in 1913. He was the first president who had worked at NHM for his whole career (his predecessor for example was a former minister). At the outbreak of the war, he did much to coordinate measures to calm the financial situation and set up an organisation (Nederlandsche Overzee Trustmaatschappij) to arrange imports in such a way that it satisfied the allied powers. After the war he put much effort in the preparation of a special trade agreement between the Netherlands and Germany, which made both imports of coal from Germany and exports to that country possible. It brought him a German honourary doctorate, of which he was very proud (he was not a stranger to vanity!). Maybe this contributed to his Eastward orientation: NHM at this time was active in placing issues of German companies and government authorities in the Netherlands. In this business a close cooperation developed with Mendelssohn & Co. and its partner Fritz Mannheimer. Van Aalst was also a member of the supervisory board of Amstelbank, the Amsterdam affiliate of the Austrian Credit-Anstalt. He held the same position with numerous other companies, in particular in the field of shipping and colonial enterprises, but also with Royal Dutch and KLM, which illustrates his central position in Dutch business and finance. The other side of his strong personality was that he had difficulty in cooperating with others, leading to the resignation of various general managers of NHM. All this resulted in a strong identification between Van Aalst and NHM. No wonder that he was held responsible when in 1934 the company suffered heavy losses on its participations in agricultural enterprises in the East Indies and he was forced to resign. Still more of a personal tragedy developed when in August 1939 his old business partner F. Mannheimer suddenly died and his firm could not be saved. What made things worse for Van Aalst was that his son had meanwhile become a partner in Mendelssohn & Co. All this was probably too much for him; he died in October 1939. Another consequence of the Mendelssohn failure was that Van Aalst's successor had to retire as president, because of the loss the company suffered from this debacle. Nevertheless, Van Aalst had contributed a great deal to the development of his bank and Dutch finance and business in general.

C. Investment bankers and domestic issues

For the domestic issue market, the years of WWI and just after were very favourable. The state had of course large borrowing needs, but this was not a very profitable business for the banks as the government mainly placed issues for its own account, with subscriptions being routed through government agencies. This was possible because the loans were mainly forced or semi-forced. Only in 1922-1924 a large banking consortium was used, because the two loans in this period were partly placed in New York. Apart from the large banks and a few banking houses (remarkably not Hope), the colonial banks were also included. When the state resumed its borrowing activities in the early 1930s, it again made use of a large syndicate, now with Hope. The colonial banks were also active in the issue of loans on behalf of the government of the Dutch East Indies, the first of which was placed in 1915. NHM, NIHB and Escompto, which had secretly agreed to cooperate, were the members of the consortium. They acted together for the following loan as well, but this time much more institutions were enlisted, probably only as a *guichet*. The small consortium also issued loans on behalf of municipalities in the Indies, but here they met strong competition from other banks like Amsterdamsche Bank and Robaver.

An area of rivalry was also the loan business of the municipalities in the Netherlands. For the larger cities we see the same issuing houses operating as before, in the smaller towns often one or two local bankers were employed, sometimes in cooperation with one of the larger houses. Fixed syndicates were not uncommon, but changes in the membership did occur. The municipality of Amsterdam, for example, made use of several combinations, one with Hope, NHM and Amsterdamsche Bank, another under Pierson (which did not preclude NHM from secretly participating in a Pierson issue in 1926), but combinations of other houses also occurred. In the syndicate for The Hague, which was traditionally managed by Wurfbain, NHM took over this position in 1919 because of its growing issuing power, whereas Lippmann, Rosenthal was included. Sometimes there were obvious reasons for a bank to be absent, such as Robaver in a Rotterdam issue in 1924, when the bank was in severe trouble.

In the private sector still more banks, private banking houses and securities firms acted as intermediaries in the new issue market. Up to 1921, the Dutch economy prospered and the stock exchange being rather strong, many companies took the opportunity to go public or to increase their capital through the issue of shares or bonds. After a few years of less activity in the mid-1920s, the market started to flourish again until 1931, with all the sectors of the economy taking part. In the first instance, it was the company's house banker which would be considered to arrange an issue, but both the company and the bank might have additional wishes. One known case is the shipyard De Schelde, whose issues had been arranged by *Finantiëele Maatschappij voor Nijverheidsondernemingen.* In 1916 the company wished to include Robaver in the syndicate, but Amsterdamsche Bank – the main shareholder of the Maatschappij – only agreed if it self would be on a par with Robaver. From then on, both banks arranged the issues.

The banks themselves called heavily on the capital market, mostly arranging their own issues, sometimes inviting friendly institutions to join. Difficult to place was the NHM share issue in 1934 after the bank's losses. With the help of Mendelssohn most of the issue was taken up by institutions abroad. In shipping, a particularly buoyant sector in the years after the war, we see the names of the older houses, Hope/Van Loon, NHM, Robaver and R. Mees & Zoonen, but also Amsterdamsche Bank, Twentsche Bank and sometimes *Nederlandsch-Indische Escompto Maatschappij* and Marx (before 1922). Industrial issues were frequently placed by quite a lot of issuing houses, too many to list. The same holds true for the many colonial enterprises which came to the market, often for the first time. The bigger companies in both sectors, of course, used the big banks that could bear larger risks and had developed a strong placing power through their country wide networks. A notable exception for a time remained Royal Dutch, which up to 1924 placed issues through its old consortium of private banks. In that year, NHM appeared among the issuing houses for the first time. NHM and Hope had, however, been involved in earlier issues of group companies. After 1924 the old houses disappear from the scene, although they remained in existence. A dollar loan in 1930 was arranged by the consortium of NHM, Mendelssohn, Pierson and R. Mees & Zoonen. A vast loan of Dfl.100 m. was issued in 1939 through the same four banks together with Amsterdamsche Bank, Twentsche Bank, Robaver, Heldring & Pierson and Schill & Capadose, the latter being the only one of the original issuing houses of Royal Dutch.

Anton Jurgens' *Vereenigde Fabrieken*, predecessor of Unilever, arranged a share issue in 1919 through Hope and Robaver in stead of Amsterdamsche Bank and Robaver. Its partner Van den Bergh's Fabrieken remained for the time being with Robaver, later on adding Pierson, NHM and Mendelssohn. The merger of Jurgens and Van den Bergh in Margarine Unie in 1927 was guided by the same four banks, which also acted when in 1929 this company merged with Lever Brothers, forming Lever Brothers & Unilever (later on: Unilever). With Philips, the third multinational dating back to before the war, we also see a broadening of its issue syndicates. Introduced in 1912 by Labouchere, Oyens, Robaver acted as its banker after the take-over of Labouchere. Robaver managed several issues (together with the smaller firms of Fred. Philips and Dunlop & Philips), but in 1929 Amsterdamsche Bank, NHM and NIHB were added, whereas in the following year the smaller firms disappeared.

The formation of *Algemeene Kunstzijde Unie* (AKU) only took place in 1929, but one of its predecessors – *Nederlandsche Kunstzijde Fabriek* (Enka) – was established in 1911. In 1919 it placed its first public issue of debentures through Robaver, later on it used a combination of Hope and Robaver. An issue of shares *Vereinigte Glanzstoffen* was placed in Amsterdam in 1929 by Hope, Teixeira de Mattos and the Amsterdam office of Deutsche Bank. When Enka and Glanzstoffen merged to AKU we see the same four banks acting: Hope, Robaver, Teixeira de Mattos and Deutsche Bank. At the end of WWI, two companies were established that would gain much importance later on: Hoogovens and KLM. The state and a number of banks had a substantial stake in both and there was no need to go public. Hoogovens shares were introduced on the stock market in 1939 by NHM, Amsterdamsche Bank, Twentsche Bank and Robaver, whereas KLM only went public after WWII.

D. Investment bankers, the stock exchange, and investors

Above we have given many names of institutions – banks, private banking houses and securities commission houses – that acted as intermediaries in the new issuing market. It should be remarked that these are only the names that appeared in publicity (prospectuses and advertisements). In many cases still more firms were involved in placing the securities, each of the syndicate members often agreeing with other houses to take up part of its participation in an issue. Also, it is not always clear whether all the houses mentioned acted as underwriters – and thus taking the risk of the placing – or only as subscription offices (*guichet*), nor how much each participated. In addition, the success of an issue is not always clear. When a syndicate was dissolved, any unsold securities were added to the banks' balance sheet item "Securities" and then sold in the market when possible. In this item – mostly 6-8 per cent of the balance sheet total – a normal trading stock was included as the issuing houses also acted as commission agents. On the floor of the Amsterdam stock exchange in 1939 Robaver and its affiliate was still the largest party (thirteen employees), followed by Twentsche Bank (twelve), Amsterdamsche Bank (ten), NHM and Incasso-Bank (seven each), compared with eight for Pierson and seven for Hope.

In preparing an issue the banks/issuing houses of course acted as advisers to companies or government bodies with regard to the possibilities of an issue, the amount, the terms, the timing etc. An important aspect was the creation of some kind of protection against unfriendly – mostly interpreted as foreign – takeovers. We saw this before in the shipping sector. An early example is also Royal Dutch, which in 1898 had already introduced preference shares (later called priority shares) with certain powers regarding the appointment of members of the board. Later on, certificates of shares in a subsidiary company that would like to go partly public were created through a trust company, which exercised the voting rights on the original shares. In other cases a separate holding company – with a name indicating 'national' or 'common' ownership – was established, which issued shares to the public, whereas the holding acquired the shares in the operating enterprise.[26] In many cases, *administratie kantoren* were used to the same end. Later on in this period – in the depression years – another aspect of *administratiekantoren* and trust companies became more prominent, the protection of the rights of the holders of shares and debentures in case of company failures. Stock exchange protection committees served the same purpose, their members coming from the various categories of issuing houses.

An indication of a growing involvement of banks in industrial affairs is the increasing number of seats in supervisory boards. We know of the position of A.C. Wertheim and M. Mees in the previous period, but now board membership seems to have become more widespread, not only by managers of the larger institutions, but also of houses outside of Amsterdam and Rotterdam.[27] This phenomenon may be related to the growing number of companies that went public; the listings of industrial enterprises for example more than doubled to about 350 in 1925/1930 (thereafter it started to decline again). During WWI leaders of the banks were strongly involved in the introduction and execution of government measures regarding the economy. Here again, not only the managers of

---

26 So the shares of Philips that were listed were those of '*Gemeenschappelijk Bezit van aandelen Philips' Gloeilampenfabrieken*', which came with an issue every time it had to take up shares in its subsidiary, the Philips works itself.

27 Joost Jonker, "Sinecures or sinews of power? Interlocking directorships and bank-industry relations in the Netherlands, 1910-1940", *Economic and Social History in the Netherlands*, 3, 1991, pp. 119-131.

the big banks like Van Aalst were engaged, but also partners of smaller houses as J.H. Kann of Lissa & Kann in The Hague, who was a member of the government commission on the stock exchanges.

What about the relations with the investors? These still mostly took place on a personal basis, in particular at the smaller houses. The banks were the first to create a separate department for investment management, serving the wealthiest clients in particular. Although investment research had yet to be introduced in the Netherlands, the banks gradually made a start with gathering and using economic information. In 1924, Amsterdamsche Bank created a statistical office, the forerunner of its economic bureau, which towards the end of the period started with the publication of an economic bulletin. At NHM one person was entrusted with studying investment problems, which in 1930 resulted in the establishment of Hollandsche Belegging en Beheer Maatschappij (Dutch investment and management company). NHM itself was, however, not involved in this pioneering company, which was run on a personal basis by the initiator. In general, the big banks refrained for the time being from entering the field of investments trusts or companies. Besides a few funds established before 1914, new initiatives around the war were also taken by smaller houses such as *Haagsche Commissiebank*, which in cooperation with H. Oyens & Zonen introduced *Nederlandsche Fondsen Maatschappij* (Dutch securities company). It would take another decade before further steps were made. In 1929 a number of private persons in Rotterdam created *Rotterdamsch Beleggings Consortium*, later known as Robeco. It remained a private venture (initially not very successful in the ensuing stock market crisis), but in 1938 its shares were introduced on the stock exchange by a consortium of Robaver, R. Mees & Zoonen, NHM and Heldring & Pierson. There were also close personal ties, managers of the banks acting as members of the supervisory board of Robeco. Also in the early 1930s, following the American example, some fixed investment trust were created, for example a fund investing in six South African goldmines, again by smaller firms.

The 1930s were not an appropriate time to invest on the stock market. Towards the end of the period, however, the outlook improved and with very low interest rates shares became more attractive. Increasing political tensions in Europe, moreover, created a need for investment in safer areas. Now the big banks joined in creating investment vehicles, in particular fixed trusts. Incasso-Bank was very active here, but also Twentsche Bank, Amsterdamsche Bank, Robaver and others introduced new funds for investment in the United States, Canada and South Africa. In this period also institutional investors (pension funds, social insurance funds, insurance companies and savings banks) became more influential. Through cooperation they tried to fix minimum conditions below which they would not take part in conversion loans. Apart from subscribing to new issues, they proceeded in taking parts of a planned issue beforehand (at somewhat better terms) and in offering private loans to large debtors. In these cases also a new kind of intermediation between borrowers and lenders arose, a field in which the firm of Labouchere was active.

E. Investment bankers through WWII

A completely new situation arose under the German occupation (1940-1945), a dramatic period in Dutch history, and in the financial field as well. The regulations aimed at excluding Jews from the business world were far-reaching, ultimately leading to deportation and genocide. The securities sector, which had a comparatively large Jewish element, was particularly hit and quite a number of Jewish firms disappeared. Jewish properties were also confiscated. For this purpose the German occupier used an institution with the old name of Lippmann Rosenthal, although it was a separate entity. All Jewish monies and securities had to be deposited with this company. The securities were then sold through the intermediation of the stock exchange. After the war attempts were made to redress this injustice, but the procedure was highly disputed and cumbersome, with a registration of all the securities in the hands of the public. Many years later this traumatic experience revived again, ending in 2000 with a public expression of regret by the banks and the securities association and the payment of a certain amount of compensation. More and more the financial sector was also constricted by the regulations of the occupier, bringing the usual business practically to a halt. Apart from a number of issues by domestic companies, four state loans were placed with amounts increasing to Dfl. 1 billion. On the instruction of the Ministry of Finance, the syndicates now included the Nederlandsche Middenstandsbank, in which the state had a substantial interest.

4. Investment banks through institutional banking changes (1945-1980)

When the first austere years after the war were over, the banking sector began to display a rather strong growth, which lasted until the mid-1970s. Roughly speaking, the emphasis fell on commercial banking activities. After the liberation in 1945 it took a number of years before the economy could again function more or less normally. The heavy damage of the war, a shortage of goods and foreign exchange and an oversupply of money required strict regulation. The banks had an enormous task in the government's money purge and foreign exchange policies and had to comply with guidelines for their lending. The capital market also was strictly regulated, whereas the stock exchange was hampered by the necessary registration of all securities, the requisition of American securities for balance-of-payments reasons and the near-disappearance of the colonial enterprises. Only in the early 1950s were the strictest regulations abolished, although international capital movements remained restricted for the time being.[28] With an improving economy the stock exchange also revived and share prices started a strong upward movement.

This did not mean, however, a return to pre-war conditions. In many respects banks and securities houses were confronted with a changed environment. First of all, government regulation would remain far more important than before. As a reaction to the depression years of the 1930s an active economic policy was pursued to stabilise the economy. This implied among other things a supervision of the banking system. A law was introduced that authorised the Nederlandsche Bank – meanwhile nationalised and subjected ultimately to the Minister of Finance – to give guidelines to the banks with regard to their lending (credit restriction when necessary) and their liquidity and solvency ratios. These could be different for various types of institutions (for example commercial banks or securities credit institutions), but it is important to note that no specific activities were forbidden. Furthermore, banks had to ask permission for mergers with or participations in other credit institutions, whereas later on a limit was agreed for larger participations in other, non-financial, enterprises. In its policy the Bank guarded the limits between banking, mortgage banking and insurance in particular. But within those limits, the banks were not restricted in their activities, so they could continue both with commercial lending and investment banking activities (with an exception for lending to purchase securities). As a result of the increased government interference, not only in the economic sphere, but also in other fields, taxes remained much higher than before the war. In particular the high rate of income tax caused problems for private banking firms, which were no longer able to build up the necessary reserves to expand their business.

Another factor was that the importance of the stock exchange for the financing of companies gradually diminished, internal financing becoming a main source of capital as the economy gained steam and wages were kept low. The further growth of institutional investors also played a part here, as those institutions began to prefer granting private loans to enterprises and municipalities. Moreover, new institutions were created for the financing of the business sector. In 1945 already the *Maatschappij tot Financiering van het Nationaal Herstel* (Recovery Bank; in 1963 *Nationale Investeringsbank*) was established by the government, along

28 The dividend restriction and the tax on speculation profits for example were terminated in 1953.

with a number of institutional investors and banks, which was aimed at granting longer-term loans to industrial companies. It also cooperated in the formation of the *Nederlandsche Participatie Maatschappij*, that could take participations in the share capital of companies, and the Export Financiering-Maatschappij for the financing of exports.

Of great importance was that the economy from the early 1950s showed an unprecedented growth, leading to rising personal incomes and the spreading of wealth among large sections of the population. This offered the banks the opportunity to approach completely new segments of clients, often with new products as well. Hire purchase and financing companies, which were mostly taken over by the banks later, paved the way for consumer credit, followed by personal loans and mortgage credits from the banks themselves. The introduction of savings accounts and easy payment facilities was also an element of this retail banking, which was supported by the establishment of many new branches all over the country. In addition, other groups of banks, in particular the savings banks and the agricultural cooperative banks, also actively penetrated this retail market, leading to a blurring of boundaries between the various categories of banks. With regard to companies, the traditional clients of the commercial banks, the growing economy cause a need for more money for investment purposes. Medium-term loans were introduced, initially granted by subsidiaries, later on by the banks themselves. New dimensions were opened by the formation of the European Economic Community in 1958, which stimulated international trade and the establishment of branches or subsidiaries abroad. On the other hand, foreign companies, in particular from the US, settled in the Netherlands. The banks followed this trend to internationalisation with own branches or subsidiaries in other countries and cooperation with banks abroad. The rise of the Euromarkets was a new impetus in this respect, also leading to the formation of international banking consortia towards the end of the 1960s.

A. Investment banks and institutional changes

It goes without saying that all these developments had a strong impact in the institutional sphere. Broadly surveying this field, we start with the unfortunate exits of two old houses, Kerkhoven and Teixeira de Mattos, which went bankrupt in 1948 and 1966 respectively. The latter, once a prominent issuing house, got involved in risky banking operations which caused heavy losses. Another old house, Lippmann, Rosenthal which was revived after the war, became Hollandse Koopmansbank Lippmann Rosenthal through a merger. A drastic overhaul occurred with the disappearance of practically all the provincial banks and commission houses, partly as a result of further take-overs by the bigger banks. Only F. van Lanschot (Den Bosch, 1737, transformed into a limited liability company in 1978) developed independently with a few larger outside shareholders. Van Lanschot belonged to a category of medium-sized banks that developed in the 1950s and 1960s. Nederlandsche Credietbank (NCB, 1918) and Slavenburg's Bank (1915) grew partly by taking over other houses, in the securities field as well. The latter merged in 1974 with Oyens & Van Eeghen, which was created some years before by an amalgamation of H. Oyens & Zonen and Van Eeghen & Co. Another institution in this group was Nederlandse Overzee Bank (NOB) – the former Nederlandsche Bank voor Zuid-Afrika – which acquired several securities firms and a few banking houses outside Amsterdam (Haagsche Commissiebank and Fred. Philips). It also obtained the Dutch business of the Nederlandsch-Indische Escompto Maatschappij after the nationalisation in Indonesia. Hollandsche Bank-Unie (HBU) – originally an overseas bank – had already started to broaden its activities before the war and after 1945 it became more involved in the securities business. In particular these smaller banks first ventured into the market for personal savings, mainly with a view to interest new clients in their services, including securities.[29] For this category of banks the growing internationalisation posed problems, which they initially tried to solve by accepting participations from foreign banks: NCB from Chase Manhattan, Slavenburg from First National Bank of Chicago, Van Lanschot from National Westminster and NOB from Continental Illinois. The firms of R. Mees & Zoonen and Hope merged in 1962, maintaining a connection with Morgan Guaranty. Some smaller houses, too, joined a foreign partner, Kol & Co. became Barclays Kol & Co. (1972) and the Rotterdam firm Arnold Gilissen was renamed Lloyds Bank International. All these alliances would be terminated in later years, however *Banque de Paris et des Pays-Bas* continued its activities in the securities field, but moved also into the general banking business. Other foreign banks – mainly American and Japanese – were more engaged in (international) banking activities.

Of the medium-sized banks some ultimately opted for a Dutch solution. NOB merged with Mees & Hope into Bank Mees & Hope (BMH), which in 1975 became a subsidiary of ABN, for the time being continuing to operate rather independently. HBU had already found the way to ABN. We have not yet mentioned the Pierson houses, Heldring & Pierson in The Hague and Pierson in Amsterdam. During the war they had concluded a profit sharing agreement, merging into a new

[29] The big banks' move into the savings market is often explained by the need to finance their medium-term lending. In 1957, however, this still took place through subsidiaries which financed themselves on the capital market, whereas the medium-sized banks were hardly engaged in this kind of loans. The big banks only started to attract savings a few years later, partly as a reaction to the moves of the smaller institutions.

entity Pierson, Heldring & Pierson (PHP) in 1958, a few years after the firm of Schill & Capadose in The Hague had been acquired. In 1975 PHP linked up with AMRO Bank. ABN (Algemene Bank Nederland) and Amro (Amsterdam-Rotterdam Bank) themselves were the outcome of the biggest mergers so far in Dutch banking, formed in 1964 by the amalgamation of NHM and Twentsche Bank and Amsterdamsche Bank and Rotterdamsche Bank respectively.[30] These four had already been active in taking over other institutions in the province. Moreover, Amsterdamsche Bank acquired Incasso-Bank in 1948, maintaining this name up to 1956, Rotterdamsche Bank took over the business of the former Nederlandsch-Indische Handelsbank. There were even participations that were not disclosed to the public: Amsterdamsche Bank bought Labouchere in 1947, NHM took over the renowned firm Wed. Tjeenk (1948). After 1964, the dominance of the two big banks was such, that the central bank objected to further mergers, with the exception of ABN/HBU in 1967. Next in size after the big two but coming before the medium-sized banks was Nederlandsche Middenstandsbank (NMB). It reached this position without major mergers, partly based on the credits to smaller companies guaranteed by the state. It also succeeded in expanding its securities business, partly by taking over a smaller banking house specialised in this field.

Slower was the entrance of the agricultural cooperative banks and the savings banks into the securities business. The former started in the 1950s to look beyond their original field of activity and joined the struggle for the retail market by opening branches in urban regions and adding new services for private customers. More or less hesitantly because of the competition with their own savings accounts, they also entered the securities business by offering intermediation for stock exchange transactions. The two central institutions of these banks – established in Eindhoven and Utrecht – both acquired a foothold in Amsterdam by buying a commission house. The merger of both central agricultural banks into Rabo Bank in 1972 laid the foundations for a later expansion. The savings banks had to cope with a loose organisation of rather independent local banks. Competition from the other banks pressed them hard and they also developed more retail services, but their entry into the securities field was slow.

B. *Investment bankers and capital market operations*

Among the various investment banking activities new issues continued to occupy an important place, at first only on the domestic market,

30 In 1947 the name Robaver (*Rotterdamsche Bankvereeniging*) was again changed into *Rotterdamsche Bank.*

from the mid-1960s also on the international markets. Initially, the capital market was regulated rather strictly with a view to economic recovery, later on to ensure a smooth functioning of the market and to support domestic monetary policy. Borrowing by the state had priority, lower public bodies had to comply with maximum interest rates (up to 1963) or were obliged to borrow from the Bank voor Nederlandsche Gemeenten (BNG, Bank for the Dutch municipalities) (1965-1975). Moreover, the banks agreed to inform the Nederlandsche Bank of proposed issues and to get a 'no objection' for the actual launching. For this purpose, the Bank used a calendar (*calandrier*), placing the applications according to date. For foreign issues, a permission was always needed, in which balance-of-payments considerations played an important part.

Early in 1946 the state was the first to call on the market with loans in various forms, mainly to absorb the money blocked in the money purge. It did not make use of a syndicate, but all the banks, including the savings banks and the agricultural cooperatives – which also held blocked accounts of the public – accepted subscriptions. For years to come the state operated in this way to issue loans. Within the limits for their borrowing, the municipalities also resumed their issue activity, including loans for conversion purposes, as did the state in connection with its cheap money policy. In addition to the big banks, in these first years we still see a number of local banks acting as intermediaries for municipal loans, which mostly had the character of *guichet* issues under the government regulations. Amsterdam used a large group of banks, including the members of the two pre-war syndicates. Rotterdam did the same, although Hope was absent in this case. Both municipalities also placed loans privately, which were later on introduced on the stock market. The rise of other issuing houses in the 1960s is illustrated by loans for these cities arranged by entirely new syndicates, including NOB, NCB, NMB, Van Lanschot, Vermeer, Th. Gilissen and others. BNG, gradually developing as the central financing institution for the municipalities, also used a large *guichet* syndicate (at first not including Hope), of which Slavenburg, NCB, NMB and Rabo also became members later on.

One of the first operations on the capital market, apart from the government, was the share issue of the Herstelbank, organised by the big banks together with the firms Lippmann, Rosenthal, R. Mees & Zoonen and Pierson (Hope was probably not interested in industrial finance), which had taken part in its foundation. Later on several loans were issued through this same syndicate. In the private sector industrial companies soon started attracting capital on the public market. In this sector Amsterdamsche Bank with its affiliate Incasso-Bank, Rotterdamsche Bank, NHM and Twentsche Bank, occupied the major place, in the first years after the war often supported by one of the smaller institutions or NIHB. From the 1950s HBU,

Slavenburg, NCB and NOB also began to appear more often. We need not give a complete survey, but only mention some interesting features of the big companies we dealt with earlier.

A major and complicated operation – because of the international and foreign exchange aspects – was the issue of Dfl. 300 m. shares and Dfl. 100 m. debentures by Royal Dutch[31] in 1947. As the securities also had to be placed abroad, a large syndicate was formed, including two Belgian banks and one each from the United Kingdom, Switzerland and France. The Dutch group consisted of fifteen members, all the institutions which earlier had been involved in capital market operations of the Group, together with Incasso-Bank and Paribas. The syndicate for the debentures was smaller, not including Dunlop, Dunlop & Philips and *Gebr. Boissevain*. There were probably historical considerations to let them take part in the share issue, which moreover had a *guichet* character, so they did not have to take risks. A new share issue in 1958 was organised in the Netherlands by a smaller group of seven banks – the big four together with Hope, R. Mees & Zoonen and Pierson, Heldring & Pierson.[32] This issue was also placed in other countries by foreign members of the syndicate.

Unilever had already dropped the smaller firms. In 1947 it used Rotterdamsche Bank and NHM, together with the newcomer Pierson, to which Amsterdamsche Bank was added in 1949. The syndicate for a placement of AKU shares in 1951 included NHM and Pierson & Co. along with its old relation Hope and Amsterdamsche Bank/Incasso-Bank, but not Rotterdamsche Bank (which was at odds with the company). In later years the syndicate consisted of NHM, PHP, Hope and Amsterdamsche Bank/Incasso-Bank. A share issue of the Philips holding company in 1948 was placed through a syndicate of Rotterdamsche Bank, NHM and Amsterdamsche Bank, together with Dunlop & Philips and Fred. Philips (the latter two being old relations) and Pierson. At the same time, a debenture issue of the Philips company itself had only the three big banks and Pierson & Co. as members. In later issues, HBU was included, together with R. Mees & Zoonen. In addition, a share issue of Hoogovens in 1947 was supported by the same four banks that acted in 1939 (NHM, Amsterdamsche Bank, Twentsche Bank and Rotterdamsche Bank), which were also the members of later syndicates. Finally, KLM was introduced

31 See J.L. Van Zanden, S. Howarth, J. Jonker and K. Sluyterman, *A History of Royal Dutch Shell, op. cit.*

32 Pierson & Co. (Amsterdam) and Heldring & Pierson (The Hague) in fact decided to merge just with a view to this issue, partly to prevent confusion abroad on the names. Joost Jonker, *MeesPierson. The Link between Past and Future. 275 years of Tradition and Innovation in Dutch banking*, Amsterdam, MeesPierson, 1997, p. 79. Incasso-Bank and Schill & Capadose had meanwhile been integrated in Amsterdamsche Bank and Pierson respectively.

on the market in 1957 by a large group of the four big banks, five old firms (Heldring & Pierson being the manager) and the smaller banks HBU and NOB.

From the mid-1960s bank concentration made further headway (ABN, AMRO, Bank Mees & Hope), as a result of which issue syndicates became less varied, whereas at the same time new parties (NMB and the agricultural banks) were gaining ground. After the leap in share prices which lasted until 1964, the stock market began to stagnate (although a further spurt occurred in 1972/1973), leading to less interest in new issues from the private sector. Meanwhile, attention had also shifted to the international markets, which grew rather strongly after the first Euro-bond issue in 1963, in which Rotterdamsche Bank participated. Earlier, however, the Dutch market had gradually resumed its role as a supplier of capital to foreign borrowers. In 1950 a large syndicate of fourteen members issued Dutch certificates for part of a 1947 dollar loan by the World Bank, followed by a direct issue of a guilder loan in 1954. The first foreign debtor to tap the guilder market was Belgium in the same year, with a loan arranged by Twentsche Bank and its subsidiary Van Mierlo & Zoon. In later years a broader syndicate was used for the Belgian issues. Paribas intermediated for several Belgian cities. Around the same time foreign bonds and shares were also introduced through the issue of certificates by various *administratiekantoren*, mostly connected with smaller institutions. An example is a DM loan by *Dortmund-Hörder Hütten Union*, for which Kol issued the certificates. More and more American companies also came on the market in the same form. In the following years debtors from other countries such as Norway, Australia and South Africa called on the Dutch market, along with international organisations.

Meanwhile, the guilder had developed into a currency not only for borrowing, but owing to its strength also for investment purposes. To prevent a large capital inflow, which could disturb the central bank's restrictive monetary policy, the euro-guilder note was created in 1969, the issue and conditions of which were strictly regulated (no investment by Dutch residents, spending of the proceeds abroad, no prospectus etc.). International organisations and foreign governments and companies as well as domestic borrowers made use of this market. The latter included both banks and the Dutch internationals. It was also these companies that tapped the market in other currencies. Here the big banks ABN and AMRO played a role as lead or co-managers of the syndicates, PHP acting as a co-manager in a number of cases. The euro-guilder market was dominated by a consortium of ABN and AMRO with their subsidiaries Bank Mees & Hope and PHP (called the "cloverleaf"). A second group consisting of NMB, Rabobank, NCB, Slavenburg and Van Lanschot played a minor role.

C. *Investment bankers and the stock market and related activities*

From the above we can see that the Dutch new issue market remained rather varied, with a few big banks and a lot of smaller houses. While older parties disappeared, mainly as a result of takeovers or mergers, new banks came forward, which challenged the established names. The big four – NHM, Amsterdamsche Bank, Rotterdamsche Bank and Twentsche Bank – did not differ much in size, although Amsterdamsche Bank was slightly in the lead. In the early 1960s they all participated in 30 to 40 syndicates per year, competition between them being rather strong, as is illustrated by the changes from time to time occurring in the composition of the syndicates. After the mergers in 1964 Amro Bank occupied first place in bringing out new issues. To give the smaller parties, including the commission houses, a better chance in the allocation of the issued securities, a new issue system was introduced in 1978. In line with the international situation, syndicates from then on consisted not only of managers and co-managers but also of a group of underwriters and sellers, in which the participants would get an allocation according to their size on the stock exchange.

With regard to the latter, many things changed in the 1960s and 1970s in trading practices, price quotation, technical equipment etc. The Amsterdam stock exchange association became a national organisation in 1972, leading to the closure of the exchanges in Rotterdam and The Hague, which had outlived themselves. Around the same time the stock exchange began preparations for an options exchange in cooperation with the Chicago Board Options Exchange. Negotiations were conducted with the London stock exchange in order to establish a common European Options Exchange, but ultimately London decided to go it alone. Nevertheless, the EOE started trading in April 1978, before the London Traded Options Market opened.[33] Although it attracted foreign parties to Amsterdam, its international ambitions did not come through, but it did much to popularise options among the investing public in the Netherlands.

New financing techniques began to be introduced from the 1950s, in addition to the traditional short-term credits of the banks. However, participations in industrial or commercial enterprises remained an exception. We saw earlier that banks were involved in the establishment of companies like Hoogovens and KLM, which were introduced on the stock exchange later on. NHM's interests in agricultural enterprises overseas came

---

33 According to Richard Roberts, *The City*, *op. cit.*, p. 86, the LIFFE in 1982 was 'the first financial derivatives exchange in Europe'.

to an end after the nationalisation in Indonesia. After the war, NHM and Twentsche Bank took part in establishing a whaling company. In addition, NHM became involved with the Fokker aircraft company, whereas Twentsche Bank created it own participation company, which was not a success. These experiences, together with the rather negative attitude of the central bank which would avoid developments in the direction of *banques d'affaires*, prevented further growth of this kind of activity by the big banks. Interesting experiments were undertaken by the smaller NOB, which entered into an agreement with Hambros Bank of London, establishing Investeringsbank Amsterdam (1963).[34] It took share participations in unlisted companies, advised on financial structures and mergers and introduced the Wimpy chain in the Netherlands. It even developed into a private equity company *avant la lettre*, acquiring enterprises and splitting them up with a view to realise the hidden reserves in immovable properties. When ABN acquired Bank Mees & Hope in 1975, it was obliged by the Nederlandsche Bank to divest this part of the company.[35] NOB was also one of the first in the field of leasing with Lease Plan (1963), which later on developed into one of the leading international leasing companies.[36] Earlier, however, Amsterdamsche Bank had introduced a sale and lease back construction for large oil tankers (1957).

The stock market recovery from the mid-1950s opened up new opportunities for investment services for clients. The increase and spread of wealth brought the stock exchange within reach for more people than before and the growth of retail banking made it possible for the banks to approach private clients for this kind of service as well. However, institutional investors became more and more dominant as the expansion of social security caused an accumulation of capital in the hands of pension and other social funds and insurance companies. Banks and commission houses, following US practices, introduced securities research, publishing news letters, market comments and company reports. The big banks could afford to establish separate departments, the smaller ones had only a few people working in this field. The reports were then used to interest clients in buying stocks, with account managers assigned to the more important relations, particularly the institutions. Investment management on behalf of clients was still rare. The 1960s were a fruitful period in the

34 A reference to this institution in G.K. Young, *Merchant Banking. Practice and Prospects*, London, Weidenfeld and Nicholson, 1966, p. 93.

35 In 1975 ABN made a bid for the Mees & Hope Groep, which was the holding of Bank Mees & Hope, Mees & Hope Investeringen/Investeringsbank Amsterdam, and Assurantie Beheer Maatschappij, which held the insurance brokerage activities of the former R. Mees & Zoonen. The latter were also sold by ABN. The time was obviously not ripe for an integrated banking/insurance concern.

36 In 2004 also sold by ABN-AMRO.

securities field, in contrast to the following decade when this sector became a burden for the banks at times, but no one dared to withdraw from it. With regard to investment funds, developments were rather slow with few new initiatives. So the independent Robeco continued to dominate, even more so after it incorporated a few smaller funds. With all the funds, diversification into foreign shares became more important. Some new specialised investment companies were created by smaller houses, but it was only in 1967/1969 that the big banks first had their own funds. When the share market began to stagnate in the 1970s, attention shifted to immovable properties and fixed interest securities, for which separate funds were created. Nevertheless, during 1950-1980 the number of investment funds and companies on balance remained more or less the same at about fifty.

5. New trends for investment banks through the liberalisation wave (1980-2000)

Following some difficult years and a recession in the early 1980s, a new phase started, stimulated by a new government policy in many countries and ending in the boom period around the turn of the century, whereas in the second the investment banking side strongly gained ground. The 1970s had been a difficult period, both in the securities field and for the economy at large. It ultimately ended in a severe crisis in 1980-1982 with an economic recession and a declining but still high rate of interest, reflecting strong inflation. From 1982 the picture started to change, and rather drastically as could be observed later on. The economy recovered strongly, inflation and interest rates came down – continuing in the 1990s – and stock prices soared, showing a rise of 170 per cent in the period 1982-1986. This first upswing of the stock exchange was followed by setbacks in later years, in particular after the crash in October 1987 and the early 1990s, but every time a new recovery set in, bringing the market to an all time high in August 2000 at the top of the ICT boom. After the ensuing steep decline the following increase was more modest, but the stock exchange climate nevertheless remained rather positive in the beginning of the new century.

A. Changes in policy

After the recession of the early 1980s the restructuring of the business sector in the decade before bore fruit; old industries were reorganised and the financial position of the remaining companies became much stronger. In this situation, also new initiatives could flourish, and completely new enterprises arose in the fields of information and communication technologies, medical instruments, pharmaceuticals and the related service sectors. Government policy contributed to the favourable development. In general policies were directed towards making room for and supporting the business sector by lowering budget deficits, decreasing the tax burden, facilitating credits and abolishing unnecessary regulations. In general terms, policy was much more market-orientated than before, which was in line with the prevailing philosophy of the time. In the Netherlands, however, it was not only a question of conviction, but also of economic necessity and influences from abroad. In the beginning of this period the pursued separation of financial sectors – banks, mortgage banks and insurance companies – had already come under pressure as a result of financial difficulties with the mortgage companies, which had ventured too far in the exploitation of commercial property. The Nederlandsche Bank had to agree with rescue operations by some banks and insurance companies, resulting in the end of the mortgage institutions as a separate sector. At the time developments within the European Union – the intended completion of the internal market by 1992 – also started to exert an influence. Later on, the preparations for the Economic and Monetary Union with a single currency (Maastricht Treaty in 1992) had a still stronger impact on the whole financial sector. This was evident with regard to the regulation of the capital market by the central bank, which was questioned more and more. The liberalisation of international capital movements made it easier for market participants to circumvent the rules by operating on the international markets, thus endangering the position of the Netherlands as a financial centre.

As a result, a deregulation of the capital market was brought about in 1986. It entailed a more flexible application of the issue calendar and the abolishment of a number of requirements with regard to conditions and practices of new issues of securities. From now on there was nearly complete freedom in redemption schemes – in particular "bullet loans" with a fixed redemption date were now allowed – and floating rate notes and the issue of short-term certificates of deposit and commercial paper were also made possible.[37] Foreign banks were given greater freedom in the management of Dutch issues. In 1994 the last remnants of the capital market regulations – the notification of new issues to the Bank – were abolished. At the same time the remaining separation between banks and insurance companies, which did not exist in the same way abroad, became gradually untenable. So in 1990 a liberalisation in this field was introduced, making possible mutual investments between banks and insurance companies and even complete mergers, albeit in separate companies and still of course with consent of the Nederlandsche Bank. Investments of banks in non-financial enterprises – which were restricted

[37] The reason for the earlier restrictions was that Nederlandsche Bank was eager to prevent the creation of short-term paper that could be considered a money substitute. In the 1980s controlling the money supply became ever more difficult, so restrictions gradually became obsolete.

under the so-called "*banque d'affaires* policy" – were likewise made easier by allowing all participations of less than 10 per cent in such companies and setting limits of 10 per cent of the banks' capital in individual cases and of 30 per cent in total. In order to facilitate financing of small (venture) companies, special Private Participation Companies, which could also be a subsidiary of a bank, were within certain limits entitled to a government guarantee for their holdings.

The stock exchange too had to conform more and more to international practices. Important in this respect was that foreign investors had already at an early stage discovered the potential of the – cheap – Dutch stock market; in fact they were the first strong buyers in 1982, with Dutch parties only following later on. With the guilder being strong and interest rates often somewhat higher than in Germany, Dutch debentures became attractive too, the financing of the large state deficits supplying ample material to deal in. On the other hand, domestic investors began to diversify their portfolios geographically and became accustomed to international habits. We already mentioned the establishment of the European Options Exchange in 1978, which started to grow strongly in the 1980s. A financial futures market was opened in 1987, making possible hedging transactions in Dutch state loans. A strongly growing turnover necessitated a permanent modernisation of the technical organisation of the exchange and of clearing and settlement procedures. The rigid commission structure came under pressure with the introduction of exemptions for larger transactions.

In 1989 a plan was launched to improve more fundamentally the competitive position of the Amsterdam stock exchange vis-à-vis other exchanges, in particular London, which attracted part of the dealings in Dutch securities. This included the lowering of transaction costs, abolishing the tax on securities transactions and improving the liquidity of the government bond market. The fixed commission structure was abolished and in 1993 a new trade system made it possible for foreign parties to participate directly in bond dealings. Floor trade was ultimately abolished on the stock exchange in 1998, followed by the options trade in 2002. Meanwhile major steps were also taken with regard to the organisation of the exchange as a whole. The old-fashioned association structure with members, a majority of which had always to agree to important decisions, was replaced by a corporate structure with shareholders and a managing board. In 1997 the stock exchange and the options exchange merged into a limited liability company, Amsterdam Exchanges, which organised all the markets in Amsterdam (securities, options, futures). Only a few years later Amsterdam Exchanges amalgamated with the bourses of Brussels and Paris, forming Euronext. The last stage in the international battle between the exchanges was the takeover of Euronext by the New York Stock Exchange, resulting in NYSE Euronext.

B. Investment banking activities

In the new deregulated and integrated financial world that emerged, investment banking activities could flourish as never before, showing strong growth in volume as well as in diversity. New supervisory regulations that were introduced at the same time did not seem to hamper this development. These regulations now originated mostly from international bodies (BIS, EU) and were devised to cope with new practices and to ensure a level playing field between the banks that operated internationally. In the Netherlands, the securities sector in particular was subjected to more stringent rules regarding integrity, trading practices, use of insider knowledge and information to investors, whereas investment companies were brought under a separate supervisory regime. A general characteristic in the field of investment banking was the increasing importance of market activities. Stock exchange turnover rocketed, in Amsterdam rising to a tenfold between 1990 and 2000. A growing merger and takeover activity, the introduction of many new companies, for example in the ICT, the growth of investment funds together with the new phenomenon of securitisation, all contributed to this trend.[38] Futures markets in financial instruments also showed strong growth. Apart from this, there was a strongly growing over-the-counter trade in new derivatives. As a consequence, market participants began to hold greater positions, not only on behalf of their clients, but also to make trading profits for themselves. For the banks this implied that their traditional source of income – interest from credits – lost in importance in favour of commissions and trading results.[39] The dominance of the market became such, that the perception of investment banking gradually seemed to be restricted to trading in financial instruments of all kind. Dealmakers and traders began to form a new caste of bankers, who did not hesitate to move to a competitor if they could earn more, with the old-fashioned credit specialists losing ground in their organisations. Nevertheless, investment banking continued to embrace a wide range of activities, even more than before.

New issue activity developed beyond the introduction of the traditional types of shares and debentures. Many more varieties were introduced, including zero coupon bonds, issues with warrants, medium-term notes and commercial paper, which might be accompanied by interest rate or

---

[38] Securitisation can be interpreted in two ways: 1. the transformation of already existing debts into marketable securities, for example mortgages or credit card debts on the balance sheet of a bank; 2. the tendency with companies to circumvent bank credits and place their own debt instruments in the market. Both have the effect of increasing the volume of negotiable paper in the market.

[39] See D. van Wensveen, "Banks prospered against the odds. Why?", *De Economist*, 156/3, 2008, pp. 307-338; here: pp. 319-322.

currency swaps. Various markets could be tapped, as a result of which also issue syndicates became more varied, often including foreign institutions to ensure a broader distribution of the securities. For example, the issues of international bodies like the World Bank and of foreign governments were now placed with the support of foreign investment banks, these being included as managing underwriters when this was made possible in 1986. Also the government introduced new kinds of debt and new issue techniques through designated primary dealers. Mergers and acquisitions took place on a larger scale, both national and international. In this field, newly created corporate finance units in banks found a fruitful existence, often approaching companies with their own proposals for an investment or, as the case might be, a divestment. Foreign banks and securities houses with their great experience and international relations were also active here. An example is the placement of the shares of the motor-industry DAF in 1989, which was led by AMRO, Credit Suisse First Boston and SG Warburg. Here we see the investment banks also in a new capacity, that of advisers to the company (F. van Lanschot) and to the selling shareholders (NM Rothschild & Sons).

Privatisation of government-owned enterprises also became an interesting and profitable field of activity. Major transactions such as the sale of shares in the former state mines DSM and NMB Postbank in 1989 were managed by ABN and SG Warburg and the other transaction by NMB/ Postbank, ABN and Goldman Sachs, with separate lead managers for various regions. A still bigger transaction was the privatisation of the telecom provider KPN in 1995. Under ABN AMRO Hoare Govett as global coordinator, there were seven to ten syndicate leaders for each of the four regions in which the world was divided. Towards the end of the period the shares of many new private companies, in particular in the ICT sector, were introduced to the market, often causing a speculative fever.

In the relations with investors, both personal and institutional, the services offered were likewise broadened. The research was widened to include foreign securities, undertaken from the domestic head office or by special teams abroad. Portfolio advice and analysis together with investment management gained ground, accompanied if necessary by auxiliary services such as custody and administrative support, in particular for smaller pension funds. Securities transactions were executed more and more through other exchanges than the local forum, Dutch banks establishing some form of presence in important financial centres abroad. The banks, but also other financial institutions like insurance companies, became very active in creating new investment companies, often specialised in one or more sectors or regions, as a result of which the number of funds increased from 50 to over 500. With the increase in personal wealth much attention was paid to servicing the private investor. The former simple advice on securities portfolios was replaced by the concept of private banking – sometimes called wealth management – embracing al types of investment and related services, and offered to clients in the Netherlands and abroad.

C. Changes in the financial sector

To cope with all these developments the organisation of the banks and securities houses was adapted rather frequently. New departments referred to as capital markets, merchant banking, private banking, asset management etc. were established as the need arose. Moreover, reorganisations and reshuffling of activities took place when adverse market developments and/or rising costs depressed the results. Integration of newly acquired (investment) banks in existing (commercial) banking groups was rather difficult, partly as a result of differing cultures and remuneration systems. In general, the whole sector underwent drastic alterations. Against the background of intensifying competition, in particular from the large foreign investment banks, size began to matter still more than before. Only big institutions had the capital and the expertise that were needed for the increasingly complicated deals in the capital market. From an international perspective even the biggest Dutch banks played a secondary role. In the international league tables of investment banking activities AMRO and ABN usually occupied a place somewhere between twenty and thirty, but their ambitions reached higher. Since domestic mergers between the large institutions were impossible for the time being, both were active in taking over banks and securities houses in other countries. International mergers, however, seemed a step too far, as was illustrated in 1988 by the failed negotiations between AMRO and the Belgian Generale Bank. The situation changed when in 1990 the Dutch authorities adapted their policy with regard to the structure of the financial sector. In a relatively short time a number of large financial concerns (conglomerates) emerged.

Rather sensational was the merger between the old rivals ABN and AMRO under the name of ABN-AMRO. This combination climbed to a position between ten and fifteen internationally. It continued expanding abroad, not only in commercial banking but also in investment banking, for example by taking over Hoare Govett in London and smaller houses in other countries. In addition, an alliance with Rothschild & Sons was concluded with a view to international capital market transactions. Building a strong position in investment banking in the US, however, turned out to be a difficult and costly effort. Although ABN-AMRO had a small insurance company, it did not develop the concept of *banque assurance*, which other groups did, with ING (*Internationale Nederlanden Groep*) most prominent. It emerged when the state-owned Postbank amalgamated with Nederlandsche Middenstandsbank, this combination being joined shortly afterwards by the insurance company Nationale Nederlanden. In 1995 ING acquired the British Barings after this had got into severe problems, followed by Bank Brussel Lambert of Belgium and the smaller Furman Salz in New York. As a cooperative institution, Rabo had difficulties in merging with another bank; it started by taking over the likewise cooperative insurer Interpolis and acquired further interests in this sector later on. To strengthen its position in investment management Rabo entered into a strategic alliance with Robeco in 1990, and obtained all the shares in 2001. In addition to its private banking subsidiary Schretlen & Co., it bought the old securities firm Stroeve, which was, however, sold already a few years later. It further acquired a Swiss private bank and established subsidiaries in other financial centres. However, efforts to create a strong investment banking business were not very successful.[40]

The old savings bank sector also broke new ground, after most local banks had joined one of two new groups, VSB (*Verenigde Spaarbanken*) and SNS (*Samenwerkende Nederlandse Spaarbanken*). VSB merged with the insurer AMEV, joined somewhat later by the Belgian AG insurance company, thus laying the basis of the Fortis group. Fortis strengthened its banking arm by buying MeesPierson from ABN-AMRO, while in 1998 it succeeded in acquiring the Belgian Generale Bank after a tough battle with ABN-AMRO. Generale Bank had entered the Dutch market in 1995, when it obtained the business of Crédit Lyonnais (which had acquired Slavenburg's Bank in 1981 and Nederlandse Credietbank in 1987). The branches of VSB, Generale and MeesPierson were combined in Fortis Bank Nederland. The other savings bank group SNS merged with the Reaal Groep consisting of a few insurance companies and savings banks. The old Hollandsche Koopmansbank/Lippmann Rosenthal also joined this group. Of the medium-sized banks mentioned earlier only F. van Lanschot succeeded in remaining independent with the help of a few large shareholders.

Many changes also took place among smaller banks and securities houses, which were often bought and sold several times. An example is Labouchere & Co., which since 1976 was a joint venture of Amro and J.P. Morgan, becoming Morgan Bank Nederland in 1984. Morgan terminated its banking operations in the Netherlands in 1992, selling Labouchere to the insurer AEGON. It was revived under the aegis of the Belgian Dexia, which in 2000 also acquired the Dutch business of the former Paribas. When Dexia withdrew from the Dutch market after severe problems with investors after the crash of 2000, it sold the latter operations to GE

---

40 Gerada Westerhuis, *Conquering the American Market. ABN-AMRO, Rabobank and Nationale-Nederlanden Working in a Different Business Environment, 1965-2000*, Amsterdam, Boom, 2008, pp. 177-209.

Commercial Finance, while Labouchere was bought out to its management and fell apart in several units. The Nationale Investeringsbank, owned by the state and a number of financial institutions, was transferred to two big pension funds in 1999, but sold to the American investor J.C. Flowers in 2005. As NIB Capital it was intended to develop into a full fledged investment Bank.

It will have become clear that the face of investment banking, in regard to both activities and institutions, was changing rapidly in the last decades of the 20th century. A Dutch survey in 1990 identified about twenty banks that practiced some form of investment banking. Dominant among them was ABN-AMRO, with Rabo and NMB/Postbank (soon to become ING) striving to gain more ground in this field. Smaller Dutch institutions were Bank Mees & Hope and Pierson, F. van Lanschot, Kempen & Co., Nationale Investeringsbank and Staal Bankiers. The list included a number of foreign names, among which Banque Indosuez, Paribas, Crédit lyonnais, Albert de Bary/Deutsche Bank, Citicorp Investment Bank, Credit Suisse First Boston, J.P. Morgan, Samuel Montague and Swiss Bank Corporation. In addition, quite a lot of smaller firms, partly from foreign origin, were active in securities trading as brokers or market makers. As indicated above, there were already a number of changes during the rest of the 1990s. The new millennium would be still more turbulent than seen, with even the big names finding themselves in trouble and changing ownership.

Box 5. Jean-Paul Votron and Fortis/*ABN-AMRO*

For a long time the leading bank managers had spent their whole careers in their own institutions. As a rule, the most senior member of the board of management became chairman of the board, which had a common responsibility for the business of the bank. (It should be noted that the Dutch governance structure consists of a board of management and a supervisory board, a so-called two tier structure). A good example is P.J. (Jan) Kalff (1937): Having joined NHM in 1964, he became a member of the managing board of ABN in 1977 and chairman of the board of ABN-AMRO in 1994, from which position he retired in 2000. His successor, Rijkman Groenink (1949), started his career with Amro Bank in 1974, where he became a member of the managing board in 1988. In 2000 he was appointed as chairman of ABN-AMRO. Although he had a typical Dutch banking career, as a chairman he developed more into an Anglo-Saxon type of chief executive officer (CEO), assuming more and more personal responsibility for the management. A good illustration of the changing management style in the banking world is Jean-Paul Votron, whose career was quite different. Born in Belgium in 1950, he started with Unilever, where he worked for sixteen years in various marketing functions. After another six years with

City Bank, he joined Abn-Amro *in 1997. When in 2001 it became clear that he would not be appointed to the board of management, he left the bank and returned to City Group. Through a headhunter he was selected as* ceo *of Fortis in 2004 with the task of repositioning and expanding this Dutch-Belgian financial conglomerate.*

As ceo *of Fortis, and supported by the chairman of the board of directors Maurice Lippens, Votron acted resolutely in improving the cohesion between the companies in the group, at the same time expanding further by taking over banks in various countries, including Russia and Turkey. Although it had been agreed that Fortis would grow outside the Benelux in particular, early in 2007 an opportunity was offered to substantially enlarge the Dutch banking side and it was too tempting to let that pass by. By that time* Abn-Amro *had gotten into a difficult position and was about to be sold. After years of mediocre performance, this bank was confronted with activist shareholders, from which it tried to escape by a merger with another European Bank, without success however. In the beginning of 2007 an intended merger with the Dutch ING group failed, and an amalgamation with Barclays was forged rather hastily. Royal Bank of Scotland and Banco Santander, however, were interested in parts of* Abn-Amro. *On the advice of Merrill Lynch, Fortis was also approached and the three banks decided to create a consortium – RBS 38.3 per cent, Fortis 33.8 per cent and Santander 27.9 per cent – that came with a higher bid than that of Barclays. The three partners intended to divide the activities of* Abn-Amro, *the Dutch retail and private banking business going to Fortis. It was a grim struggle, which seemed to become a success for the consortium when in August the shareholders of Fortis gave their consent for a share issue as a part of the financing. In October the consortium indeed took over* Abn-Amro *and started dividing the activities and integrating them in the three banks. But the tide was already turning. The ensuing international credit crisis depressed share prices and aroused suspicion against banks. Fortis also had to report losses on investments and the financing of its part of the deal became more difficult. In June 2008 it announced a number of measures – attracting new capital, selling parts of the group and passing its interim dividend – which were heavily opposed by the shareholders. In the growing unrest and uncertainty in July J.-P. Votron, who a few months earlier had received an extra bonus for his performance, was dismissed, but this did nothing to calm the situation. Major clients now began to withdraw their deposits, endangering the very existence of Fortis. A way out could only be found in October, when the Dutch state took over the Dutch banking and insurance business of Fortis and* Abn-Amro, *whereas Belgium along with the French group BNP Paribas acquired the other parts of the once proud Fortis group. It was also the end of the career of the influential Maurice Lippens, who with his AG had laid the foundations of the now extinct group.*

Conclusion

The end of Dutch investment banking?

In the boom years preceding 2000, there were – as is not uncommon in comparable periods of strong expansion – cases of fraud, improper use of insider knowledge, misleading of investors and the like. The crisis of 2000/2003, in which share prices plunged with more than 60 per cent, caused much more trouble. The banks had been overoptimistic in bringing companies – in particular those in the 'new economy' – to the market and investors in this sector were confronted with heavy losses. Through legal action they tried in a number of cases to get compensation from the companies or the banks. The aggressive selling methods of new financial products, which often entailed buying with borrowed money, came under heavy criticism when investors were left with debts much higher than the value of their securities and had to repay. Less sincere takeover practices leading to better figures came to light. After all this, one would have expected a more prudent attitude with investment bankers and investors alike. When share prices again recovered, more than doubling up to the summer of 2007, the temptation was again too strong and many took part in new promising developments. Quite a lot of advanced products were devised, mostly in the sphere of derivatives, which securities houses sold to investors or bought for their own account. At the same time hedge funds and private equity firms became much more active, in the Dutch market too, driving up share prices and pressing the management of companies for higher results. In their operations debt financing was often used to increase the return on their investments. They attracted many investors in search of better yields. Not directly related to stock exchange developments was the 2005 failure of the small Van der Hoop Effectenbank. It caused unrest among investors and savers, but did little to hamper the optimism and the wish for as high returns as possible. Even in early 2008 the somewhat higher rates paid on savings accounts by the Icelandic Icesave met with a strong response.

Towards the end of 2006 the first signs of deterioration emerged in the American housing and mortgage market, which had been a prime mover in the strong growth of derivatives. In August 2007 the Dutch NIBC had to announce a loss on its investments in American mortgage products. It was followed by others, but the impact for the time being remained small, although share prices came under pressure. The fall of Lehman Brothers in September 2008 caused much more alarm. The Dutch banks might have been able to weather the storm, had it not been for the battle concerning ABN-AMRO. From August 2008 Fortis came under heavy pressure, the fall in its share price causing unrest among depositors, who started to withdraw their money on an increasing scale. Liquidity support was not enough in the ensuing panic and both Fortis and the authorities did not see any other solution besides a takeover of Fortis. The concern was divided in a Belgian and a Dutch part, the latter (including ABN-AMRO.) going into the hands of the Dutch government. Shortly afterwards, the trouble moved to ING, with the same sequence of falling share prices and withdrawal of deposits. Here again, a capital injection by the government came as a rescue, followed by a guarantee for its investments in American mortgages. Additional measures, including participations in the capital of SNS Reaal and the insurer Aegon, together with guarantees for loans to be issued and the safeguarding of the Icesave victims, completed the rescue operation. Of the major banks only Rabo and Van Lanschot could do without government support.

It is not easy to see a way out of this complicated situation. To a large extent the crisis circled around investment banks and their operations, but as so often in cases of disaster there were many factors that coincided, contributing to the ultimate mess: low interest rate policies, the affluence of liquidity partly caused by government behaviour, high rates of leverage in the business and banking sectors, the search for ever higher yields by shareholders and other investors, the bonus system of rewarding managers, lax supervisory policies etc. More specifically, the rapid expansion of investment banking activities by financial concerns entailed problems of organisation, supervision and risk management. So, one or two measures will not suffice, action on a broad front is more appropriate. In investment banking itself, it is not so much the institutional set-up that matters, but the manner in which business is done. That should not centre around financial market operations just to make profits, but around the real or long-term needs (as distinct from the needs as presented by some investors or speculators) of their clients. Traditional relationship banking should be revived, although market operations of course remain indispensable.

Would a separation of investment banking activities from other business be a solution? In the Netherlands, too, voices were raised in favour of a division of banking into a simpler, less risky part of deposits and credits, and a more risky part of financial market operations. This country has, as we have seen, a long tradition of mixed (universal) banking, in which commercial banking, investment banking and capital market activity have always gone together. With a few exceptions problems mostly arose in commercial banking, when credits were granted on too large a scale and in a risky manner. The present crisis was aggravated by a dangerous take-over, the financing of which was not assured sufficiently. Splitting up the banks does not seem the right solution. Commercial banks will always need market activity for their liquidity management. Moreover, a separation will cause much difficulty with regard to which activities will be allowed in each of the two parts and methods of circumvention will be devised. Banks will have to find a good balance between the two kinds of activity without the dominance of investment banking of the last decades. Together with higher capital requirements – obligatory or as a result of prudent banking policy – and less dependence on the money market to finance their operations, this will contribute to a more stable banking system.

Another question is whether such a type of banking should be part of a broader financial conglomerate, including in particular insurance. There seem to be reasons to be careful in this respect because of the complicated structure of these conglomerates. As a result of the takeover, with Fortis there is already a separation between banking and insurance, and ING was forced by the European Union to separate their banking and insurance business. What might also be considered is a separation of investment advice and asset management from investment banking with a view to conflicting interests between these sectors and the use of insider knowledge. Whatever model will be used, a more stable general economic environment, with cautious policies on the side of government, companies and investors, will in any case be needed.

CHAPTER 7

The Resurgence of French Investment Banks after WWII (1948-1960)

Competitive Edge and Groundbreaking Innovation

Hubert BONIN

professor of modern economic history at Institut d'études politiques de Bordeaux & at UMR GRETHA-Bordeaux University <www.hubertbonin.com>

The competition put up by deposit banks in the field of corporate banking compelled French investment banks to improve their competitive edge. They needed to live up to their reputation as "groundbreakers" if they were to accompany and stimulate the rebirth of the French economy after WWII and help spread its influence abroad against competing US, British and German businesses at a time when France was trying to regain momentum at the international level and Paris was struggling to regain its role as an international financial and banking centre. Though investment banks had resisted the move towards nationalisation, they had been weakened by the increasing influence of State companies and the nationalisation of key clients, mainly in utilities, which deeply affected banking and financial communities and led to the loss of important positions in Eastern and Central Europe between 1937 and 1948. They had thus to rebuild their basis of activities while resisting the influence of the four big nationalised (in 1945) commercial banks, which had honed their skills in corporate banking and could take advantage of their connections with the state-owned sectors to encroach on investment bank strongholds.

First, we shall assess the strengths and weaknesses of investment banks (Banque de Paris & des Pays-Bas or Paribas, Banque de l'union parisienne or BUP, Rothschild, Lazard), analyse the emergence of new competitors (Banque de l'Indochine, Union européenne industrielle et financière, the "Francès group", etc.), and consequently, determine the strategy followed by these players. We shall, for example, specify the effects of the nationalisation of numerous big companies and the dwindling of the financial market on their issuing and brokering activities.

Second, we shall study the evolution of the portfolios of strategic activities and skills within the "classical" investment banking services. We shall gauge their ability to regain momentum in favour of corporate customers (in the areas of merchant banking, trade banking, corporate banking, and financial engineering), either national or international.

Third, we shall reconsider the "groundbreaking" activities of investment bankers on the international market of structured finance as a lever of French industrial investments abroad.

Fourth, we shall reconstitute the competitive edge of investment banks on the imperial/colonial market, and argue about the priorities fixed, either "obsolete strategies" or the involvement of colonial sectors into internationalised and modern business models.

Last, we shall tackle the issue of investment bankers as "pioneers" of the new credit and financial products and techniques which were either being mostly transferred from the US or engineered in Paris, as a way of unearthing new sectors of activity to balance those being taken over by public institutions, or as a way of building bridges to promising activities in real estate development, outlets for bourgeois building and the construction of the affluent society.

In a nutshell, our chapter will focus on the balance of power – who and which department or team played a significant role within investment banks and the financial divisions of deposit banks? Which type of bank prevailed in each field thanks to its portfolio of skills and connections? Issues of "political science" within business communities and organisations do matter and establish a further link between business history and banking history. We found new archival records at Crédit lyonnais (on the entire banking community of Paris), at the Association for the history of Paribas, at Société générale (on Bup), and at the Banque de France, which have allowed us to complement the previous wide studies about Paribas[1] and Bup.[2]

1 Éric Bussière, *Paribas, l'Europe et le monde, 1872-1992*, Anvers, Fonds Mercator, 1992. Éric Bussière, "Les banques d'affaires françaises au xxe siècle: des établissements en quête d'identité?", in Maurice Lévy-Leboyer (ed.), *Les banques en Europe de l'Ouest de 1920 à nos jours*, Paris, Comité pour l'histoire économique & financière de la France, 1995, pp. 223-235.

2 Hubert Bonin, *La Banque de l'union parisienne (1874/1904-1974). De l'Europe aux outre-mers,* Paris, Publications de la Sfhom, 2011.

1. Investment banking as a profession and a corporate culture

Our purpose is to gauge the extent to which investment banks succeed in reconstituting their competitive edge by asserting their portfolio of skills against their competitors: commercial banks practicing corporate banking and brokerage of securities. Did investment banks follow the trend of furthering the progression of high civil servants in the banking management profession, those called *inspecteurs des Finances*? Were investment banks copying the process followed by State institutions, deposit and specialised banks in building bridges between the top financial administration and the upper echelons of the banks' staff? Was there a single "model" as regards picking up and promoting top managers? We cannot embark on any kind of sociological or prosopographical survey, but we shall try to sketch the outlines of the directions taken by these two leading investment banks.

A. *Paribas' rebirth and fighting spirit*

The offensive led by Paribas against its peers and State institutions appeared "punchy" because it was headed by Jean Reyre, somewhat of a "dissenter". On the Paris market, a few banks were struggling to "change" the rules and to "contest" positions: among deposit banks, Banque nationale pour le commerce et l'industrie (Bnci) challenged cartels, informal alliances and well-established tables for credit and issuing, but it lacked the scope of investment banks. Within the "club" of investment banks, Lazard and its merchant bankers shook the profession with their flexible *modus operandi*, all the more because their tripolar base (with London and New York) helped them manage "trade operations" linked with foreign exchange and moreover the financing of exports by French firms, and more generally to foster a refreshed spirit of internationalisation among renewed teams of experts.

a. Jean Reyre: an imaginative team manager

Paribas had to react rapidly in order to rebuild its reputation of a groundbreaking team, and it was lucky to have a contestant of Jean Reyre's caliber. Though his education had been classical – law studies and the *Institut d'études politiques de Paris* – followed by a steady career within Paribas, which he had joined as early as April 1924,; he became successively *fondé de pouvoirs* (or "vice-president" in the language of the bank) in 1936, under-executive manager in 1938, deputy-chief executive manager in 1941, and chief executive manager (*directeur général*) in 1945. He had a special "profile", having been a close "junior" to Paribas' managing director, Horace Finaly,[3] during the inter-war period and

[3] Éric Bussière, *Horace Finaly, banquier, 1871-1945*, Paris, Fayard, 1996.

having imbibed "managerial culture" oriented towards openness to foreign activities – perhaps because his father had managed a trading house brokering South American coffee and cocoa, or because he had been trained himself from 1925 in the service of correspondent banking and treasury operations, for example with North America, before joining in 1933 the department in charge with "selling" the services of the bank to firms, and last, the financial department for two years.

This impressive portfolio of experience and competence, his ambitions and his relative participation to the *Résistance* (with André Debray also playing a key role in the movement) pushed him to the head of Paribas in March 1948 (for a term of twenty years) – occupying a seat freed by Henry Jahan (1937-1944) at the end of the war and Occupation time. Far from being a "bureaucratic-minded" manager, he asserted himself as a driving or "pushing" force, because he intended to turn Paribas once again into a big player on the Parisian market and in the domain of international investment and corporate banking. He also showed himself as an "innovator" by the manner in which he encouraged innovative people and teams up the hierarchy within the company's flexible structure – and this very resiliency may be seen as a mark of an investment bank, more reactive, more risk-taking, more targeted towards engineering banking and financial "products".

Under the benevolent guidance of chairmen Louis Wibratte (1944-1950) and Emmanuel Mönick (1950-1961), a top-level civil servant capable of building bridges with the financial administration), the bank undoubtedly developed a competitive edge, a fighting spirit and imagination.[4] Guy de Rothschild recalled in his souvenirs[5] that the lead team of his elder family lacked dynamism in the 1950s-1960s. Witnesses too have pointed out that BUP's competitiveness was somewhat eroded after the death of its boss Henri Lafond in the 1960s. If not decisive, the human factor has definitely played a significant role in business and banking history.

b. Layers of investment bankers

It is always difficult to catch the "fizzing" formula which turns a company resilient and performing. Our perception leads us to claim that Reyre moulded *Paribas'* structure to suit the emergence of new skills and *métiers* so as to allow the driving forces to deploy and develop their professional capabilities in full freedom, without hindrance from restrictive and bureaucratic mindsets and processes. No doubt it was Louis Bricard who managed Paribas' administrative "organisation of firm", the introduction

4 But we are still missing a comprehensive biography of Jean Reyre.

5 Guy de Rothschild, *Contre bonne fortune*, Paris, Belfond, 1983; J'ai lu, 1985, pp. 252-258.

of automation, business computing, and the rationalisation of the management of the finance department. At the same time, the investment bank avoided drifting towards some kind of an administration – by keeping its focus on its portfolio of skills, without dreaming of "universal banking". Bricard himself had a deep knowledge of finance, because he had worked as a close junior secretary to deputy CEO Wibratte in the interwar period and had engineered the reorganisation of the collapsing car manufacturer Citroën in 1934-1935 (*rapport Bricard*). He supervised the financial department and represented the bank on the board of several partner companies (even chairing a few of them).[6]

And there was room for manoeuvre because "bosses" were trusted to create "little firms" within the bank. That was the case of Bédier, a clever pioneer in the field of real estate, property development, social and mass housing and the ways of financing their growth, from the inter-war period (for a joint company between Paribas, the City of Paris and the building contractors, *Régie immobilière de la Ville de Paris*) till 1962. The "department of real estate" became a key division within *Paribas*, with links to the department of industry, but following its own imaginative path. He was joined in 1951 by René Martin, a brilliant engineer and top civil servant who had constructed large installations in North Africa[7] in the 1920s-1940s and built a wide-ranging department of industry and real estate at Paribas (wide-ranging in responsibilities and engineering abilities, but not in workforce (about two dozen employees in 1951) since 1947. François Anthoine had succeeded André Laurent-Atthalin as the specialist of African business at Paribas, and appeared as the "go-between" between bankers, financiers, industrialists and engineers to design new schemes for mining, industrial and trade projects in "French" Africa – till (and after) the independences in the 1960s. We shall show later how Bernard de Margerie set up a foreign commercial department in 1951 as a key component of Paribas' competitive edge.

All in all, the studies and the professional training of these managers was not very standardised: very few *inspecteurs des finances* – who, after WWII, were supposed to form an elite layer all over the banking business[8] – were active at Paribas (estimated at three). An "engineers'

6 Pierrefitte, *Compagnie des compteurs.*

7 *1926-1932: service des grands barrages en Algérie, 1932-1936: chef de l'exploitation du port d'Alger; 1936-1942: directeur du service des irrigations en Algérie; 1942: directeur du service de l'hydraulique à Alger; 1945: délégué à Berlin à la Mission interalliée (directeur des transports); 1946: directeur de l'Office national de navigation.*

8 About the history, prosopography, and influence of the *inspecteurs des Finances*, see the articles of Nathalie Carré de Malberg, and moreover her book: *Le grand état-major financier: les inspecteurs des Finances, 1918-1946. Les hommes, le métier, les carrières*, Paris, Comité pour l'histoire économique et financière de la France, 2011.

culture" seems to have prevailed, with the corporate culture being a mix of engineering and financial skills. Some commercial culture and expertise also gathered momentum: Reyre had set up a "commercial business unit" within each department (as well as an overall department), in order to keep in touch with corporate (or State) customers and to never forget the practice of "senior investment banking", that is, to offer a diversified offer to clients. He probably wanted to avoid the fiefdom syndrome which arose in firms in which the specialised departments forgot to co-ordinate their action, and functioned along an organisation of "silos".

Table 1. The top managers at Paribas in 1945-1960

Management of the organisation and management of finance		
Louis Bricard	*École polytechnique*, *École des mines de Paris*, law school	Joined in 1922; training through the services 1924: at the bureau des secrétaires January 1927: assistant to CEO Wibratte January 1928: chef de service February 1936: fondé de pouvoirs October 1938: *sous-directeur* July 1945: directeur adjoint January 1947: directeur; directeur du département financier February-December 1963: directeur général adjoint
Classical corporate banking		
Hervé du Bouexic de Guichen	*Hautes études commerciales* (Paris business school) (1925)	Joined Paribas on 1st May 1927 Secrétariat de la direction banque in 1927-1938 Affected to affiliate *Banque franco-chinoise* from 1st July 1938 till 1st October 1941 (*secrétaire du conseil*, then *secrétaire général*) Chargé de mission in Algeria in 1941-42 Back to Paribas on 10 September 1942 as *sous-directeur* 28 November 1945: *directeur adjoint; directeur adjoint du département bancaire.* "*Ses fonctions l'amènent à superviser la conclusion des opérations de banque pure de toute nature avec la clientèle parisienne, provinciale et étrangère et le mettent en constant rapport avec les dirigeants des milieux d'affaires français ou étrangers.*" 10 July 1952: *directeur du département bancaire* (at the same time as Margerie)

Pathbreaking portfolio of skills		
René Martin	*École polytechnique, École des Ponts-et-Chaussées*	Joined *Paribas* as manager (*directeur*) on 1st May 1947 till December 1964 1947: *directeur du département industriel* 1951: *directeur du département des affaires industrielles et immobilières*
François Anthoine	*École polytechnique,* Law school	Joined *Paribas* in September 1924 February 1936: *fondé de pouvoirs* July 1941: *sous-directeur* January 1947: *directeur adjoint* Joined the direction in charge with the assets of *Paribas* in North Africa and in the colonies; in charge with the overseas territories of the *Union française* 1954: directeur of this department
Bernard de Margerie	Law school, *Institut d'études politiques de Paris*, inspector at ministry of Finance	Joined Paribas in August 1951, *directeur adjoint*, to set up the "*département des affaires commerciales*" July 1952: *directeur; directeur du département Étranger* 1967: Deputy CEO

Source: Personal files of the managers, historical archives of the Association for the history of Paribas

Table 2. Rough draft of the organisation of Paribas in 1945-1960

<table>
<tr><th colspan="6">Direction générale (Jean Reyre)</th></tr>
<tr><td>Direction de l'organisation (firm organisation) (Louis Bricard)</td><td>Direction bancaire
(Hervé de Guichen)</td><td>Direction des affaires internationales (export and trade finance) (André Debray, then Margerie)</td><td colspan="2">Direction des affaires industrielles et immobilières (René Martin)</td><td rowspan="3">Direction chargée des intérêts en Afrique du Nord et dans les colonies, puis de l'Union française (François Anthoine)</td></tr>
<tr><td colspan="3" rowspan="2">Direction commerce extérieur (which coordinated the activities of the commercial business units of each of the specialised directions)</td><td>Département industriel</td><td>Département des affaires immobilières</td></tr>
<tr><td>Starting as fondés de pouvoir: Roger Schulz then René Martin</td><td>Pierre Bédier, deputy manager</td></tr>
</table>

Deprived of the huge tasks of managing discounting, branching and retailing organisations at a time when universal banking was not yet fashionable, investment banks were still lean organisations, and their success depended on only a few dozen managers. In 1948, Paribas' team counted only 36 main managers: five managers ("executive directors"; *directeurs*), seven deputy-managers ("senior vice-presidents"), six under-managers, and seventeen sub-managers ("assistant vice-presidents").

Table 3. The team of managers at Paribas in 1957-1959

• CEO Reyre (since 8 March 1948)
• Managers or "executive directors" (*directeurs*)
Louis Bricard, René Martin, Hervé de Guichen, Bernard de Margerie, François Anthoine, Gustave Rambaud (July 1958)
• General secretary Jean Lequime
• Deputy managers ("senior vice-presidents"; *directeurs adjoints*)
Roger Schulz, Pierre Decker, Jean Cabet, Charles Flory (human resources)
Since July 1958: Daniel Bedin, Charles Bouzanquet, Édouard Hauser, Yann Pellet
• Sub-managers ("assistant vice-presidents"; *fondés de pouvoirs*)
André Gallais-Hamonno, Jean Desmarests, Jean-Pierre Fontaine, Gérard Galichon, François Pezet, Claude Plateau, Jean Richard, etc.
• Head of divisions (*chefs de service*)

c. Banque de l'union parisienne as a challenging team

As the second largest French investment bank (till its merger with Paribas in 1974), BUP played an important role on the Parisian market, even though its management was not as striking as that of Paribas. It was headed by a brilliant and well-connected executive chairman, Henri Lafond, who was at the nexus of many connections among the public economic sector, big business, and overseas interests. He was at the heart of French business and thus a providential recruit for BUP as vice-chairman in April 1948 and as chairman in September 1951 (till his assassination in 1963). BUP's ability to penetrate deep into French business connections was enhanced when it absorbed the (French) merchant bank Mirabaud[9] in 1954, a beacon of *Haute Banque* houses: a partner and patron since the co-operative foundation of the investment bank, Mirabaud "families" and their interconnections provided it with five key top managers, among whom Jacques Monnier (as deputy director at the *département des études techniques et financières*) and Jean Lepinay (sub-director at the *direction financière*) promised to become major actors in the merchant banking field – all in all, about fifty *Mirabaud* managers (and more than a hundred employees) joined BUP.

But the main management streams at BUP came from internal promotion, which benefitted Charles Letondot, the head of financial affairs,

9 Note *Fusion Mirabaud et BUP*, 11 and 15 September 1953, Mirabaud records, historical archives of BUP.

who retained this post when he became deputy CEO in March 1946 and CEO in September 1951 (at the death of Paul Bavière, chairman and CEO) till his retirement in December 1955. Having joined the bank in 1921, he had become a managing director in 1929 and co-headed the bank ever since, becoming the head of the *Département financier et étranger* in 1936. Financial skills were thus placed at the core of the bank's portfolio of skills, in parallel with the management of corporate banking. But Lafond felt it necessary to look outside for an eventual boss in what was to become the "French way of top recruitment", bridging public and business "elites": he recruited Emmanuel Lamy, a high-level civil servant who had been active in the empire (as head of finances of the Morrocco protectorate), as deputy managing director in February 1955 and CEO in January 1956, replacing Letondot. His mission was to take into account the growing connections with the State financial and banking sectors, and to set up a relevant modus of management for a growing banking organisation.[10] Like Paribas, BUP also had a "lean management", with only 1,342 employees in 1954 and about a hundred top managers. At that time, when it did not yet have those massive departments for property trading, private banking and even trade banking, investment banking relied on a small and sharp group, dedicated to merchant and corporate banking.

Table 4. The executive team of BUP in January 1954

Executive chairman	Lafond
CEO	Letondot
Executive managing directors	5
Deputy executive managing directors	10
Sub-directors	7
Specialised managers (administration, law advice, tax advice, etc.)	5
Consulting engineers	2
Fondés de pouvoir	13
Heads of divisions	7
Chefs de service, attachés à la direction, chefs adjoints de service, sous-chefs de service	116
Total	165

At BUP, a gradual transition between the team built during the inter-war period and a new generation (recruited at the end of the 1930s and during the 1940s) was completed at the turn of the 1950s, symbolised

10 Hubert Bonin, *La Banque de l'union parisienne*, *op. cit.*, pp. 405-409.

by Jacques Burin des Roziers as head of the banking division from 1954. Roger Quentin-Bauchard, Burin des Roziers' deputy in 1952, was promoted managing director: he had entered in 1935 and climbed from being *fondé de pouvoirs* (1944) to sub-manager (1947) to deputy director (1952) and finally managing director in charge with the financial direction (*direction financière*, from 1955 till 1972),[11] where he became more and more the cornerstone of the financial activities. He developed through fresh recruitments and by refurbishing its portfolio of skills, to follow the changes sweeping through the Parisian market in the domains of corporate and merchant banking.

d. Banque de l'Indochine as an emerging challenger?

The first cracks in the overseas financial empire had immediate effects on the architecture of the Parisian banking and financial centre. There was a move towards a redistribution of the capital invested in Indochina either to some other part of the empire (mainly in sub-Saharan Africa and Morocco), or to Paris. Banque de l'Indochine, which had been only an issuing, commercial, corporate and investment bank in Asia, started a long-term process of capitalisation of its portfolio of competences and redeploying them towards French metropolitan business. Its power came from its connections to a large pool of firms, which were still active overseas but had also transferred part of their activities to Europe, like *Société française d'entreprises de dragages et de travaux publics* (public works). It thus benefitted from a captive clientele and followed its apprenticeship in corporate and investment banking.[12] But during the years 1945-1960, it had not yet risen as a challenger to Paribas and the Bup. Seeds were being sown, and the merchant bank Lazard seems to have had a premonition as unwritten testimonies relate that it tried to pick up the Banque de l'Indochine's equity discreetly on the Stock Exchange in 1952-1955, before reneging on this predatory project....

e. Merchant banks as a renewed force in investment banking?

The decline of the *Haute Banque* houses was confirmed when the leading Mirabaud bank was merged into the *Banque de l'union parisienne* in 1953 (starting in January 1954): its portfolio of stockholding, business, family and overseas connections was transmitted to the investment bank. Rothschild itself had been weakened by its Aryanisation during WWII and had to rebuild itself during the 1950s by first reconstituting a small

11 *Ibidem*, p. 421-422.

12 See Marc Meuleau, *Des pionniers en Extrême-Orient. La Banque de l'Indochine, 1875-1975*, Paris, Fayard, 1990.

team of real bankers (Robert Jablon, mainly,[13] who was the driving force behind the expansion from simple Stock Exchange operations and asset management to merchant banking), whose mission was to weave a refurbished network within the business community. But the house first bet on its portfolio of financial holdings in maritime transit, mining and as a leverage for further development, mainly overseas. Lastly, Lazard, as we shall see, remobilised its team towards transatlantic connections, with Pierre David-Weill and André Meyer leading a small team of partners or managers (Jean-Frédéric Bloch-Lainé, Jean Beauvois or Marcel Caroli, joined by Christian Valensi in 1950 and by Jean Guyot in 1952).[14] Lazard's ambitions even went so far as attempting to capture a decisive stake in the *Banque de l'Indochine* and even Paribas in 1954. Both offensives were halted and remain blurred in the memory of the Parisian market…[15]

2. How to identify investment banking as opposed to mere corporate banking?

Beyond facts and stories, beyond the history of the links between investment banks and industrial or services sectors, the key issue lies in the difference between them and deposit/commercial banking at a time when these latter practiced corporate and market and brokerage banking. Once again, the question is: Was it a difference in nature? Or was it only a difference in the degree of involvement in financial activities, merchant banking and investment banking? We will not pretend having reached a comprehensive conclusion, but we shall try and draw the outlines of a difference. Without making an exhaustive study, we hope to delimitate the spheres of influence of investment banks against those of commercial banks, to assess how and to what extent each type developed a competitive edge in the issue of syndicates and credit pools, and whether their respective positions revealed a "difference" between the portfolio of skills and a difference "in nature" or function within the French banking system.

13 See Robert Jablon, Laure Quenouelle-Corre and André Straus, *Politique et finance à travers l'Europe du xxe siècle. Entretiens avec Robert Jablon*, Brussels, Peter Lang, 2009. Jablon joined Rothschild in 1939 and became a managing director in 1956; at that time Georges Pompidou, the future French Prime Minister and President, was also an executive manager of the merchant bank and appears in a few archives (*Notes de conversations*, historical archives of *Crédit lyonnais*) when bankers negotiated about co-operative projects.

14 See "Refaire une banque", in Anne Sabouret, *MM. Lazard frères et Cie. Une saga de la fortune*, Paris, Olivier Orban, 1987, pp. 117-172.

15 *Ibidem*, p. 131-134.

A. Investment banks defined by banking regulation

The new rules set up in 1945/1946 left a specific area to investment banks: the difference was established by the regulation itself:[16] whereas deposit banks could not use more than 75 per cent of their permanent funds in investing into firms, the act of 2 December[17] allowed investment banks to purchase and hold stakes in companies, create firms and distribute middle and long term loans – while specialised institutional guarantees by the State and/or refinance by *Banque de France* were to tackle middle and long term credits earmarked for privileged sectors (small and medium sized enterprises, housing, external trade, etc.). Flexibility increased when another act broadened their portfolio of activities to all kind of "credit",[18] even short term and drafts, which allowed investment banks to assert their skills in corporate banking ("one-stop banking", or "all under the same roof"). It rapidly became obvious that investment banks needed to collect deposits to fuel short/medium term credits, even though the law stipulated that they had to focus on deposits of two years or more, and that they may only collect deposits from the firms in which they held stakes or which were their clients for credit, or from individuals

---

16 Laws of 2 December 1945, 17 May 1946, 28 May 1946. Also see: Records *Contrôle des banques*, historical archives of *Crédit lyonnais*, 129AH112, note "Analyse d'un projet de décret relatif à l'aménagement des règles de fonctionnement de certaines banques", 14 June 1946, which reconstituted the evolution of the regulation.

17 "Investment banks are banks which deal mainly with investments and the management of investments in corporations. They only accept demand or term deposits of less than or equal to one year and only from their personnel, their partners in name, limited partners, or from enterprises in which they hold at least 15% of the corporate capital or those they helped create by assuming 15% of the initial capital." 2 December act.

18 "Those banks are henceforth considered to be investment banks when their principal activity consists of investments or the management of investments and the opening of a credit line without time limit to private enterprises which would benefit from these investments or are called to benefit from." 17 May 1946 and 28 May 1946 acts. "The relative layout of the opening of a credit line is new and will result in an increase in the number of establishments classified as investment banks. The exact definition of the operations allowed to investment banks cannot be given with any precision till the long-awaited implementing order has not appeared." report of the general assembly of the *Association professionnelle des banques*, 12 May 1947. "As regards active operations, investment banks have great latitude: in the size of their participation as much as in the length of the duration of credit they can allow. Restrictions were applied only to the numbers of their borrowing clientele, and even here the imprecise terms left the door open to some serious difficulties in their application, [with] the opening of credit to enterprises which have benefited, do benefit or should benefit from the said investments [whilst] their limited deposits […] to the underwriters of the shares of companies in which they have invested, on the condition that these underwriters be the bearers of the securities custody accounts on their books." Note of *Crédit lyonnais* about banking acts, September 1949 (pp. 15-16) and February 1950 (p. 7), records *Banking regulation 1939-1983*, historical archives of *Crédit lyonnais*, 129AH112.

who held securities and were customers of the private banking division of investment banks – which in fact reflected their practices. Gradually, the implementation of these rules was also made more flexible.

B. One-stop-shopping for corporate banking?

Beyond legal boundaries, which were themselves being softened, no "Stalinist" fences hemmed investment banks into a specialised business model, because deposit bankers tended to broaden their scope from merely commercial and corporate banking to financial initiatives. They baulked at being limited to being just road companions of more "noble" bodies and to content themselves with distribution and co-financing. There was a scramble for engineering talents in corporate banking and even in merchant banking.

a. Corporate bankers as investment bankers?

Deposit banks had refurbished their financial department, because they still needed as usual bunches of securities to be brokered within their network to individual investors and within their division of private banking. Day to day interbank meetings show how far a few "investment bankers" had regained momentum within the financial departments. At Société générale, Louis Beaupère was the head negotiator for the loan and issuing projects under the guidance of CEO Maurice Lorain, with a team rich with several sub-managers (Pierre Etchecopar, etc.), meeting frequently their partners at Crédit lyonnais, who were led by Olivier Moreau-Néret, C. Bouis and Charles Brincard (for the distribution of securities), and at CNEP, by Henry Bizot.

Table 5. Corporate bankers as competitors of investment bankers in the 1950s

At Société générale	At Crédit lyonnais
Louis Beaupère[19] was a top-level academic (law, *École des sciences politiques de Paris*) who had joined Société générale in 1927 at the *Études financières* department, and he had become *fondé de pouvoirs* at the *direction financière* in 1934, sub-manager (sous-directeur) in 1939, deputy manager (sous-directeur) in 1940, manager (directeur) in 1943. He was made *directeur de département* of	Olivier Moreau-Néret[20] had been an inspecteur des Finances at the Finance Ministry and an under-manager and deputy manager at the *Mouvement général des fonds* (the Treasury) in 1923-1925, thus a high civil servant. He joined Crédit lyonnais in 1925, as the head of the General Accounting division, then as general secretary in 1926. From 1926 onwards

[19] Record from human resources archives at Société générale historical archives (thanks to archivist Sylvie Guillaudeau).

[20] Record from human resources archives at Crédit lyonnais historical archives (thanks to archivist Roger Nougaret).

the finance division in 1942 and thus Société générale's chief corporate banker. His career attained its zenith when he was promoted to *directeur général adjoint* (co-deputy CEO) in 1956 and then *directeur général* (co-CEO) in 1967-1969, before his retirement. He had also managed the investment fund and financial holding of the commercial bank, *Société financière de valeurs industrielles et de valeurs de banque* in 1936-1939.	he worked at the *Affaires financières* department (financial affairs, for the issuance of securities) – except for a while in 1940-1941. He was promoted as head of financial affairs in 1947, with the rank of co-CEO and finally as director-CEO in 1949. He ended his brilliant career as chairman of the bank in 1955-1961, thereby proving the quality of his portfolio of skills as a corporate banker.
Louis Etchecopar,[21] a law graduate from the *École des sciences politiques de Paris,* joined the *Études financières* département (financial studies) of Société générale in 1929, where he became *fondé de pouvoirs* in June 1938, *chef de service* in August 1940 and *chef de division* in September 1941, before being promoted under-manager in August 1943, deputy-manager in July 1947, head of the department in March 1958 and manager (*directeur*) in June 1961 – till his death in July 1961. He was Beaupère's partner in corporate and investment banking throughout these 1940s and 1950s, both piling up a broad capital of skills.	

Agile and inventive teams of corporate and almost investment bankers sustained competition against the specialists at investment banks. Competing against the well-established influential network of investment bankers, each team of corporate bankers entertained its own network of connections among the business communities to fuel operations. Thus, Crédit lyonnais got in touch with *Société générale d'exploitations industrielles*, some kind of a financial holding or fund, and was rewarded with financial contracts with its affiliates, like Colombes-Goodrich[22] (then Kleber-Colombes). Deposit banks followed a long term trend to complement their corporate banking

21 Record from human resources archives at Société générale historical archives (thanks to archivist S. Guillaudeau).

22 *Notes de conversations*, historical archives of *Crédit lyonnais*, 20 June 1946. When the US group Goodrich ceded a block of equity, SGEI entered the capital of Colombes Goodrich in 1946 and therefore tried to draw *Crédit lyonnais* as a house bank, at the expense of BNCI (its lead manager), Paribas and *Crédit du Nord*. The firm became Kleber-Colombes in July 1946.

division with merchant banking services, first because of the "one-stop-shop" rule and second, because of the revenues drawn from guarantee and brokerage fees (*commission de guichet*). Prestige was also at stake with banks vying for the rank of lead manager like hunting trophies. Finally, a few deposit banks had practiced some form of mixed banking in the inter-war period and had captured positions which they struggled to keep after WWII, as was the case with Crédit commercial de France (CCF)[23] and BNCI.

b. Convergence of corporate banking skills

Obviously, there was not much difference between deposit banks and investment banks in these fields. They often shared the same functions and rank within pools and syndicates. A few examples confirm our perception: at Pechiney (metallurgy and chemicals), the credit pool was "crossed" ("*crédit croisé*") between Paribas, Société générale, Crédit lyonnais and CNEP,[24] at Saint-Frères (textiles) between Paribas and Société générale;[25] at Alsthom[26] (electrical equipment), the whole range of credits was shared between Paribas, CIC, CCF and Banque commerciale de Paris (a small, emerging firm practicing corporate and private banking); at Michelin (tyres), between Paribas, Lazard, Neuflize, Banque franco-chinoise and Banque impériale ottomane, the last two being affiliates of Paribas;[27] at Bull (computers), between Paribas, Crédit lyonnais and BFCE;[28] at CSF (electronics), between Crédit lyonnais and Banque de l'Indochine on one side, and Société générale, Crédit lyonnais, Worms and Banque de l'Indochine on the other;[29] at Saviem (trucks)[30] and SN MAREP (oil equipment) with Crédit lyonnais.[31] In this case, the confusion between deposit banks and investment banks was thus complete: Crédit lyonnais had been the leading commercial bank, and all of a sudden, it learnt that Paribas had offered, negotiated and

---

23 See Jean-Pierre Daviet & Michel Germain, *CCF, 1894-1994. Crédit commercial de France, une banque dans le siècle*, Paris, Textuel, 1994.

24 Report of the board of Paribas, 31 January 1957, 28 November 1957.

25 *Ibidem*, 31 January 1957.

26 Report of the board of Paribas, 14 March 1957. See Jacques Marseille (ed.), *Alcatel-Alsthom. Histoire de la Compagnie générale d'électricité*, Paris, Larousse, 1992.

27 Report of the board of Paribas, 13 June 1957, 18 September 1958 (*crédits mobilisables, crédits non mobilisables, crédits mobilisables export, crédits documentaires*, etc.).

28 *Ibidem*, 22 May 1958.

29 *Ibidem*, 17 July 1958.

30 *Ibidem*, 18 September 1958.

31 *Ibidem*, 9 April 1959.

achieved a long term loan with the firm, of which both were partners as members of the board.[32]

Corporate banking influenced merchant banking in both types of banks. Investment banks drew on their sharp domestic corporate banking department. Because of the expertise of its documentary credit division and of the needs of clients, the BUP's team was financed trade and forex operations in oil (*Compagnie française des pétroles* and *Compagnie française de raffinage, Desmarais frères*), general trade (Gradis), rubber (Kleber-Colombes), Algerian wine, etc.

They also asserted themselves as experts in the new assemblies and credit chains which helped French firms (and also foreign affiliates in France)[33] to rebuild their productivity and modernity in the post-war period. In that regard, there was no difference between investment banks and deposit banks, but they clung to the club of corporate banking leaders and were not left behind. Mid-term credits were set up with various types of refinancing by public or semi-public institutions (Crédit national, Banque de France, BFCE-Banque française pour le commerce extérieur, the equivalent of the US Exim Bank) for the purchase of equipment in France, Europe or the US. Sometimes, investment banks were co-lead managers of such sophisticated loans, like BUP in favour of *Papeteries Aussedat* for a huge paper pulp machine (1951, five years FRF 160 million credit) or to *Port autonome du Havre* (500 million, with 11 per cent to BUP, in 1948).[34]

Conversely, commercial banks could take advantage of their ability to grant easy short-term credits (*crédits d'attente*) to firms pending the completion of an issue of securities, which allowed them to keep their customers under their umbrella against contending investment banks, thanks to the "all under the same roof" motto. Moreover, in a few cases, it seems that investment banks' business model was not cohesive enough and weakened their competitive edge. Here is one example in support of this hypothesis: when Paribas complained of its low share in the equity issue by Pathé-Cinéma in 1946 as compared to the leading role played by Crédit lyonnais, the latter proved to Reyre, Paribas' CEO, that his banking department had turned down credits to the firm, which led it to consider

32 "We have reached an agreement with Paribas regarding the division of our respective allotments. It has been agreed that, in banking, our establishment [*Crédit lyonnais*] will remain the lead underwriter, especially for initiating mid-term credit. As regards financial operations, both our establishments will be co-lead underwriters, with Paribas ensuring the secretariat for all operations concerning shares, while we fulfil a similar role in matters dealing with bond trading." *Notes de conversations*, historical archives of *Crédit lyonnais*, 12 December 1958.

33 Hubert Bonin and Ferry de Goey (eds.), *American Firms in Europe (1890-1980). Strategy, Identity, Perception and Performance*, Geneva, Droz, 2008.

34 Hubert Bonin, *La Banque de l'union parisienne*, *op. cit.*, pp. 376-377.

the offers made by Paribas' merchant banking department.[35] The more investment banks turned into "firm organisations", the more organisational and operational synergies had to be "reinvented', which put pressure on the head committee. Some kind of a "partnership" or a way of life had to be engineered, as was the case at the renewed Lazard house.

They had also to react to the resiliency of commercial banks, whose teams had, generally speaking, crossed the war and the *Libération* years and were very experienced: while Paribas had launched the *Groupement de l'électricité* as a co-operative fund issuing bonds in the name of utilities in the inter-war period and engineered the *Groupement de l'industrie sucrière* (for sugar firms) in 1946, Société générale (with Beaupère) had conceived of the *Groupement des constructions navales*, another corporative body[36] – proving the competitiveness of corporate bankers. No fixed positions could be defended, as contenders challenged the edge of investment bankers. Even day-to-day operations show that corporate bankers emulated investment bankers: at Renault, where CNEP was the lead manager,[37] banks organised a field visit[38] at Boulogne-Billancourt to get a hands-on view of the reality of investments, the modernisation, and the financial needs of the (nationalised) firm in order to engineer a huge bonds issue, fix the amount (between 800 and 1,000 million francs).[39] The operation was completed in February 1947. The complementarity between banking and finance fostered an intimate knowledge of the customers' situation and needs by deposit banks, which could then activate financial advice and engineering upstream, as "merchant bankers", thus enriching their skills and improving their rank among the best investment bankers.[40]

C. The legacy of history explaining the convergence of both business models

The presence or absence of a bank was the result of history, whether or not it had taken part in the creation, rescue or development of the firm – a thorough history of French capitalism would be required to explain the

35 *Notes de conversations*, historical archives of *Crédit lyonnais*, 8 June 1946. "Reyre replied that Paribas' finance division had ignored the refusal by the banking department. Himself surely would have associated the bank to credit, with respect to the generally applied considerations which had escaped the banking department."

36 *Notes de conversations*, historical archives of *Crédit lyonnais*, 21 and 25 September 1946.

37 *Ibidem*, 20 June 1945 (despite the fact that *Crédit lyonnais* had been lead-manager for the credit pool), 26 January 1955.

38 *Ibidem*, 9 December 1946.

39 *Ibidem*, 13, 17 December 1946 and February 1947.

40 We found such a case at *Crédit lyonnais* about *Société générale d'entreprises*, which the bank advised to launch an issue to compensate for a weakened balance sheet, *Notes de conversations*, historical archives of *Crédit lyonnais*, 15 May 1945.

presence and ranking of each bank, including those of investment banks in our study. The weight of legacy played both ways as very often, an investment bank and a deposit bank were both historical partners of a firm, as was the case at *Produits chimiques et engrais d'Auby*[41] in 1946.

a. History favouring deposit banks

On the other hand, the historical legacy could sometimes play in favour of deposit banks. Traditionally, Société générale had been much influenced by metal manufacturers, and remained for instance lead manager at *Forges & chantiers de la Marine* and at *Tréfileries & laminoirs du Havre.*[42] That was also the case at *Aciéries de Longwy* and at the *Société générale de fonderie*, where it became the lead manager for bond issues in 1945[43] and 1946[44] respectively because it had been the house-bank of the firms for decades. Société générale led operations at Vallourec, Lorraine-Escaut and Sidelor (steel),[45] whilst Ugine (a competitor to Pechiney) "was a fiefdom of CCF".[46] When steel giant Lorraine-Escaut launched its first issue, Société générale and CIC led it, because they had been dominant in the two firms which had amalgamated.[47] Société générale led financial operations at Ciments français[48] and at Rateau (electro-technical engineering).[49] The legacy of the pre-war positions had to be taken into account about the operations of the nationalised companies: Crédit lyonnais was the lead manager of the EDF issuing in 1955, and CNEP of the first GDF issuing in 1955, "to take into account the position it occupied in gas financial business before the nationalisation",[50] but a turnover was scheduled for the next operations and "Paribas brokered half the loan"[51] of GDF in 1957. Anyway the broad dimension of such issuings preserved the key role of deposit banks against investment banks, and BNCI was thus lead manager for *Charbonnages de France* in 1957.

A history of less intensive banking relations with several big firms (Saint-Gobain, Renault, etc.) explain why Paribas had to often be content

---

41 *Notes de conversations*, historical archives of *Crédit lyonnais*, 25 March 1946, for an equity issue.

42 *Ibidem*, 6 February 1959.

43 *Ibidem*, 27 November 1945 (FRF 200 million).

44 *Ibidem*, 6 February 1946.

45 *Ibidem*, 3 April 1958.

46 *Ibidem*, February 1955.

47 *Ibidem*, 17 June 1955.

48 *Ibidem*, 30 October 1946 (FRF 100 million bonds issue).

49 *Ibidem*, 31 October 1946 (FRF 40 million bonds issue). *Société générale*, sole lead manager, invited Paribas to join the pool with deposit banks *Crédit lyonnais* and CNEP.

50 *Ibidem*, April 1955.

51 Report of the board of Paribas, 7 November 1957.

with little bits of the pie – its competitors controlled the syndicates[52] and their positions were not to be shaken. A telling example was Pechiney, where Paribas had to admit that Crédit lyonnais was the lead manager for bonds issues as the deposit bank was also the leader of the credit pool (with CNEP) with Paribas and Société générale coming second – although all four had equal share.[53] Both Crédit lyonnais (from the Lyon and Alps region where Pechiney was very active) and CNEP (because of its traditional kinks with electricity and the electro-industrial sectors) had built strongholds there. Crédit lyonnais records confirm that in several cases deposit bankers were able to lead financial operations without any help or intervention of investment banks. *Crédit lyonnais* was thus the lead-manager of Duralumin (a metal-working affiliate of Pechiney) and led negotiations, Paribas being relegated to the back seat thanks to the firm itself.[54] Crédit lyonnais also managed the *Tréfileries & laminoirs du Havre* bonds issue[55] in 1946. It was also a historical house bank at the *Société lyonnaise des eaux*, which it had supported since its inception in the 1880s turned into its fiefdom.[56]

Similarly, Peugeot bond issues were led by Crédit lyonnais[57] in both 1945 and 1955 because of history and also because the family – after bearing some loss of power in the mid-1920s to a small investment banker[58] – was reluctant to give any rope to investment banks, fearing of losing its grip on the firm. Deposit banks led the issuing syndicate, with Crédit lyonnais as negotatior and Société générale and CNEP accompanying it as co-lead managers, with Paribas limited to only 6.023 per cent of the share.[59]

Though credits were shared between banks at Alsthom, the bonds and equity issues in 1946 were assumed by CNEP as sole lead-manager,

52 For instance, 2% for Sidelor (steel), report of the board of Paribas, 22 May 1958; 2.4% for Vallourec (steel pipes), *ibidem*; 1.97% for Saint-Gobain (glass and chemicals), *ibidem*, 18 September 1958.

53 Letter from Reyre, 7 August 1958, historical archives of Paribas.

54 *Notes de conversations*, historical archives of *Crédit lyonnais*, 10, 22, 28 November 1945.

55 *Ibidem*, 5 April 1946.

56 *Ibidem*, 12 September 1960, for a bonds issue, and Paribas had to satisfy itself with a 4.5% share.

57 *Ibidem*, 12 and 19 September 1945. In 1955 *Crédit lyonnais* got 30.298% of the issuing in 1955, ahead of *Société générale* 24.605%, BNCI 19.064%, CNEP 14.344%, far ahead of Paribas, with 6.923%, *Notes de conversations*, historical archives of *Crédit lyonnais*, February 1955.

58 See Jean-Louis Loubet, *La Maison Peugeot*, Paris, Perrin, 2009.

59 *Notes de conversations*, historical archives of *Crédit lyonnais*, 23 February 1956. But in 1946, the equity increase at *Société des automobiles Peugeot* was led by Société générale (33.6%) with *Crédit lyonnais* (22.4%), *Ibidem*, 20 September 1946.

involving its fellow bankers on the league table only as sub-contractors.[60] At Saint-Gobain, two deposit banks managed the equity issue in 1946, without any investment bank, because of their long-term involvement in the firm's business and because its capital was spread over 35,000 shareholders (22,000 holding less than five shares), which demanded a key role by banking networks to tackle such an issue.[61]

The legacy of history was also active locally, with commercial banks having influential and respected personalities heading their big branches in the "provincial" regions. The spectre of the productive system comprised so many medium-sized enterprises because of the stage of evolution, still escaping to the intense move of amalgamation and bids of the next decades. The fact that these companies were enjoying an upward trend in growth after the stagnation of the past fifteen years, opened doors to credits to finance the new size of their treasury needs and even their refreshed investments, to compensate for the Malthusian habits of the 1930s crisis. We cannot pretend to draw a comprehensive analysis of such development of this segment of market, all the more because the State urged the half-public bank Crédit national[62] to extend its mid-term loans. We have for example identified the case of *Cellulose du Pin*, a paper-mill in the Landes area, south-west of Bordeaux, because Société générale, through its branches in Bordeaux and Arcachon, had been, since 1943, the house banker to this medium-sized firm (1,300 employees in 1958). Through multi-page files, it gauged its programme of development and investments, its balance sheet, adding transactional banking to relational banking. It conceived and managed the issue of bonds[63] in July 1945 as well as in 1947 (with 42.5 per cent of the total, ahead of Crédit lyonnais (28.5%) and two other banks) and in 1954 (38.25% of the FRF 500 million issued). A deputy-head-manager in Paris and the head of the Bordeaux branch acted as direct partners of the company. In June 1958, a top manager at *Cellulose du Pin* met the bankers in Paris[64] to negotiate the profile of the financial package to be mobilised for a huge programme of investment which would allow the company to compete at the level of the newly formed inter-regional and even European (from the Summer of 1958) markets. Commercial bankers thus mixed once more corporate

60 *Ibidem*, 23 April 1946.

61 *Ibidem*, 7 March 1946.

62 See Patrice Baubeau, "Le Crédit national dans l'évolution des circuits de financement", in Serge Berstein et Pierre Milza (eds.), *L'année 1947*, Paris, Presses de Sciences Po, 2000, pp. 127-145. Patrick Baubeau, Arnaud Lavit d'Hautefort, Michel Lescure, *Le Crédit national. Histoire publique d'une société privée, 1919-1994*, Paris, J.-C. Lattès, 1994.

63 Historical archives of Société générale, financial direction, B8059: July 1945; B8186: January 1947; B0908 and B8653, November-December 1954 (with four other banks);

64 Historical archives of Société générale, 1613, note of 10 June 1958.

banking and investment banking from upstream, as its senior partners and originators of the financing sets, as "path-breakers" on a small regional level to help push a client into the times of competitiveness and (chemical and mechanical) innovation.

b. History favouring investment banks

At Michelin, Lazard and Paribas had been partners for decades and had altogether helped the firm rescuing and purchasing Citroën[65] – which explains that Paribas was the main banker of the car firm.[66] The same co-leadership was exerted at Paris-France, a department store chain,[67] but Lazard sponsored Schneider Radio-Télévision for its floatation in 1960 because of technological connections with US firms.[68] Paribas had contributed to the creation and development of CSF and remained its house banker. It had always entertained close partnerships with the business of electricity, either utilities or manufacturers of equipment, thus explaining its presence at Alsthom or Pechiney (a big user and producer of power), etc.

The long-standing partnership between investment banks and the *Compagnie française des pétroles* preserved their share in credit lines despite their huge size. BUP for example held a total amount of credit risks of FRF 1,284 million[69] in 1950.

Table 6. Risks of BUP at *Compagnie française des pétroles* in January-September 1950 (FRF million)

Domestic discount bills	250.5
Acceptance bills	352.5
Discount bills for imports	805
Security guarantees to *Crédit national* middle term loans	547

And both BUP and Paribas led the bonds issue of the oil firm in 1960, because "the tables of the 1942 issue served as a base for the new ones", even if afterwards the share of the brokerage reflected the might of retail banks.

65 Hubert Bonin, "Les banques ont-elles sauvé Citroën (1933-1935)? Réflexion sur la marge d'initiative bancaire", *Revue Histoire, économie, société*, 3, 1984, pp. 453-472.

66 "*Paribas est le principal banquier de Citroën*", *Notes de conversations*, historical archives of *Crédit lyonnais*, DAF 1171, 1955.

67 *Ibidem*, 24 October 1945. When the head of Paris-France wished to call *Crédit lyonnais* a lead-manager for an operation, the bank had to remind him that he had "ignored the customs", "an already ancient tradition", and asked him "to talk to the traditional co-leaders for the issue", even if, within the following brokerage pool, both investment banks (with 25.2%) are lagging behind *Crédit lyonnais*, Société générale and CCF.

68 Morgan France, *Crédit lyonnais*, Rothschild and Mallet also joined the league-table, under the guidance of Lazard, *ibidem*, 26 September 1960.

69 Hubert Bonin, *La Banque de l'union parisienne*, *op. cit.*, p. 374.

Table 7. Bonds issue by *Compagnie française des pétroles* in February 1960

Paribas	**5%**
BUP	5
Crédit lyonnais	26.775
Société générale	22.950
CNEP	19.125
BNCI (introduced for the first time)	13.130
CCF	5
Lazard (replacing Mirabaud)	3

Source: *Notes de conversations*, historical archives of *Crédit lyonnais*, 5 February 1960.

Each deposit bank and investment bank had built its own network, and neither Paribas nor BUP could be active in every company: mid and long-term history explains their presence and ranking among, with and often against deposit banks or a few smaller investment banks. Both investment banks had an advantage in the form of their property portfolio (*portefeuille-titres*) as a majority of the firms in which they held a stake brought them banking business. Thus, BUP picked up numerous opportunities of corporate banking from the companies active overseas with which it had been a long term partner, often thanks to its relationship (then merger) with Mirabaud (Optorg, SCAC, Gradis, *Phosphates & chemins de fer de Gafsa*, *Compagnie marocaine*, etc.).[70] Its privileged connections with Belgian firms and SGB fuelled BUP's operations with their French affiliates (Petrofina France, Purfina, *Raffinerie de pétrole du Nord*, etc.). In spite of the leadership of deposit banks, BUP carved out for itself substantial market shares in the banking pools which took form after WWII for thick lines of credit: its global relationship with an array of firms explain that their managers recommended the investment bank in the pool and guarantee its stake. Far behind lead manager CNEP, it got 6 per cent of the credit at Lesieur (oil) and 21 per cent at Lebaudy-Sommier (sugar).[71] Because Paribas had always had a powerful network of connections in Scandinavia, Crédit lyonnais proposed sharing the management of Ericsson's floatation in France when ITT sold its equity block in 1960: even though Stockholm Enskilda Bank had contacted Crédit lyonnais, the latter was wise to respect Paribas' legacy – especially as Paribas was in touch with US investment banks Warburg and Kuhn Loeb for this operation.[72]

On their side, even the smaller investment *Haute Banque* banks succeeded in getting a few bits of the market because of historical and personal

70 *Ibidem*, p. 372.

71 *Ibidem*, pp. 373-374.

72 *Notes de conversations*, historical archives of *Crédit lyonnais*, 12 May 1960.

links. For instance, Neuflize[73] had Worms (in naval business, leading a one billion credit to the *Compagnie générale transatlantique* to complete the *Ile-de-France* flagship (1949)), or Lazard (for credits to *Shell-Berre*, the affiliate of *Royal Dutch Shell*). Vernes had been the historical companion of *Air liquide* (chemical gas) and its group.[74] This explains why BUP absorbed the merchant bank Mirabaud in 1953 inherited from its broad "address book" and thus partly fill the gap between it and Paribas.

All in all, there was no great differentiation between investment and deposit banks in the domain of domestic commercial banking – which is not too surprising – though investment banks developed their corporate banking division to feed current cash flows and deposits, which were useful for their daily life.

D. *Investment banks depending on deposit banking for the distribution of securities*

Inevitably commercial banks, when practicing corporate banking, benefitted from the economies of scale, as the global balance sheet of investment banks lagged far behind those of their competitors. The total amount of the balance sheet of the five largest investment banks represented only a seventh of that of deposit banks. Their "strike force" for brokering securities and mobilising availabilities to fuel credits was to meet invisible ceilings when vying for position with deposit banks.

Table 8. Breakdown of balance sheets between commercial and investment banks in December 1948

	Million francs	Percentage
Total amount of balance sheet of investment banks	281,480	16.28
Among which joint-stock banks	247,939	14.30
Total amount of balance sheet of deposit banks	1,438,881	83.55
Total for all banks	1,722,987	

Source: "*Les banques d'afffaires*", Historical archives of *Crédit lyonnais*, 129AH13.

Investment banks' relatively weak brokerage force was made evident when they found themselves overloaded by securities received through issues which they later struggled to distribute through "retrocessions"

73 *Société française des aciéries de Blanc-Misseron* chose Neuflize as its lead manager for a FRF 20 million operation, before retrocessions to a few other banks, *Ibidem*, 7 December 1945.

74 Vernes was the lead manager of the bonds issue of *Société chimique de la Grande Paroisse*, an affiliate of Air liquide, *Ibidem*, 7 January 1946.

with low prices, thus spurring discontent among deposit banks.[75] Because of this imbalance in favour of deposit banks, investment banks had to sharpen their portfolio of skills to get some edge over them, to engineer new "paths" of banking or some form of financial "innovation" to prove themselves more "mobile" and reactive. Such challenges appear clearly when we assess the competitiveness of each big bank on the credit and issuing market. By basing ourselves on various archival sources,[76] we can say that the issue at stake among bankers preparing operations was mostly the rank as lead and co-lead manager of the operation, credit pool, or issuing syndicate.

No doubt deposit banks could profit from their powerful brokerage. When *Papeteries de La Chapelle*'s shares were floated, its partner Paribas thought of leading the operation, but its "friend" *Crédit lyonnais* reacted strongly, arguing for its sales force. And indeed, it sold two-thirds of its chunk through its own clientele, leaving only a third to be retroceded to stockbrokers, in contrast to Paribas which had customers for a meagre third of its part.[77] But investment banks could respond that they benefitted from an intimate relationship with insurance companies – often sponsored by merchant banks from the 19th century – and that they could use this informal network to broaden their sales pitch. After high pressure negotiations, Paribas was admitted into the group of co-contracting banks at Saint-Gobain in 1958, and its CEO "claimed that his bank was able to broker a large amount of bonds, notably through insurance companies".[78] A ceiling was nevertheless put on such processes because insurance asset managers could only absorb "good" and "solid" securities, avoiding start-ups or firms with unclear futures. On its side, BUP could rely on its connections with local banks in the province to broaden its brokering might, a network that it had retained from the inter-war period: they used the investment bank to supply them with securities packages to broker among their own clientele and pay retrocession fees to their Paris correspondent.[79]

---

75 That was the case about Pechiney issuing for BUP, Paribas and *Banque de l'union européenne*-BUE, *Notes de conversations*, historical archives of *Crédit lyonnais*, 12 January 1955.

76 We scrutinized the reports of the sessions of *Paribas* (1957-1958) and *Banque de l'union parisienne* (1945-1960) boards, and a unique and original series of *Crédit lyonnais* historical archives, called "*Notes de conversations*" (1955-1959), that is reports on exchanges between bankers, which allow historians to take part to the very arguments between banks about day to day projects and operations.

77 *Notes de conversations*, historical archives of *Crédit lyonnais*, 10 January 1957.

78 *Ibidem*, 31 July 1958.

79 Hubert Bonin, *La Banque de l'union parisienne*, *op. cit.*, p. 369-371.

Table 9. Breakdown of balance sheets between commercial and investment banks in December 1956 (million francs)

	Balance sheet		Deposit account (*comptes créditeurs*)	
		Deposit banks		
Crédit lyonnais	693.2		552.6	
Société générale	575.7		447.9	
Banque nationale pour le commerce et l'industrie	491.1		414.7	
Comptoir national d'escompte de Paris	329.6		251,8	
Crédit industriel et commercial	116.9		87.9	
Crédit commercial de France	101.9		85.4	
Total for the big six	2,304.8		1,840.3	
		Investment banks		
Paribas	139	206,5 [with affiliates *Banque française et italienne pour l'Amérique du Sud* and *Banque franco-chinoise pour le commerce et l'industrie*]	84.6	123.3 (*idem*)
BUP	65.6		43.1	
Union européenne industrielle et financière	43.9		29.7	
Banque de l'Indochine	45.7		14.3	
Banque de l'union des mines	28.6		20.8	
Total for the Big Five	322.8		192.5	
		Merchant banks (*Haute Banque*)		
De Neuflize, Schlumberger	12.9		10.4	
Vernes	8.4		6.2	
Mallet	6.6		5.9	
Hottinguer	4.1		2.7	

Source: note historical archives of *Crédit lyonnais*, 129AH13, September 1958.

In a few cases, a (secret) agreement between Paribas and Crédit lyonnais (dating back[80] to 1933 and redefined[81] in 1945-1946) proved very useful whenever Paribas met with difficulties to lodge its share of securities: its partner Crédit lyonnais was there to relieve it by selling them to its own customers.[82] But the Crédit lyonnais refused to relay BUP in the case of a huge SNPA issue[83] in 1959 because it did not have a similar relationship with Paribas' competitor. We have also to note that the Big Three kept respecting their (secret/discreet) cartel agreement (dating back[84] to 1927/1929 and renewed[85] in 1959) which stipulated that they do not contest their rankings within issuing brokerage syndicates: the attempts by investment banks to circumvent deposit banks could not but fail…. Lastly, an agreement in 1942 linked Crédit du Nord (northern and Parisian region) to Crédit lyonnais and Société générale, each one retroceding securities to the others for every operation.[86]

E. Guerrilla fighting between investment banks and deposit banks?

Year after year investment banks and deposit banks had piled agreement upon agreement and were differentiated less by the "nature" of their functions or business model and more by the position and rank inherited from banking and financial history, which helped stabilise the balance of power in each industry. But they kept their fighting spirit and tried at every opportunity to change the rules in the name of little changes in their relationship with the customers involved: gaining a larger part of the credit, joining the pool of a firm because they had been the banker of another company which had been absorbed by this one, or because once they had replaced a colleague who had difficulties mobilising funds or brokering its share of securities. "Guerrilla" tactics abounded in an unending war of position among investment banks, but far more often between investment banks and deposit banks.

a. Commercial banks' offensive

The ability of commercial banks to short-circuit investment banks is confirmed by the following case studies.

---

80 *Notes de conversations*, historical archives of *Crédit lyonnais*, 8 March 1946.

81 *Ibidem*, 20, 28 August 1945; 10 and 12 September 1945; 9, 15, 19 and 25 October 1945.

82 Several cases can be picked up thus: *Notes de conversations*, historical archives of *Crédit lyonnais*, 26 December 1945 (Saint-Frères bonds). *Paribas* had to retrocede FRF 50 million of Renault bonds, 50m Ugine, and 50m GICEL to *Crédit lyonnais*, *Notes de conversations*, historical archives of *Crédit lyonnais*, 28 May 1957.

83 *Crédit lyonnais* accepted to broker FRF 100 million of SNPA bonds of the *Paribas* share, *Ibidem*, 29 April 1959.

84 See Hubert Bonin, *Les banques françaises dans l'entre-deux-guerres*, Tome I: *L'apogée de l'économie bancaire libérale française* (*1919-1935*), Paris, PLAGE, 2000.

85 *Notes de conversations*, historical archives of *Crédit lyonnais*, 6 February 1959.

86 *Ibidem*, 6 November 1945.

The Esso Standard case

Despite Paribas' support at the birth of Standard Oil's French affiliate Esso Standard in the 1920s, it could not keep a key role in the credit and underwriting pools which went to two deposit banks led by Société générale. It had to content itself to following the lead manager in the credit and issuing league tables. But at a meeting of *Standard française des pétroles*' board in September 1945, its representative Oudot learnt that Société générale intended to deprive it of any actual role because Société générale and Crédit lyonnais wanted to be sole co-lead managers![87] Strident protests and discussions did not prevent Lorain, Société générale's boss, from limiting Paribas to the role of a mere "co-contracting" bank, under the guidance of its two competitors, with an equal share in the tables, but less for the underwriting, especially as Paribas had to retrocede part of its share because it was unable to distribute the entire amount.[88]

Table 10. Banking pools at Esso Standard in 1944-1945 (million francs)

	Break-down of the credit pool, December 1944 (FRF 300 million)	Break-down of the acceptance credit pool, 1945	Break-down of bond issues, 12 November 1945 (FRF 500 million)	
			First draft	Official final break-down
Société générale	50	45	115	135.455
Crédit lyonnais	50	45	115	135.455
Paribas	50	45	80	50
CNEP	50	45	100	84.09
CIC	25	30	40	45
CCF	20	40	30	25
BNCI	5	10	20	0
Morgan	20			
Chase	10			
Guaranty Trust	10			

Source: *Notes de conversations*, historical archives of *Crédit lyonnais*, 23 August and 13 November 1945.

BNCI as a challenger

Banque nationale pour le commerce et l'industrie (BNCI) also tried to revive the traditions of its predecessor, the mixed bank Banque nationale de

87 *Ibidem*, 3 September 1945. The boss of the firm confirmed that "Société générale and *Crédit lyonnais* should keep their privileged position" as lead-managers, ahead of CNEP and Paribas, 9 October 1945.

88 *Ibidem*, 13 November 1945. Paribas retroceded FRF 30 million, 10,455 million to *Crédit lyonnais* and *Société générale* each, and 9,090 million to CNEP.

crédit,[89] in order to challenge the leadership (and even in some fields, the cartel, since the end of the 1920s) of the Big Three. BNCI often proposed better conditions to financial head-managers (more cash to be given to the firm, if it choose the bank as lead manager instead of its historical partners), but deposit banks stipulated that they would not share the buck with it and would let it face the brokerage alone.[90] But BNCI went ahead and sometimes won the contract, mainly for medium-sized firms.[91] It also tried to assert itself in the public firms, arguing of its brokerage power, which it had proven for the State loan Emprunt de la Libération in 1945. It did manage to trouble the big banks – even though it was invited to join a few cartel-like agreements (for instance regarding the conditions of capital increase[92] in 1946) to alleviate market distortions.

b. Paribas' counter-offensive

When *Freins & signaux Westinghouse* chose Paribas[93] as lead manager in 1956, Crédit lyonnais protested because its affiliate UCINA had assumed the role for the previous bonds issues in 1942, 1946 and 1951. But Paribas argued that it had been the lead manager for the capital increase in 1952 and moreover, that UCINA had stolen its role as lead manager for bonds for the issue of 1942 and sparked a fierce debate... Later, Crédit lyonnais tried to push its group ahead of Paribas which held a hegemony on further bond issues by Freins & signaux Westinghouse, because it had engineered the financial restructuration of the firm and expected to be rewarded for its involvement.[94]

89 Hubert Bonin, *La Banque nationale de crédit. Histoire de la quatrième banque de dépôts française en 1913-1932*, Paris, PLAGE, 2002.

90 *Notes de conversations*, historical archives of *Crédit lyonnais*, several cases in November and December 1945.

91 *Ibidem*, 8 December 1945, about Charles Tiberghien textile firm (only FRF 20 million) at the expense of *Crédit du Nord*.

92 *Ibidem*, 9 November 1945. *Crédit lyonnais*, Société générale, CNEP and BNCI agreed on floor conditions for fees, for instance (with a 2.5% standard for underwriting, and another 2.5% for distribution). Another meeting, on 6 December 1946, gathering all the banks, discussed on floor conditions about bonds issues, *Ibidem*, 9 December 1946.

93 *Ibidem*, 19 July 1956.

94 In 1952, "Paribas was persuaded to come to the aid of this American group which held about a third of the French company's capital so as to facilitate its exercising its right of application and it continued to hold the corresponding new shares till very recently. On the other hand, Paribas later played a role in the reorganisation of the capital [...]. We [*Crédit lyonnais*] remarked that the company's previous loans had been managed by UCINA [a common affiliate to *Crédit lyonnais* and CNEP, specialised in middle term loans]. We understood Paribas' situation vis-à-vis the company, but also remarked that in a number of cases, the lead underwritership for capital increase and that for bond issues were not necessarily confided to the same establishment [...]. Paribas felt that after the reorganisation of the affaire, it played an increasingly greater role in the company." *Ibidem*, 24 January 1957.

Some overlapping between corporate banking and investment banking also affected the balance of power. There was jostling for manoeuvring room when SACM (electromechanics) floated a bond issue. Although Crédit lyonnais and BNCI had led the underwriting syndicate in 1952, Paribas tried to convince the firm to broaden its share "in view of the services rendered by our colleague to the company in the Middle East".[95] It succeeded in raising its share from 4.5 to 7 per cent, behind Crédit lyonnais and BNCI (30 instead of 32.5 per cent) and CCF (22 instead of 25 per cent) because its contacts at the firm demanded their bankers to admit such sales talk… The crux of the matter lay there: investment banks used their role in corporate banking abroad and international business as leverage forces to get positive fall-outs in their domestic market. A similar case occurred with Saint-Gobain in 1955 when "certain investment banks, which provided notable services to the company, especially in its foreign operations, had come forward to be included in the lists. They vigorously resumed their offensive".[96] The firm convinced leading deposit banks to grant a few shares of the issue: asking 2 per cent each, they gained 1 per cent, that is a foothold, then a final offensive by Paribas on lead manager Société générale concluded in a triumph with a 2 per cent hold…

When Paribas developed its stake as industrial partner with Poliet & Chausson (cement and materials), it tried to use its position as "financier" to reinforce its ranking as "merchant banker": "Paribas informed us that due to the structural changes in the company's equity, it would henceforth manage the bond issues with Société générale as chief underwriter, and that our establishment [Crédit lyonnais], which had been up till then the contracting party, would henceforth become the retrocessionnaire of the two chief underwriters."[97] This evoked protests from "friend" Crédit lyonnais, which ended up by regaining its rank as co-lead manager. It would thus seem that companionship did not prevent iron-fisting, and some differentiation could be detected because investment banks could profit from their status as capitalist and financial partners of firms to demand a greater role in issues.

3. Investment banks' competitive edge over deposit banks regarding corporate banking

Investment banks fought to regain a competitive edge over their challengers by rebuilding their influence in the domain of domestic growth and modernisation and by refurbishing and sharpening their

95 *Ibidem*, 26 August 1955.

96 *Ibidem*, 22 and 26 October 1955. Paribas got 2%, BUP and BUE each 1%, Worms and *Union des mines* each 0.5%, etc.

97 *Ibidem*, 3 November 1955.

portfolio of financial competences. The actual differentiation came in the financial field, in the very tradition of investment banking – part of the field of "merchant banking". Paribas mobilised the portfolio of skills of its "*départements d'affaires*" or investment banking divisions: "The investment banking divisions now had close ties with the companies in which we have interests, aiding them as much technically as financially."[98] One of them was dedicated to domestic investment banking activities. Louis Bricard (the head of the finance department) and Charles Bouzanquet, his *fondé de pouvoirs* then deputy manager, were (with his deputy François Homolle) the key "Paribas men" for the negotiations with the other banks for domestic financial operations, in connection with the corporate banking department – because each development in credit shares could help developments in the financial pools. Many meetings were held between the counterparts from each bank – and then at the Treasury to fix the issue dates in order to take into account the more important demands of the public sector and the resiliency of the market.

A. *Struggle to be lead manager for the issue of company bonds*

As deposit banks reaped profits from brokerage activities and wielded their mighty influence in that field thanks to their network of outlets and their "*service des titres*" in the big branches, they demanded high ranks and key roles in the issue of bonds. Each one had staked its own privileged positions based on the intimate relationship with this or that firm that it had entertained for decades – here too "history" had to be respected. There ensued an awkward game in which banks recognised each other's respective positions but tried nevertheless to climb up or to broaden the package of securities that they could underwrite or sell. Meanwhile, Paribas and Crédit lyonnais had concluded their 1933 agreement, still active in the 1950s. Both had agreed to share information and even every operation, provided that the historical precedence for each partner was preserved. Even though on a few occasions both banks tried to short-circuit the other, the partnership was on the whole respected – and their records are very helpful in reconstituting banks' *modus operandi*. They also offer clues that the two types of banks shared a similar portfolio of skills for managing bond issues, brokerages and even for the guarantee syndicates. Differences were found in the more traditional and important role played by investment banks in guarantee syndicates and in their ability to be lead managers more frequently.

[98] Paribas annual report, 27 May 1948.

History explains why Paribas was lead manager for the issue of bonds at CSF[99] and BULL,[100] a key broker for the account of steel companies (Forges & aciéries du Nord & de l'EST-FANE), of metallurgy, mechanics, engineering and electrical engineering (Ateliers de construction Schwartz-Hautmont, Batignolles-Châtillon,[101] Les exploitations électriques et industrielles, Fives-Lille),[102] electrical and electronic equipment (LMT, Compagnie de signaux & d'entreprises électriques),[103] oil firms (SNPA-Société nationale des pétroles d'Aquitaine,[104] SN-MAREP),[105] overseas firms (Compagnie marseillaise de Madagascar),[106] and Hachette, a long-term partner. Its long term partnership with Citroën also gave it first rank.[107]

As regards leadership, subtle ways were used to assert its competitive edge over deposit banks. For the Fives-Lille[108] bonds issue in 1955, Paribas was "co-contracting lead-manager" with CCF and Crédit lyonnais, but sole "negotiator". The three leaders received a full third of the syndicate, and only afterwards "retroceded" part of their chunk to other deposit banks. Paribas ended up keeping only 10 per cent, but enjoyed a substantial share of the 5.5 per cent fees beforehand. But elsewhere, it was Crédit lyonnais which became the negotiator, which shows that no "difference of nature" actually separated deposit banks from investment banks in the field of merchant banking, but only respective positions and strongholds – and both (with Crédit lyonnais's representative as deputy chairman) were members of the board of SICOVAM, the collective professional institution managing the clearing of securities.[109] At

99 Report of the board of Paribas, 18 July 1957 – Paribas tackled FRF 2,353 million against a total amount of 4,814 million.

100 With a part of 17.3% in 1959, report of the board of Paribas, 21 May 1959.

101 *Paribas* was the lead manager in 1955, *Notes de conversations*, historical archives of *Crédit lyonnais*, 30 June 1955.

102 *Ibidem*, 2 July 1958.

103 Paribas annual report, 27 May 1948, where a little list is thus supplied.

104 With 11.88%, report of the board of Paribas, 22 May 1958, or 11.75% for another issuing, *ibidem*, 21 May 1959 and *Notes de conversations*, historical archives of *Crédit lyonnais*, 107 May 1958. The four big deposit banks got 64 per cent, whilst Paribas and BUP got 18 per cent.

105 With 35.75%, report of the board of Paribas, 22 May 1958.

106 *Notes de conversations*, historical archives of *Crédit lyonnais*, 30 April 1946, for a bond issue.

107 *Ibidem*, 13 January 1955.

108 *Ibidem*, 19 November 1955. Finally, *Société générale* got 24.30%, CNEP 4%, BNCI 4.60%, *Crédit du Nord* 9.70%, whilst co-leaders kept 18.30% (CCF) and 28.90% (*Crédit lyonnais*).

109 *Société interprofessionnelle pour la compensation des valeurs mobilières* had been set up in 1950; Louis Bricard (Paribas) and Robert d'Eichthal (Mirabaud), then Frédéric Cruse (Neuflize-Schlumberger) represented investment banks on the board in the mid-1950s.

Bull, Paribas and Crédit lyonnais were co-lead managers of the guarantee syndicate[110] in 1956, which allowed Paribas to obtain 19.2 per cent of the brokerage (38.4 per cent for Crédit lyonnais), but Paribas had to admit Crédit lyonnais as its partner, because of the need to get access to a large brokerage network.

B. Struggle for position as lead manager for the increases in company capital

A similar balance of power existed for capital increases. Though they were a specialty of investment banks, deposit banks fought to increase their share of the fees. Thus, on numerous occasions, Paribas had to be content with meagre percentages[111] or with a weaker role in the syndicate.[112] On the other hand, Paribas' historical connection with steel companies in the northern region explains its preeminent role there (often as "*centralisateur*") and lead or co-lead manager of the syndicates. It had godfathered *Forges & aciéries du Nord & de l'Est* in the interwar period, which promoted it as the lead manager of its successor (after mergers) Usinor from the 1950s[113] – but not for the bond issues, where CNEP led operations.[114] Similarly it led or co-led operations in the oil sector, which it had sponsored since the 1920s (especially its close customer Esso Standard (the subsidiary of US Standard Oil),[115] SNPA,[116] FORENCO[117] AND SN MAREP),[118] in various fields of equipment goods[119] and at Bull[120] which it had sponsored since its inception.

Only a comprehensive survey of financial operations can establish the whole range of Paribas' influence and achievements. The result would not be very different from our analysis. The balance of power between

110 *Notes de conversations*, historical archives of *Crédit lyonnais*, 28 February 1956.

111 With for example 5.25% at Saint-Gobain, report of the board of Paribas, 10 January 1957.

112 With 39.4% at Neyrpic (electro-engineering), report of the board of Paribas, 10 January 1957.

113 As for Usinor's capital increase in 1957, with "*Paribas centralisateur de l'opération*", report of the board of Paribas, 7 November 1957.

114 *Notes de conversations*, historical archives of *Crédit lyonnais*, 11 May 1955.

115 For Esso Standard's increase of capital in 1958, Paribas was the lead manageur and the centralisateur, report of the board of Paribas, 18 September 1959.

116 Report of the board of Paribas, 16 January 1958 and 20 November 1958. See Emmanuel Terré & Alain Beltran, *Elf Aquitaine, des origines à 1989*, Paris, Fayard, 1998.

117 *Compagnie nouvelle de forages pétroliers*, report of the board of Paribas, 17 April 1958.

118 Report of the board of Paribas, 19 February 1959 (with 44.25% of the operation).

119 Delattre & Frouard, report of the board of Paribas, 17 April 1958;

120 Report of the board of Paribas, 22 May 1958 and 19 February 1959. Paribas got 64% of the shares issued in 1955, against *Crédit lyonnais* 27% and BNCI 9%, *Notes de conversations*, historical archives of *Crédit lyonnais*, February 1955.

banks was not actually "contested", their room for manoeuvre was not flexible because fixed positions were admitted by the community of banking business. Where investment banks were strong before WWII, they kept their shared strongholds: "The lists of equity increase guarantors are rather limited. They depend greatly on the past, and admitting new entries remains a dicey proposition."[121]

BUP was the French lead manager (with 21 per cent of the guarantee pool of Petrofina belge in 1950 because of its close connections to the SGB group. At *Compagnie française des pétroles*, investment banks led the moves because they had been its godfather since its inception: both BUP and Paribas were lead-managers for the equity increases in 1946 (with 26.4 per cent each) and in 1947 (to the tune of FRF 5.2 billion, with 24.8 per cent each). Conversely, at Bergougnan (rubber products), Paribas and BUP lagged (with 5.715 per cent each) far behind lead manager Crédit lyonnais (20 per cent) and the other big deposit banks (11.428 per cent each for Société générale, CNEP and BNCI)[122] because of the influence of Lyon over close Auvergne. At Vallourec (steel pipes), BUP and Société générale led operations because they had sponsored the merger of several companies to form this one during the inter-war period.[123]

C. Changes because of mergers

Structural changes could shake up respective positions, as was the case when Simca absorbed Ford France in 1955: whereas the investment banks Paribas and UEIF were its lead-managers for capital increases, they had to admit deposit bank BNCI because it was the lead-manager at Ford.[124] UEIF had to share power with BNCI for bonds issues, before also admitting the Crédit lyonnais.[125] On the other hand, whereas that latter had been the Unic's (trucks) house bank, it had to allow *Paribas* as lead manager for financial operations because the latter was the lead manager at Simca, which owned half of Unic.[126] When the two equipment engineering companies Fives-Lille and Cail merged in 1958, negotiations had to recognise the leading role played by Paribas for the first and of BUP for the second. Though both became co-lead managers, the intimacy between the two

[121] Message of *Crédit lyonnais* to Neuflize, 22 February 1955, *Notes de conversations*, historical archives of *Crédit lyonnais*.

[122] *Ibidem*, 26 January 1955.

[123] *Ibidem*, 3 April 1958. BUP had absorbed merchant bank Mirabaud in 1953, which had godfathered Vallourec.

[124] *Ibidem*, 22 March and 19 July 1956. Lazard was also invited because of its ability to lodge bonds in the US.

[125] *Ibidem*, 10 December 1958.

[126] *Ibidem*, 15 June 1956.

former companies and Crédit lyonnais led the latter to demand co-lead managership.[127] Smart calculations established an average of all banks' ranking for credits on one hand and strong capital increase on the other, balancing the weight of each amalgamated firm (77.6 per cent and 22.4 per cent) – which would lead to 25.20 per cent each for Paribas and Crédit lyonnais, 15 per cent to CCF and 10 per cent to BUP. This case study confirms our view that deposit banks' corporate banking finance departments were no different from those of investment banks: "We [Crédit lyonnais] would like to review with Mr. Bricard [Paribas] the sharing of the allocations between our two establishments regarding the financial operations, the equity increases and bond issues of the new company which can be considered as our joint creation. We think that a strict equality between our establishments in regard to this affaire should translate itself in the following manner: for the equity increases and the bond issues, the negotiations with the company should be conducted jointly by Paribas and Crédit lyonnais. The book-keeping could be taken up by Paribas for the equity increases and by Crédit lyonnais for the bond issue"[128] – even if Reyre, Paribas CEO, contended that the bigger size of Fives-Lille should push Paribas ahead of Crédit lyonnais for the equity increases. "In our view [Crédit lyonnais], the relative weight of the two venerable businesses should in no way influence the allocations and the profits, and our proposals regarding this seem to us to be equitable and in conformity with the idea of equality between our establishments and which has remained the guiding principle all through our negotiations regarding the coming together of the two companies."[129] Partners/contenders had to seize every opportunity to change the balance of power and the subtle breakdown of rankings in issue pools and investment banks did not escape that game.

D. Investment banks as merchant bankers

A practical way of asserting their position as the lead managers was to engineer the floatation of a company which they had sponsored for long. That is exactly what Paribas did with equipment goods, either mechanical (Stein & Roubaix[130] or *Forges & aciéries du Nord & de l'Est*-FANE,[131] then Usinor[132] in 1957), electro-mechanical (*Société anonyme de*

[127] *Ibidem*, 18 April 1958 and 2 July 1958.

[128] *Ibidem*, 2 July 1958.

[129] *Ibidem*, 2 July 1958.

[130] Report of the board of Paribas, 18 June 1959.

[131] *Paribas* annual report, 27 May 1948.

[132] *Paribas* annual report, 22 May 1958. See Éric Godelier, *De la stratégie locale à la stratégie globale: la formation d'une identité de groupe. Usinor, 1948-1986*, Paris, EHESS, 1995.

télécommunications),[133] new technologies (*Technicolor*),[134] or oil equipment (Forenco).[135] Bup also underwrote a few corporate floatations[136] (*Presses de la Cité*, *Soudure électrique Languepin*, Clin Byla (pharmaceutics) in 1956, *Glacières de Paris* and Meci-*Matériel électrique de contrôle industriel* in 1958, and Petersen (sea transit) in 1960. Such "blue angel" activity fuelled the life of the property assets management (*portefeuille titres*): "The increase in the share portfolio was due, in large part, to investments in the equity increases of companies in which we already had interests, and to a lesser extent, to our participation in the equity of newly created companies."[137] But family businesses were sometimes reluctant to open part of their equity to an investment bank, because they feared that would open the gates to some imperialist immixing:[138] bankers had to tread slowly and tactfully.

At the same time, the entry of an investment bank in the capital of a company opened doors to a whole range of banking and finance services which could win over the company's mid-term relations from the traditional deposit banks. Bup was a constant partner of med-sized firms like Clause (seeds) and helped increase its equity in 1946 and 1949, lending money to the family to allow it to keep control of the capital. Bup likewise accompanied a handful of other companies at the turn of the 1950s when they fought to adapt their financial ground to rapid growth: *L'Entrepôt de Grenelle*, Primistères, Blachère (trade houses), Chausson (mechanics, with Crédit lyonnais as lead manager of the brokerage pool), Morane-Saulnier (aerospace), Sirey (publishing), *Papeteries de Rives*, Campenon-Bernard (public works, this stake was its third largest asset in its property portfolio[139] in 1948), etc.[140] When Paribas purchased a stake in *Papeteries de La Chapelle*,[141] it became its financial engineer and short-circuited Crédit lyonnais, its commercial banker, which had drawn up the outlines of a program of reorganisation for the paper manufacturer in December 1955 (mid-term loan, issue of bonds, then of shares).

[133] *Paribas* annual report, 27 May 1948.

[134] *Ibidem*, 12 May 1955.

[135] Report of the board of Paribas, 19 June 1958.

[136] Hubert Bonin, *La Banque de l'union parisienne*, *op. cit.*, p. 425.

[137] *Paribas* annual report, 28 May 1953.

[138] "He would like to avoid at all costs having to take recourse to the services of an investment bank which would very likely hold an important minority bloc and could come in his way", told the head of Rivoire & Carret (food pasta) to *Crédit lyonnais*, *Notes de conversations*, historical archives of *Crédit lyonnais*, 14 March 1957.

[139] Bup records, 1947-1953, historical archives of Banque de France.

[140] Hubert Bonin, *La Banque de l'union parisienne*, *op. cit.*, pp. 365-366.

[141] *Notes de conversations*, historical archives of *Crédit lyonnais*, 10 January 1957.

Tensions escalated between the two ("friendly") banks...[142] till a gentlemen's agreement was reached. A similar situation arose with Société générale when Paribas became a share- and stake-holder at CENPA (paper) and Poliet & Chausson (cement). A dominant role in "merchant banking" helped to get a key role in investment banking (for security issues, rank of "negotiator" with the other banks and co-lead manager) and in corporate banking (with an increased part within the credit pool) – even though ultimately investment banks' share in the brokerage pool lagged behind that of deposit banks.[143]

The difference lay in investment banks' bargaining power – they could pretend playing a much bigger game thanks to their power of holding stakes in companies and using that as a lever to into corporate and investment banking. That was the case about SN MAREP (oil equipment) when Paribas tried to reap profit from its position as key stakeholder to broaden its interventions from finance to credit, instead of leaving such activity to the other partner of the firm, Crédit lyonnais. That latter had to intervene harshly and contested such move – which led to the admission of an "error" by Paribas and the confirmation of the previous agreements: "It was agreed that Crédit lyonnais, which was the oldest investment bank, would remain the lead manager in matters regarding credit, especially mid-term credit. As for the financial operations, the two of us agreed to be co-lead managers, with Paribas ensuring the book-keeping for shares operations while we fulfiled a similar role as regards bond loans."[144] Such operations on equity and floatation were, in the short term, worthwhile because they showed, to some degree,

142 "Mr. Bricard [Paribas] observed that Paribas had invested in the capital of the company and further, that it would be responsible for introducing its shares at the Paris Stock Exchange. It is because Paribas had injected funds in the company on the occasion of its increase of capital stock that it could ask for a part in the mid-term credit for which our establishment [*Crédit lyonnais*] is the chief underwriter [...]. For the past ten years we have supported the company through some difficult times and it is painful to see Paribas putting at risk, by its intervention, financial projects which we helped set up, while at the same time attribute to itself the role of chief underwriter for a bond loan for which we had already approached the company earlier. Mr. Bricard understands our position, but he has pointed out that it is at the request [of the chairman] himself that he approached our establishment regarding the loan floatation. We have not insisted upon any modification of our relationship concerning this issue and by consequence, we have accepted the role of co-chief underwriter offered to us", *Notes de conversations*, historical archives of *Crédit lyonnais*, 14 June 1956.

143 For the 1956 bonds issuing of *Papeteries de La Chapelle*, *Paribas* got 16% and BUP 4%, whilst deposit banks got 30% (*Crédit lyonnais*), 20% (*Société générale*), and 15% (BNCI and CIC), because an ultimate negotiation allowed Paribas to got 1 per cent more than BNCI and CIC , reducing BUP from 5 to 4 per cent. *Ibidem*, 14 June 1956.

144 *Ibidem*, 26 January 1959.

investment banks' competitive edge and gave them room to manoeuvre as they could use their specific skills to negotiate bigger chunks of financial operations, as a lever to broaden their scope in investment banking beyond mere corporate banking.

4. Investment banks as ground-breakers: Pioneering new products

Such a strategy needed to be followed more strongly if the big investment banks wished to retain their positions among French banking business when competition intensified after WWII. First, Bup absorbed Mirabaud and resumed its offensives which it had been forced to halt in the 1930s due to major systemic difficulties. Second, the Union européenne industrielle et financière-Ueif began to diversify its clientele: it had been the house bank of the Schneider group (steel, mechanics and electrical engineering), but it extended its relationship, even merging with the other bank of the group, Banque des pays du Nord, in 1943 and choosing the status of a *banque d'affaires* in 1946. Third, Lazard itself, prone to lean management and merchant banking, played a bigger role in international operations. Even Rothschild re-emerged from its lethargy and launched a few targeted offensives (on overseas fields, mainly). Last, but not least, big deposit banks sharpened their corporate banking department when the shock of their nationalisation wore off and the Parisian market convinced itself that they were still real banks deprived of any genuine immixing with the State into their day-to-day management. Crédit lyonnais struggled to keep its edge over its brilliant seconds and even over "dissenter" Bnci, which had launched a major offensive to shake the position of its well-off competitor. Investment banks revived their tradition of groundbreaking innovation and initiatives: they had to set up new products, new firms, to prospect new fields.

Such a pioneering process was the only way to get a direct and broad access to a rejuvenated and larger clientele, because acting as creators and partners of a large array of firms opened doors to privileged financial and even banking business with them, for about a dozen years. The second purpose was to mobilise the "sleeping" funds with institutional investors (even nationalised ones) and the assets available at deposit banks (nationalised ones also) to fuel cash into a collective or "co-operative" way of modernising and developing the Parisian market through the financing of new forms of "private" projects in finance, real estate or specialised credit, in parallel with the public circuits of the Treasury, of specialised public financial institutions and of the "Plan". All in all, public authorities increasingly favoured such a renewal of private initiative because leftists and moderates were well aware that France had to favour a model of "mixed economy" as the State could not finance and tackle every sector of growth. Investment bankers also worked with the Treasury to formulate the day-to-day changes in law which the engineering of new forms of financing and banking demanded: a community of public/private interests thus took shape from the 1950s in the name of expansion and renewal. Investment bankers were not "dissenters" at all, even if they acted on the margins of the well-established ways of practicing classical banking: they were path-breakers and pioneers.

A. *Pioneering for investment funds*

Away from the larger steps of the 1960s-1980s, financiers and bankers commenced to think of financial vehicles which could collectively manage assets brought by institutional investors, as a way of introducing some kind of "trusts" in France – a concept that had developed in the City (where laws had authorised "trusts" as early as 1887-1888, either independent or linked with banks, like at Barclays in 1910) or in the US (where 2,561 "trusts" already existed in 1924, with trust departments set up within US banks). Some kind of a "model" had been established in 1946 with the *Société nationale d'investissement*, patronised by the authorities (Acts of 2 December 1945 and 30 June 1952), which welcomed investments from the *Compagnie du canal de Suez*'s Treasury.[145] They hoped to spur the revitalisation of the Parisian market after the shock of nationalisations and to foster instruments able to subscribe to bonds issued by the nationalised utilities.

Those investment banks which were able to offer such financial vehicles could take profit from brokering their shares, from selling securities which they needed to dispose off when they had acted as members of issuing syndicates as well as indirectly with the possibility to lodge their part of the stakes in companies which had helped them to be their strategic partner. Such instruments could also receive funds repatriated from abroad when perspectives of decolonisation and nationalisation (or expropriations) enticed wealthy investors to reorient their assets from the colonial empire to Paris. Such "closed" (because unlisted till the mid-1960s) funds could not but strengthen the financial might of investment banks and their influence over investors and stock markets in Paris and abroad.

Paribas seized the opportunity offered by the Act of 1952 to launch two investment funds, *Compagnie d'investissement et de placement* (CIP), and *Société de placements sélectionnés en France et à l'étranger* (SPS): "Your establishment, which has contributed actively in their creation, will continue

145 See Hubert Bonin, *History of the Suez Canal Company, 1858-1960. Between Controversy and Utility*, Geneva, Droz, 2010.

to play an important role in their management."[146] The trend was intensified at the end of the 1950s when *Paribas* engineered[147] the *Compagnie d'investissement en France et à l'étranger* and the *Compagnie générale d'investissement* – floated on the stock market[148] in 1958. In both cases, it brought them a few lines of its own stakes in companies which it had patronised, such as the Compagnie française des pétroles, etc.[149] A few months later, when the Compagnie française des câbles télégraphiques refocused on its core industry and the latter was split into an autonomous affiliate, Paribas kept the Cfct's participations in its subsidiaries under the umbrella of Cfct, thus transforming it into an investment fund rich with numerous stakes brought by Paribas.[150] As a minority stake-holder, Paribas also took part in a few other funds like *L'Union d'investissements.*[151] Meanwhile, Rothschild also mobilised its experience in managing its own family of investments funds (*Compagnie du Nord*, Paris-Orléans, PLM) to set up, in 1953, an investment fund capable of attracting of life-insurance company assets, *Société d'investissements du Nord.*[152]

Towards the end of our study period, investment banks were busy meeting State authorities to introduce mutual funds in Paris (*fonds communs de placement*, under a Act of 28 December 1957),[153] but the plans were scuttled by deposit banks which argued that such a move could hinder the brokerage of State treasury bonds to middle class investors. Differences can be seen in the attitudes: pioneers believe in the market's resiliency stimulated by innovative products, whereas more conservative stances see a "closed-shop" market missing out on the growth in living standards and the savings due to the success of the *Reconstruction* (1945-1952) and of the so-called *Trente Glorieuses* (1945-1975, or a long-term period of steady growth).

146 *Paribas* annual report for 1952, 23 May 1953.

147 Report from the Paribas board, 21 February 1957.

148 *Ibidem*, 19 June 1958.

149 Paribas brought to *Compagnie générale d'investissement* stakes in *Compagnie française des pétroles*, CSF, Citroën, *Engrais & produits chimiques*, and BPEC, report from the Paribas board, 21 February 1957.

150 Report from the Paribas board, 7 November 1957. Paribas brought stakes (equities in *Compagnie française des pétroles*, Norsk Hydro, Hachette, Saint-Gobain, *Banque ottomane*, *Compagnie générale industrielle*, ONA, Poliet & Chausson, Citroën, Bull, SNPA, *Banque nationale du Mexique*, BFIAS-Sudaméris, *Banque franco-chinoise*, etc.) for an amount of FRF 3,129 million, thus added to assets of 871 million to constitute a holding of FRF 4 billion.

151 It joined the increase of equity from FRF 750 to 3,000 million by bringing an amount of securities of 100 million, report from the Paribas board, 21 May 1959.

152 Robert Jablon, *op. cit.*, pp. 106-109.

153 *Notes de conversations*, historical archives of *Crédit lyonnais*, 24 December 1958.

B. Pioneers of real estate schemes

Like in the other West-European countries, French growth depended on the revival of the building industry.[154] In parallel with a few imaginative "professionals" from the real estate and building industries (and sometimes competing with them), investment banks took part in the general rejuvenation of the Parisian market regarding financing real estate development. Re-igniting the innovative spirit which, in the inter-war period, had led to the establishment of a handful of real estate finance companies to build middle classe housing (in Paris: RIVP-*Régie immobilière de la Ville de Paris*, chaired by Bédier) and which had been suspended by the economic slump and the War, new "financial" products were set up through co-operative vehicles drawing institutional investors and bankers to share risks and knowledge. Paribas was a pioneer in that field with its dedicated department and team of specialists headed by Bédier.[155] Reports on their initiatives[156] date back to 1955 regarding housing for American soldiers (because of NATO) and the middle class, commercial property development (when commercial centres appeared) and employee housing (Renault, *Le Printemps*, etc.). Here too it was challenged by BUP which fought to gain a foothold on these new outlets.

The scheme was simple: while national and local public authorities invested massively in social housing, private institutions had to deal with the demand for middle class collective housing, spurred by the growth in living standards and a housing loan scheme sponsored by the State (*Crédit foncier de France*). New financial vehicles, acting as real estate developers and building companies came together to purchase and develop plots, either within Paris (replacing plants or warehouses) or in the suburbs. Bank profits rose as loans were issued by these co-operative real estate developers as treasury availabilities were managed because the interlocked partners of investment banks, especially among insurance companies, could be invited to purchase shares of the financial vehicles and later, of the buildings themselves to invest part of their reserves. A thorough "system" was therefore to ripen, and the banks capable of taking the lead would multiply cash flows, fees and ultimately, profits. On its side, Paribas associated itself with the semi-public bank Crédit foncier to create SACI-*Société auxiliaire de construction immobilière*, which gained

---

154 See Sabine Effosse, *L'invention du logement aidé en France. L'immobilier au temps des Trente Glorieuses*, Paris, Comité pour l'histoire économique et financière de la France, 2003.

155 The team comprised first of Netter, CEO of OTH, and of Martin, boss of the industry and property division, and, underneath, of Maurice, Coiffard, Coudry and Schmidt, before being extended at the turn of the 1960s.

156 *Notes de conversations*, historical archives of *Crédit lyonnais*, 22 April 1955.

momentum in the mid-1950s to become a key actor in the industry for the next several decades: handling projects for 3,000 flats as early as 1959. Paribas engineered the *Groupement d'études immobilières* by bringing together sixteen members[157] (insurance companies) who wanted to invest their assets in its programs.

Lastly (for our period of study), when the State and the business circles agreed to draw a new type of investment company dedicated to real estate which would benefit from tax exemptions, the *société immobilière d'investissements conventionnée* (SIIC or SII), investment banks began to federate their own group of companies, managed by a mother company and equipped with a portfolio of engineering and finance skills. Though competitors were to be found among wealth management specialists, real estate (*Immobilière Constructions de Paris*, within the André Weill group) and building groups, investment banks were among the earliest pioneers in that field, with Paribas launching the *Union immobilière de France*[158] in January 1959, in competition with the Banque de l'Indochine group[159] and with the BUP group (*Compagnie française pour le financement de la construction*, gathering Crédit foncier, *Groupement foncier français*,[160] several insurance companies, Neuflize).[161] Commercial banks only followed with credit because their legal and practical way of life prevented them from initiating any such move: "We do not think that, in the circumstances, the deposit banks could play the leading role."[162] The State Treasury agreed with such a stance,[163] confirmed by a meeting of deposit banks[164] when they decided to join projects without competing against each other and following a passive *modus operandi*. Differentiation prevailed in favour of investment banks, structuring groups of direct and indirect investors upstream and pools of investment and commercial banks to fuel

---

157 *Ibidem*, 5 May 1955.

158 *Ibidem*, 19 December 1958. Paribas invested by itself FRF 100 million, like is partners among banks (*Crédit foncier*, *Sous-Comptoir des entrepreneurs*, *Crédit lyonnais*) or insurers (*Nationale-Vie*, *Nationale RD*, *Assurances générales*, *Mutuelle française-Vie*, *Urbaine-Vie*, *L'Urbaine & La Seine*, *La Sequanaise*, *La Populaire-Vie* – with *Vie nouvelle* providing 50m). But affiliates of Paribas also were involved (UCB and CFEC with 25 million each), thus giving Paribas the second rank (150m) with 7.5% of the FRF 2,000 million equity, behind the *Crédit foncier* group (200 million).

159 *Notes de conversations*, historical archives of *Crédit lyonnais*, 30 July 1958.

160 *Groupement foncier français* was itself set up by insurance companies, either acting in direct, or following investment banks, *Notes de conversations*, historical archives of *Crédit lyonnais*, 11 December 1958.

161 *Notes de conversations*, historical archives of *Crédit lyonnais*, 13 November 1958.

162 *Ibidem*, 10 November 1958.

163 *Ibidem*.

164 *Ibidem*, 1st December 1958.

loans downstream. Commercial banks intervened for credit pools, for instance at *Immobilière Constructions de Paris*, where Crédit lyonnais and Société générale were lead-managers for its SII Cofimeg.[165]

At the same time, Paribas saw the opportunities opened by social housing, because Social-Christian private employers began to invest a percentage of their wage bill into housing for their employees, before all firms had to by law (1953, through what was called "*1% logement patronal*", as one per cent of the mass of wages had to be earmarked by firms to social housing for their employees). A large majority chose to orient this cash towards collective institutions, which earmarked the amounts to real estate development all over the country. Paribas' team quickly set up its engineering affiliate, *Omnium technique de l'habitation* (OTH), as early as 1947 to bring together building companies and employers' institutions. And the rebirth of RIVP-*Régie immobilière de la Ville de Paris* in the mid-1950s added momentum to that trend as both Paribas and BUP were its sponsors. BUP also jumped on the property train and set up its own handful of dedicated affiliates: the *Union parisienne pour le logement* for social housing and, in 1955, a group of centrally managed real estate companies (by COGISA-*Compagnie générale immobilière*, SOPADOG, and *Société auxiliaire de gestion & d'administration*) but adapted to each housing program, with about 2,300 flats being delivered in the second half of the 1950s and a major part invested in building a commercial centre surrounded by apartments at the centre of Rueil (west of Paris).[166]

Paribas had an entire range of financial tools at its fingers in every segment of the real estate market: "The industrial department has pursued, with the help of specialised subsidiaries such as the *Omnium technique de l'habitation* and the *Société auxiliaire de construction immobilière*, the study and realisation of several major real estate transactions: construction of buildings for public bodies and large industrial organisations, living quarters for company personnel, owner-occupier dealings, commercial or mixed construction projects, ownership of smallholdings."[167] And investment banks were happy to practice commercial banking with all these companies, either directly or, more often, indirectly through real estate companies (*sociétés civiles immobilières*) set up for each project which consumed mid-term loans pending the sale of the flats (to individual investors) or of the entire building (to insurance companies).[168]

---

165 *Ibidem*, 1960.

166 Hubert Bonin, *La Banque de l'union parisienne*, *op. cit.*, pp. 440-443.

167 *Paribas* annual report for 1952, 23 May 1953.

168 See for example report from the Paribas board, 7 November 1957, or 18 September 1958 – when the credit line to the SACI group reached FRF 927 million.

Investment banks also competed for city equipment, car garages in Paris – Bup and Paribas fought one another in that field[169] – or the emerging commercial centres hosting the first supermarkets.

C. Pioneers of specialised credit schemes

In France, investment banks played a significant role in the spread of "specialised credit", that is, credit given for specific, individual cases. No doubt credit for car purchases had already been introduced in the interwar period by Citroën and Lazard through Sovac, which saw a strong growth after WWII and commercial banks had developed mid-term credit for their corporate clients through their affiliates (Ucina for Crédit lyonnais and Cnep, etc.)[170] to short-circuit their liquidity rules. But the rapid growth of the business and household equipment market in the 1950s paved the way for new initiatives from bankers. Deposit banks were not able to assume such risks – it was only in the 1960s that they intervened directly in some segments of that field – and the differences advantaged investment banks. But two well-known "dissenters" pioneered these new credit products and sketched the outline of future investment banking groups. On one side, Jacques de Fouchier had left public administration to build (helped by a dozen of high level managers)[171] a big group of little banks oriented towards specialised credit, first for the leasing of equipment (Ufb, after the Act of 1951 had stipulated that these goods could serve as pledges for loans), second, for lending to real estate developers or families investing in their homes (Cfec-*Compagnie française d'épargne et de crédit* in 1954, Ucb-*Union pour le crédit au bâtiment*) and third, for the purchase consumer goods (Cetelem in 1953).[172]

Because these pioneering banks had no cash, they needed an increasingly extended refinancing from banks. Paribas and Bup set up pools of commercial banks under their guidance and guarantee (thus earning fees and thick layers of blocks of securities within the pools). Till the 1960s, these specialised banks did not have their own resources (deposits or bonds), and had to use the pools to finance their rapid growth, acting almost as "*établissements de place*" or "co-operatives supported by the community of Paris banks", first because this latter delayed understanding the prospects of such new "products" and relied on the former to open

[169] *Notes de conversations*, historical archives of *Crédit lyonnais*, 12 June 1956.

[170] Hubert Bonin, *Les banques françaises dans l'entre-deux-guerres*, Tome II: *Les banques & les entreprises en France dans l'entre-deux-guerres (1919-1935)*, Paris, Plage, 2000.

[171] Jacques de Fouchier, *La banque et la vie*, Paris, Odile Jacob, 1989, p. 71.

[172] *De la 4CV à la video. Cetelem, 1953-1983, ces trente années qui ont changé notre vie*, Paris, Communica international, 1983.

up the paths of innovation. Only investment banks could take the risk of setting up the pools of financing at first because their balance sheet supplied them with first-hand counterparts in case of failure[173] and because they were used to engineering and managing banking pools earmarked for fresh development along with formulas of risk syndication (*syndication des risques*), which explains the key role assumed by Paribas and BUP in the refinancing pools,[174] BUP bearing 13.5 per cent of UCB's pool of FRF 800m for instance.

At the same time, Jack Francès engineered a competing group of specialised banks for housing and real estate (Immobilia, then Banque de La Hénin) and consumer goods (Sofinco).[175] This pioneer had first levied cash by purchasing an array of little investment funds left behind by nationalised collieries or utilities and managing available assets, then by taking control of a small investment bank, Banque de l'union des mines, by being sponsored by Banque de l'Indochine – a colonial bank which had begun to redeploy its assets from Indochina to France after WWII – and finally, at the end of our period of study, by Compagnie financière de Suez[176] after it had lost its canal and embarked upon a financial career. But his group also called for refinancing at deposit banks. Both Fouchier and Francès were pioneering junior investment bankers without their own investment bank: they were investment bankers-in-the-making. They ended up presiding over investment banks, the former heading Paribas, the latter Banque de Suez & de l'Union des mines-BSUM.

The history of investment banks thus consists of these developments: a new layer of investment bankers took shape, promising a brilliant future; established investment banks headed the refinancing pools of the entire banking community because they brought their prestige, guarantee and

---

[173] "I only came to understand later, as and when I began exploring the large niches left in quasi-neglect by the French banks, the far-off origins and the recent vicissitudes which could explain their tendency towards archaism, self-satisfaction and rigidity. But there was no need for long reflection to discern the signal opportunity offered by the combination of a still private sector and a general climate steeped in governmental inhibitions to novices of my type. I had the opportunity to catch the general outlines at my very first conversations with my future partners. It was almost immediately clear that while my projects – and I myself – evoked sympathy, or even simply the desire to remain close to a promising young man, not one of them wanted to risk on their own to be at my side. The stating of modest claims to begin with, and – to speak in the language that I would soon learn – the syndication of the risks I was about to ask them to take, were the two conditions required in order to have any chance of their following me." Jacques de Fouchier, *La banque et la vie*, Paris, Odile Jacob, 1989, p. 38.

[174] See Hubert Bonin, *La Banque de l'union parisienne*, *op. cit.*, pp. 377-378.

[175] Catherine Malaval, *Sofinco, 1951-2001. Les 50 années qui ont changé la France*, Paris, Creapress, 2001.

[176] Hubert Bonin, *Suez. Du canal à la finance (1858-1987)*, Paris, Economica, 1987.

creditworthiness to fuel trust towards new types of credits which were not yet seen positively on the Parisian market. Bankers (and insurance companies, which also belonged to the refinancing pools) lacked enough legal guarantees till a succession of laws fixed these new types of loans in the 1950s-1960s. They were concerned by the fragility of borrowers, on whom very few pledges were available – a car, pieces of furniture, a TV set, a flat, etc. Scoring systems had not yet been developed and pioneering bankers bet on the "clearing" between borrowers and on their actual solvency to avoid impairing big provisions or losses, especially as they could reap the benefit of high interest rates. The "prehistory" of specialised credit thus depended mainly on two pioneering investment bankers (Fouchier and Francès) and on Lazard, and, for refinancing, on the key sponsoring role assumed by the investment banks Paribas and BUP, while deposit banks followed them within refinancing pools – which provides further clues of differentiation.

Paribas' role reached its zenith with the creation of the holding company, *Compagnie bancaire*,[177] in July 1959 to crown the entire range of Fouchier's banks.[178] It commenced buying back its affiliates' equity[179] and managing its own pool of credits to be refinanced: a general pool (FRF 1,200 million) was thus set up, complementing the 1,200 million pool dedicated to UCB and the various pools for (rediscountable or not) credits oriented towards each specialised subsidiary.[180] Totally, about five billion francs' worth of operations were authorised in 1960, which shows the extent of the "revolution" that had taken place in only a few years and which opened the doors for the listing of Compagnie bancaire on the stock market[181] in 1960.

This survey shows that investment banks were pioneers in conceiving and engineering new types of financial and banking actors on the Parisian market. Sometimes they were not really "pioneers" because they just followed the real pioneers such as Fouchier and Francès, nor did they have a monopoly on pioneering because a few financiers had acted independently (like the Weil group in property finance or Lazard who launched credit for car purchasing (SOVAC)). But they were often

177 Report from the Paribas board, 15 July 1959.

178 *Aide-mémoire exposant les justifications et modalités de la constitution de la Compagnie bancaire*, 15 April 1959, multigraphied note, historical archives of *Paribas*.

179 Paribas brought about one-fifth of its stakes in the affiliates of *Compagnie bancaire* (for an amount of FRF 359 million), report from the Paribas board, and then subscribed to the increase of equity, 21 May 1959.

180 Report from the Paribas board, 4 December 1959, 1st April 1960 or 2 June 1960.

181 *Ibidem*, 23 September 1960 (with a capital of FRF 16 million, issued from the consolidation of reserves, and with an increase in equity to FRF 41m in July 1961 – under the lead management of Paribas and *Crédit lyonnais*).

either pioneers or at least groundbreakers because they godfathered, lead-managed, and co-financed pioneering property and credit companies, and their very presence and role as "pioneering leaders" fostered the degree of trust that deposit banks and insurance companies needed at that time of laying the groundwork on these projects to join the pools of refinancing – especially as the inter-bank money market and the mortgage market were still mere concepts in the minds of the Treasury and Banque de France, a fact which increased the degree of eventual risk in the eyes of asset managers in deposit banks. New actors (Banque de l'Indochine,[182] the Suez group) and new challengers (affiliates created by insurance companies and later also by deposit banks) were to appear in the 1960s. But investment banks played a decisive role throughout the 1950s in rejuvenating the Parisian market.

One could say that investment banks' main competitive edge over deposit banks lay in their access to privileged markets or, more relevantly, as the latter did take part in credit pools, in the revenues captured by strategists, lead-managers and engineers of financial and banking products, co-operative banking or real estate "vehicles". Each time they acted as merchant bankers and came up with new ideas for financial or banking growth, investment banks earned greater responsibilities as leaders on the Parisian market and money. This helped them regain momentum on the domestic market throughout the 1950s and beyond though they were challenged in the domain of corporate banking. Differentiation was not only linked with legal statutes or historical heritage for balance of power; it was the result of the conquest of refreshed margins for manoeuvre, of new bridgeheads which refuelled flexibility within banking competition and supplied investment banks with new trump cards domestically.

5. Investment bankers on the international stage

Meanwhile, investment banks began to re-sharpen their competitive edge on the international markets and regain the name they had made for themselves in 1937-1948, mainly in eastern and central Europe. While deposit banks were more often committed to the Reconstruction and to domestic growth in keeping with the State's demands, investment banks' aim was to enhance their portfolio of skills abroad. There was one other factor: French banks had lost momentum at the international level from the mid-1930s. The economic slump had deprived them of resiliency and financial means while the State had extended its grip on international business (BFCE, COFACE, controls on FOREX, etc.). The entire French economy

182 Marc Meuleau, *op. cit.*, 1990.

and banking system lacked the required foreign currency while the US' international offensive kept the Parisian market confined to a subordinate position.[183]

No doubt commercial banks also entertained international ambitions and strategies. First, they kept their stronghold in the City (Crédit lyonnais, Société générale, CNEP, CIC) while the Société générale had established a bridgehead in New York during WWII and CNEP took advantage of its network across the Mediterranean and Australia. Second, Crédit lyonnais extended its international coverage to include Brazil (1947/48), Lebanon (1950), Peru (1952), Venezuela (1954), Argentina and Columbia (1955) and Iran (1958). FOREX and trade regained momentum, especially when international flows were somewhat liberalised at the turn of the 1950s. Crédit lyonnais showed its growing trade financing skills (through its branch in Geneva) in multilateral operations on cereals and mid-term credit for the sale of equipment abroad. Investment banks had no monopoly on international business because corporate banking as deposit banks demanded a share of the global market. But we lack the information to define the actual level of differentiation between commercial and investment banks. Still, the latter felt the growing competitiveness of their challengers at the international level and they did not take a long time to rebuild their competitive edge.

A. Investment banks and import-export flows

This explains the key role played by the small investment bank Lazard after WWII, which regained momentum by focusing on what became its specialty for a while: "To win over manufacturers, we would need to offer services which other bankers had not thought of yet, and to be the first to move – because in this area of financial engineering, as soon as someone gets an idea, some other bank puts it in practice almost immediately."[184] Thanks to its close links with the Anglo-Saxon business community, it was put in charge by the State with the function of supervising the banking pools tackling forex business for the import of raw materials, mainly for

183 See Hubert Bonin, "The challenged competitiveness of the Paris banking and finance markets, 1914-1958", in Youssef Cassis & Éric Bussière (eds.), *London and Paris as international financial centres in the twentieth century*, Oxford, Oxford University Press, 2005, pp. 183-204. H. Bonin, "Les banques françaises et le monde (depuis le tournant des années 1930)", special issue, *Banque*, December 1992, pp. 60-64. H. Bonin, "L'intégration européenne des banques françaises (1796-1996)", *Bankhistorisches Archiv. Zeitschrift zur Bankgeschichte*, 2/1996, Frankfurt, Fritz Knapp Verlag, pp. 59-85. H. Bonin, "Le rayonnement international des banques françaises (1900-1940): essai d'évaluation", in Maurice Lévy-Leboyer (ed.), *L'économie française dans la compétition internationale*, Paris, CHEFF, 2006, pp. 117-143.

184 Christian Valensi, in Anne Sabouret, *MM. Lazard*, *op. cit.*, p. 124.

wool (1949) and cotton (1952). But this differentiation was challenged at the turn of the 1950s as soon as deposit banks had revitalised their foreign trade banking department, for instance at CNEP, which financed UK commodity exports (wool, cotton, tin, etc.) to France and Brussels through its branches in London and Brussels, cotton exports through its branch in Alexandria,[185] commodity exports from India through its branch in India, while its affiliate, the French American Banking Corporation also financed export of raw materials from the US to France. Every commercial bank rushed to service the global priority to re-launch the financing of trade in consumer goods beyond the Marshall Plan. Even Fouchier started its pioneering path by first financing the import of equipment through a specialised little bank, the UFEFE (*Union financière d'entreprises françaises et étrangères*): set up in 1947, it was merged with the *Banque française d'acceptations* in 1950 to form the *Union française de banques pour l'acceptation et les financements extérieurs*. But investment banks disposed of a far larger reservoir of relationships, skills and managers, and rapidly took the lead in that segment of the market.

Differentiation took shape on the field because investment banks had re-kindled and re-mobilised their networks more rapidly than the nationalised Big Four deposit banks, especially in North-America. Though deposit banks kept their branch or affiliate active in London,[186] but Paribas and BUP quickly reactivated their international channels of action (though we do lack a comprehensive study). Paribas could rely on its strong historical positions in Belgium,[187] Latin America (through a joint-venture with *Banca Commerciale Italiana*, co-affiliate *Banque française et italienne pour l'Amérique du Sud*, or Sudameris) and it benefitted from its international outlook and dedicated team, which pushed the bank into the transatlantic business from the turn of the 1950s. Roughly speaking, investment banks were a decade ahead of deposit banks in the international field and benefited from this advantage.

André Debray led the offensive at Paribas, aided by his deputy and future successor, Bernard de Margerie. This top civil servant had been a manager at the *Finances extérieures* of the ministry of Finance after WWII and general secretary of the *Comité interministériel pour les questions de coopération européenne* in 1949-1951. His knowledge of

185 CNEP 1949 and 1950 annual reports.

186 See Hubert Bonin, *La Société générale en Grande-Bretagne* (*1871-1996*), Paris, La collection historique de la Société générale, 1996. Bernard Desjardins, Michel Lescure, Roger Nougaret, Alain Plessis & André Straus (eds.), *Le Crédit lyonnais, 1863-1986. Études historiques*, Geneva, Droz, 2002.

187 Éric Bussière, *Paribas, l'Europe et le monde, 1872-1992*, Anvers, Fonds Mercator, 1992. Éric Bussière, *La France, la Belgique et l'organisation économique de l'Europe, 1918-1935*, Paris, Comité pour l'histoire économique et financière de la France, 1992.

international and European business was thus top notch, and the *Paribas*' "genius" lay in recruiting him immediately as head of a commercial and international banking division to enhance its portfolio of skills in international corporate banking. "You will head a department which will be responsible for the negotiations of business affairs and the monitoring of the banking group's commercial ventures. Your department will also look to our interests in foreign banks as and when Mr. André Debray will place them under your care, so that in due course, all the dealings presently handled by Mr. Debray will end up under your care, excepting the petrol part which will be handled by another division."[188] With five sub-managers, Margerie extended what became in 1952 the *département de l'étranger*, which he headed (as executive manager) from July 1952, after Debray's death[189] – before becoming deputy CEO in 1967.

Margerie reignited Paribas' business networks, especially with Banque nationale du Mexique, Sudameris, Banque de Syrie & Liban, and Banque ottomane, using them all as bridgeheads to consolidate Paribas's position over international flows: "The department for commercial affairs has also cooperated with the foreign banks in which we hold interests, with a view of solving financing problems which have arisen in connection with public works to be carried out abroad by French civil engineering enterprises"[190] – along what has been called "the ping pong effect", when foreign bases help one another in mutualising business connections and ultimately favouring the growth of the headquarters. His business units therefore contributed strongly to the development of trade finance and export financing at Paribas.[191]

Investment banks practiced the usual international corporate banking operations: acceptance credits, credit lines for foreign trade agreed by foreign correspondents, documentary credit operations (with the amount of such credits jumping 40 per cent in 1954 alone),[192] transfers of currencies,[193] etc. – with large departments for documentary credit and FOREX. "We have been able to provide French importers with large currency credits required for stocking the essential raw materials thanks to our relations with foreign correspondent banks and our reciprocal business

188 Personal file of Margerie, historical archives of Paribas, August 1951.

189 Debray died at only 48: "He was a skilled negotiator with exceptional gifts of understanding and adaptability. The measure of his greatness was best exemplified in the relations which it was his special duty to maintain with the oil companies and foreign banks in which Paribas has interests", Paribas 1953 annual report, 25 May 1954 (English version).

190 Paribas 1953 annual report, 25 May 1954.

191 See Éric Bussière, *Paribas, l'Europe et le monde*, *op. cit.*, pp. 172-179.

192 Paribas 1954 annual report, 12 May 1955.

193 See Paribas 1947 annual report, 27 May 1948.

dealings."[194] Paribas' competitiveness was increased by its use of three specialised subsidiaries, *Banque cotonnière*, *Crédit sucrier & commercial* and *Banque des produits alimentaires et coloniaux*, which competed with Lazard and commercial banks' departments of financial trade for financing commodity exchanges. But its advantage lay with its Belgian branch, which Paribas said was then the first foreign institution in the country, with its Geneva and Amsterdam branches, all three acting as levers for financing foreign trade and supplying customers with credit in foreign currencies. The managers travelled extensively in Mexico, South America and Canada at the turn of the 1950s, and this resiliency helped push Paribas upward.

B. Re-fuelling structured finance

The Paribas team asserted itself as a pioneering group which boosted French industry's ability to export equipment. When the *Reconstruction* had been achieved and production capabilities rebuilt, they tried to recapture foreign outlets and attain to the same level of competitiveness that France had attained in the inter-war period or earlier in the domain of heavy equipment and engineering. É. Bussière has summed up these developments[195] when the entire portfolio of investment banking skills was mobilised with all Paribas' divisions: "Our industrial department has engaged in studies, surveys and negotiations, which have led to large banking or financial operations on the part of the other departments of the bank."[196] Thanks to a change in the law on 2 March 1950 (allowing the mobilisation at Banque de France of short term export credits covered by the public guarantee of insurance creditor COFACE and of ex/im bank BFCE) as a first step before the banks by themselves granted mid-term credit whose load they had to bear till completion of the contract, a type of a chain of loans was established and became commonplace in the 1960s.

They focused credit operations on the exporting firm (what was called "*crédit fournisseur*" or "*vendeur*"), the purpose being to divide the risks through layers of credit, each one being pledged by specific guarantees and repaid through instalments of varying maturities, thus reducing the risk on the banks involved. As early as November 1950, BUP and Paribas came together to lead a mid-term loan (FRF 3,000m, of which BUP bore 618m) to the *Irakian Petroleum Company* – in which the *Compagnie française des pétroles* had a 23.75 per cent stake – to finance its 1950-1952 investments,[197] repayable in 1953-1955. In 1957, Batignolles-Châtillon

[194] Paribas 1950 annual report, 26 April 1951.

[195] Éric Bussière, *Paribas, l'Europe et le monde*, *op. cit.*, pp. 156-180.

[196] Paribas 1953 annual report, 25 May 1954 (English version).

[197] Hubert Bonin, *La Banque de l'union parisienne*, *op. cit.*, p. 377.

(mechanics) and Ernault-Batignolles (machine tools) were granted pre-finance export credit (FRF 345 million) endorsed by BFCE, shared between Paribas and Sudameris, another credit line mobilising bills on foreign customers, and lines of discounting (shared between Paribas and UEIF-Union européenne industrielle et financière, Schneider's *banque d'affaires*).[198]

"The support that we have given to the exporting manufacturers in their negotiations and the finances that we have been able to arrange for them in order that they might meet the requirements of their foreign clients as regards the fulfilment of orders, have contributed, to a large extent, to the success of many companies with which we have worked regarding major contracts for the export of materials and equipment."[199] "The great number of projects which this department has in hand, and which have been initiated both by the exporting firms and the importing foreign authorities, is a proof of the experience it has gained in arranging financial operations of this type."[200] "Brazil's vast industrial development projects have caused us to maintain a permanent representative in that country, and we have thus had the satisfaction of contributing to the success of French firms which had proposed their services to local mechanical, electrical and petroleum industries, and which subsequently called on Paribas for assistance in the financial field."[201]

Paribas was first contacted in March 1950 to launch the process of engineering a "structured finance" project in Columbia for a steel plant at *Paz del Rio.*[202] CEO Reyre gave the green light to begin clearing such a (at this time) audacious and groundbreaking project, in which France would confronted US firms which were at that time much more influential in Latin America. The *Paz del Rio* project was altogether a school for financial, banking and engineering apprenticeship for Paribas abroad, and a mantra of the renewal of its portfolio of skills. But one key advantage edge had also been its stake in Sudameris, because its connections had eased the contacts with the Columbian authorities and circles of influence. The agreement was concluded in June 1950 after several rounds of technical and financial negotiations were held to overcome US and German competitors and favour a global joint-venture between French industrialists and bankers. Paribas was able to supply a global line of credit, which was seen as a key advantage from the Columbian point of view,

198 Report by Paribas board, 17 October 1957.

199 Paribas 1952 annual report, 28 May 1953.

200 Paribas 1953 annual report, 25 May 1954.

201 Paribas 1956 annual report, 9 May 1957.

202 See Fabrice Decourcelles, *Paz de Rio, premier grand projet sidérurgique français à l'exportation de l'après-guerre (1950-1958)*, Paris 4 University, September 1997, historical archives of *Paribas*.

while the French firm could rely on its US patents to show its edge over German contenders.[203] Two further instalments were brokered in 1952 and 1953 to supply and finance complementary equipment, supported by three-year credits (till 1957): the project had thus been extended over almost the whole decade. The *Paz del Rio* plant opened up in October 1954 and became a beacon of French renewal[204] after WWII.

The Paribas teams[205] were committed to the completion of a series of successive contracts to export plants for greenhill in Latin America and in the Middle East when a few countries bet on programs of substitution to imports for intermediaries products in metal and chemicals industries. The year 1953 was, what seems retrospectively, a turning point in the French economic rebirth abroad: in Colombia, French companies had to supply "additional material for the steel plant at Paz del Rio and for equipping mines; in Chile for the supply of rolling stock and harbour equipment; in Brazil for setting up an ammonia plant and in Bolivia for supplying transport equipment or building a sugar factory; in Turkey, for equipping several sugar and cement factories; and in Iraq for road works".[206] Paribas also was lead-manager to finance deliveries to the Chimbote steelworks in Peru, followed by a series of projects in the 1950s:

Table 11. A few case studies of businesses co-engineered and financed by Paribas abroad

– In 1955:
• Financed a sugar plant in Thailand[207]
• Iron and steel works in Columbia and Peru (*Corporacion peruana del stan*, a franco-peruvian group which contracted for the final work): a rolling mill; agreement with *Companha aços especiais Itablira Acesita*; French industry supplying rolling equipment for $12.5 million

[203] *Ibidem*. *Paz del Rio* issued middle term promissory notes to be paid only along with the deliveries of equipment, transmitted to Sudameris, then remitted at Paribas New York, then in Paris, to be mobilised by the pool of banks led by Paribas; irrevocable documentary credits were also issued in favour of exporting industrialists. The French State granted a subsidy for 20 per cent of the amount to compensate for the rebate which firms had to concede to win over US and German competitors, and public insurance credit institution Coface pledged for 90 per cent of the amount.

[204] Alsthom (with 24% of the first instalment of the project) manufactured the power plant, Districoke the coke-plant (15%), Schwartz-Haumont the wireworks (5%), Secim the rolling-equipment, Delattre & Frouard the steel plant (35%), with Fives-Lille, Stein & Roubaix, Chavannes-Brun and an group of subcontractors as co-participants (Fabrice Decourcelles, *Paz de Rio*, *op. cit.*).

[205] See Éric Bussière, *Paribas, l'Europe et le monde*, *op. cit.*, pp. 173-178.

[206] Paribas 1953 annual report, 25 May 1954.

[207] Paribas 1955 annual report, 26 April 1956.

– In 1956:

- "We financed the contracts concluded by a French firm for the designing, supply and laying of pipelines in Iran."[208]
- For the Brazilian *Mataripa* project, Paribas supplied Fives-Lille, SFAC-*Société des forges & aciéries du Creusot*) and Batignolles-Châtillon with prefinancing export credits (260m, 209m and 60m) followed by mid-term export credits (308m, 225m and 71m). They were accompanied by public works firms which included Fougerolle and CIT-*Compagnie industrielle de travaux.*[209] The latter benefitted with a prefinancing export credit (91.5m) relayed by a mid-term credit (107m).[210]

– In 1957

- Financing an export pool to Columbia for electrical engineering and equipment: *Matériel électrique* SW, SFAC, CGEE and Neyrpic
- Financing export of electrical equipment to Turkey by Neyrpic (454m)[211]
- Financing export of electrical equipment by Alsthom (173.5m) – preceded by a thick line of short term credit (1,086m)[212]

– In 1958

- Numerous customs guarantees and short term credits to chemical groups (including Saint-Gobain) for industrial projects in Pakistan (Multan) and India (*Nangal Fertilizers*)[213]
- An entire range of credits to firms involved in both projects, either to chemical companies (Saint-Gobain, *Potasse & engrais chimiques*-PEC, ENSA, Grande-Paroisse, etc.) or to firms delivering the metal structures of the plants (Batignolles-Châtillon, Ernault-Batignolles), with a chain of bills being accepted by the customer along with deliveries and refinanced by bankers – the amounts reaching 1,337m at Multan and 1,719m at Nangal, part of it being assumed in direct by Paribas, with Worms, BFCE, UEIF also committed through a series of pooled credits.[214]
- Huge contracts brokered with *Électricité de Téhéran*: lines of credit to *Compagnie générale d'entreprises électriques*-CGEE, *Compagnie générale d'électricité*-CGE, SACM and *Tréfileries & laminoirs du Havre* for exports of electrotechnical equipment (739 million);[215] followed by contracts for the grid (Alsthom, Jeumont, Geoffroy-Delore, *L'Électro-entreprise*) (163.4m in short term, followed by 171.4m in mid-term)[216]
- A power plant in Cuba, with credits to CGEE (145m, then 350m)[217]
- Hydro-electrical complex in Honduras (*Rio Li Do*): Paribas lead manager of a banking pool servicing *Compagnie française d'entreprise*, CGE, Alsthom, Neyrpic and *France engineering*[218]

---

208 Paribas 1956 annual report, 26 April 1957.

209 Report by Paribas board, 14 March 1957 and 13 June 1957.

210 *Ibidem*, 13 June 1957.

211 *Ibidem*, 28 November 1957.

212 *Ibidem*, 19 December 1957.

213 *Ibidem*, 16 January 1958.

214 *Ibidem*, 18 September 1958.

215 *Ibidem*, 17 July 1958.

216 *Ibidem*, 16 October 1958.

217 *Ibidem*, 16 October 1958.

218 *Ibidem*, 16 October 1958.

– In 1959:

- "In Brazil, within the framework of the agreement which we signed with *Companhia siderugica paulista Cosipa*, the latter has placed orders with several French concerns amounting at the end of 1959 to $15m."[219] Paribas signed a similar agreement with another Brazilian company, *Usiminas*. In Mexico, Pemex agreed for a $50m order of European equipment.
- Huge risks undertaken by Paribas on a single firm, Fives-Lille-Cail; beyond a line of credits partly shared with *Crédit lyonnais* (FRF 1,140m), export credits through complex schemes (for at least 1,626m)[220]

A pioneering breakthrough was completed in 1958 when Paribas took part in one of the first export contracts to an East-European Communist country, opening the door to a series of promising connections there for structured finance and corporate banking:[221] "Emphasis has been given to the development in trade relations with the East European countries", with a Soviet order of more than FRF 6 billion placed with the Société Fives-Lille-Cail for a large cement factory which has been in addition to contracts of more than FRF 4 billion won by CSF for the supply of various types of electronic equipment", accompanied in Poland by "a new order for the supply of a thermal power station, the framework of the financial agreement to which we were associated in 1958"[222] (with Alsthom, Stein & Roubaix and Jeumont) and "three sugar plants in the USSR by Fives-lille, Babcox & Wilcox et Delattre & Frouard"[223] in 1959. But differentiation ought to be reconsidered because the two investment banks Paribas and BUP were joined by *Crédit lyonnais* for the Fives-Lille-Cail contracts,[224] which shows the rapid rise of commercial banks and the competitiveness of the corporate banking department at investment banks: they did not lose momentum even if they had to share these markets with their competitors as regards structured finance.

On a more modest scale, even Lazard joined the fray and took part in some innovative financial engineering when oil companies set up the *Société du pipe-line sud-européen* joining Marseille, Lyon and the north of Alsace: the merchant bank was at the heart of the negotiations because it involved US oil firms and US investment funds. Its partners (Jean Guyot),

219 Paribas 1959 annual report, 16 May 1960.

220 Report by Paribas board, 15 January 1959.

221 See Hubert Bonin, "L'émergence de la coopération industrielle, bancaire et commerciale franco-soviétique dans les années 1960", in Maurice Vaïsse (ed.), *De Gaulle et la Russie*, Paris, Cnrs Éditions, 2006, pp. 229-252.

222 *Paribas* 1958 annual report, 21 May 1959.

223 *Paribas* 1959 annual report, 16 May 1960.

224 Hubert Bonin, *La Banque de l'union parisienne*, *op. cit.*, p. 448.

Paribas and *Crédit lyonnais* led the team with their German, Swiss and American counterparts.[225]

We are well aware that such types of export credits became more and more common as commercial banks began to master the processes and chains of credit products and services and rushed to broker corporate banking contracts. Even CNEP connected its *service du commerce extérieur* of its *département des relations étrangères* (with documentary credit as one of its basic activities) with a new subsidiary, the *Compagnie intercontinentale commerciale et financière*, to extend its range of credits to include equipment goods.[226] In 1961, a few commercial banks set up some kind of a co-operative tool, the GICEX-*Groupement interbancaire pour les opérations de crédit à l'exportation*, to compete with investment banks for middle term loans.

For a while, investment banks enjoyed a few years' (half a dozen? a decade?) head start because their engineers, lawyers and bankers had seen the need of companies and had responded by extending subtle schemes of successive credits in a chain mixing short-term and mid-term loans (part of them mobilised in France by the semi-governmental *Crédit national*), mobilised or non mobilised bills, guaranteed (BFCE) or not, linked with insurance credit (COFACE) or not. We can say that the 1950s were therefore a "blessed" decade for investment banks, a time when they could assert a competitive edge over deposit banks and fully express their "differentiation" owing to their portfolio of banking engineering skills. É. Bussière[227] reckoned that Paribas bore 65.6, 64.8 and 80 per cent of the pre-financing export credit amounts in 1952, 1953 and 1954 respectively, which shows how decisively Reyre and his team grabbed the opportunities at the turn of the 1950s.

C. Investment banking fostering corporate banking: The "ping pong effect"

The development of structured finance ("*crédits d'équipement*" and "*contrats de financement*" which was set up by the *département des affaires commerciales* for the completion of big industrial facilities")[228] opened the doors to a wide range of businesses. As with the other groundbreaking

225 An amount of around FRF 200 million was at stake. *Notes de conversations*, historical archives of *Crédit lyonnais*, May, 23 June and 10 November 1960. Morgan Stanley was involved in the process through Lazard's connections. Two instalments were conceived, one in France (120 million new francs, with Lazard, Paribas and *Crédit lyonnais* a co-lead-managers in February 1961), and a second one in the US.

226 This affiliate gathered commercial banks from several European countries, CNEP annual report 1958. A first credit was granted to *Petroleos Mexicanos* for equipment goods.

227 Éric Bussière, *Paribas, l'Europe et le monde*, *op. cit.*, p. 176.

228 Paribas 1952 annual report, 28 May 1953.

products, the investment banking achievements had effects on corporate banking because more and more export credits were granted by Paribas, which multiplied the issue of bills ("*effets circulant sous notre endos*") by its banking department in a snowballing effect: the more its competitive edge grew stronger abroad thanks to its competitive edge over deposit banks, the more the investment banks spread its market share on the Paris market all along the chain of credit – and that explains why Paribas split its banking department into two divisions: a domestic one and a foreign one (*département étranger*)[229] in January 1953. Regarding liabilities too, the ping pong effects were obvious: "The amount of current accounts regarding liabilities increased greatly, the movement being assisted by the enlargement of the working funds of our industrial and trading customers; it is the cash resources of these latter which form the main element in the deposits of the *banque d'affaires*."[230]

Investment bank's competitive edge spread into corporate banking, where deposit banks were very active. The intertwining branches of investment and corporate banking explains how investment banks regained momentum throughout the 1950s, helping them to forget the miserable 1930s and 1940s. The *département étranger* was headed (from 1941) by Henry Burnier, who was also in charge of Sudameris, though he needed to recruit a deputy, André Littaye[231] in 1952 and promote several managers: Pierre Decker became assistant manager in 1955, the same year as Gustave Rambaud, at the industrial department,[232] both symbolising the resiliency of investment bankers.

On the other hand, corporate banking strengthened investment banking because the more Paribas came in touch with equipment firms, the more they asked for merchant and investment banking facilities: Paribas could offer them services for equity increases, bonds issues and even direct investment in their capital. The financial nebulae which had been formed in the interwar period (around oil and steel firms) were condensed with forays into chemicals, engineering and heavy equipment companies like Fives-Lille, Delattre & Frouard, Stein & Roubaix, Neyrpic, Batignolles-Châtillon, Pierrefitte – before such nebulae were transformed into what would be called "financial groups"[233] in the 1960s-1970s.

---

229 Paribas 1952 annual report, 28 May 1953.

230 Paribas 1953 annual report, 25 May 1954.

231 Paribas 1952 annual report, 28 May 1953.

232 Paribas 1955 annual report, 26 April 1956.

233 Hubert Bonin, *Les groupes financiers français*, Paris, Presses universitaires de France, 1995.

D. In the wake of intensifying European business connections

Other path-breaking initiatives may be found in Western Europe. Internal trade and connections were resumed in the 1950s, with the involvement of the entire banking community, and investment banks could rekindle their relationships on the European markets. Their "European mindset" or "culture" was perhaps more clearly re-awakened by Paribas' and BUP's close links in Belgium – an open gate to North-Western European business. Several clues regarding European action are available at Paribas and BUP and the bilateral co-operation between West Germany and France.[234]

BUP was at the frontline for the promotion of German securities on the Paris stock exchange because one of its managers, Auguste Avon, was a pioneering banker in that niche. His portfolio of skills had been honed at the Paris branch of a subsidiary of *Société générale de Belgique*, *Banque belge pour l'étranger*, and he had joined BUP when it had absorbed the branch in 1948 along with a few other managers,[235] thus creating a "European-minded" little team, spurred by BUP's connections with its former partners, *Société générale de Belgique* and *Générale de banque*. It patronised a "*groupement franco-allemand*" and its partners seized every opportunity to develop fresh business: *Deutsche Bank* and *Dresdner Bank* proposed floating German shares in Paris with BUP as lead manager and a few banks (*Société générale*, Louis-Dreyfus, *Crédit lyonnais*, BFCE) succeeded in selling 1 per cent of *Farbenfabrik Bayer*'s capital[236] in January 1959 – which helped BUP to become the lead manager of its French financial operations.[237] Paribas and Rothschild reacted by proposing similar operations later on. With the agreement of the State Treasury, Paribas and *Crédit lyonnais* (both being partners for financial operations) along with Lazard and Rothschild set up a pool competing with the BUP to start a large project of floating US and German securities in Paris. First meetings in the US occurred at Lazard[238] as early as 1955, and the "edge" there lay with Lazard's and Rothschild's US connections as the managers of both

---

234 Hubert Bonin, "Les relations bancaires franco-allemandes (1900-1970): admiration, guerre économique et coopération de voisinage", in Jean-François Eck, Stefan Martens & Sylvain Schirmann (eds.), *Les relations franco-allemandes de 1871 à nos jours*, Paris, Publications du CHEFF, 2009, pp. 357-383.

235 Avon became director manager at BUP, and was accompanied by Henri Tourbier (deputy director), Raymond Relecom (sub-director), Henri Trulin and a *fondé de pouvoirs*. H. Bonin, *La Banque de l'union parisienne*, *op. cit.*, p. 361. File *Banque belge pour l'étranger*, historical archives of Société générale de Belgique, Archives générales du Royaume belge.

236 *Notes de conversations*, historical archives of *Crédit lyonnais*, 16 January 1959.

237 Hubert Bonin, *La Banque de l'union parisienne*, *op. cit.*, p. 426.

238 Note "Introduction de valeurs américaines sur le marché de Paris", 12 January 1955, *Notes de conversations*, historical archives of *Crédit lyonnais*.

Paribas (Serge Varangot) and *Crédit lyonnais* (Deschietere) were equals without the importance of the investment banker (in spite of Varangot having travelled in the US to prospect for business). With the help of Morgan, they succeeded in floating five shares in the second half of 1959, first on the private market of brokers (*Coulisse*) to test the feasibility, then on the official *Parquet* of the stock exchange – while Lazard floated Pechiney's shares in New York. The Paribas pool (open to BUP for brokerage, not as lead manager…) floated German shares at the same time.[239]

E. Sparkling colonial business: Investment banks as levers of imperial modernity

As it had been the case in the interwar period for investment banks – with Rothschild in New Caledonia for *Le Nickel*, Paribas in Morocco and Madagascar and BUP and merchant banks in north and sub-Saharan Africa – the French colonial empire offered large territories of business. But the rhythm of development ("*mise en valeur*") was greatly accelerated after WWII, spurred by a new imperial spirit of modernisation.[240] France needed rare natural and ore resources, the growing population had to be compensated by industrialisation schemes, themselves to take profit from the improving living standards in the colonial and local populations. Lastly, mindsets began to grow out of an autarchic framework towards open-mindedness, with foreign investments joining in to exploit the available underground wealth. Mining was the traditional milk cow, and private funds were called for to start a few African projects, especially as Indochina was teetering on the edge, fuelling the repatriation of capital towards new fields of investment and profit. But soon the oil "revolution" was at hand. At first, both sectors (mining and oil) remained under State (or its offshoots) control, intervention and even direct ownership and production. But capitalist spaces began to take shape in the 1950s, explaining the "fever" or "mania" which gripped investment bankers regarding colonial and overseas mining and oil businesses. The State itself asked them for help because such project financing required foreign direct investments, and investment banks (mainly Rothschild, Lazard and Paribas) were well placed to activate their connections abroad (mainly in North-America, and sometimes through the City).

---

239 *Notes de conversations*, historical archives of *Crédit lyonnais*, 2 June, 4 June, 5 June, 23 June 1959.

240 See Hubert Bonin, Catherine Hodeir & Jean-François Klein (eds.), *L'esprit économique impérial (1830-1970). Groupes de pression & réseaux du patronat colonial en France & dans l'empire*, Paris, Publications de la SFHOM, 2008. Catherine Hodeir, *Stratégies d'empire. Le grand patronat colonial face à la décolonisation* (*1945-1962*), Paris, Belin, 2003. Jacques Frémeaux, *Les empires coloniaux dans le processus de mondialisation*, Paris, Maisonneuve & Larose, 2002.

Paribas' manager François Anthoine[241] played a key role for many overseas projects in his post as manager for North African and overseas sectors from 1946-1947 and as "*directeur pour l'Afrique*" in 1954-1965, where Hervé de Guichen[242] welcomed proposals for development – especially those of Fouchier who, in parallel with his main activity in specialised credit lines, pioneered a few mining projects in the empire – and later, in the independent countries. While Paribas kept supervising its geographical interest "groups" overseas, it launched numerous projects favouring the "intensification" of overseas growth, either in Sub-Saharan Africa (cotton, electricity, wholesale trading when it became the main banker then stakeholder of SCOA-*Société commerciale de l'Ouest africain*), or in its Moroccan stronghold (with several developments).[243]

Paribas also contributed to the emergence of new instruments of modernisation of the empire just before the independence movements. Investment banks struggled and co-operated with each other to carry financial projects, to launch funds collecting cash from banks, especially deposit banks, and then selling shares on the stock exchange. When the oil financial vehicle COPAREX was equipped with its working capital, it increased its equity from FRF 20 million to 10 billion with Paribas as sole lead manager[244] – which shows the dimension of such instruments on the Parisian market, moved by an "oil fever" or a "REP" bear speculation in the mid-1950s – along "*recherche et exploration pétrolières*" as numerous companies were named under such an appellation, taking advantage of tax benefits given to encourage savers and investors to support oil prospection. Moreover, *Paribas* was able to use its own financial holdings (*Compagnie générale des colonies*, transformed in 1958 into *Compagnie générale de participations et d'entreprises dans les pays indépendants*, *Compagnie générale du Maroc*, and even the ex-*Banque d'État du Maroc*, deprived of its banking activities and becoming in 1959 a sub-holding, *Société internationale de financement et de placements*,[245] etc.). This range in the means of intervention clearly gave it a competitive edge over deposit banks – even if these latter spread retail banking divisions overseas, especially in sub-Saharan Africa.

---

241 Personal file of François Anthoine, historical archives of *Paribas*.

242 "Hervé de Guichen, director of the Banking Department, who played a decisive role in supporting the constitution of the 'Fouchier group' of companies to which his house belonged", Hervé Pinet, *La joie d'entreprendre. Souvenirs d'une vie professionnelles*, Paris, Éditions du Jaguar, 2003, p. 71.

243 See Georges Hatton, *Les enjeux financiers et économiques du protectorat marocain (1936-1954). Politique publique et investisseurs privés*, Paris, Publications de la SFHOM, 2009.

244 Report by Paribas board, 7 November 1957.

245 *Notes de conversations*, historical archives of *Crédit lyonnais*, 17 May 1960. The merger occurred on January 1960, thus bringing assets for FRF 62 million to Paribas.

The small merchant bank Rothschild played a key role in several projects, thanks to its already existing portfolio of skills and history, which explains its initiatives and its active presence at the bankers' meetings, in contrast to the other field studies above. André Straus has highlighted the key part played by Rothschild co-manager Robert Jablon,[246] as a pioneering investment banker who set up financial vehicles (*Compagnie financière de recherches pétrolières*-COFIREP in 1955; FRANCAREP in 1957, with Worms,[247] etc.) to collect funds from institutional investors, banks' private banking divisions, or wealthy individual investors, before investing these amounts in start-up oil companies.[248] Thanks to its portfolio of skills in mining finance, Rothschild was also able to engineer a huge iron ore mine project in Mauritania,[249] to be developed in the 1960s. The State favoured such a mobilisation of savings and assets because experts perceived in the mid-1950s that the need of prospection campaigns would outstrip forecasts.[250] The REP holdings were to supply at least FRF 30b against an estimated requirement of 200b per year between 1957-1961, of which FRF 100b would be provided by the public sector, 30b by big oil firms and 40b by the issue of bonds. Bankers realised that this bonanza could help them get deeper into savings. Other investment banks quickly followed the lead, as Paribas and BUP had piled up experience in oil business in the interwar period through the support of their favourite customer, the *Compagnie française des pétroles*, and Lazard was also involved because of its US connections (about transfers of technology or capital) – and it carried the birth of REPFRANCE and EURAFREP.[251] For example, *Société financière des pétroles*-FINAREP was established[252] in May 1954 under the guidance of Paribas leading a pool consisting of other investment banks, BUP, and some deposit banks (*Crédit lyonnais*, CCF, CIC), with *Crédit lyonnais*

246 See *Robert Jablon, op. cit.*, 2009.

247 *Notes de conversations*, historical archives of *Crédit lyonnais*, 3 July 1957.

248 When *Société des pétroles d'Afrique équatoriale française* was established to prospect oil fields in French central Africa, FINAREP held 10% and COFIREP 5% of its capital, with State institutions 81.5% and Compagnie *française des pétroles* (2.9%), *Notes de conversations*, historical archives of *Crédit lyonnais*, 20 November 1956.

249 See Jean Audibert, *MIFERMA: une aventure humaine et industrielle en Mauritanie*, Paris, L'Harmattan, 1991. Jean Servant, "Naissance de MIFERMA", in Jean Servant, Pierre Legoux & André Marelle (eds.), *Les mines et la recherche minière en Afrique occidentale française*, Paris, L'Harmattan, 1991, pp. 288-297.

250 *Notes de conversations*, historical archives of *Crédit lyonnais*, 18 April 1957.

251 EURAFREP gathered Lazard and *Banque de l'Indochine*, like REPFRANCE, with deposit banks and insurance companies, *Notes de conversations*, historical archives of *Crédit lyonnais*, 3 July 1957.

252 Paribas 1954 annual report, 12 May 1955. Paribas contributed to 23.71% to the increase of capital in 1957, Report by Paribas board, 5 September 1957.

and CCF as co-lead managers. Its capital reached FRF 3b in December 1954 and 8b[253] in 1956.

Table 12. Part respectively played by investment banks and deposit banks at FINAREP

	Brokerage of equity in January 1955	Allocation of available treasury funds in 1955 and of the relay credits in July 1956
Paribas	27.23%	36.5%
Crédit lyonnais	27.23	24.5
CCF	10.47	14.5
CIC	13.54	12.5
BUP	12.53	12

Source: *Notes de conversations*, historical archives of *Crédit lyonnais*, 4 September 1956.

Paribas took part in GENAREP,[254] COPAREX (with 21.5 per cent of the equity,[255] and OMNIREX in 1957. Its traditional customers invited *Paribas* to join their own initiatives. It thus helped Esso Standard, its historical client in France, to settle Esso rep to finance exploration in French territories and it accompanied the State's affiliates to set up their instruments, as was the case at Sogerap-Société de gestion des participations de la Régie autonome des pétroles,[256] which welcomed private investors to follow the growth of its subsidiaries where private investors were sometimes present. When the mining sector began to attract investors, Paribas was not far behind, godfathering *Société des mines de cuivre de Mauritanie* (1953). Meanwhile Lazard, well connected to US businesses, was the lead manager of negotiations regarding the financing of a huge development project in Guinea (mines, power plant, alumina and aluminium manufacturing).[257]

Even funds of funds were sketched: Paribas created one to draw investors into a large holding company which would invest its cash into financial vehicles, into oil companies or into industrial firms specialised in oil equipment or services (rigging, transport, etc.). Paribas conceived of the *Société d'investissements chimiques et pétroliers* to hold

253 *Notes de conversations*, historical archives of *Crédit lyonnais*, 4 September 1956 and 12 October 1956.

254 *Ibidem*, 8 July 1957. GENAREP was engineered by Paribas and *Société générale*, with *Crédit du Nord*, two merchant banks, Neuflize and Mallet, and insurance companies, as institutional investors.

255 Report by Paribas board, 10 March 1959.

256 *Ibidem*, 7 November 1957.

257 *Notes de conversations*, historical archives of *Crédit lyonnais*, 19 November 1955, with Jean Guyot, at Lazard, with Pechiney as main manufacturer. See Jacques Larrue, *Fria en Guinée. Première usine d'aluminium en terre d'Afrique*, Paris, Karthala, 1997.

stakes in chemicals and oil firms,[258] and Rothschild and Lazard, *Société française d'investissements pétroliers*.[259] The *Compagnie financière pour l'outre-mer*-COFIMER[260] was established in 1957 under the guidance of both Rothschild and Paribas (Reyre, Bricard, Anthoine) along with a few deposit banks (led by *Crédit lyonnais*) which hoped to get some brokerage operations, to seize opportunities in the mining and oil segments. Its first chairman was Fouchier who had engineered the upstream process of the project. The 1950s sounded like a start-up forge, before the consolidation of the 1960s-1970s, and investment banks assumed their function of co-lead managers of the "clubs" of banks gathered to evaluate projects, contribute to their equity and to their credit lines.

Conclusion

On its own, this chapter cannot fulfil our quest for reconstituting the "need" for French investment banks all through the industrial revolutions and economic growth of the past two centuries. Nevertheless, with the help of relevant and specific archives (and historians' studies already published or about to be), this case study, which focuses on a very short period of time (fifteen years), does help clear a few points. In short, it seems to us that this period was the apex of French investment banks because, in the 1930s-1940s, they had been submitted to the dire conditions of the economic slump and the war, while the 1960s-1970s saw them facing intense competition from commercial banks which rushed to adopt the "universal banking" model and, at the European level, US banks began to establish bridgeheads in the City.

Despite the difference between the retail and investment banking models, there was a "convergence" in several areas of practical banking. Deposit banks rapidly regained momentum in the fields of corporate banking, and we could even say that our paper has some bias because it uses clues from investment banks' archives more than those of deposit

[258] *Notes de conversations*, historical archives of *Crédit lyonnais*, 20 March 1959, 8 and 23 April 1959. Paribas acted with *Crédit lyonnais* (18% each), accompanied by *Société générale* (13%), BNCI (12%) and CNEP (11%), and by a dozen investment banks and deposit banks with minority stakes, and insurance companies joined the pool to lodge assets.

[259] Rothschild and Lazard were to supply each FRF 400m, *Caisse des dépôts* and *Crédit lyonnais* 100m, before calling publicly for investors and savers, *Notes de conversations*, historical archives of *Crédit lyonnais*, 12 September 1957.

[260] Report by Paribas board, 14 March 1957; *Notes de conversations*, historical archives of *Crédit lyonnais*, 9 April 1957 and 19 November 1957. See André Straus, "COFIMER et Rothschild: le rôle d'une banque d'affaires dans le financement des activités minières d'outre-mer", to be published.

banks[261] (though we did use the archives from *Crédit lyonnais* regarding inter-bank relationships (and competition)). The portfolio of skills in their departments of corporate banking, finance and security brokerage were strengthened as soon as the State gave some leeway to nationalised institutions and left "state" bankers free to compete with "capitalist" ones on the field of corporate banking, when a type of "mixed economy" matured at the turn of the 1950s. The entire banking community, whatever its statutes and owners, mobilised its range of skills to prop up French economy and help reinstate it on the European market (and farther if possible). Competition was very much there, but also a strong need for currencies to overcome the deficit of the settlements balance.

This explains that we often met commercial bankers involved altogether in corporate banking and investment banking, and that "history" or "heritage" froze inter-bank positions within credit pools which, after WWII, had succeeded the informal groups of lenders and the fixed balance of power around every big customer. Every commercial bank could now compete with investment banks over the entire range of corporate banking because they all had connections with a "club" of firms, supplying them with banking facilities and services and forging long term partnerships mainly in the domestic field or for trade banking (credit for commodities trade, documentary credit, FOREX, etc. in which they had piled up over decades a solid portfolio of skills). Investment banks were therefore not original as regards domestic loans, in particular those linked with the new types of mid-term credit for equipment and modernisation, with the support of semi-public institutions and refinancing. But they strove to stay competitive and both BUP and Paribas did not lose momentum. The investment bank "club" was even joined by "newcomers" (that is, upwardly mobile banks), mainly the *Union européenne industrielle et financière*, the *Union des mines*, Worms (extending its grip from naval finance to global investment banking) and, starting its reconversion from overseas and learning to become an investment bank, *Banque de l'Indochine*: with each disposing of its own network of connections and positions, and struggling for market shares for issue.

Regarding issues, differentiation could still be found in the function of lead management of financial operations. Investment banks kept their competitive edge regarding engineering financial operations because of the skills of their industrial and financial departments, the numerous

[261] We particularly thank bank archivists who generously opened their records for us: Roger Nougaret at *Crédit lyonnais-Crédit agricole-Banque de l'Indochine* historical archives; Pierre de Longuemar, Jérôme Lescuyer, Éloi Baylin, and Maryvonne Véjux, at *Paribas* historical archives (*Association pour l'histoire de BNP Paribas*); Marjolaine Meschaeert and her predecessors at the *Société générale-Banque de l'union parisienne-Crédit du Nord*-CFAT historical archives; and the archivists of the historical archives of *Banque de France*.

services offered to medium-sized equities being floated (growing from family business to broader capitalism), or to big companies facing creditworthiness issues because they lacked profitability and size through the acceleration of growth and production investments in the 1950s. Nevertheless, investment banks brought their reputation, expertise and, what set them apart, their ability to invest into their clients' equity to mobilise their property portfolio, and to hold these stakes durably, thus stabilising both the capital and the reputation of these firms.

Here lay a key piece of differentiation, though stipulated by the laws of 1945-1946, but also belonging to the genes of investment banks – and while not exhaustive, several cases have been quoted in our paper. From the mid-1960s, commercial banks also disposed of their own investment funds, but the financial might built in the 1950s could not be attained. Paribas and BUP were so skilful in setting up investment funds to cover, or rather, ease their commitment in a large array of interests, either through "old" firms being reconverted from their former activities (overseas or in central Europe) to new functions where they could mobilise their assets to extend their scope, or brand new funds, a few of them commencing to prospect proto-forms of "assets management" by welcoming external investors, mainly institutional investors or wealthy investors. And that leads us to one of the strong levers in the hands of investment banks: their close relationship with a "club" of insurance companies, to which they proposed stakes in investment funds, companies, bond issues – thus enhancing their brokerage ability – and last in the new activities fostered by real estate and specialised credits.

The second half of our chapter dealt with the "advances" made by investment banks – their one chance to resist commercial banks' progress lay in a thorough renewal of their portfolio of skills. Either they did that within their own departments (thanks to in-house pioneers, "geniuses" of finance, etc.), or they accompanied outside "pioneers" (real estate engineers, finance and credit conceivers, etc.) as key partners and godfathers on the Parisian market. Either way, they succeeded in broadening their field of action, increasing connections and improving financing operations throughout the 1950s, even though deposit banks later created the credit pools supporting each project. Without claiming originality (É. Bussière has already studied this point regarding *Paribas*, BUP's history is available and some books and articles have already scrutinised some of these points) our chapter deals with the modernisation spread of "structured finance" overseas in the colonial empire and in developing countries in Latin America, the Middle East and even European communist countries.

Admittedly, investment banks played a decisive role, with the support of the State economic sector, in considerably extending and renewing the Paris market's portfolio of skills for structured finance, project financing, supporting exports in capital goods, major contracts involving important risks, forex transfers and close connections with industrial firms and logistics. "Industrial banking" was thus once again in the limelight, benefiting investment banks through fees, interest revenues, investment banking's "ping pong effects" on corporate banking, etc. Such initiatives provided them with opportunities to pull ahead of their competitors in commercial banking and loosen the hegemony of US banks on the international market.

The issue of investment banks' "differentiation" and "portfolio of skills" can thus be summarised thus:

- Connections with "clubs" of companies to preserve a strong client base in corporate banking and in positions of lead manager in bond issues and capital increases;
- Renewal of the skills in finance banking to sharpen competitiveness in lead management functions for issues against commercial banks;
- Development of connections with institutional investors (and also wealthy clients of private banks) to maintain some competitiveness on the brokerage field, allowing them to keep their place within the brokerage pools for securities;
- Strong positions within the informal and formal "club" of experts and authorities managing the Parisian market to spur the development of regulations on new types of credits, funds and banking and financial "products", thus opening the doors to renewed flexibility and to the resiliency of the teams engineering new "vehicles" of action;
- Relevant advances in godfathering pioneering bankers, financiers and real estate developers and in setting up groundbreaking teams to accompany them or to compete with them (in property), thus fuelling better positions within credit pools, numerous opportunities to broker stakes in the projects, etc.
- Relevant advances in godfathering or directly engineering new types of credit products to develop the export of equipment and turn-key plants, thus fuelling fees, interest revenues and strengthening the connections with firms regarding corporate banking.
- Lastly, relevant advances in setting up investment vehicles capable of mobilising commercial banks, insurance companies, wealthy individual investors, merchant bankers, assets to be reconverted from colonial businesses to "modern" businesses, either as financial vehicles active on the stock exchanges in France and abroad, or as financial vehicles dedicated to specialised areas (mining, oil prospection and production), in association with French and foreign

companies and with State affiliates, for the development of French competitiveness in a new world organised around North-American initiatives and being reshaped by the European mindset gathering momentum from the turn of the 1950s. French investment banks asserted themselves therefore as levers of a new type of growth within an open economy,[262] following about fifteen years of near-autarchic and imperial mentalities.

262 See Hubert Bonin, "Les vertus de l'économie ouverte?", in Bertrand Blancheton & Hubert Bonin (eds.), *La croissance en économie ouverte (XVIIIe-XXIe siècles). Hommages à Jean-Charles Asselain*, Brussels, Peter Lang, 2009, p. 13-42.

CHAPTER 8

Fading Investment Banking?

Italian Banks before the Second World War

Carlo BRAMBILLA

(Insubria University, Varese)

The appearance of joint stock investment banking occurred in Italy after the unification of the country, from the early 1860s. As it happened in most Continental Europe from the 1850s, new joint stock investment banks were founded, after the example of the French *Crédit mobilier*, by private bankers and financiers eager to develop this new powerful financial tool, which enabled them to better exploit the new opportunities of investment in railways, public utilities and the related industries.[1]

As known, Italian banks largely inspired their patterns and working methods to those of the big French and German ones, that often, in fact, participated to their foundation. This notwithstanding, they soon developed peculiar banking patterns and organisational features which made them quite different from their European homologues.[2] Indeed, though the establishment of big investment banks in Italy took place relatively soon, a mere decade later than in leading European experiences, their affirmation and consolidation was a long and difficult process, marked by several crises, some of which affected the very structure of banks

1 David Landes, "Vieille banque et banque nouvelle, la révolution financière du XIXe siècle", *Revue d'histoire moderne et contemporaine*, No. 3, 1956, pp. 204-222. Rondo Cameron, *France and the Economic Development of Europe, 1800-1914. Conquest of Peace and Seeds of War*, Princeton (NJ), Princeton University Press, 1961. Rondo Cameron *et al.* (eds.), *Banking in the Early Stages of Industrialization*, New York, Oxford University Press, 1967.

2 Carlo Brambilla, "Assessing convergence in European investment banking patterns until 1914", in Patrice Baubeau and Anders Ögren (eds.), *Convergence and Divergence of National Financial Systems. Evidence from the Gold Standards, 1871-1971*, London, Pickering & Chatto, 2010, pp. 89-108.

and of the financial system. In this sense, the history of Italian investment banks before WWII can be considered as an evolutionary process in banking practices and innovations owed to the endeavour by banks to fulfil their functions while struggling for additional liquidity and trying to preserve their own financial stability. Indeed, they had to adapt to a peculiar institutional framework characterised by weak capital markets, small, volatile and segmented monetary markets, and fairly poor regulation, that tended to curtail the liquidity of the system and to make it hard for them to raise funds and to perform asset liability management.[3]

This process can be divided into two main periods by the severe financial crisis that hit the country in the early 1890s, leading to the failure of the first experiences of investment banking, to a restructuring of the banking system and to the birth of Banca d'Italia. During the 1920s, then, the evolution of universal banks and their transformation in quasi-holding companies precluded to their failure in the aftermath of the Great Crash, in the early 1930s, when the government had to intervene both in bailing them out and in promoting a radical re-shaping of the institutional and regulatory frameworks, putting an end to that paradigm.

Our chapter retraces the advent and development of investment banking in Italy during the decades preceding its failure in the early 1930s. It tries to show the activity of those banks, their evolution and the various tools they came to use in order to consolidate their ability to work and to root in a difficult institutional environment, that left them small room for raising new funds and for liquidating their assets.

1. The origins: Tilling the field

Though already in the 1850s few pioneering experiences in joint stock banking, along the lines of French *Crédit mobilier*, appeared in Piedmont and in Tuscany, at the time of unification Italy still had a fairly underdeveloped credit and banking system.[4] In fact, the financial apparatus of the new kingdom was quite segmented, with very different situations in the various

3 Maffeo Pantaleoni, *La caduta della Società generale di credito mobiliare italiano*, Turin, Utet, 1998, pp. 44ff. Giuseppe Conti, "Finanza d'impresa e capitale di rischio in Italia, 1870-1939", *Rivista di storia economica*, 10, 1993, No. 3, pp. 307-32.

4 Isidore Sachs, *L'Italie, ses finances et son développement économique depuis l'unification du royaume*, Paris, Guillaumin, 1885, pp. 699-707. Alessandro Polsi, *Alle origini del capitalismo italiano. Stato, banche e banchieri dopo l'Unità*, Turin, Einaudi, 1993, chapter 1. On the influence of France in the shaping of the Italian credit and financial systems, see Gino Luzzatto, *L'economia italiana dal 1861 al 1894*, Turin, Einaudi, 1993. Antonio Confalonieri, *Banca e industria in Italia, 1894-1906*, Bologna, Il Mulino, 1981. Bertrand Gille, *Les investissements français en Italie (1815-1914)*, Turin, Ilte, 1968.

regions and almost any presence of modern banking. While in Piedmont and in Tuscany a first core of new banks was developing and a certain articulation of the system was emerging especially in the former, thanks to the policy of *Banca Nazionale*[5] – roughly inspired to that of *Banque de France* – in the southern regions issuing banks dominated a backward environment where credit services were mostly granted by the semi-publicly owned institutions inherited from the *ancien régime*, such as pawnbroking charity bodies and rural non-for-profit bodies offering advances on crops.[6] In the central-northern regions, then, were active non-for-profit savings banks, while a community of merchant-bankers was widespread all over the country.[7] Starting from the 1860s, anyway, credit and banking saw a quite rapid development along with the first massive investments in public utilities and infrastructures – fore and foremost in railways – the establishment of new industries and, later, the first wave of industrial growth. These transformations in the financial sector and its subsequent developments were marked by a number of crises which had a relevant role in shaping the evolution of the credit system and of the new joint stock banks' patterns in particular.

After Unification, the commercial code of 1865 – partly inspired to the French one[8] – was aimed at giving a common administrative and legal framework to the new country, and tended to privilege the protection of entrepreneurs' rights and properties from possible speculators, however somehow sacrificing minority shareholders and creditors' rights to those

---

5 Leandro Conte, *La Banca Nazionale. Formazione e attività di una banca di emissione, 1843-1861*, Naples, ESI, 1990.

6 Gino Luzzatto, *L'economia Italiana*. Alessandro Polsi, *Alle origini del capitalismo italiano*. Salvatore La Francesca, *Storia del sistema bancario italiano*, Bologna, Il Mulino, 2004.

7 On the first Tuscan banks see, among others, see Giuseppe Conti, "Terra commercio e credito nella Toscana del XIX secolo", *Studi e ricerche*, Dept. of Economics, Università di Pisa, 1989. On the importance of savings banks in the Italian credit system, see Alberto Cova and Anna Maria Galli, *La Cassa di risparmio delle provincie lombarde dalla fondazione al 1940*, Milan-Rome, Cariplo-Laterza, 1991. Giuseppe Prato and Giuseppe Fenoglio, *La Cassa di risparmio di Torino nel suo primo centenario*, Turin, Sten, 1927. About the permanence of *ancien régime* banking practices and structures in Milan till the 1860s see Giandomenico Piluso, *L'arte dei banchieri. Moneta e credito a Milano da Napoleone all'Unità*, Milan, Angeli, 1999. Luciano Segreto, "I banchieri privati e l'industrializzazione italiana", *Imprese e storia*, No. 24, 2001, pp. 273-306: it underlined the relevance of merchant-bankers for the Italian credit system development during the 19th century.

8 In fact it was a sort of emendation of the Piedmontese code of 1842, in its turn derived from the *code Napoléon*. See Camera dei Deputati, *Ricerca sulle società commerciali. Linee evolutive della legislazione italiana e ordinamenti stranieri*, Rome, 1968.

of promoters.[9] Indeed, though till the introduction of the new commercial code in 1882 the government's authorisation for establishing limited liabilities firms and companies was needed, very weak measures were set up to ensure companies' and administrators' accountability. Even the short-lived experience of the *Sindacato governativo* (a sort of controlling Commission on joint stock companies depending on the ministry of Agriculture, industry and commerce) did not improve the situation, characterised by high degrees of opacity in financial and economic information on companies.[10] It was in such a context that *Credito Mobiliare Italiano* and *Banca Generale* were founded and had to work.

The former originated from the transformation of *Piedmontese Cassa del Commercio*, set up by Turin's private bankers in the 1850s as a tool aimed at mobilising their assets both by granting advances on shares and even by holding and trading them, since the stock exchanges of Turin and Genoa were still small and underdeveloped. Thus, from the mid-1850s, joint stock banks in Turin started buying large stakes from the private bankers (especially railways securities), and often modified their charters, officially embracing investment banking. Nevertheless, these banks did not comply exactly with the Crédit mobilier pattern, but were allowed to carry out both investment and deposit banking activities.[11] When in 1860 its major stockholders, the Rothschilds, withdrew their participation, Cassa del Commercio had to undergo a new reorganisation as soon as 1863, this time with the Pereires' Crédit mobilier as a partner, giving birth to Credito Mobiliare Italiano.[12] Banca Generale was founded in Milan in 1871, during the boom in banking foundations that took place at the beginning of the decade giving birth to several new joint stock banks, that nevertheless were often swept away in the following crisis of the mid-1870s.[13] The new bank was headquartered in Rome and it soon became the second largest investment bank in the country. Its promoters were some of the most prominent private bankers from Milan, Venice, Trieste and Turin, who were able to assure the participation of an

9 Giuseppe Conti, "Finanza d'impresa", *op. cit.*

10 On this body, see Franco Belli and Antonio Scialoja, "Vocazioni interventiste, miti ed ideologie del liberismo all'indomani dell'unificazione nazionale. Il controllo delle società commerciali e degli istituti di credito nell'esperienze del Sindacato governativo (1866-1869)", in Carlo De Cesare, *Il Sindacato governativo, le società commerciali nel Regno d'Italia*, Bologna, Forni, 1978.

11 Royal Decree, 3 May 1856, which approved the new charters of Cassa del Commercio (quoted in Alessandro Polsi, *Alle origini*, pp. 18-19).

12 Rondo Cameron, *France*, *op. cit.*, pp. 181-82. Among Italian founders there were also outstanding bankers, such as Bastogi and Balduino.

13 Gino Luzzatto, *L'economia italiana*, *op. cit.*, pp. 75-81. I. Sachs, *L'Italie, ses finances*, *op. cit.*, pp. 700ff.

important Austrian joint stock bank and of other Centre-European bankers, such as Goldschmidt and Bischoffsheim, to their project.[14]

Figure 1

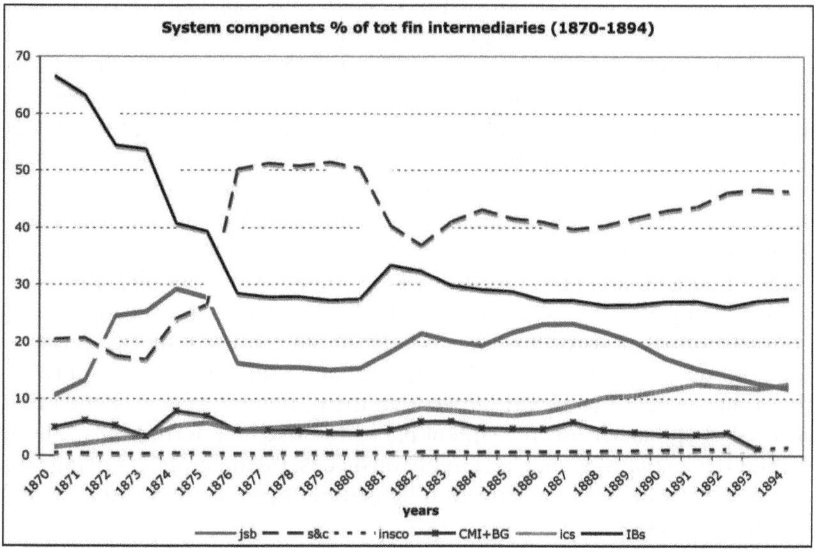

Note: banks' liabilities as a percentage of total system liabilities.

Source: calculations on A.M. Biscaini and P. Ciocca, 'Le strutture finanziarie: aspetti quantitativi di lungo periodo (1870-1970), in F. Vicarelli (ed.), *Capitale industriale e capitale finanziario: il caso italiano*, Bologna: Il Mulino, 1979, pp. 61-138; C. Brambilla, *Affari di banche. Banche universali in Italia in prospettiva comparata, 1860-1914*, Pisa: Plus-Pisa University Press, 2010.

Credito Mobiliare Italiano and *Banca Generale* were multi-purpose banks according to their charters, but they tended to be primarily, though not exclusively, committed to market activities. They emerged from the 1870s as giants in an environment of dwarf or local banks, having hardly any relations both with cooperative and savings banks and with smaller joint-stock ones. At the time, the credit market was still characterised by

14 Anna Maria Galli, "Sviluppo e crisi della Banca générale", in Enrico Decleva (ed.), *Antonio Allievi, dalle scienze civili alla pratica del credito*, Milan-Bari, Cariplo-Laterza, 1997, pp. 561-651. Gino Luzzatto, *L'economia italiana, op. cit.* Among founding partners there were the Union Bank of Vienna, the Milan banking houses Figli Weill-Schott, Pio Cozzi & Co., Ulrich & Co., Zaccaria Pisa, Cavajani Oneto & Co., the banking houses of Morpurgo and Parente, in Trieste, that were Rothschilds' correspondents; and three outstanding bankers from Turin: Ulrico Geisser, Ignazio Weil Weiss and the Fratelli Ceriana. On the financial *milieu* of the Piedmont capital, see Ivan Balbo, "Banche e banchieri a Torino. Identità e strategie (1883-1896)", *Imprese e storia*, No. 21, 2000, pp. 61-102.

the important role played by note-issuing banks (Fig. 1) that competed with other banks in offering commercial banking facilities to non financial firms and companies.

What seems to emerge from Figure 1 is that joint stock banks were quite a marginal component of the system, and that their development tended to be highly pro-cyclical and volatile: their share in the system did not change substantially between 1870 and 1894, except from ephemeral booming periods; moreover, what they had gained during the late 1870s and 1880s was not only lost in the following crisis, but it was not even regained until the mid-1900s (Fig. 2). On the contrary, non-for-profit institutions, such as savings and coop-banks experienced a steady and sustained growth that awarded to them almost half of the market. Thus, while the two largest investment banks were in fact major actors on the Italian financial and credit markets, they found extremely difficult to increase their collection, especially in the form of deposits, because of the competition of non-for-profit banks. Even state-owned special purpose institutions – mainly aimed at long term investments in agriculture, at that time – grew faster and larger than them, placing special bonds that made it even harder for investment banks to raise long term funds. These difficulties explain big banks' largely unsuccessful attempts in raising significant deposits, and their need to substitute them with correspondents' current accounts.

The segmentation of the credit system and its features, on the one hand, and the characters of the institutional and legal framework, on the other, can explain the strong ties Credito Mobiliare Italiano and Banca Generale established with the major note-issuing bank, *Banca Nazionale nel Regno d'Italia*, which sustained them whenever downturns or crises threatened their liquidity.[15] Their primary commitment to market activities can then be explained by the attempt to mobilise capital and to allocate it to long term investments while at the same time preserving their own stability in a still underdeveloped and poorly regulated economic context in which creditors suffered a lack of information. On one hand, thus, they collaborated with *Banca Nazionale* in placing risk free securities, such as national and local governments bonds; on the other, they underwrote and placed bonds and equities of railways companies and other public utilities, of basic industries such as metal works and mechanical engineering companies, essentially financing projects of national interest, that offered higher guarantees. When great infrastructural projects came nearly to an end, during the 1880s, *Credito Mobiliare* and *Banca Generale* started investing heavily in the real estate boom connected

[15] Many bankers serving as directors in the banks' boards were also sitting in the board of Banca Nazionale. Alessandro Polsi, *Alle origini, op. cit.*, p. 35.

with the renovation of main cities like Rome and Naples, relying upon a patrimonial concept of credit. Unfortunately this was not sufficient to avoid bankruptcy when the real estate bubble burst, causing frozen assets, that, together with accumulated non performing assets on industrial investments and persisting economic depression, eventually caused their failure[16] in 1892/93.

The financial crisis that hit the country in the early 1890s, during which Credito Mobiliare and Banca Generale collapsed, was extremely severe. It beheaded the Italian credit system, sweeping away not only the two major investment banks, but also many other banks, big and small, and one of the banks of issue, *Banca Romana*, while *Banca Nazionale* and the two Tuscan issuing banks were merged in the newly founded *Banca d'Italia.* This latter established itself as the dominant bank of issue, and soon as a real central bank, while the other two survivor issuing banks (*Banco di Napoli* and *Banco di Sicilia*) played a marginal role as central and issuing authorities. These outcomes had consequences on the relations between the new major bank of issue, *Banca d'Italia*, and the joint stock banks, too, as it will be seen in the next section.

2. A new phase: Growth and strengthening

The new commercial code of 1882 presented several novelties that improved the legal framework and ameliorated both the information disclosure on the part of companies and the minority shareholders' and creditors' rights as compared to the privileges of promoters and majority shareholders, improving corporate governance tools in joint stock companies, so bringing Italian institutions closer to those of the other main European countries.[17] The new code, in fact, fixed a few stricter rules on bookkeeping and made annual balance sheet publication as well as a statutory board of auditors (*collegio sindacale*) compulsory. However, the law only prescribed that balance sheets reported the exact amount of profits and losses, of capital and of reserves, but did not fix rules on the quality and quantity of information to be given on other items, in contrast with other European legislations, such as those introduced in England, Belgium and Germany, that indeed provided for more precise and

16 See Maffeo Pantaleoni, *Credito Mobiliare Italiano op. cit.* Gino Luzzatto, *L'economia Italiana, op. cit.* Antonio Confalonieri, *Banca e industria in Italia, 1894-1906, op. cit.*

17 Alberto Errera, *Il nuovo codice di commercio del Regno d'Italia*, Florence, Pellas, 1883. Giuseppe Conti, "Finanza d'impresa", *op. cit.* Raffaele Teti, "Imprese, imprenditori e diritto", in Franco Amatori *et al.* (eds.), *Storia d'Italia, Annali 15, L'Industria*, Turin, Einaudi, 1999, pp. 1211-1303. Giuseppe Carriero, Pierluigi Ciocca and Monica Marcucci, "Diritto e risultanze dell'economia nell'Italia unita", in Pierluigi Ciocca and Gianni Toniolo (eds.), *Storia economica d'Italia*, Rome-Bari, Laterza, 2004, Vol. 3-2, pp. 455-528.

accurate bookkeeping practices.[18] The statutory board of auditors, then, was elected by the same majority which expressed the board of directors; moreover, the law was very soft about shareholding syndicates, interlocking and pyramidal shareholdings; and shareholders maintained the right to withdraw from the company at any time, a threat that could be used to oppose strategic decisions such as new capital issues, mergers and acquisitions, changes in the company objects, etc.[19]

Banca Commerciale Italiana (Comit) and *Credito Italiano* (Credit) – founded after the crisis had swept away not only the two biggest investment banks, but also a plethora of other joint stock banks and, most importantly, four of the existing six issuing banks – had to cope with a framework in which *Banca d'Italia* was unable, and unwilling, to maintain the same strict, friendly relations and generous attitudes Banca Nazionale had had with the failed great banks. The main bank of issue arose from the ashes of this latter and of two regional issuing banks, having moreover taken charge of the liquidation of *Banca Romana*'s frozen assets, and displayed a more thrifty behaviour in offering refinancing facilities to the banking system.[20] Comit and Credit hybridised Central European patterns and experiences, as the composition of their groups of control confirms,[21] and, because of their origins and their universal pattern, they are often referred to as German-style mixed banks.[22] During the two decades preceding WWI, universal banks answered to the

18 Lucien Cellérier, *Études sur les sociétés en France et dans les pays voisins*, Paris, 1905. Gino Zappa, *Le valutazioni di bilancio con particolare riguardo ai bilanci delle società per azioni*, Milan, Società editrice libraria, 1910. for a wider discussion on these issues see also Carlo Brambilla and Giuseppe Conti, "Informazione e regole contabili nei rapporti tra banca e industria", in Giuseppe Conti (ed.), *Creare il credito e arginare i rischi. Il sistema finanziario tra nobiltà e miserie del capitalismo italiano*, Bologna, Il Mulino, 2007.

19 Giuseppe Conti, "Finanza d'impresa", *op. cit.* Arthur Kline Kuhn, *A comparative study of the law of corporations with particular reference to the protection of creditors and shareholders*, New York, 1912. Cesare Vivante, "Per la riforma delle società anonime", *Rivista del diritto commerciale e del diritto generale delle obbligazioni*, 2, 1913, No. 2.

20 Franco Bonelli (ed.), *La Banca d'Italia dal 1894 al 1913. Momenti della formazione di una banca centrale*, Rome-Bari, Laterza, 1991.

21 On the constitution of the two new banks see A. Confalonieri, *Banca e industria in Italia 1894-1906*, Vol. 2. Peter Hertner, *Il capitale tedesco in Italia dall'Unità alla prima guerra mondiale, banche miste e sviluppo economico italiano*, Bologna, Il Mulino, 1984.

22 See for instance Jon S. Cohen, "Financing industrialisation in Italy, 1894-1914. The partial transformation of a late comer", *Journal of Economic History*, 27, 1967, pp. 363-82. Giorgio Mori, "L'economia italiana dagli anni ottanta alla prima guerra mondiale", in *Storia dell'industria elettrica in Italia:* Vol. 1, Giorgio Mori (ed.), *Le origini 1882-1914*, Bari, Laterza 1992, pp. 1-106. Caroline Fohlin, "Relationship banking, liquidity and investment in German industrialization", *Journal of Finance*, 53, 1998, No. 5, pp. 1737-1758. Caroline Fohlin, "Capital mobilisation and utilisation in latecomer economies, Germany and Italy compared", *European Review of Economic History*, 2 (1999), pp. 139-74.

Figure 2

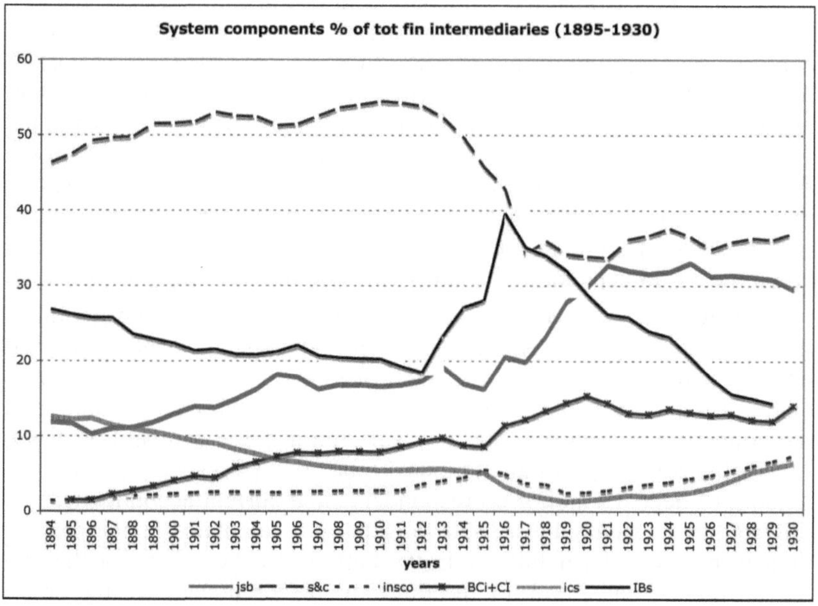

Note: banks' liabilities as a percentage of total system liabilities.
Source: see Fig. 1.

growing demand for investment banking and industrial financing induced by the upturn trend of the Giolittian years, committing themselves in financing especially new sectors such as chemicals, metal works and mechanical engineering, electricity. With the new century, the growth of industrial investments and profits, the slackening of public debt issues, and universal banks' market activities produced the first stock exchange relevant widening in listed securities and prices.[23] Compared to their Italian ancestors, they showed stronger abilities to raise funds from customers, to manage multi-branch banking, particularly from 1900 onwards, and to maintain friendly and stable relations with international financial circles: that allowed them to more easily manage demand for funding and investment banking services through the organisation of larger pools and syndicates, thus preventing a too rapid exhaustion of their means and helping preserving their liquidity.

Besides, Comit and Credit grew faster and bigger than the previous generation of investment banks, as it can be noticed from Fig. 2. Whereas

---

23 Gianni Toniolo, *An economic history of liberal Italy, 1850-1918*, London-New York, Routledge, 1990. Giovanni Federico and Gianni Toniolo, "Italy", in Richard Sylla and Gianni Toniolo (eds.), *Patterns of European Industrialization. The Nineteenth Century*, London-New York, Routledge, 1991.

Credito Mobiliare and Banca Generale remained stable throughout the period on levels around the 5 or 6 per cent of the entire system, the two big Milanese banks surpassed them already in the first years of the new century, growing quite fast – in spite of the crisis of 1907 – to a share of about the 15 per cent in 1920, then consolidating their share in the system around the 12-13 per cent throughout the decade. The late 1910s and the 1920s were also the period during which joint stock banks at large, for the first time, underwent a significant increase of their share, almost reaching that of the non-for-profit institutions, that on the contrary experienced a remarkable drop from an average of about the 50 per cent before 1914, to about the 34-35 per cent in the late 1910s and in the 1920s.

However, the still very relevant share of the credit system liabilities held by non-for-profit institutions and by note-issuing banks remained an important constraint to the growth of joint stock banking, and especially of universal banks.[24] These latter did develop branch banking and the collection of deposits, but they suffered a fierce competition from, especially, non-for-profit institutions. Figure 3 and 4 respectively plot the amount of deposits and of correspondents and current accounts held by different institutions in the 1890-1930 period, calculated as the ratio to their respective total liabilities. Both charts show these data for the two big universal banks, and for the three major components of the credit system, savings banks, coop-banks and joint stock banks.

As it emerges from Fig. 3, non-for-profit institutions, namely savings banks and coop-banks, were the only components of the system able to raise significant amounts of deposits, and, moreover, they succeeded in maintaining their deposits to liabilities ratio very stable in time, especially as savings banks are concerned. Both joint stock banks and Comit and Credit, instead, clearly found more difficult to collect savings from the public. Quite interestingly, then, is the fact that the deposits to liabilities ratio of joint stock banks fell sharply in 1900 after a significant ten-year trend of growth, and never recovered. On the contrary, after a period of relative stability on values of about the 30 per cent on average, their deposits to liabilities ratio steadily decreased further to levels near the 20 per cent.

Comit and Credit also show a positive trend till 1908, just to stabilise in the early 1910s, and to fall below the 20 per cent after the war. What seems to emerge from Fig. 3, then, are the difficulties the two big banks had in collecting deposits during their first years, most probably because of the dominant position of non-for-profit institution in this field; moreover, the war seems to have interrupted the previous growing trend for good, since in the 1920s their deposits to liabilities ratio stabilised on the

24 Issuing banks maintained the right to behave as commercial banks, thus offering credit facilities to the public, till the promulgation of the banking reform in 1936.

pre-1907 average values. Both big universal banks and joint stock banks in general, indeed, heavily substituted deposits with correspondents and current accounts, partly coming from inter-bank foreign loans, especially in the case of Comit and Credit (Fig. 4).[25]

Figure 3

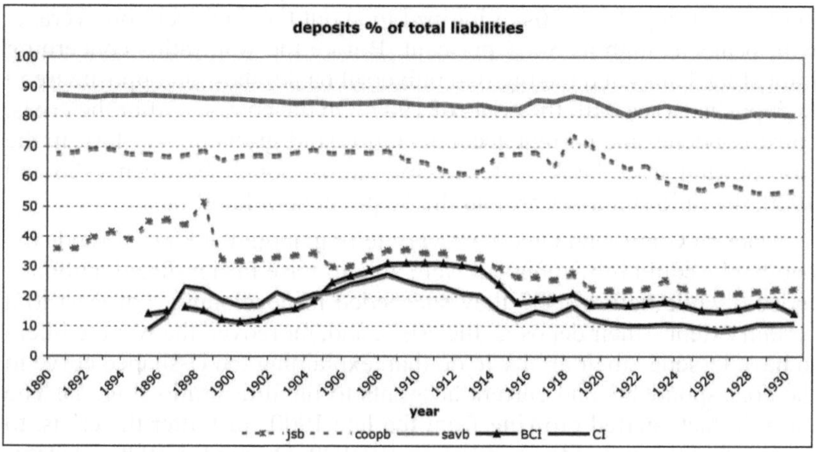

Source: calculations on F. Cotula *et al.*, *I bilanci delle aziende di credito, 1890-1936*, Rome, Laterza, 1996; Brambilla, *Affari di banche.*

Figure 4

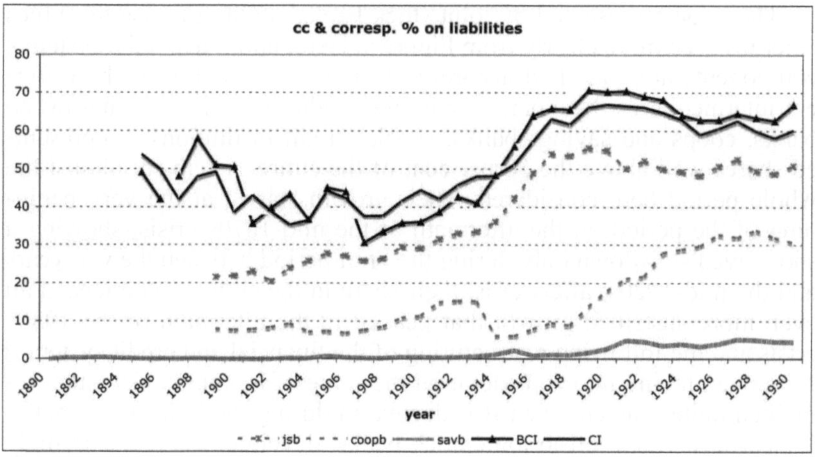

Source: see Fig. 3.

25 On the foreign inter-bank collection by Comit and Credit see Antonio Confalonieri, *Banche miste e grande industria in Italia, 1914-1933*, Milan, Banca commerciale italiana, 1994.

Fig. 4 confirms the important break represented by the war: all system components show an increase in their respective current accounts to liabilities ratios. This is true, for instance, even in the case of savings banks, where correspondents and current accounts were traditionally a very marginal means of collecting funds: before 1914, in fact, the ratio did not exceed the 1 per cent – and was on average about the 0.5 per cent – but then, during the 1920s, it jumped to about the 4 per cent on average, with peaks as high as 5-5.5 per cent. Before the war, ratios concerning joint stock banks and the big two universal banks show an opposite trend to deposits, at least till the crisis of 1907. On the contrary, after the crisis, correspondents and current accounts ratios start growing very fast. In the case of joint stock banks, after having almost double between 1906 and 1920, the ratio stabilises around the 50 per cent of liabilities.

Data on Comit and Credit are very telling about the kind of funds the two banks could rely upon and were able to raise in significant amounts. Indeed, while before 1907 they succeeded in developing – at least to a certain extent – their deposits, the crisis, and, moreover, the war are likely to have lessened their ability to do that, explaining the U-shaped curve in the correspondents and current accounts to liabilities ratio (Fig. 4). The ratio, in fact, started growing from the late 1900s just after the crisis, to peak just at the end of the conflict, in 1919/20. During the 1920s, it stabilised on values well above the 60 per cent on average (or about 20 points above the average of the pre-1908 period), denoting a worsening in the two banks financial structures.

The issue represented by joint stock banks' ability to raise resources emerges even more clearly from Figure 5. Here, liabilities of the system's components are classified according to the contestability of the different intermediaries. Non-contestable intermediaries – that is state-owned banks, coops and savings banks, special credit institutions – represented shares well above the 50 per cent of the entire system for almost the whole period here considered. Their growth started at the very beginning of the period, in the aftermath of the mid-1870s crisis, showing a short-lived slowdown only during the brief period between the war years and the mid-1920s; afterwards, their share in the system experienced an even more sustained growth that peaked in the aftermath of the 1930s crisis and the following restructuring of the financial and credit system.[26] Moreover, taking into consideration the share of issuing banks – that remained quite relevant even if it decreased during the long run – makes it clear how room left to joint stock banks' development was extremely reduced. That is to say, joint stock banks, and especially big universal

[26] It has been calculated that from 1936 onward, and till the mid-1990s, almost the 70 per cent of the credit system was represented by non-contestable intermediaries.

ones, had but very little possibilities to raise funds by means of mergers and acquisitions, simply because there were but limited preys available. This notwithstanding, Comit and Credit tried to overcome the relative shortage of funds by gradually setting up and organising a network of daughter banks, mainly situated in the area between Milan and the Ticino, in southern Switzerland, though with minor success as for their overall ability to increase deposits.[27]

Figure 5

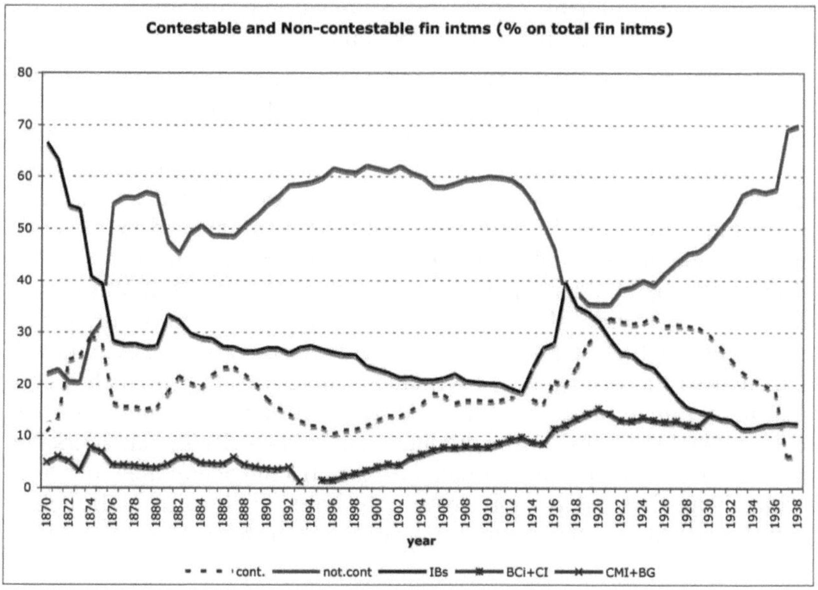

Note: banks' liabilities as a percentage of total system liabilities; contestable intermediaries: joint stock banks. Non-contestable intermediaries: state-owned banks, savings banks, coop-banks, special banking institutions (Ics).
Source: see Fig. 1.

Turning to their activities, a comparative analysis on big investment banks in Italy, France and Germany has shown as Comit and Credit tended to depart from the 'classical' pattern of universal banking represented by big German banks.[28] They in fact seem to have developed different strategies to assure 'permanent' investments to industrial companies. In Germany the legal context provided several measures to discourage speculative behaviours: higher face value of stocks; a

27 Antonio Confalonieri, *Banche miste e grande industria*, *op. cit.*

28 Carlo Brambilla, *Affari di banche*, *op. cit.*

clear separation between common and privileged stocks; a balance of power between managing bodies – such as the board of directors and the executive board (*Vorstand*) – on the one hand, and controlling bodies – such as the supervisory board (*Aufsichtsrat*) and the auditors appointed by local authorities – on the other; wider information on companies situation and deeds; and more precise provisions on managers' responsibility in case of frauds.[29] By putting their own representatives in supervisory boards, German banks had a pretty effective means for overseeing and monitoring debtors, thus strengthening their ability to promote 'permanent' capital investments and guaranteeing for effectual intermediation between savers and investors.

The new law on stock exchange of 1896, then, having banned future contracts for most securities and assured a stricter supervision over the stock exchange, brought a large share of security trading 'inside' the banks, hence fostering a stricter control by banks over the market, which enhanced their ability to assure long lasting commitment in industrial companies' financing. In Italy, the legal framework shaped by the commercial code of 1882 left important issues, such as that of the protection of minority shareholders' and creditors' rights, or that of full information disclosure, still unresolved; moreover, the stock markets were smaller and more volatile, characterised by higher speculative behaviours that discouraged the diffusion of 'permanent' investments.[30] In such a context, then, Italian banks tried to cope with information asymmetries and to strengthen their position as creditors and/or minority shareholders first and foremost by acquiring enough voting rights in general meetings as to assure themselves one or more seats in the board of directors of the debtor companies and getting effective supervision over them.[31]

---

29 Arthur Kline Kuhn, *A comparative study*, *op. cit.*, pp. 69-85. C. Vivante, "Per la riforma", *op. cit.* Walter Rathenau, "Le società per azioni. Riflessioni suggerite dall'esperienza degli affari", *Rivista delle società*, No. 5, 1960, pp. 912-947. Caroline Fohlin, *Finance Capitalism and Germany's Rise to Industrial Power*, Cambridge, Cambridge University Press, 2007.

30 Carlo Brambilla and Giuseppe Conti, "Informazione e regole contabili", in Giovanni Siciliano, *Cento anni di borsa in Italia*, Bologna, Il Mulino, 2001. Stefano Baia Curioni, *Regolazione e competizione. Storia del mercato azionario in Italia* (*1808-1938*), Bologna, Il Mulino, 1995.

31 Indeed, interlocking directorates were a practice Comit and Credit widely used. See Francesca Pino, "Sui fiduciari della Comit nelle società per azioni, 1898-1918", *Rivista di storia economica*, n.s., 8, 1991, No. unico, pp. 115-148. Caroline Fohlin, "*Fiduciari* and firm liquidity constraints, the Italian experience with German-style universal banking", *Explorations in Economic History*, 35, 1998, No. 1, pp. 83-107. Michelangelo Vasta and Alberto Baccini, "Banks and industry in Italy, 1911-1936. New evidence using the interlocking directorates technique", *Financial History Review*, 4, 1997, pp. 139-159.

This practice implied however a careful tuning in order not to excessively burden banks' securities portfolios, hence endangering their own liquidity. And indeed balance sheets data suggest that Italian great banks did not maintain significantly higher participations in industrial companies than German ones. What, on the contrary, seems to differ Italian banks' balance sheets from the others, is the amount of contangos (*riporti*) and, especially, of third parties' securities deposits (*conti titoli*), this latter being very tiny in French banks and absent in German ones. Comit and Credit securities deposits, on the contrary, amounted on average to two thirds or even more of their total assets.[32] In most French banks contangos amounted to small proportions of total assets, while on average German ones invested more on them, but still to a lesser extent than Comit and Credit. Between the 1890s and 1914, the Italian big banks invested on average the 16-17 per cent of their assets in contangos, that is to say about one third more than their German counterparts.[33] Through contangos and securities deposits Italian banks could acquire proxy voting rights, a strategy that enabled them to maintain and extend supervision and control over companies, hence securing their position as creditors or minority shareholders, at a fraction of the cost that they would have had to bear for taking stakes in them.

The international liquidity crisis of 1907 hit the Italian stock exchanges fiercely and hampered the development of Italian financial markets, that never recovered completely nor grew broader till the last decades of the 20th century, and left industrial capital supply entirely on the shoulders of the banks.[34] That had relevant consequences on the universal banks ability to fulfil their functions while preserving their own liquidity and 'freedom of movement', since it compelled them to higher commitments towards industrial financing, and hence to eventually accept heavier portfolios of securities and illiquid loans, a fact that would have soon determined an involution in universal banking patterns.

3. Roaring Twenties? The evolution in investment banking patterns after the war

The crisis of 1907 spotlighted the fragility of the Italian financial system and inspired the debate on the issues of industrial financing and banking stability that took place between 1909 and 1914, involving both

32 In some years they even exceeded total assets. Carlo Brambilla, *Affari di banche*, *op. cit.*, Appendix, tables 1-15.

33 *Ibidem*.

34 Franco Bonelli, *La crisi del 1907 una tappa dello sviluppo industriale in Italia*, Turin, Fondazione Einaudi, 1971. Giovanni Siciliano, *Cento anni di borsa*. Antonio Confalonieri, *Banca e industria in Italia dalla crisi del 1907 all'agosto del 1914*, Milan, Banca commerciale italiana, 1982.

industrialists and academics.[35] Meanwhile, the idea that a better protection to depositors was needed began to emerge, and proposals for new legislation aimed at regulating and supervising deposit-taking institutions were presented in 1908 and again in 1913, though without success.[36] It was only in 1926, however, that a new comprehensive legislation was eventually introduced.[37] Debate on industrial financing underlined the need for steady investment flows to the industrial sector and concerns about the increased difficulties banks had in asset liability management following the crisis, that left capital markets even more fragile than before.

A new scheme in industrial financing began then to emerge, pointing to the creation of special credit institutions (ICS) aimed at providing long term investments to specific industries, those characterised by the highest capital intensity, the longest investment depreciation, and differed profitability, thus relieving banks of at least the most illiquid share of their credits. Though the first of such institutes – CSVI[38] – was created in 1914, it was only after the war that their activities started eroding universal banks' scope. Alberto Beneduce, a technocrat close to Francesco Saverio Nitti[39] and to the director of Banca d'Italia, Bonaldo Stringher, promoted the constitution of several other special credit institutions, each one devoted to a peculiar end or sector.[40] Beneduce's basic idea was to raise

35 Antonio Confalonieri, *Banca e industria in Italia, 1907-1914*, *op. cit.*, Vol. 2. Carlo Pace & Giovanna Morelli (eds.), *Origini e identità del credito speciale*, Milan, Angeli, 1984.

36 Franco Bonelli, *La Banca d'Italia dal 1894 al 1913*. In the 1908 proposal, banks would have been required to create two distinct sections in order to separately manage 'savings' and 'commercial' deposits, with the prohibition to use the former for long term lending. The following project, in 1913, envisaged the introduction of liquidity and reserve ratios, and of supervision on deposit-taking institutions.

37 Giuseppe Guarino and Gianni Toniolo (eds.), *La Banca d'Italia e il sistema bancario, 1919-1936*, Roma-Bari, Laterza, 1993.

38 Created by Banca d'Italia, it discounted one signature industrial bills, making thus possible to rediscount them at the note-issuing banks, and so monetising industrial credit. Anna Maria Biscaini, Paolo Gnes and Alessandro Rosselli, "Origini e sviluppo del Consorzio per sovvenzioni su valori industriali durante il governatorato Stringher", *Bancaria*, No. 2, 1985.

39 A leftist liberal with background in economics and finance, Nitti served as minister of Agriculture, industry and commerce in 1911-1914 and as minister of the Treasury in 1917-1919, then as Prime Minister for few months in 1919.

40 Crediop (1919) and Icipu (1924) financed, respectively, public works (infrastructures) and public utilities. Credimare (1928) committed to shipbuilding financing. Pier Francesco Asso and Marcello De Cecco, *Storia del Crediop. Tra credito speciale e finanza pubblica 1920-1960*, Roma-Bari, Laterza, 1994. On Beneduce see Franco Bonelli, "Alberto Beneduce", in Alberto Mortara (ed.), *I protagonisti dell'intervento pubblico in Italia*, Milan, Angeli, 1984, pp. 329-356. Mimmo Franzinelli and Marco Magnani, *Beneduce. Il finanziere di Mussolini*, Milan, Mondadori, 2009.

savings for investments through the placement of state-guaranteed bonds issued by specialised credit institutions; these latter would have invested such funds in mortgage loans to industrial and public utilities companies. The objective was twofold: solving the mismatch between assets and liabilities typical of universal banking and channelling savings towards productive investments through the progressive development of a wide bond market, without effects on money supply.[41]

During the war, Italian industrial apparatus experienced a significant growth, especially in heavy industries related to the war effort and to the production of weapons and ammunitions, such as steelworks, shipbuilding, automotive and engineering, chemicals. Often, the development of big business led to the formation of big, vertically integrated, industrial groups, emphasising the oligopolistic features of many industries. That process was financed by large universal banks, whose liquidity constraints were relaxed thank to Banca d'Italia and to the tools it put in place to guarantee the stability of the system.[42]

Table 1. Special credit institutions

Institution	**Promoter**	**Year of constitution**	**Aims & functions**
Csvi	Bank of Italy	1914	Refinancing banks; industrial financing (short-medium term)
Crediop	Government (Beneduce)	1919	Public works and infrastructures long term financing
Spv-Csvi (later *Istituto di Liquidazioni*)	Bank of Italy	1922	Bail outs of Ansaldo and Banco di Roma
Icipu	Government (Beneduce)	1924	Public utilities long term financing
Istituto di Liquidazioni	Government	1926	Sell back industrial participation to private capitals
Credimare	Government (Beneduce)	1928	Shipbuilding long term financing
IMI	Government (Beneduce)	1931	Long term industrial financing
IRI *sez finanziamenti*	Government (Beneduce)	1933	Medium-long term industrial financing

41 For a long run perspective on 'Beneduce institutes' and on industrial credit in Italy in the 20th century, see Giandomenico Piluso, "Gli istituti di credito speciale", in Franco Amatori *et al.* (eds.), *Storia d'Italia, Annali*, 15, *L'industria*, Turin, Einaudi, 1999, pp. 505-547.

42 During the whole war the Banca d'Italia ensured a discount window to the banks, while the Csvi discounted paper not eligible to be directly discounted at the banks of issue. See Anna Maria Biscaini, Paolo Gnes and Alessandro Rosselli, "Origini e sviluppo del Consorzio".

At the end of the conflict, industrial enterprises had to face a number of issues. On the one hand, they had to cope with gigantism problems, overproduction and difficult reorganisation processes; on the other one, alternate short cycles affected their financial structure, strengthening their dependence from universal banks. The banking crisis and the financial turmoil of the immediate post-war years, to which the hostile takeover attempts on the two big Milanese banks by industrial groups were not extraneous, eventually resulted in the failure of two of the big universal banks.[43] Hence, Comit and Credit, that successfully rejected takeover attempts by, respectively, the Ansaldo group and the FIAT-SNIA groups, strengthened their primacy as the *Big Two*, increased industrial financing and market activities, as well as their role as organisers of big business corporate governance.[44] To win the battle on their own control, the two Milanese banks assigned their own equities to *ad hoc* holding companies.[45] These latter were owned by the banks themselves, directly and through "allied groups" – i.e. industrial concerns linked to the banks – and were also committed to intervene on financial markets to sustain the course of banks' stocks. Although, as mentioned, that enabled the Big Two to successfully reject hostile takeovers, and to prevent further raids by outsiders, it led to the virtual disappearance of their capital and to the removal of any form of effective control on bank managers' conduct and activities.[46]

43 Banca Italiana di Sconto, the youngest and weakest of the big banks, strictly linked with the Ansaldo group through interlocking shareholdings, failed in 1921 and was liquidated. Banco di Roma, the third bank of the country for dimension, pursued a too fast and unwise expansion during the previous years and got virtually insolvent by 1922, it was eventually rescued in 1923 by the Banca d'Italia, probably worried about the consequences its fall could have had on the stability of the system after the failure of the Bis. On these episodes see Anna Maria Falchero, *La banca italiana di sconto 1914-1921. Sette anni di guerra*, Milan, Angeli, 1990. Antonio Confalonieri, *Banche miste e grande industria, op. cit.* Gianni Toniolo, "Italian banking, 1919-1939", in Charles H. Feinstein (ed.), *Banking, Currency and Finance in Europe between the Wars*, Oxford, Clarendon Press, 1995. Piero Sraffa, "The Bank Crisis in Italy", *The Economic Journal*, 32 (126), 1922, pp. 178-197.

44 Antonio Confalonieri, *Banche miste e grande industria*. Giorgio Mori, "Le guerre parallele. L'industria elettrica in Italia nel periodo della grande guerra (1914-1919)", in Giorgio Mori, *Il capitalismo industriale in Italia. Processo di industrializzazione e storia d'Italia*, Roma, Editori Riuniti, 1977.

45 The two holding companies set up by Comit and Credit were, respectively, Comofin and Cofina.

46 In 1924 Credit had to counter a new raid by Gualino (SNIA), all managers and middle managers (from managing directors to the last branch office's cashier) resigned simultaneously compelling Gualino to withdraw. UniCredit Historical Archives (Uha), *Minutes of the Board of directors*, 28/4/1924. letters of resignation are preserved in Uha, Direzione Centrale (Dc), Segreterie Alta Direzione, Cassaforte riservata della Dc, 42, *Credito Italiano-Avv. Gualino* (*assalto 1924*). A description and discussion about changes in universal banks ownership structures and its consequences are in Stefano Battilossi, "Did governance fail universal banks?", *Economic History Review*, 62, SI, 2009, pp. 101-134. on financial holding companies in the 1920s see Stefano Battilossi, "Banche miste, gruppi di imprese e società finanziarie (1914-1933)", in Giuseppe Conti and Salvatore La Francesca (eds.), *Banche e reti di banche nell'Italia postunitaria*, Bologna, Il Mulino, 2000, pp. 307-52.

As Fig. 3 and 4 show, banks' ability to raise deposits deteriorated during the 1920s, endangering their liquidity and compelling them to heavily rely upon inter-banking accounts, especially foreign ones, exposing them to the steep oscillations that characterised international liquidity during the decade. In fact, archive records show that both banks collected between one third to one fifth of their correspondents and current accounts from abroad. Foreign funds were crucial especially to Comit, where they represented a relevant share of the bank's resources as soon as 1922, and accounted for about the 35-38 per cent of total collection between 1923 and 1926. Moreover, in 1925, Comit had to face an important withdrawal of foreign funds and turned to Banca d'Italia, obtaining advances as large as the 30 per cent of its total collection. During the second half of the 1920s, big universal banks found increasingly difficult to maintain their own liquidity owing to both the continuing haemorrhage of foreign funds and the deflationary downturn caused by the return of the lira to the gold standard, in 1926/27.[47]

Over those same years, a new Banking Act was enacted, introducing relevant changes in the institutional framework.[48] Till then, banking regulation had concerned the banks of issue alone, while commercial banks had been subject to the commercial code as any other company: for the first time, then, the 1926 legislation provided a regulatory regime to the entire system. First, it overcame the long-lasting question of note-issuing, granting the monopoly on the issue of money to Banca d'Italia; recalling the failed projects of 1908 and 1911-13, then, the new regime recognised the protection of savings as a matter of 'public interest', and it imposed to all banks capital adequacy ratios, limits to credit to any individual customer, the formation of reserves. The new legislation also introduced supervision by the central bank through direct inspections at the banks, and periodical, standardised reports of their balances. Nevertheless, no provisions were introduced on interlocking and pyramidal shareholdings, nor on the role of groups and syndicates as it emerged in bank-industry relations after the war, basically coming too late to modify the course of universal banks' behaviour and the involution in their pattern.[49]

47 Antonio Confalonieri, *Banche miste e grande industria*, *op. cit.*, pp. 560-570 and 738-743.

48 Stefano Battilossi, "Did governance fail", *op. cit.*, p. 110, notes how the introduction of the new legislation, aimed at avoiding further banking crises and at fostering the stability of the credit system, was related to the government's worries about the "viability of the restored Gold Exchange Standard".

49 Alfredo Gigliobianco *et al.*, "Innovation and regulation in the wake of financial crises in Italy (1880s-1930s)", in Alfredo Gigliobianco and Gianni Toniolo (eds.), *Financial Market Regulation in the Wake of Financial Crises, The Historical Experience*, Workshops and Conferences, No. 1, Rome, Banca d'Italia, 2009, pp. 45-73.

Facing the turbulent and adverse environment of the post-war decade, in fact, big universal banks tried to strengthen their position as creditors and shareholders by forming pyramidal groups and interlocking syndicates in order to enhance their market power and to secure control over industrial enterprises, quickly transforming into bank-holding companies at the head of financial-industrial groups.[50] Indeed Comit and Credit did not exploit the stock exchange boom of 1922-1925 to withdraw industrial participations, but rather to gain higher profits from syndicates and market activities. Both banks, then, favoured concentration and cartels formation as means to strengthen companies and to ease monitoring and control on companies, industrial groups, and on whole industrial sectors. That was especially the case of metallurgical and electrical industries, as witnessed, for instance, by the fierce struggle that oppose Comit and Credit in their endeavour to gain control over Bastogi, a quasi-bank holding company and a coffer of electrical companies relevant stocks. Fights for Bastogi control were eventually stopped in 1926, when Beneduce imposed on Comit and Credit to jointly run the holding company.[51] Often competing fiercely to get rich *affaires* and to obtain exclusive relations with customers, Comit and Credit greatly enlarged their securities portfolios, though they then concealed the bulk of these holdings filling out-of-balance 'special accounts' and daughter financial companies' portfolios with industrial stocks.[52]

Increasing commitment towards industrial financing prompted big universal banks to find new tools in order to gather information about their customers and to improve their screening and monitoring abilities over borrowers and participated enterprises. Along with interlocking

---

50 In the words of Raffaele Mattioli, Comit's managing director after 1933, this interlocking shareholding between banks and industrial groups assumed the characters of a "monstrous siamese twinship", see Raffaele Mattioli, "I problemi attuali del credito", *Mondo Economico*, No. 2, 13 January 1962.

51 Bastogi was a former railways company that after railways nationalisation in 1905 had become a sort of investment bank specialized in mechanical and electrical industries. When in the mid-1920s fights for its control were transforming in an endless war threatening the power industry and its stability, Beneduce succeeded in imposing a collaboration agreement to all contenders, transforming Bastogi in the "clearing house" of Italian financial interests, a role later performed by Mediobanca. Giandomenico Piluso, "Lo speculatore, i banchieri e lo stato, la Bastogi da Max Bondi ad Alberto Beneduce (1918-1933)", *Annali di storia dell'impresa*, Vol. 7, Bologna, Il Mulino, 1991, pp. 319-373. Giandomenico Piluso, "Un centauro metà pubblico e metà privato. La Bastogi di Alberto Beneduce a Mediobanca", *Annali della Fondazione Luigi Einaudi*, Vol. 26, Turin, Fondazione Einaudi, 1992, pp. 347-392.

52 Careful analysis of archive records allowed Confalonieri, *Banche miste e grande industria* to map quite well, even if not exhaustively, their participations and the structure of their financial and industrial 'groups'. See also Stefano Battilossi, "Did governance fail", *op. cit.*, figure 1, p. 112.

directorates and monitoring of customers' cash flows through supply of day-to-day banking services,[53] from the 1900s Comit and Credit began developing other strategies to supervise customers and strengthen their ability to collect private information about debtors. Comit organised a first nut of an industrial technical department, Credit relied upon expertise of some of its board members, namely Giovanni Battista Pirelli, an engineer who run the first and most important rubber company in Italy, and Giacomo Castelbolognesi, a banker with a long experience on international financial markets and in chemical industry. In 1915, then, Credit hired Alberto Lodolo, an electrical engineer with a relevant experience in electrical plant building and management, as general director responsible for its electrical and industrial *affaires*. Lodolo flanked Carlo Orsi as managing director in the 1920s, being especially committed to the creation of Credit's electrical group and with its financial and industrial organisation.[54] At Comit, a metallurgical engineer, Emilio Tansini, was hired in 1900 and flanked by Ferdinando Adamoli, a bank officer since 1898 and an expert in accounting and financial mathematics.[55] In 1907, they were both transferred to the newly organised Technical industrial office, Tansini being the director. This office was the core of what soon became a Technical financial office aimed at the financial and technical supervision of financed and participated enterprises. From the late 1920s it employed several young engineers and accountants, that would have worked under the direction of Giorgio Di Veroli at the bank's industrial holding Sofindit to reorganise industrial companies belonging to the "Comit group" and to coordinate the work of the bank's officers in the boards of those companies.[56] During the 1920s, the two banks' technical and financial departments, however organised, flanked their managers in securing

53 Francesca Pino, "Sui fiduciari della Comit". Michelangelo Vasta and Alberto Baccini, "Banks and industry in Italy".

54 Carlo Brambilla, "Lodolo, Alberto", mimeo, 2004. At Credit an industrial department gradually emerged in the 1910s and 1920s, devoting itself mainly with the collection of information on debtor companies. Credit also published reports on major companies (*Notizie statistiche*).

55 He taught *Banking Practice* at Bocconi University from 1904 to 1907. Guido Montanari, "Introduzione", in Archivio Storico B.C.I., *Società finanziaria industriale italiana (Sofindit)*, Milan, Banca commerciale italiana, 1991, pp. I-LI.

56 On Sofindit engineers, see Ferruccio Ricciardi, "Gestione e riorganizzazione industriale durante la crisi, da Comit a Sofindit (1930-34)", *Archivi e imprese*, No. 18, 1998, pp. 291-343. Their activities were especially devoted to the reorganisation of steel works, telephone and electrical holdings and gas companies (Terni, Ilva, Sip). After 1933 this group of experts was transferred to Iri where they went on working on the same tasks. Many of these young engineers became directors and managers in Iri's participated companies in the late 1930s, often continuing their job also in the 1950s. Alberto Mortara (ed.), *I protagonisti dell'intervento pubblico in Italia*, Milan, Angeli, 1984.

control over relevant companies and industries. The Big Two tried to impose sound financial criteria to participated companies, too, sometimes suggesting plant reorganisations and shaping holding structures, merging plants and companies to obtain more "rational" sectoral organisation, especially in metal works and mechanical engineering, electricity, gas, and chemicals. Besides, over the mid-1920s, both banks charged either their financial departments or single officers with the study of new forms of holding companies, after the example of American investment trusts, in order to implement them in Italy and to unburden their distressed balances of industrial participations, in the attempt to regain liquidity, but these projects never came to life.[57]

Especially from the second half of the 1920s, owing to the deflation following to the restored convertibility of the lira at "quota 90", the Comit and Credit had to cope with conflicting objectives: managing depreciating portfolios which threatened their own liquidity, on the one hand, and sustaining enterprises suffering the effects of deflation, on the other. When the Great depression reached Italy in 1930/31, already weakened great banks were fiercely hit by both deposit withdrawals and securities' falling prices, whose combined effects threatened their very existence. Giuseppe Toeplitz and Orsi – managing directors of Comit and Credit, respectively – search for government intervention, asking for liquidity injections and trying a financial reorganisation able to preserve their institutes' role both as great banks and as centres of the Italian financial capitalism. Between 1931 and 1932 banks were refinanced twice and their participations formally sold to *ad hoc* financial holdings, still owed and controlled by the banks. Finally, when at the beginning of 1933 Alberto Beneduce, acting as the plenipotentiary of the government, imposed a radical reorganisation, culminated in 1934 in the agreements among the three major banks, the IRI, Banca d'Italia and the government itself, Comit, Credit and Banco di Roma passed under IRI's control, along with their financial holdings and industrial participations.[58]

---

57 A few of these studies are still in the records of the Big Two's archives; see for instance Uha, Dc, Affari Finanziari, *Investment Trust* (*schema*).

58 Ernesto Cianci, *Nascita dello stato imprenditoriale in Italia*, Milan, Mursia, 1977. Gianni Toniolo, "Crisi economica e smobilizzo pubblico delle banche miste (1930-1934)", in Gianni Toniolo (ed.), *Industria e banca nella grande crisi 1929-1934*, Milan, Etas, 1978, pp. 284-352. Giorgio Rodano, *Il credito all'economia. Raffaele Mattioli alla Banca commerciale italiana*, Milan, Ricciardi, 1983. Antonio Confalonieri, *Banche miste e grande industria* reconstructed in details all complex passages of these events. Here it suffices to say that the intervention by the state through IMI (1931) and IRI (1933) had a double objective, not only preventing the failure of the three most important banks, which controlled about the 48 per cent of joint-stock industrial companies, but also to rescue Banca d'Italia, that, as lender of last resort, had found itself creditor towards the industrial sector for sums equal to about the 54 per cent of the whole monetary circulation.

The Banking Act of 1936 ratified those agreements, explicitly forbidding industrial participations to commercial banks and entrusting specialised credit institutions with medium and long term industrial credit.[59] Comit, Credit and Banco di Roma, now state-owned banks through IRI, became 'banks of national interest', preserving their nationwide network of branches and granting short term credit to (mainly large) firms.[60]

Conclusion

Modern banking arose in Italy from the 1860s, following shortly the emergence of investment banking in Continental Europe around the mid-19th century. As elsewhere in Europe, the new banks were aimed at financing public utilities and other capital intensive industries, characterised by differed profitability and high degree of risk. Between the unification of the country and the crisis of the early 1890s, big banks supported a first wave of investments that mainly interested infrastructures, while later on they were able to foster the first wave of industrial growth, occurred between the late 19th century and WWI. Through the whole period, the affirmation and consolidation of investment banking took the form of an evolutionary process of innovation during which big banks – inspired first to French and later to German experiences – tried to find out their own pattern and to root in a newly emerging financial system, tweaking to the developments of markets and institutions, as they gradually came forth, mainly in response to crises.

Nevertheless, financial innovation was not always attended and steered by 'regulative' and "institutional" innovation, thus compelling banks to adapt their strategies to the specific kinds of guarantees and risks they can rely upon and have to cope with. That affected the composition of the set of activities, the peculiar "crafts", they could opt for performing their allocative functions. In Germany, for instance, the choice for universal banking found support in the evolution of the institutional and legal framework: on the one hand, policies of the central bank were aimed at protecting banks from overly sharp fluctuations and shocks. On the other, legislation on companies and on the stock exchange enhanced banks' ability to manage

59 Sabino Cassese, *Come è nata la legge bancaria del 1936*, Spoleto, Banca Nazionale del Lavoro, 1988. Sabino Cassese, *È ancora attuale la legge bancaria del '36? Stato, banche e imprese pubbliche dagli anni '30 agli anni '80*, Rome, NIS, 1987.

60 Confirmations of a praxis of medium and long termism by these banks through the roll over of short credits are in Carlo Brambilla, "Le banche miste dopo la crisi e il risanamento (1933-1939)", *Archivi e imprese*, No. 18, 1998, pp. 345-387; and in Alfredo Gigliobianco, Giandomenico Piluso, Gianni Toniolo, "Il rapporto banca-impresa in Italia negli anni Cinquanta", in Franco Cotula (ed.), *Stabilità e sviluppo negli anni Cinquanta*, Vol. 3, *Politica bancaria e struttura del sistema finanziario*, Rome-Bari, Laterza, 1999, pp. 225-302.

riskier activities. In Italy, instead, the institutional framework proved unable to sustain and foster the widening of credit and capital markets and to promote the integration of a segmented system,[61] hence preventing banks from specialising, as happened in France, but also to adopt a "classic" universal banking pattern, as in Germany.[62] Data on liabilities of the system's components, in fact, show how difficult it was for big joint stock banks to grow larger and to raise funds, and how they suffered competition from non-for-profit segments.

Furthermore, contestable intermediaries were but a residual part of the credit system, that was indeed dominated by non-contestable institutions, hence even worsening the ability of big universal banks to develop and to adopt less risky attitudes. In addition, Italian banks had to cope with a legal system that neither enhanced minority shareholders' rights – providing, for instance, for stronger controlling bodies and institutions as in Germany – thus limiting information disclosure by companies, nor limited the speculative attitudes and prices' volatility of the stock exchanges. All that led to higher grades of opacity as for investment projects' quality and industrial undertakings' performances, and to higher degrees of risk connected with capital investments. As a consequence, Italian great banks, whose monitoring and controlling strategies implied the acquisition of larger voting rights, were more exposed to liquidity risks and to financial crises, as the experience of *Credito Mobiliare Italiano* and *Banca Generale* showed. New universal banks addressed these issues trying to overcome credit markets segmentation by developing stable relations with European great banks and bankers, and to minimise their commitments towards industry by relying upon proxy voting, as large shares of securities deposits accounts and contangos in their balance sheets shows, thus developing a distinctive universal banking pattern. Though these strategies proved effective in the medium term, they tended to improve capital markets weaknesses and instability, and after the 1907 crisis shook the system, banks' involvement in industrial companies grew, leading to their transformation in quasi-financial holdings during the 1920s and eventually to their failure at the end of the decade.

---

61 On the segmentation of the Italian banking system see Giuseppe Conti, "Le banche e il finanziamento industriale", in Franco Amatori *et al.* (eds.), *Storia d'Italia*, *Annali*, 15, *L'industria*, Turin, Einaudi, pp. 443-504. And Giandomenico Piluso, "Mercati settoriali e squilibri regionali nella formazione di un sistema bancario in Italia (1860-1936)", in Giulio Sapelli (ed.), *Capitalismi a confronto, Italia e Spagna. Atti del secondo seminario internazionale di storia d'impresa*, Soveria Mannelli, Rubbettino, 1998, pp. 83-157.

62 Marcello De Cecco, "La 'Protezione del risparmio' nelle forme finanziarie fasciste", *Rivista di storia economica*, III, 1986, No. 2, pp. 237-241.

CHAPTER 9

Maturity Mismatch and Allocative Efficiency

Long-term Financing and Investment Banking in Italy, 1936-1975

Giandomenico PILUSO

Professor in economic and finance history at the Sienna University

Our introduction will commence with the issues to determine how to cope with maturity mismatches. As is well known, banks have liquid liabilities – short-term or demand deposits – against potentially illiquid assets – longer-term loans to firms, households, and other financial institutions via the interbank market. Normally, such a "maturity mismatch" does not affect financial stability, as it is unlikely that all depositors would request their money back exactly at the same moment. Yet, when a wider lack of trust occurs, a run on the banks could occur, thereby menacing financial stability, possibly with a serious impact on capital formation and, in the end, on the long-term economic growth pace. This disparity is even emphasised by the underlying conflict of interests that usually emerges when commercial banking is associated to investment banking under the same roof. Such a problem was particularly apparent up to the first decades of the last century, when financial systems were loosely regulated and central banks were rather reluctant to intervene during liquidity crises as they were bound by the constraints of the gold standard.[1]

In the 1930s, as the financial crisis hit all the major economies hard, the maturity mismatch and the related instability issues were boldly dealt with by central authorities and lawmakers. The emerging idea was that financial intermediaries needed to be set in a more regulated environment,

1 This point has been considered by Franklin Allen and Douglas Gale, *Comparing Financial Systems*, Cambridge (Mass.), MIT Press, 2001. More recently, and provocatively, by Nouriel Roubini and Stephen Mihm, *Crisis Economics*, London, Allen Lane, 2010.

in which commercial banking was to be separated from investment banking, in order to preserve stability.[2] Typically, the US Glass-Steagall Act of 1933 was shaped according to such a broader view, rigidly separating commercial and investment banking.[3] In Italy, where a restrictive monetary policy had pre-empted the debt deflation of the Great Depression from 1926-1927, after a string of major bail-outs the Banking Act of 1936 was conceived, largely echoing the principles of the Glass-Steagall Act.[4] Up to the eve of this Act, universal banking had thus been a common feature of the Italian banking system as a whole, and was not just limited to few major banks.[5] The new banking law mirrored the vision of a small group of technocrats, intimately connected to the Bank of Italy, who directly experienced the extent to which universal banking could degenerate and produce instability, a systemic instability that could affect capital formation in the long term.[6] Up to then, investment banking activities were run by the major German-style mixed banks, and the key point was that a substantial intervention by the central bank was required[7] as

2 See Daniel Verdier, "Explaining Cross-National Variations in Universal Banking in 19th Century Europe, North America and Australasia", in Douglas J. Forsyth and Daniel Verdier (eds.), *The Origins of National Financial Systems: Alexander Gerschenkron Reconsidered*, London and New York, Routledge, 2003, pp. 23-42.

3 See Charles W. Calomiris, *U.S. Bank Deregulation in Historical Perspective*, New York, Cambridge University Press, 2000.

4 The very design of the new Banking Act was the outcome of direct experiences of failure of the universal banking as a potentially unstable business model within the financial sector. On this topic see Gianni Toniolo and Pierluigi Ciocca, "Industry and Finance in Italy 1918-1940", *The Journal of European Economic History*, XIII, 1984, pp. 113-136. Gianni Toniolo, "Italian banking, 1919-1939", in Charles Feinstein (ed.), *Banking, Currency and Finance in Europe between the Wars*, Oxford, Clarendon Press, 1995, pp. 296-314. On some echoing of the Glass-Steagall Act see Giandomenico Piluso, "From the universal banking to the universal banking: a reappraisal", *Journal of Modern Italian Studies*, Vol. 15, 2010, 1, special issue edited by Paolo Malanima and Vera Zamagni, pp. 88-89.

5 As clearly stated in a letter to the Minister of Finance Giuseppe Volpi, written in 1926 by the most influential representatives of banking and industry in Italy: "Almost all the local banks are actually mixed banks." See Archivio Centrale dello Stato (ACS), Rome, Carte Volpi, fold 4, sub-fold 32, "Promemoria Bianchini-Guarneri", Rome, 26 August 1926.

6 See Franco Bonelli, "Alberto Beneduce (1877-1944)", in Alberto Mortara (ed.), *Protagonisti dell'intervento pubblico*, Milan, Angeli, 1984, pp. 329-356. Franco Bonelli, "Alberto Beneduce, il credito industriale e l'origine dell'IRI", in *Alberto Beneduce e i problemi dell'economia italiana del suo tempo*, Rome, Edindustria, 1985, pp. 71-85.

7 See Gianni Toniolo, "Crisi economica e smobilizzo pubblico delle banche miste (1930-34)", in Gianni Toniolo (ed.), *Industria e banca curane la grande crisi* (*1929-35*), Milan, Etas, 1978, pp. 284-352.

a consequence of their difficulties in dealing with liquidity.[8] The new banking law adopted specialisation as its cornerstone, and, as a result, investment banking was rigidly separated from commercial banking, and universal banking was – at least formally – banned up to the time of the reforms of the early 1990s. Such a rigid specialisation principle, nevertheless, did not necessarily mean that commercial banks could not overcome some intrinsic limits within this principle, as was rather clear in the 1950s and 1960s when the Bank of Italy allowed a certain degree of freedom to *Banca Commerciale Italiana* and *Banca Nazionale del Lavoro*.[9] Under such circumstances, the Italian banking system seems, in the long run, to follow some general trends common to other advanced economies. As Raymond Goldsmith pointed out, in the more advanced economies financial intermediaries tended to specialise from the 1930s onwards, whilst financial assets increased as a percentage of gross domestic product, especially during the Golden Age. This aspect is confirmed by more recent studies on the relationship between finance and growth.[10]

This chapter aims to sketch a general picture of dynamics of the forms, institutions and mechanisms of long-term financing in Italy from the mid-1930s to the mid-1970s, within the regulatory scheme which emerged in order to overcome the maturity mismatch problems which were previously regarded as a major factor of financial instability. The next section offers a short illustration of the genealogy of the regulatory model and its main principles. The third section depicts the main evolutionary dynamics of the model during the Golden Age when it was regarded as substantially fitting to investments demands and those of firms'. The fourth section illustrates which factors were mainly responsible for the decreasing allocative efficiency of the model from the mid-1960s and, especially, during the 1970s when it entered a major crisis. Finally, the fifth section concludes by discussing whether the model implied a trade-off between stability and efficiency or, instead, other factors, such as monetary policy, affected the

8 This path-breaking approach has been developed by Daniel Verdier, *Moving Money: Banking and Finance in the Industrializing World*, New York, Cambridge University Press, 2003.

9 See Alfredo Gigliobianco, Giandomenico Piluso and Gianni Toniolo, "Il rapporto tra banche e imprese negli anni Cinquanta", in Franco Cotula (ed.), *Stabilità e sviluppo negli anni Cinquanta*, Vol. 3, *Politica bancaria e struttura nel sistema finanziario*, Rome-Bari, Laterza, 1999, pp. 225-302.

10 See Robert G. King and Ross Levine, "Finance and Growth: Schumpeter Might be Right", *Quarterly Journal of Economics*, 108, 1993, 3, pp. 717-737. Asli Demirguc-Kunt and Ross Levine, *Financial Structure and Economic Growth. A Cross-Country Comparison of Banks, Markets and Development*, Cambridge (Mass.), MIT Press, 2001. Ross Levine, "Finance and growth: Theory and evidence", in Philippe Aghion and Steven Durlauf (eds.), *Handbook of Economic Growth*, Amsterdam, Elsevier, 2005, Vol. 1, pp. 865-934.

efficiency of investment institutions and, in the very end, the overall allocative performance of financial intermediaries up to the late 1970s.

1. The genealogy and principles of a regulatory model, 1905-1945

The regulatory model which emerged in the 1930s with the Banking Law had a long incubation period during which its principles were tested and perfected throughout several, and sometimes even severe, trials. This model was firstly conceived when the first attempts to integrate mixed banks and the stock market, according to the German model, failed in 1907. This regulatory model was initially envisioned as an alternative to the macroeconomic tensions resulting from the attempts to integrate the German-style mixed banks with the securities market. As recently observed the integration of the German mixed banks within the stock market up to the 1914 demonstrates how hard it is to adhere to the notion that civil law systems crowd out securities markets favouring univocally large universal banks.[11] In fact, such integration was pursued by the German-style mixed banks in Italy up to the 1907 crisis by developing rather similar tools and techniques. In the years preceding the crisis, from 1900 to 1906, the Italian major mixed banks, such as *Banca Commerciale Italiana* and *Credito Italiano*, successfully developed "*riporti*" operations – or contangos: securities, shares or corporate bonds, whose market value tended to increase, were used as collateral thus allowing leverage – to a fairly large sum as a means of creating a highly liquid secondary stock market which could foster issuance operations.[12] Through issuance operations, they were able to stabilise long-term credit operations, which usually started as technically short-term credits to funded industrial enterprises which needed to re-balance their debt to networth ratio, as banks needed also to obtain a liquid portfolio.[13]

This model was not particularly favoured by the Bank of Italy whose monetary policy targets were in sharp contrast with what *riporti* implied in terms of re-financing operations. As a rule all the mixed banks used to ask systematically for generous, and increasing, re-financing in order to maintain

---

11 See Caroline Fohlin, *Finance Capitalism and Germany's Rise to Industrial Power*, Cambridge and New York, Cambridge University Press, 2007.

12 See Antonio Confalonieri, *Banca e industria in Italia, 1894-1906*, Milan, Banca Commerciale Italiana, 1975, Vol. 2, p. 192. Stefano Baia Curioni, *Regolazione e competizione. Storia del mercato azionario in Italia* (*1808-1938*), Bologna, Il Mulino, 1995, pp. 248-250. Giovanni Siciliano, *Cento anni di borsa in Italia. Mercato, imprese e rendimenti azionari nel ventesimo secolo*, Bologna, Il Mulino, 2001, pp. 18-19. Giangiacomo Nardozzi and Giandomenico Piluso, *Il sistema finanziario e la borsa*, Rome-Bari, Laterza, 2010, pp. 23-25.

13 This point is particularly stressed by Giangiacomo Nardozzi and Giandomenico Piluso, *Il sistema finanziario e la borsa*, Rome-Bari, Laterza, 2010, pp. 23-25.

their portfolios liquid.[14] These operations placed great pressure on the central bank's reserves and, in the end, a substantial reduction of the independence of monetary policy, as the long-term financing operations provided by mixed banks was not a guarantee per se that their client manufacturing firms were sufficiently able to strengthen their competitiveness to assure a sounding trade balance, like it actually occurred in the German case. Relatively low levels of industrial competitiveness in the international markets, which did not allow a surplus balance of trade, meant that the central authorities had to adopt a relatively restrictive monetary policy in order to peg the Italian currency stably to the gold standard. Theoretically, such a monetary policy could assure macroeconomic stability (i.e., stable exchange rates) encouraging non-inflationary investments which actually fostered productivity improvements through a rigorous selection of the fund-takers.

In 1905, Bonaldo Stringher, then the managing director of the Bank of Italy, made his point rather explicitly during a committee of the Bank affirming that the stock market rally supported by "*riporti*" was a menace to the exchange-rate stability just when the central authorities were preparing to peg the lira to the gold standard. Coherently, Stringher imposed a neat reduction in the total amount of "*riporti*" by limiting the acceptance of stock for re-financing. This decision paved the way for the first stern correction in the stock market. In July 1907, Stringher himself advocated that "it would not be just a mere error, but it would be a real crime if the Bank of Italy failed to protect her own reserves and circulation with efficacy" against the speculation of the stock market, the *Bourse* (in particular, naked selling).[15] This move had a harmful impact on the stock market, and even provoked a banking crisis. As a result, the restrictive monetary-policy manoeuvre, combined with the mounting international monetary crisis, marked a major shift in the Italian financial system, which, from then on, clearly became a bank-oriented system.[16]

As an alternative to the integration between mixed banks and stock market – in 1913, a new act, largely inspired by the Bank of Italy, badly

---

14 See Marco Fanno, *Le banche e il mercato monetario*, Rome, Atheneum, 1912, pp. 155-156.

15 The managing director of the Bank of Italy, Bonaldo Stringher, was clear to this regard in a letter to the managing director of the Chamber of Commerce of Genoa, published in "La situazione del mercato", *L'Economista*, 28 July 1907. Bonaldo Stringher, *Un quarto di secolo alla Banca d'Italia*, Rome, Tipografia della Banca d'Italia, 1926. On the view-point of the Bank of Italy towards mixed banks as a factor of instability see also Franco Bonelli, "Introduction", in Franco Bonelli (ed.), *La Banca d'Italia dal 1894 al 1913: momenti della formazione di una banca centrale*, Rome-Bari, Laterza, 1991, pp. 103-106.

16 See Anna Maria Biscaini Cotula and Pierluigi Ciocca, "Le strutture finanziarie: aspetti quantitativi di lungo periodo (1870-1970)", in Fausto Vicarelli (ed.), *Capitale industriale e capitale finanziario: il caso italiano*, Bologna, Il Mulino, 1979, pp. 69-71.

regulated the *Bourse* – a specialised long-term credit institution was proposed in 1911, although this was abundantly criticised. Such a proposition depicted a public special credit institution, whose long-term bonds would have financed long-term investments in industrial sectors and infrastructure, along a specialisation principle: financial institutions would have distinguished according to the maturity of the liabilities and assets, and commercial banking would be separated from investment banking. The State guarantee and special fiscal conditions would have made the bonds favour investors. The underlying basic idea was that the development of a bond market would have replaced the stock market as the centre of the financial intermediation, reducing the instability risks connected to the structural maturity mismatch, which was particularly emphasised by universal banking, as the crisis of 1907 had demonstrated.[17]

The outbreak of WWI offered a good opportunity to establish this kind of institution. Bonaldo Stringher designed the first special credit institution in 1914, the *Consorzio per Sovvenzioni su Valori Industriali* (Csvi), as a device under the direct control of the Bank of Italy which could have re-financed banks by accepting securities which otherwise would have been unacceptable to the central bank. Nonetheless, Csvi was not particularly active in re-discounting securities until the early 1920s, operated only marginally during the Great War. From the early 1910s, Stringher's close collaborator Alberto Beneduce, a statistician who published on the maturity-mismatch problems in 1915, asserted that intermediaries needed to be organised according to the maturity of their liabilities and assets. In the 1920s, following this principle, Beneduce, himself, built up a string of special credit institutions. *Crediop* (1919), *Icipu* (1924), and *Istituto di Credito Navale* (1927) were established as public special credit institutions, autonomously managed according their peculiar status.[18] These special credit institutions issued long-term bonds (with a 15 to 20 year maturity) thus raising funds that were channelled to finance long-term investments in infrastructural networks and capital goods. Finally, in the early 1930s, whilst he was pro-actively organising banking bail-out operations on behalf of the government, Beneduce conceived and established *Istituto Mobiliare Italiano* (Imi) (1931), in order to take over longer-term financing operations which mixed banks had been performing until then

17 See Antonio Confalonieri, *Banca e industria in Italia dalla crisi del 1907 all'agosto del 1914*, Milan, Banca Commerciale Italiana, 1982, Vol. 2, pp. 496-502.

18 Crediop and Icipu were acronyms for, respectively, Consorzio di Credito per le Opere Pubbliche and Istituto di Credito per le Imprese di Pubblica Utilità. See Paolo Baratta, "Alberto Beneduce e la costituzione e la gestione del Crediop e dell'Icipu", in *Alberto Beneduce e i problemi dell'economia italiana del suo tempo*, Rome, Edindustria, 1985, pp. 53-62. Pier Francesco Asso and Marcello De Cecco, *Storia del Crediop. Tra credito speciale e finanza pubblica (1920-1960)*, Rome-Bari, Laterza, 1994.

along the same lines: matching liabilities and assets maturity IMI would finance industrial long-term investments by acceding to a bond market that was increasingly intended as a public securities market.[19]

Even though IMI did not seriously grow in the 1930s, as from 1933 the *Istituto per la Ricostruzione Industriale* (IRI) took over some of its functions, it aimed at concentrating major long-term financing operations and promoting, at the same time, the development of a capital market essentially centred on a thick and liquid bond market in which the securities issued by special credit institutions and State-owned holding companies would be the core of the market itself. Such a capital market would have substituted the largest mixed banks, dismantled as universal banks by March 1934 and, to all intents and purposes, transformed into commercial banks, as the main source of long-term financing for all the major industrial enterprises. A factor of recurrent instability, universal banking, which were incompatible with the prevailing macroeconomic policy targets and views, would thus be erased, whilst the Italian economy was becoming a mixed economy in which private enterprises would be organically flanked by State-owned holding companies, such as IRI, and public special credit institutions, such as IMI.[20] This integration design would have encouraged a constant capital formation process with no financial instability phenomena similar to those previously experienced. On the whole it was a technocratic attempt to reduce both the risks and the impact of financial shocks in a catching-up economy specifically by regulating investment banking by separating it from commercial banking.[21] During the 1930s, this kind of capital market worked only partially, as can be seen in Table 1, which shows how slowly IMI grew in size in comparison to Crediop and CSVI.[22]

The rationale behind the regulatory architecture designed in the 1930s had, in general terms, a long gestation, which separated investment

---

19 IMI was the acronym for Istituto Mobiliare Italiano. See Giorgio Lombardo, *L'Istituto mobiliare italiano. Modello istituzionale e indirizzi operativi: 1931-1936*, Bologna, Il Mulino, 1998. Giorgio Lombardo and Vera Zamagni, *L'Istituto Mobiliare Italiano: 1931-1998*, Bologna, Il Mulino, 2009.

20 See Franco Bonelli, "Alberto Beneduce (1877-1944)", pp. 329-356. Marcello De Cecco, "Splendore e crisi del sistema Beneduce: note sulla struttura finanziaria e industriale dell'Italia dagli anni venti agli anni sessanta", in Fabrizio Barca (ed.), *Storia del capitalismo in italiano dal dopoguerra a oggi*, Rome, Donzelli, 1997, pp. 389-404. Leandra D'Antone, "Da ente transitorio a ente permanente", in Valerio Castronovo (ed.), *Storia dell'IRI*, Vol. 1, *Dalle Origini al dopoguerra, 1933-1948*, Rome-Bari, Laterza, 2012, pp. 167-228. Leandra D'Antone, "L'architettura di Beneduce e Menichella", *ibidem*, pp. 229-268.

21 See Douglas J. Forsyth and Ton Notermans, "Macroeconomic policy regimes and financial regulation in Europe, 1931-1994", in Douglas J. Forsyth and Ton Notermans (eds.), *Regime Changes*, Providence and Oxford, Berghahn Books, 1997, pp. 17-68.

22 See Giorgio Lombardo, *L'Istituto mobiliare italiano*, pp. 293-330.

banking and commercial banking, and thus favoured the growth of a bond market under public auspices, and satisfied a wide macroeconomic objective. Indeed, the rationale was to stabilise the financial system within a specific economic policy frame.

Table 1. Loans: IMI, Crediop, Icipu, CSVI and IRI's Sezione finanziamenti, in millions of lire at current values, 1915-1940

	IMI	Crediop	Icipu	CSVI	IRI – Sezione finanziamenti
1915				29.8	
1916				43.5	
1917				49.8	
1918				58.0	
1919				82.0	
1920		38.8		328.7	
1921		82.9		516.1	
1922		111.3		767.8	
1923		188.9		571.8	
1924		345.9		621.7	
1925		430.7	259	610.7	
1926		451.1	762	632.1	
1927		942.4	750	673.3	
1928		1,355.3	865	635.5	
1929		1,513.5	950	662.4	
1930		1,594.8	992	671.2	
1931		1,905.2	1,093	805.0	
1932	532.2	2,394.4	1,570	777.0	
1933	627.2	4,946.7	1,551	917.0	620
1934	621.1	5,064.4	1,528	1,139.0	1,052
1935	534.7	4,979.1	1,328	1,091.0	1,067
1936	565.4	4,959.9	1,272	1,420.0	1,037
1937	711.5	5,490.1	1,326	1,623.0	
1938	1,048.0	6,147.6	1,290	1,729.0	
1939	1,457.0	6,203.2	1,349	2,802.0	
1940	2,277.0	5,969.4	1,344	4,018.0	

* and to public works.

Sources: Banca d'Italia, *Relazione del Governatore, ad annos*; Banca d'Italia, *L'economia italiana nel sessennio 1931-1936*, Rome, Istituto Poligrafico dello Stato, 1938, Vol. I, p. 153, tav. 17; Anna Maria Biscaini, Paolo Gnes and Antonio Roselli, "Origini e sviluppo del Consorzio per Sovvenzioni su Valori Industriali durante il Governatorato Stringher", *Bancaria*, 1985, No. 2, p. 158, tav. 1.

Under the gold standard regime, Italy, unlike Germany, was not able to achieve trade-balance surpluses, and hence reserves were always a matter of concern for the central authorities, requiring a strict monetary policy as a prerequisite of successful macroeconomic adjustments to the international environment. A major achievement of these adjustments was the pegging of the Lira to the gold standard as a condition to lower the interest rates on the Italian public debt, thus aligning public sector and private sector interest rates.[23] This objective lay at the core of the latent conflict between Stringher and the major mixed banks, which culminated in the crisis of 1907. Furthermore, the balance of payments targets adopted by Italian central authorities to regulate their monetary policy constituted the corner-stone of a long-term view of how investments were to be realised. Investments were not to entail inflationary pressures on monetary policy by assuring a long-term equilibrium under which money would have reached a lower, cost, but the perspectives and projects of firms were simultaneously to be screened seriously, in order to support long-term income and productivity growth. Such a scheme was adapted successfully, albeit in a different international context, after WWII.[24]

2. The dynamics of the model: Dualisms in balance, 1946-1962

Within the Banking Law of 1936-37, investment banking was intended essentially as a matter of financing long-term projects in industrial sectors or infrastructure under very specific and tight regulation. In a first phase, from 1946 to 1962, investment banking as long-term financing – as it was conceived in the early 1930s – was adapted to a rather different international context, although it maintained a substantially similar balance of payments framework when defining monetary policy. This meant that the Bank of Italy pursued monetary stability, both domestically, in terms of prices, and externally, in terms of exchange rates. From 1948 to 1960 the governor Donato Menichella, who personally contributed to the Banking Act, defended the principles that monetary policy must be regarded as an autonomous task performed by the central bank in order to guarantee macroeconomic stability (prices and exchange rates under the Bretton Woods arrangements) and that commercial banking and investment banks had to remain as separate functions within the banking system. Up to the early 1960s, such objectives were, to a large extent, achieved even though some changes did affect the banking system. As investments in fixed capital robustly thrived

23 On the dynamics of interest rates up to 1914 within the international context see Stefano Fenoaltea, *L'economia italiana dall'Unità alla grande guerra*, Rome-Bari, Laterza, 2006, pp. 105-122.

24 This thesis is proposed and discussed in Giangiacomo Nardozzi and Giandomenico Piluso, *Il sistema finanziario e la borsa*, pp. 12-21.

from the early 1950s, the relative weight of special credit institutions as a whole increased both steadily and significantly as a percentage of the banking loans. It was a joint consequence of the increase in their number and of their operational development in the decade up to the 1964 (see Graph 1).

Figure 1. Ratio of special credit institutions' loans to banking system loans, 1931-1975

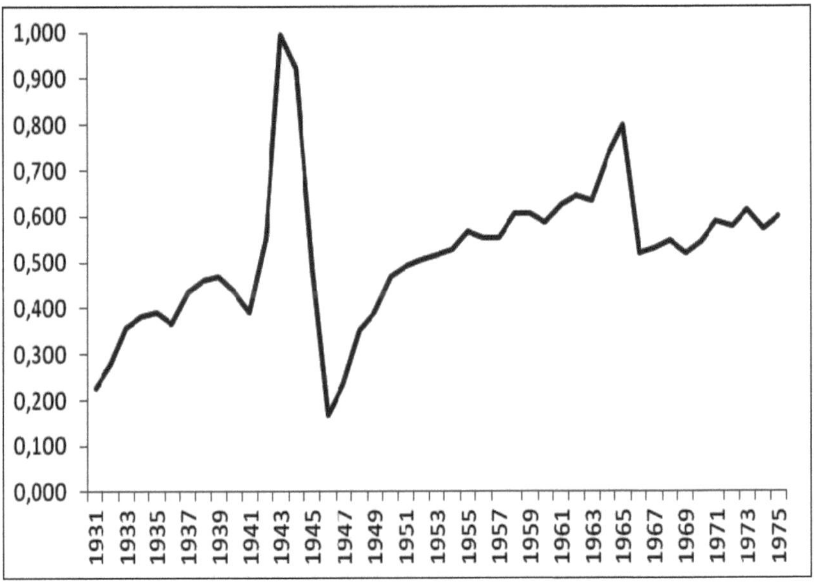

Source: Riccardo De Bonis, Fabio Farabullini, Miria Rocchelli and Alessandra Salvio, "Nuove serie storiche sulle attività di banche e altre istituzioni finanziarie dal 1861 al 2011: che cosa ci dicono?", Banca d'Italia, *Quaderni di storia economica*, No. 26, June 2012, pp. 36-37, Tav. 3.

Such a growth of the share of long-term financing operations through special credit institutions within the banking system was clearly related to the regulatory sea change of the mid-1930s as well as to the development of a domestic bond market as a fundamental part of the scheme conceived in the 1930s in order to guarantee investments in a framework of stability.[25] The power reserved to Bank of Italy to authorise bond issuances, both for enterprises and special credit institutions, was meant to improve the

[25] See Douglas G. Forsyth and Ton Notermans, "Macroeconomic policy regimes...", *op. cit.*, pp. 19-21. A particular emphasis on this specific point is given by Giangiacomo Nardozzi and Giandomenico Piluso, *Il sistema finanziario e la borsa*, pp. 57-60.

balance of issuances between these components. Governor Menichella was particularly vigilant in this regard.[26]

Although Menichella aimed to preserve the original arrangements by rationing authorisations to the establishment of new special credit institutions, lawmakers favoured a multiplication of intermediaries, fragmenting a system which was thought to be highly concentrated and controlled by the central authorities. Thus, in structural terms, a double dualism emerged. On the one hand, in spite of the original scheme, a number of regional special credit institutions were allowed by the lawmakers from the early 1950s, when *Mediocredito Centrale* was eventually admitted in 1953, which paved the way for a series of regional medium-term regional banks, generally controlled by local savings banks in which politics had a rather strong presence. Besides, all the major public banks ("istituti di credito di diritto pubblico"), such as *Banco di Napoli* and *Istituto Bancario San Paolo* of Turin, and savings banks, such as *Cassa di Risparmio delle Provincie Lombarde* (*Cariplo*), were allowed to create their own special credit sections, so that they could gradually enlarge their range of activities in longer-term operations, especially in the expanding soft loans sector. In the 1960s, following the adoption of planning economic policies, soft loans became a relevant percentage of special credit institutions' operations, particularly within the regional medium-term intermediaries segment. As soft loans had rather lax screening and monitoring mechanisms the quality of the selection processes of borrowers by credit worthiness tended to worsen significantly.[27]

Table 2. Number of special credit institutions, benchmark years, 1936-1975

	1936	1950	1960	1970	1975
industrial institutions	6	17	30	32	32
institutions	4	9	22	23	23
sections (banks)	2	8	8	9	9
land banks	12	13	15	21	21
public works institutions	-	1	9	12	12
agricultural banks	10	10	13	13	13
Total	28	41	67	79	85

Source: Vincenzo Pontolillo, "Profili del sistema di credito speciale", in Guido Carli (ed.), *La struttura del sistema creditizio italiano*, Bologna, Il Mulino, 1978, p. 288, tav. 3.

26 A fitting example to this regard is represented by the opposition to the creation of Mediobanca as documented in Archivio storico della Banca d'Italia (AS BI), Rome, Vigilanza, dossiers 9218 and 9219.

27 See Giandomenico Piluso, "Gli istituti di credito speciale", in Franco Amatori, Duccio Bigazzi, Renato Giannetti and Luciano Segreto (eds.), *Storia d'Italia, Annali*, 15, *L'industria*, Turin, Einaudi, 1999, pp. 522-523.

On the other hand, these changes were accompanied by a general increase in the number of industrial credit institutions, such as Mediobanca or *Efibanca*, or second level financial institutions, such as *Centrobanca*, a sort of central bank of the cooperative banks (see Table 2). The multiplication of special credit institutions implied a certain specialisation, even though area of cooperation within this segment were preserved. A typical form of dualism emerged as a consequence as Mediobanca tended to act as an almost private institution, whilst IMI appeared as a policy-dependent institution. This difference emerged clearly in the late 1960s and, above all, in the 1970s, when economic policies related to planning were abnormally rampant in the face of the stagflation. In fact, IMI had a prominent role in longer-term financing operations during the post-war recovery, when it intermediated Export and Import Bank funds, and, in the 1970s, when it abundantly financed the chemical sector, largely through soft loans, up to the crisis of the early 1980s. As Tables 3 and 4 show how IMI progressed from the late 1940s onwards as a result of its ability to manage special funds related to international flows, such as those provided by the American Export and Import Bank in the wake of the starting of the Marshall Plan (in the late 1940s these funds accounted for about 60 per cent of the overall operations run by IMI).[28] The other major special credit institutions which could be described as policy-dependent, Crediop and Icipu, had a large share of longer-term financing operations in the sector especially when they were engaged in infrastructural investments (motorways in the 1950s and 1960s) or in industrial investments sustained by public funds via soft loans (chemicals in the 1960s and 1970s).[29]

Both tables 3 and 4 suggest that IMI and Crediop-Icipu (as they eventually merged in the early 1980s) were, to a certain extent, the hand of public intervention in all the major investments through which the country was committed in order to catch up with the core of the industrialised economies during the Golden Age. IMI in particular, was a thriving force within this process as an effective instrument of structural economic policies meant to foster productivity improvements, via technology transfers and capital investments, and to reduce regional imbalances. Although some financial instruments, such as soft loans, entangled a certain degree of allocative inefficiency, in such a context of successful catching-up policies, they proved to be substantially effective as they sustained high capital formation and productivity growth rates.[30]

---

28 See Giorgio Lombardo, *L'Istituto mobiliare italiano. Centralità per la Ricostruzione: 1945-1954*, Bologna, Il Mulino, 2000.

29 See Pier Francesco Asso and Marcello De Cecco, *Storia del Crediop*, pp. 561-584.

30 See Giandomenico Piluso, "Gli istituti di credito speciale", pp. 519-522. Vera Zamagni, "Il credito all'industria", in Claudio Bermond, Alberto Cova, Angelo Moioli, Salvatore La Francesca (eds.), *Storia d'Italia, Annali*, 23, *La banca*, Turin, Einaudi, 2008, pp. 765-784, pp. 765-784. Giorgio Lombardo and Vera Zamagni, *L'Istituto Mobiliare Italiano*, *op. cit.*, pp. 237-251.

Table 3. Loans: special credit institutions, industrial credit institutions, Mediobanca, Crediop-Icipu, in billions of current lire, 1947-1975

	Special credit	Industrial credit*	IMI/ industrial credit	Mediobanca/ industrial credit	Crediop-Icipu/ industrial credit
1947	186	98	13.3	1.0	12.4
1948	305	185	57.8	2.1	13.0
1949	447	281	45.2	2.4	10.7
1950	637	431	32.7	2.3	8.3
1951	808	566	35.7	2.2	7.0
1952	988	697	24.8	2.7	7.6
1953	1,191	799	22.9	3.1	7.5
1954	1,412	912	23.5	3.3	8.8
1955	1,705	1,064	24.2	3.3	10.4
1956	1,963	1,197	27.3	3.8	11.4
1957	2,195	1,334	28.9	4.1	12.1
1958	2,539	1,524	25.9	4.0	14.6
1959	2,921	1,771	31.1	4.4	16.2
1960	3,501	2,160	33.5	4.4	16.9
1961	4,271	2,623	31.8	4.9	15.5
1962	5,400	3,295	30.8	5.9	14.0
1963	6,414	3,918	30.2	6.1	13.3
1964	7,360	4,592	30.1	6.5	13.7
1965	8,207	5,090	29.8	6.0	14.1
1966	9,425	5,770	29.2	6.4	13.3
1967	11,032	6,750	27.9	7.1	12.2
1968	13,026	7,850	27.7	7.5	11.6
1969	14,989	9,006	33.1	8.1	10.7
1970	16,960	10,186	33.1	9.7	9.6
1971	20,315	12,621	30.4	8.2	8.8
1972	23,413	14,891	30.7	8.4	8.5
1973	28,467	17,785	30.1	8.4	8.2
1974	31,730	20,251	30.7	10.4	8.3
1975	37,888	24,563	32.8	9.8	18.7

* and to public works.

Source: Marcello De Cecco and Giovanni Ferri, *Le banche d'affari in Italia*, Bologna, Il Mulino, 1995, table 9.

Somewhat obviously, such considerations have to be revised, as will be done in the next section, when put in a longer term. But, in the 1950s and in the early 1960s, there was a twofold stability which allowed: on the one hand, technological paradigms of the second industrial revolution to be relatively stable, requiring plain investments in capital and technology transfers for would-be catching up economies, such as that of Italy; on the other hand, under the Bretton Woods arrangements, the international monetary system guaranteed a certain stability which favoured foreign direct investments and boosted international trade.

Table 4. IMI's long-term financing operations, in billions of current lire and in percentage, 1946-1960*

	Ordinary loans**		Special loans***		Eximport Bank loans		Total
		%		%		%	
1946-47	12.2	69.3	5.4	30.7	-	-	17.7
1947-48	22.3	32.7	12.3	9.1	33.5	49.2	68.1
1948-49	42.4	38.5	16.0	14.5	51.8	47.0	110.2
1949-50	61.8	28.3	99.2	45.3	57.7	26.4	218.7
1950-51	80.2	22.7	221.8	62.9	50.6	14.4	352.6
1951-52	100.7	24.3	272.4	65.7	41.4	10.0	414.5
1952-53	136.0	29.5	289.5	62.8	35.3	7.7	460.8
1953-54	178.7	36.0	291.8	58.7	26.5	5.3	497.0
1954-55	228.5	44.0	270.7	52.1	20.4	3.9	519.5
1955-56	280.5	49.1	265.8	46.6	24.8	4.3	571.1
1956-57	335.3	54.9	252.1	41.3	22.9	3.8	610.3
1957-58	393.0	61.1	232.3	36.2	17.4	2.7	642.8
1958-59	469.0	67.8	211.7	30.6	11.4	1.6	692.1
1959-60	574.3	73.5	188.2	4.1	18.3	2.4	780.8

* 31 March each year. ** ordinary mortgages and ship-building mortgages funded by IMI.

*** included also special loans on behalf of the State from European Recovery Plan funds, in liras and other currencies, managed by IMI.

Sources: IMI, *Financial Statements, ad annos*; Istituto per gli Studi di Economia, *L'economia italiana*, Milan, 1964, p. 147, table 38.

Actually, in the 1950s the Italian economy benefited considerably from the choice of liberalising her foreign trade in 1947, especially with the rest of Europe: in this way, Italian exports took off and manufacturing firms rapidly obtained a significant easing of liquidity constraints: investments intensified in all the capital-intensive industrial sectors (steel, mechanical engineering, the car industry, oil refining, chemical), thus adding to these productivity improvements.[31] In this phase IMI financed these very sectors and contributed to the funding of new plants and new technology through up-to-date machinery. In this regard, it is worth observing that more than 60 per cent of IMI's operations were destined to firms of the thriving north-west regions of the country (see Table 5).[32]

[31] See Andrea Boltho, "Convergence, competitiveness and the exchange rate", in Nicholas Crafts and Gianni Toniolo (eds.), *Economic Growth in Europe Since 1945*, Cambridge, Cambridge University Press, 1996, pp. 107-130.

[32] See Giorgio Lombardo and Vera Zamagni, *L'Istituto Mobiliare Italiano*, pp. 173-235.

Table 5. *IMI's* long-term financing operations per sectors and geographical areas as a percentage, 1950-1980

	1955-1957	1958-1963	1964-1969	1970-1973	1974-1978	1979-1980
a) industrial sectors:						
iron and steel	26.5	27.4	20.9	29.1	26.0	3.4
mechanical engineering	37.7	36.9	24.2	25.3	26.3	53.8
chemical industry and oil refining	13.8	19.7	24.8	27.7	27.9	5.8
textiles and clothing	9.2	4.4	9.6	5.4	5.9	11.9
Others	12.8	11.6	20.5	12.5	13.9	25.1
b) regional areas:						
north-west regions	64.5	72.0	44.3	24.1	19.5	29.9
north-east and central regions	18.4	16.3	23.5	39.1	27.4	31.4
southern regions and islands	17.1	11.7	32.2	36.8	53.1	38.7

Source: Giulio Zanetti, "Il finanziamento all'industria: linee emergenti nelle relazioni tra Imi e sistema industriale nell'arco di un trentennio", in IMI, *Misure e modalità di trent'anni di sviluppo industriale in Italia*, Rome, IMI, 1986, pp. 98-99, table 1.8.

If Imi was undoubtedly the leading long-term financial institutions during the 1950s, with an increasing share of the segment, Mediobanca had to climb up the ladder as an almost private merchant bank, as it was actually owned by the three major former mixed banks controlled by Iri and regrouped under the special legal category of "banche di interesse nazionale" (*Banca Commerciale Italiana*, *Credito Italiano*, *Banco di Roma*). Thus, Mediobanca was formally a private financial institution owned by commercial banks controlled by a public agency, Iri, in a highly regulated long-term financing system, a substantially State-centred one. Established in 1946, after a long and winding negotiation with the Bank of Italy, which was worried about a surreptitious return to the universal banking practices of *Banca Commerciale*,[33] Mediobanca became a real investment bank in the 1950s. Starting as a medium-term financing institutions during the decade, under the leadership of Enrico Cuccia, Mediobanca significantly enlarged its scope and modified its ownership structure as well. In 1956, Cuccia successfully associated a string of international investment banks as shareholders, including Lazard Frères & Co. (New York) and Lehman Brothers of New York, Lazard Brothers of London, the Belgian Sofina,

33 *Mediobanca* was devised by Raffaele Mattioli, the ceo of *Banca Commerciale*, and Cuccia in Rome in August 1944, according to the reconstruction by Cuccia himself: see Enrico Cuccia, in *Ricordo di Raffaele Mattioli*, Florence, Le Lettere, 1987, pp. 11-18. See Giandomenico Piluso, *Mediobanca, Tra regole e mercato*, Milan, Egea, 2005, pp. 42-52.

and the German *Berliner Handels-Gesellschaft*. This enlargement of the shareholders to a group of high-standing investment banks entailed an agreement through which Mediobanca was able to enter international financial markets, for instance by placing corporate bonds issued by Italian firms in Europe and the US. Above all, the underlying alliance, especially the relationship with André Meyer of *Lazard Frères* & Co.,[34] gave to Cuccia a unique position, for an Italian banker, within major international financial networks.[35]

From this point onwards Mediobanca could exert its role as a merchant bank by promoting mergers and by the restructuring of firms and groups on an international scale, especially during the 1960s when, for instance, Cuccia and Meyer organised and advised a prospective merger between Citroën and Fiat in 1967 in order to promote a European player successfully able to reduce costs and compete in all market segments. As a result Mediobanca acquired a special role as a merchant bank, alongside *Banca Commerciale* which preserved some remains of its ability to syndicate and get firms listed on the stock exchange, whilst, at the same time, developing a consistent portfolio of crucial shareholdings in manufacturing firms (Montecatini, Sade, Caffaro, Finsider, Pirelli, Snia Viscosa, Fiat, Loro Parisini, Olivetti, Mondadori), finance (Bastogi and Fidia) and insurance companies (*Assicurazioni Generali* and *Fondiaria Vita e Incendio*).[36]

In the 1950s and in the 1960s, Mediobanca was rather innovative as a merchant bank, also by promoting and creating a string of specialised subsidiaries in consultancy (Progredi), accounting (Reconta), consumer credit (Compass), mutual funds (Prudentia), and export financing in Africa and Middle East (Intersomer and Tradevco). This dynamism was largely mirrored by its involvement in funding investment projects of large manufacturing firms operating in the capital and technology intensive sectors, as can be gauged by classifying medium-term financings according to the Pavitt sectoral sub-division: science-based firms accounted for 45 to 62 per cent from 1950 to 1960, whilst the total amount of both specialised equipment and science-based firms accounted for 65-75 per cent during the same period (see Table 6).[37]

---

34 See Giandomenico Piluso, *Mediobanca, op. cit.*, pp. 89-100. On Meyer see Cary Reich, *Financier. The Biography of André Meyer*, New York, William Morrow, 1983.

35 Up to eve of this only *Banca Commerciale* and its CEO Raffaele Mattioli had such an international visibility.

36 See Mediobanca, *Financial Statements*, 1955-1966; Giandomenico Piluso, *Mediobanca*, pp. 78-83.

37 See K. Pavitt, "Sectoral patterns of technical change: Towards a taxonomy and a theory", *Research Policy*, 1984, No. 13, pp. 343-373.

Table 6. Mediobanca: financing operations per sectors according to the Pavitt classification, 1949-1975

	1949	1950	1955	1960	1965	1970	1975
Scale intensive firms	10.5	6.5	3.0	7.0	18.0	11.2	12.0
Specialised equipment suppliers	23.5	21.0	18.0	26.5	26.4	17.8	15.1
Science based firms	23.6	44.6	61.6	46.5	21.3	16.3	27.1
Supplier dominated firms	39.4	26.5	11.8	11.6	17.0	13.9	25.6
Other sectors	3.0	1.4	5.6	8.4	17.3	40.8	20.2

Source: Mediobanca, *Financial statements, ad annos*. Giandomenico Piluso, *Mediobanca*, p. 217.

Table 7. Underwriting syndicates led by Mediobanca, in millions of current lire, 1957-1967

Corporate bond issuances		Equity share issuances	
Alitalia	20,000	Caffaro	7,790
Autostrada Cevo-Savona	10,000	Fiat	96,000
Autostrade – Concessioni e Costruzioni Autostrade	250,000	Finelettrica	15,000
Banca Europea Investimenti	6,000	Finsider	67,320
CIS – Credito Industriale Sardo	40,000	Ilva	34,000
Cotonificio Vittorio Olcese	4,000	La Magona d'Italia	2,000
Enel	250,000	Lanerossi	10,000
Enel-Europa	100,000	Ledoga	20,000
Fiat	84,000	Marzotto	20,000
Finanziaria Ernesto Breda	16,000	Montecatini	176,000
Finsider	100,000	Olivetti	20,000
IBM Italia	10,000	Pirelli Spa	13,300
IRI	799,400	SIP	42,946
IRI-Elettricità	15,200	Snia Viscosa	196,744
IRI-Stet	44,000	Stet	187,500
Istituto Romano di Beni Stabili	20,000	Terni Finelettrica	7,000
La Magona d'Italia	4,000	Vizzola	11,730
La Rinascente	6,000		
Lancia & C.	10,000		
Lanerossi	6,000		
Montecatini	320,000		
Olivetti	30,000		
Pirelli Spa	40,000		
RIV	12,000		
Saint-Gobain	50,000		
Snia Viscosa	56,000		
Società Generale Immobiliare	20,000		
Total	2,322,600	Total	927,330

Source: Mediobanca, Financial Statements, ad annos.

From 1957 to 1967, Mediobanca organised and led underwriting syndicates of bond and equity share issuances for the largest Italian firms, both State-owned and private ones, and for multinational Italian subsidiaries, such as IBM Italia and Saint-Gobain, thereby assuming a dominant position within the banking system: in ten years Mediobanca led underwriting syndicates that placed slightly less than 930 billion lire of equity shares and 2,322 billion lire of corporate bonds, while taking part in syndicates, usually led by *Banca Commerciale*, which placed almost 190 billion lire of corporate bonds (see Table 7).

On the whole, Italian industrial firms did not suffer from forms of credit rationing or liquidity constraints. During this period, except at some very short junctures, self-financing prevailed in funding investments, the stock market provided extra capital to the companies already listed which dominated the issuances of corporate bonds and equity shares. Thus, as the Italian stock market suffered a very low level of new listing, major listed companies absorbed an increasing amount of resources on offer, both in terms of equity shares and corporate bonds, reducing as a consequence, in relative terms, the access to external funding for the emerging enterprises not yet listed, as Menichella noted with some apprehension at the end of his governorship in the late 1950s.[38] Until the early 1960s, the capital structure of the largest firms and groups appeared balanced, to a certain degree, and, thus, had good bargaining power *vis-à-vis* commercial banks and the bond issuances offered extra funds for longer-term investment projects.[39]

3. The erosion of the model, 1963-1975

From the early 1960s, the regulatory model which had been emerging in the previous decade was being distorted significantly by legislation on subsidised funds and soft loans in particular. From the late 1950s, macroeconomic policies deeply re-shaped the overall institutional framework within which long-term financing through special credit institutions functioned. The first distorting factor in allocating financial resources was represented by economic policies aimed to rebalance the North-South divide within the country by imposing a quota

---

38 The Bank of Italy had to authorise new issuances of corporate bonds and equities. See Federico Barbiellini Amidei and Claudio Impenna, "Il mercato azionario e il finanziamento delle imprese negli anni Cinquanta", in Franco Cotula (ed.), *Stabilità e sviluppo negli anni cinquanta*, Vol. III, *Politica bancaria e struttura del sistema finanziario*, Rome-Bari, Laterza, 1999, pp. 661-663. Giangiacomo Nardozzi and Giandomenico Piluso, *Il sistema finanziario e la borsa, op. cit.*, pp. 62-67.

39 See Alfredo Gigliobianco, Giandomenico Piluso and Gianni Toniolo, "Il rapporto tra banche e imprese negli anni Cinquanta", *op. cit.*, pp. 278-281.

on State-owned enterprises' new investments (at least 40 per cent of investments had to be realised in Southern regions). A second factor was the adoption of planning policies in the early 1960s in order to stimulate economic growth through investments, under public supervision, which were meant to be consistent with the macroeconomic objectives defined at the end of the previous decade.[40] Such economic policies entailed the nationalisation of the electric power industry in 1963, a move which had a profoundly negative, depressing, impact on the domestic stock market.[41]

Hence, a sea change in economic policies drove legislation and public intervention at a turning point of the Italian "economic miracle". The planning policies that lasted up to the early 1970s required strict regulation of the choices of State-owned holding-companies, which witnessed a relapse in terms of the sectors and geographical areas financed by special credit institutions. As Table 8 shows IMI and other major special credit institutions, with the exception of Mediobanca, had to modulate their choices within their planning policies and took the decision to fund those sectors and areas which they considered as strategic to the macroeconomic objectives as defined by the central authorities through planning policies.[42]

Table 8. Special credit institutions (SCIs) as a percentage of the banking system as a whole and as GDP of geographical areas, 1951-1978

	"Mezzogiorno"			Centre-North			Italy		
	1951	1965	1978	1951	1965	1978	1951	1965	1978
SCIs/tot	35.5	52.1	53.1	25.2	32.6	32.0	26.7	36.4	35.9
SCIs/GDP	5.2	23.5	27.4	6.7	19.8	22.6	6.4	20.7	23.7

Source: Paolo D'Onofrio and Riccardo Pepe, "Le strutture creditizie nel Mezzogiorno", in Banca d'Italia, *Il sistema finanziario nel Mezzogiorno*, Rome, Banca d'Italia, 1990, p. 237, tav. 17.

Such a sea change was connected to a momentous shift in monetary policy and central banking, whose objectives were explicitly stated in May 1963 by governor Guido Carli, who succeeded Menichella at the beginning of the decade. According to Carli, himself, such a move radically modified the role of the Bank of Italy, which had previously been "an institution

40 See Fabio Lavista, *La stagione della programmazione. Grandi imprese e Stato dal dopoguerra agli anni Settanta*, Bologna, Il Mulino, 2009.

41 See Giangiacomo Nardozzi and Giandomenico Piluso, *Il sistema finanziario e la borsa*, pp. 67-71.

42 See Fabio Lavista, *La stagione della programmazione*, pp. 308-385. Giandomenico Piluso, "Banche, regolamentazione e politiche economiche (1946-1990)", in Leandro Conte (ed.), *Le banche e l'Italia. Crescita economica e società civile, 1861-2011*, Rome, Bancaria Editrice, 2012, pp. 207-237.

intent on contributing to the design of economic policy by achieving intermediate objectives, [it] became part of the government system".[43] The approach to monetary and credit aggregates that Menichella had followed (typically, a balance of payments approach) was shelved, and credit supply was not to be set in relation to the formation of savings and deposits. As Carli remarked in May 1963, the Bank of Italy held that it was "doing its duty by injecting sufficient liquidity to finance the production system at rising prices in order to avert adverse effects on the continuity of growth".[44] In fact, in 1962, the Bank of Italy had perceived that the industrial firms were entering a different phase as self-financing was rapidly slowing down: the largest firms were experiencing a shrinking self-financing capacity, and equity capital was reducing whilst debts were growing higher, especially as long-term funds were being provided by special credit institutions, as Graph 1 shows. The largest enterprises were increasingly relying upon long-term debts provided by special credit institutions and less upon equity capital and corporate bonds.[45]

In the face of this weakening within the capital structure of the largest enterprises, the Bank of Italy reacted by adopting a rather lax monetary policy. Carli justified the Bank's expansionary monetary policy with the need to accommodate the demand for funds from firms, State-owned holding-companies such as Iri, and the State. However, the inflationary pressure stemming from this credit expansion induced the governor to alter his stance on monetary policy, and the tightening of this policy in the second half of 1963, brought an end to the long period of high economic growth.[46] Subsequently, monetary policy had to become more accommodating again, to counter the first post-war recession of 1964. Between 1966 and 1969, the Bank of Italy intervened to stabilise interest rates and thereby support the bond market, given the mounting difficulty of firms to raise equity capital. The underlying basic idea was that the expansion of

---

43 See Guido Carli, *Intervista sul capitalismo italiano*, an interview by Eugenio Scalfari, Bari, Laterza, 1977, p. 38. See Leandro Conte, "L'azione della Banca d'Italia (1948-1993)", in Claudio Bermond, Alberto Cova, Angelo Moioli and Salvatore La Francesca (eds.), *Storia d'Italia, Annali*, 23, *La banca*, Turin, Einaudi, 2008, pp. 661-687.

44 Banca d'Italia, *Considerazioni finali all'Assemblea dei partecipanti al capitale della Banca d'Italia*, Rome, Banca d'Italia, 1963.

45 See Leandro Conte and Giandomenico Piluso, "Financing the largest Italian manufacturing firms. Ownership, equity, and debt (1936-2001"), in Andrea Colli and Michelangelo Vasta (eds.), *Forms of Enterprise in 20th Century Italy: Boundaries, Strategies and Structures*, Cheltenham, Edward Elgar, 2010, pp. 132-158. This change in the capital structure of the largest firms was observed also by *Mediobanca* (see Mediobanca, *Financial Statements*, 1962 and 1963).

46 See Pierluigi Ciocca, "L'istituzione e l'uomo: Guido Carli a via Nazionale", in Pierluigi Ciocca (ed.), *Guido Carli governatore della Banca d'Italia*, Turin, Bollati Boringhieri, 2008, pp. ix-xxxix.

debt would provide sufficient cover for the demand for funds from both the private and the public sector.[47]

From the late 1960s, however, mechanisms were operating that would induce the monetary central authorities, in the face of inflationary expectations, to cover the bond issues of the State-owned holding-companies (Iri, Eni, Efim) and the special credit institutions (Imi, Crediop, Icipu) that met with insufficient demand because of "double intermediation". Under this arrangement, issues not fully absorbed by the market were placed forcefully in the assets of ordinary credit banks upon the basis of administrative constraints.[48] Double intermediation effectively severed the relation between fund-raising and lending and relieved bankers of virtually all responsibility for screening both borrowers and investment projects. During the 1970s, the liabilities of the special credit institutions were thus fundamentally supported by administrative measures. Indeed, their share of lending grew sharply during Carli's governorship, and their loans were increasingly concentrated geographically in the South and sectorally in capital-intensive plants, as shown in Table 8.[49]

The decline in the efficiency of the intermediaries was bound up with the extension of the public bond circuit, the spread of soft loans and the associated administrative constraints on the management of bank assets, as well as constraints introduced in the early 1970s not only to counter rising inflation, but also to prop up the bonds of public sector entities. The central role assigned to banks in the financial system was accompanied by administrative measures that fuelled double intermediation and altered the management procedures and techniques of the intermediaries. Accordingly, it coincided with a fall in the loan/deposit ratio of the banks. Double intermediation conditioned the entire banking system through the institution, in 1973, of a ceiling on the increase in bank loans and a requirement to invest in fixed-income securities, particularly the bonds of special credit institutions and public sector entities.[50] In parallel with the

47 See Giangiacomo Nardozzi and Giandomenico Piluso, *Il sistema finanziario e la borsa*, pp. 78-93; Giandomenico Piluso, "Banche, regolamentazione e politiche economiche (1946-1990)", pp. 218-222.

48 See Francesco Cesarini, *Struttura finanziaria, sistema creditizio e allocazione delle risorse in Italia*, Bologna, Il Mulino, 1976. Renato Balducci, Mauro Marconi, Maria Luisa Marinelli and Alberto Niccoli, "L'evoluzione degli intermediari e dei mercati; 1950-1972", in Fausto Vicarelli (ed.), *Capitale industria e capitale finanziario: il caso italiano*, Bologna, Il Mulino, 1979, pp. 190-196.

49 See Paolo D'Onofrio and Riccardo Pepe, "Le strutture creditizie nel Mezzogiorno", in Banca d'Italia, *Il sistema finanziario nel Mezzogiorno*, Rome, Banca d'Italia, 1990, pp. 237-238. Giandomenico Piluso, "Gli istituti di credito speciale", pp. 523-524.

50 See Giangiacomo Nardozzi, *Tre sistemi creditizi*, Bologna, il Mulino, 1983. Riccardo De Bonis, "Ricchezza finanziaria e indebitamento dell'economia italiana dal 1950 al 2004", in *I conti finanziari: la storia, i metodi, l'Italia, i confronti internazionali*, Rome, Banca d'Italia, 2006, pp. 315-358.

rise of double intermediation, from the end of the 1960s, the share of debt in the financial structure of the companies grew rapidly and the equity capital component shrank. The contraction in equity financing intensified in the early 1970s, in response to the incentive implicit in high inflation and negative real interest rates. In the span of a decade, the expansion in borrowing on the part of firms, especially short-term bank debt, drove equity capital down to 14 per cent of total liabilities. The leverage of Italian firms reached its post-war peak.[51]

The deterioration in financial structure was greatest for large firms and State-owned enterprises, especially those of the IRI and EFIM groups.[52] Spiralling corporate leverage and the financing of debt through double intermediation and soft loans damaged the overall quality of resource allocation. The increase in the special credit institutions' share of loans corresponded to an increase in the share of loans disbursed on concessionary terms to finance investments in sectors destined to be hit hardest by the macroeconomic shocks of the early 1970s. The dependence of the special credit institutions' financing on subsidised credit, and thus on administrative approval, undermined their efficiency in allocating resources, as is clearly demonstrated by the case of IMI and the soft loans abundantly made to Nino Rovelli's SIR group.[53] Double intermediation reduced the capacity of intermediaries to assess creditworthiness and select promising investment projects, further entrenched the position of established firms, reduced the propensity to promote innovative firms and products, and made such firms vulnerable during a critical period of wide swings in relative prices and technological discontinuity. The level of the intermediaries' allocative efficiency impacted negatively on the growth of the whole economy, reducing the capacity of Italian firms to compete and innovate in the long run.[54]

In his last address as governor of Bank of Italy, on 31 May 1975, Carli launched a proposal for the conversion of corporate loans on bank assets into equity, so as to restore a balanced corporate financial structure and pin down

---

51 See Riccardo De Bonis, "Ricchezza finanziaria e indebitamento dell'economia italiana dal 1950 al 2004", pp. 320-324.

52 See Leandro Conte and Giandomenico Piluso, "Finance and structure of the state-owned enterprise in Italy. IRI from the Golden Age to the fall", in Franco Amatori, Robert Milward and Pier Angelo Toninelli (eds.), *Reappraising State-Owned Enterprise: A Comparison of the UK and Italy*, New York-London, Routledge, 2011, pp. 119-141.

53 See Vera Zamagni, *L'Industria chimica italiana e l'IMI*, Bologna, Il Mulino, 2010, pp. 107-187.

54 See Fabio Lavista and Giandomenico Piluso, "Sectoral specialisation and firm size in Italy before and after the stagflation. IRI, 1962-1991", paper presented at the Economic History Society Conference, Cambridge, University of Cambridge, Robinson College, 1-3 April 2011.

the responsibilities of intermediaries. In this way, he laid bare the contradictions that had arisen within the central banking model, which he had followed and then laboriously remoulded in order to cope with macroeconomic shocks, nonetheless observing that for him, personally, this was a cause of "profound sadness". "The Bank," Carli later had to admit, "by channelling resources to the Treasury and to the sectors indicated by the political system, played a role typical of the fiscal system, one the fiscal system was unable to play",[55] a peculiar institutional function that Carli interpreted in part as a mandate for the modernisation of Italian society.[56] According to Carli's assessment in his concluding remarks to the Bank's annual meeting for 1973, any refusal by the Bank to accommodate the financing of the public and private sectors, under those specific conditions, would have had "the appearance of an act of monetary policy", but, in substance, would have been "a seditious act" leading to "the paralysis of the institutions".[57]

This involution of special credit institutions, strongly influenced by monetary and regulatory policies, enabled Mediobanca to develop its own merchant banking activities further. Mediobanca was autonomously managed by the authoritative and charismatic Cuccia, who saved the bank from distortion practices such as soft loans, and made it a cornerstone for Italian capitalism by promoting collusion pacts and supporting the existing majority shareholders through corporate agreements and alliances amongst the largest industrial and financial groups, such as Fiat, Pirelli, and Montedison. In fact, from the mid-1960s Mediobanca as a merchant bank promoted a string of alliances and mergers. In 1966, Mediobanca acted as advisor in the momentous merger between Montecatini and Edison which led to the largest manufacturing group, Montedison. In 1967, Mediobanca, alongside with *Lazard Frères* (Paris), advised Fiat and Citroën regarding the prospect of a merger between the two carmakers, which could have resulted in a major European player, but which essentially, because of the opposition by the French President Charles de Gaulle, led to a simple alliance in the early 1970s. In the late 1960s, Mediobanca advised Pirelli and Dunlop along similar strategic lines by supporting the formation of the British-Italian alliance between these tyre-makers under the umbrella of a holding company, Union. Mediobanca affirmed its dominant position within the domestic financial market.[58]

55 Guido Carli, *Intervista sul capitalismo italiano*, an interview by Eugenio Scalfari, Bari, Laterza, 1977, pp. 36-39.

56 See Leandro Conte, "L'azione della Banca d'Italia", pp. 680-682.

57 Banca d'Italia, *Considerazioni finali all'Assemblea dei partecipanti al capitale della Banca d'Italia*, Rome, Banca d'Italia, 1974. See also Leandro Conte, "L'azione della Banca d'Italia", pp. 683-684.

58 See Napoleone Colajanni, *Il capitalismo senza capitale*, Milan, Sperling & Kupfer, 1991, pp. 160-166. Giandomenico Piluso, *Mediobanca, op. cit.*, pp. 114-127.

4. A trade-off between stability and efficiency?

For a rather long period, from the Golden Age to the stagflation juncture, investment banking was rigidly separated from commercial banking. The regulatory architecture designed in the mid-1930s substantially influenced the very way in which the banking system worked. In broader terms, the liquidity problem was solved, but an information asymmetry emerged in the late 1950s and early 1960s, even before the crisis of the 1970s. The model grew inefficient as a whole, essentially for two reasons: first, separating commercial banking and investment banking meant breaking up debtors' cash-flows, and the monitoring of credit worthiness screening activities by banks; second, and crucially, this problem was made worse because of an efficient practice of soft loans and public intervention. Until the early 1970s, rapid economic growth mitigated the repercussions of the inherent limits of a borrower selection system in which analysis of firms' payments (divided among a sizable number of ordinary credit banks) was separated from the assessment of long-term investment projects (assigned to the special credit institutions).

But, above all, factors of fragility were introduced into the allocation mechanisms. The intermediation model was not only underpinned by a number of regulatory principles (specialisation and segmentation of intermediaries), but also by the idea that credit was a public good and that banks belonged to the realm of economic policy. From the early 1960s onwards, under the pressure of legislation that steadily deformed the original model, widespread resort to forms of concessionary credit – soft loans – and the expansionary stance of monetary policy seriously eroded the standards by which prospective borrowers were assessed. In the 1970s, the fragility and limitations of the financial system emerged powerfully, as its reduced dynamic efficiency acted as a drag on growth.[59] This loss of efficiency in banking was compounded by the absence of an efficient, sufficiently deep and liquid share market.[60] In the early 1960s, economic policy decisions modified the conditions and mechanisms of resource allocation. New macroeconomic policies radically redesigned the overall framework. Economic planning, the slump of the financial markets, the first signs of decline in the self-financing of firms strained the banking system. The Bank of Italy set itself different objectives from those it had pursued in the previous decade, renouncing its autonomy in the conduct of monetary policy.[61]

---

59 See Pierluigi Ciocca, *Banca, finanza, mercato. Bilancio di un decennio e nuove prospettive*, Turin, Einaudi, 1991.

60 See Giovanni Siciliano, *Cento anni di borsa in Italia. Mercato, imprese e rendimenti azionari nel ventesimo secolo*, Bologna, Il Mulino, 2001.

61 Douglas J. Forsyth and Ton Notermans, "Macroeconomic policy", *op. cit.*, pp. 22-23.

It is not easy to assess to what extent the regulatory architecture affected the allocative efficiency of the banking system, even though we can observe much more stable dynamics in the post-war period compared to other sub-periods, as Table 9 suggests. Probably, a lower volatility of the banking system's main variables related to real variables suggests that the separation of commercial banking from investment banking and the State ownership of intermediaries were not *per se* responsible for misallocation, but, rather, bad regulation and unsuitable monetary policies introduced relevant distortions in the way in which the system worked. Having solved the maturity mismatch problem did not guarantee *per se* a superior level of efficiency, but rather just a higher stability within the banking system.

Table 9. Volatility of real and banking system's main variables (standard deviation), 1890-1973

	1890-1913	1914-1945	1946-1973	1890-1973
investments/GDP	3.130	3.654	1.191	3.172
loans/deposits	9.489	13.248	3.575	9.986
loans/total assets	8.226	9.745	3.481	7.683
liquidity	0.633	8.674	3.243	6.939
ROA	0.185	0.154	1.231	0.783
core tier	1.358	2.649	0.664	6.280
total assets/GDP	0.485	0.321	0.871	0.869
loans/GDP	1.664	1.279	1.615	1.920

Source: Giandomenico Piluso, "Financial intermediaries: their evolution and relations with firms", *Review of economic conditions in Italy*, Vol. 64, 2011, No. 2/3, p. 371, Table 1.

CHAPTER 10

The Spanish Investment Banks

From Financial Intermediaries to Company Shareholders

Luis JAVIER CORONAS-VIDA

University of Burgos (Spain)

In this chapter we shall study the constitution – people who carried out and capital origins – of a "six big banks" group in Spain during the 20th century which had dominated the financial sector until the 1970s. The very nature of them will be also analysed: relations between these banks and other companies, as well as with the State … We shall also use some accounts of the balance sheets to characterise their evolution during the interwar period and the Franco's regime. It is necessary do not forget that the State banking policy went through important changes along these years. One question we shall stand out is the Banking Regulation Act of 1962 and its interest about the banking compulsory specialisation (commercial or industrial and investment banking) in Spain, following the steps of US, France, Belgium, Switzerland … We shall study the most important industrial and investment banks set up as consequence of that act – usually promoted by the biggest banks –, its performance and that of the large banks. Finally, the effects of the 1973 economic crisis are analysed, as well as the mergers policy as a consequence of the entry of Spain in the EEC.

1. The birth of mixed-type banking in Spain

After some experiences in investment banking during the 19th century,[1] in the early 20th century, the banks of Madrid, Bilbao and Asturias acquired shares in companies and managed to establish

1 In the mid-19th century investment banks were promoted to facilitate the railways construction; the main institutions were set up by French bankers (Rothschild, Pereire and Prost), but the economic crisis started in 1864 and the railways companies problems

connections with the most important firms. From the late 19th century onward, technologies were also being developed that offered considerable economies of scale but required sizeable investments. Firms in these sectors benefited from the tariff protectionism then in force. At the outbreak of WWI, the Spanish banks were not prepared for numerous transactions which they undertook with the belligerent nations. An initial consequence of this was an increase in the branches of foreign banks in Spain, but from 1916 onward, domestic bankers began to react, creating new institutions, often by transforming existing banking houses. They also began to participate in previously unknown types of transactions, but this transformation was not accompanied by sufficient improvements to their organisational systems.[2]

The interwar period was fundamental for the consolidation of the mixed-type banking sector, as was the capital accumulated during WWI. Writing in 1973, Santiago Roldán, José Luis García Delgado and Juan Muñoz were of the opinion that the public debt had also facilitated this process since, as in 1917, a pact was made between the private banks and the Treasury Ministry under which the former took over the national debt issues, kept them in their portfolios and could "pawn" or mortgage them automatically at the Bank of Spain when they considered it appropriate. This afforded them liquidity and greater security in view of the immobilisation of their funds due to their investments in the industrial sector. More recently, Pablo Martín Aceña has shown that not all the debt remained in the hands of the banks, but that an important part ended up in private hands outside the financial sector; during the interwar period public debt was a profitable liquid asset as it was issued at market rates and the banks did not pledge it on a massive scale. However, the debt could indeed constitute a reserve offering greater

brought the liquidation of much of this system. The first genuinely Spanish business bank was the *Banco Hispano-Colonial* (founded in 1876), but the loss of Cuba, Puerto Rico and the Philippines (1898) affected it seriously. Gabriel Tortella, *Los orígenes del capitalismo en España. Banca, industria y ferrocarriles en el siglo XIX*, Madrid, Tecnos, 1973. Miguel A. López-Morell, *La Casa Rothschild en España* (*1812-1941*), Madrid, Marcial Pons, 2005. Ramon Canosa, *Un siglo de banca privada* (*1845-1945*), Madrid, 1945, pp. 31 and 51. Pedro Tedde di Lorca, "La banca privada española durante la Restauración (1874-1914)", in Gabriel Tortella and Pedro Schwartz (eds.), *La banca española en la Restauración*, Madrid, Banco de España, 1974, Vol. 1, pp. 268-270 and 396-398.

2 Santiago Roldán, José Luis García Delgado and Juan Muñoz, *La formación de la sociedad capitalista en España*, Madrid, CECA, 1973, Vol. 2, pp. 175-256. Javier Pueyo Sánchez, *El comportamiento de la gran banca en España* (*1921-1974*), Madrid, Banco de España, 2006, p. 32. Carles Sudrià, "Desarrollo industrial y subdesarrollo bancario en Cataluña, 1844-1950", *Investigaciones Económicas*, 18, 1982, pp. 137-176.

security in the case of liquidity problems.[3] On the other hand, the banks not only held shares in the capital of companies, but they also helped finance them through credit, which was officially short-term, but was successively renewed.[4]

In the 1960s, the chairmen of some of Spain's largest mixed-type banks, such as *Banesto* (Jaime Gómez-Acebo y Modet, Marquis of Deleitosa) and the *Central* (Ignacio Villalonga and Alfonso Escámez) emphasised the role of the Spanish banks in the promotion of industry throughout the 20th century, adopting a role similar to that of the German banks, although clearly on a smaller scale.[5] But while, on the one hand, the large mixed-type banks in Madrid and Bilbao consolidated their presence, those of Catalonia experienced a period of relative decadence, above all following the declaration of voluntary bankruptcy by Spain's oldest private bank, *Banco de Barcelona* (1920), in the context of the depression of 1920-1921.[6]

2. The formation of the 'big six' Spanish banks

Only one of the "big six" – as measured in terms of their equity capital – which predominated over the financial panorama in Spain until the 1970s dated back to the 19th century: Banco de Bilbao. From the 1970s *Banco de Santander* and *Banco Popular Español* joined the ranks of the big banks (by the same yardstick of equity capital), although in terms of deposits these two had been ahead of *Urquijo* bank

3 Santiago Roldán, José Luis García Delgado and Juan Muñoz, *La formación, op. cit.*, Vol. 2, pp. 246-247. Pablo Martín Aceña, *La política monetaria en España*, Madrid, IEF, 1984. Pablo Martín Aceña, *La cantidad de dinero en España, 1900-1935*, Madrid, Banco de España, 1985. Javier Pueyo, *El comportamiento*, *op. cit.*, pp. 35-38.

4 Santiago Roldán, José Luis García Delgado and Juan Muñoz, *La formación*, *op. cit.*, Vol. 2, p. 252. Maria Ángeles Pons has pointed to the difficulty of determining exactly what the activities of 'mixer' or 'universal' banking are, although in general it is understood that they involve non-banking companies: "Banca e industria en España. 1939-1985: la influencia de la banca universal en el crecimiento económico", *Revista de Historia Industrial*, 19-20, 2001, pp. 249-250.

5 Santiago Roldán, José Luis García Delgado and Juan Muñoz, *La formación*, *op. cit.*, Vol. 2, pp. 244-246.

6 Pedro Tedde, "La banca privada", *op. cit.*, pp. 430-446. Santiago Roldán, José Luis García Delgado and Juan Muñoz, *La formación*, *op. cit.*, Vol. 2, pp. 166-82 and 256-62. Francesc Cabana, *Història del Banc de Barcelona* (*1844-1920*), Barcelona, Edicions 62, 1978, pp. 163-81. Francesc Cabana, *La banca privada en Cataluña entre 1920 y 1935*, Bilbao, Archivo Histórico BBV, 1998, Series "*Informaciones: Cuadernos de Archivo*", pp. 56-57; here: pp. 31-4. Carles Sudrià, "La banca catalana en los años de Entreguerras y el debate sobre la decadencia. Una revisión", *Revista de la Historia de la Economía y de la Empresa* (*RHEEMP*), 1, 2007.

since the 1950s.[7] Banco de Bilbao was constituted on 29 April 1857 with the participation of 106 local "patricians". Among the founders, surnames connected with the metallurgical industry stand out, yet others had interests in overseas trade, and so the interests of both mercantile and industrial capitalism coincided at its launch. The bank's initial capital was two million pesetas, and – after several capital enlargements – the capital outlay in 1901 reached fifteen million, with equity capital of 19.2 million.[8] Between 1899 and 1902 there was a surge in the creation of new banks, this being the moment in which three of the 'big six' came into being; the repatriation of capitals from the Americas played an important role in this process, as did the expansion of iron and steel exports, and industrial development in the Basque Country and Asturias. Banco Hispano-Americano was created in October 1900, by a group of Spanish entrepreneurs who had made their fortunes in the Americas. The group was led by Antonio Basagoiti Arteta, who was appointed chairman of the bank. This group of businessmen had been among the most important in the Mexico of Porfirio Díaz, commanding large companies and controlling the country's biggest bank: Banco Nacional de México (Banamex). On its foundation, the Hispano-Americano could also draw on the repatriation of capitals following the loss of the remaining Spanish colonies; with them came several board members of Cuban origin. From its beginnings, the bank was particularly concerned to promote trade relations between Spain and Spanish America and to channel the repatriation of remittances from emigrants. The bank was launched with a paid-up capital of ten

---

7 Mauro F. Guillén and Adrian Tschoegl, *Santander, el Banco*, Madrid, LID, 2007. Pablo Martín Aceña, *1857-2007. Banco Santander, 150 años de historia*, Madrid, Turner, 2007. Pablo Martín Aceña and Maria Ángeles Pons, "Estructura y rentabilidad de las empresas financieras en España, 1874-1975", in Francesco Comín and Pablo Martín Aceña (eds.), *La empresa en la Historia de España*, Madrid, Civitas, 1996, pp. 325-347; here: p. 329.

8 Juan Muñoz, *El poder de la banca en España*, 2nd edition, Madrid, Zero, 1970, pp. 33-34. Juan Muñoz, *La banca privada en el País Vasco y Navarra entre 1920 y 1935*, Bilbao, Archivo Histórico BBV, 1998, series "*Informaciones: Cuadernos de Archivo*", 54, p. 19. Pedro Tedde, "La banca privada", *op. cit.*, pp. 227-230. Pedro Tedde and Gabriel Tortella, "Censo y balances normalizados de los bancos privados españoles (1874-1914)", in Gabriel Tortella and Pedro Schwartz (eds.), *La banca española en la Restauración, op. cit.*, Vol. 2. Arantzazu Galarza, *Los orígenes del empresariado vasco*, Bilbao, Beitia, 1996, pp. 208-216. José Víctor Arroyo Martín, "BBVA y sus bancos históricos", *Revista de la historia de la economía y de la empresa*, No. 1, 2007 ("Instituciones financieras en España"), pp. 61-91.

million pesetas, and by 1914 paid-up capital had risen to fifty million and equity capital to 55.2.[9]

In 1901, Banco de Vizcaya was set up by leading representatives of industry and finance in the province of that name. This new bank was born with an evident mixed-banking vocation, since in the very same year of its foundation, it lent decisive support to the creation of *Hidroeléctrica Ibérica*. The Vizcaya was born with a paid-in capital of 3.8 million pesetas, although by 1914 it was rising to 8.5m and its equity capital to 10.7m.[10] Banco Español de Crédito (Banesto) was created in 1902 following the winding up of Crédito Mobiliario Español – one of those founded in the mid-19th century, which survived –, with a paid-in capital of twenty million pesetas. The original French investors continued to exercise an important influence (30 per cent of the disbursed capital), 40 per cent belonged to Paribas and other foreign capitalists, and the remaining 30 per cent was in Spanish hands. Foremost among the board members were Gustave Pereire and Raimundo Fernández Villaverde, who became Prime Minister in 1903. Banesto came into being as the great bank serving French business in Spain, but during WWI it gradually passed into Spanish hands, with those who were to be its future controllers – particularly José Gómez-Acebo Cortina (the Marquis of Cortina) and Pablo Garnica – gaining influence. Likewise, from WWI onwards, the institution started to evolve towards a mixed-type bank. Banesto inherited, from its origins in Crédito Mobiliario Español, the latter's relations with the *Ferrocarriles del Norte*, and several other industrial and service companies.[11]

The last two banks of the "big six" to be founded appeared at the end of the second decade of the 20th century. Banco Urquijo was born

9 Jose Luis García Ruiz and Gabriel Tortella, "Trayectorias divergentes, paralelas y convergentes: la historia del Banco Hispano-Americano y del Banco Central, 1901-1965", in Juan Hernández Andreu and Jose-Luis García Ruiz (eds.), *Lecturas de historia empresarial*, Madrid, Civitas, 1994; here pp. 405-406. Juan Muñoz, *El poder*, *op. cit.*, pp. 40-41. Pedro Tedde, "La banca privada", *op. cit.*, pp. 426-430. Pedro Tedde and Gabriel Tortella, "Censo y balances", *op. cit. La banca privada en Madrid entre 1920 y 1935*, Bilbao, Archivo Histórico BBV, 1998, Series "Informaciones: Cuadernos de Archivo", 55, p. 21. Jose-Luis García Ruiz, "Noventa años de gran banca comercial. El Banco Hispano-Americano, 1900-1991", *Revista de la historia de la economía y de la empresa*, 1, 2007.

10 Juan Muñoz, *El poder de la banca*, *op. cit.*, p. 42. Pedro Tedde, "La banca privada", *op. cit.*, pp. 422-424. Pedro Tedde and Gabriel Tortella, "Censo y balances", *op. cit.* José Víctor Arroyo Martín, "BBVA", *op. cit.*

11 Pedro Tedde, "La banca privada", *op. cit.*, pp. 424-426. Ramon Canosa, *Un siglo de banca privada*, *op. cit.*, pp. 56-7. Juan Muñoz, *El poder de la banca*, *op. cit.*, pp. 43-46. Pedro Tedde and Gabriel Tortella, "Censo y balances", *op. cit. La banca privada*, *op. cit.*, p. 26. Jose Luis García Ruiz, "Banesto, 1902-1993. Auge y decadencia de un gran banco mixto", *Revista de la historia de la economía y de la empresa*, 1, 2007, pp. 141-163.

in January 1918, but as the transformation of an older banking house, *Urquijo y Compañía*. The fifty million pesetas of subscribed capital stock remained in the hands of the three brothers who had inherited the business, although originally only half the capital was disbursed. The first hallmark of the new institution was that it declared explicitly as its central aim the protection of national industry and trade. On its constitution, the three founders contributed an industrial portfolio already worth ten million pesetas, comprising companies such as like *Sociedad Española de la Construcción Naval* (SECN), *Construcciones Auxiliares del Ferrocarril* (CAF), electrical corporations, tramways.[12] Banco Central was founded in Madrid in 1919 by agreement between several local banks with the intention of constituting a more powerful institution. The core was a merger between two banking houses. In 1921, it reached a disbursed capital of sixty million, not changed in the interwar period. The first shareholder was Crédito de la Unión Minera, an institution founded in Bilbao in 1901, followed by the proprietors of the aforementioned merging houses – Aldama and *Sucesores de Jiménez* –, Banco Guipuzcoano, Banco de Santander, Banco Castellano (in Valladolid), etc. Very soon it combined commercial banking with industrial investment, for it participated in the group of companies which in 1920 founded CHADE, the company that took over AEG's subsidiary in South America, DUEG, owner of electrical and tramway companies.[13]

3. The "Big Six" up to the Civil War

Drew on information from the *Anuario Financiero y de Sociedades Anónimas de España* (1922), S. Roldán, J.L. García Delgado and J. Muñoz analysed the companies that had relations with the seven big banks in 1921, on the basis of the existence of board members from those banks who also sat on the boards of other companies (Table 1). It clearly points to the existence of some connection, but fails to determine the intensity of the relationship between the bank and the company, since

---

12 Onésimo Díaz Hernández, *Los marqueses de Urquijo. El apogeo de una saga poderosa y los inicios del Banco Urquijo, 1870-1931*, Pamplona, Eunsa, 1998. Onésimo Díaz Hernández, "El Banco Urquijo: un banco industrial fundado en el periodo de Entreguerras", *Revista de la historia de la economía y de la empresa*, 1, 2007, pp. 254-255. Núria Puig Raposo and Eugenio Torres Villanueva, *Banco Urquijo. Un banco con historia*, Madrid, Turner, 2008, pp. 33-44.

13 Jose Luis García Ruiz and Gabriel Tortella, "Trayectorias divergentes", *op. cit.*, pp. 411-12. *La banca privada, op. cit.*, p. 31. Santiago Roldán, José Luis García Delgado and Juan Muñoz, *La formación de la sociedad*, *op. cit.*, pp. 202-204. Gabriel Tortella, "El triunfo del centralismo. Breve historia del Banco Central, 1920-1991", *Revista de la historia de la economía y de la empresa*, 1, 2007. Other institutional shareholders in CHADE were Urquijo, Banco de Vizcaya, Deutsche Bank, Crédit suisse, Sofina, etc. Onésimo Díaz Hernández, "El Banco Urquijo", *op. cit.*, p. 256.

their information does not include the percentage of share capital represented in each case. Furthermore, this seat could have been on a personal basis and not on behalf of the bank. Banco Central does not appear because it was of very recent creation, while the Hispano-Colonial was to end up being absorbed by the former, and Crédito de la Unión Minera went into liquidation in 1925. The Bilbao was head and shoulders above the others, followed by Urquijo and Vizcaya, as regards relations with other companies, and the commercial vocation of the Hispano-Americano was characterised by the scarcity of its relations with other companies. These banks had representation on the boards of 7.2 per cent of all limited companies (*sociedades anónimas*), but those firms brought together 49 per cent of the paid-up capital of all such companies, situated in sectors such as electricity, railways, mining, iron and steel, tobacco, etc.[14]

Banco de Bilbao was prominent in mining (eighteen companies), railways (eleven companies), and electricity (eight companies). In the machinery sector it had also relations with eight companies, among which Babcock & Wilcox stood out, but it was also involved in the Hispano-Suiza (automobiles) and maintained relations with eight shipping companies, and with six iron and steel producers, the foremost of which was *Altos Hornos de Vizcaya* (AHV). In banking, besides controlling Banco del Comercio, it had participated in the creation of Banco de Crédito Industrial.[15] Banco Hispano-Americano began its existence promoting overseas relations. In 1904, it invested in a pre-existing Argentine institution which it transformed into Banco del Comercio Hispano-Argentino, and which, in the following year, merged with the Banco de la Provincia de Buenos Aires (the name under which it still exists). Its activities extended through Uruguay, Paraguay, Brazil, Chile and Cuba, in the search for colonies of Spanish emigrants. In Spain it acted as a commercial bank, but it also had an important securities portfolio in which the Spanish national debt had pride of place (52 per cent), followed by shares in the Banco de la Provincia de Buenos Aires (23 per cent), the rest consisting of stocks and bonds in some thirty Spanish and Spanish-American companies. The Hispano-Americano underwent a serious crisis of confidence in 1913, as a result of the Mexican Revolution, and it tended to moderate its overseas relations and more than any other institution opted for the commercial bank model. The BHA preferred involvement with electrical companies

14 Santiago Roldán, José Luis García Delgado and Juan Muñoz, *La formación*, *op. cit.*, pp. 249-253. Maria Ángeles Pons, "Banca e industria", *op. cit.*, p. 260.

15 Santiago Roldán, José Luis García Delgado and Juan Muñoz, *La formación*, *op. cit.*, pp. 328-330.

(*Hidroeléctrica Española* taking pride of place) and those promoted by the state rather than the traditional ones such as railways. It also participated in setting up Banco de Crédito Industrial.[16]

Table 1. Posts occupied in other limited companies by members of the boards of seven banks, 1921

	Number of companies with		
	Leading directors (chairman, vice-chairman, manager, managing director, chief executive officer)	Other members	Board members from these banks
B. Hispano-Colonial	20	56	49
B. Español de Crédito	16	47	47
B. Hispano-Americano	5	31	28
B. Urquijo	33	74	67
B. de Bilbao	31	97	91
B. de Vizcaya	22	128	64
Crédito de la U. Minera	18	58	55
Total	145	491	274

Source: Santiago Roldán, José Luis García Delgado and Juan Muñoz, *La formación de la sociedad capitalista*, *op. cit.*, p. 249.

Banco de Vizcaya had, from the outset, a mixed activity, and had supported industry. Before WWI it had already fully developed its relations with the electrical sector, holding shares in eleven such companies, as well as seven railway companies (including Norte, MZA and Andaluces), and the SECN (the leading firm in the shipbuilding sector). Foremost among its foreign holdings were shares in banks which had set up branches in Spanish America (British Bank of South America, Banco Francés del Río de la Plata, etc.). In 1921, the Vizcaya's board members occupied seats on fifteen electrical companies, and so it is hardly surprising that for many years it was regarded as the 'electrical bank *par excellence*'. Its degree of participation in *Cooperativa Electra Madrid* was very significant, contributing no less than eight members to its board. Similar cases were *Hidroeléctrica Española* (principal director and three other members), Viesgo (vice-chairman and seven board members) and *Hidroeléctrica Ibérica* (chairman, general manager and three members). Although its participation must have been much less significant, the Vizcaya also had directors in other important companies such as CHADE. By 1921,

[16] Pedro Tedde, "La banca privada", *op. cit.*, pp. 426-430. Jose Luis García Ruiz and Gabriel Tortella, "Trayectorias divergentes", *op. cit.*, pp. 406-411. Jose Luis García Ruiz, "Noventa años", *op. cit.*, pp. 118-120. *La banca privada en Madrid entre 1920 y 1935*, pp. 21-26. Roldán, García Delgado and Muñoz, *La formación*, *op. cit.*, p. 325.

its relations with the railway companies had shrunk to five. Other sectors with which it had relations were tramways, machinery (including Babcock & Wilcox), and above all mining (nine companies). Its relations were also significant in iron and steel (AHV), and in shipbuilding (SECN and Euskalduna).[17]

Banesto came into being to manage certain French interests in Spain, but according to Pedro Tedde, the securities portfolio did not reach an appreciable size until the 1904-1907 period, in which it participated in several loans to the Spanish Treasury, the Moroccan Government and the Barcelona City Council (in fact the aforementioned portfolio grew from 5.5 to 11.5 million pesetas between 1903 and 1904). Its initial relations with companies came about generally through Crédito Mobiliario Español and, apart from the railways (Norte and four other companies), it held shares in an insurance company (*La Unión y El Fénix*), electricity and tramways companies, and SECN. In 1921 Banesto's directors sat on the boards of nine electrical companies, the best known being Hidroeléctrica Española, Unión Eléctrica Madrileña, Sevillana and Viesgo, and on those of seven railway companies, among which were neither Norte nor MZA (the two biggest ones). Its relations with other banks extended to the Hipotecario and Banco de España; in machinery, Babcock & Wilcox stands out, and in electrical goods the Spanish subsidiary of Siemens. In 1927, Banesto completely dissolved its ties with Paribas, and opted for a more commercial line, although it retained its investments in railways, insurance, etc.[18]

Between 1918 and 1920, Banco Urquijo rapidly set up a network of subsidiaries in Asturias, Basque Country and Catalonia: Banco Minero Industrial de Asturias (Oviedo, 1918), Banco Urquijo Vascongado (Bilbao, 1918), Banco Urquijo Catalán (Barcelona, 1919), and Banco Urquijo de Guipúzcoa (San Sebastián, 1920). By 1921, Urquijo had directors also on the Hipotecario, in Banco de España and in Banco de Crédito Industrial. The main sectors in which Banco Urquijo participated were railways, including MZA and Norte (thirteen companies in 1921), iron and steel (Duro Felguera, AHV), machinery and other equipment manufacturers (SECN, CAF, etc.), electricity (*Unión Eléctrica Madrileña*, CHADE), chemicals, mining, and so on. The Urquijos always had firm links with political power, which eased their participation in legal monopolies such as the *Compañía Arrendataria de Tabacos* (CAT, 1887), *Compañía Telefónica*

---

17 Santiago Roldán, José Luis García Delgado and Juan Muñoz, *La formación*, *op. cit.*, pp. 333-334.

18 Pedro Tedde, "La banca privada", *op. cit.*, pp. 425-426. Santiago Roldán, José Luis García Delgado and Juan Muñoz, *formación*, *op. cit.*, pp. 323-324. Jose Luis García Ruiz, "Banesto", *op. cit.*, p. 144. Jose Luis García Ruiz, "Noventa años", *op. cit.*, p. 119. *La banca privada*, *op. cit.*, pp. 28-30.

Nacional de España (1924), and CAMPSA (in the distribution of petroleum derivates, 1927). In the 1930s, the bank took part in initiatives connected with transport and energy: Firestone Hispania, Worthington (hydraulic pumps), etc.[19]

Banco Central began its activity satisfactorily, since besides participating in the creation of CHADE, but from 1925 onward, its history was very convulsed as a consequence of the bankruptcy of Crédito de la Unión Minera (1925), which was the principal shareholder in the institution. Also, at that time serious internal dissension broke out, and things became worse with the entry onto the board of directors of individuals such as Manuel Pereña who abused his position in order to sell the bank several cork producers in difficulties, which affected the institution. Apart from this serious error, the Central had holdings in other companies that were profitable, although not always immediately, such as CEPSA (in petroleum refining), and in *Banco Exterior*, created at the suggestion of the state but managed by private enterprise for the purpose of operating with foreign currencies and in foreign trade. In 1930 and 1931 the Central had to be rescued with the help of the government and Banco de España, but despite everything in 1934 it reached an agreement with Banco Hispano-Colonial, which would henceforth be a subsidiary of the Central in Catalonia until its complete absorption in 1950. The monetary authorities distrusted the financial situation of the Central and in July 1936, an inspection was set in motion that could have had very serious consequences for the bank, but which was interrupted by the outbreak of the Civil War.[20]

4. Some magnitudes in the interwar period

During the interwar period, the leading Spanish bank as regards total net worth (paid-up capital, reserves and accounts payable) was always the Hispano-Americano, although in 1920 the Bilbao surpassed it in equity capital (the latter had almost sixty million pesetas in reserves, as against the just under twenty-two million possessed by the Banco

[19] Onésimo Díaz Hernández, "El Banco Urquijo: un banco industrial fundado en el periodo de Entreguerras", pp. 254-260. *La banca privada, op. cit.*, pp. 43-46. *La banca privada en Cataluña, op. cit.*, pp. 99-102. Santiago Roldán, José Luis García Delgado and Juan Muñoz, *La formación, op. cit.*, pp. 326-327. Núria Puig Raposo and Eugenio Torres Villanueva, *Banco Urquijo, op. cit.*, pp. 44-86. CAMPSA was created by a consortium of banks in which, together with Urquijo, the Hispano-Americano, the Bilbao, Vizcaya, Banesto and Banco Herrero participated.

[20] Gabriel Tortella, "El Banco Central en el período de Entreguerras o cómo llevar una empresa a la ruina", *Estudis d'Història Econòmica*, 17-18, pp. 241-272. Gabriel Tortella, "El triunfo", *op. cit.*, pp. 214-20. Jose Luis Garcia and Gabriel Tortella, "Trayectorias divergentes", *op. cit.*, pp. 414-417.

Hispano-Colonial). As for the ranking in equity capital plus deposits, only two significant changes occurred: Banesto was ahead of the Bilbao between 1925 and 1930, above all in the attraction of deposits, but also came close to the Basque institution in equity capital, by growing faster in paid-up capital and above all in reserves. On the other hand, the Urquijo, which occupied the fifth position in 1920 (slightly above the Vizcaya), had fallen by 1935 to the last place both in equity capital plus deposits, and in deposits alone, although it had a greater equity capital than the Central, a very important aspect in an industrial bank. The two banks that grew fastest in terms of equity capital plus deposits were the Hispano-Americano and the Español de Crédito, especially between 1925 and 1930.

Table 2. Financial resources of the 'big six' during the interwar period

	Equity capital (in thousands of pesetas)					
	Hispano-Americano	**Banesto**	**Central**	**Urquijo**	**Bilbao**	**Vizcaya**
1920	91,910	39,300	59,799	35,000	116,438	41,000
1925	115,181	53,999	69,385	77,724	123,000	50,500
1930	142,181	104,821	80,500	94,724	125,000	110,000
1935	164,916	121,948	83,107	90,224	144,750	110,000
	Equity capital plus deposits (in thousands of pesetas)					
	Hispano-Americano	**Banesto**	**Central**	**Urquijo**	**Bilbao**	**Vizcaya**
1920	772,848	374,780	144,527	290,388	603,177	287,082
1925	788,321	394,243	184,038	246,212	715,847	359,115
1930	1,400,502	1,307,652	405,040	468,584	898,844	667,525
1935	1,655,256	1,461,584	612,078	419,243	1,198,278	803,967

Source: *La banca privada en el País Vasco y Navarra entre 1920 y 1935*, pp. 78-79. *La banca privada en Madrid entre 1920 y 1935*, pp. 88-91.

As for total bank investment (securities portfolio, mercantile and credit paper), the evolution was logically similar to that of equity capital plus deposits (which are marked to a greater extent by deposits than equity capital), but an intense transformation took place as regards its structure. In absolute figures, commercial investment (mercantile paper and loans) grew – except in the Bilbao and the Urquijo – but this was most notable in Banesto and the Hispano-Americano. In percentage terms, the securities portfolio (government funds and industrial securities) always tended to grow, which meant that in absolute figures it grew more than commercial investment; in 1935 it was more than 57 per cent of total bank investment in all cases. Indeed the differences among the "big six" – as regards investment policy – were much greater in 1920 than in 1935. In 1935 the most voluminous portfolio (74.4 per cent) was that of the Vizcaya, followed by the Urquijo and the Bilbao.

Table 3. Structure of investment in the interwar period

	Total bank investment (in thousands of pesetas)					
	Hispano-Americano	**Banesto**	**Central**	**Urquijo**	**Bilbao**	**Vizcaya**
1920	514,598	363,048	101,590	226,437	486,830	175,003
1925	679,155	365,782	136,622	266,897	572,062	287,483
1930	1,155,348	1,111,259	282,325	467,307	780,145	601,517
1935	1,317,162	1,193,342	456,609	373,011	794,149	665,237
	Securities portfolio (public and industrial funds): % of total investment					
1920	8.3	10.7	3.7	18.2	30.4	29.8
	Government securities: % of total investment					
1925	25.3	13.5	20.5	6.1	22.7	19.6
1930	34.0	32.2	28.6	25.7	33.0	29.7
1935	50.8	46.5	38.4	21.0	43.6	48.6
	Industrial securities: % of total investment					
1925	9.0	14.2	4.8	29.6	12.9	24.1
1930	10.1	12.8	26.0	33.2	23.9	29.3
1935	7.8	10.8	19.0	46.6	19.5	25.8

Source: calculated from *La banca privada en el País Vasco y Navarra, op. cit.*, pp. 78-79; *La banca privada en Madrid, op. cit.*, pp. 88-91.

The area of the securities portfolio that grew most significantly in percentage terms was that of government funds, which, besides, enjoyed the advantage of being pledgeable in case of need; in the Urquijo, however, they fell between 1930 and 1935. Industrial securities increased significantly in relative terms in the Urquijo between 1930 and 1935, as a consequence of the already mentioned reduction of gilt-edged securities in terms of absolute values, but in this case in absolute values the growth of investment in company securities was very strong between 1925 and 1930, becoming moderate in the first half of the 1930s. Of the "big six", it was the Urquijo that had the greatest proportion of capital invested in company securities. In the case of Banco Hispano-Americano, industrial securities did not exceed 10% of total bank investment. It has been stated that "at the most, between 1921 and 1934, the big Spanish banks did not devote [...] more than a quarter of their portfolio assets to industrial securities"; their mixed nature was therefore less marked than that of the German and Italian banks.[21] In that definition, the "portfolio"

[21] Francesco Comín, "La economía española en el período de Entreguerras (1919-1935)", in Jordi Nadal, Albert Carreras and Carles Sudrià (eds.), *La economía española en el siglo XX. Una perspectiva histórica*, 3rd edition, Barcelona, Ariel, 1989, p. 107. Javier Pueyo, *El comportamiento, op. cit.*, p. 38.

included not only the securities portfolio but also the trade bills, and the data in Table 4 show that – apart from the Urquijo, which was a bank of industrial vocation – in 1930 the Central, the Bilbao and the Vizcaya amply exceeded that proportion, although by 1935 it had fallen.

Table 4. Industrial securities as a percentage of the investment portfolio (securities owned plus trade bills)

	Banco Hispano-Americano	Banesto	Banco Central	Banco Urquijo	Banco Bilbao	Banco Vizcaya
1925	12	19	8	63	20	37
1930	13	15	34	45	36	42
1935	9	13	25	59	26	30

Source: calculated from *La banca privada en el País Vasco y Navarra entre 1920 y 1935*, pp. 78-79. *La banca privada en Madrid entre 1920 y 1935*, pp. 88-91.

5. Banking policy in the early period of Franco's dictatorship

After the Civil War (1936-1939) sation, the establishment of new banks without prior governmental authorization was prohibited (with narrow restrictions until 1962), occasioning what has been called the "*status quo*". Besides, the Bank Regulation Act (*Ley de Ordenación Bancaria*) of 1946 also regulated interest rates, opening of branches, etc. The banks in fact financed industry with short-term but renewable loans, although the danger existed that any moment renewal of the loan might be refused and the company would have to declare bankruptcy.[22] These restrictions have given rise to a wide-ranging literature on the monopolistic or oligopolistic nature of the banks in Spain, and the question of relations between the banks and the state. Spain's first Bank Regulation Act (*Ley de Ordenación Bancaria*) dates back to 1921, but in the interwar period the law did not create barriers to entry in the sector, unlike the 1946 law, which represented a genuine rupture with the previous period.[23] J. Muñoz considered that the 1946 *Ley de Ordenación Bancaria* facilitated the reorganisation of the banking sector, its concentration and consolidation as mixed-type banking,[24] as well as the

22 Maria Ángeles Pons, *Regulating Spanish Banking, 1939-1975*, Aldershot, Ashgate, 2002, pp. 55-59. Esteban Maria Faus Mompart, *Regulación y desregulación. Notas para la historia de la banca española*, Barcelona, Península, 2001, pp. 136-137 and 145-155. Maria Ángeles Pons, "Banca e industria", *op. cit.*, pp. 253-254. Juan Muñoz, *El poder*, *op. cit.*, pp. 81-84.

23 Javier Pueyo, *El comportamiento*, *op. cit.*, pp. 41-46 and 79-80. See also Esteban Maria Faus, *Regulación*, *op. cit.*

24 Esteban Maria Faus, *Regulación*, *op. cit.*, pp. 153-154. Gabriel Tortella, "El triunfo", *op. cit.*, p. 224.

maintenance of monopolistic behaviours, in what has been regarded as a 'capturing' of the state by the banks.[25]

Subsequent authors have made it clear that the law, and the protection it afforded the established banks, were received with delight by the financiers, while the *Falange* (one of the groups that supported the regime) was calling for the nationalisation of the sector. The banks, in order to maintain their independence, had to agree to finance Franco's policies via the acquisition of public debt, and in exchange they were allowed to function as an oligopoly. M.-A. Pons has therefore emphasised that, rather than a "capture" of the state by the banks, or a total submission of the sector to the government, there was a 'consensus' in which the latter obtained funds in order to reallocate them while the banks minimised their risk by reducing competition.[26]

A question of great importance is the role of pledgeable public debt. The situation was similar to that before the Civil War, but in the post-war an artificially low interest rate was applied, thus making this a somewhat undesirable asset. Although obligatory coefficients of investment did not exist, the authorities found ways to persuade the banks to acquire it; for example, the National Bank facilitated better conditions to the banks which held abundant government securities. The abundant issues of pledgeable public debt with unattractive interest rates resulted in constant inflation, which led to the disappearance of this modality with the new economic policy introduced in 1959, although it was not formally prohibited until the *Ley de Ordenación Bancaria* of 1962. Those authors who defended the monopolistic role of the banks considered that the pledgeable debt favoured the power of the sector, but in reality it was floated under coercion, and could not be reassigned among the banks' own customers, unlike the situation in the interwar period.[27]

---

25 Juan Muñoz, *El poder de la banca, op. cit.*, pp. 60-69. See also Ramon Tamames Gomez, *Los monopolios en España*, Madrid, ZYX, 1967.

26 Jose Luis García Ruiz, "Banesto, 1902-1993", *op. cit.*, p. 147. Jose Luis García Ruiz, "Noventa años", *op. cit.*, p. 121. Gabriel Tortella, "El triunfo", *op. cit.*, pp. 226-228. Maria Ángeles Pons, "Banca e industria", *op. cit.*, p. 254. Javier Pueyo, *El comportamiento*, *op. cit.*, pp. 46-51 and 82-88. Esteban Maria Faus, *Regulación*, *op. cit.*, pp. 220-224. See also Pablo Martín Aceña and Maria Ángeles Pons, "Estructura y rentabilidad", *op. cit.* Maria Ángeles Pons, "Oligopolio y tipos de interés en la banca española, 1942-1975", *Revista de Historia Económica*, XIX-3, 2001, pp. 679-703. Jose Luis García Ruiz, "Los arreglos interbancarios durante el franquismo", *Revista de Historia Económica*, XX-2, 2002. Javier Pueyo, "Oligopolio y competencia en la banca española del siglo XX: concentración económica y movilidad intraindustrial, 1922-1995", *Revista de Historia Económica*, XXI-1, 2003, pp. 199-212. Javier Pueyo, "Relaciones interempresariales y consejeros comunes en la banca española del siglo XX", *Investigaciones de Historia Económica*, 6, 2006, pp. 137-168.

27 Juan Muñoz, *El poder*, *op. cit.*, pp. 60-69. Jose Luis García Ruiz, "Banesto", *op. cit.*, p. 147. Javier Pueyo, *El comportamiento*, *op. cit.*, pp. 36-38.

The "*status quo*" often prevented the banks from establishing branches in particular places, so that they were forced to acquire banking houses or small local banks in order to do so (which, on the other hand, increased the value of these businesses). On occasions, the same business name was maintained, or only a certain share in capital was acquired, giving rise to the creation of banking groups. Among the big bankers, Andrés Moreno (CEO in the Hispano-Americano) wished to maintain the rules of the English banks, where he had worked earlier. He disdained the introduction of collusive practices and the absorption of banking houses. This strategy led the Bank to lose its leadership, although it grew in the decades of the 1940s and 1950s.[28]

6. The 1962 Bank Regulation Act and specialisation

The *Ley de Ordenación Bancaria* of 1962 tried to remedy certain problems that the authorities believed needed attention. These included: improving the performance of Banco de España as a central bank (it was nationalised together with the "official banks" such as Banco de Crédito Industrial and Banco Hipotecario de España); facilitating long-term credit; and bringing about the specialisation of the banks as either commercial or industrial, so as to avoid credit discrimination in favour of the companies in which the banks held shares – but this obligatory specialisation was eliminated in 1974. The new law also gave greater facilities for the expansion of networks of branches and the creation of banks, but continued to maintain a certain control, and there was still no move to liberalise interest rates – something that only began gradually in the 1970s. Although pledgeable debt had been suppressed, since 1965 coefficients were established for investment in government securities in order to facilitate the financing of the State.[29]

The *Ley de Ordenación Bancaria* of 1962 was developed through other provisions, and it is worth highlighting that the industrial and business banks had to possess four characteristics.

- The industrial securities portfolio (private sector) was not allowed to exceed three times the amount of equity capital;

[28] Esteban Maria Faus, *Regulación*, *op. cit.*, pp. 153-155. Jose Luis García Ruiz, "Noventa años", *op. cit.*, p. 121. About another large banks absorption policy, see: Gabriel Tortella, "El triunfo del centralismo", *op. cit.*, p. 76. Jose Luis García Ruiz, "Banesto, 1902-1993", *op. cit.*, p. 146.

[29] Juan Muñoz, *El poder*, *op. cit.*, pp. 69-71. Maria Ángeles Pons, "Banca e industria", *op. cit.*, pp. 253-256. Maria Ángeles Pons, *Regulating Spanish Banking*, *op. cit.*, pp. 59-62. Esteban Maria Faus, *Regulación op. cit.*, pp. 166-74. Jose Luis García Ruiz, "Banesto, 1902-1993", *op. cit.*, p. 152. Antonio Lacomba et Gumersindo Ruiz, *Una historia del Banco Hipotecario de España* (*1872-1986*), Madrid, Alianza, 1990, pp. 445-460. Gabriel Tortella and Juan Carlos Jiménez, *Historia del Banco de Crédito Industrial*, Madrid, Alianza, 1986, pp. 123-127.

- The bank's interest in any company should not represent more than half of that company's paid-up capital;
- It should not invest more than 10 per cent of its equity capital plus deposits in any one company;
- No more than 50 per cent of an industrial bank's paid-up capital should be controlled by other Spanish banks.

Table 5. Principal industrial banks created on the basis of the *Ley de Ordenación Bancaria* of 1962

Industrial bank	Spanish promoter	Year of founding	Principal foreign associates
Banco de Desarrollo Económico Español (Bandesco)	Banesto	1963	Barclays (GB), International Finance, (USA), Morgan Guaranty Trust (USA)
Banco de Fomento	B. Central	1963	
Unión Industrial Bancaria	B. Atlántico	1963	Condotte d'Acqua (It.), Banca Privata Finanziaria (It.) De Neuflize Schlumberger (Fr.)
Banco Industrial de Bilbao	B. Bilbao	1964	
Banco de Financiación Industrial	B. Vizcaya	1964	The First National City Bank (USA), Westminster Foreign Bank. (GB), Philip Hill Investment Trust (GB),
Banco Europeo de Negocios	B. Popular	1964	Banque de l'Indochine (Fr.), Compagne privée de banque (Fr.), Crédit commercial de France (Fr.)
Banco Intercontinental Español (Bankinter)	B. Santander	1965	Bank of America

Source: Assembled from information in Muñoz, *El poder de la banca en España*, pp. 81-84 et 163-165. Guillén and Tschoegl, *Santander, el Banco*, pp. 126-127.

The mixed-type banks, for their part, were allowed a period of five years to adjust their situation to the new law, if they opted to convert to commercial banks, in which case the sum of the portfolio of industrial securities and tangible fixed assets (real estate investment and furniture and fixtures) was not allowed to exceed the volume of equity capital. J. Muñoz stated that a consequence of capital enlargements effected during the 1960s was that the mixed-type banks were transformed into commercial banks without any need to carry out divestments.[30]

In Spain in 1962 there was, properly speaking, only one industrial bank: the Urquijo, which in 1944 had sealed a collaboration agreement with the Hispano-Americano, known as the *Pacto de Las Jarillas* – after the name of the estate where the negotiations had taken place. The agreement was based on an exchange of shares, and the Hispano-Americano was thus able

30 Juan Muñoz, *El poder*, *op. cit.*, pp. 81-84, 215-223 and 389-391.

to maintain its commercial tendency in spite of government pressures for it to involve itself in industrialisation, by accompanying and financing the Urquijo in a variety of industrial promotions.[31] By 1972 there were a total of seventeen industrial banks,[32] and the most important, apart from the Urquijo, had been backed up by the large financial institutions. As the Spanish banks could not control more than 50 per cent of the capital of the industrial and business banks, the entry of foreign capital into their stock was facilitated.

7. The big banks and the promotion of companies during the Franco period

As we have already seen, the "*status quo*" favoured concentration of the banks, sometimes through absorptions and sometimes by forming groups around related interests. J. Muñoz identified several large banking groups on the basis of individual members sitting on the boards of different institutions and links between institutions in the form of first-degree family connections, which can be summed up in the following table. The group led by Banco Santander was of smaller size, but grew very fast in the 1960s, while the groups led by the Bilbao and the Vizcaya lacked directors in common but did, on the other hand, have board members related by close family ties.[33]

Table 6. Principal Spanish banking groups (balances as of 30 September 1967)

		Equity capital	Deposits	
Group	**Banks**	**Millions Ptas**	**Millions Ptas**	**Offices**
Banco Español de Crédito	9	13,177.9	122,743.1	691
Hispano-Americano / Urquijo	8	14,326.4	118,587.3	572
Banco Central	6	8,982.7	84,844.8	558
Banco de Bilbao	7	7,977.3	74,289.6	371
Banco de Vizcaya	3	6,660.5	56,503.4	282
Popular/Rumasa/Atlántico	14	5,057.4	48,256.6	259

Source: Assembled from information in J. Muñoz, *El poder, op. cit.*, pp. 142-153.

The banks exercised influence on companies in three different ways: through direct shareholdings; through having board members in common; and by exercising voting rights on behalf of individuals whose shares were deposited in the banks. Likewise, the concession

31 Jose Luis García Ruiz, "Noventa años", *op. cit.*, p. 121. Onésimo Díaz Hernández, "El Banco Urquijo", *op. cit.*, p. 261. Núria Puig Raposo and Eugenio Torres Villanueva, *Banco Urquijo*, *op. cit.*, pp. 112-14.

32 Consejo Superior Bancario (CSB), *Un cuarto de siglo de banca privada, 1947-1972*, Madrid, CSB, 1973.

33 Juan Muñoz, *El poder*, *op. cit.*, pp. 149-154. Pablo Martín Aceña, *1857-2007. Banco Santander*, *op. cit.*, pp. 134-188.

of a sizeable loan could be made conditional on the bank's placing a member on a company's board of directors, so that they might have better knowledge of the firm's situation, thus reducing information costs and uncertainty. For the companies, the connection with a bank could also be of benefit, since it provided a more reliable access to loans in times of a credit squeeze. The influence of the banks was also due to the low level of self-financing of companies and the rudimentary state of the financial system and the capital market. In any case, the industrial securities portfolios of the Spanish banks were far smaller than those of the German or Italian banks, resembling a commercial bank more than a universal bank.[34] In the case of Banesto, in the 1950s, its chairman Pablo Garnica considered that only equity capital should be invested in company securities and in immobilised capital (buildings, furniture and fixtures) – a condition that in the 1960s was imposed on the commercial banks. Besides the participation in companies that arose during the interwar period, one must highlight the intervention of Banesto together with the Spanish public holding company INI, Fiat, and several private banks, in the creation of SEAT in 1950; similarly, in the 1970s it participated in Acerinox (steel production), and likewise collaborated in the installation of Ford's subsidiary in Valencia.[35]

During the 1950s, Banco Urquijo was outstanding for its support of the automobile industry (it, too, held capital in SEAT), pharmaceuticals (*Compañía Española de Penicilinas y Antibióticos*) and chemicals: SA Cros, *Unión Española de Explosivos*, etc. In the 1960s, together with other banks, it participated in important loans to CAMPSA – which, as we have already seen, was created by a bank consortium of which the Urquijo was a member – and also fostered mergers of shipbuilding and chemical companies (giving birth to *Astilleros Españoles* and the chemical manufacturer La Seda).[36] As for Banco Central,

[34] Juan Muñoz, *El poder*, *op. cit.*, pp. 209-215, 223-230 and 266-307. Javier Pueyo, *El Comportamiento*, *op. cit.*, p. 20. Jesus M. Valdaliso, "Grupos empresariales y relaciones banca-industria en España durante el franquismo: una aproximación microeconómica", *Información Comercial Española, ICE: Revista de Economía*, 812, 2004, pp. 163-166. Esteban Maria Faus, *Regulación*, *op. cit.*, pp. 237-240. See also Maria Ángeles Pons, "Banca e industria en España", *op. cit.* Pablo Martín Aceña and Maria Á. Pons, "Spanish banking after the Civil War, 1940-1962", *Financial History Review*, 1, 1994, pp. 121-138.

[35] Jose Luis García Ruiz, "Banesto, 1902-1993", *op. cit.*, pp. 147-153. Juan Muñoz, *El poder*, *op. cit.*, pp. 209-235.

[36] Onésimo Díaz Hernández, "El Banco Urquijo", *op. cit.*, pp. 262-263. For the relations of the Urquijo, Hispano-Americano, and other related banks with the Sota and Aznar group of companies and hence with the shipbuilders Euskalduna, see Jesus M. Valdaliso, "Grupos empresariales", *op. cit.*

when Villalonga took over in the 1940s, he had to carry out a complete transformation of the institution, hiving off companies linked to the bank that were not viable. As for its relations with other banks, it is worth underlining the absorption of the Banco Hispano-Colonial in 1950, since the latter was affected by the bankruptcy of the Barcelona Traction, Power & Light Company, and its participation in the creation of FECSA, the firm that took over the assets. In the electrical sector, the bank gradually shed all its holdings in CHADE, which had once yielded it substantial profits (although after the war it lost importance), and created an important hydroelectric group in the northwest, and it likewise participated in the south in Hidroeléctrica del Chorro. The bank's last great foundation turned out to be a failure: Andaluza de Piritas, a mining company that began exploitation in 1979 and had to be sold off to the Swedish firm Boliden in 1987 at a price far inferior to what the Central had invested in it.[37]

8. Financial resources and investment

The consolidation of the great banks during the Franco period (1939-1975) is borne out by Table 7: Banesto had clearly drawn ahead of the Hispano-Americano by the start of the 1960s, since its development had been faster throughout the decade before, as was also the case of the Central and the Urquijo, but these started at a lower level. The two Basque banks (Bilbao and Vizcaya) were the only ones that lost weight during the 1940s in real terms, since although their financial resources grew, it was at a slower rate than inflation. At the end of the period they were the ones that had grown least, possibly because of their links with the mining and metallurgical industries, which were gradually losing importance, above all after the Stabilisation Plan of 1959 and the end of autarchy. The growth rate was moderate between 1947 and 1957, accelerating until 1962, and with a genuine take-off in the following years, which was particularly rapid for the Urquijo, Central and Banesto. As for the principal industrial banks (Table 9), in 1972 they were much smaller in size than the big banks, although nearly all were growing at a good pace, the leaders being Bankinter and the two industrial banks set up by the large Basque banks: Banco Industrial de Bilbao and Banco de Financiación Industrial.[38]

[37] Gabriel Tortella, "El triunfo del centralismo", *op. cit.*, pp. 223-229.

[38] Juan Muñoz, *El poder*, *op. cit.*, pp. 84-86 and 98-100.

Table 7. Equity capital of the large banks and the main industrial banks

	Large Banks. Thousands of pesetas (constant to 1995 value)					
	Hispano-Americano	**Banesto**	**Central**	**Urquijo**	**Bilbao**	**Vizcaya**
1947	33,508,497	25,233,007	18,104,575	14,052,288	27,990,196	27,843,137
1952	36,254,980	27,280,876	26,494,024	16,733,068	24,404,622	26,294,821
1957	39,507,576	36,559,318	28,156,566	19,823,232	29,021,338	29,356,061
1962	54,316,406	57,737,051	39,383,203	25,178,223	41,031,563	40,778,340
1967	128,476,776	151,430,874	101,046,434	49,608,934	84,218,456	78,324,836
1972	160,784,747	200,452,105	152,653,998	133,568,998	125,347,348	92,724,109

	Pesetas (1995 value) x 1,000			
Industrial Banks (1962 LOB)	**1964**	**1965**	**1967**	**1972**
Bandesco	4,450,390		7,005,533	13,069,696
B. de Fomento	7,363,458		10,601,093	12,145,749
B. Industrial de Bilbao	3,069,068		7,214,768	18,984,241
B. de Financiación Industrial			11,327,801	19,581,913
Unión Industrial Bancaria	10,169,492		17,138,661	17,257,085
B. Europeo de Negocios	3,389,831		6,733,648	13,353,775
Bankinter		3,894,081	5,150,273	22,937,814

Source: Assembled from information in CSB, *Un cuarto de siglo de banca privada, 1947-1972.* Data deflated with the series given by Prados de la Escosura, *El progreso económico de España (1850-2000)*, Bilbao, Fundación BBVA, 2003, pp. 686-693 (as the rest of the tables).

Table 8. Percentage represented by short-term bonds over total deposits of the industrial banks

Industrial banks	**1967**	**1972**
Banco Urquijo	14.7	2.7
Bandesco	94.5	41.2
B. de Fomento	89.1	39.5
B. Industrial de Bilbao	17.9	9.7
B. de Financiación Industrial	24.7	15.1
Unión Industrial Bancaria	48.6	51.6
B. Europeo de Negocios	78.8	41.7
Bankinter	72.3	51.9

Source: Calculated from data in CSB, Un cuarto de siglo de banca privada, 1947-1972.

In 1972, the equity capital of the smallest of the big banks (Vizcaya, 92,724 million pesetas) were four times those of the biggest of the industrial banks (Bankinter), but the differences were even greater when we compare equity capital plus deposits. The industrial banks had certain advantages as regards attraction of funds, such as the ability to pay somewhat higher interest rates and to issue short-term bonds exchangeable for shares, but their branch networks were very limited. The importance of these bonds in the totality of the industrial banks' deposits differed considerably according to each case, although it was consistently greater in 1967 than in 1972, perhaps to some extent because by the latter date they had already been exchanged for shares.

Table 9. Equity capital plus deposits of the large banks and the principal industrial banks

	Large banks. Millions of pesetas at 1995 value					
	Hispano-Americano	**Banesto**	**Central**	**Urquijo**	**Bilbao**	**Vizcaya**
1947	698,196	605,194	284,111	96,638	283,465	279,944
1952	788,809	743,124	471,859	102,862	356,702	338,720
1957	1,001,826	1,008,120	613,038	150,965	435,004	468,983
1962	1,307,462	1,393,016	813,605	182,607	697,676	671,959
1967	1,710,666	1,918,032	1,234,739	266,400	1,005,035	916,589
1972	2,584,920	3,018,004	2,490,793	677,839	2,524,480	1,757,330

	Millions of pesetas at 1995 value			
Industrial banks (1962 LOB)	**1964**	**1965**	**1967**	**1972**
Bandesco	21,400		50,220	138,031
Banco de Fomento	16,502		29,491	160,656
Banco Industrial de Bilbao	16,386		45,443	201,288
Banco de Financiación Industrial			102,507	240,139
Unión Industrial Bancaria	19,302		55,966	225,643
Banco Europeo de Negocios	17,245		46,628	141,822
Bankinter		15,115	42,950	198,562

Source: Created from information in CSB, *Un cuarto de siglo de banca privada, 1947-1972.*

As for total bank investment (bills, loans and securities portfolio), this grew at a more or less brisk rate, in pesetas at a constant value, between 1947 and 1957. Banco Central more than doubled it, though the Hispano-Americano's only grew by 39 per cent. In all cases, however, growth accelerated following the Stabilisation Plan (1959) and underwent an explosion between 1967 and 1972. In those years, total bank investments grew more in the case of the industrial banks than the big banks; particularly outstanding were Bankinter and the Banco Industrial de Bilbao.

Table 10. Total investment of the large banks and the industrial banks

	Hispano-Americano	Banesto	Central	Urquijo	Bilbao	Vizcaya
	Large banks. Millions of pesetas (1995 value)					
1947	643,997	507,901	246,946	78,096	254,796	251,911
1952	711,938	682,730	397,455	89,582	317,012	307,810
1957	896,604	873,903	545,117	131,349	380,363	425,279
1962	1,175,207	1,201,584	733,748	158,000	610,395	614,518
1967	1,521,642	1,651,901	1,055,048	223,158	891,453	786,509
1972	2,256,063	2,643,289	2,074,683	515,832	1,880,869	1,393,078
	Large banks. Index in constant pesetas (1947 = 100)					
1947	100.0	100.0	100.0	100.0	100.0	100.0
1952	110.5	134.4	160.9	114.7	124.4	122.2
1957	139.2	172.1	220.7	168.2	149.3	168.8
1962	182.5	236.6	297.1	202.3	239.6	243.9
1967	236.3	325.2	427.2	285.7	349.9	312.2
1972	350.3	520.4	840.1	660.5	738.2	553.0

	Millions of pesetas (1995 value)		1972 index
	1967	**1972**	**1967=100**
Large banks			
B. Hispano-Americano	1,521,642	2,256,063	148
Banesto	1,651,901	2,643,289	160
Banco Central	1,055,048	2,074,683	197
Banco Urquijo	223,158	515,832	231
Banco de Bilbao	891,453	1,880,869	211
Banco de Vizcaya	786,509	1,393,078	177
Industrial Banks (1962 LOB)			
Bandesco	46,451	97,746	210
Banco de Fomento	35,342	127,052	359
Banco Industrial de Bilbao	33,725	180,823	536
Banco de Financiación Industrial	64,148	171,195	267
Unión Industrial Bancaria	40,497	181,386	448
B. Europeo de Negocios	39,100	122,776	314
Bankinter	20,763	121,626	586

Source: Calculated from information in CSB, *Un cuarto de siglo de banca privada, 1947-1972.*

As for the growth of investment in the securities owned portfolio (Table 11), this was less than that of total bank investment (Table 10) in all cases relating to the big banks, but the increase in industrial stocks and shares was always stronger than that of the aforementioned portfolio. Private company securities multiplied in value, in constant terms, by a factor of around three, with the exception of the Vizcaya. In relation to the industrial banks, total bank investment grew in general more rapidly than the securities portfolio and industrial securities, but there were three exceptions: Banesco, Banco Industrial de Bilbao, and above all Bankinter.

Table 11. Growth of investment in the securities portfolio and in industrial securities in the large banks, in real terms

	Large banks. Securities portfolio. Constant values. 1947 = 100					
	Hispano-Americano	**Banesto**	**Central**	**Urquijo**	**Bilbao**	**Vizcaya**
1947	100	100	100	100	100	100
1952	101	105	144	124	119	106
1957	137	141	190	179	150	143
1962	106	119	138	185	135	141
1967	140	171	246	162	202	147
1972	191	261	530	249	441	234
	Large banks. Industrial securities. Constant values. 1947 = 100					
	Hispano-Americano.	**Banesto**	**Central**	**Urquijo**	**Bilbao**	**Vizcaya**
1947	100	100	100	100	100	100
1952	102	97	117	122	115	109
1957	127	121	105	151	173	128
1962	135	147	115	191	204	151
1967	231	265	191	186	223	113
1972	324	396	349	344	288	138

	Constant pesetas. Index: 1967=100	
	Industrial Securities	**Securities portfolio**
Industrial banks (1962 LOB)	1972	1972
Bandesco	237	286
Banco de Fomento	121	115
Banco Industrial de Bilbao	603	561
Banco de Financiación Industrial	183	115
Unión Industrial Bancaria	200	207
Banco Europeo de Negocios	158	180
Bankinter	2,349	695

Source: Calculated from information in CSB, *Un cuarto de siglo de banca privada, 1947-1972.*

Finally, let us see to what extent Spain's big banks and the industrial banks created as a result of the *Ley de Ordenación Bancaria* of 1962 behaved in accordance with what was expected from this law that was made by the commercial banks on the one hand and the industrial and business banks on the other. As Juan Muñoz pointed out, the capital enlargements and the volume of reserves led to an increase in equity capital so that the mixed-type banks had no need to carry out divestments and could acquire new shareholdings in companies at the same time as they adjusted to what was expected of them as commercial banks: in other words that their investments in industrial securities, equipment and buildings did not exceed the value of their own equity capital. The commercial stamp of the Hispano-Americano became manifest to the extent that it had always been true to that definition. In 1962 Banesto was, likewise, already well adjusted to the provisions of the new law, and the Central, too, was very close to its parameters. Prior to 1962, the Vizcaya was the bank with the most strongly mixed character, followed by the Bilbao (in both cases the ratio between industrial securities and tangible fixed assets and equity capital grew until 1957). In 1947 the Central had been the bank of most notably mixed nature, but the particular ratio was to fall gradually over the years, which was also the case for Banesto.

Table 12. The large mixed banks in accordance with the *Ley de Ordenación Bancaria* of 1962

	(Industrial securities + Furniture and fixtures + immovable assets) / Equity capital				
	Hispano-Americano	**Banesto**	**Central**	**Bilbao**	**Vizcaya**
1947	1.01	1.45	1.88	1.05	1.55
1952	0.98	1.30	1.65	1.49	1.78
1957	0.99	1.21	1.37	1.74	1.86
1962	0.80	0.88	1.03	1.36	1.58
1967	0.65	0.64	0.78	0.79	0.77
1972	0.80	0.74	0.93	0.92	0.82

Source: Calculated from information in CSB, *Un cuarto de siglo de banca privada, 1947-1972.*

As for Banco Urquijo, until 1962, its investments in industrial securities were worth twice its equity capital (the limit permitted by the *Ley de Ordenación Bancaria* of that year was three times), but after that date the growth of equity capital was far ahead of investment in private enterprise securities, so that the ratio was progressively reduced. On the other hand, the ratio for the industrial banks created after the *Ley de Ordenación Bancaria* of 1962 was always very low, except for the case of Unión Industrial Bancaria in 1972, so that we can conclude that in the 1960s and 1970s the industrial banks did not fulfil the objectives that had been expected of them; this obviously was an argument in favour of the decision to eliminate the obligatory specialisation in 1974 and the reservation on issuance of short-term bonds in favour of the industrial banks.

Table 13. The industrial banks in accordance with the *Ley de Ordenación Bancaria* of 1962 (Industrial securities/equity capital)

	1947	1952	1957	1962	1964	1965	1967	1972
Banco Urquijo	2.00	2.05	2.15	2.13			1.05	0.72
Bandesco					0.67		0.34	0.43
Banco de Fomento					0.68		1.19	0.77
Banco Industrial de Bilbao					0.12		0.24	0.56
Banco de Financiación Industr.							0.32	0.34
Unión Industrial Bancaria					0.42		0.88	1.75
Banco Europeo de Negocios					0.25		0.82	0.65
Bankinter						0.04	0.05	0.24

Source: Calculated from information in CSB, *Un cuarto de siglo de banca privada, 1947-1972.*

9. The economic crisis of 1973 and the banking crisis

The world economic crisis that was set off by the Arab-Israeli war of 1973 affected Spain very significantly as a result of problems in the country's economic structure and political problems deriving from the Transition from the Dictatorship to Democracy. The crisis affected the banking system with particular force between 1977 and 1985 and with greater virulence the industrial banks and those created after the *Ley de Ordenación Bancaria* of 1962, which were less consolidated. The problems of the private sector affected the banks through non-payments and the fall in current market values of their company shareholdings, but the crisis was also a result of causes internal to the banks. The creation of large networks of branches in the 1970s, as a way of competing to attract custom, affected the profitability of the banks. It was also a result of the lack of professionalism and risk-taking, including illegal measures, on the part of certain bankers, as well as the absence of an adequate legal framework and preventive capacity on the part of the authorities. On the other hand, in the second half of the 1970s the Central and Banesto indulged in some absorptions of banks with the sole aim of heading the ranking of the Spanish banks, which also meant these institutions were to get into difficulty. Meanwhile, the close relations between the Urquijo and the Hispano-Americano also affected the latter, since the former was very severely damaged by the crisis and by the economic liberalisation; Banco Urquijo began changing hands from 1983 onwards.

From the mid-1970s until 1986, the percentage of industrial shareholdings in the banks' portfolios was gradually reduced, while that of gilt-edged securities increased. With the upturn of the economy, from

1985 on, the financial institutions set about restructuring their investment portfolios, selling off their holdings in sectors of low profitability and increasing investments in strategic fields such as electricity, construction, chemicals and communications. All these banks had to carry out reorganisation policies, which took several years to complete. Likewise the entry of Spain in to the EEC on 1 January 1986, made it necessary to resize the banking sector, so as to be in conditions to compete with the big European institutions; thus a process of mergers began which led to the consolidation of the two big banks of the present day: Santander and BBVA.[39]

Conclusion

Among the 'six big banks', there was only a genuine investment bank, four mixed-type banks and a commercial bank. These mixed-type banking grew up in a very protectionist environment – industrial and financial – as in the interwar period foreign banks were discriminated by Banco de España, and establishment of new ones was completely forbidden during the Franco's regime. So, Spanish bankers were neither "path-breakers" nor "rainmakers" and worked in an oligopolistic system. Nevertheless, Andrés Moreno (CEO in the Hispano-Americano) used the Midland Bank model of business and organisation in Spain, and Deleitosa, chairman of Banesto in the 1960s, was in favour of importing ideas and organisation models from other European countries and the US. Relations between banks and companies were exerted by several ways. Catalonian banks had been specialised in underwriting firm issues of capital stock during the last years of the 19th century and the beginnings of the 20th century, but this model declined. Big banks of Madrid and Bilbao acquired shares and participated in the launching of some of the most important firms in Spain. They had common directors in the boards of numerous companies, and exercised voting rights on behalf of individuals whose shares were deposited in the banks. Banks also helped firms financing through short-term credit; although it was renewable, danger existed that any moment renewal of the loan might be refused.

39 Maria Pons, "Banca e industria", *op. cit.*, pp. 256-259. Alvaro Cuervo, *La crisis bancaria en España, 1977-1985*, Barcelona, Ariel, 1988, pp. 197-205. Jose Luis García Ruiz, "Noventa años", *op. cit.*, pp. 126-128. Jose Luis García Ruiz, "Banesto", *op. cit.*, pp. 154-156. Gabriel Tortella, "El triunfo del centralismo", *op. cit.*, pp. 227-232. Núria Puig Raposo and Eugenio Torres, *Banco Urquijo. Un banco con historia*, *op. cit.*, pp. 219-256. Onésimo Díaz Hernández, "El Banco Urquijo", *op. cit.*, pp. 264-265. Mauro Guillén and Adrian Tschoegl, *Santander*, *op. cit.*, pp. 47-85. José Víctor Arroyo, "BBVA y sus bancos históricos", *op. cit.*, pp. 82-84.

The Bank Regulation Act of 1962 brought the specialisation, trying to achieve facilitating long-term credit. Nevertheless, at least as company shareholders, the industrial and investment banks performance during the 1960s and 1970s did not fulfil the objectives that have been expected of them. The economic crisis of 1973, the banking Spanish crisis (1977-1985) and the entry in the EEC (1986) have changed the banks panorama in Spain. Nowadays there are two big banks which have a securities portfolio, but their nature is far from the old mixed-type style.

Part IV

International Expansion: Assessing Investment Bankers' Advantage Edge

CHAPTER 11

Investment Banking in Russia, 1890-1917

From Pioneering Finance to Universal Banking

Sofya SALOMATINA

Moscow Lomonosov State University

This chapter analyses investment banking in pre-revolutionary Russia. In the focus of its attention there are banking services on initial public offering for private companies' securities. This activity became a mass phenomenon in the 1890s for the first time. Our study reveals prerequisites of this trend stemming into the 1860s – the 1880s, peculiarities of Russian investment banking in the 1890s, this banking model's hardships in the crisis and depression period in 1899-1908, as well as integration of Russian investment banking into universal banking in the 1910s.

This research is an attempt to investigate making and evolution of Russian investment banking in the aspect of banking models' development. It proves that investment banking for private companies appeared throughout traditional activity of several commercial banks in St. Petersburg, dealing with services to public and mortgage bond market and intensive currency speculation caused by fiduciary standard. However, private companies' demand for investment banking appeared persistently in the peak of pre-revolutionary economic growth by 1895, and the Petersburg banks switched over to private stock as a new subject for exchange transactions. Investment banking in "Petersburg style" was also observed outside St. Petersburg, but rarely. In the beginning of the 20th century the crisis revealed weak points of the 1890s investment banking, and they were overcame by universal banking development by the 1910s.

The chapter summarises findings of investigations in several fields of Russian economic history: the studies of economic and industrial growth by Paul Gregory, Lev Kafengauz;[1] the equity market research by Iosif Gindin and Valery Bovykin;[2] studies of international banks' syndicates on issues of Russian securities in Russia and abroad by Boris Ananych and Sergey Lebedev.[3] The government's struggle for currency stabilisation in the period 1880s-1895 is analysed under Pavel Lizunov's monograph.[4] The principal tendencies of relations between banks and industrial companies are derived from Bovykin's research;[5] the facts and trends of Petersburg and Moscow banking are obtained from Bovykin's and Yuri Petrov's studies.[6] Summaries on Russian banks' models are based on Sofya Salomatina's research[7] as well as on analysis of Russian banks' public reports. A special attention has to be paid to a role of state in history of Russian investment banking. In what degree did banks rely on the government support or state participation in their projects? In what degree did these accounts come true? The current findings of investigations cover this issue relatively in a new way.

1 Paul R. Gregory, "Poisk istiny v istoricheskih dannyh", in Valery I. Bovykin (ed.), *Jekonomicheskaja istorija. Ezhegodnik, 1999*, Moskow, Rossiiskaia politicheskaia entsiklopediia (Rosspen), 1999, pp. 471-500. P.R. Gregory, "Jekonomicheskaja istorija Rossii: chto my o nej znaem i chego ne znaem. Ocenka jekonomista", in Valery Bovykin and Yuri A. Petrov (eds.), *Jekonomicheskaja istorija, op. cit.*, pp. 7-97 (English version of article's title: "Russian economic history: What we know and do not know. An economical appraisal". Lev Borisovich Kafengauz, *Jevoljucija promyshlennogo proizvodstva Rossii*, Moskow, Epifaniia, 1994, p. 22-23, 70.

2 Iosif Frolovich Gindin, *Russkie kommercheskie banki: iz istorii finansovogo kapitala v Rossii*, Moskow, Gosfinizdat, 1948, pp. 391-405, 444-447. Valery Bovykin, *Finansovyj kapital v Rossii nakanune Pervoj mirovoj vojny*, Moskow, Rossiiskaia politicheskaia entsiklopediia (Rosspen), 2001, pp. 93-111.

3 Sergei K. Lebedev, *S.-Peterburgskij Mezhdunarodnyj kommercheskij bank vo vtoroj polovine XIX veka: evropejskie i russkie svjazi*, Moskow, Rossiiskaia politicheskaia entsiklopediia (Rosspen), 2003, pp. 213-346, 462-475. Boris V. Anan'ich and Sergei K. Lebedev, "Uchastie bankov v vypuske obligatsii zheleznodorozhnykh obshchestv (1860-1914 gg.)", in Sergeĭ Ivanovich Potolov (ed.), *Monopolii i ekonomicheskaia politika tsarizma v kontse XIX-nachale XX v.: K probl. ist. predposylok Velikoi Okt. sots. revoliutsii*, Leningrad, Nauka, Leningr. Otd-nie, 1987, pp. 3-41.

4 Pavel V. Lizunov, *Sankt-Peterburgskaja birzha i rossijskij rynok cennyh bumag (1703-1917 gg.)*, St. Petersburg, Izdatel'stvo 'Russko-Baltiiskii informatsionnyi tsentr "Blits"', 2004, pp. 241-251.

5 Valery Bovykin, *Zarozhdenie finansovogo kapitala v Rossii*, Moskva, Izd. Mosk. un-ta, 1967, pp. 203-291. Valery Bovykin, *Formirovanie finansovogo kapitala v Rossii. Konets XIX v.-1908 g.*, Moskow, Nauka, 1984, pp. 128-156.

6 Valery Bovykin and Yuri Petrov, *Kommercheskie banki Rossijskoj imperii*, Moskva, Perspektiva, 1994.

7 Sofya Salomatina, *Kommercheskie banki v Rossii: dinamika i struktura operacij, 1864-1917 gg.*, Moskva, Rossiiskaia politicheskaia entsiklopediia (Rosspen), 2001. Sofya Salomatina, "Modeli kommercheskikh bankov v Sankt-Peterburge i Moskve, 1864-1917 gg.", in Boris Anan'ich (ed.), *Kredit i banki v Rossii do nachala XX v.: Sankt-Peterburg i Moskva*, St. Petersburg, Izd-vo SPbGU, 2005, pp. 328-343.

The four parts of the chapter analyse, firstly, the preconditions of investment banking spurt in the 1890s; secondly, Russian banking models in the period of flourishing investment banking in the 1890s; thirdly, investment banking difficulties in crisis period, and fourthly, qualitative changes in banking models in connection with transition to universal banking in the 1910s.

1. The factor of investment banking origin

This section analyses the necessary factors, concurred in the 1890s for the first time and created circumstances for spurt of investment banking for private companies. These factors can be divided into four groups for convenience. Firstly, there were industrial and banking growth; secondly, development of equity market; thirdly, making of banks, specialised on equity market services; fourthly, successful pressure on currency speculation on the Russian government's part. These factors have to be examined thoroughly for understanding of economic circumstances in which investment banking became apparent tendency.

A. Industrial and banking growth resumption in the 1890s

The modern economic growth occurred in Russia since the 1880s. General tendencies of this stage ere industrial growth, reduction of agriculture percentage and growth in service percentage; population growth increased firstly then slowed down; an income distribution's model gradually changed.[8] Russian industrial production rate was extremely fast for the last 25 years before WWI. Rate estimations varied from 5.1 per cent per Raymond Goldsmith's index to 6.65 per cent per L. Kafengauz' index.[9] By the first estimation Russian growth of large-scale industry competed with main rapidly growing countries, by the second one Russian industry grew more rapidly. But then Russia was still substantially backward in economic and social per capita indicators, although growth rates per capita revenue remained just 85 per cent from average European measure.[10]

The most rapid development was in the period from 1889-1892 to 1901-1904. These years the drastic industrial alterations were based on machinery, mechanical transport, mineral fuel, coke, cement, modern chemical materials, although this process had been started even in the middle of the 19th century. The most intensive reconstruction was held in

8 Paul Gregory, "Jekonomicheskaja istorija Rossii: chto my o nej znaem i chego ne znaem. Ocenka jekonomista", pp. 9, 13-23.

9 Paul Gregory, "Poisk istiny v istoricheskih dannyh", p. 478.

10 Paul Gregory, "Jekonomicheskaja istorija Rossii: chto my o nej znaem i chego ne znaem. Ocenka jekonomista", p. 18.

railroad facilities, industrial engineering and urban development. Before the 1890s this growth was caused by import of metals and intermediate products to a considerable degree. The demand for heavy industry production was reliably provided and the domestic heavy industry appeared at last in the 1890s.[11]

Figure 1. Russian commercial banks assets, 1865-1891

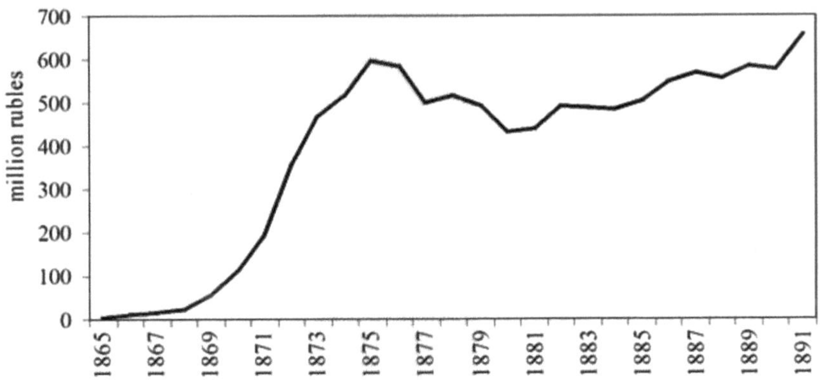

The banking system resumed growth only in the 1890s. Earlier Russian banking history had the following milestones. The modern banking system started to develop in Russia since the 1860s. The first joint-stock commercial bank was established in 1864, by 1873 there were about forty commercial banks, and roughly the same number of banks was kept until 1917. Before 1875 a situation at financial market had been relatively favourable, but since 1875 the period of crisis and long depression began. Total commercial banks' assets[12] in 1875 were exceeded only in 1891 (see Figures[13] 1 and 2). The development of earlier decades found vent in a quantitative and qualitative spurt in the 1890s. This decade became one of the most striking periods in Russian economic history before 1917.

11 Lev Borisovich Kafengauz, *Jevoljucija promyshlennogo*, *op. cit.*, pp. 22-23. Valery Bovykin, *Zarozhdenie finansovogo kapitala*, *op. cit.*, p. 201.

12 Sofya Salomatina, *Kommercheskie banki*, *op. cit.*, p. 105.

13 Sources: 1 January 1865-1916. Russkie akcionernye kommercheskie banki v cifrovyh dannyh za 1915 g. v sravnenii s 1914 g., Petrograd, Kom. s'ezdov predstavitelei akts. kom. Bankov, 1916, pp. 54-55. 1 January 1917. Svodnyj balans akcionernyh bankov kommercheskogo kredita, deistvuiushchikh v Rossii na 1 janvarja 1917 g., Petrograd, Kom. s'ezdov predstavitelei akts. kom. bankov, 1917, p. 2.

Figure 2. Russian commercial banks assets, 1865-1917

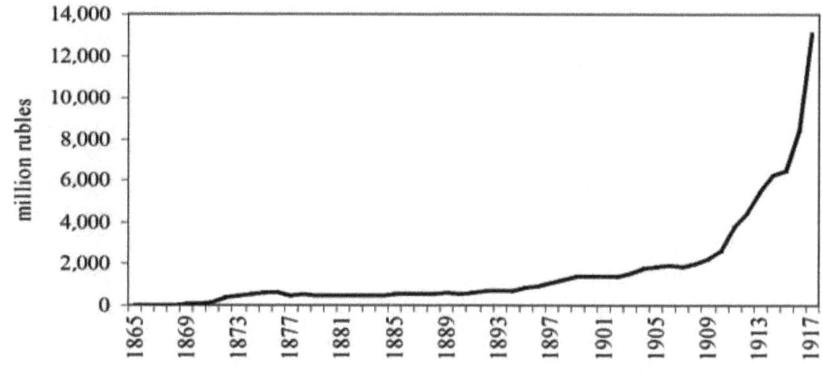

B. The Russian equity market in the 1860s-1880s

The exchange upturn occurred at the well-established equity market in the 1890s. Thereupon Russian domestic and overseas capital issues have to be kept in mind. The market gradually developed since the beginning of the 19th century, but the critical period lasted from the end of the 1850s to the middle of the 1870s, when principal exchange institutions, all types of issuers and investors came into being as well as first exchange upturns and downfalls in up-to-date sense of the word.

Table 1. Russian securities in 1893 and 1900

	Russian issuers' securities		**Russian issuers' securities, placed in Russia**		**Russian issuers' securities, placed abroad**	
	1893	**1900**	**1893**	**1900**	**1893**	**1900**
Par value, million rubles	8,231	11,990	5,369	7,445	2,862	4,545
State bonds and securities, guaranteed by state, except state mortgage bonds, %	71.1	60.9	58.4	45.8	94.8	85.7
State mortgage bonds,%	2.5	4.7	3.9	6.2	0	2.2
Private mortgage bonds, %	14.9	14.9	22.8	24.0	0	0
Municipal bonds, %	0.2	0.7	0.3	1.1	0	0.1
Private companies shares, %	11.3	18.8	14.6	22.9	5.2	12.0
Total, %	100	100	100	100	100	100

Calculated on: V.I. Bovykin, *Finansovyj kapital v Rossii nakanune Pervoj mirovoj vojny*, Moskva, Rossiiskaia politicheskaia entsiklopediia (Rosspen), 2001, pp. 102-104. These data on equity market development in 1893-1900 arranged in table 1 were put together and corrected by I. Gindin and then V. Bovykin: I. Gindin, *Russkie kommercheskie banki, op. cit.*, pp. 444-452; V.I. Bovykin, *Finansovyj kapital, op. cit.*, pp. 102-105.

Russian equity market's main features were an abundance of government and mortgage securities and a slight portion of private companies' shares, which was gradually increasing. Long-term state bonds amounted 60/70 per cent of Russian issues in the second part of the 19th century. A particular part of these securities were railway loans – state and private. The fact of the matter is that almost 90 per cent of private railway stock was guaranteed by the government in various forms,[14] therefore these securities were essentially equal to state bonds. There were two large state issuers at Russian mortgage bond market – State Peasant Land Bank (since 1882) and State Land Bank of the Nobility (since 1885).[15] Outside state equity market there was a large domestic market of private mortgage bonds, developed in the 1860s-1870s. The portion of securities of land banks and urban mortgage institutions amounted 22.8/24 per cent of domestic market in 1893-1900. Private companies' securities amounted only 11.3 per cent of Russian equity market in 1893 but this sector was just ready to grow.

In the second part of the 19th century the securities were traded at Russian exchanges: in Petersburg – at the leading Russian exchange, as well as in Warsaw, Moscow, Riga, Odessa and in some other cities. However, Petersburg exchange and Petersburg equity market played absolutely prevailing role in Russian empire, and differentiation between the metropolis and regions was considerable. Russian securities circulated also at European markets. British and French markets prevailed in the 1860s-1870s. Then, since 1884, after Rothschilds' boycott against Russian capitals these securities shifted from Britain to Europe, especially in Germany. But since 1887 tariff and trade war between Germany and Russia had begun and the role of French and Russian domestic markets started to grow. In the beginning of the 1890s unfavourable state of market impeded to amount of Russian issues, desirable by government, so positions of the domestic equity market became still stronger.[16]

The Russian market was filled with new issues. Thus there were about ten issues of long-term loans in the 1860s-1870s and six of them were distributed abroad.[17] More than ten issues took place also in the 1880s-1894, and a considerable part of them were conversions, conducted in Europe in the end of the 1880s in favourable conditions of reduction in discount

[14] Sergei Lebedev, *S.-Peterburgskij Mezhdunarodnyj*, *op. cit.*, p. 214.

[15] From here and so on – the list of original Russian banks' names in transliteration in Appendix 1.

[16] Sergei Lebedev, *S.-Peterburgskij Mezhdunarodnyj*, *op. cit.*, pp. 233, 235-236, 249, 252-255, 261, 267-272, 344-346.

[17] Estimated on: A. K. Sorokin, "Zaimy", in *Ekonomicheskaia istoriia Rossii (s drevneishikh vremen do 1917 g.): Entsiklopediia*, Moskow, Rossiiskaia politicheskaia entsiklopediia (RossPEN), 2008, Vol. 1, pp. 798-800.

rate and upsurge of securities rate.[18] The railway securities, guaranteed by state in a majority, were massively launched into market in addition to state funds. There were fifty one issues of Russian railway companies' bonds in the 1860s – the 1890s,[19] and these securities had parity with hard European currencies. In addition to that, twenty six railway companies' loans were distributed in rubles in 1886-1893.[20] By 1 January 1893 the total sum of general-purpose state loans amounted 3,178 million rubles where of 595 millions were placed abroad. Russian guaranteed railway securities amounted 2,671m rubles including 2,118m abroad.[21] Thus Russian equity market developed more than thirty years by the 1890s, though government securities, railway bonds with government guarantees and mortgage bonds dominated at this market for a while. However this market was favourable for making of commercial banks, specialised in equity market services. The next subsection deals with this trend.

C. The making of Petersburg banks' investment specialisation in the 1880s

Several commercial banks acquired wide experience from securities transactions by the 1890s. These banks' development in the 1880s has to be scrutinised. Russian commercial banks amounted 58.6 per cent of short-term credit system on 1 January 1893.[22] The largest part of them included discount banks, dealing with services to local trade and industrial firms; some of them had deposit specialisation.[23] However Petersburg, as a centre of Russian equity market, affected some metropolitan banks deeply. In the first place it concerned Petersburg International Commercial Bank and Petersburg Discount and Loan Bank – the future investment banking leaders in the 1890s. Since the 1880s these banks took part in all Russian issues – state, railway and mortgage, domestic and foreign. Russian banking system adopted techniques of paper issue via these banks. Their partners were Russian Bank for Foreign Trade and Volga-Kama Commercial Bank. A number of regional commercial banks acted as sub-participators

---

18 Estimated on: Sergei Lebedev, *S.-Peterburgskij Mezhdunarodnyj*, *op. cit.*, pp. 462-466.

19 Estimated on: Boris Anan'ich and Sergei Lebedev, "Uchastie bankov v vypuske obligatsii zheleznodorozhnykh obshchestv (1860-1914 gg.)', pp. 3-41.

20 Estimated on: Sergei Lebedev, "Peterburgskii Mezhdunarodnyi kommercheskii bank v konsortsiumakh po vypusku chastnykh zheleznodorozhnykh zaimov 1880-kh-nachala 1890-kh gg.", in S. I. Potolov (ed.), *Monopolii i ekonomicheskaia politika tsarizma v kontse XIX-nachale XX v.: K probl. ist. predposylok Velikoi Okt. sots. Revoliutsii*, Leningrad, Nauka, Leningr. Otd-nie, 1987, pp. 41-65.

21 Valery Bovykin, *Formirovanie finansovogo kapitala*, *op. cit.*, p. 105.

22 Iosif Frolovich Gindin, *Russkie kommercheskie banki*, *op. cit.*, p. 69.

23 Data on Russian banks' participation in international syndicates: Sergei Lebedev, *S.-Peterburgskij Mezhdunarodnyj*, *op. cit.*, pp. 213-346, 462-475.

in syndicates, and a part of them would develop investment banking later in the 1890s, but another part would not progress in this field. The most active sub-participators were following: Petersburg Private Commercial Bank, Moscow Merchant Bank, Warsaw Commercial Bank, Riga Exchange Bank, Petersburg-Moscow Commercial bank, Moscow Trade bank, and Riga Municipal Discount Bank.

In general the Russian equity market may be said to develop as a bank-oriented institution. International banking syndicates distributed Russian securities. Every consortium included a lot of participators and one of the powerful European banks led them. Before the 1880s Russian banks acted as just technical intermediaries. But since the 1880s they gradually became full-fledged participants having real influence on conditions of issues.

It was since the 1880s that international contacts of Russian banks are systematically revealed due to archive of Petersburg International Bank, remained relatively intact for this period in Russian State Historical Archive in Petersburg. Particularly the archive includes correspondence of bank's leaders in the 1880s-1890s. In the issue the international activity of Russian bankers can be investigated in details on these materials. S. Lebedev revealed the particularities of these secret negotiations on syndicates' questions.[24]

In the first part of the 1880s two banking groups competed for Russian issues, and it makes senses to specify just the principal participators. The first group's leader was *Disconto-Gesellschaft*, the other active members being Mendelssohn & Co, Robert Warschauer & Co. and *Deutsche Bank*. The group included Petersburg International Bank and Russian Bank for Foreign Trade from Russian side. Their rivals may be called as "Rothschilds' group",[25] including besides Rothschilds their allies: S. Bleichröder, *Berliner Handels-Gesellschaft* and Lippmann, Rothenthal & Co. In this alliance the Russian side was presented by Petersburg Discount and Loan Bank and sometimes by Volga-Kama Commercial Bank. These groups united in 1887. Russian banks' share amounted usually on third of issue in joint group. Petersburg International Bank and Petersburg Discount and Loan Bank had approximately equal shares, although International bank usually acted as a leader of Russian group and kept syndicates' accounts in Russia.

In 1888-1891 owing to barriers to Russian equities at German market the French group, led by Paribas, joined to Russian issues due to active role of banking house Hoskier E. & Cie, which had been able to opened French

24 See reference 23.

25 Rothschild Frères (Paris), M.A. von Rothschild (Frankfurt am Main), N.M. Rothschild & Son (London).

market for Russian equity throughout intermediary of International Bank in negotiation with the Russian Ministry of Finance. The Russian share in French syndicates was about 20 per cent with International Bank as the leader again. The French side included *Comptoir national d'escompte de Paris* (CNEP), *Société générale, Banque d'escompte de Paris, Crédit lyonnais* and *Crédit industriel et commercial* (CIC).

As a rule, a syndicate was usually led by bank, in which country the largest part of issue was distributed. However Petersburg International Bank and Petersburg Discount and Loan Bank acted as intermediaries between the syndicate and the Russian government, railway companies, mortgage institutions. This role provided these banks with an ample opportunity to influence on syndicates' affairs. This tendency gained strength as far as importance of domestic market was increasing. The members of the "syndicates for Russian equity" waged a fierce struggle against competitive European banking groups striven to obtain admittance to Russian issues. However serious competition occurred inside the Russian syndicates themselves: between foreign and Russian groups, inside foreign group, between International Bank and Discount and Loan Bank. The reasons why two leading Russian banks clashed against each other consisted in the same field of activity. Both banks had the similar model of operations and single-type customers.

They were simultaneously closed to the Ministry of Finance. International Bank's director Vladislav Ljasskij (1831-1889) and Discount and Loan Bank's director Abram Zak (d. 1893) played the roles of financial advisers of Ivan Vyshnegradsky, the Russian minister of Finance in 1888-1892. The minister was suspected of close connections with "Rothschilds' group". His no less close ties with International Bank arose before his appointment to ministerial post, when Vyshnegradsky executed duty of vice-chairman of the South-West Railways Society's board. International Bank provided the company with banking services. Sergei Witte, the successor of Vyshnegradsky as the minister of finance, began his private career at this railway company. International Bank enjoyed support or even auspices of government, and the bank enabled even to bring into play of the State bank's machinery for securities placement at domestic market. After Ljasskij's death in 1889 Adolf Rothstein was assigned to director's position and he enabled to retain bank's privileged positions in the time of the Witte's ministry in 1892-1903. Thus, by the 1890s Russian banking system adopted syndicate's technique. There were at least two banks which were deeply involved in international and domestic issuing transactions. The other Russian banks gradually joined to these operations, led by Petersburg International Bank and Petersburg Discount and Loan Bank.

D. The end of speculation in ruble

Russian commercial banks played an active role not only at capital market but at foreign exchange market. A fierce speculation in ruble flourished at some European financial centers in the end of the 1880s and in the beginning of the 1890s. Totals of pre-revolutionary and modern analytics on this phenomenon were summarised by P. Lizunov.[26] This period Russian currency system was based on fiduciary standard. In the first half of the 1880s paper ruble cost 0.63 conventional gold ruble or so called "credit ruble" for international transactions. Since 1885 the exchange rate was dropping until 0.50 by 16 February 1888, then it came up to 0.82 in autumn 1890 and fell again until 0.58 by 7 November 1891. The Russian currency fluctuations were very intensive even in the course of one trading session. The leading speculative centres were Peterburg and Berlin exchange. Several German banking firms specialised in ruble speculation and kept their representatives in Petersburg. The press charged banking institutions with exportation of rubles for speculation. Russian foreign economic activity suffered from unstable currency.

The Russian Ministry of Finance played European currency traders intensively. For improvement in exchange the ministry issued bills of exchange from abroad to Russia and bought up rubles at European exchanges. These operations were provided by foreign agents of the Russian government, for instance the house S. Bleichröder in 1888. The ministry carried out additional issues of rubles for drop in rate. In Vyshnegradsky's period the government didn't step in exchange affairs straightly, but after Witte's accession to office the pressure on speculators began in connection with preparation to transition to golden standard, occurred in 1897. This new course against speculation had been declared since 1893. It's important to note that bargains on term were officially prohibited in Russia, but this practice flourished informally. But in 1893 some new legislative acts reaffirmed illegality of currency transaction on term, they restricted all operations, used for currency speculation, empowered the ministry of Finance to conduct an audit of banking institution, suspected in currency speculation, the minister enabled to put pressure on exchange brokers, board members and directors of banking institutions up to liquidation of business. A custom duty on currency export was imposed on 29 March 1893.

There is no evidence on victims of acts against speculation in contemporary literature, but analysts described quiet conditions at Petersburg exchange in 1893, there were no possibilities for currency gamble any

[26] The subsection is based on: Pavel Lizunov, *Sankt-Peterburgskaja birzha*, *op. cit.*, pp. 241-251.

more. The struggle for stabilisation yielded results whether by economic or political measures. The fluctuations of the exchange rate from London to Petersburg amounted 28 per cent in 1891, 9.6 per cent in 1892, 6 per cent in 1893, 1.94 per cent in 1894 and 0.54 per cent in 1895. Petersburg bankers conversed about coming gold standard. Rothstein, International bank's director, wrote a letter to S. Bleichröder in Berlin in April 1895 and outlined alternatives of gold standard reform, known him from contacts in the ministry of Finance, and retold local rumours on this subject.[27] The epoch of fierce currency speculations came to an end.

A new trend occurred at Petersburg exchange since October 1893: the banks' stock price began to come up, then the stock of industrial companies joined to this process.[28] The 1890s upsurge had begun, and activity at the exchange resumed. This rise was concentrated on private shares unlike previous decades. Incidentally, the 1893 acts did not only prohibited futures currency transactions, but permitted bargains on term with private shares for the first time. Thereby the market trend and the economic policy delimited in 1893 two periods of equity market development in Russian empire. Thus, by 1893-1895 some factors, important for investment banking, concurred in Russia: economic growth peak; banking growth resumption; sufficiently developed equity market, where banks, experienced in domestic and even international equity market, prevailed; fiduciary standard period was at its end and set of stockjobber's tools had to be changed.

2. The boom of investment banking in the 1890s

Investment banking became a symbol of the 1890s. It evinced in mass private shares issues through intermediary of commercial banks. As a result, the period 1893-1899 became the most striking years of banks' participation in financing of Russian economic growth.

It should be noted that there were no special investment banks in Russia in the 19th century and in the beginning of the 20th century. Investment operations became one of the fields of merchant banks' activity. But in the 1890s several banks, having head offices in Petersburg, had developed investment banking so essentially, that it influenced negatively on their stability in crisis 1899-1903. The peculiarities of Russian investment banking are in the focus of this section's attention.

27 A. Rothstein to house S. Bleichröder (Berlin), 11/23 April 1895 (*Rossiia i mirovoi biznes: dela i sud'by: A. Nobel', A. Rotshtein, G. Spittser, R. Dizel': Sbornik arkh. dok.*, ed. by Valery Bovykin, translated by I. A. D'iakonova, Moskow, Rossiiskaia politicheskaia entsiklopediia (ROSSPEN), 1996, pp. C. 84-87.

28 Pavel Lizunov, *Sankt-Peterburgskaja birzha*, *op. cit.*, pp. 254-255.

Table 2 includes all data, concerning general estimation of investment banking in comparison with total investment in stock capital from 1893 to 1900. The rapid stock market growth applied to private shares in the first place in the 1890s. This peculiarity occurred for the first time. The total increase in Russian securities at the domestic market consisted of about 30 per cent (see table 1), the increase in private companies' shares amounted almost 140 per cent, and 168.4 per cent – in trade and industrial companies' shares (see table 2). In the issue, the private shares' percentage rose from 14.6 to 22.9 at the domestic market (see table 1). The largest part of private shares consisted of trade and industrial securities – 62.7 per cent (see table 2).

Table 2. Stock capital in Russia in 1893 and 1900

	1.01.1893	1.01.1900	Increase from 1893 to 1900
(1) Russian stock capital, million rubles	852.9	2,037.1	1,184.2
Including (2) Russian trade and industrial stock capital, million rubles	476	1,277.5	801.5
(2) / (1), %	55.8	62.7	6,9 pct
Heavy industry stock capital's increase, placed in Russia, million rubles			300*
Including Heavy industry stock capital's increase, placed through intermediary of commercial banks, million rubles			150**
Stock capital of foreign trade and industrial companies, operating in Russia, million rubles	69.9	281.4	211.5

Source: *V. I. Bovykin, Zarozhdenie finansovogo kapitala v Rossii*, Moskva, Izd. Mosk. un-ta, 1967, pp. 202-203, 207.

* – Estimation of V. I. Bovykin.

** – Estimation of I. F. Gindin, *Russkie kommercheskie banki: iz istorii finansovogo kapitala v Rossii*, Moskva, Gosfinizdat, 1948, pp. 90-91.

The leading issuers were mining, metallurgical, metalworking and chemical companies. These shares became the main subjects for speculative transactions at Petersburg exchange and the most popular shares for stock jobbers were following: Society of Bryansk rail-rolling, iron and engineering works,[29] Society of Putilov plants in Petersburg (metalworking), Partnership of Sergino-Ufaleysk mining and metallurgical

[29] From here and so on – the list of original Russian companies' names in transliteration in Appendix 2.

plants in Urals, Society of Russo-Baltic wagon works in Riga, Society of iron, steel and engineering works *Sormovo* in Nizhny Novgorod, Society of Maltsov plants in Kaluga province (metalworking), Oil company "Caspian partnership" and Baku oil refining society.[30] By I. Gindin's estimation, confirmed and developed by Bovykin, Russian banks took part in 150 million rubles of industrial issues from approximately 300 million of heavy industry stock, placed in Russia[31] in 1893-1900.

This figure of 150 million rubles is a rough estimate, obtained by I. Gindin by an analysis of banks' financial statements. The same publications can be used for estimation of investment activity in every bank. But unfortunately, the Russian financial statements didn't include definite investment items, therefore historians are forced to use indirect indicators. The investment activity can be studied through accounts, registered transactions with securities "not guaranteed by the Russian Government".[32]

In prerevolutionary Russia securities were usually divided into two groups: firstly, the securities, guaranteed by the government, i.e. securities of government loans, government mortgage bonds, as well as numerous railway shares and bonds, and secondly, the securities, not guaranteed by the government, i.e. all shares of industry, transport, trade and other companies, private mortgage and municipal bonds. These two groups of securities are called "guaranteed securities" and "non-guaranteed securities" in this text for convenience. Debit accounts, concerned to "non-guaranteed securities", included four items: non-guaranteed portfolio; short-term loans and credit accounts ("on call loans") against these securities, as well as correspondent *loro* accounts against them. Term loans were usually commercial credits to entrepreneurs. Credit accounts were used both by enterprises and by stock gamblers. Correspondent accounts were used for various settlements between banks, particularly *loro* accounts registered syndicates' transactions with shares.

However, three principal drawbacks should be taken into account if the investment activity is considered as the sum of non-guaranteed securities' transactions. Firstly, above-mentioned accounts were substantially broader than necessary for study of investment banking, because they included a large share of short-term commercial loans. Credit accounts were particularly controversial thereupon. For instance it is well known that credit accounts have been actively used for security trading in St. Petersburg, and for

30 Valery Bovykin, *Zarozhdenie finansovogo kapitala, op. cit.*, p. 203.

31 *Ibidem*, p. 207.

32 This principle underlies the analysis of banks' statements, developed by I. Gindin, *Russkie kommercheskie banki, op. cit.*, p. 385-386.

lending to manufacturers against their own shares in Moscow.[33] A researcher may divide credit accounts by the types of customers' activities only on ledgers in banks' archives, but not on published financial statements.

Secondly, there was no separation by types of securities in published financial statements except concept of "guaranteed/non-guaranteed", therefore we aren't able to separate trade and industrial shares, mortgage and municipal bonds inside non-guaranteed portfolio. Thirdly, and perhaps it's the main problem, not all banks indicated separately operations with government and private securities. A separate accounting of pledges required some changes in accounting practices; therefore it would make sense only when private securities became mass assets. It happened in St. Petersburg only in the late 1890s. This difference between St. Petersburg and provincial banking is indicated in table 3. The data for calculations were derived from the consolidated balance of joint stock commercial banks[34] on January 1st, 1898. This date applied to the heyday of the industrial boom of the 1890s. The balance included data on all forty commercial banks of the Russian Empire except of the Russo-Chinese Bank, because its financial statement was not sufficiently diversified by various pledges.

Table 3 surveys the accounts, registered non-guaranteed securities. However, direct comparison of these accounts in St. Petersburg and the rest of Russia appears difficult, because the provincial banks didn't provide separate accounting of pledges, as it was already mentioned. Consequently, it is obvious that private securities are underestimated in some banks. It concerns uppermost to huge credit accounts of the Volga-Kama Bank, undivided by pledges, as well as all Moscow banks, except for the Moscow Merchant Bank. But this regional comparison will be possible for operations concerning all types of securities (guaranteed and non-guaranteed by the government). In this case the result is more correct but more general because it reveals the bank's involvement in capital market as a whole. But in any case table 3 reveals that the operations with non-guaranteed securities were much larger in St. Petersburg as compared to provincial banks. It concerned three accounts, decisive for investment banking: security portfolio, credit and correspondent *loro* accounts against non-guaranteed securities. Ten banks, invested the largest assets in private (non-guaranteed) securities and all types of securities, are represented in tables 4a and 4b, and three important conclusions follow from the tables.

---

33 Information on credit accounts as a tool for stock market game see: Pavel Lizunov, *Sankt-Peterburgskaja birzha*, *op. cit.*, pp. 263-287. The importance of credit accounts for lending to enterprises in Central Russia see: Yuri A. Petrov, *Kommercheskie banki Moskvy. Konets XIX v.-1914 g.*, Moskow, Rossiiskaia politicheskaia entsiklopediia (ROSSPEN), 1998, pp. 57-80.

34 *Svodnyj balans akcionernyh kommercheskih bankov na 1 janvarja 1898 g.*, St. Petersburg, Kom. s'ezdov predstavitelei akts. kom. bankov, 1898, pp. 1-7.

Table 3. The average percentage of securities operations in banks' regional assets on January 1, 1898

	Security portfolio		Pledges on term loans		Pledges on credit accounts ("on call loans")		Pledges on correspondent loro account		Total	
	(1)	(2)	(1)	(2)	(1)	(2)	(1)	(2)	(1)	(2)
St. Petersburg banks*	2	10	0,2	1	19	24	12	19	33,2	54
Outside of St. Petersburg:										
Provincial divisions of Petersburg banks	1	4	2	5	13	17	2	3	18	29
Entirely provincial banks**	1	8	4	8	***	9	1	2	***	27

Notes:

The table contains the average values, weighted by the regional banks' assets.

(1) Private (non-guaranteed by the government) securities for banks that reported this item in their statements.

(2) Government and private securities (all types of securities).

* Data on 11 head offices and branches in St. Petersburg. Head offices: Petersburg International Commercial Bank, Petersburg Loan and Discount Bank, Petersburg Private Commercial Bank, Petersburg-Azov Commercial Bank, Petersburg-Moscow Commercial Bank, Russian Bank for Foreign Trade, Russian Trade and Industrial Bank, Crédit lyonnais (Russian headquarters). Petersburg branches: Moscow Merchant Bank, Warsaw Commercial Bank. The data on the head office of the Volga-Kama Commercial Bank were included only in calculations on all types of securities.

** 29 banks except 11 specified in note *.

*** The item was published in reports of 2 banks of 29, which is insufficient for correct calculation.

Calculated on: *Svodnyj balans akcionernyh kommercheskih bankov na 1 janvarja 1898 g.*, Sankt-Peterburg, Kom. s'ezdov predstavitelei akts. kom. bankov, 1898, pp. 1-7.

Firstly, the leading of role of head offices of Petersburg International Commercial Bank (PICB) and Petersburg Discount and Loan Bank (PDLB) is clearly revealed in any grouping of statistical data, despite the fact that they ranked second and sixth Russian banks, respectively, in terms of assets. The top ten includes banks, close to the model of operations of PICB and PDLB: Petersburg Private Commercial Bank; Petersburg-Moscow Commercial Bank; Petersburg-Azov Commercial Bank (table 4a). These five banks concentrated in investment activity 33-39 per cent of their Petersburg assets. They operated in Petersburg, having minimal number of branches in the provinces. The press and contemporary analysts started a tradition to call these banks "investment banks" or even "speculative banks". Surely this cliché made hints about *Crédit mobilier*, but it was reminiscence but not proper used term.

Table 4a. Commercial banks, placed the largest assets in private securities (non-guaranteed by the government) on 1 January 1898*

#	Banks	Operations with private securities, thousand rubles	% in bank's regional assets	Rating of assets, 1 – max
1	Petersburg International Commercial Bank (head office)	32 363	37	2
2	Petersburg Loan and Discount Bank (head office)	24 885	39	6
3	Moscow Merchant Bank (outside Petersburg)	18 636	23	3
4	Russian Bank for Foreign Trade (Petersburg head office)	14 023	28	8
5	Petersburg-Azov Commercial Bank (head office)	10 628	38	16
6	Petersburg-Moscow Commercial Bank (head office)	10 178	37	18
7	Russian Trade and Industrial Bank (Petersburg head office)	9 863	29	11
8	Petersburg Private Commercial Bank (head office)	8 931	33	19
9	Petersburg International Commercial Bank (branches)	7 438	24	14
10	Moscow Merchant Bank (Petersburg branch)	7 054	43	26

Secondly, large banks with numerous branches – Russian Bank for Foreign Trade and Russian Trade and Industrial Bank – developed investment activities in St. Petersburg in a slightly smaller share than "the investment banks" – 28/9 per cent of regional assets. Thirdly, it's curiously enough, but the two largest Russian deposit and discount banks – Volga-Kama Commercial bank and Moscow Merchant bank – dealt with investment in Petersburg in the 1890s, while in general these banks focused on lending to trade and industrial customers. The high position of these two banks in tables 4a and 4b are due to a large amount of their credit accounts, but they related mostly to the entrepreneurial lending, as other studies argue.[35] But their Petersburg divisions were statistically more similar to "investment banks" than to provincial banks. Thus, the statistics of securities transactions places on top the Petersburg banks. However, the leading Russian banks are known not only from the statistical data, but from other sources, created a broad context to the quantitative data.

35 Valery Bovykin and Yuri Petrov, *Kommercheskie banki*, *op. cit.*, pp. 117-125, 190-211.

Table 4b. Commercial banks, placed the largest assets in all types of securities on 1 January 1898

#	Banks	Operations with all securities, thousand rubles	% in bank's regional assets	Rating of assets, 1 – max
1	Petersburg International Commercial Bank (head office)	48 789	55	2
2	Petersburg Loan and Discount Bank (head office)	40 045	63	6
3	Moscow Merchant Bank (outside Petersburg)	31 799	40	3
4	Volga-Kama Commercial Bank (Petersburg head office)	31 118	59	7
5	Volga-Kama Commercial Bank (outside Petersburg)	27 460	26	1
6	Russian Bank for Foreign Trade (Petersburg head office)	20 062	41	8
7	Russian Trade and Industrial Bank (Petersburg head office)	17 518	51	11
8	Petersburg Private Commercial Bank (head office)	16 220	58	16
9	Petersburg International Commercial Bank (branches)	15 982	58	18
10	Azov-Don Commercial Bank (outside Petersburg)	13 400	20	5

* for banks that reported this item in their statements.
Calculated on: *Svodnyj balans akcionernyh kommercheskih bankov na 1 janvarja 1898 g.*, nkt-Peterburg: Kom. s'ezdov predstavitelei akts. kom. bankov, 1898.

The leader of investment banking in the 1890s became Petersburg International Bank. By the 20th century tens of industrial companies – in metallurgical, mining, oil, machinery, electrical, glass industries – entered the Petersburg stock market through this bank. At least six famous Russian companies were kept under bank's control: Russian society of Hartmann engineering works, Nikopol-Mariupol mining and metallurgical society, Russian gold mining society, Bibi-Eibat oil society, Moscow glass society, Partnership of Revel distillery. Moreover there were at least ten ascertained personal union between the banks and well-known companies, such as above-mentioned Society of Bryansk works and Society of Putilov plants, as we as Society of Tula copper-rolling and cartridge factories, Society of Russian electrotechnical works Siemens & Halske.[36]

[36] Valery Bovykin, *Zarozhdenie finansovogo kapitala*, *op. cit.*, pp. 208-260, 276-291. Bovykin and Y. Petrov, *Kommercheskie banki*, *op. cit.*, pp. 102-105. Sergei Lebedev, *S.-Peterburgskij Mezhdunarodnyj*, *op. cit.*, pp. 336-388.

Petersburg Discount and Loan bank – the junior partner and simultaneously rival of International bank – kept up with the leader. It was revealed active transactions with large holdings of stock of more than 20 industrial companies, including Baku oil refining society, Society of Gluhoozersk Portland cement plant, Doneck-Jur'evs metallurgical society, Stock-company of engineering, iron foundry and cable works 'Lessner G.A., Oil production and refining companies Mazut and Mantashev A.I. & Co., above-mentioned Nikopol-Mariupol and Sormovo societies and Russo-Belgian metallurgical society.[37]

The other three small Petersburg "investment banks" conducted the similar operations. Petersburg Private Commercial Bank was usually a partner of International or Discount and Loan banks.[38] The other two Petersburg banks belonged to quick-growing financial and industrial group of well-known businessman and banker Lazar Polyakov (1842-1914). He was a chairman of council in Petersburg-Moscow Bank and a principal shareholder in Petersburg-Azov Bank. The core of the group was Polyakov's banking house in Moscow.[39]

These five banks had a resembling model of operations in the 1890s. Security transactions brought at the average 25 per cent of gross profit per year to the banks, although this percentage could increase up to 30/35 per cent in some banks. In general, their non-credit profit (that is profit from exchange transactions and commissions) amounted 40/50 per cent of gross profit.[40]

As a rule, the resources of Russian "investment banks" included, as a rule, sizable own funds (equity and reserves): for instance in 1898 the own funds of International bank amounted 38 per sent of liabilities, Discount and Loan Bank – 23 per cent, Private Bank – 36 per cent. The other resources, used by these banks, were interbank short-term credits as well as customers' current accounts, but these banks did not attract time deposits.[41]

The term "investment bank" was also applied to Russian Bank for Foreign Trade and Russian Trade and Industrial Bank, but this cliché characterised their Petersburg head offices and it was irrelevant to their model of operations in general. These two large banks had wide branch networks in provinces (13 and 39 branches, respectively), where crediting of trade and industrial

37 Valery Bovykin, *Zarozhdenie finansovogo kapitala*, *op. cit.*, pp. 270-272. Valery Bovykin and Yuri Petrov, *Kommercheskie banki*, *op. cit.*, pp. 103-105.

38 Valery Bovykin, *Zarozhdenie finansovogo kapitala*, *op. cit.*, pp. 260-269. Valery Bovykin and Yuri Petrov, *Kommercheskie banki*, *op. cit.*, pp. 85-88.

39 Valery Bovykin, *Zarozhdenie finansovogo*, *op. cit.*, pp. 273-274. Valery Bovykin, *Formirovanie finansovogo kapitala v Rossii. Konets XIX v.-1908 g.*, pp. 141-142.

40 Sofya Salomatina, *Kommercheskie banki v Rossii*, *op. cit.*, pp. 174-181.

41 *Ibidem*, pp. 164-171.

customers brought the principal profit. Bank for Foreign Trade took part in foreign economic activity through branches in London, Paris and Genoa.

In the 1890s Russian Bank for Foreign Trade was a principal founder of Sormovo company, Russo-Belgian society, Balakhany oil society and Mantashev A. I. & Co. The bank was a partner of International bank since the 1880s. In the 1890s it collaborated in the issue of Hartmann works' shares and stock of Kolomna society of engineering works and Revel distillery.[42] Investment activity of Russian Trade and Industrial Banks was due to projects of controlling shareholders – brothers Pavel and Sergey von Derwies (von Derviz) – entrepreneurs, philanthropists and sponsors. They were sons of Pavel von Derwies – a large railway contractor at the age of Alexander II. The brothers used bank's resources for stock floatation and stock market games. The family had shares in some railway; steamship and industrial companies, including Society of Moscow electro-mechanical and engineering works (former K.A. Vejhelt), Society of Gluhoozersk Portland cement plant.[43]

The strong growth of Petersburg stock market did not skirt banks traditionally associated with deposit model in the 1890s. It concerned two banks – Volga-Kama Bank and Moscow Merchant Bank. Both banks were among the top three Russian banks together with Petersburg International Bank. Volga-Kama bank possessed numerous branches. The bank's leading operations was discount of trade bills; amounted 35/40 per cent of assets, and discount in provinces was twice as much than in Petersburg. All peculiarities of operations indicated discount and deposit bank. Its time deposits amounted 25 per cent of liabilities, and the largest part of deposits was attracted in regions. Bank had a very small stock in comparison with "investment banks" – 12 per cent of liabilities, therefore its return on equity was the largest in Russian – 34/36 per cent in the 1890s. In addition to that the bank paid the biggest dividends and market value of its stock was the highest – more than 1,000 rubles for share with nominal price 250 rubles.[44] In spite of deposit and discount model in whole, Petersburg head office was active enough at the equity market and the scale of these transactions was comparable with small "investment banks" in absolute value, but their percentage numbered just in 6.5 per cent of total assets. In the 1880s-1890s, Volga-Kama Bank took part in railway issues. Bank was not involved in

---

42 Valery Bovykin, *Zarozhdenie finansovogo kapitala, op. cit.*, p. 270. Valery Bovykin and Yuri Petrov, *Kommercheskie banki, op. cit.*, pp. 144-147.

43 Valery Bovykin, *Zarozhdenie finansovogo kapitala, op. cit.*, pp. 272-273. Valery Bovykin and Yuri Petrov, *Kommercheskie banki, op. cit.*, pp. 147-149.

44 Sofya Salomatina, *Kommercheskie banki, op. cit.*, pp. 129-135, 143, 152, 165-167, 177. Andrei Golubev (ed.), *Russkie banki: Sprav. i stat. svedenija o vseh dejstvuju-wih v Rossii gos., chast. i obwestv. kredit. uchrezhdenijah. God 1*, Sankt-Peterburg, Kom. s'ezdov predstavitelei akts. kom. Bankov, 1896, pp. 23-24.

promotion of industrial companies, but equity market brought 11/13 per cent of bank's gross profit.[45]

The Moscow Merchant bank was an old-fashioned and respectable institution for Moscow business elite, first of all for textile manufacturers of Central Industrial Region, included several provinces around Moscow. Bank possessed one of the largest bill holdings in Russia, the percentage of discount varied from 30 per cent to 50 per cent of assets in different periods. The basis of the bank's resources was time deposits (the same 30/50 per cent of liabilities). Since the 1890s the bank's Petersburg branch acted at equity market. The bank could be included in top ten banks developed investment activity, but this field was not very important for the bank in percentage – just 7.8 per cent of assets.[46]

Thus, the analysis of banks' annual financial reports for the 1890s permits to draw a conclusion that this decade the banking specialisation, related to equity market, were showed up, although there were no pure investment banks in Russia. This specialisation had evident traces in reports. Particularly, profit from exchange and commission transactions exceeded profit from short-term crediting of customers. Thereafter the assets associated with holding of securities, crediting security trading and syndicates' transactions displaced discount of bills of exchange and short-term crediting of business in whole. For instance, discount amounted in the average 14 per cent in Petersburg International Bank in 1895-1899, in Petersburg Discount and Loan Bank – 11 per cent, in Petersburg Private Commercial Bank – 15 per cent, whereas average rate for Russian merchant banks was in the range 25/35 per cent.[47] The same trends could be observed in liabilities: "investment banks" increased stock and reserves, refused from time deposits' development, the half of resources these banks attracted came via credits from correspondents.[48] This tendency was showed up at most in the model of Petersburg "investment banks", this disposition was less evident in the structure of operations of other banks, possessed Petersburg offices, and the most of regional banks were not affected by the trend at all.

It's important to note that Russian "investment banks" developed the most profitable banking model in the 1890s, even according to their public reports. For instance, the ratio of net profit to average annual assets amounted 3/4 per cent in "investment banks" in 1898. Particularly, Private Bank – 4.18 per cent, International Bank – 3.79 per cent, Discount and Loan Bank

---

45 Sofya Salomatina, *Kommercheskie banki, op. cit.*, pp. 158-160. Valery Bovykin and Yuri Petrov, *Kommercheskie banki, op. cit.*, pp. 122-123.

46 Valery Bovykin and Yuri Petrov, *Kommercheskie banki, op. cit.*, pp. 190-201. Sofya Salomatina, *Kommercheskie banki, op. cit.*, pp. 129-135, 165-167.

47 Sofya Salomatina, *Kommercheskie banki, op. cit.*, pp. 129-135.

48 *Ibidem*, pp. 164-170.

and Bank for Foreign Trade – 3.11 per cent each. This indicator for deposit banks was below 3 per cent, for instance, 2.82 per cent in Volga-Kama Bank and 2.27 per cent in Moscow Merchant Bank, and these figures were typical for regional banks. It is obvious, that in 1890s investment banks took up an option to draw profit from equity market as much as possible.[49]

Private companies stock was greatly integrated in model of "investment banks" geared the banks to rate of these securities. By the 1900s the new companies stock was kept in banks' portfolios, in pledges on customers' credit accounts and on correspondent accounts. So far there is no evidence, that some of bankers worried about possible drop in prices in the end of the 1890s; although in some way growing stock and reserves of Petersburg banks indicated the attempt to secure themselves against critical juncture.[50] It is interesting that in autumn 1898 Rothstein wrote to A. Rothschild about stress of money on Russian market, appeared these months. Particularly Rothstein mentioned that Russia "is in financial straits, as Europe", but "industry needs vast sums of money". He meant that numerous new enterprises, founded with assistance of banks, were still in their infancy. Rothstein was aware that all large plants had exhausted considerable sums on their accounts in International bank very soon and turned into bank's debtors "in absolutely unnoticeable way". Nevertheless Rothstein drew a curiously optimistic conclusion and declared that these companies had just spent their first credits and they would attract new funds through issues of bonds or shares soon.[51]

3. Investment banking difficulties in crisis, 1899-1903

However the stress of money was one of the first crisis warnings in autumn 1898.[52] In spring 1899 a tendency to price fall appeared at Petersburg exchange. In summer public opinion was agitated by bankruptcies of some well-known entrepreneurs.[53] At the end of September 1899 the general collapse was happened at Petersburg exchange. Since 1900 the total economic crisis gradually came after exchange downfall. An economic crisis had broken out in Russia in 1899-1903, it was a part of European economic recession. The hardest period fell on 1901-1902, when deep industrial fall spread to maximal number of industries. The signs of improvement had appeared since 1903, but unsuccessful Russo-Japanese War (1904-1905) and Revolution (1905-1907) did not make possible economic recovery,

49 *Ibidem*, p. 170.

50 *Ibidem*, pp. 165-166.

51 A. Rothstein to A. Rothschild, 26 October/7 November 1898, in *Rossiia i mirovoi biznes*, *op. cit.*, p. 146.

52 Sergei Lebedev, *S.-Peterburgskij Mezhdunarodnyj*, *op. cit.*, pp. 388-391.

53 Valery Bovykin, *Formirovanie finansovogo kapitala*, *op. cit.*, pp. 128-129.

these events disrupted money and credit market and in the issue the recession continued until 1908-1909 in some industries.[54] In fact the crisis was a breakdown of a new economy arisen in previous decade. The new enterprises bore the downturn especially hardly. These plants appeared in connection with railway construction and railroading, they were often founded with an assistance of foreign capital and, unfortunately, they accumulated large inventories under favourable conditions for trade and industry[55] in the 1890s.

The banks, taken part in foundation of the new economy, suffered together with their customers. Devalued stock of new companies had stuck tightly in banks' portfolios and ledgers, and suddenly banks appeared to be tied to industry in literal sense. Thereby the basis was laid for long-term relations between banks and issuers. Since the beginning of the crisis the striking wave of drops in prices, estimates of loss, banking panics and crashes washed over Russia. These events had deep public resonance. The crisis didn't confine itself to stock market downfall, but it revealed problem banks by several characteristics, including liquidity, quality of stock and credit portfolio. By 1903 the stock market had flattened at moderate level, but unfavourable events, associated with war, revolution, difficulties of state and mortgage bond market,[56] would be to follow in 1904-1908.

The Petersburg International Bank took the hardest blow of crisis. The bank's report for 1900 showed the largest loss in banking system associated with stock market downfall – 1,487.9 thousand rubles or 22 per cent of gross value in that year.[57] But general losses on various accounts amounted no less then 3.98 million rubles in 1901-1903, according public reports.[58] The bank appeared an owner of large stock holdings, particularly of Nikopol-Mariupol society and Hartmann engineering works.[59] In 1901 the audit of the ministry of Finance revealed large debts of industrial companies to the bank. The major debtors were five companies, having total debt in 14 million rubles. This list included the same Nikopol-Mariupol society, Russian gold mining society, Tula copper-rolling and cartridge factories, Moscow glass society and Zhillovskoe society of coal and iron ore mines. The audit recorded that "bank had violated its charter, placed considerable sums in arisen industrial enterprises through purchase of their stock and opening credits to them".[60]

---

54 Lev Borisovich Kafengauz, *Jevoljucija promyshlennogo proizvodstva Rossii*, p. 70.

55 *Ibidem*, p. 70.

56 Valery Bovykin, *Formirovanie finansovogo kapitala, op. cit.*, pp. 121-156.

57 Calculated on: *Vestnik finansov, promyshlennosti i torgovli*, 1901, No. 17, p. 498.

58 Calculated on 1900-1903 annual reports, published in *Vestnik finansov, promyshlennosti i torgov*li (1901-1904).

59 Valery Bovykin and Yuri Petrov, *Kommercheskie banki, op. cit.*, p. 105.

60 *Ibidem*, p. 105.

Public opinion charged the bank with passion for industrial securities, which were regarded by small shareholders as the root of all evil. Sergei Lebedev gathered striking illustrations of public hysteria concerning 1900 report at stockholders' meeting in spring 1901. *Russkie Vedomosti* (*Russian Gazette*)[61] wrote that the bank had set an example of "the most groundless, thoughtless, ignorant *Gründertum*".[62] "Every business looks like a contrivance to obtain another sinecure, material for stockbrokers' gambling and source of profiteering for syndicates headed by the same financial geniuses."[63] Small shareholders charged the directory with purchases of inflated shares, implied securities without state guarantee unlike state equity, customary for Russian *rentier*. They were made appeals to "clean the portfolios from dummy securities", purporting the same private stock and industrial capital in the first place.[64]

The State Bank relieved Petersburg International Bank and open to it the preferential credit, though the favourable attitude of minister Witte toward director Rothstein were finally damaged. Nevertheless the bank obtained a permit to keep this credit account not as separate balance account, but inside total correspondent account in the liabilities. The bank owed to report for this credit account to the Credit Office of the ministry every month. The government promised to render assistance in recovery of railway companies' accounts, which had been withdrawn because of reputation problems of International Bank. Before railway accounts would be returned the government intended to "transfer some money from the State Bank's account to the International Bank's current account for temperate interest".[65]

The situation in other "investment banks" was the same as that of Petersburg International Bank in many details, but differences also deserved consideration. Thus, Russian Bank for Foreign Trade carried out reappraisal of portfolio and revealed 1,058.24 thousand rubles of loss or 20 per cent of gross profit[66] in 1900. The bank's total loss amounted no less then 3,418.98

61 *Russkie Vedomosti* (*Russian Newspaper*, 1863-1918), represented liberal opposition to government in the end of the 19th century.

62 *Gründertum* was a period of feverish promotion of companies in Germany after Franco-Prussian war (1870-1871), a very popular term, concerning any intensive economical promotion in Russian pre-revolutionary journalism.

63 *Russkie Vedomosti*, 1901, 19 February, No. 106 (from: Serguei Lebedev, *S.-Peterburgskij Mezhdunarodnyj*, *op. cit.*, p. 394).

64 Serguei Lebedev, *S.-Peterburgskij Mezhdunarodnyj*, *op. cit.*, p. 395.

65 I.I. Levin, *Aktsionernye kommercheskie banki v Rossii*, Vol. 1, Petrograd, tip. T-va Ptgr. pech. pr-va I.R. Belopol'skogo i Ko, 1917, p. 283 (from: Serguei Lebedev, *S.-Peterburgskij Mezhdunarodnyj*, *op. cit.*, p. 398).

66 Calculated on: *Vestnik finansov, promyshlennosti i torgovli*, 1901, No. 15, p. 397.

thousand rubles[67] in 1899-1901. Nevertheless the bank restored stability due to branch network since 1902. In exactly the same way the small "investment banks" – Petersburg Discount and Loan Bank and Petersburg Private Commercial Bank – evaluated amount of loss from drop in prices and from bad credits.[68] The case of Private Bank appeared much more difficult. The bank failed to improve its assets without assistance in the 1900s. In 1910 the bank was reorganised by foreign banking group including Crédit mobilier français, J. Loste & Co., Mrs Thalmann & Co. and L. Hirsch & Co. through intermediary of the Ministry of Finance.[69]

The case of Russian Trade and Industrial Bank drew a wide public response, although the bank was not deeply involved in investment banking in comparison with the other Petersburg banks. In summer 1899 the bank's owner Pavel von Derwies became insolvent. As soon as the news had ran all over Petersburg, the bank became a victim of panic withdrawal of deposits. The bank's crush was prevented by interference of the State Bank. Later Trade and Industrial Bank recovered losses and stockholders' meeting made a decision to abandon speculation in stock and shift to trade crediting, mainly in regions[70] since 1902. The Volga-Kama Bank's total loss amounted considerable sum – 793,440 rubles in 1900, but it was just 8 per cent of gross profit.[71] The Moscow Merchant Bank's reports didn't display any serious losses in crisis period.

The Lazar Polyakov's banks turned out in the tightest situation. In 1901 it became clear, that Polykov and his banking house in Moscow were bankrupts. The Polyakov's many-millioned debts burdened his banks, and the situation appeared the worst in Petersburg. Petersburg-Azov Bank collapsed in 1902 and Petersburg-Moscow Bank shut down operations in 1904. Polyakov's banks in Russian Central Industrial Region – Moscow International Trade Bank, Orel Commercial Bank and South Russian Industrial Bank – passed under control of the State Bank, which bought out their debts. In state auditors' opinion, these tree banks were considered as viable institutions albeit burdened with their owner's debts. In the 1900s the persistent attempts to find any European investor for Polyakov's group failed, and in 1908-1909 the Ministry of Finance and the State Bank conducted a merging of three banks into new Union Bank, but 17.5m rubles from 25m of total fixed capital of three banks was spent

67 Calculated on 1899-1901 annual reports, published in *Vestnik finansov, promyshlennosti i torgov*li (1900-1902).

68 Valery Bovykin and Yuri Petrov, *Kommercheskie banki, op. cit.*, pp. 88-89, pp. 105-106.

69 *Ibidem*, pp. 91-95.

70 *Ibidem*, pp. 148-149.

71 Calculated on: *Vestnik finansov, promyshlennosti i torgovli*, 1901, No. 16, p. 470.

on cover of loss. Nevertheless a part of Polyakov's debts remained on State bank's accounts.[72]

In order to summarise the banks' difficulties in 1899-1903 it is important to underline that any bank endured drops in stock prices easier if it had kept large credit customers' network outside head office. The role of banks' reserves remains still underestimated by economic historians in risk management at the turn of the 20th century. In other words, some banks, dealing with investment banking, tried to diversify operations and accumulate reserves. Bankruptcies usually happened to not large banks, bunched various drawbacks in management, and banks which had not been saved by the State Bank.

At the same time the large banks survived crisis due to ample informal opportunities to obtain crediting of the State Bank, subordinated to the Ministry of Finance. The fact is that the Russian government always aimed to exclude crushes of large banks by all means. This policy went back to the 1870s when unfavourable juncture and problems in banking system in 1873-1875 had crystallised the government approach to banking regulation. Since then banking founding was provided with a lot of state restrictions and financial institutions were under particular control in comparison with Western Europe in the second half of the 19th century. The government considered bankruptcy as undesirable shock to domestic financial market, and they found insolvency conceivable for minor banks only, unencumbered with the large-scale liabilities to various sectors of economy.

The State Bank not only credited banks urgently at the turn of the 20th century, but it took part in syndicate, organised for interventions in Petersburg exchange. It was formed on Witte's initiative in October 1899 and it included fifteen Petersburg banks and banking houses. By June 1900 syndicate spent 4 million rubles, although its effectiveness has not studied well yet. Among the other State Bank's measures worthy of being noted there was a decision to buy shares of viable enterprises or to take their stock in pledge. This measure developed into mass urgent crediting of industrial customers of large banks.[73] Thus, the crisis revealed the principal investment banks' weaknesses: insufficient assets' diversification and lack of experience in stock market risk management. In short-term perspective the main factors in crisis management were banks' reserves and the State Bank's policy of banking liquidity support and prevention of financial panic. In middle- and long-term perspectives the banking system's recovery was provided by banks themselves. It took all the 1900s to integrate investment banking into a more stable structure of operations.

72 Valery Bovykin, *Formirovanie finansovogo kapitala*, *op. cit.*, pp. 141-142. Valery Bovykin and Yuri Petrov, *Kommercheskie banki*, *op. cit.*, pp. 243-248.

73 Serguei Lebedev, *S.-Peterburgskij Mezhdunarodnyj*, *op. cit.*, pp. 392-393.

4. Towards the universalisation of banking

Before WWI, the Russian banking system had noticeably changed. The process, caused these changes, was launched by the crisis at the turn of the 20th century, revealed risks of intensive investment activity. In the 1900s the banks had to deal with crisis management and to develop new foundations for services to industrial customers and their stock. Credit portfolios' readjustment took eight years and cost banks a lot of efforts. The banks worked out a counterbalance to stock market operations, wherefore they partly returned to traditional discount customers' networks. These customers were attracted in regions, where the metropolitan banks had rushed to build up branch networks in the 1900s. In the 1910s since the new economical upturn the percentage of discount began to drop again due to increase in stock transactions but it would not lead to the disparity observed in the 1890s.

In the pre-war period a universal bank became a prevailing model in the Russian banking system. This type of bank distributed the assets more or less evenly between discount, credit accounts and transactions with securities. The universal bank credited trade and industrial companies and simultaneously took part in new paper issues. Its liabilities included not large stock and reserves, deposits (the share of current accounts prevailed over the share of time deposits) and credits from the other Russian and European banks. The large-scale universal banks operated not only at domestic market but all over the world.[74] Abovementioned traits corresponded wholly to five largest Russian commercial banks in 1913: Russo-Asian Commercial Bank, Russian Bank for Foreign Trade, Petersburg International Commercial Bank, Azov-Don Commercial Bank, Russian Trade and Industrial Commercial Bank (see table 5a).

The tables 5a, 5b and 5c retrace evolution of banks presented previously in tables 4a and 4b, as investment banking leaders in 1890s. The grouping of banking operations with private shares, used in tables 4 for the 1890s data, didn't permit to reveal any trends in the 1910s, as if the investment banking dissolved in banking reports. But universal trends could be observed by another way, and these calculations were given in tables 5; they were carried out for every bank in whole, but not for head offices only as in tables 4. In these tables banks are grouped by following principles: firstly, the leading universal banks in the 1910s – top five banks in Petersburg and in entire Russia and the largest Moscow bank – Union bank. Secondly, Volga-Kama Commercial Bank (Petersburg) and Moscow Merchant Bank embodied deposit and discount banking even in the 1910s, in spite of securities departments at their Petersburg and Moscow offices. Thirdly, Petersburg Discount

[74] Sofya Salomatina, "Modeli kommercheskikh bankov", *op. cit.*, p. 342.

and Loan Bank and Petersburg Private Bank had been small "investment banks" in the 1890s, but they kept many "investment traits" until the 1910s.

Table 5a. The assets rating and evolution of discount

Banks	**Assets on 1.01.1914**		**Average annual discount, % of average annual assets**		**(3)-(4)**
	thousand rubles	**Rating, 1 – max**	**1895-1899, (%)**	**1908-1913, (%)**	
	(1)	**(2)**	**(3)**	**(4)**	**(5)**
Russo-Asian Bank[1]	834,941	1	–	26 (6)	–
Russian Bank for Foreign Trade	628,354	2	17 (3)	22 (1)	+5
Petersburg International Commercial Bank	617,494	3	14 (4)	20 (2)	+6
Azov-Don Commercial Bank[2]	543,540	4	25 (2)	26 (3)	+1
Russian Trade and Industrial Bank	496,245	5	21 (4)	32 (2)	+11
Union Bank[3]	333,776	7	–	34 (2)	–
Volga-Kama Commercial Bank	424,686	6	34 (3)	35 (2)	+1
Moscow Merchant	279,861	8	37 (4)	41 (7)	+5
Petersburg Discount and Loan Bank	208,029	11	11 (2)	21 (2)	+10
Petersburg Private Commercial Bank	182,741	12	15 (2)	29 (8)	+14

The tables 5a, 5b and 4c present the evolution of banking models since the 1890s up to 1913/1914; they observe the several tendencies. Firstly, former "investment banks" had increased percentage of discount by the 1910s in comparison with the 1890s (see table 5a). By the 1910s discount amounted no less then 20 per cent of any large bank's assets, whereas it went down to 11-15 per cent in the 1890s. Secondly, the total number of branches increased approximately in five times from the 1890s up to the 1910s. They were the Russian provinces who gave a stimulus to discount customers' networks growth. In addition to domestic branches large universal bank surely developed some branches abroad – in European and Asian financial centers. Thus bank evolved foreign economic activity (see table 5b). Thirdly, the percentage of stock transactions was down by 10 percentage point in universal bank, but in absolute value there was a considerable profit usually gained by large stock department, having substantial transactions turnover (table 5c).

Table 5b. Profit from security trading

Banks	1898		1913		Difference, 1913-1898	
	thousand rubles	% of gross profit	thousand rubles	% of gross profit	thousand rubles	pct
Russo-Asian Bank[1]	–	–	2,294	5.3	–	–
Russian Bank for Foreign Trade	157	12	917	3.3	+760	–8.7
Petersburg International Commercial Bank	819	24	2,619	7.6	+1800	–16.4
Azov-Don Commercial Bank[2]	52	10	1,919	6.0	+1867	–4.0
Russian Trade and Industrial Bank	367	15	552	2.1	+185	–12.9
Union Bank[3]	–	–	1,049	5.4	–	–
Volga-Kama Commercial Bank	345	11	154	0.7	–191	–10.3
Moscow Merchant	159	7	158	1.1	–1	–5.9
Petersburg Discount and Loan Bank	725	26	1,443	14.1	718	–11.9
Petersburg Private Commercial Bank	296	17	628	5.2	332	–11.8

Notes:

The head offices of all banks were in Petersburg except Union Bank and Moscow Merchant Bank, having directory in Moscow.

The sections of tables: 1) the five largest Russian universal banks and Union Bank – the largest universal bank in Moscow; 2) the largest deposit banks; 3) small □investment banks□ in the 1890s.

1 – Russo-Asian Bank was established in 1910.

2 – Azov-Don Commercial Bank was relocated in Petersburg from Taganrog by Azov Sea; it was the largest provincial merchant bank in the 1890s.

3 – Union bank was established in 1909.

4 – Azov-Don Commercial Bank possessed control stock of Banque des Pays du Nord in Paris.

Sources:

Assets on 01.01.1914 – *Svodnyj balans akcionernyh kommercheskih bankov na 1 janvarja 1914 g.*, Sankt-Peterburg, Kom. s'ezdov predstavitelei akts. kom. bankov, 1914, pp. 1-15.

Average annual discount – Sofya Salomatina, *Kommercheskie banki v Rossii: dinamika i struktura operacij, 1864-1917 gg.*, pp. 129-135.

Branch networks in 1898 – A. Golubev (ed.), *Russkie banki: Sprav. i stat. svedenija o vseh dejstvujuwih v Rossii gos., chast. i obwestv. kredit. uchrezhdenijah. God 3*, Sankt-Peterburg, Kom. s'ezdov predstavitelei akts. kom. bankov, 1899, pp. 24-40.

Branch networks in 1913 – *Akcionerno-paevye predprijatija Rossii po oficial'nym dannym*, Moskva, 1913, pp. 464-480.

Profit from security trading in 1898 – Sofya Salomatina, *Kommercheskie banki v Rossii: dinamika i struktura operacij, 1864-1917 gg.*, pp. 147, 159.

Profit from security trading in 1913 – *Russkie akcionernye kommercheskie banki po otchetam za 1913 g. v sravnenii s 1912 g.*, Sankt-Peterburg, Kom. s'ezdov predstavitelei akts. kom. bankov, 1914, pp. 32, 36

Table 5c. Branch networks evolution

Banks	In Russia		Abroad	
	Branches on 1.07.1913	Difference with 1898	Branches on 1.07.1913	Difference with 1898
Russo-Asian Bank[1]	87	–	12	–
Russian Bank for Foreign Trade	59	+49	4	+1
Petersburg International Commercial Bank	38	+35	2	+2
Azov-Don Commercial Bank[2]	69	+37	1[4]	+1
Russian Trade and Industrial Bank	96	+57	2	+2
Union Bank[3]	92	–	3	+3
Volga-Kama Commercial Bank	57	+37	0	0
Moscow Merchant	2	–1	0	0
Petersburg Discount and Loan Bank	6	+5	0	0
Petersburg Private Commercial Bank	0	–2	0	0

The pre-war universal banks had different origins. In the first place there were "investment banks" evolving into universal banks through the expansion to the provinces. It was the course of development of Petersburg International Bank, Russian Bank for Foreign Trade, Russian Trade and Industrial Bank. In the second place some new-founded banks, transformed form problem banks or rapidly developing banking houses, took up a strong position in banking system right away. These new banks began to operate initially as universal institutions. This group was represented by Russo-Asian Bank in Petersburg and Union Bank in Moscow. The deposit Volga-Kama Commercial Bank, the largest private bank in the second half of the 19th century, lost its leading position in assets rating by the 1914 and ranked sixth before WWI. The bank did not take part in issues of companies stock and preferred short-term crediting of business customers in metropolis and in the provinces.[75]

In the 1910s the alignment of forces changed in Moscow. Union Bank, newly founded on the basis of crashed Polyakov's banks, drew the previous Moscow leader Merchant Bank back to the second place. Union Bank concentrated on discount and loan operations. The bank tried to pursue a very reasonable policy towards stock market transactions, because it sought to clean its reputation from Polyakov's legacy,[76] associated with bankruptcy due to risky projects. The bank had no sufficient opportunity

75 Sofya Salomatina, 'Modeli kommercheskikh', *op. cit.*, p. 342.

76 Valery Bovykin and Yuri Petrov, *Kommercheskie banki*, *op. cit.*, pp. 249-250.

to develop time deposits by reason of this legacy, therefore it had to borrowed resources from the other Russian and foreign banks.[77]

Generally speaking there was a trend that banks, keeping any non-universal model, began gradually to lose their positions. It concerns Volga-Kama and Merchant banks uppermost. The small "investment banks" kept also many traditional traits by the 1910s and they remained at minor position at banking system. For instance, Petersburg Private Commercial bank continued to develop as "investment bank". The Petersburg Discount and Loan Bank increased discount appreciably, but any way equity market transactions brought substantially greater percentage of return to the bank in comparison with larger universal banks.[78]

All in all the "universalisation" of banks in pre-revolutionary Russia corresponded to development of powerful merchant bank having broad domestic branch network as a counterbalance to investment department in head office, and further to these units the bank possessed foreign branches subordinated to central foreign department. It was obvious that universal bank became the leading model in Russia before WW I, and banks, kept to the other models, began to go under to strong competition from powerful universal banks. But for the world war and the revolution in 1917 Russian banking system would have entered in the epoch of merges and acquisitions.

Conclusion

Our chapter reviewed the prerequisites and evolution of investment banking in pre-revolutionary Russia, placing in the focus of attention the boom of investment banking in the 1890s and transition to universal banking by the 1910s. The development of investment banking was traced from services to state and mortgage bond market in the 1880s to investment specialisation inside merchant banking in the 1890s, then up to its integration into universal banking.

The 1890s decade had passed under the sign of investment banking in Russia. It was a period of the heaviest economic growth in the pre-revolutionary period. The financial system of empire had also overcome the recession of previous two decades. In the 1890s the investment banking concerned those commercial banks that had developed specialisation in equity market services in earlier years. Russian equity market was concentrated in Petersburg to a large degree, because state bonds and securities, guaranteed by government, prevailed at the market and therefore Petersburg developed as only centre of negotiations from Russian side for Russian domestic and foreign issues.

77 Sofya Salomatina, 'Modeli kommercheskikh', *op. cit.*, p. 342.

78 *Ibidem*, p. 343.

An underwriting was typical for Russian investment banking; therefore international banking syndicates played a decisive role in Russian issues. Two banks – powerful Petersburg International Commercial Bank and middle-sized Petersburg Discount and Loan Bank – were the most active participant of international syndicates. International Bank acted usually as a leader of Russian group since the 1880s. At the same time a head office of any Petersburg bank was involved into equity market transactions, regardless of bank's model. The important changes happened at Russian currency market by the middle of the 1890s simultaneously with the economic growth and equity market development. Russian currency was stabilised and banks, drawn out of currency speculation, switched easily to investment banking for private companies.

The investment banking evolution was specified by risk management development. Investment banking emerged inside merchant banks and special investment institutions didn't appear in Russia. Before the 1890s the banking risks were mainly caused by unstable currency and competition between European and domestic financial markets. In the 1890s mass investment banking for private companies was a new phenomenon in Russia, therefore risks of investment activity turned out underestimated until the crisis, happened in 1899-1903. Uppermost there were the risk of drop in stock prices and immobilisation risk of assets, placed in industrial credits. It became obvious through the crisis that the immobilisation of banks' resources in industrial projects had reached substantial sums of money in 1895-1899. Since 1899 banks unwittingly had proved to be owners of huge holdings of unsalable industrial stock and they were reluctant to act not as investors but as governing owners of companies founded or reorganised in the 1890s.

In short-term perspective the substantial own funds and reserves of "investment banks" appeared very important in crisis management, as well as banking system's support by the Ministry of Finance and the State Bank. The government role in investment banking development deserves a special consideration. This subject doesn't refer to government contractual work to industrial companies, whose influence on market is often overestimated. The state affected investment banking deeply as the principal Russian issuer, the currency regulator, the main supervisor of companies' promotion, the lender of last resort. At the same time the by-product of state patronised policy towards financial institutions was a regular attempt of large-scale bankers to do business relying upon government participation or support, although their expectations were not always lived up. But state support was ineffective for development of middle- and long-term risk management in investment banking after crisis at the turn of the 20th century. The 1900s were spent on elaboration of a new stable banking model, which was found in universal type of bank.

By the 1910s the banks acquired broad experience of investment banking and they cleared up their relations with industrial companies. In the issue the banks integrated investment banking into universal banking. Particularly banks, concentrated on investment in the 1890s, had restored credit networks and developed numerous branches before WWI. The provincial branches became an abundant source of deposits and trade and industrial credit customers, whereas the investment activity concentrated at banks' head offices in Petersburg and Moscow. A Russian universal bank always developed international banking as well, this field was provided by strong foreign department, managed several branches abroad. In the 1910s the universal model predominated at the Russian banking system. Those banks which kept adherence to any other specialisation were gradually sidelined. The fast growth of universal banks signified forthcoming period of redistribution of forces in banking system but this trend would not be put into effect due to collapse of the empire.

Appendixes

Appendix 1. List of original Russian banks' name in transliteration

Azov-Don Commercial Bank	Azovsko-Donskoj kommercheskij bank
Moscow International Trade Bank	Moskovskij Mezhdunarodnyj torgovyj bank
Moscow Merchant Bank	Moskovskij Kupecheskij bank
Moscow Trade Bank	Moskovskij Torgovyj bank
Orel Commercial Bank	Orlovskij kommercheskij bank
Petersburg International Commercial Bank	Sankt-Peterburgskij Mezhdunarodnyj kommercheskij bank
Petersburg Loan and Discount Bank	Sankt-Peterburgskij Uchetnyj i ssudnyj bank
Petersburg Private Commercial Bank	Sankt-Peterburgskij Chastnyj kommercheskij bank
Petersburg-Azov Commercial Bank	Sankt-Peterburgsko-Azovskij kommercheskij bank
Petersburg-Moscow Commercial Bank	Sankt-Peterburgsko-Moskovskij kommercheskij bank
Riga Exchange Bank Bank	Rizhskij birzhevoj bank
Riga Municipal Discount Bank	Rizhskij gorodskoj uchetnyj bank
Russian Bank for Foreign Trade	Russkij bank dlja vneshnej torgovli bank
Russian Trade and Industrial Bank	Russkij Torgovo-promyshlennyj bank
Russo-Asian Bank	Russko-Aziatskij bank
South Russian Industrial Bank	Juzhno-russkij promyshlennyj bank
State Peasant Land Bank	Gosudarstvennyi Krest'ianskii Pozemel'nyi bank
State Land Bank of the Nobility	Gosudarstvennyi Dvorianskii zemel'nyi bank
Union Bank	Soedinennyj bank
Volga-Kama Commercial Bank	Volzhsko-Kamskij kommercheskij bank
Warsaw Commercial Bank	Varshavskij kommercheskij bank

Appendix 2. List of original Russian companies' name in transliteration

Baku oil refining society	*Bakinskoe neftepromyshlennoe obshchestvo*
Balakhany oil refining society	Balakhanskoe neftepromyshlennoe obshchestvo
Bibi-Eibat oil society	Bibi-Eibatskoe neftianoe obshchestvo
Doneck-Jur'evs metallurgical society	Donetsko-Iur'evskoe metallurgicheskoe obshchestvo
Franco-Russian society (cement plant in Gelendzhik)	Franko-Russkoe obshchestvo (tsementnyi zavod v Gelendzhike)
Moscow glass society	Moskovskoe steklopromyshlennoe obshchestvo
Nikopol-Mariupol mining and metallurgical society	Nikopol'-Mariupol'skoe gornoe i metallurgicheskoe obshchestvo
Oil production and refining companies 'Mantashev A. I. & Co.'	Neftepromyshlennoe i torgovoe obshchestvo Mantashev A. I. i K°
Oil production and refining companies Mazut	Neftepromyshlennoe i torgovoe obshchestvo Mazut

Oil company "Caspian partnership"	Neftianaia kompaniia "Kaspiiskoe tovarishchestvo"
Partnership of Revel distillery	Tovarishchestvo Revel'skogo spirtoochistitel'nogo zavoda
Partnership of Sergino-Ufaleysk mining and metallurgical plants	Tovarishchestvo Sergino-Ufaleiskikh gornykh zavodov
Russian goldmining society	Rossiiskoe zolotopromyshlennoe obshchestvo
Russian society of Hartmann engineering works	Russkoe obshchestvo mashinostroitel'nykh zavodov Gartmana
Russo-Belgian metallurgical society	Russko-Bel'giiskoe metallurgicheskoe obshchestvo
Society of Bryansk rail-rolling, iron and engineering works	Obshchestvo Brianskogo rel'soprokatnogo, zhelezodelatel'nogo i mekhanicheskogo zavoda
Society of Gluhoozersk Portland cement plant	Tovarishchestvo Glukhoozerskogo portlandtsementnogo zavoda
Society of iron, steel and engineering works "Sormovo"	Obshchestvo zhelezodelatel'nykh, staleliteinykh i mekhanicheskikh zavodov "Sormovo"
Society of Kolomna engineering works	Obshchestvo Kolomenskogo mashinostroitel'nogo zavoda
Society of Maltsov plants	Obshchestvo Mal'tsovskikh zavodov
Society of Moscow electro-mechanical and engineering works (former K. A. Vejhel't)	Obshchestvo Moskovskikh elektromekhanicheskogo i mashinostroitel'nogo zavodov (byvshee K. A. Veikhel't)
Society of Putilov plants	Obshchestvo Putilovskikh zavodov
Society of Russian electrotechnical works Siemens & Halske	Obshchestvo russkikh elektrotekhnicheskikh zavodov Simens i Gal'ske
Society of Russo-Baltic wagon works	Obshchestvo Russko-Baltiiskogo vagonostroitel'nogo zavoda
Society of Tula copper-rolling and cartridge factories	Obshchestvo Tul'skikh mednoprokatnykh i patronnykh zavodov
Stock-company of engineering, iron foundry and cable works Lessner G. A.	Aktsionernoe obshchestvo mashinostroitel'nogo, chugunoliteinogo i kabel'nogo zavodov Lessner G. A.
Zhillovskoe society of coal and iron ore mines	*Zhillovskoe obshchestvo kamennougol'nykh kopei i rudnikov*

CHAPTER 12

French Investment Banking and Bulgaria from the 1880s until 1930s

Portfolio of Skills and Strategies

Gergana TANEVA

PhD in economic history at Bordeaux University and UMR CNRS 5113 GRETHA research centre-Bordeaux University; assistant professor at Plovdiv University (Bulgaria)
<gergana.taneva@yahoo.fr>

At the turn of the 20th century, the movements of capital in Europe developed through the banking groups' intervention network. They tried to secure the financial territories that were barely or almost autonomous, by the way of negotiations; their funds aimed at developing their economy, industry and finance. Bulgaria was connected to the European banking market by the pace of foreign capital introduction.[1] Bulgarian market was often shaped by the concrete repercussions of history on its own development; the European tendencies after the Independence War in 1878 characterised a step in its progress, in the improvement of its condition.

The French banking groups occupied an important place in Bulgarian history due to their structure and their influence on social organisation. They entered the market to promote its development through a portfolio of skills. Such a study, dealing with investment banks (Paribas,

[1] See John Lampe and Marvin Jackson, *Balkan Economic History, 1550-1950: From Imperial Borderlands to Developing Nations*, Bloomington, Indiana University Press, 1982. John Lampe, *The Bulgarian Economy in the Twentieth Century*, London, Croom Helm, 1986. Kostas Kostis (ed.), *Modern Banking in the Balkans and West-European Capital in the Nineteenth and Twentieth Centuries*, Ashgate-European Association for banking history, London, 1999. Kenneth Koford and Adrian E. Tschoegl, "Foreign Bank in Bulgaria, 1875-2002" in Edith Klein (ed.), *Capital Formation, Governance and Banking*, New York, Nova Publishers, 2005.

BUP) and the financial activities of commercial banks (Crédit lyonnais, Société générale) intends therefore to examine the role and the impact of financial groups, first in the formation of a Bulgarian State, then in its institutional reorganisations. Paribas was the main participant. Soon after its foundation, it took part in controlling the issuing of loans in the Balkans, relying on a fund concentration network,[2] on security distribution organisation, and on strategic gatherings with other detail banks – Société générale or Crédit lyonnais. The organisation created by French banks, based on an underwriting syndicate (their activity on the primary and secondary market securities, collectively in underwriting or placement syndicates), which managed stock exchange investments, became an archetype of union and intervention. Its essential goal was to gather funds in order to finance infrastructures and government borrowings.

To study the impact of French financial institutions in Bulgaria means analysing their strategies and their operations on stock exchange and financial markets whose competition and collaboration represent the form of bank investments.[3] The first characteristic was a result of their integration into the Bulgarian market that led to constituting an intervention area by controlling most of the capital coming in. At the first level were the relations between the syndicates and both countries' governments – it was a kind of bank mediation. Two spheres of influence were created, purely residing in bank and politics, in which the place of financial groups was to be determined. They used different tools to intervene before WWI: In the financial sphere of influence, a local company network was formed, and that was the origin of the group capital; thanks to the second sphere and political support the groups could access railway concessions.[4] More specifically, the type of

---

2 About the historical deployment of *Paribas* see Éric Bussière, *Paribas: Europe and the World: 1872-1992*, Antwerp, Fonds Mercator, 1992.

3 See Samuel Hayes, Andrew Michal Spence & David Van Praag Marks (eds.), *Competition in the Investment Banking Industry*, Cambridge, Harvard University Press, 1983. John Peter Williamson (ed.), *The Investment Banking Handbook*, New York, John Wiley & Sons, 1988. Hubert Bonin, *Le Monde des banquiers français au XXe siècle*, Brussels, Complexe, 2000. Douglas J. Forsyth & Daniel Verdier (eds.), *The Origins of National Financial Systems*, London & New York, Routledge, 2002. Youssef Cassis, *Les capitales du capital: histoire des places financières internationales, 1780-2005*, Paris, Honoré Champion, 2008.

4 See Peter Hertner, "The Balkan Railways, international capital and banking from the end of the nineteenth century until the outbreak of the First World War", in Gerald Feldman and Peter Hertner (eds.), *Finance and Modernization. A Transnational and Transcontinental Perspective for the Nineteenth and Twentieth Centuries*, Burlington, Ashgate, 2008.

specialisation of French banks[5] (investment banks, commercial banks or universal banks) reflected a potential competition resulting from the development of interbank relations with the aim to extend a wider range of instruments for intervention in foreign markets. Thus, on this basis, the groups could minimise their risks, assess their position, strengthen their collaboration, and capitalise on the interests of both sides next to the borrowing country and the resources of the country later praetor. Our purpose is therefore to gauge the principles and convergence mechanisms of French groups in Bulgaria.

Historically, the Bulgarian market evolved thanks to foreign capital and its distribution in various fields, and the foreign participation varied in different historical periods. For instance, from 1902 to 1913 the French groups' activity was very intense in comparison with the interwar period. The market presented opportunities to seize, and the investors had to be ready to reform the system in some ways that could improve it, through their investment policies, negotiation methods, the increase of public debt, the development of trade and industry, etc. The banking portfolio and skills included therefore many parameters of analyse, such as the structure of investment, the credit structure, the structure of the monetary circulation, the importance of centralisation of capital, and so on. This analysis is both an analysis of their weight on Bulgarian finances and the identification of their expertise in management.

The investing in Bulgarian securities – related to the renovation in the administration, the creation of railway companies or the foundation of credit companies – implied an involvement on economic, financial and political levels at once. Its analysis leads to examining risks, as well as the possibilities to foster foreign capital into Bulgaria, and to assess the influence of French capital on the development of Bulgarian market.[6] The investments will be into sectors for a more detailed perception of French intervention on Bulgarian market, and to distributing the invested securities invested on French market. Secondly, we will consider the amount of investments, as a way to assess the impact of the groups according to the first method), and lastly the accumulation of Bulgarian public debt (and how regularly the loans were paid off during

5 About the difference between investment banking and commercial banking, see Hubert Bonin & Giandomenico Piluso, "Investment and merchant banking in France and Italy in the long run: Comparing models of corporate financing. Starting a research program", European Business History Association, Copenhagen, 2006, <http://boninhub.free.fr/>.

6 Maurice Lévy-Leboyer, "La balance des paiements et l'exportation des capitaux français", in Maurice Lévy-Leboyer (ed.), *La position internationale de la France, aspects économiques et financiers, XIXe-XXe siècles, op. cit.*, p. 75.

that period. Inevitably, the introduction of capital is linked to politics; each modification in political strategies led to changes in the structures of direct and indirect investments. All that determined the amount of French investments and the choice of tools for intervention. Long-term bank investments were mainly active in lucrative sectors – industry, infrastructure building or public bonds.

1. Means of banking development: Portfolio of skills and strategies

The deep economic and financial transformation in Bulgaria was only achieved after the unification process[7] between Eastern Rumelia and the Principality; a banking system was founded, basic infrastructures were built, economy and industry developed. The start of industrialisation[8] at the end of the 19th century brought about the need to develop credit, but Bulgarian bank market did not have enough credit companies with working capital. This was of great importance for Bulgarian National Bank. It used a policy of short-term credits increase, using the drop in interest rates at first, and then a stable monetary convertibility, in order to reduce investment risks and to gather capital more specialised in financing industrial and trading concerns. However, through the effect of foreign capital, Bulgarian market initiated the creation of a stronger structure and organisation for economic (industrial and trade-related) and banking business. Big foreign banking companies (French *Banque de Paris et des Pays-Bas*-Paribas and *Banque de l'union parisienne*-BUP, or Austrian *Länderbank-Banque des pays autrichiens*) created investment funds that operated in numerous sectors – transportation, trade, credit, mining industry, metal industry, light industry, and even financial reorganisation and public debt financing (through public bonds).[9] On a financial level, the introduction of foreign resources allowed an improvement of industry, which was only financed at a rate of 25 per cent by external capital invested in the foundation of firms.

7 See Charles Serkis, *La Roumélie orientale et la Bulgarie actuelle,* thèse de doctorat, Université de Paris, 1898.

8 See Alexander Gerschenkron, "Some aspects of industrialisation in Bulgaria, 1878-1939", in *Economic Backwardness in Historical Perspective: A Book of Essays*, Cambridge, Massachusetts, The Belknap Press of Harvard University Press, 1962 and 1966.

9 See Éric Bussière, "Banks, economic development and capitalism in France", in Alice Teichova, Ginette Kurgan-van Hentenryk & Dieter Ziegler (eds.), *Banking, Trade, and Industry: Europe, America, and Asia from the Thirteenth to the Twentieth Centuries*, Cambridge, Cambridge University Press, 1997.

A. *The role of French banking competition in the reinforcement of the Bulgarian market at the turn of the 20th century*

Among the countries investing in financial sector, France was one of the first.[10] In consequence, the position of banking groups depended on the local market circumstances. This process developed relationships between the banks and their clients, in our case, the Bulgarian State. In the long term it explained their competitive banking position.[11] The evolution and organisation of the French capital market allowed us to determine the importance of French banks and of their operations on the stock market and the financial market and their policy of internationalisation. The influence of French groups included Bulgarian finance through the organisation of the stock market and financial market by achieving funding for Bulgarian economy in the long term, by investing either indirectly (the issuance and placement of securities), or directly (participation in the capital of financial companies and credit companies). Their portfolio consisted with different types of bonds: industrial securities, the acquisition or concession of railways, public securities quoted to the consolidation of finance, participation of corporate finance, etc.

This was the first level for banking competition: economic and finance backgrounds and the role of banking knowledge determined business culture the banking houses. For instance, the advantage of the process of banking liberalisation and the deployment of financial instruments developed banking competition.[12] French competition included two strategies: intermediation (between French savers, Bulgarian government or credit and industrial companies) and internationalisation of financial knowledge and capital flow.[13] By using intermediation strategies French banks managed a commercial and corporate portfolio. This specialisation determined their competitive status that included three types of activities: money-market operations (operations of short term finances market), corporate finance and investment management (pre-investment activities

---

10 Robert Lengelé, *La Bulgarie économique, ses relations avec la France*, Paris, Jouve, 1921, p. 19.

11 About the banking competition, see Samuel Hayes, Michael Spence & David Van Praag Marks, *Competition in the Investment Banking Industry*, Cambridge, *op. cit.* John Peter Williamson (ed.), *The Investment Banking Handbook*, New York, John Wiley, 1988. Graeme Donald Snooks (ed.), *Historical Analysis in Economics*, London & New York, Routledge, 1993. Daniel Verdier, *Moving Money: Banking and Finance in the Industrialized World*, Cambridge, Cambridge University Press, 2002.

12 See Hennie van Greuning & Sonja Brajovic Bratanovic (eds.), *Analyzing and Managing Banking Risk: A Framework for Assessing Corporate Governance and Financial Risk*, Washington, World Bank, 2003.

13 See Daniel Verdier, *Moving Money. Banking and Finance in the Industrialized World*, *op. cit.*

(projects, studies of economic and political background, dialogues with Bulgarian governments) and investment operations (underwriting operations: issue management capital and Bulgarian corporate and public securities, public subscription of equity securities, finance Bulgarian trade and industry).[14] Thus, in terms of their structure, French investments banks (Paribas, BUP) did not have a large network of branches, as it existed in the system of commercial banks (Société générale or Crédit lyonnais). However, the mechanisms of convergence between investment banks and commercial banks were based on the specificity of their functioning in particular: commercial banks played a role rather between national savings and investment banks than in financing various projects.[15] This mediation was expressed by the participation of commercial groups in banking syndicates. Investment banks, such as Paribas or BUP, by the brokerage of securities, trade finance, industry finance, formed two types of syndicates: he selling group and the underwriting guarantee.

Table 1. Structure of banking activities and portfolio linked with Bulgaria

– *Money-market operations* (operations of short term finance market).
– *Corporate and investment management*: pre-investment activities – projects, studies of economic and political background, dialogues with Bulgarian governments) investment operations – underwriting operations (issue management capital and Bulgarian corporate and public securities, public subscription of equity securities, finance Bulgarian trade and industry.
– *Equities portfolio:* refinancing Treasury bonds or participation in the financing of the central bank or other Bulgarian banks: 5 per cent loan in 1896 for Agricultural Bank, a FRF 25m advance with treasury bills in 1900, the Tobacco company loan in 1902, and then 1904 and 1907, three advances with treasury bills in 1912-1913, and two loans in 1926 and 1928.
– *Industrial portfolio:* finance of industrial companies by participation in the board or financial flows invested in industry and economy (agriculture, mining and forestry, sugar, textiles, construction of infrastructure by BUP, *Société générale*, Paribas, CNEP.
– *Foundation of local banks and credit companies*: creating mortgage companies, deposit and discount banks – *Crédit foncier franco-bulgare* (granting of mortgage credit), *Banque franco-bulgare* (specialised in security trade, advance and industrial investment granting).

Both types of banks took part in the syndicates, investment banks (Paribas, BUP) and commercial banks, of which the activities included the

14 See Robert Raymond, "Money market and monetary policy", in Christian de Boissieu (ed.), *Banking in France*, London & New York, Routledge, 1990.

15 See Hubert Bonin & Giandomenico Piluso, "Investment and merchant banking in France and Italy in the long run: Comparing models of corporate financing. Starting a research program", European Business History Association, Copenhagen, 2006, <http://boninhub.free.fr/>.

banking operation between commercial and investment banking-deposit and loans gatherings (Société générale, Crédit lyonnais).[16] The French banking activities in Bulgaria included also the securities business: deposit and savings banking activity, intermediation in the syndicates (placement and equity issues), participation of corporate and investment managements.[17] Through the relationships between commercial and investment banking,[18] their clients' portfolio included Bulgarian state bonds (1802-1913), shares and voting rights in different credit and banking companies dedicated to Bulgaria (*Crédit foncier franco-bulgare*, *Banque franco-bulgare*), whilst three main banks practiced industrial finance (BUP, Paribas or Société générale).

B. The specialisation of French banks in securities

French investors managed their portfolio by subscribing to public loans. The securities debt was disseminated among the public, which required the intervention of financial groups.[19] Their intervention was the formation of two syndicates in which banks held a well diversified portfolio. The objective was to ensure their investment by facilitating the placement of bonds. Banks carried out the placement of securities by two methods, either *à option*, or *à prise ferme* (optional or pledged). The banks of the underwriting syndicate focused on the underwriting of securities which were not placed on the Paris Bourse at the closing date of public subscription.[20] There were two ways to guarantee the subscription of all shares of the loan: first, each bank came to the conservation of security scheduled to be placed; second, there was a bond not under the system of redistribution, but in banking participation scale in which each bank received a portion of the securities according to its proportion in the syndicate (which was the method practiced by French banks about the Bulgarian loans). The syndicate was organised by a leading investment bank (often Paribas), called also chef de file that met a few banks, still called "sub-participants", in order to ensure the operation

---

16 See Joseph Auerbach & Samuel L. Hayes, *Investment Banking and Diligence: What Price Deregulation?*, Boston, Harvard Business School Press, 1986.

17 See Joseph Auerbach & Samuel Hayes, *Investment Banking and Diligence*, *op. cit.* John Peter Williamson, *The Investment Banking Handbook*, New York, John Wiley & Sons, 1988.

18 See Rondo Cameron & Valery Bovykin (eds.), *International Banking, 1870-1914*, Oxford, Oxford University Press, 1991.

19 About the banking portfolio, the capital flow and financial securities market see Ranald Michie, *The Global Securities Market: A History*, Oxford & New York, Oxford University Press, 2006.

20 See Anjan V. Thakor and Arnoud Boot (eds.) *Handbook of Financial Intermediation and Banking*, Amsterdam & Boston, Elsevier, 2008.

through a set amount, subscription and was guaranteed à prise ferme. In general, the syndicate received a guaranteed underwriting commission which included the costs of security and of issuing securities, and that of management.[21] It might decrease along with the amount of emission. During the operation, the leading institution was compensated by its management. The brokerage fee was the commission on the counter, paid to the banks involved in the syndicate according to their proportion. The leading investment bank, Paribas, disseminated brochures with the conditions of the loans through the banks participating to the project. The relationships between the banks and the Bulgarian government were regulated by the contract of loan between the syndicate and the underwriting agreement.[22] Then each of the participants signed a banking union in order to determine their involvement (an agreement between underwriters). Finally, a settlement in the selling group agreement had to define the relationships between the banks that put the securities.[23]

Investment banks Paribas and BUP balanced short term involvement, with the financing of trade, of the Bulgarian Treasury and foreign exchange, and long-term investment.[24] The deployment of their position abroad required the development of a network of correspondents and relationships, as both were based on the relationships with the Haute Banque,[25] in which at the bottom there were different strategic coalitions, either foreign, or local.[26] The multiplicity of operators had thus to diversify their portfolios of skills and connections: By their position, the banks were inserted into strong relationships with local institutions.

---

21 John Peter Williamson, *The Investment Banking Handbook*, *op. cit.* Aswath Damodaran, *Finance d'entreprise: théorie et pratique*, Brussels, De Boeck, 2004. Alan Morrison and William Wilhelm, *Investment Banking: Institutions, Politics, and Law*, Oxford, Oxford University Press, 2008.

22 Joseph Antoine, Marie-Claire Capiau-Huart, Henri Olivier and Henri Carpentier (eds.), *Titres et Bourse*, Brussels, De Boeck Université, 1997 and 1998.

23 *Idem.*

24 Éric Bussière, "De l'internationalisation à la globalisation: la vocation des banques d'affaires en question", in Michèle Merger, Dominique Barjot & Marie-Noëlle Polino (eds.), *Les entreprises et leurs réseaux: hommes, capitaux, techniques et pouvoirs, XIXe-XXe siècles*, Paris, Presses de l'Université de Paris-Sorbonne, 1998.

25 Rondo Cameron & Valery Bovykin (eds.), *International Banking, 1870-1914*, *op. cit.* Éric Bussière, *Paribas: Europe and the World: 1872-1992*, *op. cit.* Éric Bussière, "De l'internationalisation à la globalisation: la vocation des banques d'affaires en question", in Michèle Merger, Dominique Barjot and Marie-Noëlle Polino (eds.), *Les entreprises*, *op. cit.* Hubert Bonin, *Le Monde des banquiers français au XXe siècle*, *op. cit.*

26 Éric Bussière, "De l'internationalisation à la globalisation: la vocation des banques d'affaires en question", in Michèle Merger, Dominique Barjot & Marie-Noëlle Polino (eds.), *Les entreprises*, *op. cit.*

2. French banks and the financing of the Bulgarian take-off at the turn of the 20th century

Their interests were threefold: the interbanking relationship and partnership, their position with the industrial and commercial companies, their role as intermediaries to service the public debt between French capital market and foreign countries.[27]

A. *The use of French funds in the reinforcement of the Bulgarian banking system*

The emergence of private banks led to a new step in the evolution of the Bulgarian money market, as, until 1902 in Sofia, the Bulgarian National Bank (BNB) exerted a dominant influential activity because the establishment of other banks was not known of. Some banks were created between 1904 and 1906, like *Banque générale de Bulgarie*[28] and *Banque balkanique* – this latter founded in 1906 with capital of LV 1.5m and 15,000 shares of LV 100 each. A harsh bank-related rivalry took shape as elsewhere between France and Germany, at the time of the creation of an institution managed by *Deutsche Bank* in Bulgaria.[29] On its side, *Banque franco-bulgare* specialised in security trade, advances, and industrial investment granting. The Bulgarian market was already well endowed with capital and banking companies; it still needed financial sponsors. This bank was established in Sofia during the first decade of the 20th century with FRF 1m, of which Paribas and its partners brought 60 per cent, and Bulgarian banks 40 per cent.[30] It also had a very important mission, to support the French position in Bulgaria in 1905-1906, especially its commitment to the Balkans' financial world.[31] For their future, big French banking institutions secured the capital and created an investment system on the Bulgarian market. In other terms, creating mortgage companies, deposit and discount banks allowed French capital to prop up its presence on the market – but founding an investment bank controlled by French

27 *Ibidem.*

28 The Bulgaria General Bank was founded in October 1905 with a LV 3m capital (2,400 shares, 1,250 levas each). It brought together French, Hungarian and Austrian interests (*Paribas* and *BUP* with 58 per cent, the Hungarian Trade Bank with 29 per cent, and *Allgemeine Österreichische Boden Kredit Anstalt*). Raising the capital to FRF 50m after WWI increased the French-Hungarian influence. *Economic and Financial Situation of Bulgaria, French-Belgian & Balkan Bank*, Sofia 1927, p. 139.

29 BNP Paribas archives, *Project for the creation of a French-Bulgarian bank*, 15 June 1905, file 11DFOM 221 489.

30 *Idem.*

31 *See* Éric Bussière, *Paribas: Europe and the World: 1872-1992*, *op. cit.* John Lampe and Marvin Jackson, *Balkan Economic History, 1550-1950: From Imperial Borderlands to Developing Nations*, Indiana University Press, 1982.

cash also stimulated French initiatives in the industrial world,[32] in which banks could get more interest.

The foreign groups' position was exemplified by two basic characteristics. First, the French banks participated to the boards of directors of the banks or credit companies; second, private Bulgarian banks[33] (*Bulcombank*, *Ghirdap*) collaborated or did business with French banks (Paribas, Crédit lyonnais, Bup or Cnep-Comptoir national d'escompte de Paris). Consequently, there were some projects and means of establishing banking organisms in Bulgaria – as investment bank subsidiaries, as limited partnerships (often run by Paribas or Bup), or as joint-stock limited companies, the capital merger of which was most efficient at generating investments. Investment banks tried to increase their power by appointing worthy, well-known people, in positions of responsibility, so that they surmounted market risks due to their past experience and personal merit (mostly intelligence and ambition).[34]

Until 1906, 34 banks were present on the Bulgarian market, with a cumulated capital of LV 20m and an amount of credit of LV 8.35m.[35] In this respect, foreign capital inflow was a way for Bulgaria to access European financial relations on a larger scale. Change in the trade sector allowed to broaden the scope of banking operations and thus to speed up capital circulation linked to the building of a large network of credit companies. In 1915 there were 71 banks with a capital of LV 81.4m.[36] The stagnation on Bulgarian money market from 1906 to 1910 reduced the foreign fund inflow, but in 1910-1912 a new wave of investments appeared in banks with four credit companies and in industry with four new sugar factories. The foreign capital reached LV 270m in 1900 and LV 731m[37] in 1911, among which 15m were invested in banking companies, 15m in

32 See Eric Bussière, "Banks, economic development and capitalism in France" in Alice Teichova, Ginette Kurgan-van Hentenryk & Dieter Ziegler (eds.), *Banking, Trade, and Industry: Europe, America, and Asia from the Thirteenth to the Twentieth Century*, Cambridge, Cambridge University Press, 1997.

33 See Alexandre Kostov, "La Banque bulgare de commerce (1895-1947): créateurs et leurs successeurs", in Kostas Kostis (ed.) *The Creators and the Creation of Banking Entreprises in Europe from the 18th to the 20th Century*, Athens, Alpha Bank, Historical Archives, 2002.

34 BNP Paribas archives, Project for the creation of a French-Bulgarian bank, 15 June 1905, file 11 DFOM 221 489.

35 *Jubilee Record of the Bulgaria National Bank, 1879-1929*, Sofia, State Press, 1929, p. 99, Nikola Lazarov, *A History of the Bulgaria National Bank and of Banking Activity in Bulgaria*, Sofia, Siela, 2007, p. 237.

36 *Economic and Financial Situation of Bulgaria, French-Belgian & Balkan Bank*, Sofia 1927.

37 Kiril Popov, *Economic Bulgaria, Statistical Studies*, Sofia, State Press, 1916, p. 399.

individual concerns, and 1m in trading companies.[38] Belgian investors concentrated their capital in industry and French ones in banking, along with Austrian and German capital. Three-fifths of the public debt were negotiated with French groups. Just before the First Balkan War, foreign investments amounted to LV 219m, among which 98m went to banking sector, 74m to industry, and 36m to trade.[39]

The presence and leading role of French banks was favourable for the expansion of the influence of the Paris place. They had an integrating and leading role, and helped bring together more quickly banking, industry and trade capital, which led to more trade, budget deficit recovery, credit and bank activity standardisation. French groups had defined a clear policy: to raise and invest capital in countries such as Bulgaria, they contributed to Eastern European modernisation and overall trade liberalisation. They wanted to keep up to their reputation of influential institutions that exerted authority to manage their portfolios and to guarantee safety to their funds, which was a way of adding value to their investments. Collaborating with 'friendly' banks was a way of entertaining the positive image of investment banks that knew how to develop their organisational capacities and to capitalise on their funds.[40] Part of the securities from the 'friendly' banks were retroceded to partners: for instance, for the modernisation of the Bulgarian financial system, Société générale cooperated with Paribas, Crédit lyonnais and CNEP.

More generally, investment banks (Paribas, BUP) gradually applied their policies and strategies, as well as their investment funds. Supporting the development of the Balkan region in order to reinforce French economic and political power was part of the objectives of the French Ministry of Foreign Affairs, which led to two main directions: on one hand, the political goal[41] of the French government was to gain greater influence in the Balkans; on the other hand, France had to invest in a greater economic and financial transformation of emerging countries.[42]

---

38 *Idem.*

39 Dimitar Simidtchiev, *Foreign Capital in National Economy and their Profitability*, Sofia, Miladinovi Brothers Press, 1928.

40 See Hubert Bonin, *Le monde des banquiers*, *op. cit.*

41 About the political influence and strategies in banking investments see Youssef Cassis, "Introduction: The weight of finance in European societies", in Youssef Cassis (ed.), *Finance & Financiers in European History (1880-1960)*, Cambridge and Paris, Cambridge University Press-Éditions de la Maison des sciences de l'homme, 1991.

42 Louis Léger, *Le panslavisme et l'intérêt français*, Paris, Flammarion, 1917. R. Lengelé, *La Bulgarie économique, ses relations avec la France*, *op. cit.* Raymond Poidevin, *Finances et relations internationales, 1887-1914*, Paris, Armand Colin, 1970. René Girault, *Diplomatie européenne, nations et impérialismes, 1871-1914*, Paris, Armand Colin, 1997.

B. The impact of French groups on the economic and industrial development of Bulgaria

The expansion of trade depended on trade agreements between nations in the first place, and on the improvement of infrastructures in the second place (especially between the Black Sea Bulgarian harbours and the Danube scales). The growth of economic and industrial market depends on the level of development of financial sector.[43] In this context, the policy of bank internationalisation has two methods of introduction through the financial flows invested in industry and economy (agriculture, mining and forestry, sugar, textiles, construction of infrastructure by BUP, Société générale, Paribas, CNEP), or investments in financial companies and credit insurance – corporate and housing investment (by Société générale and Paribas). The policy of bank financial intermediation included the flow of funds from the accumulation of savings (by commercial banks) for granting government loans (investment securities) and financial saving to fuel investments into economic and industrial sectors.[44] A less developed country's banking system is based mainly on the banks of deposit and discount and on some small banks that are not able to ensure "capital flow" of the economy with stability and enough scope. According to Gerschenkron's theory,[45] the various stages of financial and economic development explain that a lagging economy affect the shape of commercial and investment banks, but can be influenced by the regulations of the State.[46] Market conditions predispose economic development and financial separation of commercial banks and investment banks, even if a government tries to structure and regulate the system. The concentration of deposits depended on Bulgaria's economic situation, which evolved as elsewhere when more people started saving, thus fostering a layer of deposits at banks. The objective was to favour trade by financing infrastructures thanks to the Budget availabilities, but mainly thanks to foreign

---

43 About the relation between the financial market and economic growth, see Richard Sylla & Gianni Toniolo (eds.), *Patterns of European Industrialization: the Nineteenth Century*, London & New York, Fondazione Adriano Olivetti, 1995. Richard Sylla, Richard Tilly & Gabriel Tortella (eds.), *The State, the Financial System and Economic Modernization*, Cambridge, Cambridge University Press, 1999. Michel Lescure, "Banking and Finance", in Geoffrey Jones & Jonathan Zeitlin (eds.), *The Oxford Handbook of Business History*, Oxford, Oxford University Press, 2008.

44 See Michel Lescure, "Banking and Finance" in Geoffrey Jones and Jonathan Zeitlin (eds.), *The Oxford Handbook of Business History*, *op. cit.* Samuel Hayes, Michael Spence & David Van Praag Marks, *Competition in the Investment Banking Industry*, Cambridge, Harvard University Press, 1983.

45 See Douglas Forsyth & Daniel Verdier, *The Origins of National Financial Systems. Alexander Gerschenkron reconsidered*, London, Routledge, 2003.

46 *Idem.*

loans and credits, thus the growth of the relations between Bulgarian government and European banks.

From the 1890s new agreements based on the system of the most favoured nation led to reciprocal concessions with Bulgaria's trading partners. The French participation[47] in Bulgarian importations rose steadily from FRF 3,784m in 1886 to 4,311m in 1898. The intensification of trade contributed to the reinforcement of the agreements between European countries in the context of industrial investments. During the taking-off of Bulgarian industry, close relations between Bulgaria and western countries commenced due to beer factories in Sofia in 1884, then in Sliven in 1887, and in Gorna Oriahovica in 1892 (with Czech capital),[48] five sugar factories (with Belgian and French capital), two cotton factories, and two woollen textile factories (with English capital). The flow of French capital also went to forestry with an investment amounting to FRF 2.7m, mining with 3.7m, and sugar industry with about FRF 10m.[49] During the first decade of the 20th century, the growth of Bulgarian industrial sectors notably depended on French companies which invested FRF 2.7m in forestry and FRF 3.7m in mining, and the sugar factories in Plovdiv and Svoge received FRF 10m.[50] France and Belgium took a leading part in financing Bulgarian industry: *Société belge des tramways électriques* in Sofia (a capital of FRF 1.75m) merged with an affiliate of *Compagnie française des grands travaux* from Marseille, which provided lighting in Sofia (with a capital of FRF 3.5m).[51] The amount of industry and trade investments in the first half of the 20th century shows the great capacity of French capital to secure its presence in Bulgaria: it invested FRF 34.4m francs while Belgium invested FRF 21.35m, Great Britain 3.54m and Italy 6m.

Before 1900 various industrial companies were founded with French capital[52] like Prince Boris, a company exploiting coal in Trevnen and match factories in Kostenec. Various groups took footholds on the industrial investment market developing their activity from studies and analyses on growth perspectives. Various newly created industrial companies

47 BNP Paribas archives, Economic Europe, principality of Bulgaria and East Rumelia, 1901, 4\Cabet-1\117.

48 See Jacques Natan, *Bulgarian Economic History after the Independence*, Sofia, 1938, Nikola Lazarov, *A History of the Bulgaria National Bank and of Banking Activity in Bulgaria, op. cit.*

49 Robert Lengelé, *La Bulgarie économique, ses relations avec la France, op. cit.*, p. 20.

50 *Idem*. See Raymond Poidevin, *Finances et relations internationales, 1887-1914*, Paris, Armand Colin, 1970. Raymond Poidevin, *Diplomatie européenne, nations et imperialisms, 1871-1914*, Paris, Armand Colin, 1997.

51 Robert Lengelé, *La Bulgarie économique, op. cit.*, p. 20.

52 Dimitar Simidtchiev, *Foreign Capital in the Bulgarian Economy and Their Profitability, op. cit.*

studied the possibility to exploit and export black coal. Paribas prepared investments in the coal-mining industry: The carboniferous areas were analysed in order to be exploited. Some coal galleries expanded around Sofia, Kostinbrod, and Svoge, to try and reduce importing foreign coal.[53] The main coal supplier for domestic needs was the mine in Pernik; its very development depended on the improvement of the railway network, part of which was financed by Paribas, Société générale or CNEP. Nevertheless, the formation of industrial capital was not as important as the resources used for founding credit companies and banks, for which the advantage lied on the side of France.

According to the sources of the French Ministry of Foreign Affairs, French capital in 1902 was geographically distributed as follows:[54] Russia was endowed with FRF 6,966 billion, Romania with FRF 438m, Serbia with 201m, Greece with 283m, European Turkey with FRF 1,818 billion, making a total of 21,012b invested in Europe, against which Bulgaria stood far behind with only FRF 48m[55] in industry, trade, participation of big French banks in the launching of concerns or credit companies, and Bulgarian public bonds. After 1902, the intensity of French investments increased gradually and their role in the economic and financial development of Bulgaria became more pronounced – in 1908, French investments rose to FRF 300m in total.[56]

3. The role of French groups in the investment of Bulgarian loans, 1896-1928

Two key elements characterise the context of the expansion of French groups in Bulgaria. The first one is political, as the treaty of Berlin (14 July 1878) made it easier for Western countries to participate in the period of emergence for new Balkan countries. The second one is financial, as the main purpose was to introduce foreign capital (frequently through government bonds) and to take the risk of investing in securities. French intermediaries held a leading role in Bulgarian economy and finances, which accounted for the fact that the deposit and discount bank became a brokerage and a world-wide scale investment bank. Commercial banks took part in financing the Bulgarian market, in the midst of fear of political and economic instability and fragility, and the prospects of a still partially developed market. The development had direct, long-term influence on Bulgarian finance:

53 BNP Paribas archives, file 4 Cabet-1/102.

54 Émile Becqué, *L'internationalisation des capitaux*, doctoral thesis, Montpellier, 1912, p. 64, from the 1902 official inquiry of the French Ministry of Foreign Affairs, p. 64.

55 *Ibidem.*

56 *Ibidem*, p. 93.

a 5 per cent loan in 1896 for Agricultural Banks, a FRF 25m advance on treasury bills in 1900, a Tobacco company loan in 1902, and then two others in 1904 and 1907, three advances on treasury bills in 1912-1913, and two state loans in 1926 and 1928. French banks investment policy seemed rather open-minded, and its developments were sometimes based on competitiveness or cooperation with German or Austrian banks, alongside the opportunities and circumstances.

The strong presence held on this "niche" market was a result of their investment portfolio with their equity funds. During the industrial and financial consolidation, the introduction of French investment increased and the banking portfolio amplified. Despite the limits of the scope of Bulgarian development and the competition within big banking business, French banks relied on their capital experience, built on several bigger markets, and on their domestic networks enabling them to collect savings and thus cash for action abroad, and they rushed to conquer strong positions on the market of foreign state loans to be listed on the Paris Bourse.[57] The Bulgarian bond issues, taken in gold *levas*, were invested on various Stock Exchanges in Europe: Paris, London, Amsterdam, Zurich, Vienna, Berlin and Sofia. Each bank's profitability was assessed by a syndicate in charge of intermediating between the banks and the government in order to make sure that the business was running smoothly. The mission of French banks was clear: they invested securities and managed the security holders network (their sub-participants). The competitive edge of Paris Bourse[58] depended on its efficiency to resist crises, the terms of the external loans (interest rate, ceasing rate, commissions, charges),[59] and ability to favour coordination between bankers to facilitate their intermediation with governments.[60]

Bulgarian government bonds were a perfect example of such intermediation. They were all long-term bonds (for periods of 50 to 60 years, very often with FRF 500 notes and with a rather low interest rate – 4 to 6 per cent, which reduced the price of the capital and, of course, made benefits less profitable). They also concerned granting massive resources with strong guarantees: the bonds were invested among the public or on the Stock Exchange. The collateral system for bonds started in 1902 with the tobacco monopoly guarantee, and afterwards in 1904 and 1907 – with

57 Youssef Cassis, *Les capitales du capital*, *op. cit.*, p. 148.

58 *Ibidem*.

59 *Idem*. See also Youssef Cassis, *London and Paris as International Financial Centres in The Twentieth Century*, *op. cit.* About the banking risk, Hennie van Greuning & Sonja Brajovic Bratanovic (eds.), *Analyzing and Managing Banking Risk: A Framework for Assessing Corporate Governance and Financial Risk*, Washington, World Bank, 2003.

60 Youssef Cassis, *Les capitales du capital*, *op. cit.* See also: Pierre-Cyrille Hautcoeur (ed.), *Le marché financier français au XIXe siècle*, Paris, Publications de la Sorbonne, 2007.

customs duty or stamp monopoly. The granting technique conditions set very high interest rates, very low issuing cost and transferring cost for securities, high commissions, short-term redemption. All that led to a lower real transferring cost and a higher issuing effective interest rate, which introduced a negative idea of debt.[61] The banks tried to get a good difference between the interest rate of issued and invested securities and the profitability rate, as their intermediation bonus, which was submitted to market conditions, with circular letters based on studies about the political and economic situation of the country and its the assets influencing the value of securities.

The diversity of financial tools seemed safe enough to the negotiators who took the risk of competition. The main drawback was the search for profitable securities. Calculating the risks (interest rate risk and liquidity risk)[62] allowed to gauge their commitments on the market, with bought deals or options. Banks were innovative as they aimed at finding new types of credit companies and at favouring finance and economy in order to raise the number of savers and borrowers; they were also inspiring and incentive as they meant profit, institutional prestige or national well-ranking. The risks for investors[63] were the rise of interest rates, because of the accumulation of public debt, and the difficulties in refunding public debt, associated with the state policy regarding war financing or creditor activity paralysis. But, through the diversification of their portfolio, the evolution of international market and the mixture of financial instruments, banking groups increased the opportunities of Bulgaria to get access to foreign funds,[64] even if such developments could be perceived as the extension of some kinds of French economic and financial imperialism.[65]

Within the overall historical framework, a transition towards self-sufficiency and reinforcing Bulgarian finances were the main objective for the governments that negotiated the 1892, 1896, 1902, 1904, 1907, 1912-1913 and 1928 loans, which French banking groups are involved in.

---

61 See Jean Andreau, Gérard Béaur & Jean-Yves Grenier (eds.), *La dette publique dans l'histoire*, Paris, Comité pour l'histoire économique et financière de la France, 2006.

62 Hennie van Greuning & Sonja Brajovic Bratanovic (eds.), *Analyzing and Managing Banking Risk*, *op. cit.*

63 About the interest rate and liquidity risk, see Xavier Freixas & Jean-Charles Rochet, *Microeconomics of Banking*, Cambridge, MIT Press, 1997.

64 Hennie van Greuning & Sonja Brajovic Bratanovic, *Analyzing and Managing Banking Risk: A Framework for Assessing Corporate Governance and Financial Risk*, Washington, World Bank, 2003.

65 Jean Bouvier & René Girault (eds.), *L'impérialisme français d'avant 1914*, Paris, Mouton, 1979. Jacques Thobie, *La France impériale, 1880-1914*, Paris, Mégrelis, 1982. Jean Bouvier, René Girault & Jacques Thobie (eds.), *L'impérialisme à la française*, Paris, La Découverte, 1986.

They carried on their activities in Bulgaria with a pioneering participation to bank consortiums – German, then Austrian-French, and then properly French – from the beginning of the 20th century. International collaboration was in the first place a diplomatic step – after important negotiations bank-to-bank relations formed through capital merger. Such cooperation was a way to centralise the various parts of the operations in order to protect their position or to make various alliances. Relations of that type occurred for the granting of the 1892 loan, of Treasury bonds of the 1899, and of the FRF 2m credit in favour of BNB in 1899. The syndicate[66] set up for the 6 per cent loan in 1892 gathered Paribas (with 12.61 per cent), *Banque internationale de Paris* (with 26.29 per cent), Länderbank (21.80 per cent) and the German group (36.30 per cent) and BNB (3 per cent).

A consortium of banks, with Länderbank heading it, negotiated the LV 142.8m loan, and invested the securities on the Vienna, Paris, Berlin, London Stock Exchanges; they went to building railways building as well as to the Varna and Bourgas harbours. The agreement between Paribas and Société générale (by investing securities on the Paris Bourse), *Breslauer Diskonto Bank* (by issuing and investing securities on the Berlin Stock Exchange) and the Henry Schröder house[67] of London (which had interacted a lot with Société générale since the 1870s on the Latin American loans,[68] investing Bulgarian securities on the English market) implied six option operations during a five-year period secured by mortgage. Option rights were part of the terms of the contract: creditor banks bought a part of the bonds with fixed term and ceasing rate, against an instant premium.

The banks invested in bonds and hold portfolios packed with international securities – the more their portfolio was diversified, the more they increased their profitability. The real challenge on the market was trying and understanding its current trend while negotiating and buying securities in order to identify the risks before acting. The same mechanism was at stake during the 5 per cent loan in 1896 (financing Agricultural bank): Länderbank-Banque des pays autrichiens,[69] Banque internationale de Paris and Paribas sought strong security for their investment, which is the yield of the agricultural banks. Two groups formed – Paribas, Länderbank and Banque internationale de Paris, on one side, and Crédit lyonnais, on the other. A so called "protectorate" was created in order to establish control on loan collaterals. A Committee was in charge of directing the

66 BNP Paribas archives, Bulgarian Syndicate 6 per cent, 1892, file 4\Cabet-1\101.

67 See Richard Roberts, *Schröder: Merchants & Bankers*, London, MacMillan, 1992.

68 Hubert Bonin, *La Société générale en Grande-Bretagne*, Paris, Mission Histoire, Société générale, 1996.

69 See Bernard Michel, *Banques et banquiers en Autriche au début du XXe siècle*, Paris, Presses de la Fondation nationale des sciences politiques, 1976.

operations. In accordance with clauses it carried on the bought deals of FRF 10 and 15m, granting part of both those advances to French banks in 1896.

The negotiations organised during the issuing of treasury bills in 1899 (amounting to FRF 30m) showed a third occurrence of syndicate cooperation between banking groups – the French-Austrian banks participated with up to 62.5 per cent (Paribas, Banque internationale de Paris, Länderbank) and the German group, reaching 37.5 per cent (Deutsche Bank, Berlin Wiener Bankverein, Vienne Mitteldeutsche Creditbank, Deutsche Vereinbank).[70] The loan was collateralised with tobacco contributions and the Principality revenue. It was divided into two parts with an underwritten rate of 89 per cent and an advance of FRF 25m. Both groups (German with FRF 9.4m and French with FRF 15.6 m) collaborated to come to an agreement concerning the advance.[71] Almost the same consortium intervened for the 1899 loan of FRF 2m, granted to BNB: Banque internationale de Paris, Paribas, Länderbank, Deutsche Bank et Wiener Bankverein with a FRF 400,000 standard proportional share for each one.[72] They had to convert the 6 per cent securities of 1888, 1889 and 1892, which helped rubbing off a pile of Bulgarian bills that could have exerted a negative influence on the parity; it also diversified more the banks' portfolios, and it meant less risks for the government. Another purpose was paying off the floating debt and building railways for an amount of FRF 260m divided into 520,000 bonds with an option price of 89.5 per cent. The banks' investments were guaranteed by the Principality revenue, the receipts from railway exploitation and mortgage on some railway lines.[73]

There were three clear transformation phases in the French banks presence corresponding to three different periods. The first period (up to the 1900s) saw arbitrage between the German and Austrian interests, on one side, and the French interests, on the other. During that first step the intervention of French capital in Bulgarian finances reached FRF 110.5m in 1900 for the securities invested on the Paris Stock Exchange[74] (Banque internationale de Paris was the head of a consortium of seven French, German and Austrian banks – Paribas and Länderbank).[75] The second period (from 1902 to 1913) was a very intense one marked by the context

70 BNP Paribas archives, Treasury bonds 6 per cent 1899, file ET 1314.

71 *Ibidem.*

72 *Ibidem.* A FRF 2m credit is opened at Bulgaria National Bank.

73 *Ibidem.*

74 Simeon Damianov, *L'introduction économique de la France en Bulgarie, de la Libération à la Première guerre mondiale* (*1878-1914*), Sofia, Éditions de l'Académie des sciences bulgares, 1971, p. 120.

75 Société générale archives, Bulgarian Affairs, Scales, B 7491.

of growing French-Bulgarian relations; the evolution of the relations between the French groups and the Bulgarian government was noticeable. The third period was marked by the return of German influence, favoured by WWI; then the 1920s opened a new opportunity to the French banking houses to take part in Bulgarian economy, which was sustained by the monetary stabilisation loan in 1928.

The loans concerning budget stabilisation and army reorganisation (1902-1904) are made under the direction of the Paribas. In 1902 Société générale, Banque impériale russe, BNB and the Bulgarian Agricultural Banks contributed to the loan with the security of a monopoly on tobacco, named "Mourourié". The total loan amounted to FRF 106m in securities, with an annual interest rate of 5 per cent. It was redeemable within a period of 50 years, and the idea was to remedy to the monetary and financial situation of the state, as well as to buy back the 1900 treasury bills and pay off the external public debt. A syndicate in Paris, at the Paribas headquarters, was in charge of looking over the collateral securities (tobacco rights) attributed to the loan. It was called Établissement des délégués des porteurs de titres bulgares (Institution of the Bulgarian bond-holders representatives), and its members represented the bondholders. A subscription was launched in St Petersburg by Banque impériale russe and Paris by Paribas, Société générale, Banque impériale ottomane, Banque française pour le commerce & l'industrie, Société marseillaise de crédit and Länderbank.

The same banking circle – Paribas (as lead manager), CNEP, Société générale, Francibank, Banque ottomane, BFCI, BUP, Société marseillaise, Länderbank – managed the capital engaged in the 1904 loan guaranteed with customs revenue. In the established relations, a convergence was led by a creative spirit. CNEP followed the development of an establishment of bank-only operations, Paribas was meant to follow international affairs, and Société générale filled up the space between them two – it kept its profile of deposit and investment bank, an authority increasing with the amount of deposits. Granting the loan essentially meant a large program of development for industry (economic aspect) and greatly helps to redeem internal debt (financial aspect). The Parisian intermediaries took part of investment counters and security subscription, and held a portfolio of Bulgarian securities – part of the 1902 Tobacco loan coupons and 1904 bonds. Their characteristics were the importance of fixed benefits and the variable interests for various investment periods. The objective was to have an even more diversified portfolio so as to increase their activity and to generate a profit as well.

The economic and financial aspects of the 1907 loan comprised of a program of liberalising trade so as to increase exportations, the instauration of a legislation for mortgage and craft industry credit organised by Crédit foncier de France as an incentive for credit relations and economical and industrial development. What was implemented by the French consortium (Paribas, Société générale, CNEP, BUP, Länderbank, BFCI, Société marseillaise) was a financing programme that included three "reserves" – 50,000 bonds to convert the 1888 and 1889 loans securities, 31,000 bonds to "distribute subscriptions" and 209,000 bonds divided up among the banking houses. The French banks had a definite policy – the consortium was involved in the amount of lending securities (the tobacco monopoly-Mourourié-surplus and the stamps unused for the preceding loans), the interests on the securities (4.5 per cent), the negotiations for the issuing rate and for investing the bonds (ceasing rate of 85 per cent), amortisable within a period of sixty years by six-monthly drawings. A more direct intervention was that of a syndicate represented by the bondholders' representative:[76] a commission with three members designated especially by the French minister of Finance was established. The organisational structure of the syndicate accounted for the specific loan conditions. It was integrated into the granting process and it first needed to dilute risks, and then to be a control tool over the drawings on collaterals. The relations were based on three underwritten investments, and value was added by the participation of Société générale, CNEP and Paribas (which took up a centralising position in business operations).[77] Some other banks joined the consortium – BUP, BFCI or Länderbank.

The various means of increasing the banks' participation resided in the nominal value (security value at issuing time) of their portfolio to assess the investment level by comparing it with the market value, very often expressed by their yearly profit in relation to the registered securities, which were a useful assessment, as they reflected profits related to issuing and ceasing rates. The amount of profit was a minor indication of founding a small group of investors; as far as public bonds or government stocks were concerned, they essentially depended on the financial level of the country. The French banks, headed by Paribas, were willing to act as intermediaries, pending favourable political conditions to carry out a liquidation loan. They granted thus three security advances to the Bulgarian Treasury[78] – a FRF 25m advance in June 1912, a 40m one in November 1912, and a 10m one in May 1913. That participation revealed the coordination between various financial institutions, which highlighted the role played by French banks as well as their impact on Bulgarian market. Paribas, which had to centralise bill investments on behalf of the

---

[76] George Bousquet is the representative during the 1902, 1904 and 1907 loans.

[77] Société générale archives, Bulgarian Loan 4½ per cent 1907, file: B 2644.

[78] Société générale archives, Bulgarian Affaires, Scales, file B 7491, BNP Paribas archives, Treasury bonds 1912-1913, file 4\Cabet-1\92.

banking group, undertook to approach the bondholders and to negotiate with Bulgarian government. Société générale and CNEP committed themselves to investing bonds on the French market and then to managing a group of sub-participants.[79] The contract enhanced two objectives, reinforcing BNB's gold resources and buying 1892 Bulgarian securities on the Vienna Stock Exchange, and repaying the expenses (LV 7m) made by the Bulgarian government for the Schneider factories weaponry supplies.[80]

After WWI, the expansion of diplomatic and financial relations with French banking houses was under the good care of the Inter-Allied Commission – the repayment of the Bulgarian debt (FRF 75m in treasury bills 1912-1913) was planned under its authority – and of the League of Nations, which concentrated Bulgarian and European interests by negotiating Bulgarian finances reorganisations around 1928. The result of the dialogue between Bulgarian government and the defence committees of the French holders of Bulgarian securities was the agreement of 23 June 1925 (based on the plan prepared during the London conference in November 1924). It set repayment conditions for Bulgarian bonds concerning the loans preceding WWI.

The French committees (formed with the National Association of French stock and shareholders – *Association nationale des porteurs français de valeurs mobilières*) had been negotiating since December 1923 agreeing with the Dutch (formed with the Dutch Stock Exchange) and English (formed with the Council of Foreign Bondholders) committees. They aimed at suspending the amortisation drawings as well as issuing coupons in French francs, sterling pounds and florins in order to buy more easily securities on the various stock exchanges. In their capacity of establishments involved in the investment of securities on the Paris Stock Exchange, the French banks were to give out information on the payment of coupons concerning the loans of 1896 (Paribas, CNEP, Société générale, Banque nationale de crédit), of 1902 (Paribas, Société générale, Banque nationale de crédit, Banque ottomane, Société marseillaise), of 1904 (Paribas, Société générale, CNEP, Banque nationale de crédit, BUP, Société marseillaise, Banque ottomane), and of 1907 (Paribas, Société générale, CNEP, BUP, Banque nationale de crédit, Société marseillaise).

In 1928 the League of Nations accepted Bulgarian government's request for a loan. The agreement of 10 March 1928 set the clauses to what is known Bulgarian financial history as the stabilising loan. The loan conditions were approved by the representatives of the Financial

79 *Idem.*

80 See Agnès d'Angio, "Schneider & Cie et l'effort de la guerre de la Bulgarie, 1897-1914", *Études balkaniques*, No. 2-3, 2001 (<http://www.ceeol.com>).

Committee of the League of Nations. The amount was £4.5m – £1.8m in securities invested by British, Dutch and Czechoslovakian banks, $13m issued in the United States, Italy and Belgium. France committed itself to subscribe FRF 130m. The presence of French capital, gathered by Paribas and BUP (Paribas, BUP, CNEP, *Société générale*, *Crédit lyonnais* and *Crédit mobilier français*), suggested an financial organisation for intermediation to reach some profits through the Financial Committee stabilisation project.

Table 2. Bulgarian State bonds issued on the Paris Bourse or Stock exchanges of allied countries and their circulation in 1913: Amount of loans in circulation in 1913 (FRF million)

Loan 6 per cent 1892 (French Austrian group) quoted in London	78.9
Loan 5 per cent 1902 (French group) quoted in Paris	99.4
Loan 5 per cent 1904 (French group) quoted in Paris	95.5
Loan 4 ½ per cent 1907 (French group) quoted in London and Paris	142
Loan 4 ½ per cent 1909 (Austrian group) quoted in London	97.9
Treasury bonds 1912-1913 (Paribas) quoted in Paris	75
(*Banque russo-asiatique*) quoted in Paris	25
	Total: FRF 643m

Source: BNP Paribas archives, Bulgarian debt, file Bulgaria, 4\Cabet-1\101.

4. The commitment of French groups in financing the Bulgarian money market (1912-1930)

Before the Balkan Wars, the French position in Bulgaria was based on strong collaboration, with the granting of public loans. However, from the 1910s there is an increase in direct investments in French-Bulgarian limited liability companies as well as in the trade sector. Between 1892 and 1913, foreign securities issued on the French market amounted to FRF 24m, as compared to French securities (FRF 26 billion).[81] Just before WWI, stock and share capitalisation on the Paris Stock Exchange amounted to about FRF 150b, more than half of which were foreign.[82] Before Bulgaria

[81] Georges Gallais-Homonno & Pierre-Cyrille Hautcoeur (eds.), *Le marché financier français au XIXe siècle*, *op. cit.* p. 11.

[82] *Idem.*

entered WWI, the French contribution on the Bulgarian market, more precisely in 1914, had amounted to LV 512m, 470.5m of which were the proportional share of French capital, invested as public bonds.[83]

The structure of Bulgarian market during the period of the Balkan Wars allowed two more foreign banks to appear, with a strong participation from the French groups. They were Banque générale de Bulgarie[84] as the initiator of Crédit foncier franco-bulgare and Banque hypothécaire, which stopped functioning shortly after that, and the Balkan Bank (that included a great Austro-Hungarian part during the Balkan Wars). Some foreign banks founded before the WWI got involved in financing cereal and tobacco trade, creating concerns and industrial companies that developed their activities mainly during the war periods. The foundation project for Crédit foncier franco-bulgare planned to finance those sectors, especially with the birth of *Société balkanique d'entreprises générales*, whose headquarters were in Sofia and to the FRF 2m capital of which Société générale participated for 15 per cent;[85] 50 per cent came from the French group (BUP, Société générale and Banque d'outre-mer), 50 per cent from the Belgium group (Société générale de Belgique), among which 10 per cent were retroceded by the Bulgarian group (Banque balkanique). It was founded in 1913 to play an essential part on mortgage market, with the idea of studying the evolution of industrialisation in that part of Europe, of performing financial and credit operations and doing commercial and industrial research.[86]

The foundation of Crédit foncier franco-bulgare was the major destination of French-Belgian capital. It was a mortgage institution, even it could also serve manufacturers who needed an intermediation company. It was born in January 1912, through merging capital (amounting to FRF 12m)[87] from the Bulgarian Syndicate (in Brussels) and Crédit foncier de Bulgarie.[88] The limited liability status promoted mortgage operations and investments on the local and foreign markets, "buying, subscribing,

83 Vasil Vasilev, "Le commerce franco-bulgare pendant les dix ans qui ont suivi la Première Guerre mondiale", in *La France et les Balkans dans les années 1920*, Paris, Centre d'étude des civilisations de l'Europe centrale et du Sud-Est, 1983, p. 121-138.

84 See Assen Tchakalov, *Formes, ampleurs et l'activité du capital étranger en Bulgarie, 1878-1944*, Sofia, p. 58, Vasil Vasilev, "Le commerce franco-bulgare pendant les dix ans qui ont suivi la Première Guerre mondiale", in *La France et les Balkans dans les années 1920*, *op. cit.*, p. 121.

85 Société générale archives, Various Affairs, *Société balkanique d'entreprise générale*, Sofia, 23 septembre 1913, B 2892; Exposé, January 1913, file B 3333.

86 *Ibidem*.

87 Paribas archives, Basis suggested for the merger between two Bulgarian groups, file Bulgaria, 1910-1939.

88 Paribas archives, Board of Directors, Minutes from 25 April 1912, 4\Cabet-1\132.

discounting, accepting all stocks and shares underwritten by mortgage". A second capital merger occurred between Crédit foncier bulgare (constituted in December 1910 by Société générale with a capital of FRF 5m) and Banque hypothécaire de Royaume de Bulgarie.[89] The concentration of funds came from Société française de banque et de dépôts,[90] Banque balkanique, Banque d'outre-mer, Thalmann & Cie (Paris), and E. Paniza Frères (Vienna).

On Budapest Trade Bank[91] manager Philippe Weiss' initiative, Banque hongroise de commerce de Budapest achieved the foundation of the Banque hypothécaire du Royaume de Bulgarie in 1911 with the capital of LV 10m.[92] An institution was to integrate the capital from Crédit foncier de Bulgarie and the international consortium; the merger with the Budapest Bank, resulting in the foundation of Crédit foncier franco-bulgare exemplified the large amounts necessary to make the Bulgarian real estate market more active,[93] all the more because the country was predominantly dependant on its rural and agricultural evolution to fuel its growth and savings. The ambitions corresponded to the requirement that "the Banque hypothécaire should be the first and most powerful real estate institution in the country",[94] with "a larger base and meriting more credit"[95] owing to its founders, the big banks. The project initiators were[96] Weiss (director of Banque commerciale hongroise de Budapest) and E. Chevrant (director of Paribas), George Bousquet (representative of Paribas), Vladislav Polakovitch (director of Banque générale de Bulgarie), G. Goubidelnikov (director of Banque commerciale de Bulgarie), G. Teodorov (director of Compagnie d'assurance Bulgaria), Victor Veil, director of Banque internationale de Bruxelles, and Paul Wallich (director of Berliner HandelsGesellschaft).

Thanks to the new institutional framework, a project for a new society was set up. The result was the instauration of the National Land Bank for the Bulgarian kingdom, with a capital of FRF 10m and 16,000

89 Paribas archives, Basis suggested for the merger between two Bulgarian groups, file Bulgaria, 1910-1939.

90 *Société française de banque et de dépôts* was *Société générale* subsidiary in Belgium.

91 The Trade Bank together with Paribas found the General Bank in 1905.

92 Paribas archives, Basis suggested for the merger between two Bulgarian groups, file Bulgaria, 1910-1939.

93 *Ibidem.*

94 BNP Paribas archives, *Bulgaria Mortgage Bank*, Social capital, 4\Cabet-1\132.

95 *Idem.*

96 BNP Paribas archives, Request to the county court to register the General Bank, Sofia, 1911, file 4 Cabet-1 132.

founding shares.[97] The merger was based on the acquisition of the new institution shares by Crédit foncier franco-bulgare. However, the founder parts from Banque hypothécaire du Royaume de Bulgarie and Crédit foncier de Bulgarie were originally absorbed by Crédit foncier national.[98] Through operations of merger and purchase, a real mortgage structure was created: Crédit foncier franco-bulgare appeared as a mortgage company with headquarters in Paris. Crédit foncier national du Royaume de Bulgarie was an "auxiliary organ" representing Crédit foncier franco-bulgare in Sofia; its important mission was to study Bulgarian market, to prepare business for Crédit foncier franco-bulgare focusing mainly on the contact network and adding value to investments. Crédit foncier national had a small local managing structure (that did not even depend on the banks that had shares in Crédit foncier franco-bulgare or the Banque balkanique and the Banque générale), which held a board of directors gathering representatives from the mentioned institutions – the president represented the Banque hypothécaire du Royaume de Bulgarie and the vice-president was president of the former Crédit foncier bulgare.[99]

On the local market both banks were the main participants – Banque balkanique, which got a 1 per cent commission on each mortgage operation "brought to purchase and mortgage consideration by its organs in Sofia and other regions";[100] and Banque générale in Bulgaria. Both banks acted as agents for Crédit foncier franco-bulgare through their subsidiaries and agencies: Banque balkanique was the "only Crédit foncier franco-bulgare agent" in the towns of Northern Bulgaria, and Banque générale was the only one in the South.[101] French participation in the expansion of other foreign banks on Bulgarian market (Banque balkanique, Banque générale de Bulgarie and Banque franco-belge) can be measured by their activity developing from 1914 until 1923 (with an increase in capital from LV 35m to LV 57m), as well as the expansion of their investments, from LV 95 to 580m.[102] Cooperation between French bank (Paribas, Société générale, Crédit lyonnais) and Belgian banks (Banque belge pour l'étranger, Banque d'outre-mer) expressed itself through the foundation of Banque

---

97 Paribas archives, Basis suggested for the merger between two Bulgarian groups, file: Bulgaria, 1910-1939.

98 *Idem.*

99 Paribas archives, Basis suggested for the merger between two Bulgarian groups, file: Bulgaria, 1910-1939.

100 Paribas archives, Basis suggested for the merger between two Bulgarian groups, file: Bulgaria, 1910-1939.

101 *Idem.*

102 Simeon Damianov, "Les placements français en Bulgarie, 1878-1940", in Maurice Lévy-Leboyer (ed.), *La position internationale de la France*, Paris, Éditions de l'École des Hautes Études en Sciences Sociales, 1977, p. 327.

franco-belge. The roots of the cooperation were the clauses about the distribution of each group in the capital constitution (number of shares), in the board of directors and responsibilities. They benefited from the development of trade and industry, and they reinforced their positions by increasing their investments in both domains: they incorporated 26 industrial companies and 14 in the trade sector.

In their wake, a few other banks appeared to take profit there too of the emergence of the Bulgarian agricultural expansion and of its European exports. Brazil and South America Land Bank (Paris) and Caisse industrielle et commerciale de Paris fostered Banque franco-bulgare pour le commerce international in 1917 (capital of 10m levas. After WWI the Bulgarian Credit Bank was founded in 1918 (capital of LV 13.5m), the Banque de crédit national in 1919 (15m capital), Banca commerciale italiana & bulgara in 1919 (capital of 40m capital. International Bank started its activity in 1923 (capital of 75m), which was much larger than the capital of the other banks and a great part of which was put down by Austrian, German and French bankers. In 1923 Banque belge pour l'étranger (Brussels) and Crédit foncier d'Algérie et de Tunisie (Paris) joined to found Banque franco-belge in Bulgaria (capital of LV 25m). Banque franco-belge et balkanique was a limited liability society (capital of 150m gold levas) managed by Banque belge pour l'étrange), Bup, Wiener Bankverein, Banque générale de crédit hongrois, Société générale de Belgique and Banque de Salonique.

With the stabilisation process being achieved in 1929, the banks expanded the capital invested in industry and trade by granting credit or by investing directly, supplying 2 billions levas, that was 28.6 per cent of the whole creditor operations.[103] The investments increased in key sectors, especially after the 1928 merger between Banque franco-belge de Bulgarie and Balkan Bank (founded under French-Austrian influence by participation from Bup[104] (16 per cent), Société générale (7 per cent), Wiener Bankverein, etc.), becoming Banque franco-belge et balkanique. Through both those mergers, French interests, close to Belgian interests, on one hand, and to Austro-Hungarian interests, on the other, formed a robust network of banks integrated into the structure and business of Banque franco-belge et balkanique and Banque franco-bulgare.

Another representation of the capital introduction level was the banking activity throughout the industrial sector as, just before WWI, most foreign banks were involved in financing various industrial and economic sectors. Under the "agrarian cabinet" in the 1920s, France held on to its

---

103 *Ibidem.*

104 Hubert Bonin, *La Banque de l'union parisienne (1874/1904-1974). De l'Europe aux outre-mers*, Paris, Publications de la Sfhom, 2011, p. 273.

position in the financing and the control of companies and individual concerns on Bulgarian market, with 21.3 per cent of the assets. Afterwards, with the political trouble it brought on and the negative impact on capital circulation, especially for the financing of various branches with foreign capital, French presence was noticed in coal industry (two mines under French control: Badachté and Vulkan) and in textile industry (the Berov-Horinek factory). Foreign banks on Bulgarian market invested in tobacco sector, with the creation of manufacture and trade companies: Nikotea, granted funds by the Balkan Bank Tahandat by Banque générale, Orient Tobacco by Banque italienne et bulgare, United Manufactures of Tobacco, the most influential concern on Bulgarian market, by Banque franco-belge,[105] and Banque de crédit the tobacco export company Bulgaria. Through Banque franco-belge, French funds were furthermore used for financing the fabric manufacturing of Berov and Horinek in Sofia, as well as the Volcan company for coal extraction in Rakovski.[106] The United Tobacco Manufactures, the sugar manufacture in Rousstchouk and Izida concern were managed by the biggest French-Belgian group, with BUP (Banque franco-belge et balkanique) till they were liquidated in 1932. The intermediation by the French banking groups and partnerships favoured the creation of a French "banking model" in Bulgaria mixing commercial banking, investment banking, and investment funding – in 1931 they put down an equity capital of LV 75m equity for the industrial, commercial and banking development of the country.[107] They aimed at doing all possible prospection within the Bulgarian and Balkan industry, civil engineering, in which they could invest and make profit.

Conclusion: An assessment of the expansion of French banks in Bulgaria

One of the major consequences of the opening of Bulgarian market was the increase in banking competition.[108] The policy of internationalisation of the French groups around 1900 was an incentive to develop more strategies and influence mechanisms in order to cope with that competition. In the course of time the competition offered new partnership rules adapted

105 See Nikola Lazarov, *A History of the Bulgaria National Bank and of Banking Activity in Bulgaria*, *op. cit.* p. 273.

106 Vasil Vasilev, "Le commerce franco-bulgare pendant les dix ans qui ont suivi la Première Guerre mondiale (d'après les sources bulgares)", in *La France et les Balkans dans les années 1920*, *op. cit.*, p. 123.

107 *Ibidem*, p. 328.

108 About the banking competition see Samuel Hayes, Michael Spence & David Marks (eds.), "Investment banking competition: An historical sketch", in John Peter Williamson (ed.), *The Investment Banking Handbook*, *op. cit.*

to the progressive opening of Bulgarian market, with new condition to take into account the modifications in Bulgarian financial system. Loans could give way to financing projects in building railways or credit company creation and building a system of trust between Bulgarian authorities and French banks. The second aspect concerns the power of group power: French banks intervened with relatively massive funds that allowed them to play a key role in underwriting and distributing syndicates. They also created strong interaction relations: French savings became committed to financing Bulgarian economy. French banks, by means of their capital, took part in the process of catching up on the Bulgarian market. Their decision to start business in the Balkans was quite risky, but it went with security "ranking", and, when risks decreased, banking profitability increased. Founding a flexible organisation within the groups was therefore important; first it gave a more detailed knowledge of the local market, which helped to boost possibilities of financial intervention and participation in business; that organisation was notably possible due to the network of subsidiaries and correspondents, which was coherent for partners in negotiations as far as risk sharing was concerned.

Secondly it reinforced the potentialities of a more complete expansion; the intervention of French banks on Bulgarian financial market strengthened the means of Bulgarian state; and it set a balance to the financial system of the host country by favouring fund mobility. The financial situation in Bulgaria was significant: budgetary receipts did not manage to stimulate industry and trade; till the end of the 19th century, they included direct (tax on vineyards, road maintenance tax, military tax, etc.) and indirect taxes (custom tax, harbour tax, land tax, with forest exploitation tax), the major part of which was used to repay debt towards creditor banks.[109] The weaker the revenue grows, the more dependent the state is on its creditors. That link leads us to a second generalisation: the overall impact of debt is based on the sequence of capital transactions from a debtor country to a creditor country.

On that field, the "positive aspect" of the banks' influence was obvious. The building of a debt economy is quite complex and is based above all on the development of banking system. When the financial system of a country is still in its infancy, the most efficient means for the state to finance itself are external loans, which explains the role played by foreign banks: they became a driving force in the economic and financial development of Eastern European countries. With their assets (loans, subscription to movable securities), the banks worked in accordance with market information.

[109] The concepts of the impact of public debt and financial dependence of a country are the subject of *La dette publique dans l'histoire, op. cit.*

The advantages to French banks in taking part in the creation of credit companies or industrial concerns were numerous. They got represented in the board of directors, which allowed them to influence decisions related to financial activity and to manage their international relations. They got access to direct information about running the market in this host country and its way of business. The purpose was assessing and securing banking investment quality, which took the shape of loan movable securities or advances granted when the concern's capital increased. The loan system allowed them to get underwriting commissions, to issue securities, and to set up along a diversified range of commercial and financial products and facilities. The increase of the "foreign correspondents" accounts fostered banks' activity in Eastern and Balkanic Europe. The history of Bulgarian government loans shows the activity of French banks and the evolution in their operations. For the issuing and investment of Bulgarian securities the most widespread banking convergence forms were creating underwriting groups or security syndicates. The mission of merchant banks on the Bulgarian market played various roles: they were innovating banks as they helped setting up creating a new economic and financial structure; they were stimulating as they supplied capital in order to secure the reforms of the emerging financial and economic system. As a matter of fact, finally, despite the secondary size of the Bulgarian platform in comparison with the Russian and Ottoman operations, the deployment of French banks there broadened their geo-economic scope and brought more power to France in itself as a competing edge against its main European rivals on the field of "the balance of power".[110] Mainly Banque de l'union parisienne[111] and Paribas intensified, through their Bulgarian involvement, their array of connections and activities throughout Central, Eastern and Balkanic Europe, and Bulgaria was only a piece of that large jigsaw puzzle which they built from the 1890s till the 1930s, the Bulgarian case study epitomising somewhat such achievements.

However, a country facing the dilemma of leading an autarchic policy or turning to external financing, when forced to choose a financial protectorate, is characterised by Jean-Claude Allain as a "small power", with no

[110] Jean-Claude Allain, "La moyenne puissance: une réalité fuyante de la vie internationale", in *Enjeux et puissance, pour une histoire des relations internationales au XXe siècle. Hommages à J.-B. Duroselle*, Paris, Publications de la Sorbonne, 1986. Robert Frank, "Sur la perception de la 'puissance' économique en France pendant les années 1930", in René Girault and Robert Frank (eds.), *La puissance en Europe 1938-1940*, 1984, pp. 165-189.

[111] Éric Bussière, "The interests of the BUP in Czechoslovakia, Hungary and the Balkans, 1919-1930", in Philipp Cottrell & Alice Teichova (eds.), *International Business and Central Europe, 1918-1939*, Leicester, Leicester University Press, 1983, pp. 399-410; reedited in: Geoffrey Jones (ed.), *Multinational and International Banking*, Aldershot, Edward Elgar, 1992, pp. 406-417.

"freedom of action".[112] The only remaining solution is to opt for a lesser dependence. In Bulgaria, as far as the types of political and economic influence (which strongly lead the bank transformations in a country) are concerned, external presence (mostly of European groups) showed itself in three main axes: the Russian presence at the end of the 19th century, intensive relations with European countries, such as France, Germany, Austria-Hungary; and, third, trade relations with the Ottoman Empire that were still under the protection of powerful countries. We have studied the French intervention in Bulgaria by analysing its nature (in financial sector through the creation of banks and companies, or through public loans), the forms of that intervention, and the negotiating tools. The forms of negotiation include the nature of negotiations (between governments or between various private banking establishments), and their mechanisms (through a multinational or national alliance within a syndicate, or through collaboration between private banks and their negotiating tools). All of these represent a major factor covering and depending on political, economic, psychological and sociological matters. As for the negotiating tools, they depend on the aim of the intervention, which means the decision and the manner in which it is taken ("in a conscious manner").[113]

In order to understand the respective positions of France and Bulgaria, our research was done in a complex way. First, examining the frame of politics and diplomatic relations between Bulgaria and European countries means considering the circumstances of the financial decisions taken by the government, on one side, and by the financial groups, on the other. This type of circumstances makes French-Bulgarian relations specific: history is at the base of "imperialist ideology", which stirs the details of well-assessed strategies and interests. The specificity in French-Bulgarian relations, or rather, the influence of imperialist interests, led to an ideological confrontation in Bulgarian government circles: the choice was either leading the country with an autarchic policy (which could not encourage a country so little developed to evolve on an economic, financial, or political level), or using contacts and international relations that could guide the country. Of course, a country never wants to be financially dominated, so it seeks for means to defend its own interests at all costs: a utopian policy of opposing infrastructure building projects took shape for instance in the 1880s, when they could facilitate the access of foreign goods and had a negative influence on Bulgarian craft and industry,[114] and there were in the country strong nationalist movements.

112 *Ibidem*, p. 14.

113 Marlis Steinert, "La décision en matière de politique étrangère: un essai sur l'utilisation des théories pour l'étude des relations internationales", in *Enjeux et puissance, pour une histoire des relations internationales au XXe siècle, op. cit.*, p. 71.

114 See Elena Statelova, *La diplomatie de la Principauté de Bulgarie, 1878-1886*, Sofia, Académie des sciences bulgares, 1976.

We can draw two main conclusions from the French intervention in Bulgaria. First, the economic expansion of a country is based on its banking evolution and institutionalisation, and calling for foreign capital was a way of securing the country's financial construction. Second, the influence of French banking groups on Bulgarian banking market was an inevitable historical circumstance for the not well developed banking system in the country under which it had to reach an accumulation of development capital. An important question still needs an answer: did that influence lead to dependence of an imperialistic-type? What needs to be clarified right away is that financial dependence does not necessarily lead to imperialist relations, although it creates imperialist-looking conditions.

CHAPTER 13

Reconfiguring Multinational Banking

Deutsche Bank's Acquisition of Bankers Trust as Seen after a Turbulent Decade

Christopher KOBRAK

Professor of Finance, ESCP Europe

Deutsche Bank's acquisition of Bankers Trust in 1998 was not only a giant step in the German bank's efforts to establish an "American footprint," it was also a major event in banking history. Although Deutsche Bank's nearly 140-year long history in the United States contained many uniquely German and Deutsche Bank characteristics, Germany's largest bank's lack of major foreign direct investment in the United States and other important markets until the end of the 20th century was by far not unique, even for the largest financial institutions from other countries. Before the breakdown of Bretton Woods, networks of foreign correspondent relationships and joint ventures seemed to be an adequate or at least the most feasible way for even money-centred banks to maintain an international reach.[1] Greater macro-economic instability, foreign direct investment by bank customers, greater use of Euro (offshore) bank accounts, and the greater power of a host of relatively new financial actors such as pension funds, mutual funds, and hedge funds, provided money-centered banks with more financial interest in developing new products, performing new sorts of transactions, and coming closer to key users and providers of services, all of which seemed to require greater foreign investment in major financial centres.

[1] Christopher Kobrak, *Banking on Global Markets: Deutsche Bank and the United States, 1870 to the Present*, Cambridge, Cambridge University Press, 2008. With the permission of Cambridge University Press, this chapter is largely based on "The Bankers Trust Acquisition: Deutsche Bank Fulfills Its 'American Dream'", pp. 331-351 as well as other sections of *Banking on Global Markets*.

This chapter will put Deutsche Bank's acquisition of Bankers Trust into its historical and economic context, trace the steps of the purchase and the public reaction, and then will conclude with some discussion of its significance to international banking, especially investment banking. The story involves contemporary perceptions of how the interaction of regulatory, technological, and economic changes will shape the future of investment banking.

1. The urge to merge

For the better part of the 1980s, Deutsche Bank has been at the centre of takeover rumours, both as an acquiring or target institution.[2] In dramatic fashion, in fall 1998, Deutsche Bank radically restructured its business in the US and, by some accounts, all over the world, by acquiring a well-known, nearly-one-hundred-year-old US bank. In many senses, the purchase was not its first piece of US direct investment. Nonetheless, its acquisition of Bankers Trust represented a giant leap for Deutsche Bank and was part of a huge sea change in the nature of international banking. Unlike its other acquisitions, that of Bankers Trust led to significant changes in the structure of Deutsche Bank, its investments and its corporate governance. It was part of an enormous global reshuffling of assets in the whole financial services sector. As the world prepared for the Millennium, America remained Deutsche Bank's greatest challenge. It began the 1990s with huge real estate losses in the States. Even Deutsche Bank's handling of many financial problems in Germany met with much criticism in the United States. The bank's attempts to buy away top talent from other investment banks ended in cost overruns and finally the resignations of 100 top technology-group stars.[3]

Under competitive pressure and with a host of new, strategic opportunities, big has understandably seemed better to many bankers. In the decade preceding Deutsche Bank's acquisition of Bankers Trust, a veritable tidal wave of mergers had already run through the banking world. Like many merger waves of the past, even those of international scope, the United States have led the way in the consolidation of the banking sector.[4] From 1988 to 1997, the American market alone had lost 30 per

---

2 See "Deutsche Bank wagt Kauf in den USA", *Finanz und Wirtschaft*, 25 November 1998, for an interesting analysis of Deutsche Bank's share movements annotated by announcements of other finance sector mergers and rumors of its own interests.

3 "Für die Deutsche Bank war Amerika bislang voller Stolpersteine", *Frankfurter Allgemeine*, 30 November 1998.

4 Jane E. Hughes & Scott B. MacDonald, *International Investment Banking*, Boston, Addison and Wesley, 2002, pp. 427-428. While the number of acquisitions in the US peaked in 1995-96, the dollar volume soared to a record $350 billion in the two years ending in December 1998.

cent of its banking institutions – 510 per year – through mergers and acquisitions.[5] In Europe, the numbers were smaller but still impressive, including such well-known institutions as the above-mentioned Morgan Grenfell purchase by Deutsche Bank, the mergers of BNP with Paribas, Crédit agricole with Crédit lyonnais, and Swiss Bank Corporation with Union Bank of Switzerland. Most of these mergers have been within the national markets of the two institutions, but in the late 1990s, cross-border deals seemed to be on the upswing.[6] The wave of consolidation, moreover, included bank mergers with non-financial institutions, insurance companies, and pension funds.

By 1998, the world of mergers and acquisitions had reached unprecedented dimensions. Despite the roughly $10 billion cost of the Bankers Trust deal, it was only the 10th largest in history, merely 15 per cent of Citibank's acquisition of Travelers and well below other mega-banking deals of the late 1990s.[7] Though clearly not the first, the Deutsche Bank acquisition seemed to unleash a new chain reaction of both domestic and cross-border mergers.[8] The reasons for this wave of acquisitions are varied and in line with other waves of consolidation in history.[9] As in earlier periods, regulation played a significant role. In the US, passage of the Riegle-Neal Interstate Banking and Branching Efficiency Act of 1994 effectively removed the last obstacles to inter-state banking. In Europe, the

---

5 Eduardo Strachman *et al.*, "Worldwide concentration in the banking sector", IPEA, 2002.

6 R.V. Vennet, "Cross-border mergers in European banking and bank efficiency", Gent University, 2002. From 1995 through the first half of 2000, there were 2,153 mergers and acquisitions of credit institutions in the European Union; 1807 were domestic deals, but of the remaining 346, most were between Europe and other regions.

7 "Deutsche Bank. Aufbruch nach Amerika", *Frankfurter Allgemeine*, November 25, 1998. Nations of Bank America (1998) $60 billion, Norwest of Wells Fargo (1998) $34 billion, Mitsubishi Bank of Bank of Tokyo (1995) $34 billion, Banc One of First Chicago (1998) $30 billion, Schweiz Bankverein of UBS (1997) $25 billion. Few of the non-banking deals were cross-border, none among the banks.

8 See Stephen A. Rhoades, "Bank mergers and industry-wide structure, 1980-1994", Washington, Board of Governors of the Federal Reserve System, January 1996; and Steven J. Pilloff, "Bank merger activity in the United States, 1994-2003", Washington, Board of Governors of the Federal Reserve System, May 2004, for a list of the important bank mergers in the US 1950 to 2004. From 1950 to 1989, there were 26 considered important. During the fourteen years that followed 62, see also *The Times*, 24 November 1998.

9 The great merger waves are usually considered in the US between 1897 and 1904, 1916 to 1929, 1965 to 1969, 1981 to 1989. While the European experience is different, this periodisation roughly holds for that area too. In these other periods, technological and regulatory changes have also played an important role in stimulating the consolidations. Many analysts speculate about whether we have begun a new round of consolidation. Patrick A. Gaughan, *Mergers, Acquisitions and Corporate Restructurings*, New York, John Wiley & Sons, 1999, pp. 21-59.

Second Banking Directive – passed in 1989 but implemented in 1993 – abolished geographic restrictions on member country banks by the introduction of a single bank license and the principle of home-country control.[10] Technological changes allowed banks to have a greater scale and to extend their services. Once any institution makes the enormous investment in information technology, adding sites usually entails few costs, at least few relative to the initial investment. More transactions can be done and more internalised among widely dispersed offices in far often countries.

Indeed, the spreading of capitalism and high savings rates in many emerging market have widened the geographic plain for exchanging know-how and capital, and thereby potential economies of scale for the present on key markets. As many costs are fixed, the more transactions you do and other services you perform, the lower their total unit cost. Some activities, such as foreign exchange management, can be centralised with high-speed electronic connections, while simultaneously and relatively easily extended to customers in the farthest corners of the globe. Moreover, many of the banks' largest domestic customers have increased their foreign direct investment, while bringing together many financial services in money centers such as New York, London, and Paris, a positioning the large banks are almost compelled to follow.

Mergers helped attain several other strategic goals. By expanding internationally, big banks avoided one of their greatest risks, a lack of market diversity, becoming so large that, in the eyes of some regulators, they were "too big to fail." With a larger size, banks could add more equity capital and extend their range of services, which in turn gives banks even more market flexibility and international breadth, both for changing services and adding new equity value.[11] Many of the mergers, especially the domestic ones, promised high degrees of cost reduction, sadly often in the form of staff layoffs. But for some observers, the merger was a strategic necessity for Deutsche Bank and other banks.[12] As one analyst put it in short, "from this view point of view, the very survival of banking institutions in national markets became fundamentally dependent on their global competitive capacity".[13]

Consolidation in the banking sector was not without its critics and risks. The public and regulators feared that multinational banks would loose interest in small domestic clients and grow too powerful to be supervised adequately by their home-country regulators or even supranational agencies. There are still many legal, tax, management, and attitudinal obstacles that can prevent even the most well-reasoned mergers from

10 R.V. Vennet, *op. cit.*

11 Karina Robison, "The driving forces in bank mergers", *The Banker*, 2002.

12 Jane E. Hughes and Scott B. MacDonald, *op. cit.*, pp. 429-430.

13 Eduardo Strachman, *op. cit.*

becoming cost-effective, especially across national borders. According to some analysts, size has its limits and executive egos can be an impediment to realising gains in merging giant institutions.[14] Reaching synergies, moreover, often implies many staff reductions, and, at the very least, a great deal of post-merger complex coordination. Going from the slogans to the realisation of having worldwide reach for a large range of financial services, as Citibank aims, or being America's banker, as NationsBank intends, require enormous skill and perseverance in cross-selling as well as management knowledge of many sectors.[15]

2. Bankers Trust as a target

Deutsche Bank's announcement that it would buy Bankers Trust came at a time of general stock market frenzy or "irrational exuberance" as Alan Greenspan dubbed it. It unleashed a torrent of press speculation. Concerns mounted on both sides of the Atlantic. One newspaper metaphorically asked about the merger, "*Frosch oder Prinz für die Deutsche Bank*?" ("Frog or Prince for Deutsche Bank?").[16] At the time of the merger, "the frog or the prince" had a market capitalisation roughly one quarter of Deutsche Bank's €30 billion and 40 per cent of its 1997 assets of €500b.[17] With the final negotiations, and approval and process alone taking an addition four to five months after the first late November 1998 announcement, "frog or prince," the kiss was long – lasting the whole winter – and deep! Deutsche Bank had been on the hunt for an American acquisition for some time. Bankers Trust was not the first American bank Deutsche Bank had targeted. With one of its arch rivals (Goldman Sachs) advising it, Deutsche Bank sought new talent first at the California high-tech specialists Hambrecht & Quist and then Bankers Trust. In the fall the principals met to iron out a deal, which Goldman Sachs had code named 'Osprey,' for the large hawk that picks its prey from the water with its talons.[18] For many observers, it seemed like an expensive meal.

Established in 1903 by several leading New York banks – spearheaded by the House of Morgan – Bankers Trust took deposits of individuals and corporation during its first few years of operation with a meager staff of

[14] Ken Elkins, "Merger of egos", *Bank Director Magazine*, 2nd quarter, 1998 about the 1998 giant merger of National Bank and BankAmerica, which created an institution with a 8.1% US market share, close to the top allowed by regulation, a coast to coast US presence, the highest market share in some of the fastest growing regions in the US, and the largest pure banking operation in the US.

[15] Lisa Reilly Cullen, "Citicorp vs. Nationsbank", *Money*, 19 October 1998.

[16] *TAZ*, 25 November 1998.

[17] "Hoffnung auf Einsparungen durch Übernahme", *Die Welt*, 25 November 1998.

[18] Bloomberg-Ticker, 30 November 1998.

eight in a two-room office at 143 Liberty Street. It specialised in trust services, acting as executor and trustee for wills and administrators of estates, an activity that before 1914 was forbidden to commercial banks and one that stimulated a spurt in the growth of new trust institutions, many of which were affiliated with commercial banks in order to get around the restriction. Under the leadership of several well-known bankers – including, as mentioned earlier, Benjamin Strong, its second president and later head of the N.Y. Federal Reserve Bank – Bankers Trust became well respected in banking circles. By its 50th anniversary, with 4,000 employees, seventeen offices and $2 billion in assets, Bankers Trust was the eighth largest commercial bank in the US as measured by assets.[19] By early 1970s, Bankers Trust had expanded well beyond its original functions, even establishing a large international presence and branching out into riskier activities. In the 1950s and 1960s, it grew in part through making many acquisitions. As one of the first American banks to invest internationally, its activities were regularly tracked by the Bundesbank.[20] At a time when American banks dominated the league tables in 1962, Bankers Trust was among the twenty largest banks in the world as measured by total assets – eighth to be precise with $3.2 billion in deposits. With nearly 25,000 shareholders and 7,000 employees, it sat six places ahead of the bank that would acquire it nearly four decades later. Tellingly, with $600 million less in assets, Deutsche Bank had twice the shareholders and three times the employees.[21] The two banks had a fair amount of contact in Germany. According to Bankers Trust representatives at the time of Deutsche Bank's reunification, the two banks – that is, Bankers Trust and the three banks that became Deutsche Bank in 1957 – had a "balanced relationship."[22]

In the late 1970s, Bankers Trust was considered by many observers to be a "mediocre money-centre bank." Despite inflation, from 1975 to

19 *The New York Times*, 30 March 1953.

20 See several Vermerke, B330/5170, February 7, 1966, HABBK.

21 "98 free world banks with assets of $1 billion", *The American Banker*, 7 August 1963, p. 12. With the world still suffering the effects of WWII, Bank of America topped the league tables with $13.4 billion in assets. Ten of the top 20 were American banks. British and Canadians banks were the only others to make it into the top ten. Japanese banks were beginning to develop a very powerful position in world banking with ten on the top twenty. Deutsche Bank was by far the largest in Germany, well ahead of Dresdner Bank, but not the largest in continental Europe, an honour which Banca Nazionale del Lavoro held.

22 M.E. Gevers, 30 September 1957 file not distributed to Bankers Trust officers. HADB, K50/9/36. Bankers Trust managers seemed a little concerned about the "hot money" coming into Germany from speculators (about $1.0 billion). Managers from the two banks met regularly. The contact seemed particularly strong with Krebs and Jacobs. See also correspondence HADB, K50/9/34 and 35.

1978, Return and Equity did not exceed 10 per cent.[23] It was staggering under the weight of huge losses in real estate lending and the competitive pressures in its retail and credit card businesses. The real estate losses were particularly damaging, as Bankers Trust had positioned itself as a leader in this sector. It had to book large charges due to real estate investment trusts (REITS) even before the 1973-74 national recession and New York City municipal crisis hit in 1975.[24] The problems facing the bank's retail and credit card business were different. Whereas it had to book losses in real estate, its credit card business lacked economies of scale. Although Bankers Trust had grown these businesses over the past twenty years, its growth had not kept in pace the highly-competitive New York market. In addition, retail banking was facing a technology transformation with the introduction of automated teller machines (ATMS). Improving its weak position in the market required heavy investment outlays in new technology, for which Bankers Trust was ill-prepared.[25]

By the end of the 1980s, much had changed. Both the media and peers were lavishing heavy praise on Bankers Trust for its innovation and transition into investment banking.[26] As early as 1994, Deutsche Bank's management, for example, indicated that it had much to learn from Bankers Trust.[27] By then, that latter had been transformed from a sleepy middle-sized commercial bank to one of the most aggressively innovative financial institutions in the world. Under the leadership of Charles Sanford, the bank began a decade-long metamorphosis. Sanford recognised that changes in regulation and the competitive environment for banks left financial intermediaries, like Bankers Trust, in a precarious position.[28] The liability side of the balance sheet but not the asset side had

---

23 Bankers Trust Annual Reports, 1975-1978.

24 REITS are groups of lenders organized as mutual funds to support construction and real estate development. In 1973, real estate loans amounted to $884 million or 10 per cent or of Bankers Trust's total loan portfolio.

25 Interviews with Charles S. Sanford, Jr., 9 March 2006 (during first interview, with Gene Guill, a former Bankers Trust employee, who left to join Deutsche Bank in 1994) and 14 March 2006.

26 Shelagh Hefferman, *Modern Banking in Theory and Practice*, New York, Wiley and Sons, 1996, pp. 417-419.

27 "The battle plans of Hilmar Kopper", *Euromoney*, January 1994, Vol. 29, No. 4, pp. 28-44. Kopper singled out Charles Sanford as one of the bankers he admired most for his courage and determination in successfully turning Bankers Trust around.

28 Interviews with Sanford and Guill. A graduate of the University of Georgia (1958) and the Wharton School (1960, MBA), Sanford joined Bankers Trust in 1961 in commercial banking and then moved into money and securities trading. In joined the Management Committee in 1979, became president in 1983, deputy chairman in 1986, and chairman and CEO in 1987. See also Ron Chernow, *The Death of the Banker*, New York, Random House, 1997, for a good discussion of the evolution of banking activities.

been deregulated. A horde of new competitors had come into the financial services sector depriving traditional commercial banks of deposits, their basic franchise and lowest cost of financing. Easy access to capital markets allowed corporations to circumvent banks with commercial paper, which could be bought up (underwritten) directly by investment banks and non-bank lenders, and distributed to final investors. Without top-tier corporate relationships, Bankers Trust was particularly vulnerable with its dependence on loan business in the United States and low return on equity. Pension and other funds were switching their investment management activities away from trust departments, the crown jewel of Bankers Trust, to specialised investment managers.[29]

C. Sanford had the vision and courage to push the bank into uncharted waters. By 1993, it not only had become highly-touted for its innovative approach to risk management but also extremely profitable, posting nearly a quarter of a billion dollars in client-related risk management profits. Total business income rose from $125 million in 1985 to $634 in 1992.[30] According to many accounts, the success was directly attributable to C. Sanford's bold new approach to banking and his efforts to change the mentality of the bank.[31] By 1990, Bankers Trust had chalked up many impressive successes, including being the first US commercial bank since 1933 to underwrite commercial paper and to enter the securities business. The bank attracted clever people who were rewarded for innovative, creative products. As an agent of change, C. Sanford challenged the status quo even before becoming president of the bank. Applying an "underwrite and distribute" model of investment banking to even its lending business, Bankers Trust created loan syndications which lowered risks and reduced the percentage of assets devoted to loans.

But C. Sanford's greatest contribution may have come in the analysis and control of risky instruments. Shortly after he became executive vice-president for Resource Management, Sanford put into place a new methodology for assessing the effect of interest-rate volatility on the returns of transactions and products. This methodology – risk-adjusted return on capital (RAROC) – was eventually applied throughout the bank as a guiding principle for evaluating transactions, business units, capital allocations, and individual performance. It even influenced the control systems

29 An Address by Charles S. Sanford, Jr., "Managing the Transformation of a Corporate Culture: Risks and Rewards", 14 November 1996, Delivered as part of the 1996-97 Musser-Schoemaker Leadership Lecture Series at the Wharton School, University of Pennsylvania.

30 Bankers Trust, 1995 Annual Report.

31 "New tricks to learn", in *A survey of international banking, The Economist*, 10 April 1995, pp. 17-19.

of many competitors.[32] C. Sanford wanted to create an organisation that focused on managing global risk, but that enterprise itself was fraught with uncertainty, as became evident in short order. The banks 1987 profits had to be adjusted for the mispricing of a foreign exchange position. Although restatement of earnings net of accrued bonuses was relatively small and only the timing of the write off was challenged by regulators,[33] the experience contributed to beefing up the bank's internal controls and its methods for evaluating risk. The 1987 foreign-exchange problem added a greater sense of urgency to C. Sanford's efforts to spread the use of RAROC throughout the organisation, making it part of the bank's internal culture. Risky transactions had to beat a high hurdle rate, usually 20 per cent. Applied to individuals and whole units, the system helped management move from a pure growth strategy to a controlled one in which not all new business was treated equally. While not infallible, the system helped convince management to move away from traditional lending into new-fangled risk management and trading, whose risk-adjusted returns appeared more profitable.[34]

But by the time of the acquisition, however, some observers wondered whether Deutsche Bank had purchased tainted merchandise.[35] All the news associated with Bankers Trust's new focus was not rosy: The process and results had its critics. Bankers Trust took heat for its aggressive financing of leveraged buyouts (LBOs). Its substantial portfolio of real estate holdings and emerging market loans led some to argue that its real credit exposure had been understated, a problem certainly not confined to Bankers Trust and one that predated C. Sanford's appointment as CEO. During the late 1980s, as was the case at many banks, continued write-downs of loans made during the 1970s periodically weighed on Bankers Trust's stock price.[36]

---

32 See Robert A. Bennett, "Sanford's New Banking Vision", *The New York Times*, 17 March 1985 and interviews with Charles Sanford and Gene Guill, 12 September 2006, and Bankers Trust 1995 Annual Report. See also Gene D. Guill, "Bankers Trust and the Birth of Modern Risk Management", Financial Institutions Center, Wharton School. 2007.

33 E-mail from Gene Guill, 26 July 2006.

34 "New tricks to learn", in *A survey of international banking*, *The Economist*, 10 April 1995, pp. 17-19. It involved a system by which allocations of capital were made to transactions by allocating 99 per cent of the expected loss to the capital based on the historical loss experience of different markets. Even though the positions may be of a shorter duration, RAROC assumed that they would take a year to unwind. On this basis, expected returns were recalculated.

35 See, for example, "Die amerikanische Herausforderung", *Frankfurter Allgemeine*, 25 November 1998.

36 Shelagh Hefferman, *op. cit.*, pp. 417-418.

Worse still, the very successful transformation was marred by unfortunate publicity arising from the sale of derivative instruments. In April 1994, two of its customers, Procter & Gamble and Gibson Greetings, made charges against the bank connected with its selling the clients high-risk leveraged derivatives. Although charges were different in each case, P&G alleged, for example, that Bankers Trust representatives has had mispriced investments and promised quick profits, a charge Bankers Trust of course denied. According to senior management at Bankers Trust, the treasury staff at P&G wanted to turn that department into a profit centre without fully informing or educating its own senior management of the risks.[37] In January 1995, Bankers Trust settled with Greetings and paid a $10 million fine to several regulatory authorities. Bankers Trust sacked two salesmen and agreed to having its leveraged derivatives business, a business Bankers Trust later exited, reviewed by an outside examiner.[38] The bank booked another reserve against derivatives losses and instituted other procedures to avoid further deterioration in client defections.[39]

Nonetheless, the publicity took a heavy toll on its stock, which declined nearly 30 per cent during the second half of 1994, despite a strong market for bank stocks.[40] Even though Bankers Trust won repeated court successes against P&G and regulatory authorities took no punitive action against it, bad publicity dogged the bank. P&G continued to maintain that Bankers Trust had failed to inform fully its client of the risks of the Deutsche Mark and interest rate swaps Bankers Trust had arranged. The Cincinnati firm refused to make contractual payments. In 1996, Frank Newman, C. Sanford's successor as CEO somewhat surprisingly settled the case for an undisclosed amount, even though no court had passed judgment on the allegations and some distinguished academics publicly sided with Bankers Trust.[41]

Despite heavy trading losses in the first quarter of 1995 on Latin American leveraged positions – which contributed to a steep drop on year-to-year profits and in Return on Equity for year, Bankers Trust was one of the most profitable financial firms in the US from 1985 to 1995. Its average annual return on equity was above those of J.P. Morgan, Merrill Lynch and Citibank, for example. For six of the previous ten years, the

---

37 Interview with Charles Sanford and Gene Guill, 12 September 2006.

38 Shelagh Hefferman, *op. cit.*, p. 427.

39 *Ibidem*.

40 "Bears clawed bank-investor bulls in 1994", *American Banker*, 27 December 1994.

41 See "Judge denies award in derivatives suit against Bankers Trust", *American Banker*, 22 April 1996. At least some academics sided completely with Bankers Trust on the appropriateness of the hedge, but the case points to a management difficulty of selling highly complex products to corporate clients who may not understand or want to understand the different payouts and risks.

bank enjoyed over 20 per cent returns on shareholder equity – In contrast, from 1974 to 1986, the bank averaged 12.9 per cent, with a high of 16.6 per cent in 1985.[42] During the early 1990s, only Morgan Stanley and Bear Stearns among Bankers Trust's peers out performed Bankers Trust.[43] The bank had built strong franchises in providing financial services, especially with derivatives, syndicated loans, debt underwriting and placement, particularly financing for Leveraged Buyouts.[44] With the bank's high dividend and healthy stock price growth, from 1985 to 1995, shareholders had done well. In spite of the falling out with some of its clients, in 1994 Bankers Trust was named the best derivatives bank by a Greenwich Equity poll.[45] The confidence of many important clients remained unshaken.[46]

But in 1995, Bankers Trust's share price began a five-year long roller-coaster ride. It bounced from its 1994 high of nearly $85 a share – nearly the price Deutsche Bank paid in 1998 and above its pre-acquisition-rumour price – to a low of $50 in 1995. It then climbed to a new high of $133 before plummeting once again in 1998, loosing nearly half of its 1997 highs shortly before the acquisition despite a buoyant stock market.[47] Although by 1997 Bankers Trust had seemed to have overcome its derivative troubles of the mid-1990s, a whole set of news popped up.[48] Under C. Sanford's successor, continued some policies and strategies, but lost some of its focus and control strengths. Some key managers left. Although in 1996 and 1997, Bankers Trust's earnings and stock price growth were back on track, it pushed ahead with some risky areas some of which had even low returns, such as loans and derivatives in emerging markets, without sufficient central control.[49] In 1998, however, Bankers

42 This may not sufficiently show the contrast between the two periods. If the losses do less Developed Country Loans had been booked to the earlier years when the business was done, as opposed to 1987 and 1989, the 1974-86 average return would have been less than 1 per cent.

43 Bankers Trust 1995 Annual Report, pp. 1-5.

44 *Ibidem.*

45 *Derivatives Week*, 23 May 1994,

46 "Bankers Trust wins votes of confidence," *Pension & Investments*, 16 October 1995, p. 39.

47 Bankers Trust 1997 Annual Report for the stock price up to year-end 1997. Some analysts believed that Bankers Trust stock price stayed as high as it did during the mid-1990s only because of its high dividend.

48 E-mail from Gene Guill, 26 July 2006. Frank, Newman who had been appointed as president on 19 October 1995, assumed the position of CEO on 1st January 1996. C. Sanford, who remained as chairman until 16 April 1996, effectively relinquished operating control in January.

49 Banker's Trust's 1998 Annual Report (10-K) and Mark Yallup interview, 11 December 2006. Chief Operating Officer, ICAP, formerly of Deutsche Bank, member of Due Diligence Team.

Trust took huge write offs. Unfortunately for Deutsche Bank, the bleeding continued well into 1999.[50] With the market turmoil in Asia and Russia, Bankers Trust seemed to be in big trouble, for which the selling strategy seemed to be the best "fix."[51] Various aspects of its involvement with the 1998 collapse and bailout of Long Term Capital Management (LTCM) had been widely criticised.[52] Bankers Trust had already been approached by Bank of New York, Mellon Bank, and State Street Corp. about buying portions of its business. By the time Deutsche Bank began talks in summer 1998, the company was already in play.[53]

For these and other reasons, some observers believed that Bankers Trust was not the ideal target company. The acquisition put Deutsche Bank into several businesses it really did not want to have, such as the custodial business. Although it expected to realise eventually $1 billion per year in pre-tax savings by elimination of back office personnel in Europe and the US, the merger entailed a $1 billion charge to income for the expected pre-tax first-year costs. This was in addition to the understandable fears of layoffs and culture clashes in the major centres of the combined bank such as New York, London, and Frankfurt.[54]

Nevertheless, Bankers Trusts position was not weak compared with its larger German suitor, and perhaps even a bargain given its cost. Bankers Trust brought with it a great deal of experience in initial public offerings, management buyouts and derivatives. At least during the early 1990s, Bankers Trust had cultivated an innovate corporate culture with a great many dynamic managers. While the shares of both companies had suffered a nosedive over the previous six months and Bankers Trust's 1998 pre-tax income was roughly one-sixth that of Deutsche Bank; a year earlier they were roughly equal.[55] Deutsche Bank was buying the American bank with strong DM.; Bankers Trust was selling well below its highest share price of $133 in 1997 and at a lower price earnings ratio than many other comparable banks. Despite its troubles, Bankers Trust was a substantial American player with an extensive international presence. Nearly half of its 20,000 employees were outside of the US Even though Bankers Trust was struggling with

50 Banker's Trust's 1998 Annual Report and 1999 first and second quarter 10-Qs.

51 "Mr Fix-it aims to get bankers on the mend", *Financial Times*, 30 November 1998.

52 Roger Lowenstein, *When Genius Failed: The Rise and Fall of Long-Term Capital Management*, New York, Random House, 2001. In addition to Bankers Trust being a major lender to LTCM, Bankers Trust management was highlighted for its threatening the success of the bailout; p. 224.

53 *The New York Times*, 24 November 1998.

54 *Ibidem.*

55 *Berliner Zeitung*, 24 November 1998.

large losses, stiff competition, and its participation in the recent bailout of LTCM, it was still the eighth largest US bank. With assets of $850 billion, the combined bank, if all the negotiations and regularly hurdles were cleared, would be the largest in the world, surpassing the recently merged UBS with $778 billion in total assets. With the acquisition, Deutsche Bank made a significant step toward making further inroads in US investment banking.

3. The announcement of the merger

Long rumoured, the news of the acquisition unleashed a torrent of media coverage, speculation, and even recrimination, principally on both sides of the Atlantic but stretching to all countries where the two banks had big offices, as far away as Australia.[56] At a share price of $93 per share or $9.7 billion for the company, the initial purchase details implied a price 20 per cent over Bankers Trust's pre-acquisition market value and 2.4 times book value, making it the largest acquisition of a US banking company by a foreign firm. Much of Deutsche Bank's American staff was taken by surprise by the size and magnitude of the venture. It was very much a deal driven by Frankfurt and London management. In the face of internal and external scepticism, though, senior management appeared confident.[57]

US markets surged, at least temporarily, on this news and that of other deals. Bankers Trust shares ended the day at $84.5, up $7, but still considerably below the offering price of $93 indicating perhaps that much still had to be done or that there was much potential in the American bank. Despite regulatory hurdles and last-minute negotiations about the new structure right after the announcement, even Deutsche Bank's shares jumped 2 per cent, a welcome relief for shareholders who had seen their stock lose nearly half its value over the previous six months. The markets makers seemed to believe, at least at first blush, that the advantages of combining Deutsche Bank's healthy balance sheet with Bankers Trust's market position and know-how seemed to outweigh the cultural and other difficulties of combining a German commercial bank with an American investment bank.[58] Four days later both boards approved the deal.

---

56 See "Breuer's mating dance", *Institutional Investor*, November 1998. By the time this issue came out, Bankers Trust seemed to be the leading candidate to fulfil the Deutsche Bank's ambition to buy an American financial institution, even though Lehman Brothers and J.P. Morgan were also mentioned and despite Rolf Breuer's "non-denial" denials. R. Breuer contended that he was always talking to executives at Bankers Trust as part of normal business and that he had nothing to tell shareholders.

57 Michael Rassmann, 9 and 12 January and 7 March 2006, reporting the announcement meeting and Michael Philipp response to a question.

58 Reuters-Ticker, *Berliner Morgenpost*, and *The Times*, 24 November 1998.

Some of the initial international response was relatively favourable. The deal would make Deutsche Bank the second largest asset manager in Europe. It represented a major step in the bank's efforts to remake its hurting investment banking – especially on the equity side – more robust. Even if it was not the perfect target and difficult to integrate, the acquisition of Bankers Trust was a step in the right direction. The two banks together had many common activities, which could be serviced with roughly the same infrastructure, a tremendous opportunity to improve profits. For both, the merger represented an opportunity to diversify into new areas and strengthen areas in which they had not reached critical mass. Moreover, parts of the Anglo-American press viewed the acquisition as a trendsetter, "the most visible sign of a much broader upheaval in European finance" to deal with new competition.[59]

But those competitive pressures were not coming just from outside of Europe as many critics of globalisation claimed, but rather from Europe's own ambitions and constraints. As the *International Herald Tribune* put it two days after the announcement, "the introduction of the single European currency, the euro, in eleven countries in January has increased the pressures on national banks to reinvent themselves as European players".[60] So long as many European countries blocked foreign entry into the banking sector – for example, France – and Germany's banking system remained dominated by non-profit financial institutions, deals within Europe or in Germany itself would be difficult. The real opportunity for expansion would come from deals involving institutions outside of continental Europe.[61]

Despite the need to consolidate and develop a broad international presence, there were also many critics of the acquisition. After the initial bounce in its stock price, by the middle of the day following the announcement, Deutsche Bank's share price slid nearly 5 per cent. Quoting bankers from other institutions, several newspapers doubted whether the planned synergies could be realised and whether the purchase price could be justified. Although widely acknowledged as a courageous step, some thought that the price was a little expensive for what Deutsche Bank was getting, especially considering the problems that the merger would unleash.[62] The purchase left the combined banks at only 11th among institutions for issuing new stocks and bonds in the US and 14th worldwide. Integrating the bank would be a challenge for Deutsche Bank managers, whose problems with Morgan Grenfell in 1989 were deemed by many to be a fiasco. Earlier difficulties

59 "Deutsche deal seen as a trend-setter", *The International Herald Tribune*, 26 November 1998.

60 *Ibidem*.

61 *Ibidem*.

62 "Experten sehen Banken-Deal skeptisch", *Die Welt*, 25 November 1998.

had sparked the departure of two hundred executives. Investment bankers were still furious that the bank's structure forced them to hawk the bank's low margin services such as cash management and trade financing.[63]

4. The press' reaction

It was a busy couple of weeks for Deutsche Bank's press department. During the first days after the announcement, there were on occasion multiple articles about the acquisition in the same newspaper. On the very day of its Bankers Trust announcement, rumors appeared about how it would finance the acquisition. Two often mentioned were the sales of its DaimlerChrysler or Allianz holdings, which had market values of DM 20 and 15 billion respectively, even though both of these sales under the German tax law would lead to a sizeable capital gains tax.[64] Several German papers picked up the theme, which would have wide-ranging consequences for other German companies and perhaps the whole German financial system. Questions arose in Europe and the United States about whether Deutsche Bank would have to disgorge its large German-company share holdings, whether it had structured the deal in a tax effective manner, and whether it used accounting gimmicks to disguise the true impact of the transaction.[65] The bank faced regulatory problems in Europe and in the United States.[66] There was some speculation that Bankers Trust was only the beginning of a buying spree that would involve a French bank next.

There were a host of varied and interconnected employment issues and cultural issues. Preserving the loyalty of Bankers Trust executives would be a great challenge. Headhunters would swoop down on the best of them.[67] On another labour front, within a few days of the announcement, German and international journals began fretting about the inevitable loss of jobs as far away as Australia, where both banks had substantial staffs.[68] What was for management synergies and cost savings amounted to around 10 per cent staff reductions, potentially nearly 9,000 job losses

63 "Deutsche Bank. Aufbruch nach Amerika", *Frankfurter Allgemeine*, 25 November 1998.

64 Bloomberg-Ticker, 24 November 1998.

65 "Gemischtes Finanzierungspaket der Deutschen Bank erwartet", *Börsen-Zeitung*, 25 November 1998 and "Deutsche Bank Plans to Keep DaimlerChrysler", *The Wall Street Journal*, 26 November 1998, "DaimlerChrysler shares 'not for sale'", *Financial Times*, 26 November 1998, for example.

66 "Deutsche Bank in Belgian buy", *Financial Times*, 3 December 1998.

67 Bloomberg-Ticker, Second, 24 November 1998.

68 See, for example, "Bank-Fusionen kosten Arbeitsplätze", *Frankfurter Neue Presse*, 25 November 1998, *The Age*, Australia, 25 November 1998, and the *Herald Tribune*, 25 November 1998.

worldwide for the combined bank. At the time of the announcement, the two banks employed around 91,000 people, roughly 76,000 with Deutsche Bank and 15,000 at Bankers Trust. The sacrifices and rewards seemed unbalanced. Even the conservative *Wall Street Journal* mused over how the mind-numbing pace of mergers could mean only one thing: "Mind-numbing fees for the deal makers."[69]

Some American journals viewed the takeover as the first step in the "Americanization" of Deutsche Bank. To get real benefit out of acquiring an American niche player, *The Wall Street Journal* reasoned that the real question was how a bank that epitomised German banking style would mesh with an institution that has always done things the American way. The potential for a clash was huge. But if the results were positive, other European banks would be emboldened to try the same. The American business journal feared that the Germans would have to do the most changing, and that they were not well known for their capacity to adapt. Safety had been the watchword and strength of German banking. How would those bankers feel in a world dominated by equities and derivatives? The independence and above all high salaries demanded by the American staff might not go down well with the German public and even with some German executives trained in the belief that managers work for the institution, not themselves. Although Deutsche Bank had learned to be more flexible, "the analysts trying to determine whether the merger will work might like to take a break from their numbers crunching and watch this clash of cultures unfold."[70]

Although the *Wall Street Journal* acknowledged that the combined companied in the US might work out, if managed well to form a magnet for attracting high-quality new staff, it also mused whether Bankers Trust was the right target at all. Neither Deutsche Bank nor Bankers Trust was among the top ten advisers on announced M&A deals involving a European target through October 1998. Other American investment banks still dominated even the European terrain. Bankers Trust, for *The Journal*, was hardly the right candidate to fill the investment bank gap in Deutsche Bank's arsenal: after all, it ranked only the 26th in the US. The acquisition seemed to be a desperation move by a European bank, which like so many others, had difficulty entering the rarified world of mergers and acquisitions. Neither creating investment banking capabilities from scratch nor purchasing them seemed to be feasible. Only four European banks broached the top 10 in even European deals.

---

69 "Bankers Reap Gains as Merger Frenzy Persists", *The Wall Street Journal*, 25 November 1998.

70 "Americanizing Deutsche Bank", *The Wall Street Journal*, 25 November 1998.

The question remained: Could Deutsche Bank draw top talent to the new bank and was it willing to write the checks for them?[71] Investment banking at any one institution had become a kind of temporary partnership of highly-mobile, talented people who just seemed to divide the profits among themselves before moving on to a new firm. Even more money might have to be put in, at least in the near term. According to *The Wall Street Journal*, the new entity's greatest gains might be in Europe by expanding Deutsche Bank's clout for underwriting stocks and bonds for smaller- and medium-sized companies, a sector in which Bankers was particularly strong. Bankers was strong in some growth sectors such as new stock issues and high-yield corporate debt (junk bonds), where *The Wall Street Journal* judged that the potential for growth in Europe was higher than the saturated US market. This might become particularly important if the introduction of the Euro gave a kick-start to European issuances and trading, as many expected. In short, Bankers Trust might give Deutsche Bank's European investment banking business a boost by adding a greater window to the US markets and US banking innovations. Finally, Bankers Trust might have been Deutsche Bank's second choice, but unlike its first, J.P. Morgan, it was available.[72]

Understandably, some of the German press feared that Deutsche Bank would lose its identity.[73] In Germany, one could almost feel the sense of bewilderment as one major restructuring after another, like a tidal wave, washed over icons of the German economic scene. Within a few years Daimler, Hoechst and now Deutsche Bank were losing some of their German character. For some, the supposed synergy effects were spurious or represented a too-costly attempt to realise overly zealous goals. According to *Der Tagesspiegel*, Deutsche Bank's 76,000 worldwide employees felt that the great ship was adrift, moving from one restructuring to another. Deutsche Bank had not only lost its European power, it no longer was a force in determining national policies. The bank seemed more interested in itself than its clients. It seemed to lurch from one scandal and acquisition plan in several countries and sectors to another.[74] The next day the same paper called into question, what *Der Tagesspiegel* obviously considered an underlying assumption of the merger: whether growth had economic value considering the price. It feared that the sudden rash of mergers involving German companies was only the tip of the iceberg.[75]

---

71 "Is Deutsche Bank hunting big game with the wrong gun?", *The Wall Street Journal*, 23 November 1998.

72 *Ibidem*.

73 See, for example, "Die amerikanische Herausforderung", *Frankfurter Allgemeine*, 25 November 1998.

74 "Die Deutsche Bank. Ein Gigant im Nebel", *Der Tagesspiegel*, 24 November 1998.

75 "Wachstum um jeden Preis?", *Der Tagesspiegel*, 25 November 1998.

Some competitors rejoiced at the prospect of Deutsche Bank losing its European focus and being tangled up in a long, complicated implementation process.[76] At the very least, the move entailed enormous risks. Deutsche Bank's earlier efforts with Morgan Grenfell had proven that heavy investment did not necessarily bring exceptional rewards in the investment-banking sector. It was a massive investment requiring future cash input with unproven returns and severe integration problems.[77] Perhaps the most insightful point was raised by Peter Martin, columnist for *The Financial Times*. In an article entitled "Alice in mergerland," he sensibly posed the question of whether any of the huge mergers of the 1990s had sufficiently considered that the economies of scale realised by the mergers also entailed huge management costs, because of the new institutional complexity, which could easily reduce or eliminate the incremental economic benefit of the merger. Like "Alice in Wonderland" who grew so large she could not tie her shoes, giant companies might find it hard keeping in touch with the parts that matter.

Moreover, in some sense every acquisition was an admission of a hidden failure, failure of the target to achieve acceptable returns, failure of the acquirer to achieve adequate internal growth. What was often overlooked was whether the acquisition really provided a solution to the hidden failures. While size can rectify many ills, some research and experience indicates that despite modern technology, beyond a certain point, economies of scale are hard to realise. Designing the appropriate communication, control and remuneration structures provided a daunting challenge, whose solutions were not particularly evident in investment banking.[78] While investment banking paid high returns to executives, returns to shareholders were not quite so rich. Only three major investment-banking houses returned more than 20 per cent on equity. Neither Bankers Trust nor Deutsche Bank was among them.[79]

5. Regulatory hurdles and integration

The initial stages of the integration passed relatively smoothly. Even before the official approvals, the bank had formed committees of Deutsche Bank and Bankers Trust executives to recommend organisational and personnel changes. After years of work in London and New York, Deutsche

---

76 "Deutsche Bank Threatens Focus with US Deal", *The Wall Street Journal*, 27 November 1998.

77 "Die Deutsche Bank riskiert alles", *Handelsblatt*, 27 November 1998 and "Deutsche Bank push into US market seems to be a bumpy ride", *Wall Street Journal*, 27 November 1998.

78 "Alice in mergerland", Peter Martin, *Financial Times*, 1st December 1998.

79 "Deutsche's foray into America will offer little to its shareholders", *The European*, 30 November 1998.

Bank had within the organisation several executives with a good deal of relevant experience. There was no long wait to find out who would stay and who would go. Senior managers had learned from the bank's experience with Morgan Grenfell nearly a decade earlier. There were to be no "co-heads of businesses." Instead of leaving the "Anglo-Saxon" investment bankers as a separate, albeit very profitable entity, Deutsche Bank took steps to create a worldwide investment banking arm. Senior executives realised that it had no one in Germany who was comfortable with the equity segment of investment banking. The challenge was first to create a broad-based, young, German talent pool, then cross-national teams, which would spearhead marketing throughout Europe and the rest of the world. Like Germany, Deutsche Bank needed more of an equity culture. In bonds and M&A, Deutsche Bank was fine, but in the growing, dynamic area of Initial Public Offerings, it lacked talent and experience.[80]

Although most observers considered the Bankers Trust deal done, there were still several regulatory and other hurdles to jump to acquire Bankers Trust. American law still technically separated investment and commercial banking. In addition to European and other regulation, the Federal Reserve would have to pass judgment on whether the proposed merger violated the latest American regulations. Deutsche Bank's stakes in non-banking institutions such as its 12 per cent position in DaimlerChrysler, for example, might sound some warning bells. The acquisition might also undermine Deutsche Bank's excellent (Aa1. Moody's Investors Service) credit rating.[81]

Within a few weeks of the announcement, Germany's misdeeds during WWII threatened to derail the merger, illustrating the almost imponderable duration of home-country political risk.[82] The Comptroller of the State of New York warned that he would not approve the deal until all the claims relating to Holocaust victims had been settled by German companies. Organising American pension funds against Swiss banks had proven to be a quite successful tactic to get information and the return of Jewish funds held in Switzerland. The lawyer for the victims contended that approval of the Bankers Trust deal by federal and state authorities had no chance until his clients had been satisfied.[83] Although the approval of the US authorities came in May 1999, the hurdle for regulatory clearance was persuading survivor groups of Deutsche Bank's relatively clean record during the Third Reich and openness about its role during the Nazi period.[84]

80 Interview with Rolf Breuer, 23 January 2006.

81 *Neue Züricher Zeitung*, 25 November 1998.

82 See Christopher Kobrak, "Home-country political risk: The case of German business", Forthcoming.

83 *Financial Times*, 8 December 1999.

84 *The Economist*, 27 November 1999.

In addition to regulatory and financing issues, Deutsche Bank had to address many internal management ones. Bank prepared to make in its traditionally-cautious corporate culture and the structure of its business? How would the acquisition affect the bank's European operations. Could it and did it really want to move from a bank built on intimate relationships with customers into a more open group that provides cutting-edge services to a whole-host of customers through impersonal capital markets? At the time of the acquisition, Deutsche Bank representatives sat on more than 400 company supervisory boards. It held substantial stakes in some of Germany's best known and largest companies – for example, Allianz, 10 per cent of share capital, market value DM 10.4 billion; Daimler-Benz (before merger with Chrysler) 22 per cent, DM 14.2b; Philipp Holzmann, 25 per cent. DM 0.5b, and Metallgesellschaft, 13 per cent, DM 0.6b.[85] Could the bank attract, encourage, and tolerate the high salaries and big egos of those investment bankers it had and would inevitably have to pinch from other firms? The bank had already had many important recent defections. Was Deutsche Bank prepared to divest of some its unprofitable business sectors and push into new, higher margin ones in order to reach its aggressive goal of a 25 per cent return on equity by 2001? How could the bank, moreover, avoid the missteps, delays and squabbles associated with its Morgan Grenfell acquisition of nearly a decade earlier with a bank like Bankers Trust, which was already in relatively desperate straits?[86]

There were many priorities, some were conflicting, and many involved complicated personnel choices. Job cuts would have to come first. For those Bankers Trust executives the bank wanted to keep, however, Deutsche Bank set aside a $400 million retention pool to be spread over many people. In spite of Deutsche Bank's very serious and experience acquisition team, the acquisition suffered, though, from some glitches. Although Deutsche Bank knew the extent and quality of the assets it acquired, it was not quite sure what it wanted to do with them. Some businesses required more investment; others had to be dropped. Senior management was not yet sure which. There were some false starts. Even after another small acquisition, Deutsche Bank was deemed to be too small in what was once a core business of both banks, custodial services. Private equity, an area in which both banks were relatively strong, was dropped. Moreover, each time Frankfurt management changed its views about the configuration of businesses and the structure of the regional operations, it changed its "man" on the ground. The bank went through four regional presidents in three years. As one of them put it, "one of the major hurdles

85 "Breuer aims for the top", *Financial Times*, 26 November 1998. See also "Ein ziemlich schwerer Brocken", *Die Zeit*, 26 November 1998.

86 "The battle of the bulge bracket", *The Economist*, 28 November 1998.

for the acquisition implantation was Frankfurt's indecision about exactly what it wanted in the US".[87] Perhaps the biggest glitch came in the person of Bankers most senior management, which was to have been integrated into Deutsche Bank senior management, but lacked the confidence of key New York and Frankfurt personnel.[88]

Conclusion

With the acquisition, Deutsche Bank clearly realised some of its strategic ambitions. By 1999, Deutsche Bank was once again a leading player in investment and other banking activities. It was the fifth largest provider of syndicated loans and the largest outside of the United States, even though its activity was only 25 per cent of the world leader, Chase Manhattan.[89] With $844 billion in assets, it was the largest bank in Germany and Europe as measured by assets.[90] During the first third of 1999, it ran approximately 200 bond issues, totaling $48 billion and nearly 8 per cent market share.[91] For the first six months of that year, it led all issuers of West European corporate bonds.[92] By 1999, investment banking profits amounted to 60 per cent of the group's total.[93]

Nevertheless, the first few years of the merger brought few profits. It initiated a period of big investment not of high payouts. Unfortunately, Deutsche Bank's investment banking business was still dominated by low margin, volatile activities. The merger had bought credibility, but little immediate business.[94] Bankers Trust added something in derivatives and in leveraged buyouts (LBOs), Deutsche Bank still needed to beef up both these areas with personnel acquisitions. Much of the development of the above-mentioned capacities had to be brought in or grown internally anyway. In retrospect, the acquisition brought the bank a platform, an identity, an innovative spirit, and a perception on the Street that it was committed to being cutting edge.[95] Deutsche Bank had realised its "American Dream," but in the fast-moving world of financial services, no institution can count on long-term value creation with one investment or collection of offerings. Truly the slogan "innovate or die" applies here more than virtually anywhere else

87 Interview with John Ross, 16 January 2006.

88 *The Financial Times*, 21 June 1999.

89 Jane E. Hughes and Scott B. MacDonald, *International Banking*, Boston, Addison Wesley, 2002, p. 27.

90 *Ibidem*, p. 53.

91 *Ibidem*, p. 145.

92 *Ibidem*, p. 149.

93 *The Economist*, 27 May 2000.

94 *Ibidem*.

95 Separate interviews with Seth Waugh and Gary Hattem, 6 January 2006.

in the global economy.[96] But in light of the recent banking crisis, the axiom might be revised to read, "innovate and die."

The story of Deutsche Bank's Bankers Trust acquisition, a major step in the restructuring of international banking, especially international investment banking, points to many insights about our banking system that might be helpful in understanding the 2008 banking crisis. It highlights both the perceived economic imperatives and risks of modern banking institutions. The foreign direct investments of megabanks have helped them control vast amounts of assets by giving them access to more markets, and setting up trading and product development for new financial players, such as hedge funds. Deutsche Bank's interest in and final acquisition of Bankers Trust is testimony to the degree in which modern investment banking has become a supranational activity. Megabanks do business development, create complex financial products and trade them across borders within the same group, virtually eliminating the "frictions" that national borders once represented. To do so they have greatly expanded their balance sheets.

Many have assets that nearly equal (big countries like Germany) or even exceed (small like Switzerland) the gross national products of the countries in which they are incorporated. By European accounting standards, in 2004, Deutsche Bank's assets were roughly equal to 50 per cent of Germany's GNP. In 1913, when that bank was the second largest in the world as measured by assets, they were only 5 per cent of German GNP. Having those assets, both securities and offices, play an important role in moving money around the world quickly, sourcing and using funds where needed, and an essential role tailoring and trading sophisticated, tailor-made derivative instruments, very profitable and risky activities in which Deutsche Bank, in part thanks to its Bankers Trust acquisition, excels.

The very recent crisis (sinvr 2007/2008) has underscored the inability of regulators to even recognise how risky – let alone control – the amount and types of trading done by the kind of multinational banks created by the Bankers Trust acquisition.[97] The acquisition shows that big business and society must still deal with political risk, but of a somewhat different kind that prevailed forty years ago. The case here suggests that institutions like Deutsche Bank still suffer from what some have called "home country" political risk, and a somewhat new forms of cultural conflict. Despite Deutsche Bank's many efforts to "Americanise" its US business, approval of the acquisition was held up by actions of its own government nearly fifty years earlier.

---

96 See *The Economist*, 25 September 1999.

97 Harold James and Chris Kobrak, "From international to transnational finance: The new face of global capital markets", working paper, August 2009.

Even in its own country, the acquisition reinforced criticisms of the bank. Changes in Deutsche Bank's business culture – for example, high bonuses and lack of responsibility for companies whose securities it hawks – are regularly attacked in its own national press as part of a larger cultural problem, to which the acquisition contributed. During the first decade of the 21st century, Deutsche Bank had to confront the paradoxical and at times conflicting necessity of shoring up its position in its "domestic" market – the German or European "home countries" – while simultaneous bolstering its reputation in the highly competitive and unsentimental international capital markets. Frustrated in many of its attempts to consolidate its position in German financial services but aided by changes in German tax law, Deutsche Bank divested itself of many German holdings, freeing up capital for more profitable investment banking activities, and shed some of its German identity. But cultivating entrepreneurial managers for its key businesses in the face of some its home-country constituents, who fear the freewheeling ways of international capital markets, associated with the Wild West.[98]

In any case, both the successes and failures of the acquisition must be seen in a long historical context. Although Deutsche Bank fared pretty well in the recent crisis, both the acquisition and crisis are useful reminders of the huge management challenge inherent in adequately controlling approximately 80,000 employees in nearly 80 countries performing complicated and risky tasks, many of which senior management cannot be expected directly monitor and perhaps even ultimately understand. Circa 2007, Deutsche Bank had nearly 12,000 employees and operated over 500 entities in its North American operations alone. Despite the added complexity, megabanks like Deutsche Bank have added financial liquidity and reduced some transaction costs, by creating such a frictionless internal network. Although many have been bailed out by governments, some of the most diversified ones (both geographically and in business segments) survived with few scars. As of this writing, some that took money are paying back public funding relatively quickly and returning to high profitability embarrassingly quickly. Whether banks like Deutsche Bank will continue to thrive themselves and what overall effect they will have on system risk remains to be seen. At the very least, hopefully the story of Deutsche Bank's acquisition of Bankers Trust gives us a clearer idea the direction of multinational banking strategies and structures.

---

98 See *The Economist*, 2 February 2000 and 27 May 2000.

Part V

Conclusive Chapters

CHAPTER 14

Overall Survey of Authors' Contributions to the History of Investment Banking

Hubert BONIN & Carlo BRAMBILLA

We do not claim that the eleven contributions in this book completely answer the questions posed in the introductory chapter. Each of them has developed its own national logic and gauged its banking model at the heart of a very specific banking system, whatever be the international connections of each place and the osmosis which allowed for the interpenetration of strategic models and banking practices. Nevertheless, this chapter will rise to the challenge of showing the relative unity between them by referring to the problematics raised in the introductory chapter. Each has contributed more or less to the collective body of ideas presented by our team at a conference and given shape to in this book.

1. What differences between the business models?

Naturally, we need to begin with a section dedicated to the central issue of the "business model", now that the question of the difference between the investment bank on one hand, and the corporate or market banking business (within the commercial bank) on the other, is rather vague and has, in any case, given rise to much debate, especially when we know that in many countries, banking systems favoured the model of the "universal bank".

A. *How to pinpoint the differentiation?*

All the ambiguity regarding investment banking resides in its being practiced by both the specialised investment banks and commercial banks: the activities of the investment bank, the corporate bank, the issuing bank and even of the brokerage bank have all been assumed by the big deposit banks as part of their corporate banking services. It is difficult to even draw a clear line between the two business models! No wonder that P. Hertner has not been able to clearly specify the "boundary" between commercial and investment banks in the execution of their work as finance and capital markets banks in central and Balkan Europe. Crédit lyonnais figures among the foremost French banks, which explains the decisive role played by its technical and financial services[1] in support of its working as both a "corporate" and "financial" bank. Deutsche Ban*k* too worked in the same field – what one could call that of the "mixed" or "industrial" bank. Their financial services functioned well upstream as regards railway projects and in close conjunction with industrialists and investors in the ceded public services. Both these major banks continued at the end of the 19th century to work closely with private banking houses such as those mentioned by P. Hertner, Bardac and Bethmann – in a mix that was somewhat different from the one analysed by Youssef Cassis in London which combined stock brokers, merchant bankers and intermediary financiers.[2]

P. Geljon and T. de Graaf have made a detailed study of this osmosis between the "old banks" and the "new banks", between banking houses, stock brokers and the big commercial banks in their workings as corporate and capital markets banks. Several business models came together. Rotterdamsche Bank was an investment as well as a colonial corporate bank; Amsterdamsch Bank was a combination of a commercial and a corporate bank, while Algemeene Maatschappij is an example of the European model of the Pereire brothers' "Crédit mobilier", that is to say, a corporate-cum-market bank combo. After the spate of inter-bank mergers in the years 1960-1970, the Netherlands counted half a dozen major banking firms which practiced both corporate banking as well as investment banking: we are well on the road towards the business model of the "universal bank" which prevailed at the European scale in the years 1980s-2000s. Henceforth, the difference would become very difficult to perceive from the outside.

H. Bonin's chapter aims at determining exactly how the big deposit and commercial banks differ from investment banks as regards the workings of the corporate, capital markets or investment bank. The available archives clearly show that their corporate banking division boasted of a

---

1 Marc Flandreau, "Le service des Études financières sous Henri Germain (1871-1905): une macro-économie d'acteurs", in Bernard Desjardins, Michel Lescure, Roger Nougaret, Alain Plessis & André Straus (eds.), *Le Crédit lyonnais, 1863-1986. Études historiques*, Geneva, Droz, 2002, pp. 271-302. Bernard Desjardins, "Les Études industrielles du Crédit lyonnais, 1953-1989", *ibidem*, pp. 303-332.

2 Youssef Cassis, *City Bankers, 1890-1914*, Cambridge, Cambridge University Press, 1994. Youssef Cassis, *La City de Londres, 1870-1914*, Paris, Belin, 1987. Youssef Cassis, *Les banquiers de la City à l'époque édouardienne, 1890-1914*, Geneva, Droz, 1984. Youssef Cassis & Philip Cottrell (eds.), *The World of Private Banking*, London, Ashgate, 2010. Youssef Cassis (ed.), *Finance & Financiers in European History (1880-1960)*, Cambridge and Paris, Cambridge University Press-Éditions de la Maison des sciences de l'homme, 1991.

large portfolio of financial know-how: participating well upstream of the negotiations with investment bankers, enterprises and the Treasury for the planning and implementation of issuing and investment operations. They were often listed as joint lead managers. As relational banks, they based themselves on a core group of privileged "good clients", and a synergy sprang up between credit banking and corporate, merchant and investment banking in the name of loyalty: one would think henceforth of an actual nature of an "investment bank", oriented towards the financial interests of its layers of customers among the business communities. H. Bonin emphasises the considerable overlap in the know-how and the impossibility of finding a difference in nature if one considers only the usual business of the corporate bank (credit as an "industrial bank"; cash-management and long-term resources counseling; capital markets bank; investment bank). In fact, why retain such a separation between investment and deposit banks when no law required it till 1941/46 and when it was only structured later by legislation to exorcise the crash of 1931-1935?

This blurring of financial and banking practices was aggravated by the nationalisations of the bulk of public and communal utilities in 1937 and 1945/46 which ruptured the historical link between them and investment banks (mainly BUP and Paribas and Rothschild for the railway company *Compagnie du Nord*) and allowed commercial banks to carve themselves important positions in the bonds issue syndicates of public firms… It was only by tending to their core group of "good clients" and offering new services – as we shall see below – that investment bankers managed to retain their market share.

G. Taneva dedicates an entire section to the modalities of the differences between commercial and investment banks (Paribas, BUP). Table 1 in her chapter details the analysis criteria and the results obtained. Though it does not revolutionise the field, it does help define each type of bank and determine the points of convergence and cooperation and those of specialisation. Having said that, banks such as Société générale and CNEP sometimes exceeded their "nature" and participated in certain investment projects in addition to their activities as commercial and investment banks because solidarity was required in a highly competitive market and such portfolio commitments were hardly sustainable, except for the stakes in various banks outside France as part of transnational financial "webs".

Much later, a similar deployment strategy was employed by Deutsche Bank for its overseas expansions in Latin America and Asia (Deutsch-Asiatische Bank) before WWI. In fact, in both cases it meant deploying its portfolio of corporate banking services at the heart of a key market within the process of globalisation that was underway. C. Kobrak talks of a change in its very nature regarding its international commitments when it aspired to become, like Citigroup, a "banking and financial conglomerate" as regards its business model and a globalised bank, and to thus turn the United States into its third "domestic market" after Germany and the City – where it had acquired Morgan Grenfell: the objective was the "Americanising of Deutsche Bank". Having said that, Bankers Trust had positioned itself as, and was, a "commercial bank" and not an "investment bank" like Goldman Sachs or Lehman Brothers.

It was only at the turn of the 1990s that its strategy veered gradually towards investment banking: it entered the "securities business" market in 1990 in keeping with its strategic boss, Charles Sanford's slogan: "underwrite and distribute", a little ahead of the abrogation of the Glass-Steagall law, but completely in the spirit of the times which was favourable to the liberalisation of the banking economy. It was also the diversification strategy, of going from brokerage to underwriting for example, that was followed by Merrill Lynch. Thus, *Deutsche Bank*'s relatively clear nature began to gradually turn murky as and when it turned to corporate and investment banking, a trend that was intensified by the merger with Bankers Trust.

B. Contradictory models: Specialisation vs universal banking

The historian must finally come to admit that any systemic model corresponds to a given point in the history of a country's banking economy, and no theory, even that of the most brilliant theoretician, has succeeded in granting an absolute legitimacy to this or that system… It is a bit of the historian's revenge as only an empirical analysis can provide the criteria needed for evaluating the efficiency of a particular system in a particular country during a very specific period or cycle of development. Subsequent to the crash at the turn of the 1930s, it was the aspiration towards a theoretical specialisation, that is, as the result of a regulation, that dominated the scene.

We know that the Italian government imposed strict limits to the deployment of universal banks which, actually, were inherited from a specific history and inspired by the "German-type bank",[3] as C. Brambilla shows here and as G. Piluso recalls before WWII: he draws the contours of the corset enclosing the universal bank in his section devoted to the

---

[3] See: Caroline Fohlin, "*Fiduciari* and firm liquidity constraints: The Italian experience with German-style universal banking", *Explorations in Economic History*, 1998, Vol. 35, pp. 83-107. Caroline Fohlin, "Capital mobilisation and utilisation in late-comer economies: Germany and Italy Compared", *European Review of Economic History*, 1999, Vol. 3, No. 2, pp. 139-174. Alessandro Polsi, "The early development of universal banking in Italy in an adverse institutional context, 1850-1914", in Douglas Forsyth & Daniel Verdier (eds.), *The Origins of National Financial Systems. Alexander Gerschenkron Reconsidered*, London & New York, Routledge, 2002.

genealogy of the regulated model. And L.-J. Coronas shows in this book how the corset of specialisation constrained the Spanish banking economy for a long time (the law of 1962 especially). And yet, as in Italy, the model of the mixed or universal bank had dominated earlier for decades in the wake of "the Crédit mobilier model" – with a sister bank being established across the Pyrenées. It was thus as a function of the theoretical or empirical evaluation, according to the inspirers of regulatory[4] and specialisation reforms and the merits or demerits of the universal bank, that a change in the strategic course was decided which aimed at separating the investment bank from the commercial and deposit banks.[5]

At the same time, it would seem that French laws[6] did not put up insurmountable hurdles and H. Bonin shows clearly the overlap that existed in investment banking activities between investment and deposit banks. Moreover, before the laws of 1941-1946, a *de facto* empirical specialisation had taken shape between investment banks (banks oriented towards investment banking) and the Big Banking houses on one hand, and the commercial and deposit banks on the other as a result of the setbacks experienced between 1867 and 1889 by every "modern" deposit bank when the "universal bank" seemed to be calling all the shots. Meanwhile, G. Piluso points out that, despite the regulations imposed in Italy, commercial banks won the right to practice certain types of long-term credit on condition that they use subsidiaries that were clearly identified by their balance sheets and consequently, their risks. This presaged the first stage of the liberalisation process begun at the turn of the 1990s and the reforms to the universal bank being proposed today.

4 Charles Goodhart, "Financial supervision from a historical perspective", in D.G. Hayes & G.E. Woods (eds.), *The Structure of Financial Regulation*, London, Routledge, 2007. Charles Goodhart, Philipp Hartmann, David Llewellyn, Liliana Rojas-Suares & Steven Weisbrod, *Financial Regulation. Why, How, and Where Now?*, London, Routledge, 1998.

5 See: Alfredo Gigliobianco, Claire Giordano & Gianni Toniolo, "Innovation and regulation in the wake of financial crises in Italy (1880s-1930s)", in Ivo Maes, Alfredo Gigliobianco & Gianni Toniolo (eds.), *Financial Market Regulation in the Wake of Financial Crises: The Historical Experience*, Banca d'Italia, Seminari e convegni, No. 1, November 2009, pp. 45-74. Brias Pons, *Regulating Spanish Banking, 1939-1975*, London, Ashgate, 2002.

6 Hubert Bonin, "Crises et réglementation bancaire dans l'histoire européenne", in Loïc Grard & Pascal Kauffmann (eds.), *L'Europe des banques. Approches juridique et économique. Concurrence, réglementation, marché unique*, Paris, Pedone, 2010, pp. 81-96. Claire Andrieu, *La banque sous l'Occupation. Paradoxes de l'histoire d'une profession, 1936-1946*, Paris, Presses de la Fondation nationale des sciences politiques, 1990. Dominique Lacoue-Labarthe, "L'évolution de la supervision bancaire et de la réglementation prudentielles (1945-1996)", in *Bâle II: genèse et enjeux*, *Revue d'économie financière*, No. 73, 4-2003, pp. 39-63.

C. A denaturation of the investment bank's specificity?

Whatever be their relative advantages, investment banks began to gradually lose their hold on investment banking, capital markets banking and consulting businesses. P. Geljon and T. de Graaf have described the irresistible trend towards mergers which has led to the formation of some Dutch giants around Amsterdamsche Bank, Rotterdamsche Bank, Twentsche Bank and the NHM. Most of the "historic" houses were either absorbed by them or swept away by various crises like that of the first half of the 1920s (due to too many bad loans). New houses which entered the field during the inter-War period proved too fragile to change the course of events – even though German finance smartly used the Netherlands as a "neutral" platform from which to operate at the European scale without having to appear directly: a prime example is Mendelssohn's sister enterprise (managed by the well-known financier Fritz Mannheimer), though there were other smaller entities which linked Amsterdam to Berlin or Frankfurt (as well as Brussels).

Not surprisingly, this fragility resurfaced in the post-WWII years when competition from American banks in Europe shook the markets, especially as several market segments were now occupied by public institutions. As shown by P. Geljon and T. de Graaf, this was most evident in the Netherlands, but France too was affected and H. Bonin mentions several specialty corporate and investment banks that were bought over by the public sector (Banque française du commerce extérieur, Crédit national, etc.). The irrefutable convergence between investment and corporate banks accelerated. In the Netherlands, big foreign banks bought over the small merchant banking houses: NHM merged with Twentsche Bank in 1964; Mees & Zooen, Hope and NOB (overseas bank) merged in the years 1960-1970, and the new entity joined ABN (Algemene Bank Nederland) in 1975, the same year that Pierson & Heldring joined AMRO. Later, when ABN and AMRO merged, it became very clear that the corpus of traditions, relations and know-how of the family-owned investment banks had dissolved into the vast "corporate organisation": the uniqueness of investment bankers had helped the deployment of the corporate bank. As we shall discuss at the end of this book, it has become more and more difficult, at the end of the 20th century, to distinguish corporate banking from investment banking. Moreover, as competition intensified in the domain of corporate banking – thanks especially to cooperative banks such as Rabobank (established in the Netherlands in 1972), or the Crédit agricole in France which entered this niche in the 1970s – the corporate banking divisions of diversified groups took over the businesses handled by investment banks at every major marketplace.

It must also be recognised that the metamorphosis of national capitalism engendered by the entry of "multinational companies" justified this convergence between investment and corporate banking. A good example of this tendency may be found in the Netherlands with two Anglo-Dutch giants (Unilever, Royal Dutch Shell) and Philips. The relational networks woven all across the globe by the numerous companies under Unilever from the turn of the 1930s did not resist this capitalist and managerial aggregation, leading inevitably to the dismantling of what has become (again) "the old bank".

The move towards the "mixed bank" gathered momentum, as with AMRO in the Netherlands. Whether it be in the Netherlands or France, it was the corporate banking divisions which absorbed the investment banking cultural capital bequeathed by the investment banks absorbed by the big banks. In 2000, the "universal bank" BNP merged with Paribas which was then the largest investment and corporate bank in the country, having absorbed its chief rival, Banque de l'union parisienne, in 1973/74.[7] In fact, the "size effect" required such a cooperation of human, technological and financial resources. In the Netherlands, investment bankers had to co-manage about thirty to forty issuing syndicates every year – mainly Euro-syndicates – which meant greater risks and a significant increase in the size of the teams of experts. Similarly, in the Netherlands as elsewhere, the major trend towards the privatisation of public companies opened vast markets for investment bankers from the turn of the 1990s. This also opened the doors to new connections within the domain of relational banking capitalism and new business opportunities, though it did increase the need of a financial and a relational "surface".

Investment bankers needed some serious "firepower" in order to play in the European "big league". This required solid national bases and therefore, new mergers and streamlining in order to mobilise their power across continental Europe and achieve a better penetration at the heart of the London market, which was the determinant platform for the financial and capital markets bank. Thus we see why ABN-AMRO bought over the Hoare Govett bank and allied itself with NM Rothschild for the capital markets bank, or why ING acquired Barings and the Deutsche Bank took over the big merchant bank of Morgan Grenfell in 1986. We note that P. Geljon and T. de Graaf do not fail to show the absurd culmination of this race for size by recalling the "ABN-AMRO affaire",[8] targeted by

---

7 Hubert Bonin, *La Banque de l'union parisienne (1874/1904-1974). De l'Europe aux outre-mers*, Paris, Publications de la SFHOM, 2011.

8 See Jeroen Smit, *The Perfect Prey. The Fall of ABN AMRO, or What Went Wrong in the Banking Industry*, Amsterdam, Prometheus, 2009.

RBS, Fortis and Santander, and signaling the hubris which culminated at the height of the 1993/5-2007/2008 cyclic boom – as though the Dutch market could no longer meet the geo-banking criteria.

2. The key role played by senior bankers

One of the major differences lay precisely in the mobilisation of a team of about a dozen "senior bankers" in every investment bank: well established in their profession, these senior bankers led small teams which closely followed a company (client or business target). Materially and humanly, it was these senior bankers who justified the commission fees charged by investment banks to their client companies for the "rarity" of these intellectual and managerial "pointers". Paid by the percentage and/or at a set rate for the value addition,[9] the work by this "advisory bank" – whether it be for issuing operations, investments, reclassification of securities, mergers and acquisitions, strategic deployment, refocusing plans or for the design of structured finance – was based on "grey matter" and was paid by degrees of density which, though difficult for the historian to perceive, may be understood thanks to archival material and written and oral testimonies.

They made full use of their network of personal and institutional relations and their numerous contacts within the business communities of every major market, enlarged by specific, shared affinities outside of business and often facilitated by the adherence to a group having a good "social capital".[10] Though commercial banks also had such people, they were not as capable and moreover, they spent much of their time managing the "company's organisation". For example, Jean Reyre at Paribas, Henri Lafond at BUP and Robert Jablon at Rothschild led teams of "commando" investment bankers to form the "contact bank", far from the formal relations of the big banks – while the partner-managers at Lazard Paris maintained the tradition of the Anglo-Saxon merchant bank.[11] It is one of the major points of differentiation!

Often, these senior bankers constituted the interface between the client company (the chief financial officer, the head of treasury, communi-

---

9 See: Andrey Golubov, Dimitri Petmegas and Nickolaos Travalos, "When it pays to pay your investment banker: New evidence on the role of financial advise in M&A", *Journal of Finance*, Vol. 67, No. 1, 2011, pp. 271-311.

10 See: Chapter 2. "The network nature of investment banking", in Robert G. Eccles & Dwight B. Crane, *Doing Deals: Investment Banks at Work*, Boston, Harvard Business School Press, 1988, pp. 35-52.

11 Anne Sabouret, *MM. Lazard frères et Cie. Une saga de la fortune*, Paris, Olivier Orban, 1987. Martine Orange, *Ces Messieurs de Lazard*, Paris, Albin Michel, 2006. William Cohan, *The Last Tycoons: The Secret History of Lazard Frères & Co.*, New York, Doubleday, 2007.

cators, and of course the CEO and his/her team) and the specialised teams (issuers, research analysts, experts in finance engineering, salespeople for securities, etc.), especially for issuing operations – the keystone of investment banking. "The network in investment banks is distinctive. Because of their role in mediating the flow of assets between issuers and investors, and because of their economic characteristics and production process, investment banks have an internal network that is unusually flat and flexible. This is in contrast to many other organisations that have a more hierarchical network of ties in which communication occurs primarily up and down a relatively rigid organisation rather than across departemental lines."[12] "Relationship management"[13] was the force that accelerated and intensified the process of mobilising the "brains" within the investment bank, and this ability might be the point of differentiation with the usual commercial banks which often relied on long chains of analysis and decision, along with the famous "committees".

P. Hertner shows the value of these senior bankers' knowledge portfolio in the design of major infrastructure projects in central, oriental and Balkan Europe, with "strong" personalities emerging form among this community of investment bankers. While this analysis may seem rather "standard" because researchers like René Girault, Raymond Poidevin, Jacques Thobie[14] and Alice Teichova[15] among others have already studied these markets at the turn of the 20th century and the inter-war period – and the chapter has a long list of references –, P. Hertner adds insightful additions by meticulously reconstituting the information, influence and decision-making circuits upstream of the authorities' choice in favour of this or that actor, and how the stakeholders' informal community functioned both synergistically (in order to best share risks and minimise the danger of asymmetric information) and competitively (in order to get good

12 Robert G. Eccles & Dwight B. Crane, *Doing Deals: Investment Banks*, *op. cit.*, p. 38.

13 See: Chapter 9 "Relationship management", in Robert G. Eccles & Dwight B. Crane, *Doing Deals*, *op. cit.*, pp. 179-201.

14 Jacques Thobie, "French investments in public and private funds in the Ottoman empire on the eve of the Great War", in Philip Cottrell, Iain Fraser & Monika Pohle-Fraser (eds.), *East Meets West Banking. Commerce and Investment in the Ottoman Empire*, Aldershot, Ashgate, 2008, pp. 123-142. Jacques Thobie, *Intérêts et impérialisme français dans l'Empire ottoman (1895-1914)*, Paris, Publications de la Sorbonne-Imprimerie nationale, 1977.

15 Alice Teichova, Terry Gourvish & Agnes Pogany, *Universal Banking in the 20th Century. Finance, Industry and the State in the North and Central Europe*, Aldershot, Ashgate, 1994. Philip Cottrell & Alice Teichova (eds.), *International Business and Central Europe, 1918-1939*, Leicester, Leicester University Press, 1983. Harold James, Hakan Lindgren & Alice Teichova (eds.), *The Role of Banks in the Interwar Economy*, Cambridge and Paris, Cambridge University Press and Éditions de la Maison des sciences de l'homme, 1991.

positions as lead managers for financial operations and within the securities issue and investment syndicates). In all these processes, banking and financial intermediaries proved to be the keystones, such as René Baudouy in the years 1890; and J. Thobie achieved a high end identification of these go-betweens as regards the Ottoman finance.[16] It is clear that these senior bankers[17] participated fully in the network culture which characterised the successful company, especially those in investment and finance banks. The City, its merchant banks and its market activities also provide numerous cases of such "go-betweens" at the interface between various stakeholders: investors, enterprises, banks, governments, magazines, etc. The example of Everard Hambro has been minutely studied by J. Rutterford who, having access to his correspondence and his day-to-day life as a businessman, could do full justice to his subject.

Despite its size and a tendency towards a somewhat collective culture, the Netherlands too provides personalities who have played a decisive role in the history of investment banking: P. Geljon and T. de Graaf have drawn exhaustive portraits of Frits van Nierop, whose clairvoyant anticipation and cultural flexibility allowed him an early understanding of the links between the corporate bank, the growth of the stock market and the large enterprise's need for long-term capital, allowed Amsterdamsche Bank to make early inroads into investment banking. Meanwhile, Abraham Carel Wertheim transformed a small merchant bank into a solid corporate and investment bank, Wertheim & Gompertz (between 1858 and 1897). The latter was, among others, a pioneer, a path-breaker and a keystone in several aspects of the banking revolution. Similarly, Marten Mees was one of the key figures in the construction of the investment bank and the "modern" markets in Rotterdam (between 1858 and 1905), while Karel van Aaast build a vast corporate and investment banking division within NHM (in 1889-1930).

In the second half of the 19th century, the maturation of the modern corporate bank benefited from the network of connections between polyvalent bosses, bankers and businessmen: the embeddedness of these houses within the regional business community provided the base on which to

16 Jacques Thobie, "Intermédiaires et associés d'entreprises françaises dans l'empire ottoman finissant, 1880-1914", in Abdelhellil Temimi (ed.), *Mélanges Charles-Robert Ageron*, Zaghouan, Tunisie, 1996, tome II, pp. 133-152; reedited in Jacques Thobie, *La France, l'Europe et l'Est méditerranéen depuis deux siècles. Économie, finance, diplomatie*, Istanbul, Isis, 2007, pp. 81-103.

17 Mark Casson, "Entrepreneurial networks: A theoretical perspective", in Michael Moss, Anthony Slaven & Clara Eugenia Nunez (eds.), *Entrepreneurial Networks and Business Culture*, Seville, Fundacion Fomento de la historian economica, Publicaciones de la Universidad de Sevilla, 1998, pp. 13-28. Mark Casson, *Information and Organisation: A New Perspective on the Theory of the Firm*, Oxford, Clarendon Press, 1997.

build business relations, as is shown by L.-J. Coronas regarding Banco de Vizcaya and Banco Espanol de Credito-Banesto. He goes on to add that, after a second major stage in the history of Spanish banking, other business communities spun off other banks such as Banco Urquijo and Banco central in the years 1910s-1920s. Like after the German *Gründerzeit* or the Giolitti-Nitti years in Italy when these economies were struggling to catch up,[18] such "moments" of History gave concrete shape to the aspirations of regional business communities and linked them to efficient financial supports capable of mobilising sufficient monetary and knowledge resources while winning for themselves a new confidence and reputation and the capacity to overcome economic downturns or disappointments vis-à-vis major clients. Key figures played key roles in the rise of these banks and L.-J. Coronas talks about several of these Iberian "heroes".

G. Piluso is the author of the remarkable monograph on the merchant bank Mediobanca[19] and the pioneering role played by its boss (for several decades) Enrico Cuccia. We know that he also became the key man of Italian capitalism – "*il cavaliero blanco*" – by engineering numerous financial operations within the country and, when it gained an international reputation, with his close collaboration with Lazard and its boss, André Meyer. Cuccia was the indispensable go-between in the movement of capitalistic concentration and the design of the "solid cores" which reconciled the expansion of the financial base of listed companies and the stabilisation of the power to control their strategy and management.

Dealing with a much more recent period, C. Kobrak has minutely analysed the pioneering role played by C. Sanford, who was made head of Bankers Trust towards the end of the 1980s. Joining hands with a number of other big bankers, C. Sanford upturned the American banking model, convinced governments to liberalise the international market and bank statutes, rapidly implemented diversification strategies by building banking and financial conglomerates and, as far as we are concerned, reinvented the investment banking business. By adopting the new methods

18 See mainly: Caroline Fohlin, "Capital mobilisation and utilisation in late-comer Economies: Germany and Italy Compared", *European Review of Economic History*, 1999, Vol. 3, No. 2, pp. 139-174. Caroline Fohlin, "*Fiduciari* and firm liquidity constraints: The Italian experience with German-style universal banking", *Explorations in Economic History*, 1998, Vol. 35, pp. 83-107. Caroline Fohlin, "The balancing act of German universal banks and English deposit banks, 1880-1913", *Business History*, 43, 2001, pp. 1-24. Caroline Fohlin, "Universal banking in Pre-World War I Germany: model and myth", *Explorations in Economic History*, Vol. 36, 1999, No. 4, pp. 305-343. Caroline Fohlin, *Financial Capitalism and Germany's Rise to Industrial Growth*, Cambridge and New York, Cambridge University Press, 2007. Jeremy Edwards and Sheilagh Ogilvie, "Universal banks and German industrialisation: A reappraisal", *Economic History Review*, August 1996, Vol. XLIX, No. 3, pp. 427-446.

19 Giandomenico Piluso, *Mediobanca. Tra regole e mercato*, Milan, Egea, 2005.

of risk and profit evaluation (RAROC), he contributed to the "convergence" between investment, corporate and capital markets banking. C. Sanford greatly impressed the head of Deutsche Bank, Hilmar Kopper, and thereby indirectly contributed to the introduction of this new business model and the new paradigms of the banking economy in Europe, especially in Frankfurt and London, Deutsche Bank's major platforms for these three "modern" or "modernised" activities.

These senior bankers and their teams (lawyers, financiers, loan-, current value conversion- and balance-sheet financing experts in the various ways of banking intermediation) tied investment banking closely to innovation with a commando spirit and a largely autonomous team in the design and, often, the initial implementation of projects and operations: "Those who develop strategies are also in the best position to determine what resources are needed and what organisational structure makes the best use of the resources. From the top management's perspective, although it is responsible for setting the broad organisational design for implementing the corporate strategy, the high degree of autonomy throughout the organisation for people to determine how to organise their unit and relationships with other units means that the firm [investment bank] is a self-designing organisation."[20]

In a similar, "hero-worshipping" vein, several chapters talk of the investment bank's strategic mobility, commercial reactivity and engineering capacity. The more they felt themselves copied by commercial banks in the corporate and capital markets banking niches and "pushed against the ropes" in the competitive arena, the more they needed to compensate for the risk of losing market share. They also proved themselves to be the most innovative as regards the development of new banking and financial products – though corporate bankers in commercial banks also played the game of competitive innovation as well! Investment bankers' capacity for innovation depended on their autonomy, their scope for initiative, and one could almost use the Schumpeterian expression "creative chaos"...

H. Bonin contends that investment banks played a key role, directly or through their subsidiaries or sponsored or refinanced companies, in the introduction of new forms of credit (consumer credit, property loans for developers, leasing), new banking services (factoring, etc.) and a fundamentally novel manner of using investment funds. "Pioneers" such as Jacques de Fouchier and Jack Francès not only achieved fame on the Parisian market, but were also rewarded by being promoted to the financial group's number 1 spot. They were well and truly "path-breakers" and "trend-setters" who shook the market's *modus operandi*, if not the

[20] Robert G. Eccles & Dwight B. Crane, *Doing Deals: Investment Banks*, *op. cit.*, p. 119.

rules, by turning them obsolete. Paribas and Bup contributed in the establishment of the investment funds concept and its spread in France. They fought to introduce new legislation which would allow for the implantation of these innovations. Thus, investment banking "genes" contained numerous such innovative stimulants which helped accelerate the process of adaption of the Parisian market – and it was the same with the other markets and in many decisive epochs.

Everyone knows the decisive role played by Siegmund Warburg in his "second life" as an investment banker after his exile from Germany to the United Kingdom:[21] he stimulated the birth of "pure investment banking", merger and acquisition consultancy, the emergence of the Eurobonds market[22] and thereby, the growth of the market banking business. Another major personality of that post-war era was André Meyer[23] who, like Felix Rohatyn,[24] was one of those reputed senior bankers that the house of Lazard produced at its three centers. A little later, a third "hero", Minos Zombanakis, played a major role at a stage of the market banking revolution by "creating" the Libor: "In the 1960s, this Greek national, who had a degree in economics from Harvard, was at the head of the London subsidiary of the American bank, Manufacturers Hanover Trust. An expert in financial engineering, he set up, in 1969, the first syndicated loan of 80 million dollars by a group of banks to Iran under the Shah. "I assembled the rates that were communicated to me by the members of the consortium. I averaged them and called it *London Interbank Offered Rate*, or Libor", reminisced the financier [...]. M. Zombanakis is considered to be one of the great foreign innovators of the City along with the German Sir Siegmund Warburg, founder of the eponymous bank (which was bought over by the Swiss Ubs) and Patrick Stevenson, of France, creator of Paribas Capital Markets. His expertise, coupled with an indefatigable obstinacy, turned the City into a major centre of syndicated loans

21 Niall Ferguson, *High Financier: The Lives and Time of Siegmund Warburg*, London, Penguin Press, 2010. Jacques Attali, *Sir Siegmund Warburg, 1902-1982. Un homme d'influence*, Paris, Fayard, 1985 (English version: *A Man of Influence: Sir Siegmund Warburg, 1902-1982*, London, Weidenfeld & Nicolson, 1986). David Kynaston, Siegmund *Warburg: A Centenary Appreciation*, London, UBS Warburg, 2002.

22 See: Kathleen Burk, "Witness seminar on the origins and early development of the eurobond market", *Contemporary European History*, 1992, I, pp. 65-87. Niall Ferguson, "Siegmund Warburg, the City of London and the financial roots of European integration", *Business History*, May 2009, Vol. 51, No. 3, pp. 362-380. Catherine Schenk, "The origins of the eurodollar market (1955-1963)", *Explorations in Economic History*, April 1998, No. 35, pp. 221-238.

23 Cary Reich, *Financier: The Biography of André Meyer. A Story of Money, Power, and the Reshaping of American Business*, New York, John Wiley & Sons, 1998.

24 Felix Rohatyn, *Un banquier dans le siècle*, Paris, Saint-Simon, 2011.

to countries – a market that for long had remained informal."[25] Finally, on the Parisian market, the history of Indosuez[26] (one time thought of being able to contest Paribas' domination, if not the market banking branches of BNP and Société générale), was marked by Jean-François Lepetit,[27] a major figure in this banking revolution who helped implement one of the first French trading rooms, introduce "euronotes" and the euro-commercial paper in the 1980s.

3. Investment banks and market confidence

These senior bankers were supposed to have a capital of expertise that instilled confidence in investors. J. Flores talks of this relationship of trust in his chapter on the relations between Baring and the London market. Investors and other stakeholders strongly believed that merchant bankers had a large and solid portfolio of information: "The involvement of Baring as the historical underwriter of Argentina's bonds in London was regarded as a seal of approval by financial markets." Here we have the theme of cognitive perception which forges opinions within the financial economy of representations. Baring was one of the organisers and managers of these "beauty contests" through which "paraded" the securities to be issued on the primary market. The "selector" was expected to "stage" trustworthy "stars", despite the competitive environment or, precisely, in order to avoid the hazards of such a competition.

This relationship of trust did not depend only on quality criteria as, additionally, it also assumed the constitution of some serious guarantees: investment bankers were also lawyers looking for flying buttresses for their international financial operations in "new countries" – which meant certain risks. J. Flores has meticulously analysed the relations between investment banks and business laws, when Baring and its European syndicate negotiated a range of financial buttresses (customs revenue, etc.). But did this investment bank with its (on the whole) light assets and the structure of a managing partnership[28] have an adequate know-how in development economics? How to identify the slide of fertile investments (being repaid by the income of a sustained growth) to over-investments? This question, which is so common in the history of new countries, leads

25 Marc Roche, "M. Zombanakis, créateur du LIBOR, est considéré comme l'un des grands innovateurs étrangers dans la City", *Le Monde*, 6 June 2012. See: David Lascelles, *The Story of Minos Zombanakis. Banking Without Borders*, London, Economia Publishing, 2012.

26 See: Hubert Bonin, *Indosuez. L'autre grande banque d'affaires (1975-1987)*, Paris, Économica, 1987.

27 See: Jean-François Lepetit, *Homme de marché*, Paris, Économica, 2002.

28 See Peter Ziegler, *The Sixth Great Power. Barings, 1762-1929*, London, Collins, 1988.

to the notion of the "cantilever": the growth in production capacity and, especially, the repayment of debts, was often much slower than expected, whether it be for the country as a whole or for this or that major investment in railways, port or industry. The lower than expected gains could only lead to cash tensions, the impossibility of repaying foreign direct investments and thus of servicing the loans.

As so many banking historians have pointed out (from David Landes and Bertrand Gille to Alain Plessis and Nicolas Stoskopf, for example), the passage from the banking house of the first banking revolution (merchant banks, houses of the *Haute Banque*) to the banking enterprise of the second banking revolution required the construction of a "corporate organisation" which included setting up market research services such as those of Crédit lyonnais and Société générale in France from 1870-1890, with engineers, researchers, experts and study missions – not to speak of the actuaries used here and there in asset management for institutional investors. C. Brambilla says that "Comit organised a first nut of an industrial technical department, *Credit* relied upon expertise of some of its board members, namely Giovanni Battista Pirelli, an engineer who ran the first and most important rubber company in Italy, and Giacomo Castelbolognesi, a banker with a long experience in international financial markets and in the chemical industry. In 1915, *Credit* hired Alberto Lodolo, an electrical engineer with a relevant experience in electrical plant building and management, as general director responsible for its electrical and industrial *affaires*". Faced by the web of business and credit relations and the formation of a complex industrial economy, managers of the two entities of the corporate bank felt the need to have a robust information system which would be a source of operational stability and confidence.

Having said that, a few years earlier, the little Baring ("old bank") already had a specialist, Nicholas Bower, who went to Argentina to gather the required information, while the leading European syndicated banks ("new banks") had not made a similar effort: their "learning curve" as regards financial banking was slow and their knowledge portfolio lacked investigative talent. Only Crédit lyonnais made a comparable effort and, in consequence, abstained more or less completely from Argentinean operations....

The risk lay in "procyclic" behaviours which accentuate the tendency to boom and ultimately, to overinvestment – an open door for defaults. Thus, investment bankers ran the risk of a loss of confidence whenever they were seen to lack the information required to gauge the extent of their risk-taking. It is true that, as in every boom, inter-bank competition, between generations and types of banks and between establishments in general, resulted in a fever of investments, a race to the market, in order to prevent competitors from gaining market share, commissions and resale benefits, and also to meet the demand of equally impatient and, temporarily, unconscious investors: success begets success one would think – in a very common mass movement. When everybody wants some "paper", one runs the risk of getting "bad paper"! J. Flores talks of this fever regarding Argentina in the mid-1880s – in the wake of the studies make by A. Regalski – and shows how the agreement of 1885 with the government only succeeded in lulling bankers' and, in Europe, investors' vigilance, despite some alarming articles in the press. Thus, "Gaucho Barings", as a journalist called it,[29] managed to heap overinvestments in the Pampa: "A charge that might have been brought with justice against [Barings] was that, in their eagerness to do business, they had not considered all these enterprises coolly and wisely enough."[30]

On the other hand, putting the finger on the precise nature of the risk of a sharp economic downturn, of overexposure and overinvestment has always been a tricky affair. When we see the present debates on the risk of this or that European country defaulting or remind ourselves of the intensity of the crisis that befell Russia and South East Asia in 1997-1998, it would be unfair to talk of the "backwardness" of investment banks a hundred years ago.... Locating the point of virtual reversal, that is to say, the limit beyond which the risk would become excessive, is a recurring issue. J. Flores mentions several sharp debates on this subject regarding Argentina of the 1880s. The lure of quick gains via commissions could have helped blind some bankers, while the sharing of operations among syndicates could have diluted the perception of risk and led to the recklessness. In fact, as in the case of the recent crash of 2007-2008, it was the quality and validity of the guarantees that proved to be wayward: Paribas discovered *ex post* that the Mortgage Bank of the Province of Cordoba bonds which had served as collateral for other securities had no longer any value....

We understand that the construction of a new market from scratch constituted a challenge for investment banks: they needed to persuade their partner commercial banks, the securities brokerage networks and the various other market platforms of the seriousness of the values proposed. A good example is the Bulgarian case studied by G. Taneva. The syndicates built by Paribas and the Bup were not only technical tools, but also instruments for persuading the stakeholders: while neighbouring Greece

29 W.R. Lawson, "Barings: The sixth power", *Bankers' Magazine*, 1891, quoted by Joseph Wechsler, *The Merchant Bankers*, New York, Pocket Books, 1966, pp. 76-127; here: p. 111.

30 John Clapham, quoted by Joseph Wechsler, *op. cit.*, p. 110.

disappointed and the Ottoman Empire vacillated in the mid-1870s, the inclusion of new candidates for the issues could only happen due to the attentive sponsorship by investment bankers. This led them to have active engagements at the very heart of the Bulgarian economy, enlarge their knowledge portfolio and contain information asymmetries and nurture relational networks apt for the creation of a stable and trustworthy Franco-Bulgarian business community.

As J. Rutterford remarks pertinently, "the wet finger", the intuition, the information provided by the relational networks was not enough to convince the investment banker: "The art of evaluating balance sheets and understanding accounting was a prerequisite for the investment banker who could not rely only on his connections, a 'nose', and an intuitive perception of the situation of his clients." Despite the important of the social and relational capital in the senior banker's activity, he practiced both relational and transactional banking, even in the smaller family or partner houses. We also know the amount of work involved in the perusal of "dispatches" – letters sent by correspondents in foreign markets and all kinds technical notes written by experts on this or that structured finance project: we must not have the false idea that they were "armchair bankers". When Hambro got into the shipbuilding business, he turned himself into a specialist of the economics of this branch and the financial ratios it generated: a "man of records" as much as a "man of relations". If "his word was his bond", he needed to "manage" his reputation and trust as specific "assets" and consequently, "prune the risks" upstream by fighting against the risk of information asymmetry.

This reputation[31] was very much the issue in the share issue prospectus, not only for legal reasons, but mainly because the lead manager or managers and book-keepers were supposed to inspire confidence in the bankers taking part in the investment syndicate and especially in their "sub-participants", and, ultimately, in the institutional investors who subscribe to blocks of shares and who still lacked, in the 19th century and *grosso modo* till the years 1950s-1960s, solid teams of analysts in their asset management structure. Far from being a second rate activity or simply a technical stage in the printing of ordinary documents, the issue prospectus constituted a powerful lever for building this trust and the future success of the operation.

P. Geljon and T. de Graaf also highlight another key role played by investment banks in financial affairs: as informal supervisors of the

[31] See Monika Pohle-Fraser, "Personal and impersonal exchange. The role of reputation in banking: some evidence from 19th and early 20th banks' archives", in Philip Cotrell, Even Lange & Ulf Olsson (eds.), *Centres and Peripheries in Banking*, Aldershot, Ashgate, 2007, pp. 177-196.

quality and trustworthiness of operations. To the extent that they guaranteed the bulk of issues through syndicates in which they were lead managers, they staked not only their funds but also their reputation: risk of reputation[32] and the issue of trust converged to create implicit "norms" which acted as quasi-arbiters of the markets and led to the creation of the Association for the securities trade in 1876 in Amsterdam. It meant avoiding the famous "tragedy of commons",[33] when market players hid their shady practices and lack of know-how by taking advantage of the leaders' positive initiatives and knowledge portfolio. Investment bankers were invested with the subtle mission within their business community of maintaining collective assets, answering quality expectations and managing the risk reputation on behalf of the entire market.

The establishment of "conditions" (price of investment compared to the nominal or face value of the securities issued; rate of interest; maturity of securities) and the quality of the syndicate (greater or lesser openness of the syndicate regarding the number of banking stakeholders; quality of participants and especially of lead managers) constitute, as we know, one of the jewels in investment banks' knowledge portfolios. Even the choice of these criteria was a result of this search for quality, the product of a good "perception" by the banking, market and investor communities and ultimately, the reputation of lead managers. The "sentiment",[34] the

---

32 See: Thomas Chemmanur and Paolo Fulghieri, "Investment house reputation, information production and financial intermediation", *Journal of Finance*, Vol. 49, 1994, pp. 57-79. Also: Monika Pohle-Fraser, "Personal and impersonal exchange. The role of reputation in banking: some evidence from 19th and early 20th banks' archives", in Philip Cottrell, Even Lange & Ulf Olsson (eds.), *Centres and Peripheries in Banking*, Aldershot, Ashgate, 2007, pp. 177-196. Lily H. Fang, "Investment bank reputation and the price and quality of underwriting services", *Journal of Finance*, No. 60, 6, 2005, pp. 2729-2761. Michelangelo Vasta and Alberto Baccini, "Banks and industry in Italy, 1911-1936. New evidence using the interlocking directorates technique", *Financial History Review*, 4, 1997, pp. 139-159.

33 Garrett Hardin, "The tragedy of the commons", *Science*, 1968, No. 162, pp. 1243-1248. David Feeny, Fikret Berkes, Bonnie McCay & James Acheson, "The tragedy of commons: twenty-two years later", *Human Ecology*, 1990, No. 18, pp. 1-19. Elinor Ostrom, *Governing the Commons: The Evolution of Institutions for Collective Action*, New York, Cambridge University Press, 1990. James Acheson, "Capturing the commons: Legal and illegal strategies", in Terry Anderson & Randy Simmons (eds.), *The Political Economy of Customs and Culture: Informal Solutions to the Commons Problems*, Lanhaw UK, Rowman & Littlefield, 1993. Elinor Ostrom, Roy Gardner & James Walker (dir.), *Rules, Game and Common-Pool Resources*, Ann Arbor, University of Michigan Press, 1994.

34 See: Francesca Cornelli, David Goldreich and Alexander Ljungqvist, "Investor sentiment and pre-IPO markets", *Journal of Finance*, 2006, Vol. 61, No. 3, pp. 1187-1216.

involvement and the motivation of potential investors was at stake. What we call "book building"[35] well and truly constituted a decisive issue, and "book builders" who were "lead managers" (before becoming "book-keepers") assumed an eminent responsibility in intangible (their reputation was at stake) and concrete terms (they risked being "stuck" with lots of unsold securities).

4. Investment bankers as corporate godfathers?

A recurring debate – that continues to this day, if we consider the issues regarding the investment funds of the type "private equity funds" and LBO operations – revolves around the investment bank's economic model. Is it "natural" and in keeping with its constitution as a company and its portfolio of strategic businesses, that it maintain a portfolio of financial holdings and an asset management department? It is not just a simple question of "carrying" securities, the time to place blocks of securities issued in the primary market, to animate the secondary market in order to support a specific share, etc. It was well and truly making long-term financial investments and the allocation of a part of long-term resources towards a share-portfolio. Within the framework of the specialisation[36] between deposit and investment banks, France also had the model of the "Crédit mobilier", inherited from the Pereire,[37] which melded the corporate bank with the financial or investment company. Paribas[38] and BUP used this model for a long time and the French house of Rothschild too built itself a large holding portfolio in companies it financed, be it

[35] See: Francesca Cornelli and David Goldreich, "Book building and strategic allocation", *Journal of Finance*, 2001, No. 56, pp. 2337-2369. Francesca Cornelli and David Goldreich, "Book building: How informative is the order book?", *Journal of Finance*, 2003, No. 58, pp. 1415-1444.

[36] Maurice Lévy-Leboyer, "La spécialisation des établissements bancaires", in Fernand Braudel & Ernest Labrousse (eds.), *Histoire économique et sociale de la France*, Paris, PUF, 3, Vol. 1, 1976.

[37] See Élisabeth Paulet, "Financing industry: The *Crédit mobilier* in France, 1860-1875", *Journal of European Economic History*, 2002, Vol. 31, No. 1, p. 89-112. Élisabeth Paulet, *The Role of Banks in Monitoring Firms. The Case of the Crédit Mobilier*, London, Routledge, 1999.

[38] Éric Bussière, "Les banques d'affaires françaises au XXe siècle: des établissements en quête d'identité?", in Maurice Lévy-Leboyer (ed.), *Les banques en Europe de l'Ouest de 1920 à nos jours*, Paris, Comité pour l'histoire économique & financière de la France, 1995, pp. 223-235. Éric Bussière, "Paribas and the rationalisation of the French electricity industry, 1900-1930", in Youssef Cassis, François Crouzet & Terry Gourvish (eds.), *Management and Business in Britain and France. The Age of the Corporate Economy*, Oxford, Clarendon Press, 1995, pp. 204-213. Éric Bussière, *Paribas, l'Europe et le monde, 1872-1992*, Anvers, Fonds Mercator, 1992.

Compagnie des chemins de fer du Nord or, more and more, in mining and oil companies.[39]

J. Rutterford has re-launched this debate by opposing to it the strategy used by the merchant bank Hambro, which remained content in supporting its client companies in their issuing and stock market listing operations, but refused to practice what is today qualified as "merchant banking", that is to say, conducting M&A operations and carrying its clients' security holdings. She contrasted the Hambro model with that of J.P. Morgan in the United States, though she could have also used Morgan UK and J.P. Morgan: "J.P. Morgan invested in the companies he promoted (even if at advantageous prices) and thus provided a signal to the market." In contrast, Hambros "treated each flotation as an independent event, not having been involved in events leading up to the flotation and not being involved afterwards. For example, Hambros Bank, and Hambro in particular, were not involved in the company mergers which had led to the creation of both Thames Iron and Trollope, Colls". Having said that, a wider study could have perhaps shown that British merchant bankers had no need to commit funds directly as they could orient private trusts and other investment funds which were a speciality of the London market in the field of "wealth management" and were led by special lawyers and advisors who were themselves associated with the merchant banks which saw them as useful tools for supplying the business community with long-term resources.

There were equally intense debates regarding the strategic model of the investment bank in Italy towards the end of the 19th century when there was a scramble to find a corporate banking system which would be less fragile than the one which had just crumbled in the crash of 1892/93 (C. Brambilla): "Comit and Credit hybridised Central European patterns and experiences, as the composition of their groups of control confirms, and, because of their origins and their universal pattern, they are often referred to as German-style mixed banks. During the two decades preceding WWI, universal banks answered to the growing demand for investment banking and industrial financing." The nature of these large "modern"

39 See Bertrand Gille, *Histoire de la maison Rothschild (1817-1870)*, Droz, Geneva, 1965 & 1967. Robert Vicat-Turrell & Jean-Jacques Van Helten, "The Rothschilds, the exploration company and mining finance", *Business History*, April 1986, XXVIII (2), pp. 181-205; reedited in Geoffrey Jones (ed.), *Multinational and International Banking*, Aldershot, Edward Elgar, 1992, pp. 381-405. John McKay, "The house of Rothschild (Paris) as a multinational industrial entreprise, 1875-1914", in Maurice Lévy-Leboyer *et al.* (eds.), *Multinational Enterprise in Historical Enterprise*, Cambridge, Cambridge University Press, 1986, pp. 74-86. *A contrario*, about the British Rothschild, see: Derek Wilson, *Rothschild. A Story of Wealth and Power*, London, André Deutsch, 1988. Niall Ferguson, *The World's Banker. The History of the House of Rothschild*, London, Weidenfeld & Nicolson, 1998.

institutions seemed to tend towards the "mixed bank" – what we call today the "universal bank". But here too, one must take care to define the real identity of these houses in view of their commercial and deposit banking activities. In fact, it would seem that their intrinsic weakness lay in the lack of sufficient long-term resources which prevented them from meeting the long-term capital needs of their client companies and participating in their capital.

We see in the references quoted by C. Brambilla that our Italian colleagues have discussed at length – and often discordantly – on the issue of industrial banking in Italy in the years 1900s-1930s: He concludes that these banks did not have a bigger share portfolio than their German counterparts of the same era. On the other hand, they faced tactical uncertainties by receiving large share deposits (*conti titoli*) which served as guarantees in their loans and gave them voting rights in the general assemblies and an influence within business communities in the major North Italian markets. This could in fact pass as "holding" operations, and in any case it opened the way to a form of cooperation within the framework of corporate banking which developed into "relational banking", beyond the simple criteria of a "transactional bank" that a deposit bank must have.

Meanwhile, S. Salomatina follows the path of the cyclic boom which pushed bankers into a process of blind imitation, to enter into the life of the Saint-Petersburg market and to join the two big houses which practiced investment banking in the years 1880s-1890s. Several investment banks sprang up (such as that of Polyakov) with a slightly different model: adding asset management to "pure" investment banking. In fact, they built themselves substantial share portfolios, holding shares of companies belonging to the business group which set up the bank itself (for the Polyakov group – a little like Crédit mobilier français model) or shares of companies sponsored by the bank. Be that as it may, the "mixed bank" model took solid shape at the turn of the 20th century. The Petersburg Discount and Loan Bank, the Russian Bank for Foreign Trade, the Russian Trade and Industrial Bank and the Moscow International Trade Bank (of the Polyakov group) played a part in spreading the "Crédit mobilier" model in Russia, while the "universal banking" model (with the industrial credit bank, the securities investment bank and the deposit and retail bank) was practiced by another category of houses such as the Volga-Kama Bank and the Moscow Merchant Bank.

S. Salomatina also raises the debate on the lack of long-term resources of these banks endowed with large, long-term asset commitments. She has analysed the constitution of a powerful lever effect, by bringing together the resources of these houses to their financial commitments. Probably due to the narrowness of the modern money market in Russia and the lack of long-term savings and despite the fact that the "investment banks increased stock and reserves [...], half of the resources these banks attracted came via credits from correspondents", mainly from West European markets (often Germany, Paris, London), resulting in "a stress of money on the Russian market", wrote Rothstein to Rothschild in 1898 – before the crisis of 1899-1903 which hit several investment banks. The fragility of the Russian financial and banking structure is well known, but this reminder helps sharpen our perception of the reality of the nature and structure of investment banks.

The rebalancing that S. Salomatina has noted in the pre-War years gave rise to the more robust strategic model of the "universal bank" as it was based on a collection network of Russian cash and savings holders. And, as in Western Europe, this pooling of money with the help of banks provided a sufficient amount of long-term resources to nurture long-term credit activities and security holdings. The profile of the "industrial bank" (German style?) replaced that of the banking and finance group (*à la Crédit mobilier*), while the activities of the financial bank (on the primary and secondary share markets) saw an upturn, as at the Petersburg Private Commercial Bank or the Petersburg Discount and Loan Bank (while the model of the deposit commercial bank prevailed henceforth in establishments like the Union Bank).

If we go from North-East to South-West Europe, we can discern the contours of the mixed banking model in several modern Spanish banks, whether in the second half of the 19th century or in the inter-War period. We can conclude that it led to the building of solid share-portfolios, as studied by J.-L. Coronas regarding Banco Urquijo and Banco Central mainly, in contrast to Hispano-Americano (holder of public shares mainly). Banco de Bilbao presents the profile of an "industrial bank" characterised by its presence on the Boards of several client companies and by the holding of company securities. Banco de Vizcaya too was a resolutely "mixed bank". But our colleague has not specified the extent of the influence exerted by bankers on the enterprises they supported or their involvement in defining strategy. We have here the same issue that has been raised by colleagues regarding the connection between banks and enterprises via the Boards: was there a real "influence", even interference, which went beyond the simple expression of a partnership within a united business community and information collection networks? We know the reservations held by several of our colleagues regarding this.[40] Be that as it may, the young Spanish bank shows the characteristic contours of an

40 See: Caroline Fohlin, "Relationship banking, liquidity, and investment in the German industrialisation". *The Journal of Finance*, 1998, 53, pp. 1737-1758. Caroline Fohlin, "The rise of interlocking directorates in imperial Germany", *Economic History Review*, 1999, LII, 2, pp. 307-333.

era and of practices – and, as regards the interwar period, J.-J. Coronas' statistical tables make for fertile comparisons and reflection. Gradually, differences between banks began to appear and grew, especially after WWII – culminating in the Specialisation and Regulation Law of 1962.

Here we have the recurrent debate on the influence of investment bankers and practitioners of the universal bank and its industrial banking work. Their presence on the Board was a thorny issue and continues to divide opinion regarding the actual amount of influence exerted by these bankers. In the US, "by the end of the [19th] century, all the leading investment banks were active board participants, but they typically exerted their influence only to prevent negative behaviour; in their dealings with corporations, they were otherwise 'hands-off'. Hence, although it subsequently attracted the attention of federal investigators, it appears that investment banker activism was concerned with effective corporate governance. Investment banker board participation reflected enlightened self-interest rather than an attempt to rob corporations blind."[41]

Anyway, C. Brambilla, in the wake of his Italian colleagues, has shown that the State tended to erect specialised financial institutions which were believed to fill the lacunae that himself thinks, but also the business and employer community saw, in mixed banks. Without any direct ideological link with Fascism, it is a "need" felt by business centers; and one could suppose that a democratic-liberal government would follow the same path. In any case, the growth of interventionism and of a mixed economy injected with a good dose of state-interventionism could not but accelerate the trend – before the crash of the 1930s, which led to a substantial nationalisation of the economy. It is the eternal question: People in democracies often complain of the disproportionate clout wielded by investment bankers on the banking and financial markets, but at the same time they also complain that they do not respond to the needs of so many sectors, companies or regions.... This explains why, as C. Brambilla notes, specialised public investment banks came to complement the corporate banking sector in the interwar years.

We know how France too gave itself specialised establishments (most notably, Crédit national in 1919, which played a bigger role after WWII and Banque française du commerce extérieur in 1946), as though the government was uncomfortable having investment banks endowed with the somewhat "miraculous" power of solving all long-term financing problems of big companies and SMES... The nationalisation of financial groups such as Paribas, Rothschild and Compagnie financière de Suez in 1982 led the left to believe that it could infuse strategy and financing into an industry in crisis – before it came up against the key problem of procuring

[41] Alan Morrison & William Wilhelm, *Investment Banking, op. cit.*, p. 175.

resources for these financial groups and nationalised investment banks and their insertion in the European market and re-financing community. The idea of a public investment bank that again took shape in 2012 arose from this same hope – legitimate, but destined to come up against the same problem of limited resources.

The fact was that when the great industrial re-structuring crisis came about in the years 1970-1990, several countries dreamed of a big industrial financing bank, whether it be the French socialists when they came to power in 1981 and thought of merging investment banks and nationalised financial groups into a gigantic institution, or, in 2012, their successors who created *Banque publique d'investissement* by bringing together the fragments that had been put in place by the right in order to somehow face the challenges of the economic crisis of 2007/2008 (*Fonds stratégique industriel*, OSEO, etc.). The developing countries too went the same way with the Asian Development Bank, the African Development Bank and the American Development Bank. Bypassing reluctant or shy markets, overcoming the lack of long-term resources and containing liquidity risks were all expressions of the desire to arrest the decline of the production system and bring about its renewal.

5. The role of financial markets as a lever for the growth of investment banks

It is clear that over the long-term, cyclic movements of the economy, the growth and development of investment banks benefited greatly, even decisively, from the growth of the capital markets banking profession: issue and the placement of securities on the primary market, brokerage activities and management of stock portfolios (for own account or for clients requiring wealth management) on the secondary market, international arbitrage (as with Boissevain and Pierson in the Netherlands), reporting operations[42] – not to speak of current activities on the foreign exchange market. Thus, as and when the Dutch market expanded and companies began to grow into "big enterprises" (listed on the stock market and spreading into the colonies and internationally) and foreign (or colonial) direct investments intensified (accompanied by a mobilisation of the financial asset portfolio), differences began to appear between the family-owned businesses (Hope, De Smeth, R. Mees, Bischoffsheim, Königswarter, etc.) and the major investment banks which wielded overwhelming firepower to successfully see through major financial operations, as highlighted by P. Geljon and T. de Graaf. The movement of concentration or

[42] Well studied by historian economist Marc Flandreau for the turn of the 20th century. See Marc Flandreau & Frédéric Zumer, *The Making of Global Finance, 1880-1913*, Paris, OECD, 2004.

consolidation between rankings and the partnerships between houses and the new big banks (as around Franco-Dutch Paribas for various Dutch families, after their role in the creation of Société générale in France) was the direct result of a greater or lesser embeddedness in the life of the local and European financial markets. This was to the advantage of the more reactive institutions, which added the job of the capital markets bank to that of the investment bank (financing textile exports for Twentsche Bank).

C. Brambilla has shown how the first Italian investment banks followed a similar path (though with clear differences) by basing themselves on the formation of financial markets around the Turin and Genoa markets. In fact, these markets felt the need of such houses, both for managing a securities market and to compensate somewhat for its weakness after Italy was "characterised by weak capital markets" in the middle of the 19th century. Some of the key activities performed by these new banks – like the Cassa del Commercio in the Piedmont – consisted in the granting of loans on securities by mobilising company assets in the service of market liquidity and stimulating a credit market and the investment banking business. The burgeoning investment banks (Credito Mobiliare Italiano and Banca Generale) "tended to be primarily, though not exclusively, committed to market activities" in the years 1870-1880 – till the crash of 1892/93. This shows, by the way, that the alliance between capital markets and investment banks is not "contrary to nature", but rather, a necessity for the business of the corporate finance bank. G. Piluso also emphasises this pragmatic reality, as, despite all of the Bank of Italy's monitoring and regulatory efforts, *riporti* activities kept the wind in its sails and the specialised departments within investment and commercial banks found there the wherewithal to finance their long-term intervention operations.

A few thousand kilometers to the north, Russia presented a similar picture. In the words of S. Salomatina: "Investment banking for private companies appeared throughout the traditional activity of several commercial banks in St. Petersburg, dealing with services to public and mortgage bond market and intensive currency speculation caused by fiduciary standard [...]. Private companies' demand for investment banking was persistent at the peak of pre-revolutionary economic growth in 1895, and the Petersburg banks switched over to private stock as a new subject for exchange transactions." There emerged a sizable Russian capitalism, quite different from the proto-industrialisation which linked Moscow to the Urals or the trade and textile capitalism of the Moscow region: companies' need for shares, of a primary market for the issue and of a secondary market for their securities, opened the doors to this new type of bank, whether it came from the local banking community or benefited from West European influence and aid – while the capital markets bank itself grew thanks to the foreign exchange market.

S. Salomatina reconstitutes the formation of a veritable financial market at St. Petersburg thus: "Several commercial banks acquired wide experience from securities transactions by the 1890s." The Petersburg International Commercial Bank and the Petersburg Discount and Loan Bank played key roles in issuing and investment syndicates (which, though very traditional, were pioneering in Russia) and built inter-bank networks for scales which linked them to commercial banks whose brokerage and distribution activities became part of its core business. "Their partners were the Russian Bank for Foreign Trade and the Volga-Kama Commercial Bank. A number of regional commercial banks acted as sub-participators in syndicates. While some of them would develop investment banking later in the 1890s, others would not progress in this field. The most active sub-participators were the following: the Petersburg Private Commercial Bank, the Moscow Merchant Bank, the Warsaw Commercial Bank, the Riga Exchange Bank, the Petersburg-Moscow Commercial bank, the Moscow Trade bank and the Riga Municipal Discount Bank."

S. Salomatina has minutely examined the contours of the stakeholders on this market on the side of client companies, where a key role was played by metallurgy, oil and capital goods companies. Thus, it is less the long-term credits, the acquisition of holdings, the mergers facilitated by the M&A teams of investment banks than the issuing operations that characterised the Russian investment banks. At the same time, the brokerage activity that flourished at the heart of commercial banks was reminiscent of the French deposit banks, like Société générale and Crédit lyonnais, whose bigger branches were equipped with strong securities division which turned out to be important sources of income and turned its counters profitable.

We know to what extent the revolution of the capital markets bank from the mid-1980s and the "financialisation" of the economy propelled market activities at the heart of corporate and investment banks' business portfolios. P. Geljon and T. de Graaf have followed this transformation in the Netherlands, with the breakthrough in the income procured from underwriting fees and securities trading and the profits from trading room operations: the traditional group of investment bankers were strongly challenged by "deal makers" and traders, forming a new dualism within these houses.

The osmosis between investment banking and the life of the financial markets took material shape in the form of the market banking business (or "capital banking", as we call it today, as in "Barclay Capital", so essential to the development of investment banks) and wealth management, by using relational capital to woo savings. We understand now the importance of being embedded in the retail, institutional and banking investor communities. Several chapters deal with a detailed study of the world of investors. Investment banks spread their roots into diverse investor communities, be they middle or upper-middle class savers, seasoned wealth managers and "capitalists", institutional investors or financial portfolio and quasi-fund managers. The list of subscribers to the *Salonique-Constantinople Junction* share issue in 1893/94 reveals the extent of this penetration into the strata of capitalist investors with a number of family banks as intermediaries (*Privat Banken*). Banks themselves took substantial lots as they practiced brokerage banking downstream as a simple investment tool to gain their clients' loyalty by offering trustworthy, stable and profitable "products".

J. Rutterford has gone to the heart of the intimate relation between the shares of a client company, the merchant bank and the primary and secondary markets in the Trollope case: "What was the advantage of issuing securities using the name of Hambro? First of all, Hambro provided access to the City network of lawyers and, in particular, stockbrokers and the Stock Exchange. Hambro knew what was required for securities to be accorded a Special Settlement Day and thus to be able to be traded on the Stock Exchange. Hambro, and his broker, were aware of which issues had been successful and why. Hambro could organise underwriting, if need be. Second, Hambro acted in the short-term financial interests of the vendors, ensuring the best prices for the vendors in the reconstructions and floatations, within the requirements of the Stock Exchange and of marketability."

The investment banker, by himself, with his associates and relations, "scented" the markets and followed their course, company reputations and subtle trends beyond the measurable variations. In her chapter and in various other papers, J. Rutterford has carefully reconstituted the links between bankers, individual investors ("persons of private means") and the key role played by market intermediaries who, in this case, meant brokers. She has talked about the complicity of action between Hambro and its broker, Akroyd, especially in the listing of the Trollope-Colls securities in 1903: accessing, thanks to the archives, the day-to-day details of this operation provides at once great pleasure to the banking historian and a rare peek into the investment banker's knowledge portfolio.

6. Internationalisation vs economic patriotism

In the wake of Raymond Poidevin[43] who studied the relations of German banks, P. Hertner has sketched the contours of the European investment banking and business communities. It is this strange but understandable relation of both competition and cooperation which surprises

43 Raymond Poidevin, *Finances et relations internationales (1887-1914)*, Paris, Armand Colin, 1970. Raymond Poidevin, *Les relations économiques et financières entre la France et l'Allemagne de 1898 à 1914*, Paris, Armand Colin, 1969.

the superficial student of the European, followed by the transatlantic and now the international financial worlds.[44] *Deutsche Bank*, pivot of the deployment of West European money into Oriental and Balkan Europe, worked with Parisian, Londoner, Viennese and other German houses. G. Taneva shows that the same process took place in the establishment of syndicates for Bulgarian financial operations. This little case study also reveals the underlying trend towards a new stage of Europeanisation of French banks and investment bankers' subsequent mobilisation in this direction.

Lacking "paper" for their brokerage activities, they sought to enlarge Europe's boundaries by including the "smaller countries" (besides the main targets of Russia and the Ottoman Empire: Bulgaria, Greece, Romania, Finland) into their field of action. J. Rutterford mentions Hambro organising a Greek issue in 1925, adding that Everard Hambro directed a merchant bank from London, which was strongly connected with the New York market, including via JP Morgan, as its competition with the British house of Morgan did not prevent it from pursuing a policy of cooperation, naturally in the interests of the partners. Finally, J.-L. Coronas recalls the intimate relations that the Spanish bank entertained with the rest of Europe at the turn of the 20th century via the interpenetration of strategic models, bilateral agreements,[45] numerous financial operations and also the daily business of correspondence banking.

A common but important question needs to be addressed: did investment banks serve the interests of their country of origin and their business community in the name of "economic patriotism", or had they become so much part of the international markets that they only dealt with "international finance", managing relations and people between stakeholders in money markets that were now Europeanised, even "proto-globalised"? P. Geljon and T. de Graaf have shown how the Dutch markets quickly entered international flows and participated in foreign, especially North American, securities investment syndicates with European connections (Hope, with Mendelssohn in Germany and Hottinguer in France). At the same time, they also accompanied the government, the municipalities, shipping and other companies that were active in the Dutch Indies. Moreover, they also sponsored the big Dutch enterprises that were turning into major corporations and

---

44 See Ursel Steuber, "International cooperation and competition among banks in Europe", in Edwin Wadsworth, John-Stuart Wilson, Henri Fournier & Jean-Paul Abraham (eds.), *The Development of Financial Institutions in Europe, 1956-1976*, Leiden, Sijthoff, 1977, pp. 175-179. Ursel Steuber, *International Banking*, Leiden, Sijthoff, 1976.

45 See: José Luis García Ruiz, "Nacionalizando el capital bancario: Banesto y Paribas (1902-1927)", *Publicado en Investigaciones de Historia Económica*, 2007, No. 3, pp. 79-108.

were being listed on the Stock Market towards the end of the 19th century (Heineken in 1873; Royal Dutch in 1890) and the turn of the 20th century (Jurgens in 1906; Philips in 1912).

This community of "cosmopolitan" bankers remained firmly rooted in the community of national companies – and this characteristic was well in evidence when corporate and investment bankers came together to establish a big Dutch shipping company in 1908 in order to fight off increased foreign competition and overcome a grave crisis. P. Geljon and T. de Graaf add that, during the interwar period, these investment bankers were active stakeholders in a community which led the way towards a managerial capitalism in diverse crucial sectors to improve the country's competitivity (oil, colonial goods, chemicals, iron and steel, shipping).

When Russia embarked on its cycle of industrialisation in the last quarter of the 19th century, the banking hub at St. Petersburg capitalised on its network of expertise and resources which tied it closely to West European markets. S. Salomatina talks of the consortiums (which included several subsidiaries of West European groups: Belgian, French, German, British) that were formed for the issue of shares of Russian companies. She also refers to the voluminous business correspondence between Russian bankers and their Western counterparts, as in the Petersburg International Bank. But, as is well known, this internationalisation of business by Russian investment banks clearly favoured FDI flows and the transfer of technology and management methods from the West to the East for the ultimate benefit of several industrial bases in Russia and Ukraine.[46] This dependence on financial, banking, technological and managerial resources was constitutive of both the "imperialism" – so denounced by Leninists – and a Russian capitalism whose long term power is subject to debate, as in the case of China in the inter-war period.

Consequently, this dilemma, if not polemic, around investment banks' national and international "double nature" has remained a constant over the past century... These bankers maintained and renewed a "double culture",[47] whether personal or that of their bank: a culture which was

46 René Girault, *Emprunts russes et investissements français en Russie (1887-1914)*, Publications de la Sorbonne-Colin, 1973; Publications du CHEFF, 1995. Boris Ananich & Valery Bovykin, "Foreign banks and foreign investment in Russia", in Rondo Cameron & Valéry Bovykin (eds.), *International Banking & Industrial Finance, 1870-1914*, Oxford, Oxford University Press, 1991, pp. 253-290.

47 About corporate culture and embeddedness, see: Kenneth Lipartito, "Business culture. The embeddedness of business", in Geoffrey Jones and Jonathan Zeitlin (eds.), *The Oxford Handbook of Business History*, New York, 2007; Oxford, Oxford University Press, 2008, pp. 605-610. Isabelle Huault, "*Embeddedness* et théorie de l'entreprise. Autour des travaux de Mark Granovetter", *Annales des Mines. Gérer et comprendre*, juin 1998, pp. 73-86.

part of their country's or their market's business community and a second, more open culture, deployed on the international scale, with a consequent, permanent interaction. This constituted a relative advantage over the traditional commercial banks which lacked this integration into the globalised culture. These bankers were generally active in markets which had attained to the status of "international financial centers"[48] and which required supple and reactive individual and collective mindsets, "open" to the flow of financial innovations. When Italy lived through its "Meiji era" in the years 1890s-1910s (in the times of Giolitti and Nitti), the big banks that were created were both the outgrowth of the financial and banking North-West Europe and the levers for the construction of a strong local economy. C. Brambilla shows that the appearance of a generation of entrepreneurs at the heart of the second industrial revolution was mainly in the corporate, "universal" or "mixed" banking businesses.

H. Bonin has highlighted the "clearing" role played by investment bankers to help renew the competitivity of French enterprises in the years 1940-1950: banking "diplomats" came up with new methods of financing companies as they spread over several continents (Latin America, etc.), whether it be for the financing of exports ("supplier credit", then "buyer credit"), complex "structured financing", which anticipated the growth of such products after the 1960s, in the global race for infrastructure and FDI flows – while in France of the first half of the 20th century and pre-WWII Netherlands, it was the investment banks which drove a number of investment flows into the colonies. Midway between the imperial and the globalised economies, investment bankers turned into essential stakeholders in the finance of commodities trading, often from Geneva (for *Banque de l'Indochine*, before its successor Indosuez), but also from Brussels/Anvers and London. While their weak presence in America (at Chicago and New York) prevented them from playing a major role in the United States, their operations grew rapidly in European markets that were involved in international trade.

Several classic though revealing case studies support our reflection on this link between banks and promoting the national economy. G. Taneva talks of the solidarity of place which united bankers and industrialists in their efforts at penetrating the young Bulgarian market: though of modest scale, this outlet was a field for gathering experience and, more importantly, it formed part of the FDI and capital space at the scale of the Danube

48 See Richard Roberts (ed.), *International Financial Centres: Concepts, Development and Dynamics*, Aldershot, Edward Elgar, 1994. Youssef Cassis and Éric Bussière (eds.), *London and Paris as International Financial Centres in the Twentieth Century*, Oxford, Oxford University Press, 2005. Youssef Cassis, *Capitals of Capital. A History of International Financial Centers, 1780-2005*, Cambridge, Cambridge University Press, 2006.

and Balkan regions, and as such, every piece of the puzzle has to be handled to fill the gaps in business and connections. In a foretaste of what was to come, investment bankers in Romania, Yugoslavia, Austria and Czechoslovakia, supported by their colleagues in deposit banks, turned Bulgaria into a "money market school" in the years 1920s-1930s: they were entrusted with the mission of giving the country a banking system and framework, to sponsor commercial banks and specialised institutions (land and mortgage credit), to support the young central bank. We can thus estimate the "spillover" capacity of the Parisian market's knowledge portfolio, thanks to its investment bankers – whether working in investment banks or the investment departments of commercial banks: their work included bank engineering, structured finance, banking and financial asset management, etc. This banking art was "amortised" across several bigger or smaller markets, mainly in Europe, but also in the colonial empires (Morocco, Madagascar, Egypt, etc.).

The debate regarding banking patriotism could have touched the Frankfurt market when Deutsche Bank acquired Morgan Grenfell and Bankers Trust in the 1980s… But every German stakeholder would have clearly understood that, faced by the trans-Atlantic offensive launched by its American rivals on the London and Paris, followed by the German, markets, the strategic dilemma was clear: to remain a "regional" bank – in the sense of "regions" or parts of continents within the globalised economy – or to give oneself a global span. Paradoxically, Frankfurt's competitivity passed henceforth by its duplication at London and New York (and the other big American partner markets), not to speak of the Asian markets, the fiefdoms of HSBC, Standard Chartered and Citibank.

C. Kobrak talks of these debates, as heated in the United States as in Germany, regarding the nature of a German bank which had turned international not only in its money flows and connections, but well and truly by its "multi-localisation". Like Volkswagen, Siemens and other German *Konzerne* in the 21st century, Deutsche Bank learned to fly a "confederate" flag – in the colours of Germany and the world. A similar debate arose in France regarding the best means of maintaining the global reach of the Parisian market (within the "Paris Europlace" business association) with similar conclusions: "circling the wagons" could only have resulted in reduced competitivity, and every major French enterprise, especially in banking (BNP Paribas, Société générale) and insurance (Axa), needed to assume a multi-domestic and transnational "mixedness". The growth in the investment & corporate banking and the capital markets businesses did not fail to serve as levers of this metamorphosis – even though worries regarding funds and the risks involved in the second decade of the 21st century have forced people to rethink their international strategies and begin the process of a geographic and sectoral refocusing.

CHAPTER 15

From History to Present Times

Investment Banking at Stake?

Hubert BONIN

professor of modern economic history at Sciences Po Bordeaux & at GRETHA research centre, Bordeaux University

This final chapter presents a few conclusive and synthetic issues regarding the nature of investment banking in the light of new empirical data gathered from the rapidly growing material in the wake of the recent crisis. Strategies, *modus operandi*, risks management, ethics, nature and structures – almost everything seems to be at stake in the investment banking economy – not to speak of the connections with the "real economy" or conversely its involvement in "artificial" (?) or "speculative" (?) fields of the globalised economy of money. Without challenging economists and specialists in the field of bank management, we shall (lightly) tackle several issues regarding the "philosophy" and "paradigms" of investment banking business models.

1. Protesting regulations and differentiation in the years 1980-1990

We must remember that, in the second half the 19th and first third of the 20th centuries, there was, *grosso modo*, a convergence between commercial and investment banks as they both participated in the issue, guarantee and investment of corporate and public institution shares in almost all countries.[1] Besides, the model of the universal bank dominated in

[1] See Anthony Saunders and Ingo Walter, *Universal Banking in the US*, New York, Oxford University Press, 1994. Georges Benston, "Universal banking", *Journal of Economic Perspectives*, Vol. 8, No. 3, 1994, pp. 121-143. Eugene White, "Before the Glass-Steagall Act: An analysis of the investment banking activities of national banks", *Explorations in Economic History*, 1986, 23, pp. 33-55. Also see: James Ang and Terry Richardson, "The underwriting experience of commercial bank affiliates

Germany and later, in Italy, Belgium and Spain. It was only in the United States that the Glass-Steagall Act had forbidden commercial banks from pursuing this activity for the past fifty years or so. Almost everywhere else, as in France, despite the practical and statutory (from 1946) differences imposed, commercial banks took part in interbank syndicates for organising and carrying out share issues.

A "fad" in the mid-1980s saw a relative "liberalisation" of statutes, a kind of deregulation which, for all that, did not amount to anything like a "savage capitalism" or a complete "laisser-faire". Numerous economists challenged the advantages of the Glass-Steagall Act as regards systemic stability and reliability in the 1980s and formed a sort of informal pressure group which concluded that the Act was in no way an economic "necessity". Manju Puri has shown that towards the end of the 1920s, after scholarly studies based on apparently incontestable analytical models built on imposing equations, numerous economists had reconsidered the famous conflict of interests attributed to the mixed banking system. Groups of economists and experts joined bankers to build an interest group which based itself on elements from these academic articles.

We know that, before the regulated differentiation, commercial bankers were blamed for their double identity: on one side, they granted loans to client companies; on the other, they arranged the transactions of the securities issued by them. The risk[2] lay in the possibility of over-promoting these securities, without perhaps taking into account their quality, the risks run by the issuing company, as soon as the bank wanted its client to repay its short and medium term debts with the money raised.... The investing client would be "deceived", if not "duped", by the bank for the benefit of the borrowing and issuing client. Though there have been cases in contemporary banking history, we can contest the real magnitude of the risk of such a "conflict of interests". "First, the danger of losing a profitable relationship served to keep the investment banker honest in his dealings with a firm, even when his honesty could neither be contracted upon nor proved in court. Second, when an investment bank formed a close and public relationship with an issuer, the bank's reputation was to some extent tied up in the fortunes of the

prior to the Glass-Steagall Act: A re-examination of evidence for passage of the act", *Journal of Banking and Finance*, 1994, Vol. 18, Elsevier, pp. 351-395. W.H. Parker, "The Banking Act of 1933: An appraisal", *American Economic Review*, 24, 1934, pp. 101-110.

2 George Benston, *The Separation of Commercial and Investment Banking*, Oxford, Oxford University Press, 1990. Anthony Saunders, "Conflicts of interest: An economic view", in Ingo Walter (ed.), *Deregulating Wall Street*, New York, Wiley, 1985, pp. 207-230. Also see: Mark Flannery, "An economic evaluation of bank securities activities before 1933", *ibidem*, pp. 66-87.

issuer. We argue [thus] that this provided the bank with incentives to monitor the firm on behalf of the dispersed bondholders. As a result, a reputable lead banker sent a strong signal of quality to the capital markets, and issuers were therefore prepared to pay more for such a banker."[3]

However, critics have accumulated against what has become equated with preconceptions or false evidence. First of all, one can say that the investing client, institutional or private, will not long remain the client of a bank which only offers him "bad paper", destined to crumble on the Stock Market and to turn into a "rotten asset"… Moreover, and this is M. Puri's argument, investor confidence in the mixed commercial banks did not seem to have suffered from such conflicts of interest. In fact, it would seem that their function as "certifiers of firm value" was well maintained and respected,[4] and he gives as proof – after detailed calculations based on statistics from the years 1927/29 – that investing clients were even ready to pay more for securities proposed by commercial banks than for those sold through the intermediation of investment banks. "[Commercial] banks can convey information acquired through their loan-making activities to uninformed investors, giving rise to a certification effect."[5] On the other hand, because of their knowledge of the client and issuing company's balance sheet, commercial "banks are therefore better informed than investment houses, and their underwritings can have a stronger 'certification effect' than those of investment houses"[6] and "investors perceived banks as being valuable certifiers of firm value."[7]

"Commercial banks, as lenders to firms, can obtain better prices than investment houses, particularly when costs of information production are high, and both commercial and investment houses have similar reputations *ex-ante* […]. The long-run performance of securities underwritten by banks is superior [in the 1920s] to those underwritten by investment houses."[8] It is true that this researcher subscribes to the current of thought

---

3 Alan Morrison & William Wilhelm, *Investment Banking. Institutions, Politics and Law*, Oxford, Oxford University Press, 2007, p. 173.

4 Manju Puri, "Commercial banks in investment banking. Conflict of interest or certification role?", *Journal of Financial Economics*, 40, 1996, pp. 373-401. He used the same arguments and clues along another process of analysis in: Manju Puri, "Commercial banks as underwriters: Implications for the going public process", *Journal of Financial Economics*, 54, 1999, pp. 133-163. Also see: Amar Gande, Manju Puri and Anthony Saunders, "Bank entry, competition and the market for corporate securities underwriting", *Journal of Financial Economics*, 54, 1997, pp. 165-195. Amar Gande, Manju Puri, Anthony Saunders and Ingo Walter, "Bank underwriting of debt securities: Modern evidence", *Review of Financial Studies*, Vol. 10, No. 4, 1997, pp. 1175-1202.

5 Manju Puri, "Commercial banks in investment banking", *op. cit.*, p. 396.

6 *Ibidem*, p. 375.

7 Manju Puri, *ibidem*, p. 396.

8 "Commercial banks as underwriters", *op. cit.*, p. 135.

which would like to challenge the Glass-Steagall Act and its supposed rigidities, and that we must be cautious as regards the conclusions of any research done as part of an academic "fad" which itself has become the subject of investigation and *ex post* criticism.

Commercial banks could count on their greater "distribution power" and "syndication abilities", which allowed them to play a major role in the issue of bonds, while investment banks played a relatively bigger role in share transactions, where their partnership with client companies was based more on the relational bank than the diversified analytical system retained by their sister concerns via the transactional bank based on the analysis of balance sheets and the debt situation vis-à-vis the commercial banks themselves. A modest narrative historian's empirical remark will show that modeling economist M. Puri could also have specified that the investment bank made many advances on securities, like Goldman Sachs notably. The indirect carrying of these securities and the loan relationships helped gather information on the investments of rich equity holders in numerous companies – whether listed or not, as these advances could be guaranteed by private company shares also – which suggests that additional points of rapprochement could have reduced the differences between the two types of banks.

Be that as it may, the questionable nature of the Glass-Steagall Act and the regulated differences "dominated the scene" at the turn of the 1990s. The rigidities attributed to a statutory regulation[9] seemed to hold back the maturation of the emerging banking revolution and prevent banking centers and "national banking champions" from retaining their competitivity.[10] The concept of universal banking[11] became irresistible, as though new paradigms would serve as a framework for the reconfiguration of the national banking systems and the unification of a banking system that was turning global and intercontinental.

The major structural crisis of the production system itself seemed to call for a remodeling of the international national (or continental as in West Europe) banking systems. The renewed competitivity and company inventiveness seemed to require more reactive, open and less cartelised banks. Corporate banking's very nature needed to be remoulded as, henceforth, it needed to incorporate every type of product and technique which could

---

9 See, for example: Randall Kroszner and Raghuram Rajan, "Is the Glass-Steagall Act justified? A study of the US experience with universal banking before 1933", *American Economic Review*, 1994, Vol. 84, pp. 810-832.

10 See, for example: Donald Fair & Robert Raymond (eds.), *The Competitiveness of Financial Institutions and Centres in Europe*, Dordrecht, Kluwer Academic Publishers, 1994.

11 See: Anthony Saunders and Ingo Walter, *Universal Banking in the US*, New York, Oxford University Press, 1994. Georges Benston, "Universal banking", *Journal of Economic Perspectives*, Vol. 8, No. 3, 1994, pp. 121-143.

help gain access to liquidity, refinancing, R&D financing and FDIS. While the historic forms ("Finance in the age of canals and railroads", "Common stock finance and the rise of managerial capitalism" – to recall the titles of the chapters in the book by Jonathan Baskin & Paul Miranti)[12] were recognised, new paths needed to be created in order to renew the capacity for influence and action of corporate banking and finance teams: "Financing of centre firms"; "conglomerates and leverage-buyout partnerships".[13]

2. Just before the crash: The end of investment banks in sight?

This explains why the last dramatic surge of government intervention in financial regulatory architectures, that began from the mid-1980s both in Europe and the United States, is thought to have favoured a "convergence"[14] of financial systems towards a common model within which markets are quite efficient and their under-regulation relevant, and universal banking would replace credit specialisation.[15] Investment banks' weakness as "pure players" lay in their lack of financial surface, which prevented them from taking part in the recent "rallies" in direct investment, large credit and major issues. But they could address this weakness through alliances, like the one between the French Rothschild and the Dutch ABN-AMRO for equity issuing on the primary market or Lazard and French Savings Banks (*Caisses d'épargne*).

Of course, in this case, investment banks as independent institutions were disappearing as specialised bodies, but there was still a strong demand for investment banking and its variety of functions whenever mergers and acquisitions, take-overs and underwriting was required and needed to be organised not only at a national but also at the global level. On the other hand, more realistically, we may consider this evolution not as a "one way process", but as a sort of hybridisation of the two main models which had been more clearly separated till recent times, because the commercial banking field returned resolutely as a key player in the field of market and investment banking.[16] Big commercial banks extended their

12 See: Jonathan Barron Baskin & Paul Miranti, *A History of Corporate Finance*, Cambridge, Cambridge University Press, 1997 (paperback, 1999).

13 *Ibidem*.

14 Andrew Mullineux & Victor Murinde, "Globalisation and convergence of banking systems", in Andrew Mullineux & Victor Murinde (eds.), *Handbook of International Banking*, London, Elgar, 2003.

15 J.P. Danthine, F. Giavazzi and E.L. von Thadden, *European Financial Markets after EMU: A First Assessment*, NBER, Working Paper No. 8044, December 2000.

16 See: Ingo Walter (ed.), *Deregulating Wall Street: Commercial Bank Penetration of the Corporate Securities Market*, New York, John Wiley, 1985.

financial and market activities, as did J.P. Morgan, RBS, Barclays, ABN AMRO, Société générale, BNP Paribas, UBS, Crédit suisse and Unicredit, though a few others (Lloyds, Santander, BBVA, Wells Fargo, Raiffeisen in Germany and Austria and Rabobank,[17] for example) were less prone to evolving from the "deposit banking" model (even if it contained many aspects of "universal banking") to a model where the investment and markets banking profiles dominated (in assets and returns).

One amazing picture might thus be the involvement of commonplace commercial banks in the subprime process through a move of convergence (see table 1): mixity prevailed more and more, which explained some un-balance in the financing structures of a few banks, because they had over-extended their strategic stretch to (on middle- or short-terms) attractive activities, products and markets, despite (apparent) guarantees of refinancing like the CDS system.

Table 1. Pending subprimes loans being insured trough CDSs by AIG Financial Products in London

Name of the bank	Amount in US dollars
Goldman Sachs	12,9
Société générale	11,9
Barclays	8,5
Merril Lynch	6,8
Bank of America	5,2
BNP Paribas	4,9
HSBC	3,5
Deutsche Bank	2,6
Calyon (Crédit agricole)	2,3
CITI	2,3
Dresdner Bank-Kleinwort	2,2
ING	1,5
Wachovia	1,5
Morgan Stanley	1,2
...	
UBS	0,8
Rabobank	0,8
RBS	0,7
...	
J.P. Morgan	0,4

Source: AIG data, in Pierre Jovanovic, *Blythe Masters. La banquière à l'origine de la crise mondiale*, Paris, Le Jardin des livres, 2011, p. 84.

[17] See: Joke Mooj & Wim Boonstra (eds.), *Raiffeisen's Footprint. The Cooperative Way of Banking*, Amsterdam, VU Press, 2012.

Moreover, many facts suggest that institutional diversity could still influence the structure and functioning of national financial systems: for example, regulatory schemes, stock market efficiency, company size, ownership structure and corporate finance were different in developed and emerging economies.[18] The history of investment banks or investment banking could well have avoided "its end" because the necessity of a special relationship between senior bankers, as advisors (and co-investors) and enterprises, as customers looking for services and financial "solutions", was still an issue.

3. US investment banking as the hegemonic model?

From the 1990s, yet another challenge to European investment bankers came from their US competitors. The American deregulation in practice and then through a new law had been preceded by a move toward internationalisation[19] – which transformed US banks into global universal banks and unleashed an inter-bank world war.[20] Their breakthrough on the European M&A markets was spectacular, as can be seen in the following table which shows that six American globalised banks led European M&A operations (see Table 2).

Goldman Sachs especially had been so successful, whether in quantitative growth, diversification of activities and the geography of its activities that analysts held it up as a "super-model".[21] And its sectoral and intercontinental growth symbolised the globalisation of markets, finance and corporate banks' business portfolios. The legitimacy of its directors, its strategy and its managerial philosophy – based on an intense internal competition between teams, team leaders and "potentials" – was founded

18 R.K. Mork and L. Steier, *The Global History of Corporate Governance: An Introduction*, NBER, Working Paper 11062, January 2005.

19 See S.B. Prasad, "The metamorphosis of City and Chase as multinational banks", *Business and Economic History*, 28(2), 1999, p. 201-212.

20 See: Olivier Pastré, *La guerre mondiale des banques*, Paris, Presses universitaires de France, 2007.

21 See: Suzanne McGee, *Chasing Goldman Sachs. How the Masters of the Universe Melted Wall Street Down... and Why They'll Take us to the Brink Again*, New York, Crown Business, 2010. Charles Ellis, *The Partnership. The Making of Goldman Sachs*, New York, Penguin Books, 2008 et 2009. Lisa Endlich, *Goldman Sachs. The Culture of Success*, New York, Touchstone, 1999, 2nd edition, 2000. And on a larger public level: Tristan Gaston-Breton, "Goldman Sachs. Le pouvoir de la finance", *Les Échos*, 14 August 2009, p. 11. Julien Tarby, "Goldman Sachs. Le fil du rasoir", *Le Nouvel Économiste*, 15 December 2011, pp. 21-23. Marc Roche, *La Banque. Comment Goldman Sachs dirige le monde*, Paris, Albin Michel, 2010. Various docu-films also highlighted the power and modus operandi of Foldman Sachs.

on the house's relative resistance in the face of the shocks and the demands made by the authorities, the law and clients to settle the obvious errors in its asset investment advice.

Table 2. Classification of banks involved in European M&A in the first half of 2006, just before the turn-around of the business cycle

Ex-investment bank	Ex-commercial bank	Total value of the deals (millions euros)	Number of deals
	J.P. Morgan	326	96
	Citigroup	325	92
Morgan Stanley		297	88
BNP Paribas (merger of BNP and Paribas)		280	51
Goldman Sachs		280	77
Merril Lynch		273	53
	UBS	249	80
	Deutsche Bank	229	70
	HSBC	202	39
Rothschild		202	132
	Crédit suisse (which absorbed First Boston)	169	62
Lazard		168	90
Lehman Brothers		154	45
	Société générale	109	23
	ABN-AMRO	98	44

Source: Thomson Finance, in *Les Echos*, 28 June 2006, p. 35.

Challengers to the US leaders had to redefine their business model in order to resist their offensive. But US banks themselves were faced by an immediate pressure to define more precisely their own business model. Besides Citicorp and its retail and commercial banking base, major US investment banks were re-thinking their revenues and profits because direct and proprietary trading were growing fast, while a third activity had emerged as a powerful leverage for profits: private equity management, that is, the management of investment funds all over the world which buy out companies only to re-sell them several years later. Since then, strong arguments have shown the dire effects of such growing revenues from market banking because, more and more institutional investors, investment funds,[22] journalists and experts agree

22 See: Stéphanie Lavigne, *L'industrie des fonds de pension: les investisseurs institutionnels américains*, Paris, L'Harmattan, 2004.

that universal banks ought to aim for a return on capital employed (ROCE) superior to 20 per cent, within the new mindsets and landscape of the "financiarisation"[23] based on revenues and profiles set up each quarter, the process being intensified because of the greater influence exerted by rating agencies.

4. Investment banking through the recent crisis

All these considerations might appear useless or void because the recent crash and crisis disappointed the expectations which, for about a quarter century, had enhanced the business model in corporate, investment and market banking. The developments in the history of investment banking need to be followed by re-considering recognised truths, even by leading academics and experts who form part of the so-called regulatory authorities. Forthcoming books and articles will add to the intense debates, excellent stories and sharp investigations by journalists, members of parliaments and, henceforth, economists and business or banking historians. First reflections on the lack of lucidity and accountability[24] by so many investment bankers have opened the doors to a re-assessment of the portfolio of skills, the *modus operandi*, the corporate culture and the very rules of regulation and compliance. Functions and missions are being scrutinised to determine the extent to which investments banks are committed to a drastic restructuring of their organisation and business model.

These latter topics had already raised many arguments in the interwar period, when hearings and evidences produced in the USA between 1928 and 1935 by the Federal Trade Commission[25] delivered 84 volumes on the specialisation between investment and commercial banking! This led to the famous Glass-Steagall Act on statutory differentiation which lasted till the end of the 20th century (1999) and is still invoked by contemptuous enemies of the free-standing deregulated banking economy, which opened doors to the debates regarding

---

[23] See: Claude Dupuy & Stéphanie Lavigne (eds.), *Géographies de la finance mondialisée*, Paris, La Documentation française, series "*Les Études*", 2009. William Lazonick et Mary O'Sullivan, "Finance and industrial development", *Financial History Review*, 4, 1997, pp. 7-29 et 117-138. William Lazonick, Michel Aglietta and Antoine Rebérioux, *Dérives du capitalisme financier*, series "*Bibliothèque Économie*", Paris, Albin Michel, 2008.

[24] Hubert Bonin, *Des banquiers lucides dans le boum et la tempête? (2004-2010)*, Paris, Textuel, 2011.

[25] See: Michael Perino, *The Hellhound of Wall Street: How Ferdinand Pecora's Investigation of the Great Crash Forever Changed American Finance*, New York, Penguin Press, 2010.

the *Dodd-Frank Wall Street Reform and Consumer Protection Act* of 2010. "It included the Volcker Rule, which among other things, limited proprietary trading by banks and their affiliates. This proprietary trading ban will generally prevent commercial banks and their affiliates from acquiring non-governmental securities with the intention of selling those securities for a profit in the near term. Some have described the *Volcker Rule*, particularly its proprietary trading ban, as 'Glass-Steagall lite'."[26]

Beyond regulations,[27] risk management, compliance rules and issues of business ethics, the very scope of investment banking needs to be taken into account because national patterns do not fit the internationalised, and now globalised, dimensions of finance and banking. The traditional function of the investment bank has been to contribute to international finance, trade and import-export finance, loans to internationalised firms and open underwriting on a somewhat broader track than that followed by corporate commercial banks. Investment bankers were (are) used to international and even off-shore market-oriented systems (trade on securities) and international credit systems (trade finance, project financing through durable loans, etc.). The Paris market could not have survived without the involvement of French banks on the London market, their taking part in the issuance of international securities, reaching shares within the underwriting pools and the engineering of issuances (mainly after the 1970s), upstream of the origination process and to set up brokerage syndicates with international banks and their French partner-commercial banks to draw profit from their distribution networks.

A process of osmosis prevailed, shifting boundaries informally and with "agility". This means than no "national-minded" regulation and prudential monitoring could or can be efficient, except if the aim is to decrease competitiveness. This explains the challenges posed to internationalised regulators-to be within the European institutions (Commission and Parliament), the Basel team on the platform of the International Bank of Settlements, or through transatlantic negotiations.

---

26 From the *Wikipedia* website, April 2012.

27 See: Stefano Battilossi and Jaime Reis (eds.), *State and Financial Systems in Europe and the USA. Historial Perspectives on Regulation and Supervision in the Nineteenth and Twentieth Centuries*, Aldershot, Ashgate, 2010. Charles Goodhart, "Financial supervision from a historical perspective", in D.G. Hayes & G.E. Woods (eds.), *The Structure of Financial Regulation*, London, Routledge, 2007. Dominique Lacoue-Labarthe, "L'évolution de la supervision bancaire et de la réglementation prudentielles (1945-1996)", in *Bâle II: genèse et enjeux, Revue d'économie financière*, No. 73, 4-2003, pp. 39-63.

Pressing issues could have blurred the perception of investment banking. Business ethics were suddenly at stake with the (re-)introduction of moral values versus "shareholder value" in the midst of arguments about the business models of investment banks.[28] A second hurdle was the issue of the "Anglo-Saxon model" and "bad capitalism" versus "good capitalism". Lastly, there was a strong opposition to the rapid rise of "market banking" which grew after the invention of derivatives, the enlargement of FOREX market rooms and with the appearance of a new "species", that of the "traders" and the specificities of their mindsets and practices.[29] This aversion to globalised finance trading led to the condemnation of investment banking, as it was assimilated to (badly-considered) "market banking". Glass ceilings were broken through; hubris and greed, "moral rot" and "rampant corruption"[30] had short-circuited "sound" trading of securities, in the name of "speculation".

Investment banking was confused with market trading, often over "proprietary trading", the instant management of securities on secondary markets for their own account or for investment and hedge funds, with objectives of high-end returns on capital employed (ROCE), up to 20 to 25 per cent. Numbers attained trillions of dollars/euros. But one could claim that "history" had somehow been (once again) forgotten. This somber perception coloured the general opinion regarding corporate and investment banking (like at the French Socgen CIB or Crédit agricole CIB, for example). The trial ended with a clear condemnation of investment banking – whereas all the basically "sound" contributions by investment bankers to companies' and even the government's growth and financial life (who issued bonds thanks to them) were forgotten. The entire business of investment banking stood condemned in the eyes of the general public and a number of experts who thought that it was the cause of the speculative bubble which burst in 2007-2008.

---

28 See Gillian Tett, *Fool's Gold. How Unstrained Greed Corrupted a Dream, Shattered Global Markets and Unleashed a Catastrophe*, London, Little Brown, 2009. William Cohan, *A Tale of Hubris and Wretched Excess on Wall Street*, New York, Doubleday, 2009. Joseph Stiglitz, *Le triomphe de la cupidité*, Paris, Les liens qui libèrent, 2010. Philip Augar, *The Greed Merchants. How the Investment Banks Played the Free Market Game*, New York, Portfolio; London, Penguin, 2005.

29 See: Olivier Godechot, *Les traders. Essai de sociologie des marchés financiers*, Paris, La Découverte-Poche, 2007 (first editions in 2001 and 2005). Olivier Godechot, *Working Rich. Salaires, bonus et appropriation du profit dans l'industrie financière*, Paris, La Découverte, 2007.

30 See the column by William D. Cohan, "Ending the moral rot on Wall Street. Part 1", <www.bloomberg.com/news/print/2011-08-08> (four pages).

5. Strategic and structural issues within investment banking

Investment banking's structural and strategic risks during the cyclic boom of the years 2003-2008 and the following crisis have re-launched the debate regarding the balance between the nature of investment banks or the investment/market banking divisions within the large banking and financial enterprises.

A. Senior bankers within the business units of giant universal banks

Along with the various interpretations of the present crisis, we have to ponder the actual core contribution by investment bankers to economic history and the present resiliency of the global economy. The first few chapters of this book, as well as more general considerations, first talk of investment banks' immaterial capital. They relied on "senior bankers" – either top managers or partners, like Felix Rohatyn at Lazard, who was a legendary merchant banker in the last third of the 20th century.[31] Such people were at the heart of the capitalist and business community networks. They built, entertained and revived connections between firms, authorities, investor groups, etc. They managed economic intelligence and information collecting systems in keeping with traditions of their profession. They managed the tool-box to penetrate into the communities of investors: institutional investors, asset management firms, private banks, investment funds, hedge funds, etc. to determine the balance of values, interest rates, the capacity of the markets to absorb new securities on primary markets, to influence the development of secondary markets, etc.

These usual considerations lead to the issue of relationships, of the time devoted to customers by senior bank managers, of building "trust" in these stakeholders. The "clubbish" approach of customership has always been the leverage of differentiation, and these connections of trust grew along with the diversification of investment banks and their purpose of "cross-selling", that is, delivering the whole range of their investment and corporate banking products and services. We find there again the discussion regarding differentiation versus convergence between investment and commercial banks, within the "old" system of the second banking revolution – from the 1860s to the 1970s, with investment banking skills within the corporate banking departments of the big deposit banks – and within the "new" system of the third banking revolution (since the 1980s), with mergers between investment and commercial banks, mainly. All the chapters in this book and other studies have grappled with this issue of

[31] Felix Rohatyn, *Un banquier dans le siècle*, Paris, Saint-Simon, 2011.

"connections", as market places are markets for securities and values on one side and business news on the other.

And recent history confirmed such an appraisal: when "Barbarians" hurt "at the gate",[32] opening doors to fresh chapters of US investment banking history, "heroes" came up to rekindle finance battles on the New York marketplace but also to mobilise law, finance, banking, market skills to conceive and achieve operations in hostile bids and M&A, and to finance them through syndicated loans, Behind "bad guys" of that time (those at KKR, for instance) were gathered talented teams of investment bankers, promised to a brilliant future till the mid-2000s. And the *Barbarians* book,[33] well before its successors in investigative journalism of the 2000s, described in detail, almost week by week, the range of talents showed by the senior bankers and their teams in engineering LBOs (leveraged buy-out operations) and "bridge loans" (to finance them) in the 1980s: "A single deal could generate upfront fees of $50 millions or more, enough to save a firm's quarter."[34] Steve Waters and J. Tomilson Hill (Lehman), Peter Cohen (at Shearson-Lehman), Eric Gleacher or John Gutfreund (head of brokerage and trading at Salomon Brothers) were joined by new path-setters like George Roberts (Bear Stearns), Jerome Kohlberg and Henri Kravis, or like Bruce Wasserstein and Joseph Parella.[35] J. Gutfreund was even on the cover of *Business Week* on 8 December 1985 as the head of the most dynamic investment bank, thanks to its risk taking bond trading operations and interest rate swaps, and its promising use of "quants" experts,[36] as sole kind of a "paradigmatic bank".[37] Both latters appear *ex post* as some genius of investment banking, all the more that Wasserstein succeeded in heading a globalised Lazard house in the 2000s: First Boston house, "until the late 1970s a sleepy, second-tier underwriter, rocketed to the force of major investment banks thanks largely to the brains of chutzpah of Bruce Wasserstein and Joe Parella",[38] before they left in 1988 to set up their own boutique. Classically, each *tempo* of banking history, as of general history, is being embodied by a few personalities, all creative and innovative, but themselves durable or fragile. "This was down to the personal qualities of

32 William Burrough and John Helyar, *Barbarians at the Gate. The Fall of RJR Nabisco*, New York, Harper & Row, 1990.

33 *Ibidem*, pp. 120-130s; 180s; 200s.

34 *Ibidem*, p. 187.

35 *Ibidem*, pp. 188-190.

36 Simon Johnson & James Kwak, *13 Bankers. The Wall Street Takeover and the Next Financial Meltdown*, New York, Vintage Books, 2010/2011, p. 57.

37 See the memoirs of a Salomon banker: Michael Lewis, *Liar's Poker. Rising Through the Wreckage on Wall Street*, New York, Norton, 1989; Penguin Books, 1990 (1st edition).

38 William Burrough and John Helyar, *op. cit.*, p. 376.

particular individuals: their expertise and contacts. These so-called rainmakers worked for the banks that paid the most. Those were the banks that made the best and biggest deals."[39]

Somewhat later, investigative journalist Gillian Tett identified some "heroes" who, at the investment banking division of J.P. Morgan, were the key actors of the derivatives revolution from the mid-1980s, and who led the debates at a decisive meeting in Florida in 1994 where was decided to accelerate the growth of market banking in London and New York altogether, with "commando mindsets": Peter Voicke (a German), head of global markets, Peter Hancock (a British), head of the derivative group (a team of sales and traders) and then chief financial officer[40] till 2000, or Bill Demchak,[41] supplemented by Mark Brickell, an influential specialist in the derivatives industry. Core units and main actors were thus able to impulse changes within the organisation of firm of banks to promote "revolutions" (or accelerations) in investment banking. Such "dream teams" gathered momentum in parallel by J.P. Morgan, Merril Lynch and Bankers Trust (Peter Freund and John Crystal, true engineers of the derivatives concepts and processes). And sorting out classical (and safer) commercial banking and innovative (and riskier) investment banking might seem uneffective, as, for instance, J. Hancock was altogether the head of commercial loans and of the derivatives division, as the aim was first to bring satisfactory products to customers, not to bet on proprietary trading.[42]

In fact, the process of "securitisation" itself (or pooling credit risks) was conceived at the end of the 1990s as a way to alleviate the weight of pending clients on the accounting books of these clients, not as a speculative dark force, and the further demonisation of the "special purpose vehicles" set up in the wake of such "revolution" cannot hide the fact that they firstly contributed to a useful reshuffling of balance sheets, precisedly and decidely for the account of the clients. Only later on were piles of SPVS and else drawned out on "off-shore accounts" by banks like Lehman or else to dissimulate the huge volumes of risks pending (as "firebombs"), all the more because they had chosen to keep these assets on their own books because of greed instead of spreading them on the market. Not all bankers, like James Dimon (after the merger of Bank One and J.P.

39 Jeroen Smit, *The Perfect Prey. The Fall of ABN AMRO, or What Went Wrong in the Banking Industry*, Amsterdam, Prometheus, 2009, p. 51.

40 P. Hancock became vice-president in charge of risk supervision in February 2010, then CEO of the ex-AIG renamed Chartis, in April 2011.

41 Gillian Tett, *Fool's Gold. How Unstrained Greed Corrupted a Dream, Shattered Global Markets and Unleashed a Catastrophe*, London, Little Brown, 2009, pp. 7-8. Gillian Tett, *L'or des fous*, Paris, Le Jardin des livres, 2011.

42 Gillian Tate, *op. cit.*, p. 51.

Morgan in 2004), struggled for a "fortress balance sheet", pleading for measuring and monitoring risk.[43]

But in the meanwhile one revealing change occurred too: the relative fidelity and stability of junior and senior bankers at investment banks commenced to crumble. Surely faithful experts still existed, like Blythe Masters, Steve Black and Bill Winters at J.P. Morgan. But several "heroes" and their teams were lured by competitors or hedge funds; Deutsche Bank, for instance, attracted teams from Merril Lynch before purchasing Bankers Trust.[44] These moves favoured the spillover of innovation, fighting spirit and mindsets, for the best or the worst indeed, with a phenomenon of osmosis among the worlds of investment and market banking.

B. The matrix and business models challenged

Because of the permanent revolution in lines of products, market banking and the diversification of capital finance, investment banks could never rely on an "organisation of firm" that was as structured as in the commercial banks.[45] The international organisation had and has to give way to senior bankers' initiatives and innovative paths and to ground-breakers within the financial community. This need for "immediate contacts" and tailor-made advice was expressed within the new big banks themselves. In many of them, the "organisation of the firm" endured several reshufflings to adapt to the changing demands of markets, customers, risk-managers and compliance authorities. The investment banking unit ("corporate & investment banking", CIB) had often to be restructured and posts reshuffled because it was becoming more and more clear that customers were disappointed by the big "banking industry".

On one side, they expressed their desire to be in touch with senior correspondents able to gather all the forces of the bank at the service of the client, to act as senior advisors at the head of specialised teams whose skills were to be dedicated to the client, and not only to revenue flows enriching the specialised unit. The draught for senior advisors or bankers was a sign that "merchant banking" organisations were to be re-created within big universal banks and that the business model of the "CIB" still needed to be defined efficiently. The historian of ABN-AMRO's crisis recalls of the demand by firms to get a "state-of-the art expertise in house"[46] (thus "under the same roof") to get more efficient skills "at offering shares

[43] *Ibidem*, pp. 133.

[44] *Ibidem*, pp. 108-109.

[45] See Alan Morrison and William Wilhelm, *Investment Banking. Institutions, Politics, and Law*, Oxford, Oxford University Press, 2007.

[46] Jeroen Smit, *The Perfect Prey*, *op. cit.*, p. 51.

globally and for a better price", which led the Dutch corporate banking division to extend its investment banking portfolio in the City (Hoare Govett in 1992).[47] In parallel with ING Barings (4,000 employees in the City), ABN AMRO could rely on 3,500 employees in its London body in the 1990s (share trading, originating operations, principal activities through the purchase of securities, etc.), with a growing specific investment banking "culture" there (bonus, etc.).[48]

The failure of commercial banks to integrate the merchant bank which they purchased in the 1980s revealed the huge difference in the corporate culture and the day-to-day practices between them: Deutsche Bank had great difficulty mastering its London sister-bank, the Deutsche Bank-Morgan Grenfell and Dresdner Bank long missed the chance of a happy convergence with Dresdner Bank-Kleinwort Benson (before merging it into Dresdner Bank-Wasserstein Parella), while ABN-AMRO struggled to develop ABN-AMRO-Hoare Govett. And, in the US, Deustche Bank, with Bankers Trust, and *Crédit suisse*, with First Boston, faced high hurdles before reaching some efficient targets in the management of both American and Transatlantic CIB activities – the classical "risk of execution" imposing its constraints. Transforming itself into a "global wholesale banking", including CIB, revealed as a challenge at every European bank, hesitating between centralisation and decentralisation, pondering about risks and controls management, about seniority, etc.

At ABN-AMRO consultancies helped redefine the strategy at the turn of the 21st century, to refocus CIB activities on a target of 4,000 biggest clients[49] to accompany them European-wide and even world-wide, whilst boosting the CIB division with huge investments in means of management and 500 fresh recruits: "Investment bankers were being sought with urgency. The bank wanted rainmakers, originators who would enable the corporate business division to bring in large share issues, or supervise mergers and takeovers. The new people would be required to deliver twice as much as they had cost the bank within three years."[50] One could not imagine a big playing bank without its global-playing CIB unit – and every "universal bank" followed the same (herdist) trail throughout the 2000s till lessons being drawn from the 2007/8 krach. But ABN-AMRO failed to mix corporate and investment bankers into a single-minded team and efficiency dragged behind somewhat..., paving the way to doubts about "the wholesale adventure".[51]

---

47 *Ibidem*, p. 52.

48 *Ibidem*, pp. 94-96.

49 *Ibidem*, pp. 175-176.

50 *Ibidem*, p. 177.

51 *Ibidem*, p. 203.

For years Barclays was plagued by a disappointing corporate organisation: strategies and structures did not fit. Even the high-end "hand-book"[52] published in 1996 to commemorate the ancient origins in 1690, had a chapter called: "Reassessment, rearrangement and renewal (1993-1996)", which, in fact, did not close the door to further, more intense re-considerations of strategies and structures in the fields of investment, market and corporate banking. "Matrices" were at stake, directly concerning those fields, all the more because the bank had absorbed two securities houses, De Zoete-Bevan and Wedd Durlacher-Mordaunt in 1984 to set up Barclays de Zoete Wedd or Bzw[53] in 1986. The latter was "an integrated merchant bank and market-maker",[54] created to satisfy with "banking in advanced markets: international strategy and global ambitions", through the process of "the transition to global banking".[55] But for almost a dozen years or more, the bank struggled to devise efficient and agile ways of managing this new business model, and, at the turn of the 21st century, it was swept off and a rejuvenated and refocused strategic model took shape under the umbrella of Barclays Capital. Such were the hurdles, the narrative case study reveals, that investment bankers had to face when confronted by the challenges of managing an over-dimensioned investment bank, its array of activities and broad portfolio of skills.

Throughout the 1980s-2000s, the globalised Zurich bank Crédit suisse – a marvelous case study for the banking and business history of the last few decades – was submitted to frequent tensions between its commercial banking institution and its investment banking subsidiary, Crédit suisse First Boston, before they merged in 2005-2006: its "chief executive hopes to end infighting at the bank by bringing the investment private banking and asset management arm closer together".[56] Lastly, numerous investment banks were truly "strong characters" who did not endure for long the administrative inertia in the big banks' organisation and the monitoring and reporting systems. Throughout the 1990s-2000s, this frequently led to an instability within investment banking departments of large European banks and to a constant reshuffling at their top, because these "stars" shifted from bank to bank – far from the loyalty and partnership which symbolised the stable investment banking houses in the 19th and 20th centuries...

52 "Chapter 8", Margaret Ackrill & Leslie Hannah, *Barclays. The Business of Banking, 1690-1996*, Cambridge, Cambridge University Press, 2001, pp. 358-381.

53 *Ibidem*, pp. 302-303.

54 *Ibidem*, p. 243.

55 *Ibidem*, p. 269.

56 *Financial Times*, end of 2005.

C. The debate regarding the "all under one roof" law

What management experts frequently found was that the key managerial problem lay in a lack of synergies. There were failures in the phenomenon of "cross-fertilisation", something that had been the rule in investment banks through the art of relationship of their senior partners. Managers – often dismissed and replaced – pondered the balance between the various units of the universal bank, which tried to explorate some relevant business model able to promote the key elements of its portfolio of skills and to cement some kind of *Hausbank* business model. Expectations were oriented toward the client himself, who could pick any service required ("all under the same roof", from corporate banking to market and investment banking, a range of banking arts and ranges also named "one stop shop") owing to the best combination of specialists in each banking activity. All this was done in the name of "solutions", the fashionable term to denote to what extent service enterprises (in this case, banks) were able to satisfy the client's every need and adapt their services to every client as if he was the only one.

But the traditional ties of confidence towards reliable senior bankers within investment and corporate banking bodies were broken after the 1990s, when investment banks set themselves the motto "all under the same roof". This has been denounced by several investigative books[57] which delved into the "conflicts of interests" within this new type of investment bank (Goldman Sachs,[58] Lehman,[59] etc.) – or the investment and corporate banking departments at big global banks, like J.P. Morgan,[60] Bank of America, BNP Paribas, etc.

A major issue was for example: how to afford low cost credit to clients benefiting from the M&A department when the obvious interest of the corporate banking division was to raise the cost of credit? Traditionally, the investment banker's portfolio of skills was based on promoting the

57 The first one being *grosso modo*: Michael Lewis, *Liar's Poker*, New York, W.W. Norton & Company, 1989. William Cohan, *House of Cards. A Tale of Hubris and Wretched Excess on Wall Street*, New York, Doubleday, 2009.

58 Lisa Endlich, *Goldman Sachs. The Culture of Success*, New York, Touchstone, 1999, 2nd edition, 2000.

59 Larry McDonald & Patrick Robinson, *A Colossal Failure of Common Sense. The Story of the Collapse of Lehman Brothers*, London, Ebury Press, 2009.

60 Duff McDonald, *Last Man Standing. The Ascent of Jamie Dimon and J.P. Morgan Chase*, New York, Simon & Schuster, 2010. Patricia Crisafulli, *The House of Dimon. How J.P. Morgan's Jamie Dimon Rose to the Top of the Financial World*, Hoboken (New Jersey), John Wiley & Sons, seconde édition complétée, 2009. Gillian Tett, *Fools' Gold. The Inside Story of JP Morgan and How Wall Street Greed Corrupted its Bold Dream and Created a Financial Catastrophe*, second supplemented edition, New York, Free Press-Simon & Schuster, 2010.

interests of the client ahead of those of the corporate and commercial banking divisions. "Chinese walls" or firewalls crumbled, capping the process that ended "gentlemanly capitalism"[61] at investment banks. A key issue concerns competition: the more investment banks were turning into universal banks, the less big enterprises could tolerate the reduced competition in each type of activity. They still wanted to get advice from one investment banker and credit from another (commercial or investment) banker. They wanted their banker to give them an independent financial advice based on research teams untouched by the pressures exerted on some equity by traders within their own bank. This explains the need for "China walls" or firewalls within the bank or the sharing of the demand for "solutions" among several bankers, big or small – which opened windows of opportunity to smaller investment banks.

Chinese walls have too been set up to protect the classical activity of investment bankers which consisted with advising "investors", either wealthy families, enriched entrepreneurs having benefitting from the CIB skills beforehand, or institutional investors. The banking giants transformed into universal banks had to separate attentively wealth management and assets management on one side, and their investment banking activities on the other one, first to avoid confusion of interests and insiders conflicts, second to leave advisors free to pick up securities freely and to "not advise" the securities of the customers of the CIB departments – one pending issue being still the actual freedom of the analysts of the wealth and assets management divisions or affiliates to criticise these "friendly" securities. Covering broad assets management activities even do not seem a strategic necessity for big banks, which deprived themselves of them, like Barclays or Deutsche Bank (sales) or Société générale and Crédit agricole (common merger and filialisation, into Amundi).

D. The issue of risk management

Yet another debate arose around the capacity of the managers of these polyvalent banking mega-corporations to manage risks and to impose a sufficiently clairvoyant, lucid, binding and respected analytical system. We have seen a number of top managers of the big American banks admit their incapacity to understand and supervise many of their house's activities. One of them, from Goldman-Sachs, "was standing in the middle of all these complex, high levered, exotic trades he created without necessarily understanding all the implications of those monstrosities. Anyway, not feeling too guilty about this, the real purpose of my job is to make

61 See Philip Augar, *The Death of Gentlemanly Capitalism: The Rise and Fall of London's Investment Banks*, London, Penguin Books, 2000.

capital markets more efficient and ultimately provide the US consumer with more efficient ways to leverage and finance himself".[62]

It is the universal bank's economic model itself that is double-edged: building an immense enterprise without giving it an organisation solid enough to manage pertinent risks; multiplying pockets of extreme risk in keeping with the growth of the capital markets business – themselves prone to the risks of speculative trade – classical in nature in itself, but also a source of illusion due to the securitisation of the usual risks run by the commercial bank, as the subprime crisis and Spanish savings bank crisis have proved, both being the result of several unoriginal property loans. These risks were accentuated by the analysts' lack of autonomy and the blindness of rating agency experts – though R. Lowenstein had pointed out the risk of an excessive blind convergence of these analysts during the bubble period.[63]

Perhaps it is time to ask some common sense questions: is the business model of the big universal bank, active all over the world, with lines of globalised businesses, viable? Can anybody really manage such a vast organisation? It is one thing to produce vehicles, electronic parts, tires on a global scale, quite another to manage risks as fluid as those in banking and finance. Moreover, we know that even Toyota, the grand master of the third industrial revolution with its creed of "toyotism", was faced by reliability and quality problems for some of its cars in 2011-20012, as though crossing the seven-million-vehicles-per-year cap brought it up against glass ceilings regarding quality of supervision at this vast scale.

And so, going beyond the somewhat simplistic – though not unfounded – criticisms regarding the cupidity, hubris and the will to power of the managers of the big banks, one could simply suggest that these had become "ungovernable" because of an over-large activity and risk surface. When the directors of HSBC were compelled to admit they had been unable to detect the money laundering taking place in their American subsidiaries,[64] it was actually the managerial capacity that was at fault. According to David Bagley, head of compliance at HSBC from 2002, "HSBC's excesses were due to the bank's rapid expansion and acquisition fuelled growth." "Its risk profile grew faster than its infrastructure", he observed [to the American Senate committee investigating the affair]. According to him, he did not have the means to apply the rules as he did not have the authority […]. Stuart Gulliver, CEO of HSBC from January 2011, has repeated

62 William D. Cohan, "Ending the moral rot on Wall Street", *op. cit.*

63 Roger Lowenstein, *Origins of the Crash: The Great Bubble and its Undoing*, New York, Penguin, 2004.

64 Virginie Robert, "Blanchiment: les dirigeants de HSBC incriminent la culture du groupe", *Les Échos*, 18 July 2012.

several times his excuses regarding the bank's mistakes [...]. Compliance had become a strategic priority and the department's manpower had risen from 200 to 1,000."[65] "HSBC's compliance culture has been pervasively polluted for a long time", said Senator Carl Levin, who chairs the committee. He claimed that HSBC used its bank in the United States as a gateway into the financial system for illicit money."[66] The importance of the managerial issue is proved by the simple fact that "HSBC's new chief legal officer is Stuart Levey, previously the Treasury's undersecretary for terrorism and financial intelligence. Mr Levey said his arrival was one piece of a comprehensive reorganisation under the bank's new chief executive, Stuart Gulliver. The overhaul will allow information on suspect clients and transactions, that the bank's individual country operations had not previously shared, to be pooled."[67]

Similarly, Barclays' CEO resigned in July 2012 when the scandal regarding the recurrent manipulation of the base rate of the international interbank market (LIBOR and EURIBOR) attained gigantic proportions: it later came to light that, around 2007-2008, market heads were conducting their trans-Atlantic trading activities outside of all central control.[68] We know how many big banks found themselves "caught in the crisis of 2007-2012 because their teams had developed activities with no limits. On one hand, they had been implicitly encouraged because the universal bank's corporate culture at the heart of the boom seemed to liberate "productive forces" in the name of rapid growth – though actually wild and unrestrained. On the other – and it is this point that interests us in this present study – the central information analysis and risk management platforms in these giant enterprises were underdeveloped: their corporate organisation was thus defective.

We have already mentioned in another book[69] how the Société générale's recruiting of a top manager (for the number 3 spot) from the chemical industry to supervise the company's organisation and re-organisation signaled a decisive inflexion – though it was too late as the economic downturn was only a few months away. They were finally trying, in this bank in full boom, to reconcile the management with the two key blocks, "strategies" and "structures", that is to say, to adapt the management to the scale of a globalised universal bank and, especially, to that of a new

65 *Ibidem*.

66 "HSBC's grilling. What comes out in the wash", *The Economist*, 21 July 2012, pp. 61-62.

67 *Ibidem*.

68 Éric Albert, "Barclays, récit d'une manipulation", *Le Monde*, 4 July 2012, p. 12. "Barclays, ou la *City* déconsidérée", *ibidem*, p. 1.

69 Hubert Bonin, *Des banquiers lucides dans le boum et la tempête? (2004-2010)*, Paris, Textuel, 2011.

type of corporate and investment bank which was the result of a quarter century of the "banking revolution". Too well organised into autonomous silos" (by job and territory), the investment and corporate banking divisions of the big universal banks had often become not unmanageable but unmanaged, that is to say, not subjected to a sufficiently strict corpus of regulations, checks and ratios. This explains the difference with the houses which proved in 2007-2010 that they had been able to, *ex ante*, set up risk-management divisions with relative efficacy (like BNP Paribas, Santander or even Goldman Sachs).[70]

These considerations allow for an intermediary and simple, if not simplistic, conclusion: houses which succeeded in controlling their risks in the investment banking business (in the larger sense), felt confident and could push ahead with their strategy of international deployment. That was the case with Goldman Sachs with its fascinating success story, as well as with BNP Paribas, which announced the resumption of its program by reinforcing its investment banking position in Germany for example, in order to "compete with Deutsche Bank, HSBC and J.P. Morgan",[71] especially now that it had been able to introduce in the country the activities of the Belgian bank Fortis which it had absorbed. On the other hand, other houses had the sense to "trim their sails" and admit that they had bitten off more than they could chew. That was the case with the Japanese bank Nomura: by taking over the activities of Lehman Brothers in Europe and 8,000 employees in 2008, it thought it had gained a solid foothold in London. But it soon realised that it did not have the human, managerial and financial resources to "become a financial global giant",[72] especially in the wholesale banking business.

Earlier, the investment banks set up by the French mutual banks had been deflated by the crisis, the period of strategic refocusing and the dismantling of fragile, even incompetent, entities and businesses. The Crédit agricole group did not stop trying to control the activities, the senior bankers, the feudalism and the risks of its subsidiary, born of the union of the investment bank Indosuez and the corporate and investment banking divisions of Crédit agricole and Crédit lyonnais to form Crédit agricole-Indosuez, later Calyon[73] and finally CACIB. The learning curve proved rather steep and long, and a strategy of withdrawal capped the failure of the somewhat over-ambitious growth strategy. The same course had to be

---

70 See "Chapter 4. L'art du contrôle au coeur du boum", *ibidem*, pp. 59-77.

71 Jean-Philippe Lacour, "BNP Paribas veut entrer dans le Top 5 des banques d'affaires en Allemagne", *Les Échos*, 17 August 2012.

72 Yann Rousseau, "Nomura va alléger ses effectifs en Europe", *Les Échos*, 7 September 2012.

73 See Marc Michaux, "Calyon, toujours pas à la hauteur", *L'Expansion*, No. 710, July-August 2006, pp. 60-62.

adopted by Natixis, the BPCE group's corporate and investment banking subsidiary and the Parisian division of Caisses d'épargne and Banques populaires, created in 2007 in the euphoria of the economic boom, characteristic of the mentality of the time.

Almost everywhere, big banks set up entities, systems, checks and risk-management controls aimed at adapting the management of structures to strategic requirements. It is nevertheless surprising that so many "big managers", trained in transatlantic universities and matured over years of steadily increasing responsibilities, took so long to see the necessity of "tightening the screws", "taming" what had begun to resemble "wild beasts": the short-term asset management platforms (cash investments, trading raw materials and energy resources, securitisation transactions, etc.) and, sometimes, those of long term assets (real estate investments, hedge funds, private equity funds). "J.P. Morgan wants its treasury department to fall into line",[74] but only after a big loss was deplored by its London branch in 2012, which had to be taken up again *ex post* with some humility, if not shame. These managers' maneuvering room was in fact, "as large as the risk checkers, generally installed on a different floor, were indifferent to what went on within the treasury, the backwater of banking activities".[75]

Ultimately, too great an externalisation of the risk analysis may seem, *a posteriori*, to have been one of the causes of investment bankers' overconfidence during the last economic boom. They were too taken up by the conclusions arrived at by rating agency experts who delivered reports that, *ex post*, can only be called deplorable – like that of Standard & Poor's on 6 June 2006: *Banking Industry Country Risk: These are the Good Old Days*.[76] Without going into the conflict of interest between internal analysts and asset managers, it would seem that the latter had their vigilance blunted by such assuaging reports from rating agencies or, worse, from brilliant academics. In short, "the critical sense" needed to be rehabilitated, which leads us to conclude that, if the different investment, corporate, wholesale & markets banking models are to be judged rigorously, their implementation needs to be judged within the framework of the famous "execution risk", which obviously includes the constraints of a drastic risk management and an intolerant system of compliance vis-à-vis the risk of any individual or collective excess.

74 Marc Roche, "J.P. Morgan veut faire rentrer dans le rang son département trésorerie", *Le Monde*, 9 September 2012.

75 *Ibidem*.

76 Scott Bugie, John Chambers, Ryan Tsang and Matthew Pimie, *Banking Industry Country Risk: These are the Good Old Days*, Standard & Poor's, RatingsDirect®, 6 June 2006 <www.standardandpoors.com/ratingsdirect>.

E. Giant investment banks vs boutiques?

Does it then mean that such an organisation of giant corporations can only lead to a metastasis of risk? A sign of the dissatisfaction regarding the model of the big, integrated investment bank is given by a strange phenomenon that arose at the turn of the 21st century and that went right contrary to this movement of integration between investment and commercial banks. On one side, large "universal banking" institutions prospered (with the motto: "one stop shopping", to lure customers for all their banking needs under a single roof). But the new trend promoted small "boutiques",[77] where grandees in the field of investment banking and M&A refurbished the "*banque d'affaires*" or merchant banking business model. Whether because senior bankers were uncomfortable in large banking firms and wanted to rediscover the agility, flexibility, reactivity and relational banking that rule in a smaller house; or whether clients wanted to work with smaller, specialised and innovative teams, more open to their needs and less preoccupied by managing vast trading rooms and trading innovations.

Boutiques have ever conquered some niches on the big market places, as did, for exemple, the Albert Kahn house in Paris in the 1890s-1920s, or, more decidedly, Forstmann Little & Co[78] in New York in the 1970s-1980s, where it reached the No. 2 ranking for the LBO specialty behind KKR, before Wasserstein-Parella was founded in 1988 by about twenty of the topbrass of First Boston.[79] Today, small houses in partnerships unearthed "niches" between the big banks to practice fine-tuned advice, embeddedness, relationship management, etc. A leading boutique was Bryan-Garnier, active both in London and Paris. The French Aforge Finance, created in 1995, allied itself to the ancient (since 1789) German '*Privat Bank*' Sal-Oppenheim in 2006 – before the latter's eventual collapse.... The French *Toulouse & Associés* joined the Italian Banca Leonardo in 2006, set up by an ex-partner of Lazard, whilst the little Bucephale Finance joined the fray. In the US, Jefferies[80] and MF Global emerged as competing mid-sized boutiques, capable of giving independent assessments. Even the Lazard and the Rothschild groups restructured their organisation according to global (the former) and Europeanised (the latter) schemes and re-founded their historic business cycle by imagining a role in the new globalised banking economy.

77 See Virginie Robert, "Le retour des boutiques", *Les Échos*, 1st March 2006.

78 William Burrough and John Helyar, *Barbarians at the Gate*, *op. cit.*, 1990, pp. 238-239.

79 *Ibidem*, pp. 376-382.

80 See "Jefferies and Leucadia. There's the beef. The strange combination of a conglomerate and an investment bank", *The Economist*, 17 November 2012.

Recently, the tycoon banker Joseph Parella has just established his own house, Perella Weinberg Partners, to re-invent investment banking and focus on M&A.

Nevertheless, the key question concerns the competitivity of these "boutiques" and the degree of openness of this investment banking market. Were the "rights of entry" low enough to allow the ingress of a sufficient number of serious competitors on every major banking and financial hub? What were the real barriers to entry? We understand that the investment and corporate banking divisions of the big universal banks benefited from the "size effect" afforded them by the immense technical and geographic span, a robust and diversified business and knowledge portfolio and a vast "captive" clientele in the form of the enterprises which were already clients of the commercial banking division and which would be happy to avail of services "under the same roof". On the other hand, these client-oriented companies might also want bring in some competition between their banking and financial service providers: this would open the doors to more mobile (or "agile"), more inventive and more reactive actors, especially as, often, the experts working in these boutiques were dissidents from the big investment banks.

One striking event of the recent years has been the "reinvention" of Lazard:[81] the effective amalgamation of the Paris, London and New York units, the retirement of bigwigs (F. Rohatyn, etc.) and family tucoons (Michel David-Weill), the repositioning of the strategic portfolio of activities, all in all lead to another "paradigmatic model" quite different from the Goldman Sachs one – even if its M&A units remain as an emblematic competitive edge. And the Paris Rothschild house followed the same path when it rebuilt its banque d'affaires from the 1990s.[82]

6. Still pending: What is investment banking today?

Everybody now knows that the balance (within the portfolio of strategic activities, balance-sheet figures and revenue sources) between market banking, investment banking and corporate banking had been subject to intense pressures (greed, blindness, internal balance of power, sheepish

81 See Anne Sabouret, *MM. Lazard frères et Cie. Une saga de la fortune*, Paris, Olivier Orban, 1987. Martine Orange, *Ces Messieurs de Lazard*, Paris, Albin Michel, 2006. Pierre de Gasquet, *Antoine Bernheim. Le parrain du capitalisme français*, Paris, Grasset, 2011.

82 Martine Orange, *Rothschild, une banque au pouvoir*, Paris, Albin Michel, 2012.

mindsets,[83] etc.) in a framework of "irrational exuberance".[84] Carlo Brambilla, co-editor of this book, expressed a clear opinion: "The source of profits is a good tool to discriminate between investment banking activities and banking activities: profits from fees and capital gains are typical investment banking profits, while banks rely on monetary intermediation (gap between borrowing and lending rates). The profit source is a feature that distinguishes – I think – the nature of banks." Such a "conservative" position might respond to the present debates when experts are confronted by the very definition of the activities which have to be regulated, supervised, corralled or even forbidden for some types of deposit banks, for example. One thus often differentiates between the "real economy" and the "capital markets bank" or the financial economy,[85] and discusses the negative effects of the "casino economy" – to use Keynes' expression – on the production system, as though in the eyes of the general public, the investment bank had joined the ranks, if not of "monsters", at least of bizarre "zombies"…

A. Towards "good investment banking"?

On a more serious note, it is the time of History that was lost during the boom years in the first decade of the 21st century, as though the notions of "reversal", excessive leverage or debt overload we no longer legal tender. Sure, "this time is different",[86] and one staked all on the efficiency of these "modeling machines" to prevent any excess. Even phrases like "free-wheeling" and "free-for-all" were used frequently during this "era of financial supermarkets". In the wake of its predecessor (*Liar's Poker*, which appeared in 1990), J. Knee's memoirs[87] talk of this short-sighted-

---

83 See, among many others books: William Cohan, *House of Cards. A Tale of Hubris and Wretched Excess on Wall Street*, New York, Doubleday, 2009. Alistair Milne, *The Fall of the House of Credit: What Went Wrong in Banking and What Can Be Done to Repair the Damage?*, Cambridge, Cambridge University Press, 2009. Alan Greenberg (with Mark Singer), *The Rise and Fall of Bear Stearns*, New York, Simon & Schuster, 2010. Gretchen Morgenson and Joshua Rosner, *Reckless Endangerment. How Outsized Ambition, Greed, and Corruption Led to Economic Armageddon*, New York, Times Book, Henry Holt & Co., 2011.

84 Robert Shiller, *Irrational Exuberance*, 2nd edition, New York, Broadway Books, 2005; Princeton, Princeton University Press, 2005.

85 See Christopher Houghton Budd, *Finance at the Threshold. Rethinking the Real and Financial Economies*, Aldershot, Ashgate, series "Transformation and Innovation", 2011.

86 Carmen Reinhart & Kenneth Rogoff, *This Time is Different. Eight Centuries of Financial Folly*, Princeton & Oxford, Princeton University Press, 2009.

87 Jonathan Knee, *The Accidental Investment Banker. Inside the Decade that Transformed Wall Street*, New York, Oxford University Press, 2006. Michael Lewis, *Liar's Poker. Rising Through the Wreckage on Wall Street*, New York, Norton, 1989; Penguin Books, 1990 (1st edition).

ness – "I'll be gone, You'll be gone" or IBG, YBG – that reigned in the mid-2000s and which we might consider, somewhat naively, to be completely contrary to the spirit of investment banking which is oriented towards the long-term and a certain wisdom regarding trust in business relations. But we must also note that the crash which sank a number of badly-managed and speculating banks did not necessarily incriminate the legitimacy of the banking business, especially that of investment banks in their role as corporate or capital market banks.

We join here, in all modesty, the ongoing debate between experts and bankers on what constitutes a "good bank".... "Progress is everyone's business", said Goldman Sachs in 2012 in its institutional communication campaigns,[88] where it also developed the historic core of the investment banking business, that of financing infrastructure projects ("project financing"), as though to suggest that the capital markets bank – seen as the "bad bank" – was nothing more than a tool at the service of the "good bank". On the other hand, we are too quick to denounce "the bad bank": one learned of the huge profits garnered by market banking activities, which had out-paced those of the traditional investment bank (brokerage, issuing and underwriting, M&A) but at the same time raised concerns regarding risk management (for example at Goldman Sachs).[89]

B. "Good" merchant banking?

We can only note that "the good merchant bank" constituted an essential hub in investment banking activities at the start of the 21st century. However controversial they might be, market leaders largely practiced "good banking", that is to say, a number of corporate and M&A advisory banking activities.

They can point to their beneficial role in helping companies refocus, in the sale of their assets in the course of their refocusing or breakup and in helping them fight off hostile takeover bids. An institutional communication from the Bank of America-Merril Lynch affirmed: "It ended with a successful takeover defence. It started with trust. When everything was on the line for our long-time client Airgas, they called on us. Together, we set one of the most important precedents in modern M&A history, leveraging hostile raid defence tactics and global industry insight. More important, shareholder value was protected throughout. Taking your opportunity further. That's return on relationship."[90] The tradition of senior bankers in

88 See <www.goldmansachs.com/progress>.

89 See: Peter Thal Larsen, "From pit to pinnacle: Why traders are calling the shots on Wall Street", *Financial Times*, 15 June 2006; "Goldman Sachs. On the Top of the World", *The Economist*, 27 April 2006.

90 Ad in *The Economist*, 19 November 2011, p. 43. *Idem*, 5 November 2011, p. 72.

advisory banks was thus retained, with its cohorts of engineers, lawyers and financiers specialised in this high-flying business. And a Lazard team (Jean-Louis Girodolle, Jean-Yves Helmer, both partners, and Matthieu Pigasse, a CEO) played a consistent role in advising the (failed) project of merger between air-industrialists EADS and BEA in the Fall 2012, thus keeping alive the spirit of merchant banking.

Table 3. Classification of banks by global M&A operations in the first nine months of 2012 (billions of dollars)

		Total value of transactions supervised	Fees perceived (millions of dollars)
1	Goldman Sachs	394.5	1,120
2	J.P. Morgan	348.2	825
3	Morgan Stanley	334.2	
4	Deutsche Bank	269.4	
5	Barclays	264.6	
6	Crédit suisse	263.8	
7	Citi	260.8	
8	Bank of America-Merril Lynch	220.3	
9	Rothschild	145	
10	Lazard	122.4	

Source: Dealogic, in *Les Échos*, 26 September 2012, p. 28.

Table 4. Classification of banks by M&A operations in France in the first nine months of 2012 (billions of dollars)

		Total value of transactions supervised
1	Rothschild	23.9
2	BNP Paribas	23
3	Lazard	20.5
4	Barclays	17.5
5	Morgan Stanley	16.7
6	Nomura	14.7
7	Ondra partners	12.9
8	Société générale	11.3

Source: Thomson-Reuters, in *Les Échos*, 29 September 2012, p. 28.

Among "good" investment banking would reign the advisory bank! Wise investment bankers offer their considered opinion (at a cost…) to companies wanting to grow externally or to defend themselves from hostile raids, widen their capital base with the help of "friendly" investors – like the Middle Eastern investment funds shunted by Rothschild towards the Parisian market – and finally, for asset disinvestments as part of a strategic refocusing. Still, we must not forget that this advisory banking business, however noble it might seem, was also the target of intense criticism: investment banks have conducted hostile operations in the course of bloody stock market wars, prompting cries of "Barbarians".[91] Banks have helped foreign enterprises to take control of the nation's flagship industries, in stark contrast to the custom of "economic patriotism", as when Société générale helped the Anglo-Indian Mittal group in its offensive against Arcelor, the world No. 1 in steel, not to speak of numerous other cases (Pechiney taken over by the American multinational Alcan, etc.). And we know how the attack mounted by RBS, Fortis and Santander on their Dutch colleague ABN-AMRO[92] constituted a drama in the history of the investment banker… which, by the way, turned out to be a tragedy, with the fall of three of the four protagonists.… What is seen as "good" and less "risky" contains no fewer "poison pills", if we talk of "good" and "bad" financial practices.

A last point lies with the ever issue of the balance between "greedy" mindsets or "bad practices" even at the heart of "good" investment banking, when M&As are concerned: the recent IPO for the account of the IT Facebook firm appeared as a relevant case study: investment bankers at Morgan Stanley struggled to promote sales at a high value with high fees, such a "good" team has been in charge with almost half of the IT IPOs in the US in the 2010s, and its primary operation was crowned with success, just before the fall of the stock value on the secondary market: fueling Manju Puri's analysis, what was questioned was the capital of skills and information of Morgan Stanley to reach a durable success in this IPO…, and even its "bad practices" throughout a "good" operation, because its analysts did not respect the relevant firewall isolating them from the issuers.[93]

C. "Bad" market banking?

Having said that, all these debates between regulatory authorities, parliamentarians in charge of developing regulatory texts, consulting firm experts and academics reveal the wide differences regarding the definition of "the good bank" and the "good" business model. One hears talk of an excessive complexity in the management of the big universal banks and even retired bosses suggest that "mega-banks should be broken up"…[94]

91 William Burrough and John Helyar, *Barbarians at the Gate. The Fall of RJR Nabisco*, New York, Harper & Row, 1990.

92 See: Jeroen Smit, *The Perfect Prey. The Fall of ABN AMRO, or What Went Wrong in the Banking Industry*, Amsterdam, Prometheus, 2009.

93 See Lucie Roquebain, "Morgan Stanley mis à l'amende pour son rôle dans l'IPO de Facebook", *Le Figaro*, 19 December 2012, p. 27.

94 "Universal banking. Together, forever? The enduring marriage of investment and commercial banking", *The Economist*, 18 August 2012.

Reports and experts denounce "the isolation of risky market activities. No doubt it is good intentioned, but the daily cash management for the client or the bank, the interventions on the derivatives market for the short-term valuation of client assets (production enterprises or investment funds), holding securities during issues on the primary market, managing secondary market liquidity by the purchase and sale of securities for client enterprises, "market making" activities on behalf of clients, FOREX and "swapping" activities for multinational companies wanting to cover themselves against FOREX risks, are all very traditional activities which harbour the risk of "malpractice" (taking speculative positions, concealing numbers and flows) as well as risks in any case, in the normal sense of the word. Banning these activities – according to this humble French academic – would be attempting the impossible. "We do not know exactly how much these trading activities represent", confides an expert.[95] "All activities are potentially risky, the risks are different." Historically, "the information-creation activities of many investment banks rely increasingly up their secondary market presence as traders and principal investors [which] requires a sizable capital investment"[96] arm (like a venture capital body) and even proprietary trading, as supplementary trump cards to fix a big firm as a durable (and satisfied) client.

Still, segregating these so-called "risky" activities to subsidiaries having their own funds and compensatory ability is no doubt the ideal solution.[97] We understand the intensity of the debates around the American ("Paul Volcker Rules"), British ("John Vickers Report") and European ("Erkki Liikaen's report" in September 2012) reports – not to speak of the French Moscovici law at the turn of 2013. "Banks have to often issue (initiate) an operation for their client as a share or bond issue and then resell the paper to institutional investors. To separate them [these activities] would mean that henceforth the client would have to do business with two different entities" rued a banker.[98] "There are ambiguities regarding the choice of instruments which will be seen solely as one's own account and those as that of balance sheet management and liquidity."[99] And we could

---

95 Nicolas Madelaine, interview with Nicolas Véron, from the Bruegel think tank, "On ne sait pas combien exactement représentent ces activités de trading", *Les Échos*, 3 October 2012, p. 27.

96 Alan Morrison & William Wilhelm, *Investment Banking. Institutions, Politics and Law*, Oxford, Oxford University Press, 2007, p. 21.

97 Pending numerous academic studies, and among so many day-to-day articles, see: Ninon Renaud, "Huit idées reçues sur la séparation des activités bancaires", *Les Échos*, 20 June 2012, p. 29.

98 Réjane Reibaud, "Les premières critiques des banquiers à l'égard du rapport Liikanen", *Les Échos*, 4 October 2012, p. 26.

99 Interview with Rémi Legrand, from Eurogroup Consulting, *ibidem*.

add that "the information-creation activities of many investment banks rely increasingly upon their secondary markets presence as traders and principal investors",[100] in a quite normal complementarity and osmosis.

In fact, observers have noted that it is the hyper-growth of market banking activities which has contributed to the false perception of the investment banking business. "The *Liikanen report* shows that it targets banks whose trading activities cross 15 to 25% of total assets or a total figure of more than 100 billion euros. It so happens that several universal banks fall in this category and may be seen as excessive, if not dangerous, as regards their trading activities. "According to these criteria, five banks already come under the scanner as their risk assets account for more than 30% of their total balance sheet. Deutsche Bank and the Royal Bank of Scotland top the list with a little more than de 50%, ahead of Barclays (around 43%), BNP Paribas and *Société générale* (close to 33%)."[101] Harsh arguments oppose the defenders of broad markets banking oriented towards customers and the "extremists" or uncompromising bodies (anti-free banking organisations, like Finance Watch) who doubt about the reliability of such a distinction between "good" market banking in favour of "customers" and "bad" market activities, dedicated to mere speculation and high-end profits. And no clear-cut answers seem to be defined, despite regulating laws and strategic reconsiderations within big banks.

D. From immediate history to present future?

These arguments should incite the academic to exert great caution as he approaches the end of this book.... "There is very little to explain precisely what it is that investment bankers add to economic life", said a colleague,[102] insisting on two key qualities: "human experience and judgment".[103] We shall see what the present holds for the immediate history of investment banking because, today, the very business model of the investment bank is being re-considered all over the world – which is stimulating to historians,[104] who question the relevance of a business model for every key period of a sector's history. Perhaps our book will help foster historical arguments and clues on present perspectives!

---

100 Alan Morrison & William Wilhelm, *Investment Banking, op. cit.*, p. 21.

101 Renaud Honoré, "Quatre questions autour d'une réforme très attendue", *Les Échos*, 3 October 2012, p. 26.

102 "Introduction", Alan Morrison & William Wilhelm, *Investment Banking, op. cit.*, p. VII.

103 *Ibidem*, p. 8.

104 See: Christopher Kobrak & Mira Wilkins (eds.), "The '2008 Crisis' in an economic history perspective. Looking at the twentieth century", *Business History*, Vol. 53, No. 2, April 2011, pp. 175-192.

Whatever the issues, strategic screening has been crowned as the cornerstone of the new CIB philosophy. As regards asset management on the relatively middle term, investment banks themselves have begun to reduce their strategic range, especially in the United States, and we already underlined the sale or filialisation of assets management activities by several big banks. In parallel, a few of them have got rid of their hedge[105] or private equity funds – as BNP Paribas had done earlier by externalising PAI, a stakeholding entity, just as Lazard France externalised its corporate investment arm, Eurazeo. But should universal banks' investment banking business still include subsidiaries for the promotion and investment in real estate (like at Société générale and BNP Paribas)? A veritable sieving and sorting operation began in earnest in every national and continental banking system – the whole also under the constraints of capital ratios, which meant embarking on a serious asset allocation operation by business line, that is, by subsidiary, if this process of externalisation truly takes off. The evaluation of "weighted risk" by (Basel II, II bis or III) appropriate ratios ("risk adjusted capital", at S&P, for example) should help in the re-evaluation of the portfolio of strategic activities and business models as regards "investment, corporate, wholesale and markets banking".

Market banking also include the classical function of "market management" (in French, "*teneur de marché*"), where banks manage the liquidity of the markets, either for FOREX operations or for securities flows. But such activities are rich with risks, open doors to speculative moves, and, moreover, as recent trials showed, open lateral doors leading to covered practices (on the *Euribor* or the *Libor*, for instance, etc.). Anyway bankers are striving to convince of the legitimacy of their corporate & investment banking activities: "The main aim of BNP Paribas' teams is to develop and maintain long-term relationships with clients. They provide support for clients' expansion or investment strategy as well and handle their day-to-day transactions, and deliver integrated solutions to meet clients' financing, advisory and risk management needs."[106] Refocusing on customers-oriented mindsets is now onward the leverage communication and action driving force – with the concurse of consultancies and under the pressure of regulation rules.

Strategic repositioning might appear as the motto of the new decade among big banks. Specialisation around "cash cows" and "strengths" is being achieved everywhere, through "loss-weighting treatments". For instance, UBS stopped its platform in bonds trading, oriented towards its Swiss clients and its own-accounts trade, whilst BNP Paribas sticks to its

---

[105] See: Simon Lack, *The Hedge Fund Mirage: The Illusion of Big Money and Why It's Too Good to be True*, New York, John Wiley & Sons, 2012.

[106] BNP Paribas, booklet *2012 at a Glance*, p. 13.

bonds trading platform as its worldwide size and its ranking help it being more oriented towards forms of "industrial banking" – with "low-key" profits piling up to amortise expenses and provisions for risk-taking – and services to firms (for their classical issues of bonds, BNP Paribas being the leading bank for the issues labelled in euros). But the UBS group is being refocusing on high end asset management ("wealth management", private banking) in parallel with its day to day deposit and commercial banking activities: "The Zurich-based bank said on October 30 that it was largely withdrawing from fixed income trading, reducing its funded balance sheet by SFR 300 billion ($319 billion) or a third over three years, and cutting headcount across the group by 10,000 or 16 per cent of the total. Some 2,000 front office investment bankers will be axed."[107]

On other fields where French banks had extended a leading grip, they had to fold up their strategic portfolio for the sake of the Basel leverage rules, among which the liquidity risks[108] and regulating requirements. That was the case first about loans to financial bodies investing in planes and renting them to air-transport companies, and to the commitment to project financing – and the same for trade financing, a historical stronghold for French banks (from their basis in Geneva, Paris or London dedicated to loans to commodities trading firms). BNP Paribas had been the world leading bank for the giant market of financing of infrastructures (oil and gas equipments, roadways, bridges or tunnels, etc.) in 2007, and had to drift away from that market in favour of Asian competitors,[109] even if innovative paths can be followed (desintermediation through assets

---

107 Neil Sen, "Where UBS goes, other banks may soon follow. Other bulge bracket investment banks are watching UBS closely to see if they should follow the Zurich-based bank's strategy", *The Economist*, 6 November 2012. ",There has to be an element of doubt about whether you can run a successful investment banking division and equities business without fixed income, but strategically it makes sense to allocate capital to the strongest parts of the bank such as wealth management', says Andrew Stimpson, banks analyst at Keefe, Bruyette & Woods in London. Some senior rival investment bankers doubt that UBS can make a success of a firm shorn of a core product. 'Most clients are multi-product users and some might choose to move to a genuine universal bank. This is fraught with execution risk, and it's great news for the rest of the industry', says one wryly. One the other hand, if it is a success, other big banks with relatively weak units might be tempted to emulate UBS, or Royal Bank of Scotland's investment banking business which exited its equities business piecemeal in the first quarter of this year. Citigroup, for instance, as new CEO Mike Corbat will note, has a comparatively small equities business that produced only about a fifth of the $3.7 billion generated by fixed income, currencies and commodities." See Frédéric Thérin, "Le recentrage d'UBS pourrait faire réfléchir ses concurrents, *Les Échos*, 31 October 2012, p. 24.

108 See Shin Hyun Song, *Risk and Liquidity*, series "Clarendon Lectures in Finance", New York, Oxford University Press, 2010.

109 Anne Drif, "Infrastructures: les banques françaises supplantées en Asie", *Les Échos*, 7 November 2012, p. 27.

management bodies or through funds of debts). Such a reorientation might fuel the argument about the side-effects of re-regulatory moves, as they could also drive CIB out of some fields of "real economy". But it might seem naive to imagine that "risky" (and often criticised) activities of market banking could be sacrified on the altar of strategic refocusing (and "develeveraging"): at Société générale, for example, derivatives, which had fostered prosperity during the boom,[110] remain one core activity of the investment banking division, because of its useful role for clients in search of coverage products. Contradictory clues might therefore been picked up from the very recent turnarounds of CIB strategies.

Comparing both tables in our introductive chapter (chapter 1, table 1) and here under (chapter 15, table 5) could help ponder about "traditions", "path dependancy" or the very durability of core skills of banks involved in corporate and investment banking, with the growing reservation about the impossibility of separating both types of banking, except about a breeding ground of "boutiques" and specialised and tiny investment banks (Lazard, Rothschild, mainly family or partnership bodies). "There is very little to explain precisely what it is that investment bankers add to economics life", pondered a handbook about investment banking, of which is author concluded: "We argue that the investment bank's central activity is informational."[111] And the author recalls what our own collective book had insisted on through its various chapters: "human experience and judgment", "reputational capital", "the information-creation activities", "information network", "liquidity network", fixing property rights (on commodities or securities) at price relevant to available information, etc. – investment bank's "human agency" functions being to be "a gatekeeper to its network".[112] "Business rests on relational contracts", for instance about security issuance or syndicated loans.

Throughout history, in other books and in our book, the ambiguous overlapping between corporate banking, merchant banking and investment banking has resisted analysis, which hinders historians and present regulators to define precisely the limits between "good" (helping firms and institutions within the "real economy" – to use the words of the Human Watch association) and "bad" (over-risky) banking, and also between good and bad practices. Did investment banks stumble on far-reaching innovations and over-leveraged operations? Or merely on a dire lack of transparency, shadow (off-shore or off-balance sheet) accounting,

110 Isabelle Ehrhart, "Société générale: les dérivés portent l'activité de banque d'investissement", *Les Échos*, 7 November 2001, p. 28.

111 Alan Morrison & William Wilhelm, *Investment Banking. Institutions, Politics and Law*, Oxford, Oxford University Press, 2007, p. 4.

112 *Ibidem*, p. 79.

tricky balance sheets, Let us recall that, in the 1930s, Hoover did not start investigating into investment banks because of their ranges of activities but because of their malpractices on Wall Street securities markets, which led to the Securities Act of 1933 and then the Securities and Exchange Act of 1934, and to the creation (by splitting off) of securities firms (First Boston, Morgan Stanley, Brown Harriman, etc.).[113]

Table 5. "Good" investment banking activities at French big banks? Issues of the present times

Specialties	**Present issues to reorient recent history**
Portfolios of immaterial skills	
Advice in mergers & acquisitions, and in splitting operations	Still good positions in France and Europe, but being seriously contested by American giants and even tiny boutiques or agile merchant banks
Advice in issues of bonds (fixed income) Among which: Advise on timing and execution to public issuers on debt capital markets, in euros or dollars; main book-running and co-management of bonds issuings for transnational companies (US dollars, pounds, Swiss francs, yens, euros) (corporate finance)	Challenge to balance historical issuing functions (syndication and prime brokerage) and management of liquidity on secondary markets
Advice and completion of syndicated credit operations	Challenge of the leveraging issues against permanent funds or liquidity tensions on the refinancing markets
Management of money flows	
Management of market platforms for bonds, securities, FOREX	Concerns raised by rules about permanent funds as basic counterparts for risks
Global management of means of payment and transfers	Needs of huge investments into IT and global platforms of cash management and transaction banking
Financing operations	
Project financing and financing infrastructures	Concerns raised by rules about permanent funds as basic counterparts for risks = leaving top ranking in "structured products" to Asian banks
Financing financial bodies investing in planes or ships	Consuming too much dollars to foster the loans, thus constraining French banks to cut into their historical positions on this field

113 *Ibidem*, pp. 204-212.

Specialties	Present issues to reorient recent history
Global trade finance loans	Gaining lead arranger mandates for global trade finance loans (in partnership with other banks)
Syndicated loans	Leading functions of bookrunner and mandated lead arranger for syndicated loans, with a trend to drift from European weakening markets to Asian and Middle East dynamic markets
Market banking (global equities and commodity markets) (secondary markets)	
Derivatives markets; interest rates derivatives, etc.	Keeping strong positions whilst struggling against regulating interference
Management of platforms for cash products, swap in interest rates, FOREX (exchange prime brokerage, etc.), and derivatives products at the service of institutional and financial investors Providing solutions for the coverage of risks about the liquidity of fixed income products (debt capital market)	Growing investments in IT systems and platforms ("industrialised" back offices)

(We used the annual reports of BNP Paribas to pick up clues of CIB activities in 2009-2012)

And that real competition was at last imposed in the late 1930s about the call for bids in favour of "opened" underwriting business, at railway companies and utilities, beyond department stores or medium-sized firms which had benefitted from such competitive practices since the start of the century, before the huge trial (November 1950-May 1953) set up by Harold Medina against the investment banks' cartel[114] also tackled the issue of the lack of competition (and transparency) among them. This raised once more the argument about the repetitive critics: are the crafts, professions, skills, specialties at stake? Or merely bad practices and ill-managed risks in these activities? Should regulation refurbish the whole CIB profession and bodies, or only fix rules, impose drastic "accountability"? Such dilemma has ever been the cornerstone of debates and ruling, and is still fostering harsh arguments among stake holders of the reform, supervision and management of the marketplaces.

E. *A sole certainty: No investment bank is sure of its future*

Re-reading *Barbarians at the Gate*,[115] what is striking is that a large number of the investment banks quoted about the brilliant or tepid financial

114 *Ibidem*, pp. 220-222.

115 William Burrough and John Helyar, *Barbarians at the Gate*, *op. cit.*, 1990.

operations of the 1980s have now disappeared: Dillon-Read,[116] which could be perceived then as some "queen" of Wall Street, Lehman Brothers (regaining momentum at that time), DBL (Drexel Burnham Lambert), the inheritor of the Drexel house – part of Wall Street history on the long term – or Bear Stearns have all been swept off the market by the successive crisis on Wall Street, in 1987-1993, or more recently (2007-2008), if we except Lazard Brothers. Barriers to entry might be somewhat high, but ("buffer") barriers to exit are very low indeed... A very few crossed turmoils and tsunamis, like Morgan Stanley (headed in the 1980s by Eric Gleacher),[117] that had advised NJR to merge with Beatrice instead of ceding to KKR's power.

If we focus on the 1980s, the decade of the rekindling of the "fighting spirit" among investment banking was marked by a wave of amalgamation among houses: EF Hutton and Shearson Lehman (itself resulting from the aggregation of Lehman and Kuhn Loeb), as a rival to Morgan Stanley and First Boston, all being the leaders of that time, far ahead Goldman Sachs. Later on, in the 1990s, mergers favoured Morgan Stanley, absorbing Dean Witter-Discover and jumping from 4,000s employees in 1985 to 53,000 in 2004, equal to Merril Lynch (51,000). Two lever forces acted in favour of differenciation: first, the ability to jump efficiently but also rapidly and massively from "safe and boring banking" (fixed income on the stock exchanges, corporate finance, M&As) to "risky and high-yielding banking" (market banking, derivatives, money marketfunds, etc.); second, the capacity to face with reactivity, anticipation, lucidity and durability the risks created by such a jump – as the case of RBS proved it: it had succeeded in reaching the top brass of investment banking – competing with rebound Barclays Capital and powerful transoceanic HSBC – in the mid-2000s, but collapsed through the krach.[118] A commonplace remark could be that victors of a "historical period" can be seriously challenged by their internal errors and misfits, or by renewed competition and innovation – all the more that a "global financial system"[119] might be on the making, thus intensifying competition and differentiation moves.

---

[116] Robert Sobel, *The Life and Times of Dillon Read*, New York, Dutton, 1991.

[117] William Burrough and John Helyar, *op. cit.*, p. 99. See Patricia Bear, *Blue Blood & Mutiny. The Fight for their Soul of Morgan Stanley*, New York, Harper Perennial, 2007.

[118] See "Investment banking. Too small for their boots. British investment banks have lost their swagger. That is bad news for the country", *The Economist*, 6 October 2012.

[119] Glenn Morgan and Michel Goyer, "Is there a global financial system? The locational antecedents and institutionally bounded consequences of the financial crisis", in Glenn Morgan & Richard Whitley (eds.), *Capitalism and Capitalisms in the Twenty-First Century*, Oxford, Oxford University Press, 2012, pp. 119-145.

Final Considerations: Are Investment Bankers the Issue?

Hubert Bonin

After the rather dense and complex academic exercises, we shall now embark on a more simple discussion regarding the brand image and the nature of investment banks and investment bankers.

A controversial brand image

The years 2007-2014 have seen investment bankers come under severe criticism. They have been called irresponsible, greedy, reckless and blind by economists, business analysts, rating agencies and even by experts in the academic world.[1] In short, they were judged to have been incapable of handling the economic freedom that the process of liberalisation had given them. The question is, did we pay too high a price for this liberalisation,[2] and was it not in itself too audacious, the result of too great a deregulation? Instead of moving forward on a path of healthy emulation, beneficial to both national and international economies, did we stray into a battlefield of unbridled competition and excesses due to hubris and risk-taking which vitiated the proper functioning of the market economy?[3] But these exact same journalistic and academic discussions had taken place in the 1970s and 1980s when the "new investment bank" had taken shape![4]

1 Ewald Engelen, Ismail Erturk, Julie Froud, Sukhdev Johal, Adam Leaver, Michael Moran and Karel Williams, "Misrule of experts? The financial crisis as elite debacle", *Economy and Society*, Vol. 41, No. 3, August 2012, pp. 360-381.

2 Joseph Auerbach & Samuel Hayes, *Investment Banking and Diligence: What Price Deregulation?*, Boston, Harvard Business School Press, 1986.

3 Alistair Milne, *The Fall of the House of Credit: What Went Wrong in Banking and What Can Be Done to Repair the Damage?*, Cambridge, Cambridge University Press, 2009.

4 For example: Samuel Hayes, Michael Spence and David van Praag Marks, *Competition in the Investment Banking Industry*, Boston, Harvard University Press, 1983. Samuel Hayes, "Investment banking: Power structure in flux", *Harvard Business Review*, No. 49, 2, 1971, pp. 136-152. Samuel Hayes, "The transformation of investment banking", *Harvard Business Review*, No. 57, 1, 1979, pp. 153-170. Irwin Friend, James R. Longstreet, Michael Mendelsohn, Erwin Miller & Arleigh Jess (eds.), *Investment Banking and the New Issues Market*, Cleveland, World Publishing Company, 1967.

In fact, people thought that they knew everything about investment banking, thanks to the in-depth books and manuals written on the subject.[5] Also, the cyclic upswing of the economy had lulled all the big players (governments, regulatory authorities, central banks, analysts, economists, CEOs in every sector, etc.) while the more lucid bankers remained a minority[6] in these times of irrational exuberance.[7] The crisis provided surprising, if not shocking, insights into the inner life of investment banks – the tensions and rivalries, the power struggles[8] which often determined the strategic choices and management methods which opened the door to too much "facility". A new category of "bad" investment bankers was defined: greedy,[9] predatory, irresponsible, brash, brutal, impatient, immoral, sometimes even playing against his own clients' interests…

Such negative evaluations are reminiscent of the bad press received by the American robber barons in the years 1880-1910,[10] and the recurrent condemnations of the "gods of capitalism" who defied the wisdom of Olympus.[11] In fact, similar reactions had also attended French bankers

---

5 See Alan Morrison and William Wilhelm, *Investment Banking: Institutions, Politics, and Law*, Oxford, Oxford University Press, 2008. Anjan Thakor and Arnoud Boot (eds.) *Handbook of Financial Intermediation and Banking*, Amsterdam & Boston, Elsevier, 2008. Michel Fleuriet, *Banques d'investissement et de marché: les métiers des banques d'affaires*, Paris, Économica, 2007. Jane E. Hughes and Scott B. MacDonald, *International Investment Banking*, Boston, Addison and Wesley, 2002. John Peter Williamson (ed.), *The Investment Banking Handbook*, New York, John Wiley, 1988.

6 Hubert Bonin, *Des banquiers lucides dans le boum et la tempête? (2004-2010)*, Paris, Textuel, 2011.

7 Robert Shiller, *Irrational Exuberance*, 2nd edition, New York, Broadway Books, 2005; Princeton, Princeton University Press, 2005.

8 For example: Patricia Bear, *Blue Blood & Mutiny. The Fight for the Soul of Morgan Stanley*, New York, Harper Perennial, 2007. Gretchen Morgenson and Joshua Rosner, *Reckless Endangerment. How Outsized Ambition, Greed, and Corruption Led to Economic Armageddon*, New York, Times Book, Henry Holt & Co., 2011. William Cohan, *House of Cards. A Tale of Hubris and Wretched Excess on Wall Street*, New York, Doubleday, 2009.

9 See Joseph Stiglitz, *Le triomphe de la cupidité*, Paris, Les liens qui libèrent, 2010.

10 Matthew Josephson, *The Robber Barons: The Great American Capitalists, 1861-1901*, New York, Harcourt, Brace, Jovanovich, 1934. Hal Bridges, *"The Robber Baron Concept in American History"*, *Business History Review*, Vol. 32/1, Spring 1958, pp. 1-13. John Tipple, *"Anatomy of Prejudice*: Origins of the Robber Baron Legend", *Business History Review*, Vol. 33, No. 4, Winter 1959, pp. 510-523. Burton Folsom, *The Myth of the Robber Barons: A New Look at the Rise of Big Business in America*, Hemdon (Virginia), Young's American Foundation, 6th edition, 2010 (first: 1987).

11 Michel Villette & Catherine Vuillermot, *From Predators to Icons. Exposing the Myth of the Business Hero*, Cornell University Press, 2009. Matthew Josephson, *The Money Lords, The Great Finance Capitalists, 1925-1950*, New York, Weybright & Talley, 1972.

and financiers in 1880-1900 and again in the 1930s (sometimes mixed with anti-Semitism), giving rise to a degree of hatred which makes it difficult today to conduct a purely objective analysis.

Apart from these "moral" controversies regarding the attitudes of businessmen and business ethics, the "bad" investment bankers were also subjected to other more technical criticism: they did not have a skills portfolio in keeping with their takings on operations,[12] and, especially, their transaction costs were too high relative to their capital of skills, within the "financialisation" of the economy. And despite her colleagues' harsh criticism of her conclusions,[13] Julie Froud[14] and her team concluded that these "financial elite" were at the heart of the causes behind the recent crisis and capitalism's failure as a whole. William Lazonick's analysis seems to suggest that it was their role in financialisation and the complete disorder in an artificial economy relative to the "real economy" which explain the jolts that shook the production system.[15]

As with every financial and banking crisis, investigative journalists[16] were fascinated by the power wielded by investment bankers, their "hidden", or at least, discreet clout, like in the investment or merchant banking

---

12 See Lily Fang, "Investment bank reputation and the price and quality of underwriting services", *Journal of Finance*, No. 60, 6, 2005, pp. 2729-2761.

13 Matthias Beck, "New financial elites, or financial dualism in historical perspective? An extended reply to Folkman, Froud, Johal and Williams", *Business History*, Vol. 52, No. 7, décembre 2010, pp. 1027-1047. Geoffrey Wood & Mike Wright, "Wayward agents, dominant elite, or reflection of internal diversity? A critique of Folkman, Froud, Johal and Williams on financialisation and financial intermediaries", *Business History*, Vol. 52, No. 7, December 2010, pp. 1048-1067.

14 Julie Froud, Colin Haslam, Sukhdev Johal & Karel Williams, "Shareholder value and financialization: consultancy promises, management moves", *Economy and Society*, Vol. 29, No. 1, 2000, pp. 80-110. Hengyi Feng, Julie Froud, Sukhdev Johal, Colin Haslam & Karel Williams, "A new business model? The capital market and the new economy", *Economy and Society*, Vol. 30, No. 4, 2001, pp. 467-503. Julie Froud, Sukhdev Johal and Karel Williams, "Financialisation and the coupon pool", *Capital & Class*, Autumn 2002, Vol. 26, No. 3, pp. 119-151. Julie Froud and Karel Williams, "Private equity and the culture of value extraction", *New Political Economy*, Vol. 12, No. 3, 2007, pp. 405-420. Peter Folkman, Julie Froud, Sukhdev Johal and Karel Williams, "Working for themselves? Capital market intermediaries and present day capitalism", *Business History*, Vol. 49, No. 4, 2007, Special Issue: "Comparative Perspectives on the 'Managerial Revolution', pp. 552-572.

15 William Lazonick and Mary O'Sullivan, "Finance and industrial development", *Financial History Review*, 4, 1997, pp. 7-29 et 117-138. William Lazonick, *Sustainable Prosperity in the New Economy? Business Organization and High-Tech Employment in the United States*, Kalamazoo (Michigan), W.E. Upjohn Institute for Employment Research, 2009.

16 See the two excellent books by Martine Orange, *Ces Messieurs de Lazard*, Paris, Albin Michel, 2006. Martine Orange, *Rothschild, une banque au pouvoir*, Paris, Albin Michel, 2012.

regarding the M&A. *Goldman Sachs*, "The Bank"[17] (being the symbol of the trend leading investment banks towards capital market banking), made such an impression that people began to imagine a network of influence, a network of former directors who had entered into public institutions[18] and set up a network of connivance. At the same time, we had the image of J.-P. Dimon as king of universal banks who opened the floodgates to his market bankers, including Blythe Masters, whose power over the markets surpassed that of *Morgan Stanley*'s Zoe Cruz.

How to redress the bar: "Good market?"

The fall of the big bankers who, mainly because of their market banking activities had doomed their banks to failure or major losses, reignited moral issues, with investigative journalists, parliamentary commissions (especially the American Senate) and politicians weighing in with their two bits. The legal authorities too (again, especially in the United States and to a lesser extent in London) attempted at "purging" the market of bad practices such as taking market positions against clients, manipulating prices (LIBOR, etc.). These processes led to agreements or fines amounting to billions of dollars or euros), as it happened to Goldman Sachs (whose trader Fabrice Tourré was arraigned in the Spring of 2013), HSBC and *J.P. Morgan & Chase*. In the United States, an inquiry was initiated by the 200-member strong *Residential Mortgage Backed Securities Working Group*, under the aegis of the *Financial Fraud Enforcement Task Force*. Experts combed through recent data files in order to detect malpractices within rating agencies, investment banks and the investment banking and capital market banking branches of universal banks.

The idea was that one could still "trust the market" if the required transparency and good practices were imposed. The quasi-complete liberalisation allowed for a drastic re-regulation around regulatory and legal bodies and good management codes based on clear, strict ratios defined in the Basle laws (Basle II, II bis, III and further IV). One could believe in the "virtues" of the market provided its actors were monitored and supervised and that they built themselves a community of values. This explains the resumption of the debates regarding the "ethics of money" which had appeared in books and reviews of the 1990s – for example, the *Rapport moral sur l'argent dans le monde*, launched in 1992 and *Comment penser l'argent?*[19]

---

[17] Marc Roche, *La banque. Comment Goldman Sachs dirige le monde*, Paris, Albin Michel, 2010. *Arte* TV channel, *Goldman Sachs, la banque qui dirige le monde*, 2012.

[18] Marc Roche, "La 'franc-maçonnerie' européenne de Goldman Sachs", *Le Monde*, 16 November 2011, p. 2.

[19] Roger-Pol Droit (ed.), *Comment penser l'argent?*, proceedings of the third Forum Le Monde-Le Mans, Paris, Le Monde Éditions, 1992.

Once again, ethics was the key for exiting the market crisis, and investment bankers needed to assimilate these individual and collective ethical codes in order to conduct "responsible finance" and put an end to this "crisis of financial legitimacy".[20] We already know that for the past quarter century, *corporate social responsibility* and ethics have been fertile fields for extensive structured analyses – with even a *Business Ethics Circle* in France.[21] We shall return to the values and practices linked to the "beliefs", as in every major stage in the history of money, as shown by Jacques Le Goff regarding the Middle Ages, before philosophers took up the relay (till Georg Simmel) and a sort of "moral philosophy of the market bank" was given shape to by people like John Plender,[22] André Orléan and Pierre-Noël Giraud among others who were taken up by the excesses in derivatives, the offences committed by inside-men, the double accounts and other excesses, like those of Keynes' famous "casino economy".

"Good investment bankers?"

To come back to our main theme, every stakeholder had dreamt of a "good investment banker" and a "good investment bank". These investment bankers were thus justified if we recall the number of merger-acquisition files that they put away, the rules that they themselves followed in keeping with their personal values – like François Henrot,[23] one of *Rothschild Paris*' big active partners in the years 1990-2000. Even *Morgan Stanley*, which had been so harshly criticised for its commission on the *Facebook* IPO in May 2012, can justify the high price set ($38), because the subsequent fall[24] was wiped out by a steady rise that saw the price return to its original level in July 2013. Even the 500 million dollars of the investment banking syndicate[25] seems less shocking in hindsight…. Today, specialists in every branch of activity, at the continental and

20 Claude Bébéar, "Pour une finance responsable" (pp. 59-66); John Plender, "La crise de légitimité de la finance" (pp. 67-72), Association d'économie financière, *Rapport moral sur l'argent dans le monde, 2003-2004*, Paris, AEF-Caisse des dépôts et consignations, Paris, 2004.

21 See the journal *Entreprise Éthique*, published by *Éthique Éditions*.

22 See John Plender, *Going Off the Rails. Global Capital and the Crisis of Legitimacy*, New York, John Wiley, 2003.

23 Roger-Pol Droit et François Henrot, *Le banquier et le philosophe*, Paris, Plon, 2010.

24 See Don Jeffrey, "Morgan Stanley, Goldman Sachs sued over Facebook IPO", *Bloomberg*, 23 May 2012 <www.bloomberg.com/news/2012-05-23/morgan-stanley-goldman-sachs-sued-over-facebook-ipo.html>.

25 The syndicate gathered Morgan-Stanley as its "representative", Goldman Sachs, JP Morgan & Chase, Bank of America-Merril Lynch, Barclays Capital, and a small boutique, Alba & Co. <*www.alba-andco.com*>.

intercontinental scales are required to better support the growth strategies of companies or to advise governments on managing their debt. Such was indeed the case of Michael Grimes, Managing Director and Co-Head of *Global Technology Investment Banking* at Morgan Stanley and a specialist in companies dealing with emerging technologies, who supervised this IPO.

Tensions within the refinancing markets (for those lacking liquidity or dollars) and the pressure of new regulations allowed investment banks to "recover" by donning "new clothes".[26] The national and (upcoming) European regulatory authorities, the Basle codes, the banking laws (France, United States, etc.), the nomination of new management teams, the bigger roles played by some Boards and even the measured voice of analysts, experts and academics made universal banks pass their investment banking and capital markets banking activities through a fine sieve. Even a banker such as Jean-Pierre Mustier, so emblematic of the excesses of investment banking when he was director at the *Société générale*, scrubbed steel wool over the financial and market activities of his new bank, *Unicredit*: "Keeping things simple is the new banking mantra."[27]

The key word was refocusing, based on the constraints imposed by capital and leverage ratio requirements. The "corporate" in "corporate and investment banking" began to dominate in many houses, that is to say, in the range of "transaction banking" services offered to clients: cash management, export finance, FOREX and its cover. Several European banks cut back in areas like aircraft finance, structured credit, capital-intensive trading, etc. Proprietary trading activities were also curtailed by many of them (Deutsche Bank, etc.) with J.P. Morgan even deciding to spin off its prestigious commodities trading activities, which had been raised to such a height by the brilliant Blythe Masters. The process of recovery in houses like Société générale, RBS and Deutsche Bank involved a substantial pruning of their investment banking and capital market banking teams. RBS itself lost some 900 billion Pounds between 2008 and 2013.

"Investment banking rediscovered the virtues of traditional banking activities such as loans, payment, guarantees and letters of credit. The restrictions imposed by regulators regarding extra capital over market activities, leverage ratios, and the increased financing costs gradually (or sometimes in fits and starts as in UBS and Crédit Agricole) pushed them to develop the activities of a financing and investment bank. The

26 Anat Admati and Martin Hellwig, *The Bankers' New Clothes*, Princeton, Princeton University Press, 2013.

27 Patrick Jenkins, "Keeping things simple is a new banking mantra", *Financial Times*, 7 July 2013.

derivatives businesses, which weighed heavily on the balance sheet, migrated towards simpler, more standardised products, with less leverage and mainly using clearing houses in order to limit the credit risk between counterparties. Banks were more and more seen as intermediaries rather than the final risk takers on such products. Financial activities were refocused on the bank's target clients and so managed as to allow client profitability by taking into account cross selling near or slightly higher than the capital costs."[28]

In France, the big *deleveraging* movement (the only known remedy for the disbalances caused by the cyclical booms)[29] amounted to only 15% reduction in the balance sheet regarding the available funds – and the inability of finding more CRR/CDIV and CRR ("cash reserve ratio") norms in the United States, or the *Basel III* (and the imminent *Basel III bis*) norms, depending on the house's location. Meanwhile, the expected cleanup was in the order of 25 per cent of asset reduction.[30] A number of regulatory changes took place between 27 June and 10 July 2013 in Brussels, in the United States, Basle and even Paris, with the little law of 26 July. Three main requirements were defined: the financial leverage ratio, an integrated European supervision and the "integrated resolution" subjected *ex ante* to the European Commission's *DGComp* (General Direction of Markets and Competition): this regulation necessarily comprises of a creditor's *bail in*.

It goes without saying that consulting firms, both general (e.g. the BCG) or specialised (like Équinox Consulting-Cognizant), played a significant role in these streamlining and re-focusing campaigns for a better implementation of these "slimming cures", integration of the new regulations and implementation of deleveraging ratios, both at the strategic as well as structural reorganisational levels (as part of "strategy and structure"). It could be that when the residual portfolios of lower quality assets acquired during the crisis were sufficiently amortised, the profitability of corporate and investment banking would be greater than the capital costs allotted to it, provided its transformation is accompanied by a significant reduction in pay scales as at present, the employees have too large a share of the remainder relative to the shareholders.

This transformation of corporate and investment banking has been under way since 2010: every house is busy not only redrawing its business model but also its overall philosophy. Should it "run after" the market,

28 Jean-Pierre Mustier, "Investment banking en 2013: Back to the future", email sent to Hubert Bonin, 15 August 2013.

29 See McKinsey Global Institute, *Debt and deleveraging: The global credit bubble and its economic consequences*, July 2011.

30 Details supplied by Professor Dominique Lacoue-Labarthe, August 2013.

try and be a free-for-all-trades, fight for ranking points, look for massive profit margins in every activity and on every quarterly and annual basis? And finally, after the "lessons" of the recent crisis, what kind risk structure should the bank assume? Well, we know that despite the historian's fond dreams, enterprises and banks seem impervious to the "lessons of History"[31]... and that, every cyclical boom results in renewed risk-taking because one thinks that this time it's different![32]

---

[31] Eugene White, *Crashes and Panics: The Lessons from History*, New York, Dow Jones-Irwin, 1990.

[32] Carmen Reinhart & Kenneth Rogoff, *This Time is Different. Eight Centuries of Financial Folly*, Princeton & Oxford, Princeton University Press, 2009.

Index of People

Presentation of the two editors of the book

Hubert Bonin is professor in modern economic history at *Sciences Po Bordeaux* and a member of the GRETHA research centre at Bordeaux University. He is a specialist of the history of services companies (Suez canal company, colonial and overseas trading houses and their maritime affiliates), and moreover of French banking history (regional banks. Paris deposit, corporate and investment banks, with several monography books and a few handbooks). He is preparing a large history of French *Société générale* (from 1864 to the 1940s) in a few volumes (the first published in 2006), and developing histories of the French global economy of investment banks and of the action of French banks in Eastern Asia and in Greece. As a specialist in business history, he has co-guided the research programs *Ford in Europe* (*1903-2003*) (published in 2003), *American Firms in Europe* (published in 2008), *Old Paternalism, New Paternalism, Post-Paternalism* (published in 2013), *Investment Banking History* (published in 2014) and *Imperial Banking History* (to be published) and he is taking part to several programs in banking and business history along French, European, or Asian perspectives, especially about investment banking, merchant and trade banking, economic patriotism, entrepreneurship and European business. At the Bordeaux University, he is driving the researches of doctorate PhD students, mainly from Central Europe and Africa.

Carlo Brambilla teaches Economic history at the University of Varese and at the University of Milan-Bicocca. He did his PhD at the University of Pisa under the supervision of Giuseppe Conti. He then has been post-doctoral fellow at the University of Bologna and research fellow at Bocconi University, Istitute of Economic History. He participated in a number of international research projects such as "The Performance of European Big Business in the 20th Century" led by Youssef Cassis, Business History Unit-LSE; and "Normes, institutions et territoires du crédit en France et en Italie (fin XIXe-fin XXe siècles)" led by Giuseppe Conti, University of Pisa, and by Olivier Feiertag, Université Paris X-Nanterre. He has published several articles in financial and economic history, among whom are: with E. Bussière, "Les banques d'affaires en France et en Italie: la banque mixte en question (1870-1970)", in Gisueppe Conti and Olivier Feiertag (eds.), *Le crédit et la nation en France et en Italie, 1860-1980*, forthcoming; with Giandomico Piluso, "Are banks procyclical? Evidence from the Italian case (1890-1973)", *Quaderni del*

Dipartimento di economia politica, No. 523, December 2007, University of Siena; with G. Conti, "Banche, mercati e orientamenti dei sistemi finanziari in una prospettiva storica", and "Informazione e regole contabili nei rapporti tra banca e industria", in G. Conti (ed.), *Creare il credito e arginare i rischi. Il sistema finanziario tra nobiltà e miserie del capitalismo italiano*, Bologna, Il Mulino, 2007; "Grandi banche e modelli creditizi in Italia, Francia e Germania tra XIX e XX secolo", *Imprese e storia*, 29, 2004; "Italian Multinational Banking: Banca Commerciale Italiana and Credito Italiano Between 1930s and 1940s. A Case Study", in H. Bonin *et al.* (eds.), *Transnational Companies. 19th-20th Centuries*, Paris, PLAGE, 2002; "Le banche miste all'estero negli anni Trenta", *Annali di storia dell'impresa*, 12, Bologna, Il Mulino, 2001; "Le banche miste dopo la crisi e il risanamento (1933-1939)", *Archivi e imprese*, 18, 1998.

The program in economic history of the UMR CNRS 5113 GRETHA research centre published at Peter Lang, Brussels:

- Bertrand Blancheton & Hubert Bonin (eds.), *La croissance en économie ouverte (XVIIIe-XXIe siècles). Hommages à Jean-Charles Asselain*, 2009.
- Hubert Bonin, *Banque et bourgeoisies. La Société bordelaise de CIC (1880-2005)*, 2010.
- Hubert Bonin, Bernard Lachaise & Christophe-Luc Robin (eds.), *Robert Boulin. Itinéraires d'un gaulliste (Libourne, Paris)*, 2010.
- Hubert Bonin, Luciano Segreto, (eds.), *European Business: Corporate and Social Values*, 2011.
- Hubert Bonin, Luciano Segreto, Andrzej Kozminski, Carles Manera et Manfred Pohl, (eds.), *European Business and Brand Building*, 2012.
- Hubert Bonin and Paul Thomes (eds.), *Old Paternalism, New Paternalism, Post-Paternalism*, 2013.

EUROCLIO – Published Books

N° 80 – *Christian Democrat Internationalism. Its Action in Europe and Worldwide from Post World War II until the 1990s. Volume II: The Development (1945-1979). The Role of Parties, Movements, People.* Jean-Dominique Durand (ed.), 2013.

N° 79 – *Christian Democrat Internationalism. Its Action in Europe and Worldwide from Post World War II until the 1990s. Volume I: The Origins.* Jean-Dominique Durand (ed.), 2013.

N° 78 – *Investment Banking History. National and Comparative Issues (19th-21st centuries).* Hubert Bonin & Carlo Brambilla (eds.), 2014.

N° 77 – *Citizenship and Solidarity in the European Union. From the Charter of Fundamental Rights to the Crisis, the State of the Art.* Mariana Canotilho, Pedro Madeira Froufe & Alessandra Silveira (eds.), 2013.

N° 76– *The OSCE: Soft Security for a Hard World. Competing Theories for Understanding the OSCE.* Roberto Dominguez (ed.), 2013.

N° 75 – *Euroscepticism, Europhobia and Eurocriticism. The Radical Parties of the Right and Left vis-à-vis the European Union.* Cesáreo Rodríguez-Aguilera de Prat, 2013.

N° 74 – *Fermer les mines en construisant l'Europe. Une histoire sociale de l'intégration européenne.* Nicolas Verschueren, 2013. N° 74 – *Fermer les mines en construisant l'Europe. Une histoire sociale de l'intégration européenne.* Nicolas Verschueren, 2013.

N° 73 – *Reflets de la construction européenne. Réflexions, références et refus du débat sur l'Europe.* Bertrand Vayssière (dir.), 2012.

N° 72 – *The International Relations of Local Authorities. From Institutional Twinning to the Committee of the Regions: Fifty Years of European Integration History.* Fabio Zucca, 2012.

N° 71 – *Histoire du Conseil de l'Europe (1949-2009).* Birte Wassenberg, 2012.

N° 70 – *The EU, Security and Transatlantic Relations.* Finn Laursen (ed.), 2012.

N° 69 – *Européanisation au XXe siècle. Un regard historique / Europeanisation in the 20th Century. The Historical Lens.* Matthieu Osmont, Émilia Robin-Hivert, Katja Seidel, Mark Spoerer & Christian Wenkel (dir./eds.), 2012.

N° 68 – *Consensus and European Integration. An Historical Perspective / Consensus et intégration européenne. Une perspective historique*. Daniela Preda & Daniele Pasquinucci (eds./dir.), 2012.

N° 67 – *Générations de fédéralistes européens depuis le XIXe siècle. Individus, groupes, espaces et réseaux*. Geneviève Duchenne et Michel Dumoulin (dir.), 2012.

N° 66 – *Raymond Aron, penseur de l'Europe et de la nation.* Giulio De Ligio (dir.), 2012.

N° 65 – *Europe Twenty Years after the End of the Cold War. The New Europe, New Europes? / L'Europe vingt ans après la fin de la guerre froide. Nouvelle Europe, nouvelles Europes?* Bruno Arcidiacono, Katrin Milzow, Axel Marion & Pierre-Étienne Bourneuf (eds./dir.), 2012.

N° 64 – *Aux origines de la diplomatie européenne. Les Neuf et la Coopération politique européenne de 1973 à 1980.* Maria Gainar, 2012.

N° 63 – *Europe and the Middle East. The hour of the East?* Birte Wassenberg & Giovanni Faleg (eds.), 2012.

N° 62 – *Quelle architecture pour un code européen de droit international privé ?* Marc Fallon, Paul Lagarde, Sylvaine Poillot-Peruzzetto (dir.), 2011.

N° 61 – *La construction d'un espace euro-méditerranéen. Genèses, mythes et perspectives.* Houda Ben Hamouda et Mathieu Bouchard (dir.), 2012.

N° 60 – *Innovations et transferts de technologie en Europe du Nord-Ouest aux XIXe et XXe siècles.* Jean-François Eck et Pierre Tilly (dir.), 2011

N° 59 – *Novel Outlooks on the Marshall Plan. American Aid and European Re-Industrialization.* Fransceca Fauri & Paolo Tedeschi (eds.), 2011.

N° 58 – *Europe in the International Arena during the 1970s. Entering a Different World / L'Europe sur la scène internationale dans les années 1970. À la découverte d'un nouveau monde.* Antonio Varsori & Guia Migani (eds./dir.), 2011.

N° 57 – *Cultures nationales et identité communautaire. Un défi pour l'Europe ? / National Cultures and Common Identity. A Challenge for Europe?* Marloes Beers & Jenny Raflik (dir./eds.), 2010.

N° 56 – *Les trajectoires de l'innovation technologique et la construction européenne. Des voies de structuration durable ? / Trends in Technological Innovation and the European Construction. The Emerging of Enduring Dynamics?* Christophe Bouneau, David Burigana & Antonio Varsori (dir./eds.), 2010.

N° 55 – *L'OTAN et l'Europe. Quels liens pour la sécurité et la défense européenne ?* Birte WASSENBERG, Giovanni FALEG et Martin W. MLODECKI (dir.), 2010.

N° 54 – *The Road Europe Travelled Along.* Daniele PASQUINUCCI and Daniela PREDA (eds.), 2010.

N° 53 – *Vivre et construire l'Europe à l'échelle territoriale de 1945 à nos jours.* Yves DENÉCHÈRE et Marie-Bénédicte VINCENT (dir.), 2010.

N° 52 – *De l'esprit de la Résistance jusqu'à l'idée de l'Europe. Projets européens et américains pour l'Europe de l'après-guerre (1940-1950).* Veronika HEYDE, 2010.

Réseau européen Euroclio
avec le réseau SEGEI

Coordination : Chaire Jean Monnet d'histoire
de l'Europe contemporaine (Cehec)
Collège Erasme, 1, place Blaise-Pascal, B-1348 Louvain-la-Neuve

Allemagne
Jürgen Elvert
Wilfried Loth

Belgique
Julie Cailleau
Jocelyne Collonval
Yves Conrad
Gaëlle Courtois
Pascal Deloge
Geneviève Duchenne
Vincent Dujardin
Michel Dumoulin
Roch Hannecart
Pierre-Yves Plasman
Béatrice Roeh
Corine Schröder
Caroline Suzor
Pierre Tilly
Arthe Van Laer
Jérôme Wilson
Natacha Wittorski

Espagne
Enrique Moradiellos
Mercedes Samaniego Boneu

France
Françoise Berger
Marie-Thérèse Bitsch
Gérard Bossuat
Éric Bussière
Jean-François Eck
Catherine Horel
Philippe Mioche
Marine Moguen-Toursel
Sylvain Schirmann
Matthieu Trouvé
Laurent Warlouzet
Emilie Willaert

Hongrie
Gergely Fejérdy

Italie
David Burigana
Elena Calandri
Eleonora Guasconi
Luciano Segreto
Antonio Varsori

Luxembourg
Charles Barthel
Etienne Deschamps
Jean-Marie Kreins
René Leboutte
Robert Philippart
Corine Schröder
Gilbert Trausch

Pays-Bas
Anjo Harryvan
Jan W. Brouwer
Jan van der Herst

Pologne
Józef Laptos
Zdzisiaw Mach

Suisse
Antoine Fleury
Lubor Jilek